# On Organizational Learning

# On Organizational Learning

*Second Edition*

CHRIS ARGYRIS

Copyright © Chris Argyris 1992, 1994, 1999

First published 1992
First published in the USA 1993
Reprinted 1993, 1994
First published in paperback 1994
Reprinted 1995(twice) 1996, 1997
Second edition 1999
Reprinted 1999, 2000

Blackwell Publishers Ltd
108 Cowley Road
Oxford OX4 1JF
UK

Blackwell Publishers Inc.
350 Main Street
Malden, Massachusetts 02148
USA

*British Library Cataloguing in Publication Data applied for*

ISBN 0– 631– 21308–2 (hbk); ISBN 0– 631– 21309–0 (pbk)

*Library of Congress Cataloging-in-Publication Data*

A CIP catalogue record for this book is available from the British Library.

Typeset in 10 / 11pt Ehrhardt
By Pure Tech India Ltd., Pondicherry, India
        http://www.puretech.com
Printed in Great Britain by MPG Books Ltd, Bodmin, Cornwall

This book is printed on acid-free paper

# Contents

# — List of Figures —

# List of Tables

# —— Acknowledgments ——

The author and publisher gratefully acknowledge the following for permission to use the material in this book.

Chapter 3, originally published as "How Learning and Reasoning Processes Affect Organizational Change," in Paul S. Goodman & Associates (ed.), *Change in Organizations: New Perspectives on Theory, Research, and Practice*. Copyright 1982 by Jossey-Bass, Inc., Publishers. The author would also like to thank Donald Schön, Viviane Robinson, and Lee Bolman for their helpful comments.

Chapter 4, originally published in R. Quinn & K. Cameron (eds), *Paradox and Transformation*, Cambridge, Mass.: Ballinger, 1988, pp. 255–78.

Chapter 5, originally published in the *Journal of Management Studies*, 4, 1, February 1967, pp. 31–55. Reprinted by permission of Blackwell Publishers.

Chapter 6, reprinted by permission of *Harvard Business Review*, "Teaching Smart People to Learn," by Chris Argyris, May/June 1991. Copyright 1991 by the President and Fellows of Harvard College; all rights reserved.

Chapter 7, originally published in The *University of Wales Business & Economic Review*, 1, Summer 1987.

Chapter 8, originally published in *Accounting, Organizations and Society*, 2, Chris Argyris, "Organizational Learning and Management Information Systems," Copyright 1977, Pergamon Press Ltd.

Chapter 9, originally published in *Organizational Dynamics*, a publication of the American Management Association, August 1989. Reprinted by permission.

Chapter 10, originally published as "Dealing with Threat and Defensiveness," in Johannes M. Pennings & Associates (ed.) *Organizational Strategy and Change*. Copyright 1985 by Jossey-Bass Inc., Publishers.

Chapter 11, reprinted with permission from *Accounting, Organizations and Society*, 15, Chris Argyris, "The Dilemma of Implementing Controls: The Case of Managerial Accounting," Copyright 1990, Pergamon Press Ltd. The author would also like to express his thanks to Professors Robert Anthony, Kenneth Merchant, and Robert Simons for their helpful comments.

Chapter 12, reprinted by permission of *Harvard Business Review*, "Human Problems with Budgets," by Chris Argyris, Jan/Feb 1953. Copyright 1953 by the President and Fellows of Harvard College; all rights reserved. The author would like to note that the research which led to this article was carried out under the auspices of the Controllership Foundation. Dr Schuyler D. Hoslett, Director of Executive Program in Business Administration, Columbia University, was in overall charge of the project. Mr Frank B. Miller of Cornell University assisted the author. The entire research is reported in *The Impact of Budgets on People*, New York: Controllership Foundation, 1952.

Chapter 13, originally published in *American Psychologist*, 42, 5, 1987. Copyright 1987 by the American Psychological Association. Reprinted by permission of the publisher. The author would also like to thank Dianne Argyris, Edward Bowman, Richard Murname, Robert Putnam, Donald Schön, and Diana Smith for their helpful comments.

Chapter 14, originally published in *Harvard Business Review*, July–August 1994. Reprinted by permission of *Harvard Business Review*.

Chapter 15, originally published in *Research in Organizational Change and Development*, 1. Copyright 1987 by JAI Press Inc. Reprinted by permission of the publisher. The author would also like to express his thanks for the help received from Dianne Argyris, Victor Friedman, Philip McArthur, Robert Putnam, Peter Raymond, Diana Smith, and Professor Donald Schön. The author also would like to express his gratitude to the OD consultants who, given commitments of anonymity, cannot be identified by name.

Chapter 16, reprinted with permission from NTL Institute, "Inappropriate Defenses against the Monitoring of Organization Development Practice," by Chris Argyris, pp. 299–312, *The Journal of Applied Behavioral Science*, Vol. 26, No. 3, copyright 1990. The author thanks Professor Richard Walton, the four anonymous JABS reviewers, and all the anonymous seminar participants who read this article and offered comments on it.

Chapter 17, reprinted with permission from NTL Institute, "Do Personal Growth Laboratories Represent an Alternative Culture?" by Chris Argyris, pp. 7–28, *The Journal of Applied Behavioral Science*, Vol. 8, No. 1, copyright 1972. The author should like to express his gratitude to Clayton Alderfer, Robert Barbieri, Douglas Hall, and Roy Lewicki for their generous assistance.

Chapter 18, originally published in the *Journal of Applied Behavioral Science*, 32, 4, December 1996. Reprinted by permission of *Journal of Applied Behavioral Science*.

Chapter 19, originally published in the *Journal of Social Issues* as the Kurt Lewin Award Lecture, 1997, The Society for Psychological Study of Social Issues, 1997. Reprinted by permission of the *Journal of Social Issues*.

Chapter 20, originally published in *Organization Science*, 7, 1, Jan–Feb 1996. Reprinted by permission of *Organization Science*.

Chapter 22, originally published in *The Handbook of Industrial and Organizational Psychology*, Copyright 1976 Marvin D. Dunnette (ed.). Reprinted by permission of the editor. The author wishes to express his appreciation to Professors Clayton Alderfer, Robert Cooper, Douglas Hall, Edward Lawler, Benjamin Schneider, and Gerrit Wolfe for their helpful comments.

Chapter 23, originally published in *American Psychologist*, 24, 10, October 1969. Copyright 1969 by the American Psychological Association. Reprinted by permission of the publisher. The author wishes to thank Clayton Alderfer, Lee Bolman, Richard Hackman, Douglas

Hall, Edward Lawler, Roy Lewicki, Benjamin Schneider, and Gerrit Wolf for their helpful comments.

Chapter 24, originally published in *American Psychologist*, 30, 4, 1975. Copyright 1975 by the American Psychological Association. Reprinted by permission of the publisher. The author would like to thank Clayton Alderfer, Richard Hackman, and William Torbert for their many helpful comments.

Chapter 25, originally published in E. E. Lawler III & Associates (ed.), *Doing Research that is Useful for Theory and Practice*. Copyright 1985 by Jossey-Bass Inc., Publishers. The author wishes to thank Dianne Argyris, Robert Putnam, and Diana Smith for their many helpful comments.

Chapter 26, originally published in *American Behavioral Scientist*, 32, 5, May/June 1989, pp. 612–23. Reprinted by permission of Sage Publications Inc.

Chapter 27, originally published in *Psychological Bulletin*, 70, 3, 1968. Copyright 1968 by the American Psychological Association. Reprinted by permission of the publisher. The author wishes to express his appreciation to his colleagues Douglas Hall, Richard Hackman, Edward Lawler, Lyman Porter, and Betty Ann Nunes for their many helpful suggestions.

# Preface

The premise of this book is that organizational learning is a competence that all organizations should develop. The reasoning underlying this premise is that the better organizations are at learning the more likely it is they will be able to detect and correct errors, and to see when they are unable to detect and correct errors. Also, the more effective organizations are at learning the more likely they will be at being innovative or knowing the limits of their innovation.

An error is any mismatch between plan or intention and what actually happened when either is implemented. The book provides insights into what creates mismatches or errors and how to begin to correct them. The ideas should be applicable to detecting and correcting mismatches that are technical, administrative, or human (that is, individual, group, intergroup, and organizational).

I place a heavy emphasis upon detecting and correcting errors that are potentially or actually embarrassing or threatening to the participants, be they acting as agents for the organization (and its components such as group or intergroup or departments) or for themselves. One reason for this emphasis is that experience shows that organizations have the most difficulty at learning when the problems are difficult, and embarrassing or threatening, in short, precisely when they need learning most. A second reason is that there is in the research literature little focus upon these conditions.

I have recently conducted an examination of the organizational research literature about business, government, and education organizations. I found many books and articles that described barriers to organizational learning at all levels and for all kinds of problems. I also found that the researchers did not focus upon producing actionable knowledge on how to reduce or lower these barriers. In those cases when they did, the advice was either disconnected from the world of practice or, when examined carefully, the advice could actually strengthen the very barriers that were supposed to be overcome (Argyris, 1990). And when the data were available, it appears that the writers were often unaware of the gaps. Those who aware of them often cited norms in the scientific community against such research. The most powerful norms in research are around describing the world as is, to be descriptive. If you are to follow normative practice, you advise human beings and organizations on how to be effective within the world as it exists. The idea of designing new or rare worlds is not rewarded significantly if one can judge from published research.

In Part I, I focus on organizational defenses which I believe are one of the most important barriers to learning. An organizational defense is a policy, practice, or action that prevents the participants (at any level of any organization) from experiencing embarrassment or threat, and at the same time, prevents them from discovering the causes of the embarrassment or threat. Organizational defenses (which include groups, intergroups, and interpersonal relationships) are therefore anti-learning and overprotective. In this part, I illustrate some of the most important origins of organizational defenses.

In Part II, I explore the barriers to organizational learning around several of the key managerial functions. I see each function such as managerial accounting and budgeting, strategy, and information systems as based upon explicit theories and methods as to how to design and implement each. For example, it is possible to specify how to produce an economic analysis of costs founded upon activity-based cost accounting theory and methods. The specifications are so explicit that if two individuals using the same data and methods arrive at different conclusions then it is possible to say that someone made an error. It is also possible to test this assertion by tracing backwards to find the error. Thus, activity-based cost accounting is designed to be as rigorous as possible. Its effective implementation requires what I call productive or rigorous reasoning.

There are two features of the rigor that, I suggest, are crucial. One, it makes as explicit as possible the causal reasoning that underlies its methodology. Causal reasoning is key in everyday life. As Shoham (1990, p. 214) states: "If causal reasoning is common in scientific thinking, it is downright dominant in everyday common sense thinking." The second feature of rigor is that it deals with causal reasoning by making its premises and inferences explicit and by subjecting its conclusions to continual tests in the world of practice. I call this productive reasoning.

Productive reasoning may seem obvious and taken for granted by scholars such as those who design activity-based cost accounting, strategy, information systems and other similar managerial functional disciplines. The point that I believe they often miss is that by designing in productive reasoning their methodologies require such reasoning in order to be implemented. How is that a problem?

Making the effective implementation of these disciplines dependent upon the use of productive reasoning becomes a problem when the advice and actions that they recommend are embarrassing or threatening. Under these conditions defensive reasoning is activated. The causal reasoning is not made explicit. The premises and inferences are often tacit. The tests of the conclusions tend to be nonexistent or self-sealing. The organizational defenses built to protect the defensive reasoning and actions help to assure that little learning will occur that questions the causal reasoning.

I do not mean to imply that the designers of theories and methodologies of accounting, strategy, and information systems are free from responsibility for some of the problems they face when their ideas are difficult to implement. Indeed, they would agree that there are gaps and inconsistencies in their theories and methods that should be closed and corrected. Errors due to those gaps are due to lack of knowledge. Like all scholars they are dedicated to reducing errors due to lack of knowledge.

I am suggesting that errors occur around the implementation processes and that they are by design (not ignorance). They are designed to protect the players from embarrassment or threat. Moreover, since most formal managerial theories or stewardship do not condone designed error, the players have to cover up such practices, and to really protect themselves, they cover up the cover-up.

In Part III, I examine in more detail the human resources function. I especially examine experiential learning, organizational development and change practices. Practices like these are intended to reduce the barriers to organizational learning. I try to show that the ideas and practices in good currency around these human resources activities are much more counter-productive than has been realized, especially by the organizational development and managerial education professionals.

Part IV focuses on how the ideas on conducting descriptive rigorous empirical research unintentionally reinforces the organizational defenses and defensive reasoning of practitioners. I try to illustrate how those of us who conduct research may have our own set of organizational (read community) intergroup and group defenses that are likely to reinforce the barriers to learning around issues that are embarrassing or threatening to us as well as to those that we study.

Reflecting on these ideas, I think it is fair to say that we are intentionally creating a world full of self-reinforcing, anti-learning processes that will overprotect the players so that it will be difficult to detect and correct difficult and embarrassing problems. Moreover, thanks to the organizational defensive routines – with their accompanying sense of helplessness, cynicism, and doubt about any change – the anti-learning and overprotective features will eventually be taken for granted. They will be viewed as necessary evils of organizations. For example, not only will limited learning capacity, quasi-resolution of conflict, and "satisficing" be seen as core attributes of everyday life (with which I agree), but the descriptive theories that help us to see that will not be much help in learning how to change them.

These views are based on the assumption that social science should not only describe reality as accurately, comprehensively, and economically as possible, it should also pay attention to producing knowledge about virtual worlds that provide liberating alternatives. By liberating alternatives I mean organizations and societies that endow human beings with competencies to reverse and undo the self-fueling, anti-learning, overprotective processes that are a major focus of this book.

In making this statement, I am not asserting that human beings must accept these liberating alternatives, simply that scholars have some obligation to, at least, make them available. Underlying this assumption is that worlds that encourage the production of empirically testable knowledge, the enhancement of informed choice, and the strengthening of personal responsibility are worth designing and trying to implement. These basic values are not new. What is likely to be new is that we can help to create worlds where they are not rare but part of the practice in everyday life.

In most of the chapters, I present some ideas and short illustrations of the interventions conducted to create the rare conditions and integrate them in everyday life. Unfortunately, the most thorough study illustrating our progress was not available as this book went to press. Fortunately, I can now say that it will be available (Argyris, 1993).

# References

Argyris, C., 1990, *Overcoming Organizational Defenses: facilitating organizational learning*, Needham, MA, Allyn Bacon.

Argyris, C., 1993, *Actionable Knowledge: especially for changing the status quo*, San Francisco., Jossey-Bass.

Shoham, Y., 1990, "Nonmonotonic reasoning and causation," *Cognitive Science*, 14, pp. 213–302.

# Introduction

## The Evolving Field of Organizational Learning[1]

We divide the literature that pays serious attention to organizational learning into two main categories: the practice-oriented, prescriptive literature of "the learning organization," promulgated mainly by consultants and practitioners, and the predominantly skeptical scholarly literature of "organizational learning," produced by academics. The two literatures have different thrusts, appeal to different audiences, and employ different forms of language. Nevertheless, they intersect at key points: their conceptions of what makes organizational learning "desirable," or "productive;" their views of the nature of the threats to productive organizational learning; and their attitudes toward whether – and if so, how – such threats may be overcome.

In the following sections, we describe the main currents of thought at work in the two branches of the organizational learning literature, and identify some of the controversial issues to be explored in chapter 1.

## The Literature of the "Learning Organization"

Although this literature takes many forms, its underlying conception of a central ideal is broadly shared. This ideal includes notions of organizational adaptability, flexibility, avoidance of stability traps, propensity to experiment, readiness to rethink means and ends, inquiry orientation, realization of human potential for learning in the service of organizational purposes, and creation of organizational settings as contexts for human development. Different authors articulate the ideal in different ways and single out different issues as central to its realization.

For example, David Garvin's (1993) review of literature on the learning organization pays special attention to ideas of systematic experimentation, movement from "superficial knowledge to deep understanding," "comprehensive frameworks" for the evaluation of progress, and the "opening up of boundaries [to] stimulate the exchange of ideas." In their review article, Ulrich et al. (1993) also emphasize, in contrast to demonstration projects that too often become "sequestered showcases," the importance of the "ability to move lessons learned from experience and experiments across boundaries" – including boundaries of time and geography, levels of hierarchy, functional units, and links in the supplier–firm–customer value chain. These authors focus on continuous improvement, competence acquisition, experimentation, and boundary spanning. They stress the need for managers to make a visible commitment to the generation and the generalization of organizational learning by incorporating it in strategic intent, measuring it, monitoring it, investing in it, talking about it in public, and giving it symbolic expression.

Within such a broadly shared background of assumptions and values, views of the learning organization differ according to the organizational functions to which the authors give primary attention. In each subfield, authors tend to stress different features of the ideal and to concentrate on different enabling prescriptions for its achievement.

## Sociotechnical Systems

Sociotechnical systems – also known as the Quality of Work Life, or Industrial Democracy Movement – grew out of the postwar activities of the Tavistock Institute in England. It was extended in the 1960s and 1970s by the work of Einar Thorsrud, David Philip Herbst, and their colleagues in Norway along with Fred Emery in Australia and many others. Gradually, the status of sociotechnical systems has shifted from fringe movement to established profession.

Its conception of a learning organization focuses on the idea of collective participation by teams of individuals, especially workers, in developing new patterns of work, career paths, and arrangements for combining family and work lives. According to this view, individuals, workers and their supervisors, can and must learn to redesign their work, and upper-level managers must learn to create the contexts within which they can do so.

## Organizational Strategy

This field, some 25 years old, created by management consultants and academics in schools of business and management, takes its root metaphor from the military: organizations, like nations, engage in warlike games of competition for markets. Organizational strategy was originally conceived as a kind of planning aimed at formulating broad policies based on appreciation of a firm's position in relation to its markets, competitors, technologies, materials, and skills. As the field matured and the idea of strategy penetrated governmental and nonprofit sectors, concepts of the strategic game have become dynamic. Effective strategy tends now to be seen as requiring continual development of new understandings, models, and practices. Attention has shifted from planning to implementation of plans and then to the interaction of planning and implementing in a process explicitly described as organizational learning.

In a recent review of the literature on corporate strategy, Edward Bowman (1994) traces the intellectual development of the field, asking "how people in organizations . . . can understand and/or prescribe decision processes." Bowman makes a broad distinction between "rational" and "natural" approaches to the analysis of strategic decision making. For Bowman, the rational approach, which he associates mainly with economists and management scientists, adopts a "Cooks-tour" view of planning where all is calculated in advance. The "natural" approach uses the narrative, case-based methods of behavioral theory to describe a "Lewis-and-Clark" view of planning that follows the "habitual, unfolding, trial-and-error, learned, isomorphic pattern of decision processes." Bowman argues for an integration of the natural and the rational through a synthesis of economic and behavioral theory.

## Production

In the 1970s and 1980s, as the United States slowly and painfully became aware of the competetive challenge posed by Japan, Germany, Korea, and other nations, and as attention focused on the need for continual improvement in the quality of products and production processes, authors in this field began to speak of learning.

For example, *Dynamic Manufacturing* (1988) by Hayes et al. carries the subtitle "Creating the Learning Organization," which the authors apply not only to the production process but to the performance of the organization as a whole. The authors claim that

> companies that are quick both to learn new things and to perfect familiar things, that adapt imaginatively and effectively to change, and that are looked up to by their competitors because of their ability to lead the way into new fields, tend to have certain attributes in common. Moreover, companies with these attributes tend to be excellent throughout. (p. 25)

## Economic Development

After World War II, the field of economic development, in close connection with the rise of international development agencies like the World Bank, emerged. This field has been dominated by economists, especially macroeconomists, but a few of its influential practitioners have emphasized the development of institutions on which national economic development depends.

Albert Hirschman's *Exit, Voice and Loyalty* (1970) is subtitled "Responses to Decline in Firms, Organizations and States." Hirschman sees all such institutions as inherently subject to deterioration in the form of "lapses from efficient, rational, law-abiding, virtuous or otherwise functional behavior" (p. 1). He is concerned with two principal mechanisms of recuperation: the "exit" option, through which "some customers stop buying the firm's products or some members leave the organization," and the "voice" option, through which

> the firm's customers or the organization's members express their dissatisfaction directly to management or to some other authority to which management is subordinate or through general protest addressed to anyone who cares to listen.

In both cases, the basic schema is that of signal and response: customers or organization members signal their dissatisfaction by exit or voice and managers respond.

The recuperative processes with which Hirschman is concerned have many of the attributes of the organizational learning processes described above: they affect the organization as a whole, they operate continually throughout the life of the organization, and they involve the detection and correction of decline, deterioration or dysfunction. Hirschman's view of development – of organizations, regions, or societies – contains an elusive theory of social learning, one that evinces itself most clearly in the three books that grew out of his experience as an economic development consultant (see Rodwin and Schön, 1995). In Hirschman's normative, practice-oriented theory of development, his diagnoses and prescriptions hinge on what would now be called "structural enablers" – institutional structures of incentives that compel or attract individuals to learn to produce behavior conducive to development.

## Systems Dynamics

The systems modeling discipline first developed by Jay Forrester in the 1960s on the basis of servomechanism and control theory – and applied in grand sequence first to industry then to cities and finally to the world – has turned in recent years to organizational learning. Peter Senge, one of Forrester's best-known followers, has published The Fifth Discipline (1993), subtitled "The Art and Practice of Organizational Learning." Senge's treatment of the subject unites systems thinking with organizational adaptation and with the realization of human potential in a mixture that has a distinctly Utopian flavor. On the one hand, he asserts that "the rate at which organizations learn may become the only sustainable source of competitive advantage." (p. 3). On the other hand, he envisages learning organizations where

> people continually expand their capacity to create the results they truly desire, where new and expansive patterns of thinking are nurtured, where collective aspiration is set free, and where people are continually learning how to learn together. (p. 2)

Senge's prescriptive approach combines the methodology of systems dynamics with certain ideas adapted from our theory-of-action perspective, notably an awareness of the importance of the "mental models" held by organizational practitioners, including those that constrain or facilitate reliable inquiry into organizational processes.

## Human Resources

In recent years writers in the field of human resources have picked up the language of the learning organization, stressing the development of human capability for questioning, experimenting, adapting, and innovating on the organization's behalf. Characteristically, writings in this subfield emphasize the mutually reinforcing interactions between enhanced opportunity for individual development within organizations and enhanced organizational capability for competitive performance.

For example, Jones and Hendry (1992), researchers at Warwick University in England, base their review of the literature on a pivotal distinction between "an incremental approach" to training and development and a "fundamental mind shift." They envisage a stage of "transformation" toward the latter where "learning focuses on managing personal change and self-assessment," management structures flatten, managers become more like coaches, thinkers and doers come together, everyone learns to go after the root causes of problems rather than assigning blame, and "the whole organization becomes committed via personal involvement." Beyond this stage the authors describe an as-yet-unrealized ideal of "transfiguration" in which people give priority to a concern for society's general welfare and betterment. They question why organizations exist in their present forms and treat their organizations as representing "a way of life to be cherished because of its values."

## Organizational Culture

"Organizational culture" is a term whose currency among practitioners in present-day organizations rivals that of "organizational learning". Managers have learned to speak of "our culture" as familiarly and with as little sense of the problematic as they speak of "our kind of people." Edgar Schein's Organizational Culture and Leadership (1985) offers the most careful attempt to provide a clear analysis of the meaning of organizational culture, and its second edition (1992) links organizational culture to the ideal of a learning organization. Schein argues that in a world of turbulent change, organizations have to learn ever faster, which calls for a learning culture that functions as "a perpetual learning system" (p. 372). The primary task of a leader in contemporary organizations is to create and sustain such a culture, which then, especially in mature organizations, feeds back to shape the leader's own assumptions.

Schein defines leadership as "the attitude and motivation to examine and manage culture" (p. 374). He regards the organization as the group, and analyzes organizational culture as a pattern of basic assumptions shared by the group, acquired by solving problems of adaptation and integration, working "well enough to be considered valid and, therefore, to be taught to new members as the correct way to perceive, think, and feel in relation to those problems." In organizational learning, basic assumptions shift in the heads of the group members. The job of a learning leader is to promote such shifts by helping the organization's members to "achieve some degree of insight and develop motivation to change" (p. 390).

A learning leader must assess the adequacy of his organization's culture, detect its dysfunctionality, and promote its transformation, first by making his own basic assumptions into "learning assumptions" and then by fostering such assumptions in the culture of his organization. Among the most important learning assumptions: people want to contribute and can be trusted to do so; one should advocate one's own not-knowing, becoming a learner and trying to get others to do likewise, thereby diffusing responsibility for learning; and "the process of learning must ultimately be made part of the culture." Leaders can foster a learning culture by envisioning it and communicating the vision, by rewarding those pockets in an organization that represent the desired assumptions, and by fostering their creation through cultural diversity.

Acting in these ways is a large part of what Schein means by "managing the culture." He believes cultural change *can* be managed, although he is aware that it also depends on changed assumptions found to work in effectively adapting to the external environment and producing "comfort" in the internal one. Schein does not address the possible conflict of these managerial strategies (for example, promulgating a vision versus accepting one's own not-knowing) nor what happens when changed assumptions fail to work.

Schein seems to be aware that managing a culture contains a hint of internal inconsistency (cultures are usually seen as growing up and evolving, rather than as objects of direct control), and he tries to argue simultaneously that the culture of an organization can be shaped by its leader, evolves in response to selective pressures exerted by external and internal environments, and can persist in the face of its not working. To some extent, Schein tries to reconcile these propositions by reference to different stages in an organization's life cycle. Specifically he recognizes that the culture of a mature organization may contain dysfunctional, taken-for-granted assumptions, products of past successes that "operate as silent filters on what is perceived and thought about" (p. 382). He observes, for example, that

> the overt and espoused values that are stated for [organizational] solutions (e.g., TQM) often hide assumptions that are not, in fact, favorable to the kind of learning I have described.

When a culture becomes dysfunctional, learning leaders must be careful to "look inside themselves to locate their own mental models and assumptions before they leap into action" (p. 373). In order to avoid "unwittingly undermining [their] own creations," leaders must cultivate insight into their unconscious conflicts as well as into their conscious intentions. Consultants, in turn, can foster such insight, by "helping the leader make his own sense of what is going on in himself and his organization," functioning as "cultural therapists" who help the leader figure out "what the culture is and what parts of it are more or less adaptive" (p. 387).

But Schein does not grasp the full burden of paradox inherent in the idea of managing a culture toward the ideal of a learning organization. He focuses on the danger that organizational cultures are inherently stability-seeking. He does not focus, directly and critically, on the issue of the *controllability* of a culture – the degree to which it may be subject to design causality – nor does he specify how learning assumptions such as not-knowing, trust in others, and "Theory Y assumptions about human nature" can actually be imparted to human beings. He addresses the limits of culture management mainly through his notion of "cultural humility," i.e. the recognition that culture is partly affected by powerful forces which may lie beyond a leader's direct control.

Some writings on the learning organization – like those of Schein, Senge, and the sociotechnical theorists – make significant contributions. They describe a range of types of organizational learning. They offer prescriptions that are useful at least as guides to the kinds of organizational structures, processes, and conditions that may function as enablers of productive organizational learning – for example:

- flat, decentralized organizational structures;
- information systems that provide fast, public feedback on the performance of the organization as a whole and of its various components;
- mechanisms for surfacing and criticizing implicit organizational theories of action, cultivating systematic programs of experimental inquiry;
- measures of organizational performance;
- systems of incentives aimed at promoting organizational learning; and
- ideologies associated with such measures, such as total quality, continuous learning, excellence, openness, and boundary-crossing.

On the other hand, the literature on the learning organization is inattentive to the gaps emphasized in the arguments of the learning skeptics. It ignores the analytic difficulties posed by the very idea of organizational learning. It treats the beneficence of organizational learning as an axiom. It does not give serious consideration to processes that threaten the validity or utility of organizational learning. And it gives short shrift to the difficulties of implementation, the phenomena that undermine attempts to achieve the ideal or cause such attempts to be short-lived.

These gaps and difficulties are fundamentally dependent on the behavioral worlds of organizations that make for limited learning systems. Writers on the learning organization tend to focus on first-order errors, due to mistaken or incomplete action strategies and assumptions of the sort that practitioners ordinarily detect and try to correct. They tend to be selectively inattentive to second-order errors, which are due to the organizational designs that make people systematically unaware of the behavioral phenomena that underlie the production and reproduction of first-order errors. We refer here, for example, to defensive routines, mixed messages, taboos on the discussability of key issues, games of control and deception, and organizational camouflage. As we have argued throughout this book, reflection on such phenomena and the theories-in-use that underlie them, is essential both to the task of explaining the limitations of organizational learning and to the design of interventions that can overcome those limitations.

driven by internal commitment, strong identification with company goals, intrinsic satisfaction from work... elicited by a variety of managerial appeals, exhortations, and actions... In short, under normative control it is the employee's self... that is claimed in the name of corporate interest. (p. 11)

Finally, some authors criticize organizational learning because they claim that much of it, perhaps even the greater part, is in the service of stability rather than change. On this view, organizations learn to preserve the status quo, and learning of this sort is the enemy of organizational change and reform (Fiol and Lyles, 1985; Leavitt and March, 1988).

All such criticisms rest on the idea that organizational learning is not a value-neutral activity but proceeds from values, has implications for values, and is subject to critique in terms of a conception of what is good or right, and for whom. These implications, which seem obvious once they are stated, come to light only when organizational learning is stripped of its normative aura and considered as subject to evaluation in particular contexts on the basis of particular criteria of goodness or rightness. In short, we cannot escape the need to declare what kinds of organizational learning we will take to be desirable or undesirable and why.

### Do Real-world Organizations Learn Productively?

In order to speak of an organization learning, we must see it as a more or less coherent agent. And we must also see it as capable of acting rationally, at least in the sense of being able to remember past events, analyze alternatives, conduct experiments, and evaluate the results of action. But some authors claim that these attributions have little or no validity for organizations as we find them in the world. We categorize their doubts in terms of threats to coherent action, valid inference, and efficacy.

**Threats to coherent action** Some theorists have argued that organizations are actually pluralistic systems, little more than stage settings for performances by agents such as professions, disciplines, or social groupings that by their very nature cut across organizational boundaries. Some authors see organization as political systems, made up of subgroups, each with its own interests, freedoms, and powers, crucially engaged in battles for control or avoidance of control and incapable of functioning holistically as agents of learning (Crozier, 1963). In his middle period, March, along with various coauthors (Cohen and March, 1974; March and Olsen, 1976), proposed that organizations are inherently chaotic, at best organized anarchies. His "theory of the garbage can" presents decision-making in terms of ideas, interests, images, and values in search of problems, rather than in terms of problem solvers actively searching for ideas, images, and values. Where the garbage can is in operation, it is hard to see how organizations can be considered capable of coherent action or inquiry.

Again, these lines of argument appear to have had more weight 20 years ago in the full flush of the reaction against unreflective theories of organizational rationality (e.g., Perrow, 1979) than they do at present. Although attributions of organizational incoherence still present themselves as sources of doubt about claims made in the name of organizational learning, they tend no longer to be taken a priori as reasons for outright rejection of the idea. Rather, it seems, there is a growing sentiment that the degree of coherence manifested in organizational action or inquiry is an empirical matter to be ascertained at particular places and times. A case in point is March's transition from viewing organizations as "organized anarchies" to the far more modulated position he has expressed in his more recent writings, where he suggests that there are periods in which institutional reform can be pursued through "integrative processes . . . that treat conflict of interest as the basis for deliberation and authoritative decision rather than bargaining" (p. 142).

**Threats to valid inference**   Across the wide-ranging descriptions of organizational learning processes presented in scholarly literature, there is a consistent emphasis on rational inference, inference in the form of lesson drawing from observations of past experience, inference about the causal connections between actions and outcomes, and inference from cycles of trial and error. A number of authors, including some of those noted above, base their skepticism on "threats to valid inference" which seem to them to make real-world organizational learning a dubious proposition.

March, who defines organizational learning as "encoding inferences from history into routines that guide behavior" (Leavitt and March, 1988, p. 319), has been prolific in identifying threats to the validity of such inferences. For example (pp. 322–3), he underlines the importance of "competence traps," wherein organizations falsely project into the future the strategies of action that have worked for them in the past. He calls attention to various sources of ambiguity that undermine organizational judgments of success or failure:

> The lessons of experience are drawn from a relatively small number of observations in a complex, changing ecology of learning organizations. What has happened is not always obvious, and the causality of events is difficult to untangle. What an organization should expect to achieve, and thus the difference between success and failure, is not always clear. (p. 323)

He describes instances of "superstitious learning" that "occur when the subjective experience of learning is compelling, but the connections between actions and outcomes are misspecified" (p. 325).

March also identifies a "dilemma of learning" that constitutes a family of threats to valid inference. When learning proceeds gradually through "small, frequent changes and inferences formed from experience with them," then a likely outcome is the reinforcement or marginal change of existing routines. Such behavior "is likely to lead to random drift rather than improvement" (Lounamaa and March, 1987). On the other hand, when organizations learn from "low probability, high consequence events," then inferences about them are often "muddied with conflict over formal responsiblity, accountability, and liability" (Leavitt and March, 1988, p. 334). The upshot is that

> learning does not always lead to intelligent behavior. The same processes that yield experiential wisdom produce superstitious learning, competence traps, and erroneous inferences. (p. 335)

In this line of argument, March treats learning in the narrow sense of drawing lessons from history as an alternative to other models of decision making, such as rational choice, bargaining, and selection of variations. He argues that under some circumstances learning may prove inferior to its alternatives; although he adds the caveat that the alternatives may also make mistakes, and it is, therefore, "possible to see a role for routine-based, history-dependent, target-oriented organizational learning" (p. 336). (From our point of view, all of March's alternate strategies may enter into the processes of *inquiry* around which we build our broader approach to organizational learning. The relative vulnerabilties of lesson drawing from history would be relevant, not to the general question of the cognitive capability for learning in real-world organizations, but to the problem of choosing, in any given context, what strategy of inquiry to pursue.)

A very different kind of threat to the validity of inference in organizational inquiry stems from the observation that organizational learning depends on the interpretation of events, which depends, in turn, on frames, the major story lines through which organizational inquirers set problems and make sense of experience. Framing is essential to interpretive judgments, but because frames themselves are unfalsifiable, organizational inquirers may be trapped within self-referential frames. Padgett (1992) writes that "the collectively constructed frame or 'membrane' through which information and rewards are assembled and received" is an "axiomatic construction of the world" that is "reciprocally tied to the constitution of the observer." Communication across divergent, self-referential frames is bound to be problematic.

However, Schön and Rein (1994) explore the frame conflicts that underlie persistent policy disputes, for example, those that revolve around welfare, homelessness, or the costs and benefits of advanced technology. They argue that in actual policy practice inquirers may be capable of reflective inquiry into the frames that underlie their divergent positions and can sometimes hammer out, in particular situations, a pragmatic resolution of their conflicting frames.

**Threats to effective action**   Even if organizational inquirers are sometimes able to draw valid inferences from historical experience or current observation, their inferences may not be converted to effective action. A number of contemporary researchers (Fiol and Lyles, 1985; Kim, 1993) call attention to the fact that learning outcomes may be fragmented or situational and may never enter into the organizational mainstream. In earlier research, proponents of the "behavioral theory of the firm" (Cyert and March, 1963; Simon, 1976) described dysfunctional patterns of organizational behavior that undermine productive organizational learning. They noted that organizations depend on control systems which set up conflicts between rule setters and rule followers, which leads to cheating and that in such an organizational world, "everyone is rational and no one can be trusted."

"Fragmented" learning outcomes are closely related to the "conditions for error" that we described in part II. And the dysfunctional, defensive patterns of behavior described by Simon, Cyert, and the early March are closely related to the patterns we have ascribed to limited learning systems. The question is how we should view such phenomena. Should we consider them along the lines of the behavioral theory of the firm, as pervasive and inherent features of organizational life which it is the business of organizational researchers to "discover" rather than to change? Or should we treat them as critically important impediments to productive learning that call for and may be malleable in response to, double-loop inquiry?

## CONCLUSION

Our review of the two-pronged literature of organizational learning leaves us with challenges to the beneficence, the feasibility, and the meaningfulness of organizational learning. Proponents of the learning organization are not worried about the meaningfulness of organizational learning and take its desirability to be axiomatic. They prescribe a variety of enablers through which they claim that organizations can enhance their capability for productive learning, but they do not inquire into the gaps that separate reasonable prescription from effective implementation.

Skeptical researchers into organizational learning present, from a variety of perspectives, important reasons for doubt. Some of them have raised questions about the paradox inherent in the claim that organizations learn, which hinges on assumptions about relationships among individual, interpersonal, and higher levels of social aggregation. Other writers have challenged the desirability of organizational learning, arguing that organizations may learn in ways that foster evil ends or reinforce the status quo, or arguing that the ideal of the learning organization may be used to support a subtler and darker form of managerial control. Still other researchers observe and categorize phenomena that function as impediments to valid inference and effective action.

The problems raised by the two branches of the literature are largely complementary: what one branch treats as centrally important, the other tends to ignore. Both branches do concern themselves with the capability of real-world organizations to draw valid and useful inferences from experience and observation and to convert such inferences to effective action. But authors of prescriptive bent tend to assume, uncritically, that such capabilities can be activated through the appropriate enablers, and learning skeptics tend to treat observed impediments as unalterable facts of organizational life.

In the next chapter we consider these challenges in the light of the theory-of-action perspective.

## Notes

1   Draws heavily from Chris Argyris and Donald Schön (1996).

## References

Argyris, C. and Schön, D. 1996, *Organisational Learning II*, Reading MA., Addison-Wesley, pp. 180–98.

Bendix, R., 1956, *Work and Authority in Industry*, New York, Harper and Row.

Bowman, E., 1994, "Next Steps for Corporate Strategy," *Advances in Strategic Management*, Shrivastava, P., Stubbart, C., Huff, A., and Dutton, J., (eds), Greenwich, Conn,: JAI Press, Inc.

Burgelman, R., 1994, "Fading Memories: A Process Theory of Strategic Business Exit in Dynamic Environments," *Administrative Sciences Quarterly*, 39, March, pp. 24–56.

Campbell, D., 1969, "Variation and Selective Retention in Socio-Cultural Evolution," *General Systems*, 16, pp. 69–85.

Cohen, M. D., and March, J. G., 1974, *Leadership and Ambiguity*, Princeton, Carnegie Foundation for the Advancement of Teaching.

Crozier, M., 1963, 1964, *The Bureaucratic Phenomenon*, Chicago, Ill., University of Chicago Press.

Cyert, R. M., and March, J. G., 1963, *A Behavioral Theory of the Firm*, Englewood Cliffs, N.J., Prentice-Hall.

Fiol, C. M. and Lyles, M. A., 1985, "Organizational Learning," *Academy of Management Review*, 10, pp. 803–13.

Garvin, D., 1993, "Building a Learning Organization," *The Harvard Business Review*, July–August, 71, 4, pp. 78–91.

Hayes, R. H., Wheelwright, S. C., and Clark, K. B., 1988, *Dynamic Manufacturing: Creating a Learning Organization*, New York, The Free Press.

Herrnstein, R. J., 1991, "Experiments on Stable Suboptimality in Individual Behavior," *Learning and Adaptive Economic Behavior*, 81, 2, pp. 360–4.

Hirschman, A., 1970, *Exit, Voice, and Loyalty: Responses to Decline in Firms, Organizations, and States*, Cambridge, Mass., Harvard University Press.

Holland, J. H., and Miller, J. H., 1991, "Artificial Adaptive Agents in Economic Theory," *Learning and Adaptive Economic Behavior*, 81, 2, pp. 365–70.

Huber, G. P., 1989, "Organizational Learning: An Examination of the Contributing Processes and a Review of the Literature," prepared for the NSF-sponsored Conference on Organizational Learning, Carnegie-Mellon University, May 18–20.

Jones, A. M., and Hendry, C., 1992, *The Learning Organization: A Review of Literature and Practice*, Coventry, U.K., Warwick Business School, University of Warwick.

Kim, D., 1993, "Creating Learning Organizations: Understanding the Link Between Individual and Organizational Learning," OL&IL Paper v3.5, MIT Sloan School of Management, Massachusetts Institute of Technology, Cambridge, Mass.

Kunda, G., 1992, *Engineering Culture*, Philadelphia, Temple University Press.

Leavitt, B., and March, J. G., 1988, "Organizational Learning," *Annual Review of Sociology*, 14, pp. 319–40.

Lounamaa, P., and March, J. G., 1987, "Adaptive Coordination of a Learning Team," *Management Science*, 33, pp. 107–23.

March, J. G., and Olsen, J., 1976, *Ambiguity and Choice in Organizations*, Bergen, Norway, Universitetsforlaget.

March, J., and Olsen, J., 1995, *Democratic Governance*, The Free Press.

Marin, D., 1993, "Learning and Dynamic Comparative Advantage: Lessons from Austria's Postwar Pattern of Growth for Eastern Europe," paper prepared for the 17th Economic Policy Panel, Copenhagen, April, 22–23.

Minsky, M., 1987, *The Society of Mind*, New York, Simon and Schuster.

Nelson, R., and Winter, S. G., 1982, *An Evolutionary Theory of Economic Change*, Cambridge, Mass., The Belknap Press of Harvard University Press.

Padgett, J. F., 1992, "Learning from (and about) March," *Organization Science*, 3, February, pp. 744–8.

Perrow, C., 1979, *Complex Organizations: A Critical Essay*, New York, Random House.

Polanyi, M., 1967, *The Tacit Dimension*, New York, Doubleday (Anchor).

Pressman, J., and Wildavsky, A., 1973, *Implementation*, Berkeley, University of California Press.

Rodwin, L., and Schön, D. A. (eds), 1995, *Rethinking the Development Experience: Essays Provoked by the Work of Albert Hirschman*, Washington, D.C., The Brookings Institution.

Schein, E., 1985, 1992, *Organizational Culture and Leadership*, San Francisco, Jossey-Bass.

Schön, D. A., and Rein, M., 1994, *Frame Reflection: Toward the Resolution of Intractable Controversies*, New York, Basic Books.

Senge, P., 1993, *The Fifth Discipline: The Art and Practice of the Learning Organization*, New York, Doubleday.

Simon, H., 1976, *The Sciences of the Artificial*, Cambridge, Mass., MIT Press.

Ulrich, D., Jick, T., and Von Glinow, M. A., 1993, "High-Impact Learning: Building and Diffusing Learning Capability," *Organizational Dynamics*, Autumn, pp. 52–66.

Van Maanen, J., 1988, *Tales of the Field*, Chicago, University of Chicago Press.

# Part I

*Organizational Defenses*

a new chip set). These opportunities, initially recognized or tolerated by top management, were, according to Burgelman, internal variations. They were eventually selected by Intel's internal environment, and they eventually contributed to the technological basis for its microprocessor business. Intel also learns to shift its scarce manufacturing capacity from DRAM to microprocessor technology, and Intel's top management eventually learns to redefine Intel as a microprocessor company.

But, as Burgelman tells it, the Intel story is also one of failure to learn or of inertial delays in learning. Burgelman frames this side of the story in terms of six puzzling questions around which he structures his analysis. We focus on four of these.

1  Why did Intel, the first successful mover in DRAMS, fail to capitalize on and defend its early lead?
2  How did it happen that the bulk of Intel's business had shifted away from DRAMS, and DRAM market share was allowed to dwindle, while top management, even in 1984, was still thinking of DRAMs as a strategic business for the company?
3  How was it possible that middle-level managers could take actions that were not in line with the official corporate strategy?
4  Why did it take Intel's top management almost a year to complete the exit from DRAMs after the November 1984 decision not to market 1 Meg DRAMs? (pp. 29–30)

These questions point to a series of strategic mistakes that Intel seemingly made and to inertial delays in its attempts to reconcile its formal strategy to changing competitive conditions and to convert its new strategic intent into action. Such mistakes and delays are to be understood as failures in the timely detection and correction of significant errors (surprises or mismatch of outcomes to expectations). However, there is some ambiguity and perhaps ambivalence in Burgelman's treatment of his puzzles. He certainly does frame them in terms of Intel's apparent failure to take effective, timely action or to match its thought to a changing reality. But he also suggests that in certain respects Intel's delayed responses were functional. He speculates, for example, that Intel

> would probably have done worse if it had simply divested the DRAM business and entered the new business through acquisition . . . [because it would have thereby] failed to capitalize on the full potential of its distinctive competencies in DRAMs, [some of which] could be effectively deployed in the microprocessor business . . . (p. 52)

This ambiguity plays an important role in the discussion that follows.

Burgelman's approach to his puzzles has both an historical and a systems dimension. He argues that Intel secured a strong competitive advantage in the early days of the DRAM business on the basis of its distinctive technical competence in designing, building, and manufacturing the DRAM technology. He argues further that the early successes of DRAM caused Intel's corporate strategy to be dominated by its DRAM technology. He postulates a microtheory of success and failure along the lines of March's "competence trap": When a pattern of factors is clearly related to a firm's understanding of its success, this pattern tends to be reinforced and thus to persevere, even after it ceases to be effective in the competitive business environment.

Burgelman describes several phenomena that reinforced established patterns associated with Intel's earlier success:

● the self-interest of business unit heads who had considerable latitude for decision-making yet had no interest in putting themselves out of business;

- the "bounded rationality" that kept top or middle managers from anticipating the competitive market dynamics of product and manufacturing technology that would squeeze out Intel's share of the DRAM market; and
- top management's "emotional attachment" to the DRAM business, which made it reluctant to get out of that business, just as Ford would be reluctant to "decide that it should get out of the car business." (p. 41)

In contrast to the factors that kept Intel's top management from letting go of its attachment to the DRAM business and its image of Intel as a "memory company," Burgelman postulates an "internal selective environment" made up of "structural and strategic contexts shaping strategic actions" on the part of middle managers. In the Intel case, middle managers used their discretionary freedoms to take actions that had the effect of opening up new business opportunities. For example, they pursued the development of technological off-shoots of the DRAM business that would lay the groundwork for microprocessors. And they allocated scarce manufacturing capacity to favor microprocessors over DRAMs, making use of the established corporate rule that manufacturing capacity should be allocated so as to "maximize margin-per-wafer-start" (p. 43), even while top management continued to support the view that Intel should remain in the DRAM business. In these and related ways, middle managers gradually undermined the position of the existing DRAM business and helped "dissolve," as Burgelman puts it, the earlier strategic context of the firm.

Burgelman calls his perspective "inside-out." He tells how Intel's external business environment created conditions – changes in the market and DRAMs becoming a commodity – to which Intel responded with decreasing effectiveness. But he treats the "inside" as crucial. Unlike other writers, especially economists, who relegate inside activities largely to a black box, Burgelman opens up the box. He sees that as Intel sought to maintain its competitive advantage by acting in ways that were consistent with its perception of its distinctive competence, it did and failed to do things that actually led to its competitive disadvantage. For example, although Intel's top managers did realize that DRAM had gone from a premium-priced to a commodity product (the price signals were rather clear), they persisted in believing that they could regain the lead by applying their traditional strengths in process technology to come up with innovative products that would be premium-priced niche products at first but would have to be adopted eventually by the entire market. The moment DRAMs became a commodity, Intel's strategy of being the first to introduce premium-priced products into the market became outmoded. Yet top management acted as if this were not the case.

In addition, Burgelman suggests that middle managers believed top management was closed to constructive confrontation about their emotional attachment to the DRAM business. From our perspective, the middle managers were making attributions about top management's openness to learning. From the data in the case, we infer that they never tested these attributions. In a discussion with Argyris, Burgelman confirmed this inference. He said, in effect:

> Given the status and power of the process development people, anyone who went into a meeting to propose a view different from theirs would be unlikely to carry the day. Furthermore, top managers were seen by middle managers as believing that Intel could not make changes away from DRAMs. Top management was seen as unsure.

This behavior provides a partial explanation of top management's "blindness": they were never confronted with data that would help them realize the impact of their behavior. Burgelman's explanation focuses on the top management's uncertainty and, in the face of that uncertainty, its resistance to change. We would focus, in addition, on middle managers' actions that helped to keep top management from realizing the full implications of the shift in the DRAM business, which, in turn, let top managers act in ways middle managers explained as resistance to change. Burgelman focuses on the self-sealing processes of the top managers, not on those created by the middle managers. If an intervention were designed to interrupt the limited learning processes revealed by the Intel case, it would fail if it were one-sided.

Burgelman reports that Intel's top management encouraged constructive confrontation. Andy Grove (then COO, now CEO) told managers at all levels that decisions should be data-driven and that power and emotional biases should play no role in decision-making. We hypothesize, nevertheless, that middle managers' attributions to the top were not openly discussed and analyzed in ways that would test their validity and allow them to be corrected if they proved mistaken.

Burgelman describes an additional domain of undiscussables. He notes that when DRAMs became a commodity, manufacturing capability became the dominant success factor. Yet process development (TD) people continued to downgrade manufacturing and distance themselves from it. TD people continued to frame problems in mainly scientific terms, treating manufacturing people as "tweakers." The manufacturing people reacted by developing a "not invented here" (NIH) syndrome. Gordon Moore, then CEO, reacted to this interdepartmental rivalry by placing both groups in geographical proximity in order to foster greater cooperation between them. Moore had experienced similar problems at Fairchild and wanted to avoid them now at Intel, an attempt to learn from his earlier experience. Burgelman reports that this strategy was at first effective but became much less effective when competitive pressures made the differences between TD and manufacturing much more salient.

Burgelman also observes organizational defenses at work in the relationship between upper-level middle managers and the Board. By 1980, when the company's total market share in DRAMs was less than 3 percent, these managers saw the handwriting on the wall. Yet they would learn of board meetings where Moore, then CEO, and Gelbach, the head of marketing, would defend continued expenditures on DRAM – Moore, because he saw DRAMs as the company's "technology driver" and Gelbach, because he believed Intel had to offer its customers a one-stop semiconductor shopping list. Andy Grove (then COO) remained silent. As a result of such board-level interactions, middle managers were frustrated.

These multileveled undiscussables reinforced by organizational defensive routines would make Grove's advocacy of "constructive confrontation" sound more like espoused theory than theory-in-use, namely, his view that "one of the toughest challenges is to make people see that their 'self-evident truths' are no longer true," or "organizations should practice creative destruction of routines that are no longer effective."

Burgelman told Argyris that top management recognized the organizational defensiveness which they saw as existing primarily at the level of some middle managers. As far as we can tell, top management did not examine this defensiveness directly and forthrightly with the middle managers. If so, we have top managers acting to reinforce middle managers' unawareness of their impact on those at the top.

Top management attempted to deal with interdepartmental conflicts by bringing departments into geographic proximity, defining rules to reduce the conflicts, and providing incentive systems that would do so. Over the long haul, none of these strategies worked, although some of them were effective in the first instance.

**Burgelman's analysis analyzed**   We would say that there is only partial truth in Burgelman's hypothesis that top management persisted in its commitment to the DRAM business because of emotional attachment to it and uncertainty about its importance. What is needed is an explanation of how subordinates colluded with their superiors to create domains of undiscussables that would inhibit learning around these issues.

Like Burgelman, we also try to understand how it comes about that organizations do not detect and correct significant errors, but we seek to go further. We want to understand how it comes about that Intel or other organizations are unaware that they are unable to detect and correct significant errors. The inability to detect and correct error is skilled because we can connect it to a theory-in-use; hence, it is "skilled incompetence". The existence of skilled incompetence means the unawareness of the inability, and unawareness is also connected to a theory-in use – hence, it is "skilled unawareness".

We would ask, for example, what is included in this concept of "emotional attachment"? What is the theory-in-use that produces such behavior? Is Burgelman using the concept to mean that emotional attachment always causes blindness? If not, what would be the difference between the two types of emotional attachment?

We would add an additional puzzle to those queries with which Burgelman begins his paper: How could the conditions named in his four puzzles hold when top management espoused a theory of management intended to prevent them from occurring?

To solve this puzzle would require much more directly observable data about what was actually said when people at Intel discussed these issues. For example, how did the middle-level managers craft their conversations? Did they ease in so much that their points were obscured? Or did they become so confrontational that the others could discount their views because they were obviously emotional?

Did the middle managers engage top managers in a dialogue about the attributions they were making about them? Did they explore their attributions that these issues were undiscussable, and their undiscussability also undiscussable? Did they explore their attributions that even if these issues were discussed, top management would be uninfluenced? Did they ever explore whether the top managers were unaware of the "blindness" that middle managers attributed to them?

Burgelman states that Grove did not at first believe that the lag time was as long or the inertia as deep as Burgelman concludes they were. To his credit, however, Grove conducted his own investigation and found that Burgelman's estimate was better than his own. We might ask, then, what Grove actually did. He questioned the relevant players and, months after the decision to exit the DRAM business, they gave him information they had not told him or that he had not listened to before.

Burgelman's explanations of the puzzling phenomena of delayed or failed organizational learning do not account for such phenomena developing in an organization in which cultural context, top management support, and the sheer brightness of the Intel managers would seem to militate against their occurring.

If Intel failed to capitalize on and defend its early lead in the DRAM business, for example, what actually produced the failure? To say that it was top management's emotional attachment to DRAMs is to pinpoint a small group within an abstract explanation. How did top management actually behave? How did the middle-level managers confront top management's emotional attachment, if they actually did? How did they attempt to change it? In other words, we hypothesize that the puzzling phenomena of delay and inertia were caused both by top management's emotionality and blindness and by middle managers' ways of dealing with them, that is, by bypassing these issues and acting as if they were not doing so.

We would also suggest that an operational definition of a more complete explanation of the puzzles could be used to design actions to change the causes of inertia. The causes Burgelman identifies – such as top management's emotional attachment to DRAMs, interdepartmental rivalries between TD and manufacturing, self-reinforcing processes that maintained outmoded strategic frames – are stated at a level of abstraction that cannot be used to change the organization or to enable the organization to learn to detect and correct its errors.

In our view, the fifth puzzle we introduced, how it came about that Intel's management was unaware of its inability to detect and correct its errors, underlies the other four.

Burgelman concludes his analysis by advancing a set of propositions, some of which, in the light of our own analysis, we find misleading. His first proposition states:

> The stronger a firm's distinctive technological competence, the stronger the firm's tendency to continue to rely on it in the face of industry-level changes in the basis of competitive advantage. (p. 48)

We would add, however, that this proposition holds or holds more strongly whenever organizational defensive routines at top- or middle-management levels or between departments reinforce the failure to face up to industry-level changes and to legitimize the bypassing and cover up of such reinforcement.

Burgelman's third proposition states:

> Firms whose internal selection criteria accurately reflect external selection pressures are more likely to strategically exit from some businesses than firms whose internal selection criteria do not accurately reflect external selection pressures. (p. 50)

We would add:

> Firms whose internal selection criteria reflect and deal with external selection pressure should be observed to have minimal defensive routines (of the sort we have described earlier).

Burgelman's sixth proposition states:

> Firms that have strategically exited from a business are likely to have a better understanding of the links between their distinctive competences and the basis of competition in the industries in which they remain active than firms that have not strategically exited from a business.

We believe this proposition is valid under the condition that organizational defensive routines dominate the examination of errors that are embarrassing and threatening to key players. It should not hold for firms that are not dominated by such defensive routines; these firms should have a better understanding before, rather than after, exit.

In sum, Burgelman's analysis of the Intel case focuses on puzzles rooted mainly in the organization's failures to detect and correct error:

- its failure to follow up its early lead in the DRAM business;
- its delay in matching its strategic ideas and self-image to the changing business reality; and
- its inertia in completing its exit from the DRAM business once it had decided to do so.

Burgelman's explanations of these puzzles hinge on the phenomena of top management's emotional attachment to the DRAM business, its bounded rationality and blindness concerning the mismatch of its strategic context to the changing business reality, the power and self-interest of business-unit managers associated with the DRAM business, and the rivalry between technological development and manufacturing departments. But each of these causes raises questions related to another puzzle: how did it happen that Intel's managers were unaware of their inability to detect and correct their errors? This question points, in turn, to the layer of organizational phenomena that we regard as critically important both to the explanation of existing patterns of organizational learning and to the design of interventions aimed at changing those patterns, that is, the organizational defensive routines, and the O-I processes that constrained interpersonal inquiry between top- and middle-level managers, and between departments, thereby reinforcing a lack of awareness of the gap between Intel's strategic context and its changing business reality.

In a private communication to the authors in which he responds to an earlier version of our discussion of his article, Burgelman stresses the uncertainty with which Intel's top managers were dealing at the time they were grappling with the possibility of exiting from the DRAM business. He argues that their inertial delays and the defensive routines that reinforced those delays were actually functional since they enabled Intel to exploit in their microprocessors certain technological advances made by the DRAM process developers and also to prevent TD/DRAM people from leaving the company. He observes, in part:

> I like to emphasize that one of the key points of my study is that it is very difficult for top and middle managers to examine at length what the strategic situation is [that is] faced by an organization in very dynamic environments. So much is going on simultaneously that the kind of exhaustive "airing out" of the strategic situation is probably unachievable. So, while I believe your hypothesis is a plausible one and that perhaps more effort should be spent on airing out strategic situations, I also believe (1) that we do not know enough yet about how "defensive routines" come about (perhaps my study contributes to precisely that!) and (2) that it is improbable that there is no cost at all associated with removing defensive routines. I submit that trying to remove defensive routines altogether might very well paralyze organizations operating in dynamic environments.

In this passage, Burgelman argues, as he further notes, that in dynamic and uncertain environments there may be considerable value in "strategic neglect."

The weakness we find in this argument is the following. We agree that inertial delays in a firm's response to a mismatch between its formal strategy and its actual strategic situation may be retrospectively discovered, on occasion, to be functional. But these delays may just as easily prove to be dysfunctional. How are managers to distinguish between functional and dysfunctional strategic neglect so long as they keep themselves unaware of their discordant beliefs and keep the crucial and threatening issues undiscussable?

Why, moreover, should we assume that the opening up of defensive routines would make it impossible to achieve deliberately the same benefits as those that were inadvertently achieved (through lack of awareness)? For example, Intel's top management could have chosen to keep its TD/DRAM capability on the very grounds of its uncertainty about its possible future utility, even in the face of a clear decision to exit the DRAM business.

Why then should we assume that the airing out of the strategic situation would have to be exhaustive (certainly, a recipe for paralysis!) when it could be limited to just those dilemmas that constituted the main bone of contention between top- and upper-level middle managers? One need not know just how defensive routines come about (although we believe our theory offers some insight into that question) in order to see how they constrain productive inquiry into critically important strategic issues.[3]

### Main Points Drawn from Our Analysis of the First Two Studies

Reviewing our discussion of these two retrospective studies of "naturally occurring" organizational learning, we find:

losses might be delayed until the next quarter. Upper management responded to such discoveries by introducing tighter controls and information systems.

These consequences are more general. Whenever bypasses and cover-ups are discovered, the usual remedial action is to tighten controls, usually by including more detailed specifications. The difficulty with this strategy is that as the specifications mount, they:

1   violate the idea of profit center autonomy and responsibility; and
2   become so cumbersome that they tend to fall of their own weight.

We conclude, then, that as organizations move from centralized to decentralized policies and practices, a characteristic sequence develops over time:

1   Superiors and subordinates tend to report satisfaction and enhanced performance because of their newly delegated decision rights. A minority may resist taking charge because they are doubtful that top management "really means it" and/or because they are not yet confident of their own abilities.
2   As time goes by, issues surface over which strong differences in views come into play and cause conflicts. These consequences activate the participants' Model I theories-in-use and the organizational defensive routines that accompany them. They lead to superiors taking charge, thereby appearing, in the view of subordinates, to violate the concept of decentralization. The subordinates, in turn, may distance themselves and cover up. This, in the eyes of superiors, violates the responsibility they must assume if decentralization is to be effective. How often have we heard superiors warn subordinates that there must be "no surprises"? This warning applies not only to performance results but also to the use of organizational defensive routines.
3   Model I social virtues become strengthened. This, in turn, strengthens the defensive routines at all levels of the organization. For example, managers help and support by telling others what they believe will be positive and, therefore, reduce their hurt feelings. Managers show respect by not confronting the reasoning processes other managers use. Individuals who strive to be strong (advocating their positions in order to win), to be honest (not to lie), and to show integrity ("stick to one's principles"), will likely do so around issues that are relatively objective or where the control procedures make such action transparent. Whenever issues go underground and become undiscussable, Model I views of strength, honesty, and integrity lead to polarized positions that inhibit double-loop learning at the interpersonal level.
4   A perverse sense of trust – namely, trust coupled with mutual distancing – develops, making that distancing undiscussable.
5   This produces a space of free movement that allows behavior that violates organizational norms to emerge – specifically, ways of achieving results that meet the letter but violate the spirit of the policy.
6   When upper-level managers become aware of these consequences, they tighten controls, in turn violating the concept of decentralization.

Since Cordiner's time, advances in information technology have made it possible to develop tighter and more efficient controls and bring to the surface actions that would otherwise remain underground. As the rigidities of the self-fueling, antilearning processes become increasingly difficult to hide, upper-level managers are beginning to realize that managerial practices, if they are to succeed, require reeducation that includes a focus on individuals' Model I theories-in-use. It is at this point that organizational theories-in-use and interpersonal theories-in-use become interdependent.

It is ironic to note that when the connection between the organizational and interpersonal theories-in-use was not made, the reeducational programs became known as "charm schools." Now, when the connection is seen as more crucial than before, one often hears, "This is too difficult!" or "Is it really necessary?" or "Isn't this dangerous?" In the early days, the superficiality inherent in an incomplete approach to reeducation not only led to limited learning, it was also used by superiors and subordinates to cover themselves. Today superiors and subordinates may seek to protect themselves by raising the specter of "danger" and "Pandora's box." We believe that if concepts such as decentralization, empowerment, and personal responsibility are to preserve and encourage continuous improvement, the connection between the organizational and the interpersonal will have to be made.

## Activity Costing

The following is an account of Robert Kaplan's attempts to introduce firms to activity-based costing (ABC), an information system aimed at improving organizational performance by enabling more precise attribution of costs and profitability to product lines (Argyris and Kaplan, 1994). Kaplan and his colleagues have developed an explicit structure for sponsoring and implementing an ABC project. Typically they begin with an activity-based cost model of organizational expenses and profitability which often reveals "many unexpectedly higher cost activities, processes, products, and customers" (p. 7) and proceeds to an action phase in which "management acts on the insights revealed by the ABC model to produce improved organizational performance" (p. 8). Kaplan and his colleagues distinguish key roles in this process: advocates for change, sponsors who have the ability to approve the required changes, change agents who take on the task of proving the concept and developing the more accurate information it requires, and targets, "the person or group whose behavior . . . is expected to change based on the newly revealed information" (p. 8).

Kaplan and his colleagues learned that they would regularly encounter resistance to action on improved information made available by ABC. Successful introduction of the system in one division of a firm was often followed by failure to disseminate it throughout the firm. One of Kaplan's manager-clients told him:

> I'm not convinced yet that the organization is geared to making difficult decisions based on information. It took us five years to drop a product line that we knew was not making money for us. If we're not prepared to take tough decisions, we don't need a fancy new information system.

In response to such resistance, Kaplan worked with some of his clients to develop "organizational enablers," such as performance measures keyed to incentives, formation of task forces and introduction of group training exercises. But these enablers often proved insufficient to elicit managers' internal commitment to the changes necessary for successful implementation of ABC. Subtle forces still exist inhibiting the acceptance of new ideas whenever technical theories challenge existing organizational norms and long-established ways of doing business, thereby threatening or embarrassing "people who have much of their professional and self-feelings identified with decisions, actions, and organizational structures implemented in the past" (p. 13). For example, the analysis may reveal that "certain favored product lines or customers are highly unprofitable," and product managers responsible for introducing and maintaining these lines or the account managers responsible for the highly unprofitable customers "become threatened by the quantitative and defensible evidence of their value-destroying activities" (p. 16). Or managers may be embarrassed "by the explicit recognition of excess capacity in areas under their authority," or more generally, by the recognition that their traditional cost and performance measurement systems have "led to bad decisions...and a lack of focus on wasteful activities" (p. 17). The experience of threat or embarrassment typically gives rise to defensive reasoning, as illustrated by the following.

- It is better to fail with existing procedures than to fail trying something new, especially where business is okay and no one is really up against the wall. Believe me, I know.
- People are more used to managing expenses than the behavior that drives the expenses. That's the reality of organizational life.

When champions of ABC seek to overcome such defenses, they often adopt strategies of change that exacerbate the defenses. In one instance, a top manager bypassed divisional managers, going directly to the factory to develop the ABC model, without seeking divisional managers' approval or precommitment to the changes that would be required once the large number of unprofitable products were revealed. He avoided early confrontation with these managers by concentrating on building a defensible model of operations, inoculating himself against the resistance he anticipated by asking the controller and data processing manager to make an independent confirmation of the analysis. Ultimately, the division's executives still rejected the analysis. And by framing the debate as "a conflict between an analytic, rational approach versus the executives' ignorance and resistance to change, he provided himself with an excuse that absolved him from blame for the lack of effective action," which he had anticipated (p. 17).

Argyris and Kaplan conclude their analysis by observing:

> In every change that involves the introduction of a new technical theory of action whose correct implementation could be embarrassing or threatening, the advocates, sponsors, change agents, and targets who use the generic implementation approach will still face the challenge of dealing with the defensive reasoning of organizational participants, including themselves. (p. 18)

## Studies of TQM

Total quality management (TQM), introduced in Japan by W. Edwards Deming just after World War II, has had a 50-year history. Its transfer to the United States began in earnest in the early 1980s, following American management's awakening to the fact that Japan was outperforming US industry not only in costs but in quality and that Japan's superior performance was due, in no small measure, to its practice of continuous quality improvement based on Deming's theory and methods. Throughout the 1980s, TQM grew steadily in its scope of adoption and prestige. By the early 1990s, however, its popularity had peaked, and what Beer (1994) describes as a "literature of disillusionment" had begun to appear.[4] We discuss two examples of recent essays in which the authors reflect on the mixed record of TQM interventions, the nature of the resistance TQM has provoked, and the limits of the TQM methodology.

Schneiderman (1992) writes as a professional TQM advocate and teacher, drawing on long experience in teaching organizations to implement TQM. His article is addressed to the naysayers, but it also reveals a thoughtful analysis of TQM's limits. He begins with a now familiar description of TQM which includes three main elements:

1  identification and flowcharting of component organizational processes, such as manufacturing, product development, filing, and telephone answering;
2  framing each such process as a partnership of supplier and customer and accompanying it with explicit metrics and standards for its performance; and
3  involving all workers engaged in a process in continuous, unrelenting process
   improvement through the identification and elimination of defects.

Next, Schneiderman reports on his study of "nearly 100 cases of exemplary use of the
PDCA (Plan-Do-Check-Act) cycle." These are some of his main findings:

- The rate of improvement was constant, which Schneiderman interprets in terms of
  the concept of "half-life." A half-life of six months for a process improvement activity
  means that there is a 50 percent reduction in defect level every six months (p. 6).
- As process complexity increased, the rate of continuous improvement declined. This
  was especially true where the "complexity" was "organizational." "With multiple
  managers who are not part of the team and often have conflicting goals, the improvement process slows" (p. 11).
- The complexity of processes most in need of improvement in an organization
  increases with organizational level. Success of the quality movement in Japan led to
  "the natural desire to move improvement activity to the ranks of management," but
  "QC Circles were trained to avoid, if possible, problems that involved human
  behavior, particularly when the behavior was that of others outside of the team, and
  to focus instead on machines, materials, and methods" (p. 21).
- TQM tools applied to complex management problems may produce a "false sense of
  rigor." They seem to "cut through the ambiguity that surrounds complex problems.
  But the ambiguity is real; it is the forced solution that is unreal" (p. 27). Managers like
  other workers "repeatedly make good decisions in complex situations based on their
  experience or gut feel ... [Their solutions] are often better than the descriptions that
  we force-fit into our analytical frameworks" (p. 27). But managers are often caught in
  dilemmas they find unacceptable when their intuitions put them at odds with the
  consensual conclusion that has been reached by a TQM team.
- A more fundamental limit of TQM, as practiced today, is that it fails to address the
  dynamic interactions that exist in complex systems, interactions that make it difficult
  to answer questions about the relative importance of multiple causes of defects in a
  process. Top management struggles with critical processes in which causal linkages
  are at best obscure. Consider the proposition that "increasing compensation will
  reduce labor turnover." What if job satisfaction, not compensation, is the real issue,
  and employees, not wanting to burn their bridges, camouflage the real causes of
  unwanted attrition? Or consider the proposition that "centralization improves efficiency." Why, then, do most reorganizations follow a pendulum that swings between
  centralization and decentralization?

Schneiderman concludes that TQM, as presently practiced, is limited. He even leans
toward Ackoff's (1981) argument that "most current processes are so outdated and incapable of being improved in a timely way that they should be scrapped and replaced with
idealized redesigns." Nevertheless, he believes "the improvement process remains the
same" (p. 35). He states that cross-functional problems of medium complexity can be
remedied, in some cases, through the use of advanced TQM tools (the "7-management
tools"), though "it is important to use them thoughtfully," and "we must remember that
consensus doesn't always lead to the best answer." Finally, he suggests that highly complex,

interactive, dynamic problems which "seem to create the greatest amount of pain both inside and outside our organizations," might yield to the increased use of simulation modeling (p. 39).

Mallinger (1993) describes his experience as "change agent" in a company that proved relatively ineffective in its attempts to implement TQM. He spent a one-year sabbatical as participant/observer of a manufacturing division in a multibillion dollar Fortune 500 company. The corporate CEO, in response to financial and schedule pressures, announced a reorganization that drastically reduced management levels from 9 to 5 and cut management personnel by about 2000 people. The CEO then ordered the manufacturing division to implement TQM.

After five months of training and attempted implementation and an expenditure of $11 million, the TQM program was halted, Mallinger reports, because of "a noticeable lack of transfer of TQM skills presented in training to the rework and delivery schedule problems faced by the company" (p. 11).

A year later, with a much-reduced training staff, the TQM intervention was begun again on the basis of of an iterative approach to data gathering and intervention design. This time, a "lack of tribal knowledge" held by experienced managers, due in part to the lay-offs, led to a rise in skepticism about the process. Mallinger reports, based on numerous discussions with the division vice presidents, that TQM was not a priority and was seen, indeed, as an obstacle. "Although they each acknowledged the need for change, their actual behavior was quite different from their stated objectives" (p. 15). In one case a division vice president who indicated a desire to incorporate TQM as one of his five department goals for the year left a meeting after telling his human resource liaison staff to work out the plan to "fix my people." Apparently, the vice president saw TQM as a set of training techniques to improve the productivity of first-line managers rather than as a "commitment to mutual, proactive team planning." This individual seemed to think he would meet his obligation to be a TQM department, as ordered by the corporate CEO, by head count.

Middle managers also expressed skepticism and distrust, as indicated by comments such as, "Programs come and go around here, as do the people who support them." Shop floor people became increasingly discontented when the lay-offs began and advertised changes failed to occur. They felt their union leaders were joining their managers in taking them "down the road to hell." In one department, upper-level managers who had agreed to become active participants in the transformation process, dropped out of training meetings after the first hour of a twenty-four hour training program, claiming they had emergency meetings to attend. The first-level supervisors inferred that TQM had low priority for senior management and that they themselves had little value for the organization. They increased their skepticism of TQM and their distrust of their senior bosses. "No significant changes in performance within the business unit were reported two weeks, one month, or five months after training, and the intervention was curtailed" (p. 19).

As job insecurity increased with continuing lay-offs, the TQM team were increasingly seen as "hitmen on the prowl for fodder for the next round of reductions-in-force."

Mallinger reports further that he found no evidence that a "risk-taking, empowered environment" was in place. On the contrary, he found a pervasive climate of fear. This was illustrated by a meeting that the TQM team head, the human resources general manager, and the human resources vice president held with the president to brief him on the progress of the Phase II TQM model. The primary agenda was to sell the TQM design to the president rather than address issues of resistance such as those just described. Mallinger states:

> The meeting took on a "we've got the answer now" message. I observed both the VP and GM
> agreeing with the president's philosophy and responding to each of his questions regarding

TQM in a way that suggested that we've got the "bases covered." It was evident to me that the project leader, who made the presentation, was uncomfortable raising substantive issues for fear of embarrassing his bosses. (p. 23)

Mallinger's report of his own behavior at the meeting is also of interest. He states that he "felt a responsibility not to collaborate in the ruse" but was also careful not to discomfort the HR managers. In hindsight, though, he felt he should have been more direct. What he did was to:

indicate to the president that the culture may be resistant to the changes that TQM advocates. His response was immediate: "First you change the system, then the culture will follow." ...The GM strongly agreed with the president, and the discussion of organizational culture ended." (p. 24)

The underlying meaning of what took place in the meeting, as Mallinger saw it, was to "not bring bad news to the President," a pattern he later observed at all levels of management.

The lessons Mallinger draws from this example are several. The include the need to form partnerships between the business unit under study and the elements outside it, to increase organization members' ownership of the TQM process by giving them greater input into its planning, and to encourage subordinates to engage in open discussion of troublesome issues in TQM implementation and in open expression of their fears and hopes for the process. However, Mallinger stops short of suggesting how, in corporate cultures like the one he observed, such lessons might actually be put into practice.

### Roth's Study of Business Process Reengineering in Business Service Companies

George Roth's doctoral dissertation, written at MIT's Sloan School of Management (Roth, 1993), is a detailed analysis of attempts in two business service companies to improve productivity and quality of service through interventions that combined the introduction of new information technology with "business process reengineering". Roth defines this term, following CSC Index Inc., as "the concept of fundamentally changing the way work is performed in order to achieve radical performance improvements in speed, cost, and quality."

Roth undertook a year-long study of the introduction of imaging systems coupled with process reengineering in two insurance company subsidiaries. One of these, which he calls Dover Service Company, managed mutual fund investments for a financial services operation; the other, Harwick, provided service for life insurance policies. Both of these companies had similar work activities: processing paper-based information, answering customers' telephone inquiries, and performing business transactions on computer systems. Both were engaged in reengineering customer service and paper-processing operations through the development of imaging system applications which were intended to take the place of paper processing and were based on the same image system technology.

Roth organizes both of his studies around a stage model of the reengineering process that begins with strategy formulation and proceeds through phases of systems selection, preparation, implementation, and observation of use and outcomes. As he traces the development of the two projects through these stages, he describes the roles, activities, and views of four stakeholder groups:

1   *executives* (CEOs, presidents, COOs, and senior vice presidents), who had a role in formulating strategy and making decisions about imaging systems;

2  *managers*, who had line responsibility for daily business operations,
3  *technologists*, who were responsible for systems specification, development, installation, and operation, and
4  *workers*, the users of the imaging technology, who processed documents, responded to phone calls, and serviced customer requests.

Although the contexts of the two companies and their patterns of systems development and implementation are somewhat different, Roth's findings in the two cases are basically similar.

He finds in both studies that the anticipated benefits in service quality, speed, and productivity did not materialize. At Dover he writes:

> A year later in May 1993, there were many changes but little effect on technological change outcomes. Use of the new account imaging application never resumed. Managers were still uncertain of where imaging system benefits would occur and how they would have a greater role in specifying changes. The Processing Department was allowed to hire only one person and assigned one manager part-time to work on imaging system developments. A new project to front-end scan all incoming documents in the mail room was undertaken and completed. This imaging application provided good statistics and management reports, but it did not produce productivity benefits, and documents continued to be processed in paper form. (p. 167)

At Harwick, Roth reports on outcomes across some eight sub-projects. Across the board, he writes, staffing levels in the two departments he focused on (Customer Service and Universal Life) were reduced by 23 percent, and "imaging system implementation effects on work, workers, and managers were not auspicious" (p. 244).

In Customer Service, Roth reports that one project, "UltraFind," designed to assist consultants in servicing customers over the phone, was found five months after implementation to provide capabilities required by "only one out of fifteen customer calls" (p. 249) and that "UltraFind was simply too slow to provide benefits for consultants' work" (p. 251). In the case of TIP, a paper processing system for company reps, Roth found that "reps required 3.3 times longer to process documents on TIP than to use paper documents and TAA (the preexisting system) (p. 256).

At Universal Life, an image processing application, ULIP (Universal Life Image Processing), replaced paper documents in workers' processing of cash items, franchise updates, loans, and the like. Roth reports that "workers' initial enthusiasm for ULIP waned when they were unable to process documents faster than their previous paper-based methods" (p. 261). Document processing time increased by a factor of 1.8, and questionnaire data showed "deterioration in workers' attitudes and work perceptions" (p. 265). Roth characterizes one application, CC (Correspondence Creation), designed to help word-processing workers by allowing them to select form letters from a menu, as successful. Correspondence consultants showed a 26 percent increase in productivity, and their responses to open-ended questions were more positive than those of any other workers (p. 275). Roth points out, however, that these responses were the exception rather than the norm for workers and managers.

What is especially interesting is not so much that Roth found an absence of anticipated increases in measurable productivity, quality of service, and worker attitude and performance, outcomes that may or may not be typical of the consequences of most business process reengineering, but that he described the interactions among stakeholder groups in the reengineering processes to which he partly attributes the disappointing project outcomes. Roth states that:

The two organizations' inabilities to create conditions in which stakeholders could communicate with one another led to fundamental difficulties in managing technological change and
unexpected negative consequences. Stakeholders in technological change processes were unable
to reconcile underlying assumptions, avoid miscommunications, or create shared meaning for
imaging systems and their organizational implications. As a result, the more powerful stakeholder groups' ideas and agendas were promoted through imaging system activities. Technologists dominated the technological change process. (p. 299)

Roth gives many examples of what he means by "fundamental difficulties" of interaction.
At Dover, for example, a line manager said that "he did not trust technologists because they
withheld information and were unwilling to listen to his suggestions" (p. 157). He found that
the technologists could not be influenced. He wanted his own specialists to help refine and
adapt the application, but he was unable to secure resources for them to do so. Another
manager complained that he relied on the technologists because they had chosen the imaging
system and knew how to implement it, but "they applied [the system] broadly across the
business process, without regard for whether it was appropriate, or for what business changes
were required" (p. 158). Still another manager said that when change issues surfaced, "there
was no process in place for deciding them," meetings were unsatisfactory (because they were
dominated by technologists), and "there was no dialogue outside of the meetings."

What is striking about both of Roth's case examples is that, in spite of the disappointing
data reported by managers and workers and independently ascertained by him, the top
executives declared their projects to be resounding successes. Dwyer, the COO at Harwick,
who had been hired to make organizational improvements, told Roth that "although she was
aware of some difficulties," she believed that business objectives had been met, and she
touted the project's success to the industry at large. At Dover, Bryant, the president, had a
similarly positive evaluation of his reengineering project. Managers believed that Bryant
held this view because he was fed only positive information; the problems were kept from
him. They also believed that Bryant colluded with the masking of negative information
because "he did not create conditions of intense scrutiny and involvement among his staff"
(p. 138). And when lower-level managers tried to blow the whistle on this reporting process,
they were punished. One manager said that she was floored when she saw a report indicating
that the system had "98 percent up time," since she had her own experience of system
failure. The technologist she first approached told her that, if she had problems with the
reporting, she should call the project manager. When she did so, she was told that "it was
reported that way because Craig (the CEO) wanted it that way." This manager concluded
that Bryant had only received information that the project was going well and that the
imaging system's problems and its real impact were never discussed at Bryant's staff
meetings. The manager eventually "withdrew her attention from the imaging project
because 'we aren't getting anywhere with [it] and I have other things to do'" (p. 138).

Roth concludes his analysis as follows:

Technologists had enough power in both organizations to coerce workers and managers to
accept and use applications, but not enough power to assure applications' success. Technologists did, however, wield enough power to report mostly successful results despite contrary
evidence in outcomes. (p. 302)

## Beer's Study of His SHRM Intervention at Alpha Medical

Michael Beer's account of his intervention in the Alpha Medical Corporation (Beer, 1994) is
an unusually full and frank exposition of an attempt to develop, not a one-time change, but

an organization capable of the kind of "continuous learning" suited to "the kind of strategic change required by competitive forces" (p. 6). Beer deliberately sought to bring about the internalization of a continuing organizational learning process that would link "hard" and "soft" elements of the organization. In his view, such a process must be systemic and iterative; it must establish a partnership between upper and lower levels of the organization; and it must "find some means for making normally hidden organizational and managerial behavior transparent" (pp. 7–8). In short, Beer's intervention was directly addressed to the kinds of behavioral resistances the authors, cited earlier, said they encountered when they undertook or observed attempts to undertake interventions based on decentralization and management empowerment, TQM, or reengineering. It can also be seen as an attempt to create what Schein (1992) calls a "learning culture."

In Beer's Strategic Human Resource Management (SHRM) intervention, he hoped to link strategic change to a continuing process of organizational learning in the sense that "experience in implementing the new [strategic] design [would be] used to redesign the organization to align with limitations in human capabilities, or further changes in the environment discovered along the way" (p. 8). Beer began with "strategic profiling," and went on to assess "organizational ability to reframe and implement new strategy matched to changing business realities" (p. 9). These and later steps were conducted by an employees task force made up of "the unit's best employees one or two levels below the top team." This team operated within structures that were designed to promote the discussion of findings and issues that might otherwise remain undiscussable. In the early profiling meeting:

> While management listens, the [task force] sits in the middle of the room and discusses their findings [from investigations of the organization's ability to implement its new strategy], organized into themes. This "fishbowl" discussion, interrupted at the end of each theme for questions of clarification from the top management team, typically goes on for several hours. (p. 10)

The organizational diagnosis, jointly conducted by the task force and top management, went on to identify "key design levers and human resource policies within the unit, including the top team itself, which are at the root of the problems identified by the task force." Subsequently, the participants worked out a vision, philosophy of management, organizational design, and action plan for implementing and managing strategic change (p. 11). Among the "barriers to implementation" identified in this process were several that Beer believes to have been "undoubtedly responsible" for the failure of such enabling interventions as total quality management, reengineering, and employee involvement, including unclear or conflicting strategic priorities; difficulties in how the top team works together, top-down management style, poor interfunctional/divisional coordination, poor up/down communication, and deficiencies in career development and management competencies.

Participants in the SHRM intervention reported that it "allowed us to discuss the undiscussable...[putting] things on the table that would have taken [us] years," giving rise along the way to a sense that "we didn't know what we were getting into" and anxious jokes about the messenger being shot. Beer believes that because the project's data had been generated by employees whom the managers had chosen as the best, the managers accepted the data "as valid and relevant, despite the fact that many issues point to their own effectiveness as managers" (p. 15).

Over the longer term, however, the outcomes of this intervention were viewed as mixed. Some intended objectives were achieved; others were not. Beer's surveys and interviews showed the following pattern. There was high commitment to the process of change at the top of the organization but less at the bottom (p. 16), and there was only modest change in overcoming barriers and accomplishing strategic tasks. The most change was in top-team effectiveness and cross-functional coordination; the least, in employee perception that top management rewards and promotes employees on the basis of their skill in managing and leading others and on their willingness to raise difficult issues with higher management.

Clearly, Beer concludes, top management "had not created a partnership with employees and a sense of group responsibility for producing strategic results" (p. 18). SHRM remained invisible at lower levels of the organization and remained limited by "hierarchical assumptions about how decisions should be made" (p. 17). In all but a few instances, higher management did not review SHRM results and follow them up, mainly, Beer believes, because of "their own discomfort and lack of skill in discussing difficult issues with subordinates" (p. 19). Beer observes that such discussion:

> requires interpersonal competence and management values that the process itself is designed to develop . . . Though SHRM successfully opens a window for open dialogue, it apparently does not develop interpersonal and organizational capability to sustain that dialogue. (p. 20)

Beer's final word on his intervention is that a competitive world requires organizational capacity for self-design, which calls for management processes and skills to "engage in an open, fact-based conversation" about "difficult and often painful" issues. Such skills "have not yet been invented," he believes. They require "interpersonal behavior regarded by many managers as an 'unnatural act' " (p. 22). It remains to be seen, he concludes, "whether these skills can be developed and/or whether organizations must obtain them through selection" (p. 23). In either case, Beer asserts that these are "core skills for an effective organization," whether managers and their consultants recognize them to be so, and "they will be in greater demand as organizational adaptability becomes important in a more competitive world" (p. 23).

## LESSONS FROM THE TWO SETS OF STUDIES

### The Two Gaps

We have examined two sets of studies: the first deals with episodes in the lives of business firms in which organizational learning or adaptation occurred "naturally;" the second deals with interventions designed around various types of enablers that were intended to enhance organizational capability for productive learning.

The first set of studies (Van de Ven and Polley, 1992; Burgelman, 1994) reveal a *gap of explanation*. In both of the organizations studied, there were mixed results; there was some evidence of productive organizational learning, coupled with evidence that the organization had made only a partial or delayed response to data that could and should have been interpreted as calling for a significant change of course. Dynamically conservative, these organizations tended to persist in their previously established patterns of thought and action, and in so persisting, failed to act on what some of their members knew. During critical periods of decision, managers exhibited some patterns of inquiry that were distorted, overly constrained, and ineffective. The researchers take notice of these patterns, but they stop short of emphasizing or exploring them.

The two studies provide incomplete explanations of their mixed results. They do not fully explain first-order errors, such as the firm's failure to bring managerial attention to bear on signs of trouble that were known to insiders in the early stages of the TAP case, or in Burgelman's study, Intel's lagging response to the shift in the DRAM market and its competitive position in that market. They do not at all explain the second-order errors that underlie first-order errors, namely, how key managers remained individually and collectively unaware of the firm's lagging response to important mismatches between the assumptions that guided organizational action and the changing patterns of internal or external reality, and how the organization kept undiscussable the issues raised by knowledge already privately held by some of its members.

The second set of studies (of decentralization during the Cordiner regime at GE, activity-based costing, TQM, reengineering, and SHRM) reveals a *gap of implementation*. The studies show that mixed results also followed from attempts to introduce enablers of productive organizational learning, that is, techniques and information systems (ABC), new formal structures (decentralization and flattening, creation of inquiry units, as in SHRM), principles and procedures for the development of a learning culture (TQM, reengineering, and SHRM). These interventions resulted in only partial or temporary improvement in organizational performance. For example, Cordiner's introduction of decentralization at GE was subverted, over time, by organizational games of authority, deception, and control. The diffusion of activity-based costing was stymied by the defenses it stimulated on the part of managers who were threatened or embarrassed by the information it would bring to light. The study of TQM interventions showed a declining rate of improvement in performance where the issues involved problems of behavior, such as conflicting goals and interests held by multiple managers, especially at higher levels of the hierarchy.

The studies of TQM, reengineering, and SHRM document the gap of implementation. Some of them (Beer, Schneiderman) point directly to the importance of constrained and/or distorted organizational inquiry but offer no general theory to account for it. In some instances, the researchers suggest hypotheses to account for the observed results of the interventions they studied, but their attempts to explain mixed outcomes by reference to cognitive limitations, interest theory, management values, and political games are only partly satisfactory. These hypotheses do not fully explain the first-order errors the researchers have identified in their cases. And they do not at all explain the second-order errors *we* find in their cases: the organization's being unaware of its inability to act on what it knew or to detect and correct error.

We have argued that the mixed outcomes and the limits of productive learning revealed by both groups of studies are attributable to the persistence of Model O-I learning systems, reinforced by the Model I theories-in-use of individuals whose thought and action are partly constrained by these systems. Under conditions of embarrassment or threat, these O-I systems distort processes of organizational inquiry. They give rise to defensive routines that block inquiry, they make critically important issues and dilemmas undiscussable, they prevent organizations from acting on what some of their members know, and they reinforce organizational awareness of the ability to detect and correct error.

We turn now to a discussion of the implications of our analysis for the principal challenges to a theory of productive organizational learning. We explore how our theory-of-action account of the gaps of explanation and implementation bears on the several doubts raised by learning skeptics about organizational learning:

- its meaningfulness;
- its desirability;
- the capability of real-world organizations to engage in productive versions of it; and
- the efficacy of interventions aimed at enhancing it.

## The Paradox of Organizational Learning

The meaning of "organizational learning" hinges, as we have seen, on the crucial issue of the levels of aggregation at which organizational phenomena are described and explained and at which prescriptions for organizational action are directed. Our analyses of the two groups of studies show that one cannot account for the observed higher-level phenomena of organizational learning, that is, those that seem important to researchers concerned with strategy making or technological innovation, without referring to individual and interpersonal processes of inquiry. The feedback loops contained in our cause-maps and models of O-I learning systems show crucially important causal linkages among three levels of aggregation: interpersonal inquiry, interactions among organizational subunits, and the patterns of action and learning characteristic of whole organizations. We have argued that we should also treat as organizational the kinds of processes that shape the phenomena we take to be organizational in the first instance.

Unless we refer to the level of interpersonal inquiry, we cannot:

- explain the empirically discovered phenomena of limited organizational learning;
- resolve plausible but conflicting explanatory hypotheses about limited organizational learning;
- produce an explanation useful for redesigning practices so as to overcome barriers to productive organizational learning.

## The Meaning of "Productive" Organizational Learning

What do these examples of mixed results tell us about the nature of productive, especially double-loop, organizational learning?

They indicate the occurrence of some double-loop changes in organizational outcomes at the level of theory of action. But these changes are only temporary (one-shot) or affect only a part of the organizational theory of action and not others. In both groups of examples, the organization's theory-in-use for organizational inquiry did not undergo double-loop change. Although in Beer's case the intervenor did seek to inject Model II values into organizational inquiry, the injection did not last beyond the period of intervention.

It is clear, then, that it is possible for limited double-loop learning to occur at the level of outcomes in organizational theory of action without double-loop learning in processes of organizational inquiry. We have argued that whatever values may be espoused for organizational learning – single-loop, instrumental improvement in organizational performance, or double-loop change in the criteria by which organizational improvement is measured – their sustained achievement depends on the organization's continuing ability to engage in double-loop organizational inquiry. The Model II values that govern double-loop organizational inquiry are essential to the sustained achievement of other criteria for productive learning, for example, sustained and timely adaptive learning in technological innovation (Van de Ven and Polley), the timely reconciliation of formal strategy with a changing strategic situation (Burgelman), or the maintenance of the productive effects of enablers, such as decentralization and management empowerment (as in Cordiner at GE), or of structures for enhanced organizational inquiry (as in Beer's SHRM intervention).

The Model II values that govern double-loop organizational inquiry are foundational to sustained productive organizational learning. By the same token, as we have shown in each of the studies we have discussed, double-loop organizational inquiry with its

Model II values is required in order to disrupt the defensive routines that preserve the organizational status quo in situations of ambiguity or uncertainty by keeping threatening issues undiscussable and by keeping participants unaware of how they help to perpetuate those routines.

Our emphasis on Model II values for double-loop inquiry does not obviate the issue of learning for evil ends. In any given instance, the objectives of organizational learning and the values that inform those objectives must be examined. We would argue, however, that double-loop inquiry, which seeks to illuminate issues and dilemmas we might otherwise suppress or of which we might otherwise remain unaware, offers the most likely route to such examination.

## Threats to Productive Organizational Learning

In chapter 10 we will discuss three kinds of threats: to coherent organizational action, to cognitive capability for learning, and to effective implementation of lessons drawn from experience.

The issue of coherence arises in several of the cases we analysed in this chapter, most obviously in Van de Ven and Polley's and Burgelman's cases. In all of these cases, there was evidence of incoherence in relationships between middle and top management, as well as among divisions at the level of middle management. Top and middle managers or divisions such as R&D and Fabrication, diverged from one another, enacted contrary policies, or engaged in a kind of parallel play, pursuing independent policies without coordination. Burgelman now argues that in the early stages of his example this lack of coherence proved actually to be useful since it allowed DRAM development to go on beyond the point when at least some people in the company clearly saw that Intel no longer had a competitive edge in the DRAM business. The result was that the company could eventually take advantage of the unanticipated benefits of that development for the microprocessor business that it was (by then) coming to see as the wave of the future. In this case, if we accept Burgelman's analysis, a vein of technological development undertaken for the sake of one business proved unexpectedly to be useful for another business. Such things happen. But the outcome might have been less rosy. At crucial moments in Van de Ven and Polley's story of the TAP development and in Roth's story of business processes reengineering at Dover and Harwick, analogous situations arose when TAP's development and the reengineering processes continued beyond the points at which they should have been subjected to critical scrutiny. In these instances, according to the authors, the results were negative.

What lessons should we draw from such occurrences? We certainly should not conclude that all programs of technological development undertaken for the sake of a business now seen as obsolescent should be continued because they might turn out to be useful for another business. On what basis, then, should one distinguish projects worth supporting from those that ought not to be supported? Even to raise this question is to pose the issue of awareness. If organizational inquirers are not aware of an existing incoherence in policies enacted by different levels or groups of managers and if they are not capable of subjecting that incoherence to public scrutiny, then how could such discrimination be made? In both the Van de Ven and Polley and Burgelman cases, managerial awareness and public discussion of disjointed policies would have required double-loop inquiry into the issues that provoked threat or embarrassment and triggered organizational defensive routines – inquiry comparable to the inquiry undertaken by the CEO and directors of the management consulting firm described in chapter 9. The incoherence that might be taken as evidence of lack of capability for productive learning in real-world organizations, giving rise to generalizations of the kind that March and like-minded scholars have proposed, could also be seen – and is in fact seen, from the theory-of-action perspective – as an occasion for double-loop inquiry.

All of the cases we have considered in this chapter provide evidence that could be attributed to *limited cognitive capability for productive organizational learning*. The question is how we ought to interpret this evidence.

In several of these cases, threats to valid inference arose. In most of them, uncertainty and ambiguity surrounded the causes of some critically important effects of organizational action. In some instances (Intel), managers faced with uncertainty fell into competence traps or engaged in superstitious learning. In other instances (TAP), managers failed to focus concerted attention on signs of trouble that ought to have cast doubt on the assumptions that underlay established organizational policies. In most of the cases of attempts to introduce enablers to improve organizational capability for productive learning, managers persisted in a course of action about which some members of the organization had significant grounds for doubt, yet the information and interpretations held by these managers did not give rise to a concerted, public critique of the assumptions that underlay organizational action.

Should we argue, as March and others have done, that such instances of first-order error provide further evidence for the general proposition that organizations lack cognitive capability for productive learning from experience? Our position is that such instances do not, of themselves, reveal limited cogitive capability. Rather, a close inspection of the evidence compiled by the authors of the case studies reveals a pattern of organizational defenses that reinforce a prevailing blindness to first-order error, a blindness that makes such errors uncorrectable and their underlying, mistaken assumptions self-sealing. The question of cognitive capability must remain moot since during the time periods in question, the fact that organization members were unaware of or unwilling to discuss the relevant issues, prevented the organization from applying to them whatever cognitive capability it had. There is, indeed, some evidence, from the authors' account of patterns of inquiry carried out in the later stages of the Intel and the TAP cases, that both organizations possessed the ability to engage in complex and refined exercises of error detection, causal analysis, and error correction.

There is, of course, no guarantee that if the managers in these cases had been aware of their first-order errors and had subjected them to public discussion and critical analysis, they would have succeeded in correcting them. In the world of management, as of science, there is no guarantee against persistent error. But there is also no a priori reason to attribute persistent first-order error to the limits of cognitive capability *when there is manifest evidence that a prevailing pattern of defensive behavior blocks the exercise of that capability, whatever its strengths or limitations may be*. The much more important issue raised by our analysis of the case material is the need and potential for double-loop inquiry into the patterns of second-order error, the limited learning systems whose persistence makes first-order error unassailable. This issue is central to the gap of implementation and critical to the design of interventions aimed at enabling productive organizational learning.

Moreover, from the perspective of scholarly research on organizational learning, a robust test of propositions about the cognitive capability of organizations depends on making organizational actors aware of, and helping them to overcome, the defenses that blind them to first-order errors. For in the absence of such an intervention, how could one tell whether an organization's vulnerability to such threats to valid inference as competence traps and superstitious learning is due to the organization's limited cognitive capability or to the effects of its organizational defensive routines?

Conceivably, researchers might argue along the lines of the behavioral theory of the firm that defensive routines are unalterable facts of organizational life that should be "folded into" the attribution of limited cognitive capability. We would agree that patterns of organizational defensiveness are widespread and deeply embedded in the behavioral worlds of organizations. But an intervention of the kind reported in chapter 9 and others like it (see Argyris, 1990, 1993), stand as existence proofs of the possibility of double-loop inquiry that breaks through the constraints of O-I behavioral worlds. In the wide-ranging universe of organizational life, such episodes must be counted as rare events. Nevertheless, they cast doubt on the validity of any general attribution of limited cognitive capability and point the way to future programs of intervention and research.

## Overcoming Impediments to Productive Organizational Learning

Our analysis of case material related to decentralization, TQM, activity-based costing, reengineering, and SHRM, indicates that organizational enablers can induce productive organizational learning, leading even to temporary double-loop outcomes at the level of organizational theory-in-use, when the issues are neither embarrassing nor threatening. But under conditions of embarrassment or threat, we find that the O-I learning systems of the organizations tend over time to subvert the enabling interventions.

We believe that our analysis helps to explain the characteristic life cycles of such organizational fixes as TQM, flat organization, reengineering, and management empowerment. In each such instance, a prescription for organizational reform appears on the horizon, supported by plausible-sounding theory and stories of successful implementation by early adopters. Often at the core of the reform there lies a significant insight, for example, managers *should* be freed up to take on greater responsibility and make greater use of local knowledge, or organizational processes *should* be rethought in the light of the possibilities opened up by advanced information technology. Usually, however, the prescription is converted by its advocates and the consultants who undertake its dissemination into a readily understandable package of procedures. Not infrequently, the package is accompanied by an ideology that takes on quasi-religious overtones. Organization managers, thirsty for solutions to the persistent predicaments in which they find themselves and impatient with calls to wrestle with the complexity of the predicaments or with their own possible collusion in reinforcing them, latch onto the package. A bandwagon effect ensues as managers adopt the package because managers around them are adopting it. Then over time, as experience with the reform builds up and as good intentions are subverted by organizational defensive routines and their associated Model I theories-in-use, a literature of disillusionment begins to appear. Then normal cynicism begins to reassert itself. Lower-level managers begin to mutter that those at the top never really meant it, and top-level managers express frustration at the intractable resistance to change exhibited by those below them. People begin to say, "We tried that!" and a readiness for the next reform package begins to take shape.

Nevertheless, as we have argued, there are examples of rare events in which individual members of organizations show themselves willing and able to engage the complexity of the limited learning systems in which they operate, to examine their own skilled contributions to the maintenance of those systems, and to learn to move toward the Model II values, strategies, and assumptions that enable them to disrupt prevailing organizational defensive routines. Perhaps as Beer and others have suggested, some managers who have not experienced such rare events but have experienced the reforms described in literatures of disillusionment are growing in readiness to wrestle with complexity and to explore the patterns of thought and action through which they contribute to their own disillusionment.

These conclusions hold important implications for practice and research.

Practitioners who want to increase their organization's capability for continuing productive learning, especially of the double-loop variety, should learn to improve the performance of organizational inquiry, which requires double-loop learning in their own theories-in-use.

Researchers who want only to explain the phenomena of limited organizational learning should attend to the directly observable data of organizational inquiry which must, in turn, be linked to higher levels of aggregation. This strategy of attention is all the more appropriate for researchers who want to produce usable knowledge that can help practitioners build organizational capability for productive learning. In both cases, researchers would do well to reframe their research as action research undertaken in collaboration with practitioners who seek to build capability for enhancing and expanding the rare events of productive organizational learning.

## Notes

1   Draws heavily from Chris Argyris and Donald Schön (1996).
2   In order to test their hypotheses, the authors decompose their case into "events," which they define as "critical incidents when changes were observed to occur in the innovation idea and activities, personnel appointments and roles, innovation unit relationships with others, environmental and organizational context, and outcomes" (p. 99). They adopt a monthly interval for the aggregation of events, collecting some 325 of them over a five-year period. They code outcomes of events as positive or negative or mixed, depending on their embodying good news or successful accomplishments, bad news or instances of failures or mistakes, or combinations of these. They seek to test their hypotheses by ascertaining correlations or lack of them, between positive, negative, and mixed events, on the one hand, and, on the other hand, continuation or change in a prior action course, resource controllers' interventions, shifts in outcome criteria, or events (judged significant) in the external context.
3   Burgelman's argument here is reminiscent of Hirschman's famous "principle of the Hiding Hand." Hirschman (1958) proposed that ignorance of dangers to come can actually foster the success of a development project because those who underestimate the dangers also tend to underestimate the creativity that may be brought to their resolution. However, in his later writings, Hirschman also recognized the difficulty of distinguishing instances in which the Hiding Hand proves to be beneficent from those instances in which it does not prove to be beneficient!
4   See Michael Beer, 1994. On page 2, Beer writes that "70% of all corporations report that TQM has not lived up to their expectations."

## References

Ackoff, R., 1981, *Creating the Corporate Future*, New York, John Wiley and Sons.
Argyris, C., 1990 *Overcoming Organizational Defenses*, Needham, MA, Allyn-Bacon.
Argyris, C., 1993, *Knowledge for Action: A Guide to Overcoming Barriers to Organizational Change*, San Francisco, Jossey-Bass.
Argyris, C., and Kaplan, R., 1994, "Implementing New Knowledge: The Case of Activity-Based Costing," *Accounting Horizons*, 8, 3, pp. 83–105.
Argyris, C., and Schön, D., 1996, *Organisational Learning II*, Reading, MA., Addison-Wesley pp. 200–42.
Beer, M., 1994, "Developing an Organization Capable of Implementing Strategy and Learning," Harvard Business School Working Paper, September.
Burgelman, R., 1994, "Fading Memories: A Process Theory of Strategic Business Exit in Dynamic Environments," in *Administrative Sciences Quarterly*, March, 39; pp. 24–56.
Hirschman, A. O., 1958, *The Strategy of Economic Development*, New Haven; Yale University Press.
Mallinger, M., 1993, *Ambnoh Along the TQM Trail*, Mulieo, Malibu, Calif., Pepperdine University.

Ross, J., and Staw, B. M., 1986, "Expo 86: An Escalation Prototype", in *Administrative Science Quarterly*, 31, pp. 274–97.

Roth, G., 1993, *Business Process Re-Engineering in Business Service Companies*, doctoral dissertation, Sloan School of Management, Massachusetts Institute of Technology, Cambridge, Mass.

Schein, E., 1985, 1992, *Organizational Culture and Leadership*, San Francisco, Jossey-Bass.

Schneiderman, A. M., 1992, "Are There Limits to Total Quality Management?", mimeo, Analog Devices.

Schön, D. A., 1967, *Technology and Change: The New Heraclitus*, New York, Delacorte Press.

Van de Ven, A., and Polley, D., 1992, "Learning While Innovating", in *Organization Science*, 3, 1, February, pp. 92–115.

# — 2 —

# Tacit Knowledge and Management

The argument of this chapter is that tacit knowledge is the primary basis for effective management and the basis for its deterioration. Stated briefly, the reasoning for this claim is as follows. The primary basis for effective management is to define and transform, as much as possible, the behavior required to achieve the organization's objectives into routines that work (Argyris 1990, 1993; Argyris and Schön 1996; Nelson and Winter, 1977). Routines are implemented through skillful actions. Actions that are skillful are based largely on tacit knowledge. Such actions become self-reinforcing of the status quo. The self-reinforcing features tend to reduce inquiry into gaps and inconsistencies in the tacit knowledge. When these surface, they are often embarrassing or threatening. Individuals deal with embarrassment or threat with another set of skillful – hence tacit – actions. These actions are counterproductive to effective management.

## EFFECTIVE MANAGEMENT DEPENDS ON TACIT KNOWLEDGE:
### A SCENARIO

1   All organizations are designed to achieve the objectives intended by the founders. Managing is the crucial process in implementing the design.
2   All designs specify the intended objectives and the actions required to achieve the objectives. Designs are therefore specifications intended to be generalizable and comprehensive.
    Designs intended to manage the complexities of everyday life in organizations will always contain two types of gaps. First, no a priori design is likely to cover all the specifics and uniqueness of the concrete case. Managers will always be faced with gap filling. Second, no design is likely to activate all the energies and cognitive capacities of the human beings. Motivating individuals is likely to require that attention be paid to differences in individuals and contexts.
3   In order to minimize the gaps, managers specify ahead of time the jobs and roles of the players as completely as is possible without the specifications being so complex that they immobilize performance. The rewards and penalties intended to activate the energies and cognitive abilities are also specified ahead of time.
4   The roles are usually specified by reference to the functional managerial disciplines such as human resources, information technology, finance, managerial accounting,

marketing, and operations. Each of these disciplines is a theory of action; that is, each specifies the actions required to achieve their particular objectives (which, in turn, are connected to the overall objectives) as well as the conditions under which the specifications hold. Each functional managerial discipline is therefore a causal theory about how to get something done.

5    All designs of managerial theories of action aspire to make their requirements explicit and specific so that they can be taught to human beings and their causal claims can be tested in the world of practice.

For example, activity-based costing is part of the larger discipline of accounting. It specifies, among other things, the importance of diagnosing accurately the cost drivers by focusing on the activities used to produce a product or service. It specifies the sequence of steps to be taken in order to identify the activities that drive the costs. Two individuals using the same numbers and following the activity-based costing specifications should always come up with similar answers. If they do not, they can trace their actions backwards and ultimately identify where the discrepancy or error occurred. Such possibilities are tests of the *internal validity* of the causal specifications.

Activity-based accounting also specifies the relationship of costs to more comprehensive managerial goals such as profit. These causal claims are part of the *external validity* of activity based costing.

6    The aspiration of the designers of all managerial functional disciplines is to produce propositions that exhibit high internal and external validity. Such explicitly stated propositions make the discipline transparent and therefore teachable.

7    The objective of teaching the discipline is to make the professionals skillful at carrying out their specifications. Individuals are skillful to the extent that they produce the specifications, automatically and with a low requirement for deliberate thought. Indeed, if they had to focus explicitly on what they were doing they would likely lose their skill. Individuals do focus deliberately on their skillful behavior when they produce errors, that is, when they are not behaving skillfully. Skillful actions are automatic and taken for granted.

## THE FUNDAMENTAL ASSUMPTIONS MADE BY MANAGERIAL FUNCTIONAL DISCIPLINES ABOUT THEIR IMPLEMENTATION

Embedded in the managerial disciplines is what may be described as a "micro-causal theory" of implementation.

- If individuals know the specifications,
- if they have the skills to produce them,
- if they wish to produce them,
- if they are enabled to produce them (e.g., by management, organizational norms, informal employee norms)

then they will do so...

The second fundamental assumption is that ineffective performance can be traced to errors or mismatches. Errors can be corrected by acquiring new information and skills or by reformulating the theory of action of the discipline. Underlying this assumption is a third one. Errors will not be produced knowingly because to do so is an illegitimate transgression from the specifications (i.e., unprofessional behavior). Individuals will not violate their professional stewardship embedded in their jobs, roles, and other features of their contract with management.

A fourth assumption is that it is management's responsibility to monitor the implementation of the managerial disciplines to assure the organization that the individuals are not violating the first three assumptions. This monitoring activity is carried out as follows. As many actions as possible are pre-defined and routinized. Management focuses on identifying any exceptions to the routine in order to correct them (the activity is called management by exception).

To summarize. Roles are defined and enablers (such as policies) are created that, if followed, will produce, in theory, the intended consequences. The employees are coached until they perform the role requirements skillfully. Once the appropriate level of skill has been achieved, the actions become automatic, routine, and hence manageable. They also become tacit. Hence the claim that effective management depends upon the effective use of tacit knowledge.

## ORGANIZATIONAL DEFENSIVE ROUTINES

In real life, most organizations exhibit powerful organizational defensive routines. They are activated when the participants are dealing with any business or human problems that are embarrassing or threatening. A defensive routine is any action or policy intended to prevent the players from experiencing embarrassment or threat, and does so in ways that makes it difficult to identify and reduce the causes of the embarrassment or threat. Defensive routines are overprotective and anti-learning. Defensive routines are activated under conditions when they are likely to be most counterproductive.

Defensive routines are created because the participants believe that they are necessary in order for themselves and the organization to survive. This creates a bind. On the one hand, defensive routines are used to cover up errors that are important to correct if the organization is to perform effectively. Such a cover-up violates formal managerial requirements and stewardship. Participants are not supposed to bypass errors. Moreover, the bypass is undiscussable. And, in order to produce undiscussable behavior that persists, the undiscussability must also be undiscussable. On the other hand, if the errors, their undiscussability, and the cover-ups are surfaced, the participants are subject to criticism for acting in these ways.

How does such behavior arise and how does it become so powerful? There are two fundamental sets of causes. They are the theories for effective action that individuals learn early in life and the defensive routines that they create in organizations when the theories are implemented correctly.

## DESIGNS FOR ACTION: MODEL I

Human beings have programs in their heads on how to act effectively in any type of interaction, be it as a leader, as a follower, or as a peer. We call these programs their theories of action. These theories of action are, in effect, causal theories of how to act effectively.

Human beings hold two types of theories of action. There is the one that they espouse. It is usually expressed in the form of stated beliefs and values. Then there is the theory that they actually use. This can only be inferred from observing their actions, that is, their actual behavior. To date, most human beings studied have the same theory-in-use. There is diversity in espoused theories but not in theories-in-use. A model of the theories-in-use (that we call Model I) is as follows (Argyris, 1982, 1990, 1993; Argyris and Schön, 1996).

Model I theory-in-use is the design we found throughout the world. It has four governing values:

1   Achieve your intended purpose.
2   Maximize winning and minimize losing.
3   Suppress negative feelings.
4   Behave according to what you consider rational.

The most prevalent action strategies that arise from Model I are the following:

1   Advocate your position.
2   Evaluate the thoughts and actions of others (and your own thoughts and actions).
3   Attribute causes for whatever you are trying to understand.

These actions must be performed in such a way that satisfies the actors' governing values – that is, they achieve at least their minimum acceptable level of being in control, winning, or bringing about any other result. In other words, Model I tells individuals to craft their positions, evaluations, and attributions in ways that inhibit inquiries into and tests of them with the use of independent logic. The consequences of these Model I strategies are likely to be defensiveness, misunderstanding, and self-fulfilling and self-sealing processes (Argyris, 1982).

Model I theory-in-use requires defensive reasoning. Individuals keep their premises and inferences tacit, lest they lose control. They create tests of their claims that are self-serving and self-sealing. The likelihood of misunderstanding and mistrust increases. The use of defensive reasoning prohibits questioning the defensive reasoning. We now have self-fueling processes that maintain the status quo, inhibit genuine learning, and reinforces the deception.

For example, a superior believes that the performance of his subordinate is below standard. He also believes that saying so in a forthright manner will lead the subordinate to become defensive and hence close off learning. The superior therefore attempts to ease in and to be diplomatic. He does not say that he is acting in these ways because that would upset the subordinate. The subordinate senses the easing in and the diplomacy. He covers up what he is sensing and acts as if he is not doing so.

After the session, the superior and subordinate were interviewed separately to assess how well the session had gone. The superior responded that all went well until the subordinate became defensive. Then the superior backed off in order to be constructive. Similarly, the subordinate responded that that all went well until he began to disagree with the superior. At that time, in the eyes of the subordinate, the superior became defensive. The subordinate backed off lest he get into trouble.

When each was asked if he had surfaced his evaluations about the other's actions, the response was, in effect, "Are you kidding? That is a cure that would make the illness worse". The result was that each individual reinforced his attributions about the other. Neither tested the validity of his views because both believed them to be true and an attempt at a genuine test would only make things worse. Hence, we have a situation of minimal learning, self-sealing positions, and increasing mistrust.

Human beings learn their theories-in-use early in life and therefore the actions that they produce are highly skilled. Little conscious attention is paid to producing skilled actions. Indeed, conscious attention could inhibit producing them effectively. This leads to unawareness of what we are doing when we act skillfully. The unawareness due to skill and the unawareness caused by our unilaterally controlling theories-in-use produce a deeper unawareness, namely, we become unaware of the programs in our heads that keep us unaware.

The results are skilled unawareness and skilled incompetence. For example, when individuals have to say something negative to others (your performance is poor) they often ease in, in order not to upset the other. Two of the most frequent easing-in actions that we observe are non-directive questioning and face-saving approaches. In order for these to work, the individuals must cover up that they are acting as they are in order not to upset the other. In order for a cover-up to work, the cover-up must be covered up.

Under these conditions, we find that the recipients are wary of what is happening. They sense that there may be a cover-up. Since they hold the same theory-in-use, they too cover up their private doubts. The result is counterproductive consequences for genuine problem solving. All of the above occurs with the use of skillful behavior. Hence the term skilled incompetence.

When organizational worlds become dominated by these consequences, human beings become cynical about changing the self-fueling counterproductive process. Not surprisingly, they learn to distance themselves from taking responsibility, losing, and suppressing negative feelings, especially those associated with embarrassment or threat. Individuals use behavioral strategies, consistent with these governing values. For example, they advocate their views, they make evaluations and attributions in such a way as to assure their being in control, winning, and suppressing negative feelings.

In short, individuals learn theories-in-use that are consistent with producing unilateral control. It is true that organizations are hierarchical and based on unilateral control. It is equally true that individuals are even more so. Place individuals in organizations whose structures are designed to be more egalitarian, and individuals will eventually make them more unilateral and authoritarian. The most massive examples of which I am aware are the "alternative schools" and communes of the 1970s. Most have failed and slowly have faded away.

For example, in a study of five alternative high schools that I conducted, I found that the schools were (1) given adequate funding, (2) permitted to re-design their curriculum, (3) staffed by teachers who volunteered because they believed in the concept of the school, and (4) attended by students who had the same views. All went well until the teachers began to conclude that academic performance was falling. In several attempts to correct the situation, they were attacked by the students. The students accused them of being traditional, top-down, and authoritarian. The teachers distanced themselves from students and vice versa. Soon, the teachers requested that the experiments end or, in two cases, the respective school boards did so (Argyris, 1974).

## ORGANIZATIONAL DEFENSIVE ROUTINES

Organizational defensive routines are any action, policy, or practice that prevents organizational participants from experiencing embarrassment or threat and, at the same time, prevents them from discovering the causes of the embarrassment or threat. Organizational defensive routines, like Model I theories-in-use, inhibit genuine learning and overprotect the individuals and the organization (Argyris, 1990).

There is a fundamental logic underlying all organizational defensive routines. It can be illustrated by one of the most frequently observed defenses, namely, sending mixed messages. "Mary, you run the department, but check with Bill." "John, be innovative but be careful." The logic is as follows.

1   Send a message that is inconsistent.
2   Act as if it is not inconsistent.

3   Make 1 and 2 undiscussable.
4   Make the undiscussability undiscussable.

An illustration of what happens when organizational defensive routines dominate can be seen in this case of cost reduction. Twelve foreman were trying to uncover where cost reductions might be made. In an hour or so, they were able to identify more than 30 areas. Next, they ranked these areas for possible action. Finally, they selected six areas on which they promised to take action.

After three months, the foremen met to report their accomplishments. Objectives for all six area had been achieved. Management estimated the likely savings to be about $210,000.00. Everyone was delighted. The mood was understandably festive. The group turned to champagne and dinner that top management had provided.

However, a crucial question had not been asked. Indeed, the manager who led the discussion said that he would not have even thought of asking the question. An outside observer studying these cost-reduction meetings asked:

OBSERVER:  Do you remember the list of areas that you identified three months ago?
FOREMEN:   Of course.
OBSERVER:  How long did you know about these lists?
FOREMEN:   We don't understand. What are you driving at?
OBSERVER:  How long did you know that these problem areas existed?
FOREMEN:   From one to three years. It was common knowledge.
OBSERVER:  What led you not to take action until these seminars? What prevented you from taking these actions without the stimulation from the seminar?
FOREMEN:   Are you kidding? Are you serious?
OBSERVER:  I am not kidding; I am serious. What prevented you from correcting problems that you knew about for years?
FOREMEN:   Be careful. You're opening up a can of worms! (*Turning to the top management representative*) Do you want us to answer that question? It could spoil the evening.

Reflecting on this story, we see that the criterion for success was a fix that was quick and easily measurable. The cost-reduction program was judged a success. However, the big question was not asked by those who managed it.

Organizational defensive routines are caused by a circular, self-reinforcing process in which individuals' Model I theories-in-use produce individual strategies of bypass and cover up, which result in organizational bypass and cover up, which reinforce the individuals' theories-in-use. The explanation of organizational defensive routines is therefore individual *and* organizational. This means that it should not be possible to change organizational routines without changing individual routines, and vice versa. Any attempts at doing so should lead to failure or, at best, temporary success.

## THE CHALLENGES IN PRODUCING CHANGES IN ORGANIZATIONAL DEFENSES

If this self-reinforcing process is valid, then researcher–interveners face at least two challenges when trying to help both individuals and their organizations deal with these issues. The first challenge is that individuals' senses of competence, self-confidence, and self-esteem are highly dependent upon their Model I theories-in-use and organizational defensive routines. This dependence practically guarantees that when individuals are acting to learn, the consequences will be skillfully counterproductive because the Model I theories-in-use will not allow Model I governing values to be changed. This illustrates skilled incompetence. This message is not likely to be met with joy by the clients or subjects. Indeed, it is likely to create additional conditions of embarrassment and threat. Thus, one of the first messages required for reeducation will likely trigger the very organizational defensive routines the intervener is asking participants to change. The researcher–intervener does not ignore this dilemma but sees it as an opportunity for learning based on here-and-now data. So far, most of the individuals with whom my colleagues and I have worked have indeed become defensive upon hearing this message, but most of them have learned from their defensiveness (Argyris, 1982, 1993; Argyris and Schön, 1996).

The second challenge is that individuals through acculturation define social virtues such as caring, support, and integrity as consistent with Model I. For example, to be caring and supportive, say what you believe individuals would like to hear; do not act in ways that make them defensive. This means that they are not likely to recognize the counterproductive consequences of Model I theories-in-use.

## MODEL II: THEORIES-IN-USE

To help them recognize their skillful Model I blindness, the intervener introduces Model II theories-in-use. Model II theories are, at the outset, espoused theories. The challenge is to help individuals transform their espoused theories into theories-in-use by learning a "new" set of skills and a "new" set of governing values. Because many individuals espouse Model II values and skills, these traits are not totally new to them. However, the empirical fact to date is that very few individuals can routinely act on their espoused values and skills; yet they are often unaware of this limitation.

The governing values of Model II are valid information, informed choice, and vigilant monitoring of the implementation of the choice in order to detect and correct error. As in the case of Model I, the three most prominent behaviors are advocate, evaluate, and attribute. However, unlike Model I behaviors, Model II behaviors are crafted into action strategies that openly illustrate how the actors reached their evaluations or attributions and how they crafted them to encourage inquiry and testing by others. Productive reasoning is required to produce such consequences. Productive reasoning means that the premises are explicit, the inferences from the premises are also made explicit, and finally conclusions are crafted in ways that can be tested by logic that is independent of the actor. Unlike the defensive reasoning, the logic used is not self-referenced. As a consequence, defensive routines that are anti-learning are minimized and genuine learning is facilitated. Embarrassment and threat are not bypassed and covered up; they are engaged (Argyris and Schön, 1974; Argyris, 1982).

To the extent that individuals use Model II theory instead of merely espousing it, they will begin to interrupt organizational defensive routines and begin to create organizational learning processes and systems that encourage double-loop learning in ways that persist. These are called Model II learning systems (Argyris and Schön, 1978).

## DESIGN OF THE RESEARCH–INTERVENTION ACTIVITIES

There are a few design rules that follow from the theoretical framework described above that can be used to design the research and the intervention activities.

- Discover the degree to which the clients' theories-in-use are consistent with Model I.
- Discover the degree to which the clients use defensive reasoning whenever they deal with embarrassing or threatening issues.
- Discover the designs (rules) the clients have in their heads that keep them unaware of the discrepancies among their espoused values, their actions, and their theories-in-use.
- Discover the degree to which the clients discourage valid reflection on their actions while they are acting. To put this another way: discover how the clients create designs for action that they do not follow but that they believe they do follow, while they are also being systematically unaware of this discrepancy and are behaving in ways that prevent them from discovering the discrepancy and the causes of their unawareness.
- Discover the defensive routines that exist in the organization and that limit learning. Develop maps of these organizational defensive routines, specifying the actions that lead to limited-learning consequences and cause them to persist even though the directors wish to be free of them.

In order to reach these goals, re-education and change programs should produce relatively directly observable data about these clients' reasoning and actions. The clients must accept responsibility for creating these data, and these data must be in a form from which the clients' theories-in-use can be inferred (for example, recorded conversations).

- Encourage the clients to examine inconsistencies and gaps in the reasoning that underlines their actions.
- Surface and make explicit the rules that "must" be in their heads if they maintain there is a connection between their designs for action and the actions themselves.
- View any bewilderment or frustration that results as further directly observable data that can be used to test the validity of what is being learned.
- Produce opportunities to practice Model II ways of crafting actions that will reduce counterproductive consequences.

In principle, the kind of research of which I speak can begin with identifying either the theories-in-use or the organizational defensive routines. It does not matter which because one will necessarily lead you to the other. I usually make the choice on the basis of which of the two is most likely to generate the participants' internal commitment to the research and to the eventual intervention.

## THE LEFT- AND RIGHT-HAND COLUMN CASE METHOD

We often use a case study instrument to get at theories-in-use and organizational defensive routines. The case method described below is one of several instruments used in our action science research (Argyris et al., 1985). The key features of all the research methods and this case method in particular are as follows.

1  It produces relatively directly observable data such as conversation. Such data are the actual productions of action and therefore can become the basis for inferring theories-in-use.
2  It produces data in ways that makes clear the actors' responsibility for the meanings produced. When used properly, the respondents cannot make the research

instrument causally responsible for the data that they produced (e.g., "I didn't *really* mean that"; or "I didn't understand the meaning of that term").

3  It produces data about the respondents' causal theories, especially those that are tacit because they are taken for granted.

4  It provides opportunities for the respondents to change their responses without hindering the validity of the inferences being made. Indeed, the actions around "changing their minds" should also provide data about their causal reasoning processes.

5  It provides opportunities to change their actions as well as actions of groups, intergroups, and organizations over which they have some influence.

6  It provides such knowledge in ways that are economical and do not harm the respondents or the context in which they are working.

The directions to write a case are given to each individual. The directions request the following.

1  In one paragraph describe a key organizational problem as you see it.

2  Assume you could talk to whomever you wish to begin to solve the problem. Describe, in a paragraph or so, the strategy that you would use in this meeting.

3  Next, split your page into two columns. On the right-hand side write how you would begin the meeting; what you would actually say. Then write what you believe the other(s) would say. Then write your response to their response. Continue writing this scenario for two or so double-spaced typewritten pages.

4  On the left-hand column write any idea or feeling that you would have that you would not communicate for whatever reason.

In short, the case includes:

- a statement of the problem;
- the intended strategy to begin to solve the problem;
- the actual conversation that would occur as envisioned by the writer;
- the information that the writer would not communicate for whatever reason.

Some of the results can be illustrated by reference to a CEO and his executive group. The executives reported that they became highly involved in writing the cases. Some said that the very writing of the case was an eye opener. Moreover, once the cases were distributed to each member, the reactions were jocular. The men were enjoying them: "That's just like...."; "Great,...does this all the time"; "Oh, there's a familiar one" "All salesmen and no listeners"; "Oh my God, this is us."

## CASES AS AN INTERVENTION TOOL

What is the advantage of using the cases? The cases, crafted and written by the executives themselves, become vivid examples of "skilled incompetence." They illustrate the skill with which each executive tried not to upset the other and to persuade them to change their position. They also illustrate the incompetence component because the results, by their own analysis, were to upset the others and make it less likely that their views would prevail.

The cases are also very important learning devices. If is difficult for anyone to slow down the behavior that they produce in milliseconds during a real meeting in order to reflect on it and change it. The danger is that others will grab the air time and run with it. Moreover, it is difficult for the human mind to pay attention to the interpersonal actions and to the substantive issues at the same time.

Here is a collage from several cases. They were written by individuals who believed the company should place a greater emphasis on customer service.

| Thoughts and feelings not communicated | Actual conversation |
| --- | --- |
| *He's not going to like this topic, but we had to discuss it. I doubt that he will take a company perspective, but I should be positive.* | **Self:** Hi Bill. I appreciate the opportunity to talk with you about this problem of customer service versus product. I am sure that both of us want to resolve it in the best interests of the company.<br>**Bill:** I'm always glad to talk about it, as you well know. |
| *I better go slow. Let me ease in.* | **Self:** There are an increasing number of situations where our clients are asking for customer service and rejecting the off-the-shelf products. My fear is that your sales people will play an increasingly peripheral role in the future.<br>**Bill:** I don't understand. Tell me more. |
| *Like hell you don't understand. I wish there was a way I could be more gentle.* | **Self:** Bill, I'm sure you are aware of the changes (and explains).<br>**Bill:** No, I do not see it that way. It's my sales people that are the key to the future. |
| *There he goes, thinking as a salesman and not as a corporate officer.* | **Self:** Well, let's explore that a bit . . . |

The dialogue continues with each person stating their views candidly but not being influenced by what the other says. To give you a flavor of what happened, here are some further unspoken comments: "*He's doing a great job supporting his people. I better be careful*"; "*This guy is not really listening*"; "*I wonder if he's influenceable*"; "*This is beginning to piss me off*"; "*There he goes getting defensive. I better back off and wait for another day*".

If I presented a collage of the cases written by individuals who supported the opposite views, it would not differ significantly. They too tried to persuade, sell, cajole their fellow officers. Their left-hand columns would be similar.

## REFLECTING ON THE CASES

In analyzing their left-hand columns, the executives found that each side blamed the other side for the difficulties, and they used the same reasons. For example, each side said about the other side: "*You do not really understand the issues*"; "*If you insist on your position, you will harm the morale that I have built*"; "*Don't hand me that line. You know what I am talking about*"; "*Why don't you take off your blinders and wear a company hat?*"; "*It upsets me when I think of how they think*"; "*I'm really trying hard, but I'm beginning to feel this is hopeless.*"

These results illustrate once more the features of skilled incompetence. Crafting the cases with the intention not to upset others while trying to change their minds requires skill. Yet, as we have seen, the skilled behavior they used in the cases had the opposite effect. The others in the case became upset and dug in their heels about changing their minds.

## REDESIGNING THEIR ACTIONS

The next step is to begin to redesign their actions. The executives turned to their cases. Each executive selected an episode that he wished to redesign so that it would not have the negative consequences. As an aid in their redesign, the executives were given some handouts that described Model II set of behaviors. The first thing they realized was that they would have to slow things down. They could not produce a new conversation in the milliseconds that they were accustomed. This troubled them a bit because they were impatient to learn. They kept reminding themselves that learning new skills does require that they slow down.

One technique they used was that each individual crafted by himself a new conversation to help the writer of the episode. After taking five or so minutes, they shared their designs with the writer. In the process of discussing these, the writer learned much about how to redesign his words. But the designers also learned much as they discovered the gaps in their suggestions and the way they made them.

Practice is important. Most people require as much practice to learn Model II as is required to play a not-so-decent game of tennis. But, the practice does not need to occur all at once. The practice can occur in actual business meetings where they set aside some time to make it possible to reflect on their actions and to correct them. An outside facilitator could help them examine and redesign their actions just as a tennis coach might do. But, as in the case of a good tennis coach, the facilitator should be replaced by the group. He might be brought in for periodic boosters or to help when the problem is the degree of difficulty and intensity not experienced before.

There are several consequences of this type of change program. First, the executives begin to experience each other as more supportive and constructive. People still work very hard during meetings, but their conversation begins to become addictive; it flows to conclusions that they all can own and implement. Crises begin to be reduced. Soon the behavioral change leads to new values and new structures and policies to mirror the new values.

This in turn leads to more effective problem solving and decision making. In the case of this group, they were able to define the questions related to strategy, to conduct their own inquiries, to have staff people conduct some relevant research, to have three individuals organize it into a presentation that was ultimately approved and owned by the top group. The top group also built in a process of involving their immediate reports so that they could develop a sense of ownership, thereby increasing the probability that all involved will work at making it successful.

In a recent study (Argyris, 1993) of what is now an 11-year program, the key to change is practice and use of Model II theory-in-use plus productive reasoning in solving major difficult problems. This means that the participants select key meetings in which to continue their learning. These meetings cannot be scheduled in a lock-step fashion.

It also means that the change program that began at the top is spread to the next levels as the competence of those above them becomes persistent. This has led not only to changes in the internal management of the firm (which is a managerial consulting firm) but to the development of new services for their clients.

One might ask, do interventions go wrong and how are the errors corrected? I hope that my description above illustrates that the participants are made continually responsible for their participation in the program. One of their main responsibilities is to monitor the actions so that if errors occur, they are corrected. Moreover, they are free to stop a program at any time they deem it necessary. To date, no program had been stopped. However, there is variance in the degree of enthusiasm individuals may have for managing through the use of Model II. In a few instances where these differences occur, it would violate the governing values of Model II for one sub-group to require the others to act consistently with Model II. What is required is that the doubters be open about their doubts and that they do not use their power to prevent further dialogue, especially by subordinates or peers.

## BASIC CRITERIA FOR SUCCESS IN DIAGNOSING AND CHANGING
## AT ANY LEVEL OF THE ORGANIZATION

There are four criteria that we found central to both the design diagnostic instruments and interventions in organizations.

1   The criterion for success should not be change in behavior or attitudes. We must get at the causes of behavior and attitudes. The criterion should be changes in defensive reasoning and the theories-in-use that produce skilled unawareness and skilled incompetence and the resulting organizational defensive routines.
2   The changes just described should unambiguously lead to reductions in the self-fulfilling counterproductive activities, at all levels of the organization.
3   It is not possible to achieve criteria 1 and 2 without focusing on the actual behavior of the participants. The trouble with the old criteria is that they began and ended with behaviors. The new criteria begin with behavior in order to get a window into the mental maps and type of reasoning that the individuals use and the organizational culture that they create.
4   The success of programs is *not* assessed by measuring insight gained or learning reported by the participants. Individuals often report high scores on insight and learning yet have not changed their defensive reasoning, their theories-in-use, their skilled unawareness and incompetence, and the organizational defensive routines.

Most experiential learning, at its best, helps individuals to change their behavior without changing their defensive reasoning or their theory-in-use. They accomplish this primarily by helping individuals behave in the opposite manner than they presently use. If they dominate, they learn to become more passive. If they talk most of the time, they learn to listen more. Being passive or listening more is not a change to a new theory-in-use. It occurs by suppressing the old one. Such changes usually wash out the moment the individual is bewildered, threatened, or feels betrayed.

Most large corporations expose their executives to various kinds of leadership programs where the fundamental criterion is to present knowledge in an interesting manner, in a way that leads to action and in a way that is not disquieting to the audience. For example, recently I participated in a one-week program on leadership attended by the top 40 executives of one of America's largest corporations. The presenter, one of the most sought after speakers, talked about the difference between managing and leading. He advised the top executives to focus on being leaders and less on being managers. He used cases, video tapes, simulations, and skillful questioning. He generated a great deal of interaction and enthusiasm. The presentation was rated as one of the best.

The next day, I met with the CEO and his immediate reports. They discussed how to become more effective. As the discussion began to get into the undiscussables the dialogue became cautious – individuals spoke abstractly. They cautioned about changes that were too dramatic and quick. Soon the group members produced a remarkable example of managing these issues rather than leading. No one appeared to realize the inconsistency they were creating. Or, if they did, they were not saying. A month later I had a chance to meet the presenter. We got into a discussion about education for leadership. I then told him the story above. It did not surprise him. After all, he asked, how much can one accomplish in a few hours? How much can one examine senior managers' inconsistencies without getting in trouble? After all, aren't the most effective change attempts incremental? The argument that he was making to defend his own practice was consistent with managing and not leading in his practice.

## CONCLUSION

Management of human activities is importantly based on the Model I theories-in-use and the organizational defenses that the Model I theories-in-use create. The theories-in-use and the organizational defensive routines combine to create conditions of limited learning throughout the organization. The actions and the routines are internalized and produced skillfully. Skillful actions are tacit.

It is possible to intervene to help managers learn a Model II theory-in-use. Once the theories-in use are activated they reduce the organizational defensive routines that, in turn, lead to more effective organizational learning.

## References

Argyris, C., 1974, "Alternative Schools: A Behavioral Analysis," *Teachers College*, Record 75, 4, 429–52.

Argyris, C., 1982, *Reasoning, Learning, and Action*, San Francisco, Jossey-Bass.

Argyris, C., 1990, *Overcoming Organizational Defenses*, Needham, MA, Allyn-Bacon.

Argyris, C., 1993, *Knowledge for Action*, San Francisco, Jossey-Bass.

Argyris, C., and Schön, D., 1974, *Theory in Practice*, San Francisco, Jossey-Bass.

Argyris, C., and Schön, D., 1978, *Organizational Learning* Reading, MA, Addison-Wesley.

Argyris, C., and Schön, D., 1996, *Organizational Learning II*, Reading, MA, Addison-Wesley.

Argyris, C., Putnam, R., and Smith, D. M., 1985, *Action Science*, San Francisco, Jossey-Bass.

Nelson, R. R., and Winter, S. G., 1977, *An Elementary Evolutionary Theory of Economic Change*, Cambridge, MA, Belknap Press of Harvard University Press.

# — 3 —

# Why Individuals and Organizations Have Difficulty in Double-loop Learning

Change in behavior is considered a primary criterion for effectiveness by organizational development researchers and practitioners. One way to alter behavior is through direct behavior modification. Learning theorists have been especially vocal in this approach. Another way is to understand the meanings people create when they deal with each other. Cognitive psychologists and sociologists, many ethnomethodologists, and existentialists have been primary contributors to this line of inquiry (see Argyris, 1980b; Argyris and Schön, 1974, 1978).

The experientially oriented theorists have tended to be biased towards the second approach, one that might be called the individual and social construction of reality. Donald Schön and I have attempted to build on this approach in several ways. We have suggested that there are important differences between the meanings created when people espouse their views and when they act them out. Moreover, individuals are often unaware of these differences. They can best be discovered by observing people in action and inferring the meanings embedded in their actions. Finally, we have suggested that the source of meanings is in the theories of action people use (not those they profess to hold), and that the learning systems of society reinforce these theories. Hence, behavior change that is more than a "gimmick" requires changes in the theories that people use and in the learning systems of the organization.

In this chapter, I would like to describe some recent research results. They suggest that equally, if not more, fundamental to the theories of action that people use are their reasoning processes. Reasoning processes are those activities by which we create premises which are assumed, or are proven, to be valid and from which we draw conclusions about how to act. Popper (1969) has suggested that it is these reasoning processes that are at the core of how individuals construe reality.

## ORGANIZATIONAL LEARNING: SINGLE- AND DOUBLE-LOOP

Learning is defined as occurring under two conditions. First, learning occurs when an organization achieves what it intended; that is, there is a match between its design for action and the actuality or outcome. Second, learning occurs when a mismatch between intentions and outcomes is identified and it is corrected; that is, a mismatch is turned into a match.

Organizations do not perform the actions that produce the learning. It is individuals acting as agents of organizations who produce the behavior that leads to learning.

Organizations can create conditions that may significantly influence what individuals frame as the problem, design as a solution, and produce as action to solve a problem. Individuals, on the other hand, may also bring biases and constraints to the learning situation that are relatively independent of the organization's requirements. An example of constraint is the human mind's limited capability for information processing. An example of bias is the theories of action with which people are socialized and which they necessarily bring to the organization. These theories significantly influence how individuals and groups solve problems and make choices, as we shall see below.

Whenever an error is detected and corrected without questioning or altering the underlying values of the system (be it individual, group, intergroup, organizational or interorganizational), the learning is single-loop. The term is borrowed from electrical engineering or cybernetics where, for example, a thermostat is defined as a single-loop learner. The thermostat is programmed to detect states of "too cold" or "too hot," and to correct the situation by turning the heat on or off. If the thermostat asked itself such questions as why it was set at 68 degrees, or why it was programmed as it was, then it would be a double-loop learner.

Single-loop and double-loop learning are diagrammed in figure 3.1. Single-loop learning occurs when matches are created, or when mismatches are corrected by changing actions. Double-loop learning occurs when mismatches are corrected by first examining and altering the governing variables and then the actions. Governing variables are the preferred states that individuals strive to "satisfice" when they are acting. These governing variables are not the underlying beliefs or values people espouse. They are the variables that can be inferred, by observing the actions of individuals acting as agents for the organization, to drive and guide their actions.

The diagram indicates that learning has not occurred until a match or a mismatch is produced. From our perspective, therefore, learning may not be said to occur if someone (acting for the organization) discovers a new problem or invents a solution to a problem. Learning occurs when the invented solution is actually produced. This distinction is important because it implies that discovering problems and inventing solutions are necessary, but not sufficient conditions, for organizational learning. Organizations exist in order to act and to accomplish their intended consequences. Another reason this distinction is important is related to our recent research which suggests that significantly different designs, heuristics for action, and criteria for success are used when individuals discover and invent *concerning an issue* than when they discover and invent in order *to produce an outcome about* the issue (Argyris and Schön, 1978; Argyris, 1980b).

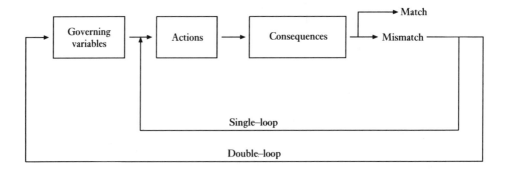

**Figure 3.1**  Single-loop and double-loop learning

Finally, single- and double-loop learning are required by all organizations. One might say that one of the features of organizations as a social technology is to decompose double-loop issues into single-loop issues because they are then more easily programmable and manageable. Single-loop learning is appropriate for the routine, repetitive issue – it helps get the everyday job done. Double-loop learning is more relevant for the complex, non-programmable issues – it assures that there will be another day in the future of the organization. (There are times, however, when single-loop learning may be relevant to long-range survival. For example, one of Europe's leading organizational research institutes was having difficulties with certain important clients because some of its interventionists failed to meet deadlines, to be on time for meetings, and so on.)

This chapter examines the reasoning processes people use when they are attempting to double-loop learn for themselves or for the organization. We will show that the reasoning processes people use for double-loop learning are actually counterproductive to such learning; that people are unaware of the counterproductive features of their own actions but usually quite aware of such features in others; that the lack of awareness exists in all subjects, and hence, may be due to a program in people's heads of which they must necessarily be unaware.

## The Importance of Double-loop Learning to Science and Practice

The overwhelming number of organizational changes reported in organizational development, political science, management information systems, and organizational sociology represents single-loop changes (Argyris, 1972, 1973, 1976b; Argyris and Schön, 1978). Reviews by Hage (1980) and Lammers (1980) appear to arrive at similar conclusions. The emphasis on organizational single-loop learning may be at least partially due to the fact, as noted above, that most organizational activities are single-loop; that is, decomposing complex tasks into simpler tasks which produce the intended result when correctly carried out.

But several unintended consequences result when social scientists study primarily single-loop change. Although single-loop actions are the most numerous, they are not necessarily the most powerful. Double-loop actions – the master programs – control the long-range effectiveness, and hence, the ultimate destiny of the system.

## Some Gaps in the Change Models Currently in Good Currency

Lewin, many years ago, developed a model of change that has been used for single- and double-loop organizational learning. The model suggested three stages: unfreezing, introducing the new values and behavior, and then refreezing. This model has been developed further by several writers (e.g., Schein and Bennis, 1965). Essentially, most of these models assume that unfreezing is produced by showing that actions lead to unintended inconsistencies (i.e., the impact is not what is intended). They also assume that human beings abhor such inconsistency, and hence, seek to learn new actions and values so that they do not repeat such errors. Finally, practice or experimentation with the new actions is assumed to lead to attitude and value change, as well as behavioral change.

At the outset, Donald Schön and I used essentially the same model to describe our views on change (Argyris and Schön, 1974). But we soon learned that the model was useful primarily at an abstract level of discourse and for single-loop learning. When we attempted to help individuals unfreeze the old in order to produce double-loop learning, we found that were several crucial gaps in the model.

The first gap was that the old model assumed that individuals had the skills to learn the new behavior, or at least the skills to learn the new skills. It now appears that this is not necessarily the case for double-loop learning. For example, we believed that if individuals were able to experience an inconsistency in their actions, they would correct it. This belief proved valid only when the individuals could alter their actions without examining their governing variables (e.g., listen more, or ask specific questions). But if the error was of a magnitude to produce mistrust rather than trust, correcting it was not simple. In order to produce trust, individuals must entrust themselves to others; they make themselves vulnerable. Before they are willing to take such action, they must examine their fears about what others may do to them, or their fears about designing their own vulnerability. Such an inquiry will lead to the underlying assumptions and values they hold which, in our language, are part of the governing variables of their theory of action. It is important for social scientists to study double-loop change because if they focus only on single-loop change, they may unwittingly become servants of the status quo (Argyris, 1972, 1980b; Moscovici, 1976).

This consequence holds negative outcomes for social science as a science. It is becoming evident that there may be a paradox embedded in the goal that social science should be descriptive of the world as it is. If social scientists aspire to study individuals and systems as they are, they will inevitably fall short of their goal: a complete description of things as they are would have to include a valid description of the capacity to make significant changes, and of the mechanisms by which these changes will occur. Knowledge of these mechanisms will also produce valid generalizations about constraints to double-loop organizational change. Such significant changes require changes in the organizational governing variables and master programs, that is, double-loop changes. But double-loop changes cannot occur without unfreezing the models of organizational structures and processes now in good currency. These models, in turn, cannot be unfrozen without a model of a significantly different organizational state of affairs; otherwise, toward what is the organization to change? If these models are genuinely new, then they do not now exist. If they do not now exist, then their invention and their use is an act of proscription, a normative stance. Yet if the logic is correct, the normative stance is needed to get at the inner nature of the present double-loop features and potentials of the organization. Hence, a full description of the world as is requires the intervention of stimuli from a world that presently is largely theoretical.

This leads to the second gap, namely, the pervasiveness with which individuals are unaware that they do not have the skills that they may value. The gap is, as we shall see, compounded by the fact that the lack of awareness may not be due simply to some void or missing knowledge, but may actually be tacitly designed, largely automatic, and hence, a highly skilled action.

The third gap is related to the belief held by many of us dealing with experiential learning that unawareness is primarily related to some form of suppression, especially of feelings. We assumed that if individuals could learn to get in touch with, and to express, their relevant feelings, then the scope of their unawareness would decrease and the probability of producing competent actions would increase. Again, as in the case of the other assumptions, this is partially valid but incomplete. It appears that the basis for individuals not being in touch with their feelings, or being reluctant to express them, is not simply defensiveness or resistance. Rather, human beings may use reasoning processes that unknowingly distort the necessity to be in touch with and express their feelings. In other words, in order to express feelings we must first alter reasoning processes.

A fourth gap is the assumption that one can understand the values individuals have by asking them to state them. If individuals do not behave consistently with the values they espouse, then that is usually seen as an error to be corrected. It now appears that a somewhat more complex interpretation is more valid. If an error is a mismatch between intentions and actual consequences, and if individual actions are designed, and if they are free of situational constraints on their design and implementation, it is not possible for individuals to knowingly design and execute an error. If A decides to act in a way that will produce dysfunctional consequences, then such "errors" are intended, and hence, there is a match, not an error.

If such errors are not errors, then they must be the consequence of some design. If this is so, then individuals must have some sort of map, schemata, micro-theory, that they use to inform their design. Since this design or theory is different from the one they espouse, a differentiation must be made between espoused values and theory on the one hand, and the theory-in-use. Social scientists have focused for many years on the inconsistencies between espoused values and actual behavior. What has hardly been discussed are the values, or the theory-in-use, that explain the inconsistencies, i.e., that show how the inconsistent is consistent.

These gaps suggest that the differences in complexity between single- and double-loop learning may be more profound than previously anticipated. If so, the programs for organizational double-loop learning may require more effort than those designed for single-loop learning.

Some recent data may help to illustrate the points made above, as well as to set the foundation for our view about designing organizational double-loop learning.

## THE CASE OF X AND Y: GETTING AT THE UNDERLYING
## REASONING PROCESSES

Fifty-three local and state government officials (25 percent women and 19 percent other minorities, ranging in age from early 30s to late 50s) were given an excerpt from a conversation between Y and X. Y, the superior, had been asked to "help X change his attitudes and behavior so that he could improve his performance." Although the organization was genuinely interested in keeping X, he would probably have to be dismissed if his attitudes and performance did not improve.

Y made the following comments to X.

- X, your performance is not up to standard (and moreover . . .)
- You seem to be carrying a chip on your shoulder.
- It appears to me that this has affected your performance in a number of ways. I have heard words like "lethargy," "uncommitted," and "disinterested" used by others in describing your recent performance.
- Our senior professionals cannot have those characteristics.
- Let's discuss your feelings about your performance.
- X, I know you want to talk about the injustices that you believe have been perpetrated on you in the past. The problem is that I am not familiar with the specifics of those problems. I do not want to spend a lot of time discussing something that happened several years ago. Nothing constructive will come from it. It's behind us.
- I want to talk about you today, and about your future in our system.

Each participant was asked to answer three questions:

1  What is your reaction or diagnosis of the way Y helped X?
2  What advice, if any, would you give Y to improve his performance when helping individuals like X?

3   Assume that Y met you in the hall and asked, "What did you think of the way I handled X?" How would you respond? Please write up your response in the form of a scenario, using the right-hand side of the page. On the left-hand side of the page, write any thoughts or feelings that you might have during the conversation which you would not, for whatever reason, communicate to Y.

All but two (97 percent) of the respondents diagnosed Y's actions as largely counter-productive to helping X. Two believed that Y behaved only partially effectively since he did make a few errors "in the manner that he talked with X." Hence, the first feature of the diagnosis was that there was near consensus that Y's actions were not effective. If consensus is an indication of valid information, then the respondents were getting at what they believed to be the truth.

The second feature was that the reasoning processes used to construct the diagnosis involved inferences that were at varying distances from the directly observable data (i.e., the transcript sentences). Comments that appeared to be directly inferable from the transcript were "Y cut off X," "Y criticizes X's attitudes," and "Y quoted others to illustrate his points." There were also such statements as "Y was too blunt," "Y did not give X an opportunity to defend self," "Y prejudged X." These sentences may well be correct inferences but their validity is not self-evident. For example, Y may believe that he was not too blunt, that he did give X an opportunity to defend himself, and that he did not prejudge X. Y could maintain he was appropriately blunt in order to be honest, that he did not give X an opportunity to defend himself because he did not wish to open up the past, or that he expressed a judgment made by top management about X's performance, a judgment of which X was aware.

In the comments above, the respondents were making inferences about the meanings Y was producing when "helping" X. A third, and higher level of inference, is evidenced in the respondents' sentences that went beyond meanings and attributed motives to Y, presumably to explain his actions. For example, "Y was not interested in getting at the truth," "Y was aggressive, cold, detached," and "Y was unwilling and not interested in understanding X."

Examining some simple quantitative data, we find that in every individual diagnosis, the largest number of comments was at Level III, the highest, most abstract level of inference, the second largest number of comments was at Level II, and that there was a significant drop-off to the most direct inferences at Level I. Of 114 scorable sentences in the respondents' written diagnoses, 60 percent were Level III, 36 percent were Level II, and 4 percent were Level I. The important point is that the diagnoses with which the respondents framed the answer contained primarily attributions and evaluations that required complex levels of reasoning about the sentences spoken by Y. Less than 15 percent of the respondents illustrated these inferences with direct evidence.

The point we are making is that the different levels of inference made by individuals became their premises. They then generated their conclusions from these premises. For example, if Y was described as "blunt" or "not interested in getting at the truth," then it followed (given a tacit theory of defense) that he would probably upset X, and hence, little learning would occur. The inferences from the premises appear valid. The problem is that the premise is subject to question. It is doubtful, for example, that Y would agree with it. If so, it is also doubtful that they can help Y by using premises whose validity he may doubt. In other words, the premises should be subject to test.

When we examine the scenarios they wrote as to how they would communicate with Y, they did not attempt to test their premises. The participants assumed that their premises were valid, and obviously so. "Anyone reading this conversation can see that Y was insensitive and blunt" is a representative comment. And the near-perfect consensus of views described above appears to support this claim.

Before we explore why individuals did not bother to test their premises, a word about the instructions given to the participants. Some readers may wonder if the words "reaction" and "diagnosis" may not trigger different responses. We have tried each word separately, jointly, and in combination with other words (e.g., "Give us your views of Y's effectiveness" or "How effective do you believe Y was with X?") To date, the different combinations have not led to different results. In the early studies, when we interviewed respondents about the instrument, the overwhelming number of them interpreted our intent as learning their evaluation of Y's effectiveness with X. In this connection, our difficulty is not that Y made evaluations or attributions; indeed, we asked for such reactions. Our point is that all the respondents assumed that their evaluations and attributions were obvious, concrete, and required no testing.

The fourth feature is that embedded in the diagnoses was a micro-causal theory of what happened between Y and X. For example, if Y is:

blunt and negative;
judgmental and offensive;
threatening and lacking in sensitivity;
not interested in understanding X;
dominating X;
*then* X will feel: rejected, prejudged, unfairly treated, and defensive.

If the above is true, *then*: there will be little learning going on between Y and X so that X is helped.

Another way to describe what the respondents did is as follows. When asked to give their reactions to the sentences, the respondents organized the meanings inferred from the sentences into a causal sequence to explain the probable effectiveness of Y with X. In so doing, they enacted, or constructed, reality; that is, the diagnoses represented their view of what happened. All appeared to enact reality by creating a causal view that contained Levels II and III (attribution and evaluation) from which conclusions were drawn (X would feel defensive) and that little learning would occur.

Embedded in this causal analysis is that, if the respondents communicated their diagnostic frames to Y, they would be creating the same conditions for Y that they condemn Y for creating with X. For example, to tell someone that they are "blunt," "cold," and "insensitive" could be experienced by the receiver as blunt, cold, and insensitive. In other words, the respondents (all of them, including the two who had expressed some ambivalence) used reasoning processes (i.e., premises and conclusions) that produced a causal analysis of Y's impact on X. There was a high degree of agreement that, if the analysis were told to Y, it would create the very conditions that they deplored.

When this puzzle was pointed out, the participants reacted in two ways. The initial reaction of the majority was to deny that this was the case, and to try to prove that the logic used by the instructor was incorrect (see Argyris, 1982). But the further the discussion progressed, the greater the number of respondents who agreed with the faculty member. Moreover, an increasing number pointed out that their reactions to the faculty member's comments, and each other's, contained the same type of reasoning (e.g., attributions and evaluations that were neither illustrated nor tested) that they used with Y. They pointed out that the faculty member was also making attributions and evaluations about their actions. He was, however, illustrating them and testing them publicly.

When the faculty member asked the class what they were now thinking and feeling, all those who replied (about 50 percent) used such words as "surprised," "shocked," "disbelief." When asked if anyone had a different set of reactions, no one described any.

The sixth feature of the diagnosis was that the respondents were unaware of the inconsistencies. Otherwise, why the surprise and shock? This attribution by the faculty member appeared to help some of the participants formulate a new reaction. They reported that, while the attribution might be true, many of them had no intention of telling Y what was in their diagnostic frame. They intended to censor the ideas in their frame. A few did say that they did not expect to censor the content. They believed that someone had to be direct and forthright with Y, just as they believed that Y had to be direct with X. We will call this group the "direct" or "forthright" group. They represented about 11 percent of the respondents.

An overwhelming number of the respondents (89 percent) took what may be described as an "easing-in" approach. Primarily through questions, and what some described as "neutral" statements, they would get Y to realize his errors. The easing-in approach meant that Y would be asked questions by which, if correctly answered, he would discover what the "helpers" had been keeping secret in their diagnostic frames. As we shall see, if Y could answer these questions in the manner considered appropriate by the framers, he might not have acted toward X as he did.

The reasoning behind the easing-in approach appears to be as follows. The respondents hold a micro-theory of defensiveness (Y's) that they use to design their actions. The theory of defense suggests: do not prejudge, do not evaluate, do not upset, do not appear negative. There are four troublesome characteristics of this micro-theory.

1  It does not tell an actor what to do; it informs him what not to do.
2  It advises the actor not to do what he is already doing, or has already done. In this case, the participants have already prejudged, have evaluated negatively, etc. Hence, the advice to hide what they have done.
3  The advice is at such a high level of inference that the recipients can violate it without being aware of the violation.
4  The organizational reality was that Y had to be evaluated and judged.

Let us turn to an example of the easing-in approach. Keep in mind that the scenario and the thoughts and feelings were written by the same person.

## Example A

| Unexpressed thoughts and feelings | Conversation |
|---|---|
| *Let him commit himself first, so I can see what he thinks happened.* | Y:  Did you read my memo on the X meeting? |
| | ME: Yeah, looks like it was quite a meeting. |
| *"A guy like X"... there's my cue.* | Y:  So how do you ever know if you got through to a guy like X? |
| | ME: You didn't write much about what he was like. |
| | Y:  He didn't talk a lot. Wouldn't look directly at me when he was talking. |
| *How much planning did Y do?* | ME: What were you thinking he'd say? You know, before the meeting. |
| | Y:  I expected he'd complain a lot but I cut him off when he started in on it. |

| | |
|---|---|
| *Apparent from your memo.* | ME: If he didn't talk much, how come he opened up with you to complain? |
| | Y: I asked him what he felt about his past. |
| *Let's see if he catches on by himself.* | ME: (pause) |
| | Y: Then I turned right around and cut him off. That wasn't very smart. |
| *Agree with him a little before you lead him into the big question.* | ME: It's hard to know how much of the past to listen to. But you must have some idea where he went wrong. |
| | Y: Everybody tells me he has a terrible attitude. I kept trying not to pay attention to how defensive he was. But he sat back kind of smug and – |
| *Get his attention back on his own problem of dealing with X.* | ME: (breaking in) What do you think of this assignment anyway? |
| | Y: Almost hopeless. |
| *Should I take him into the "what if fire" or the "what if succeed"? I'll go this way first, come back again.* | ME: You could be right. But what would happen if you did succeed? |
| | Y: Management – and old Z – would pat me on the back and then forget it. And I'd still have X. |
| *Give him a little sympathy. Then let's see if he knows what he's got here.* | ME: Sounds like the guys have been razzing you about X. But really, if you do turn him around, won't he be of some value? He must have been at one time. |
| | Y: Yes, I suppose if he wasn't management wouldn't keep him around. I should have told him that, too. |
| *You've got it. I won't rub it in. However, there's another one to mention.* | ME: I don't know, Y. It sounds to me like you didn't do enough homework. How can you work on this guy if you don't know what made him so good up until three years ago? |
| *Now he's getting enthusiastic. That's better.* | Y: That's for sure. |

From the material on the left-hand side, we infer the writer was always "in control." She had diagnosed Y as ineffective, and her task was to get Y to gain this insight without telling him directly. She did not suspend her diagnostic frame but used it covertly to judge and evaluate Y's responses. Note her unexpressed thoughts are not non-directive, do not ease in. The easing-in feature is primarily related to the questions she asked and the comments that she made. However, these comments may not have had the impact intended.

An analysis of Example A scenarios (see table 3.1) includes other reasonable interpretations. Column 1 contains the "left-hand," unexpressed thoughts. Column 2 contains my inference of the meaning embedded in the column 1 material. Column 3 is what the writer of the case actually said. Column 4 contains my inference of Y's possible interpretation of what was said to him in column 3. Column 5 contains near quotes of how Y responded to the column 2 conversation.

It is important to keep in mind that gaps between what the helper intended and the meanings Y could have inferred were found in all the cases. The content of the gap may have varied, but the existence of the gap, and unawareness of the gap, did not vary.

Table 3.1 An analysis of an easing-in case

| Thoughts on the left-hand side of the case | Meaning inferred by the writer | What the respondent said | Possible meaning to Y as inferred by the writer | Y said |
|---|---|---|---|---|
| Let him commit himself first so I can see what he thinks happened. "A guy like X" – there's my cue. | I would like to get Y's view without telling Y that this is my intent. I'll use Y's unillustrated evaluation of X to get him to commit himself about what he thinks happened. | "Yeah, looks like it was quite a meeting." "You didn't write much about what he was like." | I wonder what she means by that. Can I get her to commit herself without telling her my intent? "You have not communicated to me your view of X." I wonder why she says that? What is she trying to find out? | "So how do you ever know if you got through to a guy like X?" "He didn't talk a lot. Wouldn't look directly at me when he was talking. |
| How much planning did Y do? | I'll try another way of discovering his view of the situation. I wonder if he thought through the approach. | "What were you thinking he'd say? You know, before the meeting." | What is she getting at? Doesn't anyone expect a guy in trouble to complain and find fault with others? | "I expected he'd complain a lot but I cut him off when he started in on it." |
| Apparent from your memo. | I know you cut him off. I have to get you to see your errors. | "If he didn't talk much, why did he open up with you to complain?" (Pause) | What is she getting at? I initiated that by asking him about the past. | "I asked him what he felt about his past." |
| Let's see if he catches on by himself. | (Meaning is covert) His inconsistencies are so obvious that perhaps with a pause he will reflect on them. | (Pause) | I guess she wants me to say that I cut him off and that was not effective. I'll admit that so maybe I can learn what she's driving at. | "Then I turned right around and cut him off. That wasn't very smart." |
| Agree with him a little before you lead him into the big question. | Softsoap Y a bit to prepare him for what is a threatening question. | "It's hard to know how much of the past to listen to. But you must have some idea where he went wrong." | I'm glad she sees my dilemma, but if she does, why has she asked me all those questions? Of course I have an idea of where he went wrong. It was his attitude. What is she driving at? | "Everybody tells me he has a terrible attitude. I kept trying not to pay attention to how defensive he was. But he sat back kind of smug and –" |

| | | | | |
|---|---|---|---|---|
| Get his attention back on his own problems of dealing with X. | I've got to get him back to what I think is the problem, namely, the way he dealt with X. | (Breaking in) "What do you think of this assignment anyway?" | She must know this is almost a hopeless case. Why is she asking me such obvious questions? What does she *really* have in mind? | "Almost hopeless." |
| Should I take him into the "what if fire" or the "what if succeed"? I'll go this way first, come back again. | Maybe I can get him to see the possible payoff if he is able to succeed with X. | "You could be right. But what would happen if you did succeed?" | She doesn't think I'm right. I believe it is hopeless and hence believe that the best that can come of this is that Z will feel good and I'll be stuck with X. She is trying to get me to either see something or say something. | "Management – and old Z – would pat me on the back and then forget it. And I'd still have X." |
| Give him a little sympathy. Then let's see if he knows what he's got here. | Sympathize with him in order to get him ready for my confrontation. | "Sounds like the group has been razzing you about X. But really, if you do turn him around, won't he be of some value? He must have been at one time." | No one is razzing me. Z and others are depending on me. She does not understand me. Of course if you turn X around it would be of value – but I think that it is hopeless. I'm feeling that it is hopeless to understand her or to get her to understand my views. | "I suppose. If he wasn't, management wouldn't keep him around. I should have told him that, too." |
| You've got it. I won't rub it in. However, there's another one to mention. | Finally you see it. I'll lay off that problem and go to another. | "I don't know, Y. Sounds to me like you didn't do enough homework. How can you work on this guy if you don't know what made him so good up until three years ago?" | Finally! She believes that I did not do a good job. I know what made him so good up until three years ago. The trouble is that he doesn't have it and he refuses to see it. Not much sense in arguing with her. | "That's for sure." |
| Now he's getting enthusiastic – that's better. | He finally sees what I have seen all the time. | | | |

## Example B

| *Respondent asked* | *Y could have thought* |
|---|---|
| What kind of reaction did you get from X? | She knows that he resisted. I wonder what she is driving at. |
| Did you discuss specific examples of poor performance that X could undertake to correct? | Of course I discussed this poor attitude. What is she driving at? |
| Did you talk about any specifics, such as his lateness in meeting deadlines? | I had to keep it general, lest we get into his rehashing old alibis. I wonder why she does not see that. |
| Do you think it would have been helpful to him to know exactly what it is he is doing that fails to meet the standards we expect? | She should know that. Besides, I wish, that I knew what specifics she is driving at. |

## Example C

| | |
|---|---|
| Well, I'm not sure. What were you trying to accomplish in the meeting? | I'll bet he knows and is not saying. |
| Do you think he left with that understanding? | Of course I do. I wonder if he thinks so. What is he driving at? |
| I wonder if X isn't concerned about whether he'll really have a fair chance this time. | Of course that is the way X will feel. Whose side is he on? What is he driving at? |
| It's probably difficult for X to understand your genuine interest in understanding his problems and providing him with a fresh start. I think you could have emphasized this a little more. | Of course that's X's trouble. He is blind to those who wish to help him. Now I'm beginning to see what he is driving at. |

To summarize, although the respondents appeared to hold tacitly a micro-theory of client defensiveness that led them to conclude that unilateral control, prejudging, and unilateral attributions were counterproductive, they acted in ways to produce these conditions *and* simultaneously advised Y not to produce these conditions, yet they were unaware of this inconsistency.

If one criterion of incompetence is to act in a way that one advises others not to act, then the actions of the respondents may be judged as incompetent. But there is an additional, and perhaps more troublesome, inference. Whenever individuals state propositions about how all should act under given conditions, and when they themselves do not act in accordance with that proposition, yet appear to believe that they are, they are then creating conditions of injustice. It is unjust to say that under condition A all individuals should behave B, when the person who states this proposition acts "not B" (opposite of B) when in condition A, and acts as if that is correct.

### Advice given to Y by the respondents

Finally, let us examine the advice that the respondents wrote they would give Y. Again, there was a high degree of consensus. For example, the comments below illustrate advice given by all the respondents. No advice is excluded that might have contradicted the comments below.

The advice that the respondents gave in their papers may be categorized as advice about processes that are internal and external to the actual interview. Advice about the internal processes was primarily advice about how Y should behave toward X in order to help X improve his performance. Advice about processes that are external to the actual interview included advice that Y should have studied X's file more thoroughly, made it clear that management wanted to keep X, and jointly defined with X specific assignments, measureable goals, and a timetable.

## Examples of advice about how Y should have behaved toward X
Y should have:

- encouraged X to candidly discuss his view of his successes and failures;
- found out from X what he feels are his strong points and where he needs improvement;
- helped X express his prior problems (without getting into personality issues);
- given him the feeling that he was wanted, that the senior staff saw good potential in him;
- ended the conference on a positive, upbeat note;
- expressed a genuine concern for X's future in the organization;
- listened genuinely to X's version of the problem;
- showed that he (Y) had an open mind;
- been more tactful to indicate the hope for a more cordial relationship;
- helped X vent his feelings in order to release his frustrations;
- been more specific and constructive in feedback concerning X's performance;
- motivated X toward improved performance;
- drawn out from X his ideas as to what he (X) perceived as his needs on the job and needs of supervision;
- avoided making subjective statements.

## Examples of advice about what Y should have brought to the session
Y should have:

- given X an indication that everyone was behind him to succeed; that they wished to give him a genuine fresh start;
- reviewed X's past history and performance in detail in order to discover when and why X's performance deteriorated;
- developed jointly with X specific assignments, measurable goals, and a timetable for completion;
- developed jointly with X regularly scheduled reviews;
- established jointly with X a system which would monitor improvement and, if essential, prepare for an ultimate dismissal;
- welcomed X to his department, and explained to X how important his job was, and how important it would be for him to succeed at his job.

The gap between the advice and producing the action is not large in the second or "external" category. Most respondents would know how (i.e., have the required skills) to study X's performance, to inform X that the company is behind him, and to define specific tasks, goals, and timetables.

The gap in the first category of advice is, as we have seen, large. That is, the respondents who recommended this advice had difficulty applying it themselves, and were unaware that this was the case.

It is not clear to us why most individuals completing these cases are able to produce advice easily, yet are unable to follow their own advice when they write their scenarios, and why they appear unaware that this is the case. We think that part of the answer is, again, the way they frame their advice. They may be unaware that their advice involves a very high level of inference.

## THE GENERALIZABILITY OF THESE RESULTS

Some readers may find the lack of variance troublesome. Everyone seems to create diagnostic frames that contain the same features they advise others not to use, and when they act, everyone seems to get into difficulties of inconsistency, incompetence, and injustice. I, too, was troubled by these consistencies, because I assumed variance is a necessary feature of the universe. Indeed, such consistent data could illustrate a poor theory or flawed empirical work.

Every time a new experiment was attempted, we tried to be aware of, and deal with, ways that our instruments and methods might be creating these results. I might add that we had enthusiastic support from the subjects because they did not like the inconsistencies that they were producing nor their apparent inability to correct them. If they could show that the results were somehow forced by the methods (including the behavior of the faculty), then they would feel greatly relieved.

To date, we have collected data using the X and Y case from 17 groups, with nearly 600 respondents (including respondents from Europe, South America, Africa, the Near East [Israel and Egypt] and India). The results are highly consistent. Indeed if we include the results obtained from the 3,000 individuals using different cases, the results are still the same. Why the high degree of consistency in the data?

### Treating High Levels of Inference as Concrete Reality

A possible answer to the question of why there is so little variance in the reasoning processes and actions of the respondents is that all individuals must distance themselves from the relatively directly observable data in order to design and manage their actions. It is not possible to react in an organized manner without first extracting from, and organizing from, what occurs. This is what is meant by "constructing or enacting reality." High levels of inference are necessary because they make possible on-line management of reality. In this connection, one is reminded of Simon's (1969) view that the environment is more complex than the human mind can deal with directly, and of Miller's (1956) work which states that the human mind may be able to process, at a given moment, seven (plus or minus two) units of information. Beyond this number, new and more abstract concepts are needed which subsume the lower level units of information. The work of both men suggests that there is a hierarchy of concepts which makes it possible to organize, make sense out of, and enact reality.

However, there is nothing in their work that requires this hierarchy of concepts be attributions or evaluations that are not illustrated or tested. That is, it may well be that it is the human mind that must use concepts requiring high levels of inference from the raw data. But why must individuals use concepts that contain such a high probability of miscommunication? And why do individuals use such concepts when they advise others not to do so? And why, in many cases, do they do so when they are simultaneously advising others not to do so (e.g., "The trouble with you is that you are putting the other person down.")? Scholars working with attribution theory have frequently documented that individuals act like naive scientists. They create causal explanations to explain what they observe. More often than not, they tend to blame others for errors, and they tend to attribute any positive consequences to themselves (Kelley, 1979; Kruglanski, 1980). But again, the question is why?

## Model I Theory-in-use

A second cause of the consistency in results is related to the fact that the focus is not on predicting the actual words or behavior individuals will use. These factors may vary widely, as do the values that people espouse. The focus is on understanding the master programs in individuals' heads so that we can predict the kind of meanings and behavioral strategies they will or will not produce.

Donald Schön and I have proposed a theory of action perspective which assumes that human beings design their actions (Argyris and Schön, 1974, 1978). Since it is not likely they can design complex actions *de novo* in every situation, individuals must hold theories about effective action which they bring to bear on any given situation. We suggest that there are two kinds of theories of action. The first are espoused theories. The advice that the respondents gave to Y were aspects of espoused theories of effective action. But as we have seen, few respondents acted congruently with those espoused theories. Moreover, most of them seemed to be unaware of the gap between their espoused theory and their actions. Such discrepancies are not new in social science.

The theory of action perspective does not stop there. It suggests that the unawareness is designed. It suggests that the incongruence is designed. It suggests, in other words, that human beings must have a theory of action that they use to produce all these difficulties. We call this type of theory their theory-in-use. If we can make explicit the theory-in-use, then we can explain, predict, and have the basis for changing these findings.

One of the difficulties with the present view of the attribution theorists is that they imply that individuals act as they do (e.g., make attributions that are untested) because they have to; it is "human nature." We could agree that it is human nature if we call it theory-in-use. We have been able to devise other theories-in-use which, once learned, allow individuals to behave other than according to the prediction of attribution theory (Argyris, 1976b; 1976c). This work suggests, therefore, that the cause is not a static human nature but rather that human nature is significantly alterable.

We have created a model of theory-in-use that most individuals appear to use to use. A Model I theory-in-use has four governing variables, or values, for the actor to "satisfice:"

1   strive to be in unilateral control;
2   minimize losing and maximize winning;
3   minimize the expression of negative feelings; and
4   be rational.

Along with the governing variables is a set of behavioral strategies such as:

1   advocate your views without encouraging inquiry (hence, remain in unilateral control and hopefully win); and
2   unilaterally save face – your own and other people's (hence, minimize upsetting others or making them defensive).

These governing variables and behavioral strategies form a master program which influences the diagnostic and action frames that individuals produce. Hence, when Y behaved as he did, he violated the governing variable of not eliciting negative feelings and the behavioral strategy of unilaterally protecting others and one's self. Such actions would not assist Y to win because winning, in this case, was defined as helping X change his attitude.

This theory-in-use, which we call Model I, is held by all of the individuals studied so far (Argyris, 1976a, 1976c; Argyris and Schön, 1974, 1978). Model I individuals are able to behave according to Model I, the opposite to Model I, or an oscillating Model I (i.e., A unilaterally controls B, and then B does the same to A, and so on). The behavioral strategies, once learned, are highly skilled, meaning that the action achieves its objectives. Although complex, it is performed effortlessly; actions are produced so fast that they appear automatic.

At the moment, our hypothesis is that Model I has been learned through socialization. This hypothesis, which has yet to be proven directly, is inferred from the following types of experiences. We observe many different individuals in many different settings using Model I. When we ask them when they learned to act as they do, the reply is, in effect, that they have been acting so ever since they can remember. When we ask them to try another model of action in their organization, they quickly point out that no one would understand them, that they might be seen as deviants, or that such an attempt might be held against them. When they decide they do want to learn to act according to a different model, and after they understand that model, they are still unable to behave according to it because automatic responses learned early in life get in their way. In order to overcome their automatic responses, they must go through experiences where they identify the rules – the theories – behind their responses. When they identify the rules, they can frequently identify that they learned them early in life.

We may now hypothesize that the respondents enacted the diagnostic frames that they did because they were being consistent with Model I, and being so made it possible for them to make recommendations and take action. But being programmed with Model I theory-in-use, they also made unillustrated attributions and evaluations; they saw no reason to test their attributions and evaluations because they believed they were true. They were unaware of the many inferences that were embedded in their reasoning processes because, according to their Model I theory-in-use, everything they thought and said was not only true, it was obvious and concrete. But the reason that it was obvious and concrete is that they had learned throughout life (i.e., in socialization) that most people would agree with them. This expectation was confirmed by the data in this case. Recall that 97 percent of the respondents had a similar diagnosis, and the remaining 3 percent were in partial agreement.

To summarize, the respondents made inferences that were at high levels of abstraction, whose validity was problematic. They acted as if their inferences were not abstract but concrete, and that the validity of their views was obvious.

These actions and thoughts are congruent with Model I theory-in-use. What is also predictable from, and congruent with, Model I is that such thoughts and actions will lead to unrecognized inconsistencies, self-fulfilling prophecies, self-sealing processes, and hence, escalating error. This, in turn, will lead to a world that may be said to be unjust. Unaware of what many of these consequences are, most individuals have no hesitation in advising others how to deal with Y, yet they will not be able to produce the actions that they themselves recommend. Injustice is a double-loop problem, precisely the learning domain in which human beings are programmed to be less than effective.

The thrust of the analysis above is that human beings have theories-in-use that make it likely that they will inhibit their own and others' double-loop learning; that they are largely unaware of these theories-in-use; and that both the unawareness and the counterproductive actions are due to highly skilled, internalized, and hence, tacit, automatic reactions.

If individuals reflected on their actions correctly (which is unlikely because of their theories-in-use), they would become aware of the counterproductive aspects of their action.

Human beings are said to be programmed to act automatically and tacitly in ways that are counterproductive to their espoused theories and to the advice they give others. They are not unaware of the inconsistencies in others' behavior, but they are programmed to with-hold feedback on this lest they be held responsible for upsetting others.

## FACTORS THAT INHIBIT ORGANIZATIONAL DOUBLE-LOOP LEARNING

If it is true that all these consequences are due to highly skilled and programmed, and hence, automatic reactions, then it follows that individuals will carry these skills into any social system, be it a private or public organization, family, school, union, hospital, and so on. If it is also true that individuals who act as agents for systems do the learning, then they will necessarily create conditions within the systems that inhibit double-loop learning. This prediction should not be inaccurate, even if individuals are placed in systems where the internal environmental conditions encourage double-loop learning and the external envir-onmental conditions are at least benign.

Such conditions may be said to exist in the temporary systems created in the semester classes or week-long seminars designed specifically to facilitate double-loop learning. To date, the hypothesis has not been disproven. All individuals who have entered such new learning environments, who have become aware of their Model I theories-in-use, who have learned about a theory of action that can facilitate double-loop learning, who have chosen to learn to act according to it, and who try to do so under supportive conditions, are unable to do so when left to their own devices.

For example, a group of six executives kept producing Model I actions after nearly 30 hours of attempts to alter their actions by themselves (Argyris, 1976a). In five different classrooms (ranging in size from 40 to 100 advanced graduate students) students were unable to produce actions that facilitated their own double-loop learning (Argyris, 1976b). A group of 12 executives was similarly thwarted after 12 hours of learning over a period of two days, each day separated by several months (Heller, 1982).

In all cases, it was the participants who diagnosed their own failures, and in all cases the faculty member was able to produce actions that satisfied most students (to date, more than 95 percent in any group) that it was possible to produce actions that facilitated double-loop learning. This suggests that the students had learned a new theory of action that they could use to identify facilitative actions, and that facilitative actions were producible.

If it is unlikely that double-loop learning will occur in organizations specifically designed for double-loop learning, it is plausible that double-loop learning will not occur naturally in organizations whose structure is congruent with Model I. For example, the three underlying assumptions of formal pyramidal structure are specialization of work, unity of command, and centralization of power, with information flow following the structure of power. These conditions are congruent with the Model I theory-in-use of unilateral control, win-lose competitive dynamics, and a focus on rationality of ideas to the exclusion of rationality of feelings (Argyris, 1970).

Does this mean that we are predicting that organizations should not be observed to produce double-loop learning? The answer is yes. Does this mean that organizations should not be observed changing their underlying values and norms? The answer is yes for those values that are related to how human beings deal with each other. The answer is "not necessarily" for organizational policies. Double-loop changes in substantive areas may occur, but *not* because the present participants detected and corrected errors (which is our definition of learning). The changes could occur by fiat or unilateral imposition. For example, the Pentagon Papers may be viewed as a beginning act of double-loop learning about organizational policies and practices. Those chosen to write them had the technical skills and access to the relevant information required to accomplish the task. But these inquiries were ordered by the top. Indeed, the case could be made that there were participants who held the views eventually described in the documents, but those views, previous to McNamara's edict, were undiscussable, and their undiscussability was undiscussable. Did the Defense Department learn how to deal with undiscussables and their undiscussability? I would venture the answer is no.

But at the core of this management information system were several interpersonal values, such as "valid information is a good idea." The difficulty was that (as is the case in most organizations) that the theory-in-use about valid information tends to be that valid information is a good idea when it isn't threatening. The moment any substantive or technical information is threatening, our Model I theories-in-use are automatically engaged.

When the requirements of our Model I theories-in-use are contrary to the technical requirements, a conflict occurs. The predisposition of the participants is to hide the clash, yet play the Model I political games that they have learned to "cover themselves." They will, in effect, violate the formal technical requirements and conceal the fact that they are fighting them. If successful, they will create a situation where the executives on top and the staff in charge of the management information systems will not know about the games, the camouflage of the games, or the camouflage of the camouflage.

Elsewhere we have tried to show how these features will necessarily have to occur in any organization whose participants are programmed with Model I (Argyris and Schön, 1978). We suggest that human beings programmed with Model I theory-in-use will create and impose an O–I (organizational Model I) learning system on any organization in which they participate.

Briefly, we attempted to identify the cognitive features of information that would tend to facilitate and inhibit the production of error. We hypothesized the following continua:

Conditions that enhance the probability of:

| [Error] | | [Learning] |
|---|---|---|
| Information is vague | _____ | concrete |
| unclear | _____ | clear |
| inconsistent | _____ | consistent |
| incongruent | _____ | congruent |
| scattered | _____ | available |

Donald Schön and I then suggested that when individuals programmed with a Model I theory-in-use strive to solve difficult and threatening problems for which available information nears the left end of these continua, they will create conditions of undiscussability, self-fulfilling prophecies, self-sealing processes, and escalating error. These conditions act to reinforce vagueness, lack of clarity, inconsistency, and incongruity, which in turn reinforce the use of Model I (i.e., people strive harder to be in unilateral control, to minimize losing and maximize winning, etc.).

At the same time, we suggested these conditions tend to create win–lose groups and intergroup dynamics with competitiveness dominating over cooperation, mistrust overcoming trust, and unquestioned obedience replacing informed dissent. They also lead to the coalition groups and the organizational politicking that have been described by Allison (1971), Bacharach and Lawler (1980), Baldridge (1971), Cyert and March (1963), and Pettigrew (1973).

Under these conditions, it is difficult to see how structural and policy changes will lead to double-loop learning. In order for this to occur, individuals must be able to alter their theories-in-use and to neutralize the O–I learning system while simultaneously, and probably under stress, acting according to a new theory-in-use (e.g., Model II; see chapter 9, pp. 000–0), and creating an O–II learning system. Unless they alter the Model I features, they will use their automatic, highly skilled Model I responses. This may be an explanation for the findings described above: individuals who value Model II and wish to learn it, who are economically autonomous and powerful, are unable to produce Model II actions during the early phases of learning, even though they are in an environment that approximates Model II.

These findings also imply that structural changes that are congruent with Models II and O–II will not work until they become part of the theory-in-use of individuals, and until people act in ways to create conditions congruent with O–II learning systems. This is one reason that I believe interventions should begin at the highest levels of power in the organization. If the top people don't implement the new actions and learning system, it is doubtful that those below can do so.

We hypothesize, therefore, that the automatic reasoning processes that lead to the inconsistency and the escalating error will be triggered off, no matter whether the problem being discussed is about long-range investments, internal resource allocation, or marketing strategy, and no matter whether the unit involved is groups, intergroups, or organizations. The major conditions that should exist are:

1    individuals are programmed only with Model I;
2    they are embedded in an O-I learning system; and
3    the subject matter is individually or systematically threatening.

The hypothesis above should not hold if the error in question is easily and objectively identifiable and/or the cost of hiding it is greater than the cost of violating the Model I values and behavioral strategies. Also, to the extent the error is easily illustrated, and the illustration difficult to discredit, individuals may violate the hypothesis above. Indeed, one may suggest that one reason management information systems (in the broadest sense) are becoming popular is that management hopes they will make it easier to surface error and more difficult to hide it, and hence, will lower the cost to individuals for surfacing it and raise the cost for not doing so.

The coverage of the hypothesis is broad, intentionally so. Simultaneously, it is easily falsifiable. All one has to do is present a case where individuals programmed with Model I theories-in-use, and embedded in O-I learning systems (in any social organization), dealt with a double-loop threatening issue (excluding the exceptions noted above) in such a way that errors did not escalate. The empirical illustrations contrary to this hypothesis are presently more easily obtained from organizations that deal with double-loop issues and whose problem-solving processes are more likely to be subject to inquiry; for example, governmental decision-making (Argyris, 1976a), and schools (Argyris, 1974). Illustrations from industry do exist (the Firestone tire, the Ford Pinto) but to date they are more difficult to document.

I am presently observing and tape-recording problem-solving and decision-making meetings in several organizations. At the time of this writing, a model has been developed of how the reasoning processes and the inconsistencies seen in cases like X and Y also are found when individuals are trying to solve investment problems, new product problems, or to alter marketing strategies. The model is based on the assumption that it is possible to raise the level of abstraction of the X and Y case to a point where:

1   the individuals involved have different views regarding the problem and its causes; the differences are directly related to basic values and underlying assumptions;
2   the different views imply that if one side is correct, the other side is incorrect (and hence, the differences imply faulty reasoning and inadequate competence on some one's part);
3   the implication of inadequate competence and faulty reasoning is experienced as threatening;
4   the parties involved must continue to work with each other in order to achieve specified goals.

In the substantive problems studied so far, there are five that approximate the conditions described above, where the differences are based on different views of the world and involve questioning and threatening the governing values of the organization and coalition groups. A pattern is beginning to emerge as to the dynamics of problem-solving and decision-making under these conditions.

First, after individuals frame the nature of the technical problem (let us say, a new investment policy), they explore it with others in order to learn the reactions of relevant participants. Let us assume that they find strong opposition to the investment policy because it implies changes in the organization's existing policies and governing values. As these differences become explicit, coalition groups are formed. Each side views its approach as the correct one, and depending on the position, the other side is viewed as liberal or conservative, forward-looking or backward-looking. These attributions become symbols around which intergroup rivalries are formed and maintained. They also serve in an individual's diagnostic frame as guides of how they will deal with, and interpret, the actions of others (as in the case of Y). For example, the forward-looking members tend to see the status quo members as well-meaning individuals who are blind to the future. The status quo members see the forward-looking group as alarmists and fuzzy thinkers.

Whenever each side meets by itself and produces a new set of recommendations that it believes the other side will disagree with, it generates an action frame for its members to use when they meet with the opposing group.

1   Do not do or say anything that will make the other side defensive. Do not discuss, and do not test, the attributions made by the other side's incompetence and counter-productive reasoning.
2   Focus on the negative consequences of the present (or projected) policies.
3   Do not polarize or overstate the case. Present the case, as much as possible, as one that is based on present governing values and does not represent a major change.

During the meeting, the liberal members present their views by continually emphasizing that their plan:

● is not a panacea;
● will help the organization do better what it is already doing (the plan is building on existing practice);
● is experimental;
● should be monitored by a group representing a wide range of views.

The group representing the conservative or status quo faction appears to take advantage of this action frame by continually pointing out how glad they are that the liberals realize their plan is not a panacea; that they conceive of it as an extension of, and hence, consistent with, present organizational values; that it should be experimental; and that it should be monitored by a group with a variance of views. The double-loop features are, in effect, translated as much as possible into single-loop features. The other side emphasizes, and whenever possible magnifies, the single-loop features.

Finally, the agreement is written up, with much wrangling over language to protect whatever gains each side believes it has achieved. The words eventually agreed on tend to be at a high enough level of inference that each side can use them to protect their respective position if it is attacked.

The precise way in which the implementation of each decision is monitored varies in specifics but not in underlying strategy. Each side appears to hold the other to the commitments made in writing. But as in the case of Y, there comes a time when the high level of inference language no longer hides the actions. Whenever, for example, the actions indicate that the forward-looking group is violating the agreed-upon limits by going beyond them, or that the status quo group is preventing implementation, the offended group complains of a misunderstanding, "unfair," "betrayal and dishonesty." When the reactions are intense, the problem is typically bucked up to the next level where a superior is asked to make the final judgment. So far, we find that most superiors attempt to take an easing-in approach that induces the warring factions to cooperate. It may be this type of action and consequence that leads to the coalitions and intergroup dynamics which create the basis of the political approach described by Allison (1971), Bacharach and Lawler (1980), Baldridge (1971), Cyert and March (1963), Pettigrew (1973) and the intergroup approach described by Alderfer (1977).

Gisele and Göran Asplund (1980) have presented cases where the interpersonal issues are intimately related to marketing issues. For example, in order to correct major marketing errors, it is important to discuss the errors. Yet major errors were a taboo subject. In order to examine the marketing errors, the Asplunds had to help the clients explore such questions as: what is it about failure that makes this client unable to discuss it?; how and why did failure become a forbidden topic?, and what is the cover-up process doing to the client's capacities to double-loop learn about major marketing issues?

In conclusion, our answer to the question of why organizations will be unlikely to learn is that the participants are programmed with a Model I theory-in-use and therefore create and/or are embedded in an O-I learning system which, in turn, requires or sanctions a Model I theory-in-use. A circular, self-reinforcing system is created that leads to self-fulfilling, self-sealing, escalating error whenever double-loop issues are involved.

The analysis above may seem pessimistic. But we are optimistic for several reasons. Many people espouse actions and values related to Model II. Hence, they would prefer such a world if it could be created. Second, none of the multi-level, self-sealing, error-escalating processes that we have identified appear to be due to unconscious or "deep" personality factors. They are related to skills and people can learn new skills. Third, although any given actor is unaware of his counterproductive action, his fellow actors are not. Hence, cooperation is a necessary condition for learning. Fourth, we have found that as people learn Model II, they necessarily create an O-II learning system which feeds back to reinforce the new theory-in-use. Fifth, change cannot occur without putting one's premises to test and that can lead to an increasing sense of trust. Sixth, after the first few days of trying to learn quickly, most of our participants relaxed and slowed down. They realized that learning Model II was going to be at least as difficult as learning to play, moderately well, a musical instrument or a sport. Moreover, the very requirement for extended practice provides everyone with an opportunity to test each other's sincerity. So far, the few who have tried to learn Model II action strategies in order to use them with Model I governing variables have been confronted on the inconsistency. It is hard to fool individuals about a theory-in-use they can implement well.

## CAN ORGANIZATIONS BE HELPED TO DOUBLE-LOOP LEARN?

Elsewhere we have illustrated our attempts to help organizations become double-loop learners (Argyris, 1976a; Argyris and Schön, 1978). I will briefly outline the process. The first step is to help individuals become aware of their Model I theories-in-use and automatic reasoning processes that lead to counterproductive skilled responses.

The second step is to help them see how they create and/or maintain features of O-I learning systems which, in turn, feed back to sanction Model I theories-in-use. The second step will necessarily begin to occur as the first one is taken. For example, we have asked top management groups to write cases (in the format of the X and Y case) on issues that are currently important in their organization. Some wrote about problems of evaluating marginal performers, others about limiting the power of financial personnel (power obtained through design and control of the financial system), others about the difficulty in making certain investment decisions or marketing decisions. They met for several days to discuss their cases. The discussions typically began by examining the way individuals dealt with these difficult issues. As the cases were discussed, the executives began to identify patterns in the way they solved problems. They began to see how issues became undiscussable, and how the undiscussability was covered up with games, or even new policies. In short, they began to infer the features of the learning system that existed in their organization. Whenever there were differences of opinion, new cases were generated to illustrate the respective views, and this led to a richer map of the O-I learning system. Whenever differences in view persisted, executives designed ways to test the competing views.

The third step is to help individuals learn a new theory of action (in our case, called Model II) in such a way that they could use it in an on-line manner under zero to moderate stress, thereby providing evidence that their new theory of action has become not only an espoused theory but also a theory-in-use. Incidentally, this does not mean that individuals learn to discard Model I. Quite the contrary. They develop rules that state under what conditions Model I and Model II theories-in-use would be preferable.

The fourth step is to introduce their new actions into the organization and simultaneously help others to learn them also. They may have staff individuals create learning environments to provide others with the same learning opportunities that they had. But in the final analysis, the subordinates' learning will be reinforced or extinguished by the actions of their superiors.

As both levels learn a new theory-in-use – hence can produce new actions – they necessarily also produce new learning systems. This makes it more likely that individuals can alter organizational features such as reward and penalty systems, evaluation, and control procedures. Simultaneously, the re-education of the next lower level will begin, and learning will spread throughout the organization. (An operational definition of "gimmick" from this perspective is any change in behavioral strategies without concomitant change in governing values. For example, if individuals combine advocacy with inquiry in order to win and not lose, they will soon be manipulating others and close themselves off from inquiry.)

There are two implicit assumptions in this stage theory of organizational double-loop learning that should be made explicit. The first is that intervention should begin at the highest levels of the organization, that is, at a level that has the required autonomy to implement the learning. The key criterion is that the individuals have enough power and autonomy to assure themselves, and others, that they are not kidding themselves or others when they strive to learn new theories-in-use and create new learning systems.

The second assumption is that organizational double-loop learning must begin at the individual level and then spread to the organizational level. This assumption implies another, namely, that it should not be possible to alter Model I theories-in-use and O-I learning systems by intervening at the organizational level with a new structure or policy. This is predicted to be the case because, even if a world is created that encourages Model II actions, individuals should not be able to produce such actions even if they wish to do so. Recall that this is what has happened so far in every Model II learning environment. The participants persevered in Model I until the faculty member intervened. This does not prove, however, that individuals can never learn Model II by themselves. It only illustrates that they have not been able to do so within the seminar time restrictions.

Our approach, which begins – and I should like to emphasize *begins* – with individuals, must do so because ironically we are dealing with one of the most successful and powerful socializing processes identified to date. Recall that we have found variance in espoused theories (e.g., many individuals espoused Model II), we have found variance in behavioral strategies (e.g., a Hitler and a domineering mother have different strategies of unilateral control), but we have found almost no variance in theories-in-use. We find, therefore, that even across cultures, individuals hold a Model I theory-in-use (although the Africans, South Americans, Indians, and others that have participated were all highly educated, many in Western school systems).

Individuals are walking social structures. The socialization is so extensive and efficient that individuals will normally not act in ways to undermine it. They can be left alone because they are programmed with automatic responses which as we have seen are highly skilled. The irony is that successful socialization probably cannot be altered without beginning at the individual level. Those who suggest that it is possible to conceive of organizations as individual, group, or organizational phenomena (Bidwell and Abernathy, 1980) probably are correct if they limit their propositions to steady states or self-maintaining patterns. The moment one focuses on double-loop learning the individual becomes the basic social structure, and supra-structures cannot be changed without beginning with the individual.

## CONCLUSION

Individuals appear to be programmed with Model I theories-in-use that make it unlikely that they will produce double-loop learning and highly likely that they will create O-I learning environments within organizations that will inhibit double-loop learning. The theories-in-use and learning systems interact not only to maintain and reinforce these consequences, but also to keep individuals unaware of the degree to which they are causally responsible for contributing to, and reinforcing, these consequences.

The individual-level phenomena of almost no variance in theories-in-use is probably evidence of effective socialization processes. Yet to change such extensive socialization processes, one must paradoxically begin by altering the individual automatic skilled reactions of socialization.

Individuals are walking social structures who cannot undergo double-loop learning without reflecting on their actions. As we have seen, this includes reflecting on their diagnostic and action frames. Such reflection requires examining the validity of the reasoning processes they use. But to test for such validity requires a commonly accepted view of a process, and criteria for testing and falsification. Moving from Model I toward Model II, therefore, requires the existence of a way to test that the move is occurring effectively. This means that we depend on another successful socialization result, namely, that individuals can agree on the logic of falsifiability.

Double-loop learning at the individual and organizational levels also involves the important issues of competence and justice. As we have seen, it is not just for individuals to define certain actions as incompetent and unjust, and then act as if the incompetence and injustice do not occur when they behave in the same way. Double-loop learning must also deal with undiscussability, the undiscussability of the undiscussable, and the puzzling fact that most individuals are unaware of their own causal contribution to these organizational features, yet are aware of the causal contributions of others.

Research on intervention suggests that it is possible to help individuals learn new theories-in-use and to create new learning systems. The intervention requires the creation of a dialectical learning process where the participants can continually compare their theories-in-use, and the learning system in which they are embedded, with alternative models. This requires that interventionists make available alternative models with significantly different governing values and behavioral strategies. To the extent that social scientists remain rigorously descriptive of the world as is, they will unintentionally reinforce the status quo and add yet another set of factors to the difficulty individuals and organizations have in double-loop learning.

# References

Alderfer, P., 1977, "Group and Intergroup Relations," in Hackman, J. R., and Suttle, J. L. (eds), *Improving Life at Work*, Santa Monica, CA, Goodyear, pp. 227–96.

Allison, G. T., 1971, *Essence of Decision: Explaining the Cuban Missile Crisis*, Boston, Little Brown.

Argyris, C., 1970, *Intervention Theory and Method*, Reading, MA., Addison-Wesley.

Argyris, C., 1972, *The Applicability of Organizational Sociology*, Cambridge, Cambridge University Press.

Argyris, C., 1973, "Some Limits on Rational Man Organizational Theory," *Public Administration Review*, June.

Argyris, C., 1974, "Alternative Schools: A Behavioral Analysis," *Teachers College Record*, 75, May pp. 429–52.

Argyris, C., 1976a, *Increasing Leadership Effectiveness*, New York, Wiley-Interscience.

Argyris, C., 1976b, "Theories of Action That Inhibit Individual Learning," *American Psychologist*, 31, 9, September.

Argyris, C., 1976c, "Single- and Double-loop Models in Research on Decision-making," *Administrative Science Quarterly*, 21.

Argyris, C., 1980b, *Inner Contradictions of Rigorous Research*, New York, Academic Press.

Argyris, C., 1982, *Reasoning, Learning and Action*, San Francisco, Jossey-Bass.

Argyris, C., and Schön, D., 1974, *Theory in Practice*, San Francisco, Jossey-Bass.

Argyris, C., and Schön, D., 1978, *Organizational Learning*, Reading, Mass., Addison-Wesley.

Asplund, G., and Asphund, G., 1980, "The IDS: An Integrated Development Strategy for Effective Organizational Adaptation," mimeograph, Stockholm, Sweden.

Bacharach, S. B., and Lawler, E. J., 1980, *Power and Politics in Organizations*, San Francisco, Jossey-Bass.

Baldridge, J. V., 1971, *Power and Conflict in the University: Research in the Sociology of Organizations*, New York, Wiley.

Bidwell, C., and Abernathy, D., 1980, "Structural and Behavioral Theories of Organizations: A Bibliographic Review," mimeograph, School of Education, University of Chicago.

Cyert, R. M., and March, J. G., 1963, *A Behavioral Theory of the Firm*, Englewood Cliffs, NJ: Prentice-Hall.

Hage, J., 1980, *Theories of Organization: Form, Process, and Transformation*, New York, Wiley-Interscience.

Heller, J., 1982, *Increasing Effectiveness in Colleges and Universities: Theory and Practice*, San Francisco, Jossey-Bass.

Kelley, H. H., 1979, *Personal Relationships: Their Structures and Process*, Hillsdale, NJ, Lawrence Erlbaum Assoc.

Kruglanski, A. W., 1980, "Lay Epistemologic Process and Contents: Another Look at Attribution Theory," *Psychological Review*, 87, 1, pp. 70–87.

Lammers, C., J., 1980, "Comparative Sociology of Organizations," *Annual Review of Sociology*, Annual Review, Inc., 4, pp. 485–510.

Miller, G. A., 1956, "The Magical Number Seven, Plus or Minus Two: Some Limits on Our Capacity for Processing Information," *Psychological Review*, 63, pp. 81–97.

Moscovici, S., 1976, *Social Influence and Social Change*, translated by Sherrard C., and Heinz, G., London, Academic Press.

Pettigrew, A. M., 1973, *The Politics of Organizational Decision Making*, London, Tavistock.

Popper, K. R., 1969, *Conjectures and Refutations: The Growth of Scientific Knowledge*, 3rd edn rev., London, Routledge & Kegan Paul.

Schein, E. H., and Bennis, W., 1965, *Personal and Organizational Change Through Group Methods*, New York, John Wiley.

Simon, H. A., 1969, *The Sciences of the Artificial*, Cambridge, Mass., MIT Press.

# — 4 —

# Crafting a Theory of Practice: The Case of Organizational Paradoxes

If paradoxes are an important phenomenon for administrators, (Argyris, 1985; Barnes, 1981), why is it that the prominent theories of administration or organization do not have them as a central focus? What would it require to craft theories where paradox has a primary role?

## LOGICAL AND BEHAVIORAL WORLD PARADOXES

I should like to differentiate between logical paradoxes and paradoxes that result from human action. Philosophers have focused on logical paradoxes for many years. A logical paradox occurs when the meaning embedded in the words used contains its own contradiction. For example, suppose that if I say "I am lying," then that statement is true. But if the statement is true, I am not lying; then the statement is false. In this example, the existence of the paradox can be identified by examining what the person said. We need no further data. The contradiction is embedded in the statement "I am lying."

The paradoxes that exist in the behavioral world, strictly speaking, do not have the same properties. Most paradoxes that I have observed occur because individuals designed and produced inconsistent meanings and disguised the fact that they were doing so. The resultant actions appear to be paradoxical because we do not know all the facts.

For example, assume that A said to B "I trust you." Assume also that A did not trust B but hid his true views because he did not wish to upset B. We have a situation where the "action" has at least three components. The first is what A said. It could be caught accurately by a tape recorder. If we stopped with the first component, the statement by A that "I am lying" is true. We then have the basis for the logical paradox.

The second component of the action was what A thought and did not say. A knew that he did not trust B, but he did not say so because he did not wish to upset B.

The third component was that A acted as if he were not withholding any views. He acted as if he were not lying. If we focus on components two and three, then A is still lying. However, there is no paradox because the thoughts and actions explain the cover-up. The behavior appears paradoxical because we did not know what was covered up.

One step further. Let us assume that A covered up because he intended not to upset himself by being responsible for upsetting B. Under these conditions, it is likely that A will not allow any discussion of the cover-up because to discuss it would upset B and A and would lead to a contradiction. Let us also assume that B senses that the cover-up cannot be discussed and he goes along, but B also covers up what he senses. We now have two individuals acting in ways that are undiscussable, and their undiscussability is undiscussable.

All these consequences not only maintain the original action paradox, but they make it unlikely that the paradox will ever be discussed. The actions are not only self-maintaining; they are also self-sealing. But if they are self-maintaining and self-sealing, and if this cannot be discussed, and if their undiscussability is undiscussable, then they are not manageable.

We now have a second-order paradox. The intention of management is to manage, yet it is not possible to manage actions that are not manageable.

We must study these actions paradoxes because, I believe, they are endemic to the way most organizations are managed. Organizations are designed and managed in order to make management less difficult but human beings act in ways that make management more difficult. I am suggesting that unlike the physical science universe where Einstein insisted that nature would not play tricks, in the universe of the behavioral world, tricks may be a key characteristic. How does one theorize about a tricky universe? Are there features of the tricks that can be stated in the form of disconfirmable propositions? If so, in what sense are they tricks?

## WHERE TO STUDY PARADOXES

Paradoxes of the kind that concern us develop as a result of programs in peoples' heads and norms in the culture in which they are embedded. What would lead individuals to produce such actions?

One of the richest hunting grounds for paradoxes is in the routines that exist to defend against embarrassment or threat, be it at the individual, small group, intergroup, or organizational levels. Organizational defensive routines may be defined as any policy or action that prevents someone (or some system) from experiencing embarrassment or threat, *and* simultaneously prevents anyone from correcting the causes of the embarrassment or threat. Organizational defensive routines are anti-learning and overprotective.

Although they are related, it is important that we differentiate organizational defensive routines from the well-known individual psychological defenses that clinicians have identified. Organizational defensive routines differ from psychological defensive routines in that:

1   they are taught through socialization;
2   they are taught as strategies to deal effectively with threat or embarrassment;
3   they are supported by the culture of the organization; and
4   they exist over time even though the individuals (with different psychological defensive routines) move in and out of the organization.

### An Example of an Organizational Defensive Routine: Mixed Messages

Built into any organization is the age-old dilemma of autonomy versus control. Subordinates wish to be left alone but held accountable. Superiors agree but do not want surprises. The subordinates push for autonomy asserting that leaving them alone is the best sign that they are trusted by top management. They push for a solution that combines trust with distancing. The superiors, on the other hand, push for no surprises by using information systems as controls. The subordinates see the control feature as confirming mistrust.

The point is not how to get rid of the dilemma. That will never occur; it is built into the concept of decentralization. The point is how to deal with it effectively.

Mixed messages are the most frequently used strategy to deal with this dilemma (see Argyris, 1985). The top keeps saying "We mean it – you are managing your show." The divisional heads concur that the message is credible except when the division or corporation gets into trouble or when a very important issue is at stake. In the eyes of the divisional heads, the corporation begins to interfere precisely when they want to prove their metal. In the eyes of the corporation, they intervene precisely when they can be of most help, that is when the issue "requires a corporate perspective."

Divisional heads described the mixed messages they received as: "You are running the show, however...."; "You make the decisions, but clear with...."; "That's an interesting idea, but be careful...."

Mixed messages contain meanings that are simultaneously: ambiguous and clear; imprecise and precise. Anyone who deals with mixed messages experiences the dilemmas that are embedded in them. The designers know that constructing a message to be clearly ambiguous requires skill and knowledge about the receiver. They know that to be vague and to be clear is inconsistent. Furthermore, to be clearly vague is not only inconsistent, but designed inconsistency. To design inconsistency makes the designer vulnerable unless the receiver does not question the inconsistency.

There are therefore four rules about designing and implementing mixed messages:

1  Design a message that is inconsistent.
2  Act as if the message is not inconsistent.
3  Make the inconsistency in the message and the act that there is no inconsistency undiscussable.
4  Make the undiscussability of the undiscussable also undiscussable.

The first-order consequences of mixed messages – which are based on rules that require inconsistent actions – is that they produce advice that is paradoxical: to be consistent, act inconsistently, and act as if that is not the case. To manage, act as if you are not managing. To make some issues discussable, make others undiscussable, and act as if this is not the case.

In order for human beings to act, they must first understand what is going on and why. In the case of defensive routines, this leads to a second-order consequence. Individuals create attributions to explain each others' actions. The attributions are often wrong, or at least incomplete. But, following the logic of mixed messages, the attributions are neither discussed nor tested publicly. As a result, any distortions or errors that may result are not corrected; indeed, they are often magnified and enlarged. This feeds back to reinforce the use of mixed messages as well as the rules about undiscussability and nontestability.

The third-order consequence is that the organizational defensive routines, in this case mixed messages, become unmanageable and uninfluencable. This, in turn, leads to a fourth-order consequence which is a set of operating assumptions or beliefs about defensive routines. Individuals express, on the one hand, a sense of despair and cynicism about the defensive routines ever being changed. On the other hand, individuals may come to believe that engaging defensive routines can be dangerous, because doing so will open a Pandora's box. Consequently, individuals distance themselves from engaging the defensive routines. The rule is to bypass them and act as if you are not bypassing.

The fifth-order consequence is that defensive routines take on a life of their own. They maintain, reinforce, and proliferate themselves; hence, they become unmanageable.

## WHAT ARE THE FEATURES OF THEORIES THAT DEAL WITH PARADOXES?

A theory about paradoxes must explain why human beings create a world that is contrary to the world they intend, or if they do intend the world, then how do they explain their actions by asserting that they are forced to act as they do? In either case, we are dealing with inconsistencies that appear to be designed. The first feature, therefore, of a theory to understand paradoxes that result from defensive routines is to describe the differences between what human beings espouse and how they act. After all, if the consequences are not what they intend, then what did they intend? What beliefs or theory of their practice do they hold and espouse?

The discrepancy between what human beings espouse and what they actually produce should be viewed as the result of a describable, systematic, nonrandom process. In other words, if paradoxes exist, if individuals behave in accordance with them, if their behavior is contrary to what they espouse, then there must be some theory of action in which this contradictory behavior is not contradictory.

The fundamental assumption, to return to the Einstein remark, is that there is a rational theory to explain the tricks even though the individuals may not be aware of it. One such theory is presented in the next section.

A theory that purports to explain human paradoxes is also a theory about self-responsibility. Human beings are causally responsible for their actions. The theory must help to explain the reasons that underlie human beings' reported denial of personal causal responsibility in creating and maintaining paradoxes. For example, the theory should explain the predisposition to blame others for the defensive routines, to insist that one is helpless to change them, and to be unaware of one's own causal contributions.

The theory should make explicit the relationship between personal causal responsibility and the creation of the larger social entities such as groups, intergroups, and organizations. There are at least two important types of explanations that the theory should provide. One is how the individuals create a universe that is consistent with and protects the inconsistency and the bypassing required by defensive routines. This explanation should also provide the basis for empirical research that would disconfirm important aspects of the theory. For example, it should not be possible to observe individuals producing defensive routines, and at the same time, producing them in a context that does not reward or sanction such defensive routines.

The second explanation should be related to the conditions under which a change in the context that does not sanction defensive routines would indeed reduce them. For example, if individuals are personally causally responsible for their actions, if they are "against" creating defensive routines, if they necessarily create systemic conditions that support the defensive routines, how could changes in the systemic features of defensive routines alter how the individuals act?

Again, the processes that answer these questions should lead to ways to test the theory empirically. For example, it should not be possible to get individuals to reduce defensive routines without providing them with a new set of skills and a theory of action that they can use to reduce defensive routines. Supplying these features should not be easy, because even if we knew what they were, their effective use would go against the skills that human beings presently use.

The theory that can be used to explain paradoxes should be part of a more general theory of human behavior in the context of administration and organization. Paradoxes exist in a universe where there is much that is nonparadoxical. The theory should deal with both sets of phenomena.

## A THEORY OF ACTION

In chapter 3 (see pp. 81–3) we detailed the development of the theory of action containing Models I and O-I theories-in-use. Models I and O-I can be used as an explanation of the source of paradoxes. The explanation stated simply is as follows.

- Human beings seek, in an interaction, to control the relationships in such a way as to attain their intended consequences (Bandura, 1977; de Charms, 1968; Heider, 1958; Strong and Claiborn, 1982).
- The theory of control embedded in Model I and reinforced by O-I is one of unilateral control. We gain control by taking it away from others. No one should be able to use the reciprocal of Model I theory-in-use and design actions that are consistent with Model I.
- Acting in ways to control that takes away the control of others triggers others' defensive routines. These, in turn, protect the parties involved, and at the same time, blunt the defensive routines or inhibit the attempts of individuals to act effectively. All parties now use defensive routines that escalate error, and create self-fulfilling and self-sealing processes.
- The result of mutually reinforcing defensive routines is to combine wishful thinking (Jones, 1977) (systematic overestimation) with anticipatory face-saving (systematic underestimation) which, in turn, results in systematic distortions. These distortions result in paradoxical consequences because, as we have seen, they result in conditions where individuals (or social entities) are effective and ineffective; they experience success and failure; the consequences are productive and counterproductive.

All theories of human nature are based upon a thesis of rationality or reasonability. Human beings are rational in that they keep their actions in consonant alignment with their beliefs. They coordinate their actions and expectations in the light of the best information they have (Rescher, 1977, p. 85). Our view is that there is rationality in the espoused theories and in the theories-in-use. The rationality of actions is to be uncovered by examining the theory-in-use. This makes understanding rationality more complex because, as we have seen, the rationality embedded in the theories-in-use is often counter to the rationality embedded in the espoused theories.

A theory of reasonability assumes that we are not systematically perverse. We do not act counter to or in disregard of our beliefs. Yet our research suggests that we are systematically perverse. A theory of reasonability also assumes that we do not act counter to, or without regard for, our intentions. Yet our research suggests that we do.

The apparent violation of the thesis of rationality and reasonability can be explained by differentiating between espoused theories and theories-in-use at the individual and organizational levels. It is the latter theory that makes us perverse, and at the same time, leads to defensive routines that prevent situational rupture but may lead eventually to systemic rupture.

## DEALING WITH THE BYPASS PHENOMENON

Defensive routines are created to bypass embarrassment or threat to individuals or systems such as groups, intergroups, or organizations. In order for them to work, the individuals acting as agents for the systems must act as if they are not bypassing. In order to accomplish these requirements, individuals must be highly skilled, and the context in which they are operating must reward such actions. If the actions are highly skilled, and if they are culturally sanctioned, then they will be taken for granted. This means that not only the bypassing will be taken for granted, but the bypassing of the bypassing will also be automatic and taken for granted.

Social scientists who intend to focus on paradoxes require theories that alert them not to take for granted the bypass activities that are taken for granted. Let me give an example. During a meeting of the top line and corporate staff officers in a large decentralized organization, the chief executive officer (CEO) asked why line and staff were having problems in working effectively. As a result of the discussion, at least four causes were identified by all present.

1   The philosophy and policies about how the organization is managed are inadequate.
2   Corporate staff roles overlap and lead to confusion.
3   Staff lacks clear-cut authority when dealing with line.
4   Staff has inadequate contact with top line officers.

The CEO appointed two task forces to come up with solutions. Several months later, the entire group met for a day and hammered out a solution that was acceptable to all.

There are two important features in this story. First, the staff-line problems are typical. Second, the story has a happy ending: the causes of the problems were reduced.

However, there is a bypass problem here. Why did line and staff officers adhere to, implement, and maintain policies that were inadequate, roles that produced confusion, and contacts that were insufficient?

But why address this question if we have solved the problem? If we have not reduced the defensive routines that made it possible for executives to adhere to, implement, and maintain what, by their own judgment, were errors, these organizational defensive routines will remain alive and healthy, ready to undermine this solution or to cover up other problems.

For example, some corporate staff members said that they tried to discuss these issues with line but felt the line did not wish to discuss them. Some line officers denied ever hearing such a request. Some staff officers acknowledged this by admitting that they asked "indirectly." Other line officers reported that they heard the request and deflected it because they had experiences where the staff went to the CEO after a visit to the divisional officers and communicated information they should not have passed on. The CEO looked surprised and asked why people censored their conversations. Because, responded some line officers, he (the CEO) tended to shoot from the hip, causing unnecessary trouble. The divisional presidents had learned how to shape messages and how to time them correctly; the staff unknowingly sabotaged this.

All these actions are highly skilled; they are based on concern for people, on what the administrators conceive of as being realistic, and they are all self-sealing.

When dealing with any issues that contain defensive routines, we must study the substantive problem, be it technical or human. We must also study the bypass problems to learn why individuals adhere to, implement, and maintain the causes over time.

## WHAT DRIVES DEFENSIVE ROUTINES IN ORGANIZATIONS?

By their very nature, organizations will produce conditions that tend to activate Model I theories-in-use and especially the bypass phenomenon. First, the theory-in-use of the pyramidal structure is consistent with Model I. For example, unilateral control over others is central to the concept of superior–subordinate relationships.

Second, most organizations are managed by the rule of exception. The rule instructs superiors to define performance standards and to manage the employees by inspecting carefully those who deviate from the performance standards. The performance of an effective organization, under this rule, would always tend to cluster around the standards already defined – there would be no surprises. Under these conditions, individuals would seek to protect themselves from deviant performance. And, as the world is unlikely to produce no surprises, individuals then have to protect themselves against this possibility. Protection tactics include camouflaging surprises, bypassing them and acting as if not doing so, and surfacing them in a form that is acceptable, which usually means down-grading the surprise.

Third, surprises can also be produced by the very finiteness of the human mind. It is difficult to know everything that may be required. There are always gaps of information and, hence, there is vulnerability. Model I theories-in-use tend to produce distorted information and escalating error; this exacerbates the vulnerability.

The human mind must assemble information by using abstractions to aggregate many individual cases. For example, management information systems take on the "chunking" feature of the human mind. But in doing so, they may eventually create a world of injustice which, in turn, will be threatening to the players, which, in turn, will activate the bypass mechanisms, which, in turn, can lead to a distortion of valid information, which would produce consequences contrary to those intended.

Let us examine the nature of information required by those who use it at the highest levels versus those who use it at the lowest levels of the organization. The top, who are distant from the point of action, require information that is abstract, objective, in which the logic is explicit, and in which the data can be compared and tracked. The first line or local level use data that is concrete, subjective, in which the logic is tacit, and in which the data cannot be compared or tracked. These information characteristics produce worlds with different views about what is effective and what is just. The relevant parties, using the logic inherent in the information they use, create conditions of misunderstanding and distancing from each other. The difficulties and injustice escalate as the rationality deteriorates (see chapter 8).

We may now examine two other assumptions that are embedded in organizations that create more puzzles and a higher likelihood of vulnerability. First, hierarchies are based on the rule that exceptions are major errors and that effective management means few or no major errors. Surfacing major errors will not be threatening.

Second is the assumption of a puzzling view of trust. The superior will trust the subordinate as long as errors are not produced. The subordinates, in turn, will feel trusted if the superior leaves them alone. The puzzle is that trust appears to exist under the unlikely conditions that errors will not be produced. If errors are produced, the superior will stay away (precisely when he or she intends to intervene and may be of help).

## WHAT CHANGES WOULD BE REQUIRED IN THE PRACTICE OF CRAFTING AND TESTING THEORIES?

The nature of theory would not change – a theory would still be a set of logically interrelated concepts that were operationally defined in such a way that any hypotheses derived from the theory could be tested by a set of operations that were independent of the theory. Theories of action would therefore still be concerned with issues such as threats to internal and external validity.

Social scientists will have to pay more attention to creating theories about universes that do not exist currently, normative theories about how to produce rare events, such as the reduction of mixed messages.

Normative theories, by the way, do not automatically become prescriptive in the sense that they advise administrators how to act. In the first stage, a normative theory has to be tested. The individuals use the theory tentatively in order to see if it works, and if it does, there may be unintended consequences. Only after they are satisfied that the consequences are desirable would the normative theory become prescriptive.

Theories that purport to explain paradoxes may require different views about human nature than those presently held. For example, I believe that most scholars assume that the actors should be able to produce what they intend if they have the requisite skills, if they wish to do so, and if the context in which they are embedded does not create insurmountable barriers. These theories assume a sense of personal causality (de Charms, 1968; Deci and Ryan, 1985; Heider, 1958) and efficacy (Bandura, 1977).

Our research indicates a more complex relationship. On the one hand, we too accept the notion of personal causal responsibility, which, in turn, assumes that the actors' intentions are relatively transparent and that a sense of self-efficacy is crucial in designing whatever the actors consider appropriate actions. On the other hand, we are also suggesting that holding a Model I theory-in-use and being embedded in an O-I learning system often makes individuals unaware of the discrepancy between their espoused theories and their actions *and* of the mental theory-in-use programs that keep them unaware. The result is a paradox. The individuals have designed nontransparency and a built-in tendency for a reduction in self-efficacy as a result of a design to maintain and increase self-efficacy. They are personally causally responsible for acting in ways that reduce their sense of personal causal responsibility, yet they are, in fact, causally responsible. For example, recall that individuals express a sense of hopelessness and cynicism about changing defensive routines, the same routines for which they are responsible.

Paradoxes are related to meanings that are contradictory. Therefore, we must first identify the meanings. Because it is empirically true that there are systematic, nonrandom differences between the meanings people espouse and those embedded in their actions, and because it is also the case that actors are unaware of these discrepancies, then it is the researchers' responsibility to differentiate between meanings embedded in attitudes, espoused values, and beliefs from those embedded in actual behavior.

The first modification, therefore, would be the emphasis placed upon the importance of conversation or other relatively directly observable actions (from which meanings could be inferred). The theory-in-use can only be inferred from what individuals actually say and do as observed by others or as audio or video tape-recorded.

Conversations would no longer simply be anecdotal events to be somehow analyzed and scored according to a preestablished scheme of categories. Every act of conversation with meaning is the result of a micro-causal theory in the mind of a creator. Meaning produced in the form of conversation is never random; it is systematic.

All conversation, in turn, has at least two meanings embedded in it. The first is the meaning that comes from asking the question: what did he actually say? For example, a superior and a subordinate can both agree that the superior's words on tape were such and such. They could also agree, for example, that the superior was telling the subordinate that his performance was inadequate. The subordinate could disagree on that conclusion and still agree that the superior communicated that meaning.

The next level of meaning would be the inferences made by either party on the effectiveness with which the first meaning was communicated. For example, it could have been done thoughtfully or bluntly.

The first meaning (your performance is unacceptable) is the result of a design and an implementation of that design by the superior. Embedded in that design is a micro-causal theory about what the superior believed he had to say to the subordinate. The second meaning is the result of a causal theory in the superior's mind about how to communicate the message effectively.

So far we have found that the micro-causal theories are not infinite in variety. They all appear to be derived from the theory-in-use held by the actors. Because there is very little variance in the theory-in-use, it becomes possible to develop generalization across actors and contexts as well as within a given actor in various contexts.

Recall that defensive routines are the result of complicated patterns of processes. The patterns should be described in enough detail to explain how they maintain and proliferate themselves.

For example, in Model I, there are action strategies such as making attributions or evaluations without illustrating them or testing them publicly. In our early research, we developed quantitative patterns of such behavior based on interobserver reliability score of over 90 percent accuracy. These scores were used to illustrate quantitative patterns of categories of Model I.

We learned, however, that the scores by themselves told us little about how these categories developed into patterns of organizational defensive routines, how the defensive routines led to paradoxes, how the paradoxes were bypassed, and how the bypassing activities were bypassed. In other words, the quantitative pictures of the frequency of the units of behavior kept in a black-box status; the causes of the defensive routines, the processes by which they maintained themselves, and the processes that produced the paradoxes. From the point of view of a science of paradoxes, the most important information had yet to be developed.

The same was true from the clients' viewpoint. For those who wanted to change their Model I behavior, the quantitative picture provided them with information that they already knew. Changing their actions required the very information that was kept in black-box status.

There is another important issue that we are currently facing in trying to decide what are the appropriate units of analysis. This issue surfaced as we observed what units of analysis humans used whenever they tried to act on our data. As scientists, we were interested in the covariance of variables. For example, did changes in untested evaluations vary systematically with changes in untested attributions? We were able to plot many such relationships.

As we fed these data back to the individuals who wished to alter their actions, we learned that variance of variables remained within Model I theory-in-use. Once they understood the reasoning processes and the skills they used to produce Model I actions, providing them with quantitative relationships of various combinations that were consistent with Model I proved redundant.

We are now asking ourselves the following question: If Model I theory-in-use is what actors use to organize, store, and retrieve information in order to act, then is knowledge of the ways the variables within Model I vary empirically redundant? For example, individual A may have a pattern of 20 percent unillustrated attributions and 80 percent unillustrated evaluations. He could have quantitative figures reversed. From the point of view of creating defensive routines, the reversal of the scores makes no difference, because both patterns are Model I action strategies that lead to defensive routines.

Perhaps individuals require two different types of information. One is those quantitative patterns which, if they existed, would lead to a change in Model I. But that, according to our theory (and so far it is not disconfirmed by our research) is not possible. No imaginable combination of Model I variables can lead to states that are so different that they reduce defensive routines and their resulting paradoxes. Model I actions are self-sealing.

The second type of information is a model of the processes that produce the defensive routines and the subsequent paradoxes; a model of a new set of processes; and a model of how to get from here to there.

In short, we are beginning to believe that the units of study should be maps of processes from which it is possible to produce predictable consequences, not quantitative maps of how the variables such as action strategies within a given model might vary empirically.

The fifth change in emphasis will be a move toward producing maps of these multi-level processes (Argyris, 1985; Argyris, et al., 1985). Let us take an example of a map an individual developed to understand her pattern of bypassing and bypassing the bypass pattern (figure 4.1). The map describes the context, the action strategies, and the consequences. The map purports to describe the bypass routines and the paradox that results, namely that the individual acts in ways that are counter to her own intentions of being helpful.

The map may be used in several ways. First it organizes a set of complicated processes into an explanatory model. Second, the model can be more easily stored and retrieved from the human mind. The map may also be used to predict that the individual will continue to behave in these ways because there are no actions that can be used to interrupt and to reduce

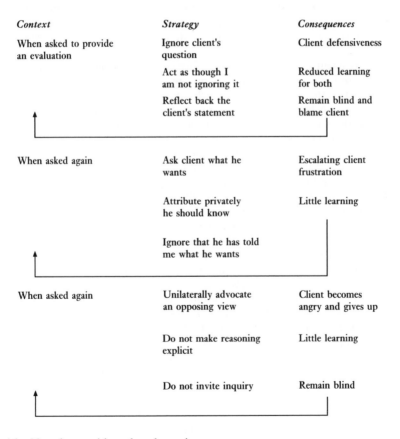

**Figure 4.1**   Nested propositions about bypassing

the counterproductive features of her pattern. All the feedback processes reinforce the pattern. The prediction not only helps the individual understand the consequences of the model: it becomes a test of the validity of the map. For example, we could observe or tape-record the individual's behavior in similar situations, after the map was developed by her (with the help of others). We should observe action strategies that are consistent with those described in the map. We should not observe action strategies where she engages the client's questions productively. These tape-recordings could be analyzed by competent analysts who have no idea of the map as well as by the individual and those helping her to change. The analysis would be made separately.

These types of analysis are now standard operating procedure in our work. We use them to test features of the theory and to help individuals reflect on their practice, to organize their reflections in the form of maps that explain and predict their actions. Finally, we also use the maps as the basis for changing the actions.

In evaluating the toughness of the test, we should keep in mind that in most cases, individuals believe that they can alter the actions once they have mapped them. The tape recordings indicate otherwise. Their prediction that they could alter their actions was disconfirmed even though the actors created the maps, knew about the changes, and intended to produce the changes.

These types of maps can also be crafted for groups and other social systems. For example, a group of personnel administrators (PAs) in a very large organization complained that the line managers acted in ways that disempowered them. They complained that the PAs were often asked by the line to perform inappropriate tasks and that the PAs' role had a low status.

The vice president of human resources formed a 20-person task force to study the problem. After some 15 hours of deliberations, the task force found that it had documented the complaints but that it did not know what to do about them. They explained their dilemma by their disbelief that line management would wish to change. Asked one, "What's the sense of working to produce ideas for change if you know the ideas are not likely to be taken seriously by the line?"

With their assistance, we implemented the following experiment. We asked the task force members to assume that they could have access to any line manager they wished, and to assume also that the line managers would be willing to listen genuinely to their ideas. We then asked them to write a case that would illustrate what they would actually say and do if they had this opportunity (see Argyris, 1982; Argyris and Schön, 1974). What actions would they take to change the line managers?

The PAs then met to discuss their cases. In every instance, the PAs concluded that the actions designed in their cases were counterproductive. They decided that if given an opportunity to change line managers, they would act in ways that disempowered them-selves. As one PA put it, "I now realize that we shoot ourselves in the foot."

We then analyzed the tape recordings of these sessions and developed a map of how the PAs disempowered themselves (figure 4.2). The map was distributed to the PAs for their confirmation or disconfirmation. Some of the PAs showed the map to other PAs and to other line managers for their reactions. There was no one who disagreed with the para-doxical results predicted by the map. The only changes that were made were editorial or additional examples.

The PAs decided that it would be highly unlikely that they could reverse the processes described in the map without some reeducation. This decision was significant: they had to say in the report to the vice president, "Not only do we disempower ourselves while trying to reduce our disempowerment, but we do not believe we have the requisite skills to change this situation." The PAs requested a reeducation program.

| Situational givens | Consequences | | Strategies to deal with barriers | Strategies about strategies | Dilemmas | Consequences |
|---|---|---|---|---|---|---|
| High ambiguity | Frustration | | Tear/wear them down | | | |
| Organization in time of transition | Tension | | Showdown: stand up to God | | If I confront line they may distrust me and maintain their negative view | Confirm line's prejudice about Personnel |
| | | | Be the Lone Ranger | | | Does not model for line strategies they don't already know |
| | | | Work my needs | Keep use of strategies private | If I maneuver around line, I do not challenge line's negative view of Personnel and they maintain it ⟶ | Does not create opportunities for PAs to learn about how they may contribute to line's negative view |
| Personnel Administrators report to two different bosses who often have conflicting view of what PAs should do | Desire to change role of PAs to be change agents and to raise status of Personnel in the organization ⟶ PAs encounter barriers to their intended change, particularly from line | | Maneuver around them ⟶ | Base beliefs about effective strategies on feelings ⟶ | sense of ⟶ disempowerment | |
| | | | Don't confront if I get my way | Do not test | If I maintain one style, I may reduce the range of managers with whom I can work | Does not create opportunities for line to learn how they create barriers for PAs |
| Personnel is perceived as low status | | | Wait for time to pass | | | Neither line nor Personnel learns about any validity in their view of each other |
| PAs asked to do inappropriate tasks | | | Match my style to the manager | | If I switch styles, I may weaken my own and others' sense of Personnel identity | Reinforces fragmented "chameleon" identity of Personnel |
| PAs asked to function as peacemakers; to smooth over conflict; to apply bandaids to symptoms instead of getting at root causes | | | Privately time interventions | | | May create skepticism on both line and Personnel's parts and Personnel can become change agents |

Figure 4.2  PAs disempowering themselves

The vice president was delighted for two reasons. As a line executive for many years he always felt that the PAs were their own worst enemy but he did not deal with this issue openly because he could not see a constructive consequence. But, if the PAs did develop the skills, then they could use them to change the line managers who, the VP agreed, did treat the PAs unjustly.

The PAs now had a map that described their actions that disempowered them. How can this map be tested?

The first test of the map is to observe the tape recorded interactions between line and PAs. The tapes should show either actions that do disempower or actions that are not relevant to the issue. The tapes should not indicate any actions that would engage defensive routines in ways that reduce disempowerment. The second test of the validity of this description is to ask the PAs who participated in the seminar to confirm or disconfirm its validity. In our experience, individuals in the position similar to the PAs do not confirm the map easily. Their self-esteem is on the line; confirming the map indicates that they are not as competent as they should be. They are, after all, human resources specialists who are supposed to help others, not to create conditions of disempowerment.

A third test is to show it to other PAs who did not help to develop the map. A fourth test is to show it to line managers. All the test situations are tape-recorded.

The tapes can be used for further tests. First, if the map is disconfirmed, then we must examine carefully the reasoning behind the disconfirmation. Second, under certain conditions, the reaction used to test the map could be a test. For example, in some cases PAs who did not participate in producing the map disagreed that they disempowered themselves. The way they disagreed with their fellow PAs led to conditions of disempowerment between them. Moreover, the examples that they used and the way they defended them illustrated defensive routines. Third, the tape recordings can be available to fellow researchers who might wish to listen to the processes by which we assert the maps were not disconfirmed.

Another series of tests is developed by studying the training program designed to reeducate the PAs. For example, the participants develop their own maps based on their individual experiences. The actions to be changed are then derived from the map. If, for example, the PAs learn the new skills, then they should be able to design new actions that they agree are more effective. They could test these inferences by role-playing with each other or by inviting in some line managers.

A more powerful test would be to tape-record or observe the PAs in action with the line managers in nontraining situations. This is not difficult, because PAs have regularly scheduled meetings with their line superiors. The PAs introduce the tape-recorder or the observer by saying that they are participating in a training program to increase their effectiveness. So far, individuals in the position such as line managers have cooperated. Indeed, many of them become intrigued and involve themselves in learning about how they create defensive routines.

## THE VALUE OF CRAFTING THEORIES THAT DEAL WITH PARADOXES

There are science-building and practice-building reasons for crafting theories that deal with paradoxes. A comprehensive theory of administration and organization includes the understanding of paradoxes because they are part of the universe. Social scientists would not be fulfilling their stewardship if they did not describe the universe as is. If paradoxes are especially activated when attempts are made to change the underlying patterns in our universe, then a full description of the universe as is would require the production of propositions about how the patterns react to varying degrees of change.

Descriptions of how the status quo reacts to fundamental change is part of the description of the world as is.

Turning to the practice-building reasons, if the future problems of administrators will focus especially around gaps, inconsistencies, dilemmas, and paradoxes, then we have an obligation to help human beings understand and solve these types of problems. Dealing with paradoxes may lead to significantly different theories of explanation and change. For example, the "inhumane" features of formal organizations that I described in *Personality and Organization* (Argyris, 1957) were caused, in important ways, by human features of human beings such as the information processing limits of their minds (Argyris, 1978). This awareness not only led to a different set of propositions about the world as is; it also led to different theories of intervention.

## THE DILEMMA TO CONDUCT ACTION SCIENCE

There is an important dilemma that social scientists will have to face if paradoxes are to be studied and reduced. The dilemma is created by the fact that the theory-in-use of normal science actions to minimize threats to internal and external validity (Campbell and Stanley, 1963) are consistent with Model I. Social scientists may be producing generalizations that have the same features of mixed messages and defensive routines (Argyris, 1980). In order to overcome this dilemma, we may have to focus on research that conceives of subjects as clients to be helped to reduce the defensive routines and therefore combines description with intervention. The intervention becomes the context for testing the description.

Several years ago, I conducted a colloquium with faculty and graduate students on intervention. After a while, the concerns of the faculty and graduate students about intervention began to surface. Most of the concerns, it seemed to me, were defensive routines. For example, would not interventions cost more because they take longer? We compared their budgets with mine, and mine were significantly less. Moreover, the organizations that I have studied were willing to pay more if we remained.

Did the interventionists become biased by the organization that paid them? I had published an analysis of the work of such scholars as Blau, Perrow, and Thompson. Although the work that I cited was primarily supported by government funding agencies, their theories, I tried to show, were more consistent with traditional managerial values than were the theories of scholars like Likert, McGregor, and myself (Argyris, 1972).

A young female assistant professor raised what I believe to be a critical question. She said that the problem she had in combining description and intervention was that she was never trained to do it, and it scared the hell out of her. Donald Schön and I have been conducting seminars in European and American universities during the past ten years on conducting action science. We have found that her comments reflected the causes better than the other concerns.

During the past ten years, we have also been conducting seminars to teach graduate students and younger faculty action science skills. To date, these students experience three surprises early in the seminars. First is our insistence on meeting the normal science criteria of generalizability and disconformability. We do seek to change the role of subjects to clients, for example, but not at the expense of muddling the research. The second surprise is that their theory-in-use is consistent with Model I; that they experience the same embarrassment, bewilderment, and frustration that their prospective clients do when faced with this finding.

The third surprise is that the skills for dealing with defensive routines, their own as well as the clients', are learnable, and with about as much or as little difficulty as they experienced in learning regression analysis. The key issue was whether they genuinely wanted to create research conditions where they would experience a greater sense of vulnerability than would be the case when conducting research where the task was primarily descriptive. We have begun to design graduate seminars where students can be exposed to learning the skills and then make up their minds as to what directions to take in their own future research (Argyris, et al., 1985). In our experience to date, most strive to include features of intervention in an incremental manner. They design action science research that is consistent with their skills. As the research succeeds, then they up the ante.

# References

Argyris, C., 1957, *Personality and Organization*, New York, Harper and Brothers.

Argyris, C., 1972, *The Applicability of Organizational Sociology*, London, Cambridge University Press.

Argyris, C., 1978, "Is Capitalism the Culprit?" *Organizational Dynamics*, Spring, pp. 21–37.

Argyris, C., 1980, *Inner Contradictions of Rigorous Research*, New York, Academic Press.

Argyris, C., 1982, *Reasoning, Leaning and Action*, San Francisco, Jossey-Bass.

Argyris, C., 1985, *Strategy, Change, and Defensive Routines*, Boston, Pitman Publishing.

Argyris, C., and Schön, D., 1974, *Theory in Practice*, San Francisco, Jossey-Bass.

Argyris, C., Putnam, R., and Smith, D. M., 1985, *Action Science*, San Francisco, Jossey-Bass.

Bandura, A., 1977, "Self-Efficacy: Toward a Unifying Theory of Behavioral Change," *Psychological Review*, 85, pp. 191–215.

Barnes, L., 1981, "Managing the Paradox of Organizational Trust," *Harvard Business Review*, March/April, pp. 107–16.

Campbell, D. T., and Stanley, J. C., 1963, *Experimental and Quasi-Experimental Design for Research*, Skokie, III, Rand-McNally.

de Charms, R., 1968, *Personal Causation*, New York, Academic Press.

Deci, E. L., and Ryan, R. M., 1985, *Intrinsic Motivation and Self-Determination in Human Behavior*, New York, Plenum Press.

Heider, F., 1958, *The Psychology of Interpersonal Relations*, New York, Wiley.

Jones, R. A., 1977, *Self-Fulfilling Prophecies: Social Psychological and Physiological Effects of Expectancies*, Hillsdale, N.J., Lawrence Erlbaum Associates.

Rescher, N., 1977, *Methodological Pragmatism: A Systems-Theoretic Approach to the Theory of Knowledge*, New York, New York University Press.

Strong, S. R., and Claiborn, C. D., 1982, *Change Through Interaction*, New York, John Wiley.

# — 5 —

# Today's Problems with Tomorrow's Organizations

There is a revolution brewing in the introduction of new organizational forms to complement or to replace the more traditional pyramidal form. I believe, on the basis of some recent research, that the new forms are basically sound. However, because of the methods used to introduce them and because of those used to maintain them, many of the unintended self-defeating consequences of the older structures are re-appearing.

Two major causes for this revolution are the new requirements for organizational survival in an increasingly competitive environment and the new administrative and information technology available to deal with complexity. W. L. Wallace (1963) summarizes these requirements as (1) the technological revolution (complexity and variety of products, new materials and processes, and the effects of massive research), (2) competition and the profit squeeze (saturated markets, inflation of wage and material costs, production efficiency), (3) the high cost of marketing, and (4) the unpredictability of consumer demands (due to high discretionary income, wide range of choices available, and shifting tastes). To make matters more difficult, the costs of new products are increasing while their life expectancy is decreasing.

## REQUIREMENTS OF TOMORROW'S ORGANIZATIONS

In order to meet these challenges, modern organizations need:

- much more creative planning;
- the development of valid and useful knowledge about new products and new processes;
- increased concerted and cooperative action with internalized long-range commitment by all involved; and
- increased understanding of criteria for effectiveness that meet the challenges of complexity.

These requirements, in turn, depend upon:

- continuous and open access between individuals and groups;
- free, reliable communication;

where

- interdependence is the foundation for individual and departmental cohesiveness; and
- trust, risk-taking, and helping each other is prevalent;

so that conflict is identified and managed in such a way that the destructive win–lose stances with their accompanying polarization of views are minimized and effective problem-solving is maximized.

These conditions, in turn, require individuals who:

- do not fear stating their complete views;
- are capable of creating groups that maximize the unique contributions of each individual;
- value and seek to integrate their contributions into a creative total, final contribution rather than needing to be individually rewarded for their contributions;

thus finding the search for valid knowledge and the development of the best possible solution intrinsically satisfying.

Unfortunately these conditions are difficult to create. Elsewhere (see Argyris, 1962, 1966) I have tried to show that the traditional pyramidal structure and managerial controls tend to place individuals and departments in constant interdepartmental warfare, where win–lose competition creates polarized stances, that tend to get resolved by the superior making the decisions, thereby creating a dependence upon him. Also, there is a tendency toward conformity, mistrust, and lack of risk taking among the peers that results in focusing upon individual survival, requiring the seeking out of the scarce rewards, identifying one's self with successful venture (be a hero), and being careful to avoid being blamed for or identified with a failure, thereby becoming a "bum." All these adaptive behaviors tend to induce low interpersonal competence and can lead the organization, over the long run, to become rigid, sticky, less innovative, resulting in less than effective decisions with even less internal commitment to the decisions on the part of those involved.

Some people have experimented by structuring the organization in such a way that people representing the major functions (marketing, engineering, manufacturing, and finance) are coerced to work together. Unfortunately, the pyramidal structure does not lend itself to such a strategy. As Wallace (1963) points out, the difficulty is that typically each function approaches the business problems inherent in the product from a somewhat different point of view: marketing wants a good product at a low price; production, a product that is easily produced; engineering, a product that outclasses – engineering wise – all other products, etc. None of these stances tends to lead to the resolution of conflicting ideas into a decision that tends to integrate the best of each view.

## THE MATRIX ORGANIZATION

One of the most promising strategies to induce cooperation and integration of effort on crucial business problems is the development of project teams and the matrix organization. These administrative innovations were created initially to solve the complex problems of coordination and scheduling of large defense projects. They have been adapted and used by many other organizations because of their potential promise. The future role of the team approach and matrix organization is, in my opinion, an important one for administration.

A project team is created to solve a particular problem. It is composed of people represent-ing all the relevant managerial functions (e.g., marketing, manufacturing, engineering, and finance). Each member is given equal responsibility and power to solve the problem. The members are expected to work as a cohesive unit. Once the problem is solved, the team is given a new assignment or disbanded. If the problem is a recurring one, the team remains active. In many cases especially in the defense programs, the project manager is given full authority and responsibility for the completion of the project including rewarding and penalizing the members of the team. An organization may have many teams. This results is an organization that looks like a matrix; hence the title of matrix organization (Figure 5.1).

| Representatives of | Project 1 | Project 2 | Project 3 |
|---|---|---|---|
| Manufacturing | | | |
| Engineering | | | |
| Marketing | | | |
| Finance | | | |
| | Team 1 | Team 2 | Team 3 |

**Figure 5.1**  Matrix organization

### Problems with the matrix organization

How effective are the project teams and the matrix organizations? In order to begin to answer that question, I have been conducting some research in nine large organizations utilizing a matrix organization structure. In preliminary interviews the executives reported that the matrix organization and team approach made sense, but that they found them very difficult to put into actual practice. People still seemed to polarize issues, resisted exploring ideas thoroughly, mistrusted each other's behavior, focused on trying to protect one's own function, overemphasized simplified criteria of success (e.g., figures on sales), worked too much on day-to-day operations and short-term planning, engaged in the routine decisions rather than focus more on the long-range risky decisions, and emphasized survival more than the integration of effort into a truly accepted decision.

Others found fault with the team approach for not providing individuals enough opportunity to get recognition in their own functional departments for their performance on the team. Still others insisted that individuals sought to be personally identified with a particular accomplishment; that it wasn't satisfying for them to know that their group (and not they) obtained the reward. Finally, some said that during their meetings the teams got bogged down in focusing on the negative, i.e., what had not been accomplished.

Why are these new administrative structures and strategies having this trouble? I do *not* believe the concept of the matrix organization is inherently invalid. I believe the answer lies in the everyday behavior styles that the managers have developed, in the past, to survive and to succeed within the traditional pyramidal organization. The behavior styles needed for the effective use of the matrix organization are, I believe, very different. Also, the group dynamics that are effective in the pyramidal structure are different from those that will be effective in the matrix organization. Thus I do not agree that the comments above are "natural" for all people. They are "natural" for people living under the pyramidal concept. For example, groups *can* be created where individuals gain success from seeing integrated decisions; where recognition *does* come more from success and less from compliments from others, where overcoming barriers and correcting faults and failures are not perceived as negative (Argyris, 1965; Schein and Bennis, 1965).

A second important cause for the ineffectiveness of the matrix type organization lies in the very processes that have given it birth. Again, the difficulty has been that the birth processes used were more applicable to the pyramidal than to the matrix organization. In short, I am suggesting that a basic problem has been that a new form of organization has been introduced in such a way as to make difficulties inevitable and that the leadership styles that the executives use to administer the matrix organization, on the whole, compound the felony. In order to illustrate my point I should like to take one of these nine studies and discuss it in some detail. The case that I have selected to discuss approximates the other eight. The variance among the cases was not high. More importantly, the establishment of a project and program approach had the most careful thought and analytical competence brought to bear on it by the top management. It is a study of a multimillion-dollar organization that decided to reorganize its product planning and program review activities into a team approach which resulted in a matrix organization. These two activities have been the ones most frequently organized into a matrix organization. The study lasted about one year. I interviewed all the top executives involved (25), asked them to complete questionnaires, and observed, taped, and analyzed nearly 35 meetings of the teams, ranging from 45 minutes to two and half hours in length.

## THE NATURE OF PRODUCT PLANNING AND PROGRAM REVIEWS

The responsibility of product planning program reviews was to collect and integrate, and maintain up to date information of the progress of any given activity in the organization. Under this concept, the top men could go to one source to get complete information on the organization's present plans, progress against plans, etc. The staff group had no authority to order any of the line executives. It was their task to analyze what the problems were and to get from the line executives their plans as to how they were to be solved. If the line executives were unable to agree then the problem was taken to the chief executive for his decision. In the manual of this company there existed a sentence which stated, "the president retains the authority for final decision and can ordinarily expect that his product planning staff will achieve the agreement of all other departments before plans are presented." Still later, "product planning provides team leadership to a team made up of appropriate, fully responsibly representatives of the (line) departments. The Product Planner as team leader encourages, challenges, and insists upon mature, complete and competent coverage by these representatives. Encouragement of better communication between departments is necessary and vital."

The assumption behind this theory was that if objectives and critical paths to these objectives were defined clearly, people would tend to cooperate to achieve these objectives according to the best schedule that they could devise. However, in practice, the theory was difficult to apply. Why? Let us first take a look at the processes by which these new concepts were introduced.

The management strategy for implementing this new program was primarily one of pushing, persuading, and ordering. The objective was to overcome the forces in the organization that were resisting change thereby pushing the level of effectiveness upward. However, the way this was done added, unintentionally, to the resisting forces. For example, 76 percent of the subordinates interpreted the processes of a small elite group planning the changes and then management unilaterally installing the activities by persuading the people to accept them as implying that they (subordinates) had not been competent in the past and that they could not be trusted in making changes. These feelings were strengthened by the fact that the new activities required greater control over subordinates, more detailed planning, and more concrete commitments which could get the subordinate in trouble if they did not fulfill them. These activities of fear and mistrust still exist. For example:

> Sometimes I wonder if the real impact of program reviews isn't to teach people that we don't trust them. I think that the top people have got to have faith in the people, and eliminate some of these constant and repetitive type of meetings, just to check being checked. I think we can get management to get themselves pretty well informed just through a nominal report type of thing, rather than all this paper work that we have.

The increasing lack of cooperation, hostility, resistance to meeting program plans, were recognized by the people responsible for the activities. They responded by making the controls even tighter. They asked for more detailed reports, for a wider distribution of minutes, and they used the minutes as evidence that agreements were arrived at that were binding. But again the impact was not completely what was expected. For example:

> Do we need these complete minutes. We still have a number of people in the organization who feel that they have to document everything in terms of a letter or memo. To me this is an indication of fear.

> The more trouble the programs got into the more paper work that we had to complete.

It was not long before the completion of the paper work became an end in itself. Seventy-one percent of the middle managers reported that the maintenance of the product planning and program review paper flow became as crucial as accomplishing the line responsibility assigned to each group. For example:

> I'm afraid that we program the most minute things and the more we program, the less work we get done. I have tried to get this across to the president, but have not been very successful.

> One problem I find is the amount of paper work that this system generates. I dare say out of the five-day week it would take you three quarters of a day or a day of your week to just keep up with the paper work. All of the paper work you get does not affect you, but you have to go through it to find out what does and what does not.

> In all honesty I think we waste too damn much time around here. These program reviews are especially costly in time. Why one of the fellows the other day said that he received and sends out approximately 50 thousand pieces of paper a month.

The final quotation illustrates the next problem that arose. Since each individual had his regular job to accomplish in addition to his role as product planning and program reviews, the load became very heavy. The executives increasingly felt overworked and overloaded with activities that were not leading to increased effectiveness (83 percent). For example:

> I believe – held a scheduling type meeting, and they do call ordinary meetings, and then all the vice presidents call their people together for a meeting, so that one little meeting at the divisional level has a heck of a lot of man hours tied up into it for the background.

> The number of jobs to be done. The sheer volume that has to be turned out. Sometimes you feel as though you are on a treadmill and you can't get off it because no matter what jobs you can see getting accomplished, there are so many more ahead of you that you know you are behind schedule, and it seems to drive you crazy at times. Everyone has the same feelings.

In spite of these difficulties the level of effectiveness eventually stabilized. But now the resisting forces became much stronger. Also the level of organizational pressure rose.

Most of the lower level managers reported that they did not tend to like to be associated with the restraining activities, because they saw such alliance as an indication of disloyalty. I believe that one way to resolve these dissonant feelings about themselves was to strengthen their personal opinions about the negativeness of the program by finding faults with it and by knowingly (and unknowingly) acting so as to make it less effective.

Another mode of adaptation was to withdraw and let the upper levels become responsible for the successful administration of the program. "This is their baby – let them make it work." At the same time much hostility could be released safely by constant joking about "everything is programmed." For example, people were asked had they programmed their sex life or had they defined the critical path to the toilet, etc.

These attitudes threatened the upper levels. They saw them as suggesting that the managers were not as loyal and committed as they should be. The executives reacted by involving the potential wrath of the president. ("He really means business – let's climb on board.") Soon the president found himself in the position of being cited as "the" reason the programs may not be questioned. Also, his immediate subordinates encouraged him to speak out forcefully on the importance of these functions. The president began to feel that he must defend the programs because if he did not, the restraining forces may begin to overcome the management pressure for change. For example:

> Make no mistake about it, this is the president's baby. Have you ever tried to talk to him about it? He listens for a few minutes and then soon lets you know that he isn't going to tolerate many questions.

> No, we have pretty much resigned ourselves to the fact that the president is really behind this, and you might just as well forget it. You are entitled to a personal opinion, of course, but beyond that, you better not take any action.

The increasing number of control activities and the increasing feelings of pressure led the subordinates to feel that product planning and program reviews had become dominant in the organization. They unknowingly or knowingly placed less attention upon their original line function activities. This reaction increased the probability that failures would occur, which increased the pressures from the president and in turn his staff people, which infuriated the line managers, and the loop was closed. The top management forces tended to increase, the middle and lower management resistance also tended to increase (even though such action may have made them feel a sense of disloyalty), the tension and pressures increased, and the effectiveness of the program was at a lower level than was potentially possible.


## EFFECTIVENESS OF PRODUCT PLANNING AND PROGRAM REVIEW
## MEETINGS

To make the situation more difficult the majority of the participants reported that, in addition to the process of introduction being a dissatisfying one, they also reported overall dissatisfaction with the way the programs were being carried out. For example, the meetings (1) tended to suppress individuality, (2) polarized issues into win–lose stances, (3) censored bad news to the top and (4) immobilized the groups with unimportant issues.

## Overall Dissatisfaction with Small Group Meetings

Dissatisfaction was found to exist with the product planning and program review meetings. The dissatisfactions increased as one went down the chain of command. Thus 64 percent of the top executives and 83 percent of the middle managers expressed dissatisfaction with the group meetings.

> These committees are not the best way to administer an organization. We tend to make little problems into big ones and ignore the nasty ones. We also eat up a lot of time. People don't come in to really listen; they come in to win and fight not to lose.

> I think the simple fact is even now there is probably less true acceptance of the product planning function than there was. And I think in truth there is quite fundamental and sincere non-acceptance of the role of planning in the function, not the general idea of —. I've talked to people about this quite a bit.

> [Researcher: Why is that?]

> Because the fact remains that we do have a schedule, and someone is after them for their answer at that point. And I guess that's tough for most of us to accept Maybe this game of having an objective and planning their work accordingly and then say what you are going to do. Management is flexible, you're so right. They know we run a high risk here, and the top management never beat them over the back for this kind of stuff.

## Suppressing Individuality

The members reported that in practice, the groups functioned so that individuality was not optimized; conformity and non-risk-taking predominated (71 percent). "Playing it relatively safe" seemed to be a common activity. For example:

> During a heated session about program reviews A accused B of being a coward for not standing up for his view. A replied "Listen mister, when you have to live with these people as I do, then you can talk. If I really stuck to my views I'd be hated by everyone – and I'd come to hate myself.

> Yes, I think the choice that we have been asked to make between no decision and one not so good is a negative choice. Most of the time it is an eleventh-hour thing that they arrive at. You either can take it this way or you won't have it for another six months.

> [Researcher: What prevents a person from sort of digging in and saying no, I don't want anything else?]

> Well, there is a lot of pressure. We've got commitments made to the management that where we charge a certain amount of dollars for the dollars they have allowed us to invest in this business."

## Polarizing Issues

At the lower levels, there was a good deal more heated argument which caused the issues to be polarized and people felt that they were neither being heard nor were they communicating. This tended to lead to a decrease in the faith in the group's processes and, at the same time, increased the probability that people would tend to come to the meetings with prepared positions (83 percent).

For example:

We have a great deal of people jockeying for position.

There are certain things that people are not willing to stick their necks out about. Particularly when it comes to a new program. When it comes to a new program everyone has preconceived positions, and they adhere to them.

I think at times people will take an extreme position one time, and another time be very compromising. To take the — committee as an example, there are occasions where they do not agree and they say. "Too bad we couldn't agree, we'll set up a meeting at the next level."

## Censoring Bad News to the Top

Another major problem was that some of the more difficult issues developed at the lower levels were watered down by the time they were transmitted to the top. People had learned not to describe to their superiors the complete differences in views and the difficulties in discussing the issues in as strong terms as they experienced them (71 percent).

By the way, there is an awful lot of time spent at the lower level and people getting information ready to beat the people at the upper level. And I would say in all honesty that we don't give all the information to the people on top. If we do present them with all the problems it would probably bring this place to a screeching halt.

When you have an overly protected meeting the people upstairs don't really get the facts. For example, you soon learn that in a review you take all the things out that might be arbitrary or that might raise difficulties with somebody else.

## Immobilizing the Group with Unimportant Details

Still another frequently reported problem was the immobilization of the group with countless small decisions (63 percent). Some department representatives brought everything to the meetings partially to make certain that the program review group took the responsibility for all activities. Other department representatives raised many issues when they were upset with the direction a particular decision was taking or when they wished to delay the making of a decision until further data could be obtained. For example:

Some people also don't mind flooding the committee with agenda items. And once there is an item on the agenda the board is committed to study it, whether it is important or not. I think it can be an awful expense of money and time.

If you looked at these minutes of our meetings, and you haven't attended any yet, of course, the number of topics we take up is fantastic, and to the point where we feel that too many people aren't deciding at lower levels, and bucking it is up to us.

The members of a review group could postpone action or prevent themselves (and their department) from being held responsible for a decision by asking the group to make it. This was guaranteed to take time since those in the group who did not specialize in that particular technical area had to be briefed.

To summarize, the product planning and program review committees were viewed as plagued with ineffectiveness and win–lose dynamics. An executive who kept account of how people described these committees concluded that the two most frequent categorizations were "Committee management at its worse" and "Moscow delegates" (i.e. delegates who couldn't make a contribution without checking with their department).

The same managers freely admitted that they could not see any resolution, "any time you run a company by a committee, you'll always have trouble," or "it's human nature for people to lie and fight when they believe they are being exposed." Such pessimistic diagnoses will not lead to action for correcting the situation. On the contrary, such diagnoses probably provide ideal rationalization why "things cannot be changed" and why they can go on feeling and behaving as they do.

As in the problems presented in the previous section, management's reaction was not to deal with the issues openly. More subtle and covertly controlling actions were typically taken. Meetings were scheduled with greater precision, presentations were made both with viewgraph and written script, and even more detailed minutes were taken. The hope was that with tighter outside controls, the groups would tend to operate more effectively. If we may judge from the comments reported above as well as from the observations, the group dynamics have not been altered – indeed, one could argue with some justification that the group defenses are becoming stronger. Thus we conclude again that although the members are aware that the relative ineffectiveness of the group is a crucial problem, they are not able to solve the problems. Moreover, most of the action taken actually helps to increase the members' feeling of being unduly controlled and mistrusted.

## WHY DID THE PROBLEMS ARISE?

The explanations for problems like these are multiple and complicated. One way to begin to organize our thoughts is to view the problems as arising from a long causal chain of actions where one action causes several others, which in turn, breeds further actions, etc. I believe that at the beginning of this complicated causal chain lie the basic values or assumptions that executives have learned to hold about how to organize human effort effectively. These values once internalized, act as commands to coerce the executives to behave in specific ways when they meet to solve problems. Elsewhere (Argyris, 1962) I have shown that executives tend to hold three basic values about effective human relationships within organizations. They are:

1  Getting the job done. "We are here to manufacture shoes, that is our business, those are the important human relationships; if you have anything that can influence those human relationships, fine."
2  Be rational and logical and communicate clearly. Effectiveness *decreases* as behavior becomes more emotional. "Gentlemen, let's get back to the facts," is the classic conference table phrase, or in other words, if you want to be effective, be rational, be clear. If you want to be ineffective, focus on the emotional and interpersonal.
3  People work best under carefully defined direction, authority and control, governed by appropriate rewards and penalties that emphasize rational behavior and achievement of the objective.

In figure 5.2, I should like to illustrate what I believe may be one underlying causal chain leading to the problems described above. Let us assume that an organization, at any given point in time, may be described, as having particular level of effectiveness; that there are forces pushing upward to increase the effectiveness (e.g. top management); and that, since the level is somewhat stable, there are forces pushing downward resisting or restraining the level from going higher.[1] A balance of forces exists.

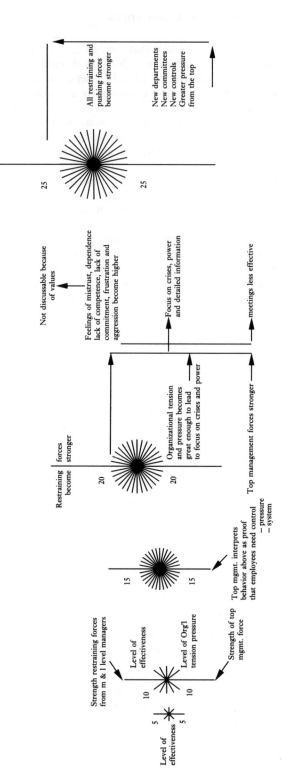

**Figure 5.2** Escalating anti-learning forces

Now, let us assume that management wants to increase the level of effectiveness (by developing new product planning and program review activities as in this case, or by any other change the reader wants to imagine). I am suggesting that the underlying strategy for, and the processes of change will tend to be greatly influenced by values the executives hold that have been described.

For example, because of the emphasis on objectives and rationality, the executives will tend to assume that the way to get a new organizational activity accepted by the members of the organization is to show them clearly how it fits with the objectives of the organization and to explain rationally the advantages of the new activity over the old one. "We need tighter controls," "effectiveness must be increased," "I'm sure all of us want to manage in the best way available," "we must always remain alert for new management innovations." These comments are seen by the subordinates as management feeling compelled to sell them a bill of goods; an implication that they resent. They see little need (if they are effective managers) for someone to tell them effectiveness should be increased, new concepts should be tried, etc. Indeed, many resent the implication that they are not doing this already.

In terms of our diagram, the strategy for change is to overcome the restraining forces by strengthening the pushing forces. This is done by management selling, pushing, and ordering. As we can see, at the second set of forces in our diagram, the level of effectiveness does increase.

But the resisting forces are also increased. The resistance increases because of (1) the negative interpersonal impact the necessity to sell the program had upon the managers, (2) the mistrust and condemnation of the subordinates implied by the new program, (3) the inhibition of the questions and fears the subordinates wished to express *before* they were "sold", (4) the feeling of being manipulated by the fact that the changes were kept a secret while they were being planned, and (5) the dependence and submissiveness caused by the unilateral management strategy.

As can be predicted from knowing that management is uncomfortable in discussing negative feelings openly, the restraining forces are not dealt with directly. The result so far is an increase in the level of effectiveness, an increase in resisting forces, and an increase in what we might call the gross organizational tension level (notched marks in figure 5.2).

Remaining true to their values the top executives respond by creating new rational forces (a new sales pitch on the values of the program); bringing to bear new controls, and issuing new orders to overcome the resistance. This tends to coerce the subordinates to suppress their confusion, feelings of distrust, and tension related to the new program, especially when interacting with the superiors. However, these feelings and tensions cannot be suppressed forever. They may erupt during the meetings that are part of the new change activities thereby guaranteeing the ineffectiveness of these meetings.

The increased management pressure, the increase in controls through paper work, the overload of work, all act to increase the forces pushing the level of effectiveness upward. The mistrust, tension, ineffective meetings (in our case of product planning and program reviews), the willingness on the part of lower level management to make the top responsible for the change ("this is their baby") become examples of how the restraining forces are increased. The organizational tension also increases. This, in turn, stimulates management to develop new controls, check points, new courses to explain the importance of the program, etc. These actions further increase the upward forces, which, in turn, increases the resisting forces, which in turn increases the organizational tension. The loop is now closed.

At some point the difficulties and tensions reach a breaking point among the members. The top executives usually sense this and typically call for a one- or two-day meeting away from home base "to take out the kinks in the program." In my experience most of these meetings were not very effective because the subordinates feared bringing out their real feelings and the true difficulties. One interesting sign that the true problems did not come out in these meetings was the degree to which the participants assigned the causes of their problems to conditions that were typical under the pyramidal organizational structure. For example, people may spend time trying to find out who was the one person responsible for decision-making; they craved identification of their individual contribution; they competed in win–lose battles, etc.

The difficulties with these meetings is illustrated in the example below. Three years after the reorganization plan went into effect developing a team approach, marketing and manufacturing were still having difficulties defining their roles and responsibilities. Manufacturing doubted that it needed marketing and vice versa. (If I included all the data we would see that engineering also had its doubts). In reading the example, it is useful to note how many of the problems raised and the solutions suggested are typical of the traditional organizational climate and not those endemic of the matrix organization. Each group worried more about trying to show that it was truly "the" most responsible. There was little attempt by the participants to help each other and to try to build a cohesive team where the whole was more important than any one part. Also when personality issues were ever so gently brought out (toward the end), the leader changed the subject.

A: Just the same way that the R and D department resents it and marketing man says "my technology manager" and he says "my manufacturing team."

D: You know I don't resent that at all because I talk about my marketing manager.

C: Some of us do. We're all getting over it but at the beginning we all tended to be sensitive.

A: Rather than the marketing manager's decisions, the direction of the company should not be contingent upon the company's decision for these market opportunities?

B: I'd like to reply to that because strategy is knowing the customer. The big deal the whole part of it is knowing what the hell your competition's in. If you don't know your competition, you don't really know what the hell to do and who helps you play the strategy defense. It's got to be manufacturing. They've got to know their competing existing technology. They're the people that tell you what dollars ... they give you a good share of the judgements that you can apply to strategy.

D: An example to support your point is product X. This is a real good example because this is where the manufacturing team set, looked at all competitive economics, all known producers, all possible methods by which X could be produced, and came up with what we might call an equilibrium sales price. This is a price at which somebody could over the next ten years afford to put in new capacity so this came out as an average sales price. Now that really established the basic strategy level, so we then compare all the methods by which we could apply ourselves to producing our requirements on this product and looked at the comparative economics of these and their performance in the in-use areas for all of the uses of the product. So all the market technology teams contributed to this area. But the prime mover in the whole thing and really the one who was developing the whole base for the decision was a manufacturing team who were drawing together all of these inputs on competitive products and competitive economics, long-range planning, but the decision as it was arrived at was a completely composite decision in the different marketing areas where the products were going to be sold.

C: I don't have very much experience the way the other guys do, but I don't see how you can, there is no separation between our groups.

E: You fellows may not like this, but I really think that basically the company still sets the price beyond which profit can be made and it's the agents who are selling the goods from this company who still are responsible to maximize profit.

D: Well, what do you think this is? I can't see where we're in any conflict with manufacturing.

B: Like hell!

A: I think this is probably right and may be this is because we don't agree with manufacturing's mandate, the whole group down there on the boon docks don't really understand what marketing's function is. That's why we're gathered around this table, to try to understand that. It's obvious that there are a lot of people that don't understand what marketing's function is because that's why we've got it on the agenda.

B: Well, maybe if we understand your point of view, maybe we can help you to understand us.

A: Manufacturing has to understand what every marketing group, how every marketing group understands their own job. If you're not going to be the same, then the manufacturing group has to understand how you understand your job and how everyone understands their job.

C: Let me ask this – maybe you can help clarify it. Suppose marketing technology's out of this thing and then just have the manufacturing team and the sales department – could you operate on that basis? Do you need this marketing group?

A: It is a good question. The answer is probably no. We were almost doing this once before, before the reorganization and obviously it wasn't working successfully. The thing we've got now is a good bit more successful.

B: This terminology really leaves me cold. What do you mean "more successful?"

E: It's semantics, that's all.

B: The guys down at the boon docks now think that marketing should look at the sales department as a bunch of peddlers. These are the terms that are being thrown around.

D: I think this all helped. We understand each better, so what's the next topic? This is the thing that I want to avoid, that we bring personalities into this. It was nothing personal. It was simply a statement that you made that I was having trouble understanding.

B: Everybody's getting involved and yet the problem's not being solved. We talked about this last week. The manufacturing managers talked about this. All of us are talking and that's about all.

Some readers may wonder how typical is this situation. In my experience the confusion and conflict is quite typical. The meeting was more open than usual which permitted us to get a rich specimen of the conflict. By the way, I do hope that these observations will help top managements pause and question their belief that the best way to plan a reorganization is to appoint a top committee (with all the appropriate help) to develop a reorganization plan and then "sell" it to the organization. The lower level managers soon hear about the meetings and see them as the first sign of mistrust. The reasons usually given for this strategy are that to get wider participation may upset people and make it more difficult to sell the new plan. In my experience people become doubly upset with the secrecy and the anxiety built up around the rumors related to the reorganization. The time necessary for getting the program truly accepted is easily doubled. (In some recent research with governmental bureaus the time is extended till the next reorganization.)

I also hope that these data will raise question with the advice that some recent theorists suggest that people's behavior can be changed by changing the organizational structure. If the data from these nine examples are valid, then we may conclude that their view is over simplified. I would agree with them that changes in organizational structure do bring about intended changes in people's behavior. (In our figure the effectiveness level was increased.) However, they also bring about unintended behavioral changes; the restraining forces are strengthened and the organizational tension level is greatly increased. To my knowledge the proponents of this approach have never shown an example where by changing the organizational structure the restraining forces and tension levels were also not increased.

These results suggest that, in addition to organizational structural changes, one should also focus on altering the basic values of the executives so that they can develop change strategies that may minimize the unintended consequences. (One example will be discussed below.) Our approach is not to be viewed as taking sides in an argument of change in structure versus changes in people: our view is changes in structure *through* changes in people's values. Nor does the approach imply a blanket condemnation of the change strategy illustrated in figure 5.2. Such a strategy may be necessary where (for whatever reason) people refuse to alter their values; to become fully involved in the change; to take on their share of creating the change. If there is a lack of time for the more involving change process then one may use the more unilateral one depicted in figure 5.2 but may consider being quite open about the possible negative consequences and asking the people to help to reduce them.

## WHAT TO DO

I should like, at the outset, to repeat my view that project teams and matrix organizations are fundamentally valid. I believe that they are the most effective organizational structures for decisions that are complex and risky, that require the integration of many different inputs, and that depend on the continuing, long-range commitment of everyone involved without the organization's being saddled with excess and unneeded structures. (Once the project is complete, the team can be disbanded or a new project be assigned to it. See Argyris, 1964.)[2]

### A New Philosophy of Organizing and Managing People

One of the most important first steps is to communicate to the people that the matrix organization is not a simple extension of the traditional pyramidal structure. The pyramidal structure acquires its form from the fact that as one goes up the administrative ladder (1) power and control increase, (2) the availability of information increases, (3) the degree of flexibility to act increases, (4) the scope of the decisions made and the responsibilities involved increase. Implicit in the matrix organization are almost opposite tendencies. For example, power and control are given to the individual and/or to the groups who have the technical skill to accomplish the task, no matter what their organizational level. Thus a team could be composed of five people representing all different levels of authority (on the traditional chart), who are equal. The group could be chaired by the individual with the least organizational authority. The individual or groups are given responsibility and authority to make decisions of the widest necessary scope.

If we may extrapolate to the probable matrix organization of the future Forrester (1965) suggests that the organization will eventually eliminate the superior–subordinate relationship and substitute for it the individual self-discipline arising from self-interest created by a competitive market mechanism within the system. The individual would negotiate continuously changing relationships. Each individual would be a profit center whose objective would be to produce the most value for the least activity; who would have the freedom to terminate as well as to create new activity, who would have access to all the necessary information. The organization of the future would be rid of internal monopolies which is the usual status of most traditional departments.

Although I would agree with Forrester, I believe that the organizations of the future will be a combination of the old and the new forms of organization. I believe that the old forms are going to be more effective for the routine, non-innovative activity that requires little, if any, internal commitment by the participants. However, as the decisions become less routine, more innovative and require more commitment, the newer forms such as the matrix organizations will be more effective.

In addition to being able to differentiate clearly between the old and the new forms, the future executive must also be able to know the conditions under which he will use the different organizational forms.[3] Moreover, he will need to become skillful in several different kinds of leadership styles, each of which is consistent with a particular form. For example, an authoritarian leadership style is more consistent with the traditional structure; a participative style with the link pin organization defined by Likert and a style that develops risk-taking and trust for the matrix organization.

## Leadership Style and Matrix Organization

If recent research is valid, then the majority of executive leadership styles conform to the traditional pyramidal style. This is not surprising since leadership styles and organizational design would naturally go together. The findings that did surprise us were (1) the degree to which the executives believed in leadership styles that were consonant with the matrix organization, and (2) the degree to which they were unaware that they were *not* behaving according to their ideals (Argyris, 1966).

Another important first step therefore is to help executives become more aware of their actual leadership style. Unless they develop such awareness, they are not going to be able to unfreeze their old styles, develop new ones, and most importantly, switch from one style to another as the administrative situations and the organization structure used is changed. Unless the switching from one style to another can be clearly identified by the person and the receivers, confusion will result. (For some concrete examples of how this may be achieved, see Argyris, 1966.)

Another finding that surprised us about executive decision making was how many executives focused on keeping people "happy." Indeed, the most frequently cited reason for not being open with another was the fear that it might upset the receiver (and thus upset the sender). The most frequently cited reason for not bringing two groups together who are locked in inter-departmental warfare was that it would simply "involve personalities and nothing but harm could come of it." Although the executives that we studied were happiness-oriented in their behaviour, they were not in their attitudes. They believed in strong leadership that could call a spade a spade and let the chips fall where they may. Again according to the observations, the spades were called spades and the chips placed on the line, but in private settings where few could be witnesses, or by such deft and diplomatic processes that few people, including the targets, were aware of what was happening. I cannot refrain from adding that there seemed to be a strong correlation between those executives who were critical of the field of "human relations" as one whose objective was to make people happy and the degree of their blindness to the fact that they tended to do the very same thing when they were actually leading.

## The Management of Tension

Executives in the matrix organization will also need to learn, if I may be permitted to oversimplify, that there is productive and unproductive or crippling tension. The unproductive or crippling tension is tension that a person experiences but which he cannot control. The reason he cannot control the tension may be external (pressure from his superior) or internal (inability to control his own demands on himself, plus the accompanying feelings of impatience and guilt aimed at himself).

Productive tension is that tension that the individual can control and which comes from accepting new challenges, taking risks, expanding one's competencies, etc. These are the very qualities that are central to the matrix organization. Thus the executive of the future will have to learn how to define internal environments that challenge people, stretch their aspirations realistically, and help them face interpersonal reality. Some examples are financial controls that reward people for risk taking; organizational situations that are optimally undermanned; incentive systems that reward excellence (not average performance), work that is designed to use people's complex abilities. To put this another way, we need to develop competence in manipulating the environment but not the people. (They should have the freedom and responsibility to choose if they will enter the new environment.)

## The Management of Intergroup Conflict

The matrix organization is composed of teams which in turn are populated by representatives of the traditional line functions. As we have seen, this leads to much intergroup conflict within the team as well as between teams.

Instead of trying to stamp out intergroup conflict as bad and disloyal, the executives need to learn how to manage it so that the constructive aspects are emphasized and the destructive aspects are de-emphasized. This means that the organization needs to put on the table for diagnosis the interdepartmental fires, the incidents of throwing the dead cat over into the other department's yard, the polarized competitive warfare where success is defined by the participants in terms of which side won rather than the contribution to the whole. The executives will have to learn how to bring the groups together, where each discusses and seeks, in private, to agree on its views and attitudes toward the other and toward self, then the representatives of both groups talk together in the presence of the other group members, followed by private discussion to establish the way they are perceived by others in order to develop (through representatives) an understanding of the discrepancy between their and other's views (Blake, et al., 1965).

## Executive Educational Activities

Most organizations send their executives to university executive programs or to internal executive programs usually designed following the concept of the university. I do not want to get into philosophical discussions about the nature of university education at this point. I would like to point out, however, that there may be a discrepancy between the characteristics of university education and the needs of the matrix organization.

The university has typically assumed that learning (1) is for the individual, (2) occurs when it is given, (3) is tested by contrived examinations of the knowledge acquired, (4) need not be relevant to any immediate problem, (5) should be designed and controlled by the educator; it is the task of the educator to define the problems, develop ways to solve them and define the criteria for evaluation who passes and who does not. The matrix organizations require education (1) that focuses on individuals in team systems, (2) occurs where the problem is located, (3) is learned by the use of actual problems, (4) is tested by the effectiveness of the actual results, and (5) is controlled by those participating in the problem (aided by the educator as a consultant).

Executive education in the matrix organization will focus on system effectiveness. This means that the central educational department will now become an organizational development activity. It will have systems as its clients. A small team of consultants will enter the system and develop a diagnosis of its human and technical effectiveness. These data will then be fed back to representatives at all levels of the system to generate, at the grass-roots level, action recommendations. A steering committee composed of representatives of the client system and the organizational development will then prepare a long-range educational program designed to increase the immediate as well as the long-range effectiveness of the system.

Classes may then be held at the plant location or at a central facility, depending upon the resources needed, the time available, the availability of the "students," as well as the faculty. Teams and not disconnected individuals will study together for the majority of technical and management subjects. These teams will be actual working teams. This will place pressure on the faculty to develop learning that is valid for the real problems of the team and motivate the students to learn, since it is their problems upon which the education is focusing.

To put this another way, education will be for organizational and system diagnosis, renewal and effectiveness. It will be held with groups, subject material, and faculty that are organic to the organization's problem. One of the dangers of this education is the possibility that it will focus on the trivial, short-range problems. The quality control in this area will depend partially on the diagnostic competence of the faculty. In defining the problem they can help the organization to get to the underlying and basic causes. The students can also help by being alert to the validity of the education that is being offered to them.

Some critics wonder if teams of people working together can be pulled away from work. The answer, in my experience, is affirmative. The fear, for example, that the company will be in trouble if the top team leaves for a week, has been quietly exploded in several cases. The explosions have been quiet lest, as one president put it, "it was learned how well things ran while the top management was away."

More importantly, this new type of education is central to the work of the system. Thus, the team is not being pulled away from work. Indeed, in many cases, it is pulled away *in order to work*. Systems, like cars, need to have their organizational hoods opened and the motor checked and tuned. Unless this maintenance work is done, the system will deteriorate as certainly as does an automobile.

Finally, the concern of being away physically from the location should be matched with the concern about the number of hours being consumed needlessly while at work. In the studies listed previously, I have found that as many as half the meetings and as much as three quarters of the time spent at meetings are not productive and worse than unnecessary.

## ORGANIZATIONAL CHANGE

Anyone who has planned major organizational change knows (1) how difficult it is to foresee accurately all the major problems involved, (2) the enormous amount of time needed to iron out the kinks and get people to accept the change, (3) the apparent lack of internal commitment on the part of many to help make the plan work, manifested partly by people at all levels resisting taking the initiative to make modifications that they see are necessary so that the new plan can work. In preparing this chapter, I reviewed my notes from 32 major reorganizations in large organizations in which I played some consulting and research role. I did not find one that could be labeled as fully completed and integrated three years after the change had been announced (and in many cases had gone through several revisions). That is, after three years there were still many people fighting, ignoring, questioning, resisting, and/or blaming, the reorganization without feeling a strong obligation personally to correct the situation.

As I mentioned above, I believe the reasons for this long delay are embedded in the change strategy typically used by management. To refer to the diagram, the basic strategy has been for the top management to take the responsibility to overcome and outguess the resistance to change. This strategy does tend to succeed because management works very hard, applies pressure, and if necessary knocks a few heads together (or eliminates some). However, as we have seen, the strategy creates resisting forces that are costly to the organization's effectiveness, to its long-run viability and flexibility, as well as to the people at all levels.

What would happen if management experiments with the strategy of reducing the restraining forces by involving, at least, the management employees at all levels in the diagnosis, design, and execution of the change program? For example, in one organization a plan of reorganization was begun by getting all levels involved in diagnosing the present problems of the organizations. Groups were formed (which met only twice for several hours each time) to diagnose the effectiveness of the present organization. These groups were initially composed of people from various functions but holding positions of about equal level. Each group brain-stormed as much as it desired to get out of the problems. They were not asked to suggest solutions at this time because (1) no one group would have a total picture of the organization, and therefore (2) its recommendations could be incomplete and misleading, with the added danger of each group becoming attached to their suggestions, and finally people tend to be hesitant about enumerating a problem if they are asked for solutions and do not have any.

The results of these diagnostic sessions were fed to a top level steering committee which contained representatives of all the major managerial levels. This committee had the diagnoses collated, analyzed, and developed into an integrated picture. Wherever they found holes and inconsistencies in the diagnoses they made a note of them. Eventually they had compiled a lengthy list of major questions to be answered before the overall diagnosis could be accepted as valid. These questions were fed to small task forces whose composition was specifically designed to be able to answer the questions. Thus, in this phase, the groups were composed of managerial personnel from many functions and levels who were relevant to the question being asked. These task forces were disbanded as soon as they provided the answers to the questions.

The third phase was one where the steering committee tried to develop a new organizational structure. In achieving this objective the steering committee began, for the first time, to suggest arrangements of individuals and groups tasks that could be threatening to various interests. This led to the members becoming more involved, cautious, and at times, defensive. Members who, up to this point, had felt free to be objective were beginning to feel themselves slipping into the role of protecting the groups toward which they had the closest attachment.

At this point, the task force went to the education group and asked for a course in such subjects as how to deal with intergroup rivalries and issues, with emotionality in groups, and with hidden agendas. This course was quickly but carefully planned. The steering committee members reported that it was a great help to them. It was especially helpful in welding them into a more fully functioning open, confronting of issues and risk taking, group. They also reported that as the members' confidence and trust in their group increased, the more willing they were to invite, at the appropriate time, members of departments whose future roles were being discussed so that the problems could be discussed and solved jointly.

The fourth phase was the preparation of a final but still tentative plan. It was fully discussed with the top executives until it represented a plan that they liked. This plan was then discussed systematically with key representatives of all the departments. Alterations were invited and carefully considered. Two members of the steering committee were members of top management who had authority to represent the top in approving most changes.

During the fifth phase two kinds of data were collected. First a questionnaire was sent to all who had participated asking them for any individual comments about the plan as well as any comments about the effectiveness of the process of change to date. This diagnosis uncovered, in several cases new ideas to be considered as well as several suggestions to be re-examined because they were developed in groups where individuals felt that they had been pushed through by a small but powerful clique.

The final plan was then drawn up with a specific timetable (which had been discussed and accepted by the people below.) The top management, with the help of the steering committee, then put the new organizational plan into action. These phases took nearly 17 months. However, once the plan became policy (1) the resisting forces and the tensions were much lower than expected on the basis of previous experience, (2) wherever they existed there were organizational mechanisms already established and working to resolve them, (3) the internal commitment to the new policy was high (it is ours not their) and thus (4) changes were made as they became necessary without much fanfare or difficulty.

One of the most important outcomes of this type of change strategy was that it provided a living educational experience for individuals and groups on how to work together, on how to develop internal commitment among the members of the organization, and how to reduce the unnecessary and destructive win–lose rivalries. Thus the change program became an opportunity for education at all levels. The result was that a new system had been created which could be used for future changes and to increase the capacity of the organization to learn.

Even with these results, I have encountered some managers who wonder if an organization can take this much time for changing organizational structure. In my experience, although time is a critical factor, it is a false issue. Time will be taken, whether management is aware of it or not, by people to ask all the questions, make all the politically necessary moves, develop all the protective devices, and create all the organizational escape hatches that they feel are necessary. The real issue is whether the time will be used constructively and effectively so that the organization can learn from its experiences thereby increasing its competence in becoming a problem solving system.

## Notes

1   The model is taken from Kurt Lewin's (1947) concept of quasi-stationary equilbria. For readers interested in organization theory, I mean to imply that people holding the three values above will always tend to create the problems original depicted in Lewin's model. I am suggesting an explanation to Lewin's question as to why he found change activities in our society tended to take one form.

2   In the same book I try to support the view that the matrix organization more nearly approximates the essential properties of organization than does the pyramidal organization.

3   Elsewhere I have suggested some examples of the decision rules that could be developed within the organization so that all concerned could be clear when to use the different structures. See Argyris (1964).

## References

Argyris, C., 1962, *Interpersonal Competence and Organizational Effectiveness*, Homewood, Ill., Irwin & Co.

Argyris, C., 1964, *Integrating the Individual and the Organization*, New York, John Wiley & Sons.

Argyris, C., 1965, *Organization and Innovation*, Homewood, Ill., Irwin & Co.

Argyris, C., 1966, "Interpersonal barriers to decision making," *Harvard Business Review*, April.

Blake, R. R., Shepard H. A, and Mouton, S., 1965, *Managing Intergroup Conflict in Industry*, Houston, Texas, Gulf Publishing Co.

Forrester, J. W., 1965, "A New Corporate Design," *Industrial Management Review*, 7, 1, Fall, pp. 5–18.

Lewin, K., 1947, "Frontiers in group dynamics," *Human Relations*, 1, 1 & 2, pp. 2–38.

Schein, E., and Bennis, W., 1965, *Personal Growth and Organizational Change Through Group Methods*, New York, John Wiley & Sons.

Wallace, W. L., 1963, "The Winchester-Western division concept of product planning," Olin Mathieson Chemical Corporation, January, New Haven, pp. 2–3.

# — 6 —

# Teaching Smart People
# How to Learn

Any company that aspires to succeed in the tougher business environment of the 1990s must first resolve a basic dilemma: success in the market place increasingly depends on learning, yet most people don't know how to learn. What's more, those members of the organization that many assume to be the best at learning are, in fact, not very good at it. I am talking about the well-educated, high-powered, high-commitment professionals who occupy key leadership positions in the modern corporation.

Most companies not only have tremendous difficulty addressing this learning dilemma they aren't even aware that it exists. The reason: they misunderstand what learning is and how to bring it about. As a result, they tend to make two mistakes in their efforts to become a learning organization.

First, most people define learning too narrowly as mere "problem-solving," so they focus on identifying and correcting errors in the external environment. Solving problems is important. But if learning is to persist, managers and employees must also look inward. They need to reflect critically on their own behavior, identify the ways they often inadvertently contribute to the organization's problems, and then change how they act. In particular, they must learn how the very way they go about defining and solving problems can be a source of problems in its own right.

I have coined the terms "single-loop" and "double-loop" learning to capture this crucial distinction. To give a simple analogy: a thermostat that automatically turns on the heat whenever the temperature in a room drops below 68 degrees is a good example of single-loop learning. A thermostat that could ask, "Why am I set at 68 degrees?" and then explore whether not some other temperature might more economically achieve the goal of heating the room would be engaging in double-loop learning.

Highly skilled professionals are frequently very good at single-loop learning. After all, they have spent much of their lives acquiring academic credentials, mastering one or a number of intellectual disciplines, and applying those disciplines to solve real-world problems. But ironically, this very fact helps explain why professionals are often so bad at double-loop learning.

Put simply, because many professionals are almost always successful at what they do, they rarely experience failure. And because they have rarely failed, they have never learned how to learn from failure. So whenever their single-loop learning strategies go wrong, they become defensive, screen out criticism, and put the "blame" on anyone and everyone but themselves. In short, their ability to learn shuts down precisely at the moment they need it the most.

The propensity among professionals to behave defensively helps shed light on the second mistake that companies make about learning. The common assumption is that getting people to learn is largely a matter of motivation. When people have the right attitudes and commitment, learning automatically follows. So companies focus on creating new organizational structures – compensation programs, performance reviews, corporate cultures, and the like – that are designed to create motivated and committed employees.

But effective double-loop learning is not simply a function of how people feel. It is a reflection of how they think – that is, the cognitive rules or reasoning they use to design and implement their actions. Think of the rules as a kind of "master program" stored in the brain, governing behavior. Defensive reasoning can block learning even when the individual commitment to it is high, just as a computer program with hidden bugs can produce results exactly the opposite of what its designers had planned.

Companies can learn how to resolve the learning dilemma. What it takes is to make the ways managers and employees reason about their behavior a focus of organizational learning and continuous improvement programs. Teaching people how to reason about their behavior in new and more effective ways breaks down the defenses that block learning.

All of the examples that follow involve a particular kind of professional: fast-track consultants at major management consulting companies. But the implications of my argument go far beyond this specific occupational group. The fact is, more and more jobs – no matter what the title – are taking on the contours of "knowledge work." People at all levels of the organization must combine the mastery of some highly specialized technical expertise with the ability to work effectively in teams, form productive relationships with clients and customers, and critically reflect on and then change their own organizational practices. And the nuts and bolts of management – whether of high-powered consultants or service representatives, senior managers or factory technicians – increasingly consists of guiding and integrating the autonomous but interconnected work of highly skilled people.

## How Professionals Avoid Learning

For 15 years, I have been conducting in-depth studies of management consultants. I decided to study consultants for a few simple reasons. First, they are the epitome of the highly educated professionals who play an increasingly central role in all organizations. Almost all of the consultants I've studied have MBAs from the top three or four US business schools. They are also highly committed to their work. For instance, at one company, more than 90 percent of the consultants responded in a survey that they were "highly satisfied" with their jobs and with the company.

I also assumed that such professional consultants would be good at learning. After all, the essence of their job is to teach others how to do things differently. I found, however, that these consultants embodied the learning dilemma. The most enthusiastic about continuous improvement in their own organizations, they were also often the biggest obstacle to its complete success.

As long as efforts at learning and change focused on external organizational factors – job redesign, compensation programs, performance reviews, and leadership training – the professionals were enthusiastic participants. Indeed, creating new systems and structures was precisely the kind of challenge that well-educated, highly motivated professionals thrived on.

And yet the moment the quest for continuous improvement turned to the professionals' *own* performance, something went wrong. It wasn't a matter of bad attitude. The professionals' commitment to excellence was genuine, and the vision of the company was clear.

Nevertheless, continuous improvement did not persist. And the longer the continuous improvement efforts continued, the greater the likelihood that they would produce ever-diminishing returns.

What happened? The professionals began to feel embarrassed. They were threatened by the prospect of critically examining their own role in the organization. Indeed, because they were so well paid (and generally believed that their employers were supportive and fair), the idea that their performance might not be at its best made them feel guilty.

Far from being a catalyst for real change, such feelings caused most to react defensively. They projected the blame for any problems away from themselves and onto what they said were unclear goals, insensitive and unfair leaders, and stupid clients.

Consider this example. At a premier management consulting company the manager of a case team called a meeting to examine the team's performance on a recent consulting project. The client was largely satisfied and had given the team relatively high marks, but the manager believed the team had not created the value-added that it was capable of and that the consulting company had promised. In the spirit of continuous improvement, he felt that the team could do better. Indeed, so did some of the team members.

The manager knew how difficult it was for people to reflect critically on their own work performance, especially in the presence of their manager, so he took a number of steps to make possible a frank and open discussion. He invited to the meeting an outside consultant whom team members knew and trusted – "just to keep me honest," he said. He also agreed to have the entire meeting tape-recorded. That way, any subsequent confusions or disagreements about what went on at the meeting could be checked against the transcript. Finally, the manager opened the meeting by emphasizing that no subject was off limits – including his own behavior.

"I realize that you may believe you cannot confront me," the manager said. "But I encourage you to challenge me. You have a responsibility to tell me where you think the leadership made mistakes, just as I have the responsibility to identify any I believe you made. And all of us must acknowledge our own mistakes. If we do not have an open dialogue, we will not learn."

The professionals took the manager up on the first half of his invitation but quietly ignored the second. When asked to pinpoint the key problems in the experience with the client, they looked entirely outside themselves. The clients were uncooperative and arrogant. "They didn't think we could help them." The team's own managers were unavailable and poorly prepared. "At times, our managers were not up to speed before they walked into the client meetings." In effect, the professionals asserted that they were helpless to act differently, not because of any limitations of their own but because of the limitations of others.

The manager listened carefully to the team members and tried to respond to their criticisms. He talked about the mistakes that he had made during the consulting process. For example, one professional objected to the way the manager had run the project meetings. "I see that the way I asked questions closed down discussions," responded the manager. "I didn't mean to do that, but I can see how you might have believed that I had already made up my mind." Another team member complained that the manager had caved in to pressure from his superior to produce the project report far too quickly, considering the team's heavy work load. "I think that it was my responsibility to have said no," admitted the manager. "It was clear that we all had an immense amount of work."

Finally, after some three hours of discussion about his own behavior, the manager began to ask the team members if there were any errors they might have made. "After all," he said, "this client was not different from many others. How can we be more effective in the future?"

The professionals repeated that it was really the clients' and their own managers' fault. As one put it, "They have to be open to change and want to learn." The more the manager tried to get the team to examine its own responsibility for the outcome, the more the professionals bypassed his concerns. The best one team member could suggest was for the case team to "promise less" – implying that there was really no way for the group to improve its performance.

The case-team members were reacting defensively to protect themselves, even though their manager was not acting in ways that an outsider would consider threatening. Even if there were some truth to their charges – the clients may well have been arrogant and closed, their own managers distant – the *way* they presented these claims was guaranteed to stop learning. With few exceptions the professionals made attributions about the behavior of the clients and the managers but never publicly tested their claims. For instance, they said that the clients weren't motivated to learn but never really presented any evidence supporting that assertion. When their lack of concrete evidence was pointed out to them, they simply repeated their criticisms more vehemently.

If the professionals had felt so strongly about these issues, why had they never mentioned them during the project? According to the professionals even this was the fault of others. "We didn't want to alienate the client," argued one. "We didn't want to be seen as whining," said another.

The professionals were using their criticisms of others to protect themselves from the potential embarrassment of having to admit that perhaps they too had contributed to the team's less-than-perfect performance. What's more, the fact that they kept repeating their defensive actions in the face of the manager's efforts to turn the group's attention to its own role shows that this defensiveness had become a reflexive routine. From the professionals' perspective, they weren't resisting; they were focusing on the "real" causes Indeed, they were to be respected, if not congratulated, for working as well as they did under such difficult conditions.

The end result was an unproductive parallel conversation. Both the manager and the professionals were candid; they expressed their views forcefully. But they talked past each other, never finding a common language to describe what had happened with the client. The professionals kept insisting that the fault lay with others. The manager kept trying, unsuccessfully, to get the professionals to see how they contributed to the state of affairs they were criticizing. The dialogue of this parallel conversation looks like this:

PROFESSIONALS: The clients have to be open. They must want to change.
MANAGER:             It's our task to help them see that change is in their interest.
PROFESSIONALS: But the clients didn't agree with our analyses.
MANAGER:             If they didn't think our ideas were right, how might we have convinced them?
PROFESSIONALS: Maybe we need to have more meetings with the client.
MANAGER:             If we aren't adequately prepared and if the clients don't think we're credible, how will more meetings help?
PROFESSIONALS: There should be better communication between case team members and management.
MANAGER:             I agree. But professionals should take the initiative to educate the manager about the problems they are experiencing.
PROFESSIONALS: Our leaders are unavailable and distant.
MANAGER:             How do you expect us to know that if you don't tell us?

Conversations such as this one dramatically illustrate the learning dilemma. The problem with the professionals' claims is not that they are wrong but that they aren't useful. By constantly turning the focus away from their own behavior to that of others, the professionals bring learning to a grinding halt. The manager understands the trap but does not know how to get out of it. To learn how to do that requires going deeper into the dynamics of defensive reasoning – and into the special causes that make professionals so prone to it.

## DEFENSIVE REASONING AND THE DOOM LOOP

What explains the professionals' defensiveness? Not their attitudes about change or commitment to continuous improvement; they really wanted to work more effectively. Rather, the key factor is the way they reasoned about their behavior and that of others.

It is impossible to reason anew in every situation. If we had to think through all the possible responses every time someone asked, "How are you?" the world would pass us by. Therefore, everyone develops a theory of action: a set of rules that individuals use to design and implement their own behavior as well as to understand the behavior of others. Usually, these theories of action become so taken for granted that people don't even realize they are using them.

One of the paradoxes of human behavior, however, is that the master program people actually use is rarely the one they think they use. Ask people in an interview or questionnaire to articulate the rules they use to govern their actions, and they will give you what I call their "espoused" theory of action. But observe these same people's behavior, and you will quickly see that this espoused theory has very little to do with how they actually behave. For example, the professionals on the case team said they believed in continuous improvement, and yet they consistently acted in ways that made improvement impossible.

When you observe people's behavior and try to come up with rules that would make sense of it, you discover a very different theory of action – what I call the individual's "theory-in-use." Put simply, people consistently act inconsistently, unaware of the contradiction between their espoused theory and their theory-in-use, between the way they think they are acting and the way they really act.

What's more, most theories-in-use rest on the same set of governing values. There seems to be a universal human tendency to design one's actions consistently according to four basic values:

1   to remain in unilateral control;
2   to maximize "winning" and minimize "losing";
3   to suppress negative feelings; and
4   to be as "rational" as possible – by which people mean defining clear objectives and evaluating their behavior in terms of whether or not they have achieved them.

The purpose of all these values is to avoid embarrassment or threat, feeling vulnerable or incompetent. In this respect, the master program that most people use is profoundly defensive. Defensive reasoning encourages individuals to keep private the premises, inferences, and conclusions that shape their behavior and to avoid testing them in a truly independent, objective fashion.

Because the attributions that go into defensive reasoning are never really tested, it is a closed loop, remarkably impervious to conflicting points of view. The inevitable response to the observation that somebody is reasoning defensively is yet more defensive reasoning. With the case team, for example, whenever anyone pointed out the professionals defensive behavior to them, their initial reaction was to look for the cause in somebody else – clients who were so sensitive that they would have been alienated if the consultants had criticized them or a manager so weak that he couldn't have taken it had the consultants raised their concerns with him. In other words, the case-team members once again denied their own responsibility by externalizing the problem and putting it on someone else.

In such situations, the simple act of encouraging more open inquiry is often attacked by others as "intimidating." Those who do the attacking deal with their feelings about possibly being wrong by blaming the more open individual for arousing these feelings and upsetting them.

Needless to say, such a master program inevitably short-circuits learning. And for a number of reasons unique to their psychology, well-educated professionals are especially susceptible to this.

Nearly all the consultants I have studied have stellar academic records. Ironically, their very success at education helps explain the problems they have with learning. Before they enter the world of work, their lives are primarily full of successes, so they have rarely experienced the embarrassment and sense of threat that comes with failure. As a result, their defensive reasoning has rarely been activated. People who rarely experience failure, how-ever, end up not knowing how to deal with it effectively. And this serves to reinforce the normal human tendency to reason defensively.

In a survey of several hundred young consultants at the organizations I have been studying, these professionals describe themselves as driven internally by an unrealistically high ideal of performance: "Pressure on the job is self-imposed." "I must not only do a good job; I must also be the best." "People around here are very bright and hardworking; they are highly motivated to do an outstanding job." "Most of us want not only to succeed but also to do so at maximum speed."

These consultants are always comparing themselves with the best around them and constantly trying to better their own performance. And yet they do not appreciate being required to compete openly with each other. They feel it is somehow inhumane. They prefer to be the individual contributor – what might be termed a "productive loner."

Behind this high aspiration for success is an equally high fear of failure and a propensity to feel shame and guilt when they do fail to meet their high standards. "You must avoid mistakes," said one. "I hate making them. Many of us fear failure, whether we admit it or not."

To the extent that these consultants have experienced success in their lives, they have not had to be concerned about failure and the attendant feelings of shame and guilt. But to exactly the same extent, they also have never developed the tolerance for feelings of failure or the skills to deal with these feelings. This in turn has led them not only to fear failure but also to fear the fear of failure itself. For they know that they will not cope with it super-latively – their usual level of aspiration.

The consultants use two intriguing metaphors to describe this phenomenon. They talk about the "doom loop" and "doom zoom." Often, consultants will perform well on the case team, but because they don't do the jobs perfectly or receive accolades from their managers, they go into a doom loop of despair. And they don't ease into the doom loop, they zoom into it.

As a result, many professionals have extremely "brittle" personalities. When suddenly faced with a situation they cannot immediately handle, they tend to fall apart. They cover up their distress in front of the client. They talk about it constantly with their fellow case-team members. Interestingly, these conversations commonly take the form of bad-mouthing clients.

Such brittleness leads to an inappropriately high sense of despondency or even despair when people don't achieve the high levels of performance they aspire to. Such despondency is rarely psychologically devastating, but when combined with defensive reasoning, it can result in a formidable predisposition against learning.

There is no better example of how this brittleness can disrupt an organization than performance evaluations. Because it represents the one moment when a professional must measure his or her own behavior against some formal standard, a performance evaluation is almost tailor-made to push a professional into the doom loop. Indeed, a poor evaluation can reverberate far beyond the particular individual involved to spark defensive reasoning throughout an entire organization.

At one consulting company, management established a new performance-evaluation process that was designed to make evaluations both more objective and more useful to those being evaluated. The consultants participated in the design of the new system and in general were enthusiastic because it corresponded to their espoused values of objectivity and fairness. A brief two years into the new process, however, it had become the object of dissatisfaction. The catalyst for this about-face was the first unsatisfactory rating.

Senior managers had identified six consultants whose performance they considered below standard. In keeping with the new evaluation process, they did all they could to communicate their concerns to the six and to help them improve. Managers met with each individual separately for as long and as often as the professional requested to explain the reasons behind the rating and to discuss what needed to be done to improve, but to no avail. Performance continued at the same low level and, eventually, the six were let go.

When word of the dismissal spread through the company, people responded with confusion and anxiety. After about a dozen consultants angrily complained to management, the CEO held two lengthy meetings where employees could air their concerns.

At the meetings, the professionals made a variety of claims. Some said the performance-evaluation process was unfair because judgements were subjective and biased and the criteria for minimum performance unclear. Others suspected that the real cause for the dismissals was economic and that the performance-evaluation procedure was just a fig leaf to hide the fact that the company was in trouble. Still others argued that the evaluation process was anti-learning. If the company were truly a learning organization, as it claimed, then people performing below the minimum standard should be taught how to reach it. As one professional put it: "We were told that the company did not have an up-or-out policy. Up-or-out is inconsistent with learning. You misled us."

The CEO tried to explain the logic behind management's decision by grounding it in the facts of the case and by asking the professionals for any evidence that might contradict these facts.

Is there subjectivity and bias in the evaluation process? Yes, responded the CEO, but "we strive hard to reduce them. We are constantly trying to improve the process. If you have any ideas, please tell us. If you know of someone treated unfairly, please bring it up. If any of you feel that you have been treated unfairly, let's discuss it now or, if you wish, privately."

Is the level of minimum competence too vague? "We are working to define minimum competence more clearly," he answered. "In the case of the six, however, their performance was so poor that it wasn't difficult to reach a decision." Most of the six had received timely feedback about their problems. And in the two cases where people had not, the reason was that they had never taken the responsibility to seek out evaluations – and, indeed, had actively avoided them. "If you have any data to the contrary," the CEO added, "let's talk about it."

Were the six asked to leave for economic reasons? No, said the CEO. "We have more work than we can do, and letting professionals go is extremely costly for us. Do any of you have any information to the contrary?"

As to the company being anti-learning, in fact, the entire evaluation process was designed to encourage learning. When a professional is performing below the minimum level, the CEO explained, "we jointly design remedial experiences with the individual. Then we look for signs of improvement. In these cases, either the professionals were reluctant to take on such assignments or they repeatedly failed when they did. Again, if you have information or evidence to the contrary, I'd like to hear about it."

The CEO concluded: "It's regrettable, but sometimes we make mistakes and hire the wrong people. If individuals don't produce and repeatedly prove themselves unable to improve, we don't know what else to do except dismiss them. It's just not fair to keep poorly performing individuals in the company. They earn an unfair share of the financial rewards."

Instead of responding with data of their own, the professionals simply repeated their accusations but in ways that consistently contradicted their claims. They said that a genuinely fair evaluation process would contain clear and documentable data about performance, but they were unable to provide first hand examples of the unfairness that they implied colored the evaluation of the six dismissed employees. They argued that people shouldn't be judged by inferences unconnected to their actual performance, but they judged management in precisely this way. They insisted that management define clear, objective, and unambiguous performance standards, but they argued that any humane system would take into account that the performance of a professional cannot be precisely measured. Finally, they presented themselves as champions of learning, but they never proposed any criteria for assessing whether an individual might be unable to learn.

In short, the professionals seemed to hold management to a different level of performance than they held themselves. In their conversation at the meetings, they used many of the features of ineffective evaluation that they condemned: the absence of concrete data, for example, and the dependence on a logic of "heads we win, tails you lose." It is as if they were saying, "Here are the features of a fair performance-evaluation system. You should abide by them. But we don't have to when we are evaluating you."

Indeed, if we were to explain the professionals' behavior by articulating rules that would have to be in their heads in order for them to act the way they did, the rules would look something like this.

1   When criticizing the company, state your criticism in ways that you believe are valid; but also in ways that prevent others from deciding for themselves whether your claim to validity is correct.
2   When asked to illustrate your criticisms, don't include any data that others could use to decide for themselves whether the illustrations are valid.
3   State your conclusions in ways that disguise their logical implications. If others point out those implications to you, deny them.

Of course, when such rules were described to the professionals, they found them abhorrent. It was inconceivable that these rules might explain their actions. And yet in defending themselves against this observation, they almost always inadvertently confirmed the rules.

## LEARNING HOW TO REASON PRODUCTIVELY

If defensive reasoning is as widespread as I believe, then focusing on an individual's attitudes or commitment is never enough to produce real change. And as the previous example illustrates, neither is creating new organizational structures or systems. The problem is that even when people are genuinely committed to improving their performance and management has changed its structures in order to encourage the "right" kind of behavior, people still remain locked in defensive reasoning. Either they remain unaware of this fact, or if they do become aware of it, they blame others.

There is, however, reason to believe that organizations can break out of this vicious circle. Despite the strength of defensive reasoning, people genuinely strive to produce what they intend. They value acting competently. Their self-esteem is intimately tied up with behaving consistently and performing effectively. Companies can use these universal human tendencies to teach people how to reason in a new way – in effect, to change the master programs in their heads and thus reshape their behavior.

People can be taught how to recognize the reasoning they use when they design and implement their actions. They can begin to identify the inconsistencies between their espoused and actual theories of action. They can face up to the fact that they unconsciously design and implement actions that they do not intend. Finally, people can learn how to identify what individuals and groups do to create organizational defenses and how these defenses contribute to an organization's problems.

| *Defensive* | *Productive* |
|---|---|
| Characteristics | |
| – soft data | – hard data |
| – tacit, private inferences | – explicit inferences |
| – conclusions not publicly testable | – premises explicit, conclusions publicly testable |
| Supported by | |
| – tacit theory of dealing with threat | – (explicit or tacit) theory of strategy formulation |
| – set of tacitly interrelated concepts | – set of directly interrelated concepts |
| – set of tacit rules for using concepts to make permissible inferences, reach private conclusions, and private criteria to judge the validity of the test | – set of rules for using concepts to make permissible inferences, reach testable conclusions, and criteria to judge the validity of the test |

Once companies embark on this learning process, they will discover that the kind of reasoning necessary to reduce and overcome organizational defenses is the same kind of "tough reasoning" that underlies the effective use of ideas in strategy, finance, marketing, manufacturing, and other management disciplines. Any sophisticated strategic analysis, for example, depends on collecting valid data, analyzing it carefully, and constantly testing the inferences drawn from the data. The toughest tests are reserved for the conclusions. Good strategists make sure that their conclusions can withstand all kinds of critical questioning.

So too with productive reasoning about human behavior. The standard of analysis is just as high. Human resource programs no longer need to be based on "soft" reasoning but should be as analytical and as data-driven as any other management discipline.

Of course, that is not the kind of reasoning the consultants used when they encountered problems that were embarrassing or threatening. The data they collected were hardly objective. The inferences they made rarely became explicit. The conclusions they reached were largely self-serving, impossible for others to test, and as a result, "self-sealing," impervious to change.

How can an organization begin to turn this situation around, to teach its members how to reason productively? The first step is for managers at the top to examine critically and change their own theories-in-use. Until senior managers become aware of how they reason defensively and the counterproductive consequences that result, there will be little real progress. Any change activity is likely to be just a fad.

Change has to start at the top because otherwise defensive senior managers are likely to disown any transformation in reasoning patterns coming from below. If professionals or middle managers begin to change the way they reason and act, such changes are likely to appear strange – if not actually dangerous – to those at the top. The result is an unstable situation where senior managers still believe that it is a sign of caring and sensitivity to bypass and cover up difficult issues, while their subordinates see the very same actions as defensive.

The key to any educational experience designed to teach senior managers how to reason productively is to connect the program to real business problems. The best demonstration of the usefulness of productive reasoning is for busy managers to see how it can make a direct difference in their own performance and in that of the organization. This will not happen overnight. Managers need plenty of opportunity to practice the new skills. But once they grasp the powerful impact that productive reasoning can have on actual performance, they will have a strong incentive to reason productively not just in a training session but in all their work relationships.

One simple approach I have used to get this process started is to have participants produce a kind of rudimentary case study. The subject is a real business problem that the manager either wants to deal with or has tried unsuccessfully to address in the past. Writing the actual case usually takes less than an hour. But then the case becomes the focal point of an extended analysis.

For example, a CEO at a large organizational-development consulting company was preoccupied with the problems caused by the intense competition among the various business functions represented by his four direct reports. Not only was he tired of having the problems dumped in his lap, but he was also worried about the impact the interfunctional conflicts were having on the organization's flexibility. He had even calculated that the money being spent to iron out disagreements amounted to hundreds of thousands of dollars every year. And the more fights there were, the more defensive people became, which only increased the costs to the organization.

In a paragraph or so, the CEO described a meeting he intended to have with his direct reports to address the problem. Next, he divided the paper in half, and on the right-hand side of the page, he wrote a scenario for the meeting – much like the script for a movie or play – describing what he would say and how his subordinates would likely respond. On the left-hand side of the page, he wrote down any thoughts and feelings that he would be likely to have during the meeting but that he wouldn't express for fear they would derail the discussion.

But instead of holding the meeting, the CEO analyzed this scenario *with* his direct reports. The case became the catalyst for a discussion in which the CEO learned several things about the way he acted with his management team.

He discovered that his four direct reports often perceived his conversations as counterproductive. In the guise of being "diplomatic," he would pretend that a consensus about the problem existed, when in fact none existed. The unintended result: instead of feeling reassured, his subordinates felt wary and tried to figure out "what is he *really* getting at."

The CEO also realized that the way he dealt with the competitiveness among department heads was completely contradictory. On the one hand, he kept urging them to "think of the organization as a whole." On the other he kept calling for actions – department budget cuts, for example – that placed them directly in competition with each other.

Finally, the CEO discovered that many of the tacit evaluations and attributions he had listed turned out to be wrong. Since he had never expressed these assumptions, he had never found out just how wrong they were. What's more, he learned that much of what he thought he was hiding came through to his subordinates anyway – but with the added message that the boss was covering up.

The CEO's colleagues also learned about their own ineffective behavior. They learned by examining their own behavior as they tried to help the CEO analyze his case. They also learned by writing and analyzing cases of their own. They began to see that they too tended to bypass and cover up the real issues and that the CEO was often aware of it but did not say so. They too made inaccurate attributions and evaluations that they did not express. Moreover, the belief that they had to hide important ideas and feelings from the CEO and from each other in order not to upset anyone turned out to be mistaken. In the context of the case discussions, the entire senior management team was quite willing to discuss what had always been undiscussable.

In effect, the case study exercise legitimizes talking about issues that people have never been able to address before. Such a discussion can be emotional – even painful. But for managers with the courage to persist, the payoff is great: management teams and entire organizations work more openly and more effectively and have greater options for behaving flexibly and adapting to particular situations.

When senior managers are trained in new reasoning skills, they can have a big impact on the performance of the entire organization – even when other employees are still reasoning defensively. The CEO who led the meetings on the performance-evaluation procedure was able to defuse dissatisfaction because he didn't respond to professionals' criticisms in kind but instead gave a clear presentation of relevant data. Indeed, most participants took the CEO's behavior to be a sign that the company really acted on the values of participation and employee involvement that it espoused.

Of course, the ideal is for all the members of an organization to learn how to reason productively. This has happened at the company where the case-team meeting took place. Consultants and their managers are now able to confront some of the most difficult issues of the consultant–client relationship. To get a sense of the difference productive reasoning can make, imagine how the original conversation between the manager and case team might have gone had everyone engaged in effective reasoning. (The following dialogue is based on actual sessions I have attended with other case teams at the same company since the training has been completed.)

First, the consultants would have demonstrated their commitment to continuous improvement by being willing to examine their own role in the difficulties that arose during the consulting project. No doubt they would have identified their managers and the clients as part of the problem, but they would have gone on to admit that they had contributed to it as well. More important, they would have agreed with the manager that as they explored the various roles of clients, managers, and professionals, they would make sure to test any evaluations or attributions they might make against the data. Each individual would have encouraged the others to question his or her reasoning. Indeed, they would have insisted on it. And in turn, everyone would have understood that act of questioning not as a sign of mistrust or an invasion of privacy but as a valuable opportunity for learning.

The conversation about the manager's unwillingness to say no might look something like this.

PROFESSIONAL A: One of the biggest problems I had with the way you managed this case was that you seemed to be unable to say no when either the client or your superior made unfair demands. [Gives an example.]

PROFESSIONAL B: I have another example to add. [Describes a second example.] But I'd also like to say that we never really told you how we felt about this. Behind your back we were bad-mouthing you – you know, "he's being such a wimp" – but we never came right out and said it.

MANAGER: It certainly would have been helpful if you had said something. Was there anything I said or did that gave you the idea that you had better not raise this with me?

PROFESSIONAL C: Not really. I think we didn't want to sound like we we're whining.

MANAGER:              Well, I certainly don't think you sound like you're whining. But two
                      thoughts come to mind. If I understand you correctly, you *were*
                      complaining, but the complaining about me and my inability to say
                      no was covered up. Second, if we had discussed this, I might have
                      gotten the data I needed to be able to say no.

Notice that when the second professional describes how the consultants had covered up
their complaints, the manager doesn't criticize her. Rather, he rewards her for being open by
responding in kind. He focuses on the ways that he too may have contributed to the cover-
up. Reflecting undefensively about his own role in the problem then makes it possible for
the professionals to talk about their fears of appearing to be whining. The manager then
agrees with the professionals that they shouldn't become complainers. At the same time, he
points out the counterproductive consequences of covering up their complaints.

Another unresolved issue in the case-team meeting concerned the supposed arrogance of
the clients. A more productive conversation about that problem might go like this.

MANAGER:              You said that the clients were arrogant and uncooperative. What did
                      they say and do?
PROFESSIONAL A:  One asked me if I had ever met a payroll. Another asked how long I've
                      been out of school.
PROFESSIONAL B:  One even asked me how old I was!
PROFESSIONAL C:  That's nothing. The worst is when they say that all we do is interview
                      people, write a report based on what they tell us, and then collect our
                      fees.
MANAGER:              The fact that we tend to be so young is a real problem for many of our
                      clients. They get very defensive about it. But I'd like to explore
                      whether there is a way for them to freely express their views without
                      our getting defensive. What troubled me about your original responses
                      was that you assumed you were right in calling the clients stupid. One
                      thing I've noticed about consultants – in this company and others – is
                      that we tend to defend ourselves by bad-mouthing the client.
PROFESSIONAL A:  Right. After all, if they are genuinely stupid, then it's obviously not our
                      fault that they aren't getting it!
PROFESSIONAL B:  Of course, that stance is anti-learning and overprotective. By assuming
                      that they can't learn, we absolve ourselves from having to.
PROFESSIONAL C:  And the more we all go along with the bad-mouthing, the more we
                      reinforce each other's defensiveness.
MANAGER:              So what's the alternative? How can we encourage our clients to express
                      their defensiveness and at the same time constructively build on it?
PROFESSIONAL A:  We all know that the real issue isn't our age; it's whether or not we are
                      able to add value to the client's organization. They should judge us
                      by what we produce. And if we aren't adding value, they should get
                      rid of us – no matter how young or old we happen to be.
MANAGER:              Perhaps that is exactly what we should tell them.

In both these examples, the consultants and their manager are doing real work. They are
learning about their own group dynamics and addressing some generic problems in client–
consultant relationships. The insights they gain will allow them to act more effectively in the
future – both as individuals and as a team. They are not just solving problems but
developing a far deeper and more textured understanding of their role as members of the
organization. They are laying the groundwork for continuous improvement that is truly
continuous. They are learning how to learn.

# — 7 —

# A Leadership Dilemma:
# Skilled Incompetence

Most of us dread incompetence. We do not wish to perform poorly or to undercut our objectives. Yet perhaps the most frustrating incompetence of all is that which is repetitive. As one CEO stated it: "In my opinion, the best sign of an incompetent executive, or organization for that matter, is one who keeps producing consequences that he or she does not intend."

Ordinarily we attribute such repeated failure to a lack of skill. But in this chapter I am going to argue just the opposite. I hope to show that the incompetence that is most difficult to correct is tightly coupled with skilfulness.

In particular, I will focus on those occasions when executives try to solve problems that are potentially threatening, and they try to do so in a way that communicates caring and respect for the other. In handling these problems, the executives use highly honed skills yet create consequences they do not intend. Hence, their skilfulness is tightly coupled with incompetence. Moreover, this skilled incompetence not only operates at the individual level, it permeates the entire organizational culture as well.

During the past decade, I have been studying small- to medium-sized, fast-growing organizations. Typically they have been started by an entrepreneur who brought together a bright, dedicated, hard-working group of colleagues to market a new service or a new product. All of them have, and some continue to, grow at high rates ranging from 30 to 60 percent per year.

Not surprisingly, they all reach a stage when they must try to manage their growth and their organization more rationally or many of them will burn out and their company could get into deep administrative trouble. The CEO of one such company said recently:

> Right now we offer products that clients can use that are prepackaged, off the shelf. The people serving those products are primarily sales oriented. We also offer custom–designed professional services. The people producing these services are oriented toward professional help.
>
> The product side is more profitable than the custom side. Yet the custom side is more challenging and helps us to design and produce new and better products. Our major problem is to decide what kind of company are we going to be. We need a vision and a strategic plan.

I met with the CEO and his immediate reportees. They agree with him that they must develop a vision and make some strategic decisions. They also told me that they have already held several long meetings. Unfortunately, the meetings ended up in no agreement and no choice. "We end up drawing up lists of issues but not deciding," said one vice president. Another added: "And it gets pretty discouraging when this happens every time we meet." A third warned: "If you think we are discouraged, how do you think the people below us feel who watch us repeatedly fail?"

This is a group of executives who are at the top; who respect each other; who are highly committed; and who agree that developing a viable vision and strategy is long overdue. Yet whenever they meet, they repeatedly fail to create the vision and the strategy they desire.

If we go back to the criteria of incompetence described at the outset, their actions are incompetent in the sense that they produce what they do not intend, and they do so repeatedly, even though no one is forcing them to do so.

## EXPLANATIONS

### The Executives Explain Their Difficulties

At first, the executives believed that the reason they could not formulate and implement a viable strategic plan was that they lacked sound financial data. They hired a senior financial executive who, everyone agrees, has done a superb job.

The financial vice president reports: "Our problem is not the lack of financial data. I can flood them with data. We lack a vision of what kind of company we want to be and a strategy. Once we produce those, I can supply the necessary data." The other executives reluctantly agreed.

After several more meetings of failure, a second explanation emerged. It had to do with the personalities of the individuals and the way they work with each other when they meet. As the CEO said:

> This is a group of lovable guys with very strong egos. They are competitive, bright, candid, and dedicated. When we meet, we seem to go in circles; we're great at telling the others how wrong they are or how to solve the problem, but we are not prepared to give in a bit and make the necessary compromises.

I question the usefulness and validity of this explanation. For example, should the top management develop weaker egos or become less competitive? Maybe these are the qualities that helped to build the company in the competitive marketplace.

Next, how valid is it? We have studied top management groups that are not good at problem-solving and decision-making precisely because the participants have weak egos and are uncomfortable with competition. More important is that executives have learned to act more effectively without taking the personality route (Argyris, 1977).

The best that I can say for a personality explanation is that it prevents executives from thinking about changing their behavior, because it understandably makes little sense for them to undergo some kind of therapy. It is an explanation, in other words, that may inhibit learning, while at the same time, it may overprotect the executives.

### A different explanation: the source of the incompetent consequences is skill

Let us begin by asking: is the behavior that is counterproductive also natural and routine? Does every player seem to be acting genuinely? Do they get in trouble even though the players are not trying to be manipulative and political in the negative sense of the word?

The answer to all these questions, for the executive group, is yes. That means that their motives are clean and their actions represent their personal best. If it is the best that they can do, then their actions are skillful in the sense that they are produced in milliseconds, and that they are spontaneous, automatic, and unrehearsed.

How can skillful actions be counterproductive? Skill is usually associated with producing what we intend. One explanation is that the skills they use help not to upset each other. However, these very skills may inhibit working through the important intellectual issues embedded in developing the strategy. Therefore, the meetings end up with lists and no decision.

This conclusion is not only true for this group of executives. It is true for executives in all kinds of organizations regardless of age, gender, educational background, wealth, or position in the hierarchy (Argyris, 1977).

## Organizational Defensive Routines

One of the most powerful ways people deal with potential embarrassment is to create organizational defensive routines. I define these as any action or policy that prevents human beings from experiencing negative surprises, embarrassment, or threat, and simultaneously prevents the organization from reducing or eliminating the causes of the surprises, embarrassment, and threat. Organizational defensive routines are anti-learning and overprotective. (For a more detailed description, see Argyris, 1985.)

These defensive routines are organizational in the sense that individuals with different personalities behave in the same way; and people leave and new ones come into the organization, yet the defensive routines remain intact.

In chapter 4 (see pp. 93–4) we discussed the problems of mixed messages in some detail. The "logic" of these ambiguous strategies is encapsulated in the following four rules:

1  Design a message that is inconsistent.
2  Act as if the message is not inconsistent.
3  Make the inconsistency in the message and the act that there is no inconsistency undiscussable.
4  Make the undiscussability of the undiscussable also undiscussable.

Individuals follow such rules all the time and do so without having to pay attention to them. In this sense they have become highly skillful at enacting such rules. The paradox is that this skillfulness is inextricably intertwined with incompetence. As the next section shows, the skillful use of mixed messages leads to a range of unintended and counterproductive consequences.

### Inconsistencies and Dilemmas Created by Defensive Routines

To see the impact the defensive routines are having, let's return to the division heads who are being managed by mixed messages. The division managers must find ways to explain the existence of mixed messages to themselves and to their subordinate. These explanations often sound like this:

Headquarters never *really* meant decentralization.

Headquarters is willing to trust divisions when the going is smooth, but not when it's rough.

Headquarters is concerned more about Wall Street than us.

The managers rarely test their hypotheses about corporate motives with top managers. If discussing mixed messages would be embarrassing, then publicly testing for the validity of these explanations would be even more so. But now division heads are in a double bind. On the one hand, if they go along unquestioningly they may lose their autonomy, and their subordinates will see them as not having significant influence with corporate. On the other hand, if the division executives do not comply; headquarters will think they are recalcitrant, and if it continues long enough, disloyal.

Top management is in a similar predicament. It senses that division managers are both suspicious of their motives and covering up their suspicions. If the top were to accuse the subordinates of being suspicious and covering up their suspiciousness, that could clearly upset the division heads. If the top does not say anything, they could be acting as if there is full agreement when there is not. Most often, the top covers up its bind in the name of keeping up good relationships.

Soon, people in the divisions learn to live with their binds by generating further explanations. For example, they believe headquarters encourages open discussions, but basically they are not influenceable. They may eventually conclude that openness is actually a strategy top management has devised to cover up its impermeability to influence.

Since this conclusion assumes that headquarters is covering up, managers won't test it either. Since neither headquarters nor division executives discuss or resolve either the attributions or the frustrations, both may eventually begin to distance themselves from each other. A climate of mistrust arises that, once in place, makes it more likely that the issues become undiscussable.

Now both headquarters and division managers have attitudes, assumptions, and actions that create self-fulfilling and self-sealing processes, that each sees the other creating, but work from both the top and the bottom.

Under these conditions, it is not surprising to find that superiors and sub-ordinates hold optimistic and pessimistic views about each other. For example, they may say about each other:

They are bright people and well intentioned
*but*
they are narrow and have a parochial view.

They are interested in the financial health of the company
*but*
they do not understand how they are harming earnings in the long run.

They are interested in people
*but*
they do not pay enough attention to the development of the company.

It is unlikely that there is a way to build on the positive features without overcoming the negative features. But in order to begin to overcome what we don't like, we must be able to discuss it, and this violates the undiscussability rules embedded in the organizational defensive routines.

Back to the idea of skilled incompetence. Producing mixed messages, we have seen, requires highly honed skills. The mixed messages, in turn, produce unintended, counter-productive consequences that create the incompetence.

### All Too Familiar Routines

Wherever I have described these results, I get instant recognition from executives. They are able to give examples from their own organizations. Many ask: "Is there any organization that does not have these hang-ups?" Recently, numbers of researchers have made pleas to managers to get back to basics and be continually alert to counterproductive actions. They provide many, many stories of organizational rigidity and poor performance (Peters and Waterman, 1984).

The stories are excellent examples of organizational defensive routines. It is important, as the authors suggest, to correct the errors caused by the defensive routines (Peters and Austin, 1985). But, they do not go far enough. They do not deal with the organizational defensive routines.

For example, in one story, an organization required a new item to go through some 270 checks before production, which understandably cut into its capacity to innovate. After isolating those checks for which no good reason, business or not, could be found, management reduced the checks to fewer than 75. Because it solved a business problem, the reduction was a step forward. But it didn't go far enough. The authors do not ask why the players adhered to and implemented these unnecessary checks in the first place.

As we all know, management learns a lot by talking directly with customers. Often the outcome is so rewarding, managers wonder why they never thought of doing it before. But what are the organizational and personal defensive routines that prevented them from talking to customers in the first place? What norms did people learn that would blind them to the obvious?

I can see why the authors place much of the responsibility for reducing organizational defensive routines on the CEO. Without the support of people at the top, no one is likely to confront organizational defensive routines.

The freedom to question and to confront is crucial, but it is inadequate. To overcome skilled incompetence, people have to learn new skills, to ask the question behind the question. When CEOs I observed declared war against organizational defensive routines and demanded that people get back to basics, most often the new ideas were implemented with the old skills. People changed whatever they could and learned to cover their own positions even more skillfully.

Defensive routines exist; they are undiscussable; they proliferate and grow in an under-ground manner; the social pollution is hard to identify until something occurs that blows things open. If the defensive routines then surface, it is difficult for those with the steward-ship to do much about them. They have been skillful at going along with, not at questioning or confronting the routines.

We do not have the choice to ignore the organizational problems that these self-sealing loops are creating. Management today may be able to get away with it, but it is creating a legacy for those who will have to manage organizations in the future.

## WHAT CAN BE DONE

The top management group with which we began this decided to begin to change their organizational defensive routines by beginning with the ones that they create in their own meetings.

The first step toward change was a two-day session away from the office. The agenda of the sessions were the cases that they were asked to write ahead of time.

The purpose of these cases was two fold. First, they allowed us to develop a collage of the kinds of problems thought to be critical by the group. Not surprisingly, in this particular group, at least half wrote on issues related to product versus customer service. Second, the cases provided a kind of window into the prevailing rules and routines used by the executives.

The form of the cases was as follows.

1   In one paragraph describe a key organizational problem as you see it.
2   Assume you could talk to whomever you wish to begin to solve the problem. Describe, in a paragraph or so, the strategy that you would use in this meeting.
3   Next split your page into two columns. On the right-hand side write how you would begin the meeting; what you would actually say. Then write what you believe the other(s) would say. Then write your response to their response. Continue writing this scenario for two or so double-spaced typewritten pages.
4   In the left-hand column write any idea or feeling that you would have that you would not communicate for whatever reason.

In short, the case includes: a statement of the problem; the intended strategy to begin to solve the problem; the actual conversation that would ensue as envisioned by the writer; the information that the writer would not communicate for whatever reason.

The executives reported that they became highly involved in writing the cases. Some said that the very writing of the case was an eye opener. Moreover, once the cases were distributed to each member, the reactions were jocular. The men were enjoying them:

That's just like . . .

Great, . . . does this all the time.

Oh, there is a familiar one.

All salesmen and no listeners.

Oh my God, this is us.

### Cases as an Intervention Tool

What is the advantage of using the cases? The cases, crafted and written by the executives themselves, become outstanding examples of skilled incompetence. They vividly illustrate the skill with which each executive tried not to upset the other and to persuade them to change their position. They also illustrate the incompetence component because the results, by their own analysis, were to upset the others and make it less likely that their views would prevail.

The cases are also very important learning devices. If is difficult for anyone to slow down the behavior that they produce in milliseconds during a real meeting in order to reflect on it and change it. The danger is that others will grab the air time and run with it. Moreover, it is difficult for the human mind to pay attention to the interpersonal actions and to the substantive issues at the same time.

Why not have an outside person act as a facilitator to make the conversation more effective? I did act as a facilitator for a while. But this is not a sound solution for several reasons.

If facilitators are successful, it is because they act as traffic cops; rephrase the conversation whenever it is necessary; clarify issues; point out messages that may be upsetting others, and so on. This is a short-term solution. The long-term solution is for the executives to learn to do these things well. In other words, a facilitator is ultimately a person who helps the group bypass its defensive routines instead of helping them to learn to engage them in order to get rid of them.

Why not have the group sit down and talk about the strategy issues? The answer is that they told us that they tried this several times and it did not work.

One reason for this lack of success may be that it is unlikely that individuals will make public, in a regular meeting, what is on their left-hand columns. Yet, as we shall see, what individuals choose to censor has an important impact, because the individuals not only cover up that they are censoring something they also strive to cover up the cover-up. The irony is that the others sense this but they too cover up that they sense it, and they too cover up their cover-up.

Here is a collage from several cases. It was written by individuals who believed the company should place a greater emphasis on customer service.

| *Thoughts and Feelings Not Communicated* | *Actual Conversation* |
|---|---|
| *He's not going to like this topic, but we have to discuss it. I doubt that he will take a company perspective, but I should be positive.* | I: Hi Bill. I appreciate having the opportunity to talk with you about this problem of custom service versus product. I am sure that both of us want to resolve it in the best interests of the company. |
|  | BILL: I'm always glad to talk about it, as you well know. |
| *I better go slow. Let me ease in.* | I: There are an incresing number of situations where our clients are asking for custom service and rejecting the off-the-shelf products. My fear is that your sales people will play an increasingly peripheral role in the future. |
|  | BILL: I don't understand. Tell me more. |
| *Like hell you don't understand. I wish there was a way I could be more gentle.* | I: Bill, I'm sure you are aware of the changes (and explains). |
|  | BILL: No, I do not see it that way. It's my sales people that are the key to the future. |
| *There he goes, thinking as a salesman and not as a corporate officer.* | I: Well, let's explore that a bit . . . |

The dialogue continues with each person starting his views candidly but not being influenced by what the other says. To give you a flavour of what happened, here are some further left-hand column comments:

*He's doing a great job supporting his people.*

*This guy is not really listening.*

*I wonder if he's influenceable.*

*This is beginning to piss me off.*

*There he goes getting defensive. I better back off and wait for another day.*

If I presented a collage of the cases written by individuals who support the product strategy, it would not differ significantly. They too would be trying to persuade, sell, cajole their fellow officers. Their left-hand columns would be similar.

## Reflecting on the Cases

In analyzing their left-hand columns, the executives found that each side blamed the other side for the difficulties, and they used the same reasons. For example, each side said about the other side:

You do not *really* understand the issues.

If you insist on your position, you will harm the morale that I have built.

Don't hand me that line. You know what I am talking about.

Why don't you take off your blinkers and wear a company hat?

It upsets me when I think of how they think.

I'm really trying hard, but I'm beginning to feel this is hopeless.

These results illustrate once more the features of skilled incompetence. Crafting the cases with the intention not to upset others while trying to change their minds requires skill. Yet, as we have seen, the skilled behaviour they used in the cases had the opposite effect. The others in the case became upset and dug in their heels about changing their minds.

I can now add an additional finding. These individuals and all the others we have studied to date should not be able to prevent the counterproductive consequences until and unless they learn new skills. Nor will it work to bypass the skilled incompetence by focusing on the business problems, such as, in this case, developing a business strategy.

Several executives in this group did not agree. The dialogue began with one asking: "Okay, so what's new? This is exactly what I have been saying for years." "That's right," added another, "no surprises."

"What surprises me," said the CEO, "is how these cases have captured the issues beautifully. That's us and that's what we must work on."

"No, I do not agree with you," responded another officer to the CEO. "If we are not to waste the two days, we ought to focus on something concrete. We ought to focus on the practical and urgent business problems we have of managing our growth and creating a business strategy that will unite us."

The group split into two factions. About half agreed with the executive above. The other half agreed with the CEO. Their view was represented by one executive who said: "But how are we ever going to listen to each other if we hold the views that we have about each other, and if we talk the way we talk to each other the way we do in the cases?"

Note the executives are recreating the dynamics that get them into difficulty. I intervened and made a suggestion. Let us begin by trying to answer the questions about what kind of a company they wish to be, and what should be their strategy. If that did not work, then they could change to examining their cases.

The executives agreed and asked that I act as the facilitator. As the reader might expect, I had my hands full acting like a traffic cop. I did succeed a bit in keeping some degree of order, asking clarifying questions, and clearing up misunderstandings. The executives did begin to listen to each other more effectively. However, some unexpected results occurred. Every time a concrete suggestion was made that they agreed on, someone would point out that the system, policy, or financial information just requested was already in place or something similar could easily be in place. If so, then why were they having these problems?

One explanation that they discovered was that the policy, rule, or system in place was often violated in the name of meeting a deadline or breaking a blockage. Often the violations were not discussed with all those involved because there was no time to meet or people were out of town. Later, when the "other side" was told, they often did not agree with the way it was handled or that it was even a crisis.

### Redesigning their actions

The next step was to begin to redesign their actions. The executives turned to their cases. Each executive selected an episode that he wished to redesign so that it would not have the negative consequences. As an aid in their redesign, the executives were given some handouts that described a different set of behaviors. The first thing they realized was that they would have to slow things down. They could not produce a new conversation in milliseconds as they were accustomed to doing. This troubled them a bit because they were impatient to learn. They kept reminding themselves that learning new skills does require that they slow down.

One technique they used was that each individual crafted by himself a new conversation to help the writer of the episode. After taking five or so minutes they shared their designs with the writer. In the process of discussing these the writer learned much about how to redesign his words. But, the designers also learned much as they discovered the bugs in their suggestions and the way they made them.

The dialogue was very constructive, cooperative, and helpful. Typical comments were:

If you want to reach me, try it the way Joe just said.

I realize that your intentions are clean, but those words push my button (for such and such reason).

I understand what you are trying to say, but it doesn't work for me because ... How about trying it this way?

I'm impressed as to how my new designs have some of the old messages. This will take time.

Practice is important. Most people required as much practice as is required to play a not-so-decent game of tennis. But it does not need to occur all at once. The practice can occur in actual business meetings where they set aside some time to make it possible to reflect on their actions and to correct them. An outside facilitator could help them examine and redesign their actions just as a tennis coach might do. But, as in the case of a good tennis coach the facilitator should be replaced by the group. He might be brought in for periodic boosters or to help when the problem is the degree of difficulty and intensity not experienced before.

There are several consequences of this type of change program. First, the executives begin to experience each other as more supportive and constructive. People still work very hard during meetings, but their conversation begins to become additive; it flows to conclusions that they all can own and implement. Crises begin to be reduced. Soon the behavioral change leads to new values, and new structures and policies to mirror the new values.

This in turn leads to more effective problem-solving and decision-making. In the case of this group, they were able to define the questions related to strategy, to conduct their own inquiries, to have staff people conduct some relevant research, to have three individuals organize it into a presentation that was ultimately approved and owned by the top group. The top group also built in a process of involving their immediate reports so that they could develop a sense of ownership, thereby increasing the probability that all involved will work at making it successful.

# References

Argyris, C., 1977, "Double Loop Learning in Organizations," *Harvard Business Review*, Sept/Oct, 55, 5, pp. 115–25.

Argyris, C., 1985, *Strategy, Change, and Defensive Routines*, Boston, Ballinger.

Peters, T., and Austin, N., 1985, *A Passage for Excellence*, New York, Random House.

Peters, T., and Waterman R. H., 1984, *In Search of Excellence*, New York, Warner.

# Part II

*Inhibiting Organizational Learning and Effectiveness*

# — 8 —

# Organizational Learning and Management Information Systems

In a recent review of the literature on management information systems (MIS) implementation, I found the major theme to be unmet expectations and disappointments, especially when MIS technology was used to deal with the more complex and ill-structured problems faced by organizations. The authors' explanations for the implementation gap could be broken down into eight different categories:

1  MIS were not well understood by line management;
2  top line management was not involved in persuading and selling the use of MIS to the users in the organization;
3  MIS were not as foolproof as they could be;
4  MIS were technically too complex and too costly to create and utilize;
5  MIS specialists and line managers did not understand each other's job requirements, perspectives, and pressures;
6  MIS ignored line managers' cognitive styles;
7  the implementation of MIS was too narrowly conceived; and
8  MIS were not humanized adequately.

The purpose of this chapter is to suggest that there are other and perhaps deeper reasons for the implementation gap. If the reasons are valid then the explanations above would provide solutions that contain inner contradictions and counterproductive consequences.

In order to get at the inner contradictions we must view MIS as part of a more general problem of organizational learning. An organization may be used to learn to the extent that it identifies and corrects errors. This requirement, in turn, implies that learning also requires the capacity to know when it is unable to identify and correct errors.

There are two types of learning that are important. They are single- and double-loop learning.

## SINGLE-LOOP AND DOUBLE-LOOP LEARNING

When a thermostat turns the heat on or off, it is acting in keeping with the program of orders given to it to keep the room temperature, let us say, at 68°. This is single-loop learning, because the underlying program is not questioned. The overwhelming amount of learning done in an organization is single-loop because it is designed to identify and correct errors so that the job gets done and the action remains within stated policy guidelines. The massive technology of management information systems, quality control systems, and audits of the quality control systems is designed for single-loop learning.

The trouble arises when the technology is not effective and when the underlying objectives and policies must be questioned. Let us examine the first case. A budgetary control system is designed to increase the likelihood that certain objectives will be met. If the objectives are not met but the causes can be corrected without questioning the original objectives around which it was designed or without questioning the competence and loyalty of those using it, then the error will, in all likelihood, be corrected. However, if the underlying objectives require re-examination or if someone or some department is going to get in trouble, it will be much more difficult to identify and to correct the errors. The former case is the equivalent of the thermostat following its program and orders. The latter is the equivalent of the thermostat questioning its order: that is what is meant by double-loop learning.

Most organizations, often without realizing it, create systems of learning that suppress double-loop inquiry and make it very difficult for even a well designed information system to be effective. Take the case of the top management of a large newspaper. Their relationships at work were primarily competitive and win–lose; however the majority insisted that what they needed to become more effective was a clear organizational structure and a tighter financial information system. With these in place, they argued, the win–lose competitive dynamics would be reduced or neutralized. I doubted this would occur. The top management insisted and I helped them to obtain the appropriate technical advice. One year later, after a new structure and a new financial information system were in place, certain errors did disappear. The more difficult ones, however, were now camouflaged within the new financial system. The top managers who were most vociferous against working on the win–lose dynamics now admitted that the new financial systems did not reduce the former; indeed they made it less likely that they could be dealt with since they were intertwined in and camouflaged by the new system (Argyris, 1974).

The trend to build quality control checks in order to tighten things up also fails for another reason. The quality control activities are housed in little organizations. Soon they, too, have their quality control problems and they, too, use the same management theory to correct their errors. At best they are also only partially successful. The depth of their ineffectiveness is kept as covered as possible because how can a unit monitor other units when it is having the same difficulties?

If any of these factors are to be corrected, they require double-loop learning. Yet the basic concepts used to design and manage organizations and the type of capabilities that people bring to work regarding dealing with double-loop problems make it unlikely that double-loop learning will occur.

## THE INNER CONTRADICTIONS EMBEDDED IN THE BASIC CONCEPTS OF MANAGEMENT

Organizations require, as a minimum, employees who have the skills to produce a product or a service. How do people acquire and use skills? A skill to perform some action is acquired by remembering and using the answer to previously solved problems, and remembering and avoiding the traps previously fallen into (Sussman, 1973, p. 178). Developing skills for even simple activities such as riding a bicycle is an extremely complex process for the human mind. The human capacity for information processing is quite limited in comparison to the demands of the environment in which it is embedded (Simon, 1968). Human beings may be said to have learned a skill when the use of the program necessary to perform the requisite actions is so much under their control that the control over the performance of the skill does not have to be conscious and explicit. This frees the individuals to use their finite information processing capacity for other kinds of problem-solving.

But in order to use these skills effectively, the programs must be "ruthlessly generalized and stored" (Sussman, 1973, pp. 178–9). Thus the workers not only make their skill-programs tacit but once they do they must make them rigid and not easily alterable. Only when errors are made will the programs become explicit, but then their rigidity must also be dealt with if corrections are to be made.

Managers are therefore faced with the task of monitoring employee actions that are guided by programs that are hidden from the actor, yet ruthlessly generalized and held tenaciously. The manager is held responsible for the workers' performances, yet neither he, nor the workers, have direct access to the programs that produce the performance. Moreover, if correction is necessary, the manager will encounter employees who will tend to hold on to their programs tenaciously. The manager is in the predicament of being held responsible for errors, yet he (and the workers) may have great difficulty in discovering and correcting errors.

This uncertainty created by the nature of human information processing capacity is cumulated and expanded because the managers are also finite information processing systems. They, too, must manage by making their programs tacit and then holding them ruthlessly. Even with the capacity to make programs tacit, there is a limit to how much information they can cope with. Hence there is a need for managers to monitor managers.

Although managerial control is necessarily incomplete and problematic, managerial responsibility for results is not. Managers must find ways to reduce the probability and cost of error. One strategy to minimize the cost of errors is to simplify jobs as much as possible. If a tacit and rigid program has to be surfaced in order to be corrected, it should be one that is as simple as possible.

The second strategy is to define production or work standards plus tolerances for errors related to achieving the standards. If performance exceeds the tolerances, then corrective managerial action will be taken. This strategy is called management by exception. At the core of this strategy is the creation of gaps of knowledge about employee performance coupled with a continual sampling for errors. Implicit in the effectiveness of management by exception is that managers must have valid information only when workers deviate from standards. But, since managers are finite and since they are monitoring the work of many human information processors, the data that they obtain about the performance of their subordinates must be comprehensive yet manageable. In order to be both, information must necessarily be abstract. The information cannot take into account the unique aspects of each situation because it would be too complex to use to manage.

So now we have workers with tacit programs ruthlessly generalized that are difficult to control directly, managed by superiors who use information that is abstracted from the unique situation for which they are held responsible. The superiors, in turn, create tacit programs that are also ruthlessly held. They, in turn, must be managed, and the problems of tacitness, incompleteness, and abstractness become replicated.

The managers who are most distant from the local level are held most responsible for what happens at that level. In order to manage effectively, they too, must design gaps in their knowledge yet be held responsible for these very gaps. Hence the need to assure themselves that they can institute programs to detect and correct error; hence the increasing power as distance from the local point increases. We now have the beginnings of the pyramidal structure with the top-down unilateral control feature.

The pyramidal structure creates a continuum of information systems ranging from local (immediate to the activity of producing the service or product) to distant from that point. These information systems are designed to be, in effect, programs to detect and correct errors. But assuring themselves that they have the prerogative to create programs to detect and correct errors is one thing; to assure that errors will be detected and corrected is another. The information system designed to detect and correct has in it properties that inhibit its effectiveness.

Why is this so? The characteristics of local management information systems (MIS) include:

- concrete descriptions of the unique situations;
- representations of the actual processes, whether they are rare or repeatable;
- connection of the performance to the processes in the situation;
- implicitly rational logic, in that the rules for defining categories, for making inferences, for confirming or disconfirming evaluations are private; and
- tacit knowledge and tacit processes.

Such MIS may be effective for local immediate management but they also are:

- uneconomic for generalizations from one setting to many settings;
- unusable by others than their creator (because they are not easily scalable, convertable, comparable, and trend-producing);
- uninformative about the general characteristics of settings; and
- unvalidatable by objective knowledge and objective procedures that go beyond the capacity of any given individual.

These limitations are in the very areas where top management especially requires valid information in order to identify important overall errors and to design and execute new actions. Therefore, in order for the top to manage competently, they cannot depend directly upon the MIS used at the local levels. Moreover, since the local MIS tend to be private, intuitive, subjective, ungeneralizable, uncomparable and non trend-setting, if the top based their MIS on these characteristics, they would find it difficult to manage employees in a just manner.

In order for top management to manage through the use of information, they require MIS that:

- contain abstract, quantitative descriptions of key performance indicators;
- represent stable variance;
- represent the results or the outputs of complex processes, and not the processes themselves;
- contain explicitly rational logic in that they attempt to satisfy the logical systematic rules for defining categories, making inferences, and confirming or disconfirming evaluations publicly; and
- exclude as much as possible, tacit knowledge and tacit processes.

Information systems with these properties tend to be:

- economic for generalization from one setting to many settings;
- usable by others than their creators;
- informative about the general characteristics of a setting;

- validatable by objective knowledge and objective processes that go beyond the information processing capacities of any given individual.

The characteristics of distant and local MIS emphasize different ways of thinking, different ways of dealing with people, different concepts of dealing with causality, and above all, different conceptions of how order is defined and managed. Some of these differences are:

| *Distant MIS induces individuals* | *Local MIS induces individuals* |
|---|---|
| To think abstractly and rationally | To think concretely and intuitively |
| To conceptualize stable variance and general overall conditions and trends | To conceptualize variable processes and specific conditions |
| To distance self from processes that produce results, and focus primarily upon the results or the performance | To become close to the processes that produce results, and focus on them as much as on the results |
| To identify errors that are exceptional | To identify errors and correct them before they become exceptional |
| To infer causality from information lacking specifity of causal processes or mechanics. | To infer causality from information rich with situational causality related to specific mechanisms. |

The distant MIS will tend to reward abstract conceptualization, impartiality, publicly verifiable rationality, distancing from individual cases, and inferring personal responsibility from abstract data and overall trends. The local MIS will tend to reward concrete thinking, intution, privately verifiable rationality, closeness to the individual case, and inferring personal responsibility from concrete specific processes.

People who live over periods of time in either of these worlds may come to hold different conceptions of the meanings of responsibility, competence, causality, and the requirements for effective order. Human beings' sense of justice may be a function of their concepts of responsibility, competence, and the requirements for effective order.

For example, we may learn by observing the operations of our courts that justice requires that all parties have equal access to the same information and an equal opportunity to confirm or disconfirm it. Yet top managers have access to different information than the locals; the locals rarely have the opportunity to confront the information used by the top; and if the locals were to have such an opportunity, it is questionable whether they would have the information processing competences required to deal with it effectively. Justice also requires that errors be directly and unambiguously coupled to individuals actions (the smoking gun). Yet, the top MIS do not attend to such rules of evidence.

The sheer information processing requirements and the costs that would be necessary to assure minimal misunderstanding and injustice may be so high that such assurances would not be possible. Employees who are responsible and loyal understand these constraints but, in doing so, place themselves in a dilemma. If they accept the high probability of injustice as necessary then they have acted to legitimize injustice. If they do not accept the necessity of injustice, they would be seen as disloyal. Those at the upper levels may find it necessary to defend themselves from the dilemma of having to be unjust in order to make the organization effective.

We may ask, how do people deal with the dilemma of being exposed to necessary and self-legitimated injustice? Some possible adaptive activities at the lower levels may be as follows.

- They may consider the basis for, and the meaning of, justice to be embedded in the nature of their type of MIS. But such an action leaves them open to potential conflict with the top because, as we have suggested above, each MIS implies a different conception of order.
- They may reduce their risks by withholding information or sending doctored information upward.
- They may reduce the tension of living in a world of unpredictable and uncontrollable injustice by withdrawing their energies and commitments, and hence, feeling less personal responsibility.

Reactions such as these reduce the probability that the top will get the information they need and the commitment they desire, on the part of the lower levels, in order to manage effectively. This may lead the top to strive to make the MIS (1) more complete and detailed, (2) more tamper-proof, and (3) more oriented toward unilateral control over others. These reactions will probably require, in turn, a reduction of the gaps permitted by the top and an increase in the frequency of their interventions into the lower levels.

To compound the top's problems is the previously stated possibility that they may be forced to be unjust even when they do not wish to be. They may react to this possibility by developing attitudes and values such as that they must be tough because, as one president said: "Five percent of the people work; 10 percent think they work; and 85 percent would rather die than work." Another set of attitudes usually developed is that lower level managers and employees can be trusted only to the extent that they can be monitored.

These attitudes and values, combined with the top management's reactions described above, may lead to at least three counterproductive tendencies:

1  The lower level managers may become more fearful, take fewer risks, and increase their defensive protective activities.
2  The actions may deepen the degree of penetration management must take into the local MIS. This can lead to confusion because the properties of the top MIS are incongruent with the properties of the local MIS.
3  The action may increase the probability that the subordinates will attempt to turn the top MIS into a way of getting even with, or generating some control over, the top. For example, air traffic controllers can "strike" simply by following the defined procedures rigorously.

To summarize: in order to manage through the use of information, it becomes necessary for the top to manage with incomplete information. Management by optimal gaps may be a critical characteristic of effective management. The gaps are managed by making the lower levels responsible for them and by the top intervening when standards are not met. If such management is to be effective, each level must use an MIS that has significantly different properties from the other. This leads to different conceptions of responsibility, competence, and order which, in turn, may influence each group's view of justice. Each group protects itself against being accused of being unjust by creating protective activities that reinforce the factors that cause the problem in the first place.

If the above is true, then organizations seem to have the capacity to learn primarily those lessons that are self-sealing because they maintain the status quo. It is therefore important to examine organizational learning more closely.

## ORGANIZATIONAL LEARNING

Organizations learn through individuals acting as agents for them. The individuals' learning activities, in turn, are facilitated or inhibited by an ecological system of factors that may be called an organizational learning system.

Figure 8.1 represents a model of the learning system that mirrors the conditions in all the organizations that we have studied (Argyris and Schön, 1978). The model begins with inputs of information. The substance of the information is relevant; it may vary from inaccessible to accessible, ambiguous to unambiguous, vague to clear, inconsistent to consistent, and incongruent to congruent.

When such information interacts with individuals utilizing Model I theories-in-use (see chapter 3, pp. 81–3), a primary inhibiting loop for learning is created because the tendency of these individuals will be to reinforce whatever degree of inaccessibility, ambiguity, vagueness, inconsistency, that exists in the information. By inhibiting loop, I mean simply that the consequences of the interaction between columns 1 and 3 in figure 8.1 are loops that tend to maintain and reinforce the original conditions that produce error. Feedback is positive in that it reinforces the original qualities of the information; it is not corrective. (Feedback is represented by arrows that return to a previous condition.)

I am asserting that people studied so far manifest similar theories-in-use which are oriented toward unilateral control and lead to single-loop learning. There are four consequences of this (column 5). People tend to be unaware of their impact upon error discovery and correction. If A makes an error and others tend to hide the impact it has on them, then A will not be aware of the impact. A second result of primary inhibiting loops is that people tend to be unaware that they are unable to discover-invent-produce genuinely corrective solutions to problems. A third result is defensive group dynamics (e.g. little additivity in problem-solving, low openness and trust, and high conformity and covering up of threatening issues). A fourth result is intergroup dynamics that are also counterproductive.

These four results create secondary inhibiting loops. They are called secondary inhibiting loops because they arise out of interaction with the primary inhibiting loops. Secondary inhibiting loops also feed back to reinforce the primary inhibiting loops and the previous conditions that predispose error (columns 2, 3, 4 and 5).

What kinds of errors tend to be correctable and uncorrectable under these conditions? Errors that tend to be correctable (see top of column 7) include errors: (a) whose existence is known and available to the relevant actors; (b) whose discovery and correction pose a minimal threat to the actors; and (c) whose discovery and correction is threatening but whose camouflage or noncorrection is more threatening. Errors that tend not to be correctable (see bottom of column 7) include: (a) errors whose discovery is a threat to the individual's system of hiding error and his or her inability to correct error, (b) errors that predispose primary inhibiting loops because they are threatening Model I values (e.g. win–don't lose, suppress feelings, etc.); and (c) errors whose correction violates organizational norms.

The errors that tend to be uncorrectable are camouflaged; the primary and secondary inhibiting loops associated with them are camouflaged; and the camouflage is camouflaged with the development of protective activities such as "j.i.c. files" (just in case the superiors ask) see column 8. Again, the conditions described in columns 7 and 8 feed back to reinforce the previous conditions.

The conditions described in column 8 also tend to increase the predisposition of competitive win–lose games, deception, not taking risks, the potency of the attribution that the participants will make to the effect that their organizations are brittle and

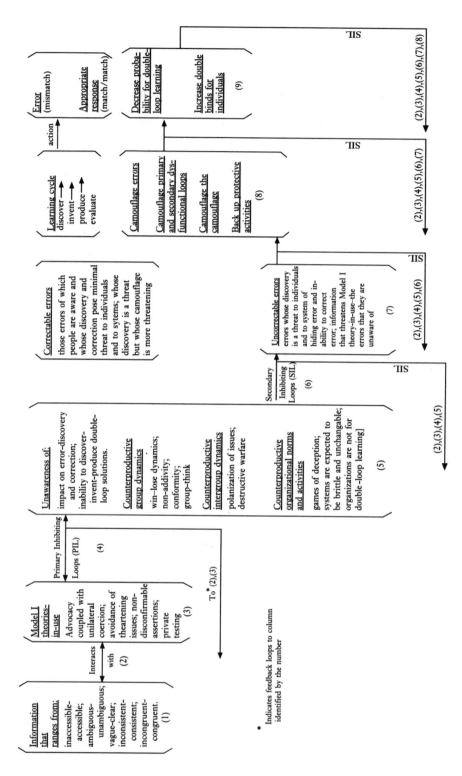

**Figure 8.1** Organizational learning systems that inhibit error detection and correction

unchangeable, and the potency of their expectation that organizations are not for double loop learning (see column 9). These conditions feed back to reinforce the previous error-producing conditions and simultaneously tend to reduce the probability that the organization will examine effectively the processes of how it examines and evaluates its performance. And again, this feeds back to reinforce the previous conditions. Every time the previous conditions are reinforced, the consequences that follow are also reinforced. Hence, we have a system that is not very likely to learn except when dealing with those problems that are correctable (top of column 7). The participants will tend to experience double binds. If they follow the requirements of the system, little learning will occur about issues that question the underlying objectives and policies. If they consider changing the system, they will tend to take on a task that they consider foolhardy and dangerous to their survival.

In the previous sections, I concluded that inherent in the use of information to manage organizations are two interdependent worlds: one predisposed to escalating error and the other to escalating injustice. In this section I conclude that organizations manifest learning systems that inhibit the detection and correction of errors that involves the questioning of the existing learning system. Hence, organizations have difficulty in learning to correct those factors that inhibit critical learning.

## IMPLICATIONS FOR CORRECTING THE IMPLEMENTATION OF MIS

In the light of this analysis let us re-examine the recommendations found in the literature to make the implementation of MIS more effective.

### Recommendation 1

Make MIS more understandable to the executive.

In the literature, the meaning of "more understandable" ranged from packaging in readable form (that is, an emphasis upon cosmetics) to an emphasis upon making explicit and clear the underlying assumption of the MIS. These suggestions would appear to make sense.

However, they may imply some unanticipated consequences. For example, as the underlying assumptions are made clear, as the impact of MIS is made explicit, and as its potential for managing behavior becomes clear, the users of the MIS (especially at the lower levels) will also realize the potential of MIS to reduce their space of free movement, to increase psychological failure and to reduce their feelings of being essential to the organization.

Given the Model I theories-in-use and the defensive behavioral world, these consequences will not tend to be discussed. To do so would run the risk of being seen as a deviant or a trouble-maker. Moreover, if these undiscussables were surfaced, the risk of surfacing the games of deception and camouflage would also be increased greatly. Bureaucracies have ways of punishing people who are responsible for such consequences and who are inept enough to make them public.

### Recommendation 2

More involvement by management so that they can persuade others to value and use MIS.

Again, such a recommendation appears to make sense, especially to a war-weary, exhausted MIS specialist. But there are unanticipated consequences. The predominant philosophy of management (in public and private sectors) is one that may be described briefly as unilaterally controlling others in order to get them to do what the organization requires, while at the same time, controlling possible confrontations of management authority (Argyris, 1970; Haire, et al., 1966; Likert, 1967).

It is this theory of persuasion and management that reinforces Model I theories-in-use. Model I theories-in-use in turn produce primary inhibiting loops. Hence, the recommendation could increase the potency and scope of the very factors that make effective implementation of MIS more difficult.

## Recommendation 3

Make MIS as foolproof as possible.

The emphasis of this recommendation is upon better ways of detecting error and the potential for error while simultaneously reducing the flexibility at the local level to edit, forgive, and correct errors privately. This recommendation tends to appeal to top line management because it responds to one of their greatest anxieties, namely, their concern over control. As one may hear at the management levels: "nothing gets done unless I check on it;" "people respect what you inspect;" and "management must be on top of things."

There are several unanticipated consequences that may occur if this recommendation is implemented. An MIS that aspires to be foolproof also indicates lack of trust on the part of the user and sanctions unilateral control by the top. These messages will be heard clearly by subordinates. In the world that we have just described, subordinates' reactions will tend to be to continuously make management's assertion that they must be monitoring and controlling a self-fulfilling prophecy. The employees may also reduce their sense of responsibility for monitoring and tend to produce at the safest minimum level. There are cases on record where employees have watched an MIS produce errors; they have permitted the errors to get into the management process; and they have watched while the financial and human costs escalated.

## Recommendation 4

Simplify the models and the data needed to make them work so that costs are reduced and usability may be increased.

Serious MIS specialists recommend less elegant models and a reduction of statistical information required in order to speed up the construction and to increase the use of the model (Wagner, 1974). Again, this recommendation appears to be useful. However, our perspective alerts us to the possibility that such simplifications may leave untouched the problems described above.

## Recommendation 5

Better education of line and staff (especially staff) to make each more sensitive to the other's problems.

Education is a laudatory response. But in none of the discussions could one find any awareness of the primary inhibiting loops with which people are programmed. These loops do not impair the staff from hearing, let us say, about the pressures upon line management. Indeed, I found that staff specialists understood these pressures and sympathized with the line managers (Argyris, 1971). But they also felt that some of these pressures were self-in-flicted, that their MIS might help to reduce them, and that they too were under pressure, especially pressure created by line managers. Moreover, MIS specialists tended to be unaware when they were making their line managers defensive. There were many cases observed where the MIS individual was making things worse by utilizing a strategy that he had hoped would make things better. The phenomenon of unawareness was equally valid for line managers.

Recent research suggests that even if people became aware of the "other's" views; if they became aware of new behavioral alternatives; if they accepted these alternative behaviors; and even if they learned them well, they still would *not* be able to use them in everyday life. The unfreezing of the old and the development of new values and skills is very difficult (Argyris, 1976a). Moreover, changing the learning system outlined in figure 8.1 is far from easy.

## Recommendation 6

Design MIS to take into account the cognitive styles of line executives.

This recommendation is just beginning to appear in the literature. However, our model raises the possibility that the dysfunctional loops may so reinforce each other that the impact of the styles of thinking may be swamped by the dysfunctional loops. Keen (1975), one of the researchers who has studied cognitive style, recently has raised the question of the potency of this factor under the conditions described above.

## Recommendation 7

The introduction of MIS should be seen as part of a total organizational development program.

This recommendation, especially emphasized by Keen (1975) and Ginzberg (1975b), comes closest to grappling with the problems of overcoming the negative effects of the learning systems described in figure 8.1. However, we may say that based upon other studies of organizational development programs, very few focus on individual theories-in-use and the learning system. At best, they focus on altering attitudes and behavior. But altering these two factors without altering theories-in-use and the learning system runs the risk that the organizational changes will become gimmicks, and therefore, not particularly credible in the eyes of others (Argyris, 1971).

None of the recommendations deals with the fact that there are inner contradictions embedded in organizations that cannot be eliminated because they are inherent in the use of information to manage organizations and in the limited capacities of individuals for information processing. Managers are rarely effective in dealing with paradoxes or dilemmas because, being programmed with Model I theories-in-use, they believe that the effective way to deal with them is to eliminate them or to choose one side of a dilemma. If my analysis is correct, the paradoxes are not eliminatable and dilemmas based on inner contradictions do not become resolved by choosing one horn or another.

It is not possible to close this chapter with recommendations that would overcome the problems that have been presented, because to my knowledge the research needed to provide viable recommendations has not been carried out. I recommend therefore, an alliance among line executives. MIS professionals, and behavioral scientists to conduct research on how to develop MIS that are more effectively implementable.

I have attempted elsewhere to indicate one type of research program that may be useful (Argyris, 1976b). Emphasis is placed on detailed case studies that are informed by theory (so that generalization is possible) and are coupled with attempts to redesign the MIS so that they are used more effectively. The attempts to produce a more effective MIS would not only be of value to the practitioner but they could provide the basis for resting theories on organizational learning such as utilized in this chapter.

# References and further reading

Ackoff, R. L., 1967, "Management Misinformation Systems," *Management Science*, 14, 4, pp. B147–56.

Albrecht, L. K., 1973, *Organization and Management of Information Processing Systems*, London, Macmillan.

Argyris, C., 1966, "Interpersonal Barriers to Decision Making," *Harvard Business Review*, 44, 2, pp. 84–97.

Argyris, C., 1970, *Intervention Theory and Method*, New York, Addison-Wesley.

Argyris, C., 1971, "Management Information Systems: The Challenge to Rationality and Emotionality," *Management Science*, 17, 6, pp. B275–92.

Argyris, C., 1973, *Organizations of the Future*, Sage Professional Papers, Administrative and Policy Study Series, no. 03–006, Vol. 1.

Argyris, C., 1974, *Behind the Front Page*, San Francisco, Jossey-Bass.

Argyris, C., 1976a, *Increasing Leadership Effectiveness*, New York, Wiley.

Argyris, C., 1976b, "Organizational Learning and Effective Management Information Systems: A Prospectus for Research," Harvard University, program on Information Technologies and Public Policy, Working Paper.

Argyris, C., and Schön, D., 1974, *Theory in Practice*, San Francisco, Jossey-Bass.

Argyris, C., and Schön D., 1978, *Organizational Learning*, Reading, Mass., Addison-Wesley.

Bean, A. S., Neal, R. D., Radnor M., and Tansik, D., 1974, "Structural and Behavioral Correlates of Implementation in US Business Organizations", unpublished manuscript, Northwestern University.

Berg, I., 1974, "Information, Management, and the Status Quo," in Jardine D. A. (ed.), *Data-Base Management Systems*, North-Holland Publishers, Amsterdam.

Churchman, C. W., and Scheinblatt, A. H., 1965, "The Researcher and the Manager: A Dialectic of Implementation," *Management Science*, 11, 4, pp. B69–87.

Davis, G., 1974, *Management Information Systems: Conceptual Foundations, Structures and Development*, New York, McGraw-Hill.

Gardner, J., 1968, "America in the Twenty-Third Century," *New York Times*, July 27.

Geertz, C., 1975, "Common Sense as a Cultural System," *Antioch Review*, 33, 1, pp. 5–26.

Ginzberg, M. J., 1975a, *A Process Approach to Management Science Implementation*, unpublished PhD thesis, MIT.

Ginzberg, M. Jay, 1975b, "Implementation as a Process of Change: A Framework and Empirical Study," Center for Information Systems Research, Report 13.

Grayson, C. J., 1973, "Management Science and Business Practice," *Harvard Business Review*, July/August, pp. 41–8.

Haire, M., Ghiselle, E. E., and Porter, L. W., 1966, *Managerial Thinking: An International Study*, New York, Wiley.

Huysmans, J. H. B. M., 1970, *The Implementation of Operations Research* New York, Wiley-Interscience.

Kantor, D., and Lehr, W., 1975, *Inside the Family*, San Francisco, Jossey-Bass.

Keen, P. G. W., 1975, "A Clinical Approach to the Implementation of OR/MS/MIS Projects," Working Paper 780–75, Sloan School of Management, MIT.

Lewin, K., 1951, *Field Theory in Social Science*, Dorwin Cartwright (ed.), New York, Harper & Row.

Lewin, K., Dembo, T., Festinger, L., and Lears, P., 1944, "Levels of Aspiration," in *Handbook of Personality and the Behavioral Disorders*, Hunt, J. McV. (ed.), np: Ronald Press.

Likert, R., 1967, *The Human Organization*, New York, McGraw-Hill.

Lucas, H. C. Jr, 1975, *Why Information Systems Fail*, Columbia University Press.

Mason, R. O., and Mitroff, I., 1973, "A Program for Research on Management Information Systems," *Management Science*, 19, 5, pp. 475–87.

Murdick, R. G., and Ross, J. E., 1975, *Information Systems for Modern Management*, 2nd edn, Englewood Cliffs, NJ, Prentice-Hall.

Oettinger, A. G., 1964, "A Bull's Eye View of Management and Information Systems," Proceedings of the 19th ACM National Conference, ACM Publication P-64, pp. B1–1–14.

Polyani, M., 1958, *Personal Knowledge*, Chicago, University of Chicago Press.

Sapolsky, H. M., 1972, *The Polaris System Development: Bureaucratic and Programmatic Success in Government*, Boston, Harvard University Press.

Simon, H. A., 1968, *The Sciences of the Artificial*, Cambridge, Mass., MIT Press.

Small, J. T., and Lee, W. B., 1975, "In Search of an MIS," *MSU Business Topics*, 23, 4, pp. 47–55.

Steele, F., 1975, *The Open Organization*, New York, Addison-Wesley.

Sterling, T. D., 1975, "Humanizing Computerized Information Systems," *Science*, December, pp. 1168–72.

Sussman, G. J., 1973, "A Computational Model of Skill Acquisition," MIT Artificial Intelligence Laboratory, AI TR–297, August.

Wagner, H. M., 1971, "The ABCs of OR," *Operations Research*, 19, 6, pp. 1259–81.

Wagner, H. M., 1974, "The Design of Production and Inventory Systems for Multifacility and Multiwarehouse Companies," *Operations Research*, 22, 2, pp. 278–91.

Wyatt, J. B., and Zeckhauser, S., 1975, "University Executives and Management Information: A Tenuous Relationship," *Educational Record*, 56, 3, pp. 175–89.

Zand, D. E., and Sorensen, R. E., 1975, "Theory of Change and the Effective Use of Management Science," *Management Science Quarterly*, 20, 4, pp. 532–45.

# — 9 —

# Strategy Implementation: An Experiment in Learning

From 1985 to 1989, several of us worked on an executive program whose focus was the design and implementation of strategy. It now appears that it is possible to combine management education and organizational development through the vehicle of getting a job done; a job that is recurring because strategy is an on-going process. In this chapter we describe the theory that was used to design the report (see also Argyris and Schön, 1974, 1976) and to illustrate how it is being implemented (see Argyris, 1985).

## A BIT OF HISTORY

David Ashton, the academic director of the executive programs at Chelwood, approached me several years ago about trying to implement the type of management education and organizational development that was based on a crucial and recurrent management activity (in this case, strategy) and was intended to make implementation of the knowledge being taught a key objective. Professor Maurice Saias joined us as the representative of strategy. After Ashton left (to become Dean at the University of Lancaster), James Butler took his place as academic director.

The idea was simple and had often been described in the literature, yet to our knowledge it had not been implemented. We wanted to bring managers and their immediate reports to the Chelwood seminars to learn about strategy and the problems of implementing it. We wanted the learning to occur as the participants were formulating and implementing their actual strategy for the coming years. The end product, therefore, was (1) a strategy, (2) a definition of some of the human problems (within the executive group, above and below it) involved in implementing it, (3) formulation of steps to overcome the problems, and (4) monitoring its implementation during the remainder of the year. The first three purposes were accomplished during an initial five-day workshop plus some pre-visits by members of the faculty to help the participants prepare. The fourth purpose was accomplished when the entire team returned six months later for three days.

Not surprisingly, all of the teams were monitoring the implementation process the moment they returned to their home locations. They spent three days therefore largely in identifying those difficult strategy and implementation problems that required careful deliberation by the group with the help of their outside consultants. Also they spent time thinking about future plans. Anticipating a bit, the participants no longer see the second workshop as the end. They now speak of returning next year even though most reported that when they arrived for the first session, they never thought that they would recommend that these sessions become annual events.

To turn now to the theory of learning that was the basis of the program. It is a behavioral theory that is intended to be relevant for the implementation of strategy or any other managerial activity (e.g., cost accounting or human resources).

## A LEARNING THEORY FOR IMPLEMENTATION

Learning is the detection and correction of error. An error is any mismatch between our intentions and what actually happens. If I intend to talk with you in ways that do not upset you yet I do upset you then that is a mismatch. If a department does not make its budget, that too is a mismatch. If the organization is unable to implement its strategy that is also a mismatch.

Behind this view of learning is a view of human nature and organizations. Human beings design their intentions and their actions. They are designing systems. Organizations design their strategies and they design the implementation of the strategy.

If this view is true then something else is also true. Individuals or organizations cannot knowingly design and produce an error. If I say that I am going to upset you and I succeed then that is a match. In another sense, however, if the organization designs an implementation process, carries it out and it fails, that too is a match. In these two examples, the consequences occurred when I (or the organization) implemented the design. The outcome – success or failure – occurred *by design*. We have to reflect on the implementation process to find out what was wrong with the design *and* why we were unaware that it was wrong.

### Causes of Designed Error

One cause of designed error is that we are skillful at what we do. Actions that are skillful work; they are produced automatically; little or no attention is paid while producing them; indeed to pay conscious attention may be distracting and lead to a loss of skill. If my backhand shots at tennis are hitting the mark then it is distracting for someone to interrupt my swing to comment on it.

As you shall see, the same thing happens in strategy implementation. Companies develop routines on how to implement strategy. These are commonly accepted practices that are so ingrained in everyday life that they are taken for granted by the players. Indeed, to question them is to activate disbelief or stony glances. "We have always done it this way." "Let's not tamper with an implementation process that works."

As we observed these processes "that worked" and that were taken for granted we found some interesting things. For example, line executives often felt that the strategic plans were often complicated with unnecessary paper work; that strategic professionals often thought like "techies" and not like line managers; that they strove to be rigorous and precise and could not see when progress would be made if the ideas were expressed with rigorous sloppiness. Strategy professionals, on the other hand, often felt that line executives did not "really" understand the importance of analytical rigor; that they nit-picked the plans; and that they asked questions that required more, not less, paper work.

Finally, and most importantly, both acted as if this was not the case. That is, they bypassed the potential embarrassment or threat that would be involved in discussing the attributions that they were making of each other. And they acted as if they were not bypassing. They covered up the bypass.

Whenever such actions occur they are likely to indicate that organizational defensive routines are operating (see Janis, 1989). An organizational defensive routine is any policy, practice or action that prevents embarrassment or threat to the players involved, and, at the same time, prevents learning how to reduce the causes of the embarrassment or threat.

Organizational defensive routines are over protective and anti-learning, usually activated in the name of not upsetting others or not opening up a can of worms, all in the name of being realistic. The trouble with this rationalization is not that it is false. The trouble is that it does not alert the manager that the reason it is true is that the organization is defensive and cannot allow candid inquiry. In organizations full of defensive routines, truth is not such a hot idea because it can be threatening. The players are being realistic but the realism is in the service of organizational defenses.

Recently, I observed 40 first-line supervisors develop a list of factors that produced poor quality products and added unnecessarily to costs. They then designed ways to reduce these factors. Three months later they came together at a dinner meeting to celebrate the fact that they saved $210,000 in implementing their ideas. Everyone was pleased.

After a few drinks, I asked the supervisors to reflect on their diagnosis and their actions. I asked, "How long did they know that these causes of poor quality existed?" At first they seemed bewildered. Finally, one individual said, "Hell we have known this for years." That means that first-line supervisors had, for years, designed implemented actions that they knew were counterproductive. This is an example of designed error.

I asked: if they had known of these causes for years, what prevented them from taking corrective actions years ago? How come they needed the workshop to get things out in the open. Not surprisingly, one supervisor said, "Are you sure you want an answer to that question? You'll open up a can of worms. And everyone is having such a good time."

The senior executive present agreed that he did not want to dampen the festive mood. But, he did not want to leave the question unanswered. For the next several hours the first-line supervisors gave what the senior executive said was an "earful." He realized that they had saved $210,000 for which he was grateful. He also realized that the organizational defensive routines that were operating to have caused the costs and to prevent them from being reduced had not been touched. They were ready for the next battle.

### The "Human Way" to Control Embarrassment or Threat

We have found that human beings have master programs in their heads about how to deal with embarrassment or threat. Although the specifics vary with age, education, position in the company, or functional discipline, the underlying master programs are the same. Indeed, they do not differ across cultures such as North America, South America, Western Europe, Africa, India, China, and Japan. One fundamental set of rules in these master programs is:

1   Bypass embarrassment or threat whenever possible.
2   Act as if you are not bypassing them.
3   Don't discuss 1 or 2 while it is happening.
4   Don't discuss the undiscussability of the undiscussable.

Individuals who adhere to these rules also use defensive reasoning. For example, they keep their premises and inferences tacit. They rarely test their conclusions or when they do, they do so by using the very reasoning that produced the conclusion. For example: "Believe me, I know what I am talking about. If you confront so and so on that strategic issue, you'll get into trouble." The person stating the conclusion is saying, in effect, "I know it is correct because I believe it is correct." That is a self-sealing logic.

### *Strategy as a Control Activity*

Strategy is also an activity designed to help executives make their world more manageable. It contains a core set of ideas about how to define the business, define victory, the best analytical techniques to analyze the external environment and external capabilities, to generate alternative choices, to identify strategic options, to develop scenarios, and to test options. The use of these concepts requires productive reasoning. For example, premises are made explicit, data are collected rigorously, inferences and conclusions are tested by logic that is not self-sealing.

## THE TENSION BETWEEN THE TECHNICAL AND HUMAN THEORIES OF CONTROL

In short, we have two theories of how to be in control especially when the environment is threatening. The technical core ideas of strategy requires that the actors be rigorous, analytical and test their ideas in ways that are not self-sealing. The core ideas that human beings have to deal with threat requires reasoning that is almost the opposite. To complicate matters, when line or strategy professionals frustrate each other, both activate their respective human theories of control which is likely to escalate defensiveness, increase frustration, hasten the bypass and deepen the cover-up.

The dilemma is that the ideas on how to be "in control" over embarrassment and threat are themselves embarrassing. The implementation of the human theory of control violates the technical theory of control. Whenever this occurs, it creates more embarrassment and threat which leads to further bypass and covering up. All these actions and reactions are highly skillful and hence actors are often unaware of their impact. Or, if the actors are aware of the negative impact they blame the organizational defensive routines. They report that they are in a double bind, helpless but to act as they do.

Our learning experience is designed to deal with this built-in puzzle and dilemma. The course was designed to teach "the best" in strategy. The course was also designed to help the participants see how they unrealizingly shoot themselves in the foot (as well as their strategy) whenever they deal with embarrassment or threat. Finally, the course was designed to help the individuals correct these errors *and* learn how to reduce such errors in the future.

It follows that the design of the educational activities should include:

- The core concept of competitive strategy.
- The conditions under which the implementation of the concepts will be relatively straightforward.
- The core concepts in the human theory of control.
- The conditions under which their activation will necessarily lead to the distortion, if not sabotage, of the strategic concepts.
- Connecting these four domains of learning with every individual as well as with the actions of these individuals as a team and to help the individuals to become aware of their particular theory of human control; their team's and their organizational defensive routines; and how these tend to hold effective strategy formulation and implementation hostage to designed error.

I will now turn to a brief description of a learning environment created for four top management groups. Each group had the authority to design and (with approval of the top board) implement the strategy that they designed.

## The First Step: Collecting Data

The faculty member responsible for teaching strategy visited each top management team at their respective locations. The teams outlined their thoughts about the strategic issues that they wished to solve. They worked out what knowledge they should produce to bring to the conference center. Several weeks before the session, the teams sent a document to the faculty member outlining the work they had done and the work they intended to accomplish during the five-day session at the conference center.

At the same time, each member was asked to write a brief case about an important human problem that he or she would face in implementing the strategy. The completed case was mailed to me about three weeks before the sessions were to begin.

The two faculty members met for one day before the session in order to identify the key strategic and human problems. This exercise influenced what ideas each would present at the outset, and where each could connect with the other's discipline when describing his own views.

## The Second Step: Strategic Control and Human Theories of Control

During the first day, the faculty focussed on providing the key concepts of their respective disciplines as they related to the problems inferred from the cases. The first three-hour sessions were on strategy. I attended the sessions especially to note any challenges the participants raised regarding the implementability of the strategic concepts being taught. For example a participant might say: "These ideas make sense but we could not use them in our organization." The strategy faculty member would inquire into what might prevent their use. The behavioral faculty member would follow up with questions about individual and organizational defenses implied in the question or the answer.

The second three-hour session was on organizational defensive routines: how they can lead to limited learning; how limited learning, in turn, can lead to discussions about strategy that contain gaps and inconsistencies that are either unrecognized or, if they are recognized, are undiscussable. There was a spirited discussion often punctuated with examples from their respective organizations. Towards the end of the session, one of the directors remarked how important it would be if "All of us could commit to reducing these defenses. Personally, I believe they are my nemesis around strategy, indeed around most of the difficult issues that we discuss."

## The Third Step: Formulating and Implementing Strategy and Reflecting on Both Processes

Each organic team went into their respective small rooms in order to begin their work of formulating and designing implementation strategies. When, and if, defensive routines (organizational or individual) arose they would become a matter of legitimate inquiry.

The examination of the impact of organizational and individual defensive routines occurred faster than expected. For example, Group A began with the general manager

(GM) reviewing the strategic thrust that had been developed so far, the questions yet to be answered, the implementation issues to be discussed, etc. After he finished his introduction he asked for any comments.

One executive asked: "Are we to take the ideas on organizational defensive routines seriously?"

GM:     Of course, if you recall I was the one who ended the plenary session by saying they were important. Indeed, I think I called them my nemesis.
EXEC:   Yes, I was pleased to hear you say that and I wanted to check to make sure you still felt that.
GM:     I most certainly do.

The executive then said that in the spirit of making undiscussables discussable he wanted to question the direction of the strategy developed so far. As he continued to speak, it became clear that he was asking for a major change.

The GM became very upset and asked, "What the devil was going on. I thought the major directions of our strategy had been agreed upon."

The facilitator intervened to ask the executive what he was feeling and thinking as he heard the GM's reaction. The executive said that the GM's response confirmed his fears. The GM wanted individuals to be candid, up to a point. "I think that I may have made an error in raising the question."

The GM apologized. He said that he now realized that he was violating what he espoused in the plenary session and in his first response to the executive's question, "But you know," he said, "it is not easy to hear this." "Yes," responded the executive, "and it is not easy to say so."

The GM then encouraged others to speak. Several agreed with the executive. The facilitator asked: "What goes on during these meetings that leads individuals normally to hold back on such data." The responses were candid. They described several organizational defensive routines about how to "go along" with a superior when one believes that the superior is wrong but that he is also emotionally committed to his position. For example:

I saw you as wanting this strategy. This is your baby. The strategy makes good sense and thus is not easy to refute it. I figured given your strong commitment and the lack of support that I would get from others, that it made sense to go along I must say, I did not realize until now that others had similar doubts.

Reflecting on the incident, we see a group describing its own defensive routines that "caused" several members to withhold technical ideas about strategy. They also described defensive routines that prevented them from testing their attributions about what was discussable.

The GM's automatic reaction of dismay and bewilderment was an example of the individual defensive routines. He reacted inconsistently with what he had been espousing, and the reaction was automatic and skillful. As the discussion continued, some group members also became aware of their individual protective reactions which were to withdraw and distance themselves from conversation that could be embarrassing or threatening.

Other examples, perhaps not as dramatic, could be presented. In all groups non-trivial alterations were made about the technical thrust of the strategy after certain relevant defensive routines were surfaced. This especially occurred around the issues of implementation. It appeared that when some players disagreed with substantive features of strategy that they felt could not be easily confronted, they waited until the moment came to discuss their implementation. They could then raise questions about the viability of the technical ideas.

Often, this led to examining organizational defensive routines that had not been yet surfaced. For example, a GM did not knowingly support a strategic thrust that he believed was not likely to be implemented. When he learned of the probable organizational resistances it compelled him to rethink his position. With the help of the facilitator they also examined why some did not realize the resistances that might occur; also, why some felt that they had to confront the technical ideas by waiting until the discussion of implementation. Often that meant hours later with a lot of dialogue about technical issues appearing solved.

## The Fourth Step: Examining the Implementation Cases

A concurrent agenda was the discussion of the cases that were written by the participants. (What went on during such sessions has been described in detail in publications listed in the reference section of this chapter.) To summarize, the participants became aware of their personal human theory of control, especially how it makes them poor learners under the conditions where learning is important. They also became aware of how unaware they were about the discrepancy between their intended outcomes and what they actually produce.

The learning occurred at different depths. The first level was about the inconsistencies and gaps that they produced.

For example:

| *Participants believed* | *Participants acted* |
|---|---|
| It was important to be candid, forthright and straightforward. | They were candid and forthright in a way that discouraged others to be the same and they were unaware of this consequence while producing it. |
| It is a good idea to identify error in order to correct it. | They were often unaware often unaware when they were producing interpersonal errors *and* that they were unknowingly communicating to others that they were unaware. |
| It is a good idea to test the validity of their ideas, especially if they were controversial. | The tests that were used were weak, and often self-serving. |

The second level of learning was to realize that they were routinely unaware of the inconsistencies and the gaps that they were producing and they were unaware that others saw them as unaware. They also learned that the others did not discuss their inconsistencies and gaps because since they were seen as being unaware, to discuss them could be embarrassing.

The others covered up all of this and acted as if this was not the case. Sometimes their cover-ups succeeded. Other times they did not. In almost all the cases where they did not the target of the cover-up also covered up that he sensed that he was a target.

The third level of learning was to realize the dilemma and paradoxes that resulted. For example, the participants who acted unilaterally (whether they realized it or not) did so because it was consistent with their personal theory of human control. However in order for that feature of their theory of control to work the recipient would have to act in a submissive manner which is behavior that the first actor considers ineffective.

The fourth level of learning was that the actions at these levels combined to create group and organizational defensive routines that lead to self-reinforcing patterns.

The fifth level of learning was that the first four combined to cause individuals to massage, distort, and censor technical information related to strategy. This produced conditions where important technical and business information tended to be inaccessible, ambiguous, and vague. Productive reasoning was taken over and dominated by defensive reasoning.

Identifying these consequences in their case-team groups and in their own organic group was itself liberating because most participants believed that they were undiscussable. Examining what made the subjects undiscussable and their undiscussability undiscussable led individuals to make public their private views about what was acceptable behavior in the group and the organization whenever the subject contained potential for embarrassment or threat. The very discussion of what was undiscussable made it possible to interrupt the cycles that were, up to this point, seen as not interruptable. Moreover, it made it possible to define ways not to get into these self-sealing ruts again.

Finally, individuals began to learn how to craft their conversations so that they could act consistently with the new norms and be helped to see when they were not.

All this learning was continually tested against the task of solving business topics related to strategy. Whenever someone wondered "if all this is really necessary" the answer was explored in such terms as: "If we do not change how would we transfer business information that is now inaccessible, ambiguous, and vague into accessible, unambiguous, and clear."

By the way, once these new norms were created, once ongoing learning was legitimized about reducing the counterproductive features of their personal human theories of control and the organizational defensive routines, the learning was transferrable, within these groups, to any business subject.

## The Fifth Step: Continued, Iterative Learning

As the week progressed the boundaries of the technical and behavioral began to become blurred. For example, in several groups members changed their substantive positions on strategy significantly. They had enough successful experiences in their "behavioral" sessions dealing with organizational defensive routines that they began to confront issues, in their strategy group, that they had previously covered up.

As they talked about running silent and deep they brought important technical information to the surface that changed the input into the strategy formulation. By the third day, the integration between the behavioral and the strategic had out-distanced the capacities of the two faculty members. We found ourselves being scheduled during lunch through dinner, and into the late hours of the evening.

## The Sixth Step

The groups returned to their respective locations and began to implement features of their strategy which in turn changed their designs.

## The Seventh Step

The groups returned for a three-day session. Several groups added new members. The faculty designed a mini crash course in strategy and human behavior. That turned out to be an error because we short-changed these players. They did not have the in-depth learning that had been available to their colleagues. The next time we will allocate the appropriate amount of time.

It is fair to add, however, that the "new" members were able to learn something faster because they were in a group that had developed skills for on-line learning and norms to permit reflection in action.

During these sessions the groups continued to modify other strategic plans and especially monitor the implementation. In one group several senior executives focused on how frustrated and concerned they were about the impact on their group. They believed that the new organizational structure of sales might well be counterproductive. They also discussed how unaware they were of some of the consequences. It took six months of implementation to see problems that they had not foreseen.

I should like to highlight two features of these discussions. First, they discussed as a group what would have been undiscussable a year ago. The sales executives, for example, would have been hesitant to discuss openly, in their group, how blind they had been about the problems of implementation. They would have also been hesitant to admit how the implementation frustrations were leading them to change their minds about the technical strategic thrusts to which they had agreed.

The second feature was a discussion of "deeper" problems. For example, with the help of the faculty the CEO and several others were able to say that the reason they were hesitant to take the sales executive's concerns about strategy seriously was that they were attributing fear to him, feeling that he was frightened about the changes. They did not wish to base changes in strategy on reasoning used by an executive who was, by their attribution, frightened. Moreover, the CEO and several others were apprehensive about discussing such issues especially because they believed the sales executive was unaware about how frightened or apprehensive he sounded.

The sales executive was indeed surprised to hear this. He insisted however that he was not frightened. Indeed he was apprehensive but not about himself as much as about the impact the new strategy was having on the organization. Having learned from the session, he asked his fellow team members what it was he said or did that led them to believe that he was personally apprehensive. They were able to provide him with concrete examples which helped him to think about how to craft his conversation in order to express more accurately his apprehension about the organization.

## NOTES ON EFFECTIVENESS

The systematic answer to effectiveness will have to await the results of the research. However, there are several observations that may be made at this time that stem from how the participants have "voted" through their actions.

First, in all cases except one, the strategies were implemented and monitored in ways that the participants described as effective. It is difficult to make an assessment of the fourth case since the company was sold and never returned.

Second, the leaders of the three teams communicated to their superiors that the learning experiences were helpful. They recommend further financial and time investment, even though both were non-trivial. Moreover they recommended that their superiors (and their group) attend. Two of these superiors have made such a commitment.

Third, the participants see the learning process as ongoing. For them the boundaries between education, team development, organizational development, and the strategies have become fuzzy and irrelevant. The educational experience, in their eyes, respects the wholeness they must deal with. It is the first time in the history of this corporation that senior line managers are pressing the educational professionals to expand the program. It is also the first time that they are applying pressures at the corporate level to educate professionals who are members of the corporation to emulate the skills of the two consultants.

# References

Argyris, C., 1985, *Strategy, Change, and Defensive Routines*, New York, Ballinger/Harper & Row.

Argyris, C., and Schön, D., 1974, *Theory in Practice*, San Fransisco, Jossey-Bass

Argyris, C., and Schön, D., 1976, *Organizational Learning*, Reading, MA., Addison-Wesley.

Janis, I. L., 1989, *Crucial Decisions*, New York, The Free Press.

# — 10 —

# How Strategy Professionals Deal with Threat: Individual and Organizational

Most writers on strategy agree that implementation is a crucial problem (Lorange and Vancil, 1977; Yavitz and Newman, 1982). Some have tried to specify what may be required to get genuine involvement (Ansoff, 1979; Bourgeoiss and Brodwin, 1982; Mason and Mitroff, 1981). Naylor (1978) and Pettigrew (1973) have described intergroup rivalries and political in-fighting within organizations. Ansoff (1979) suggests that strategy formulation and development will threaten managers who (1) hold personal power by virtue of private knowledge, (2) may be incompetent, and (3) may not be able to make the required shifts in outlook from an introverted, historically familiar view of the world to an extroverted, unfamiliar, and therefore threatening perspective (p. 179). It is these types of conditions that help to create undiscussable organizational defenses. If we can help organizations to face up to and reduce the undiscussables, we may provide them with help that is rarely offered, namely the ability of the organization to learn to detect and correct errors and continue to do so.

In this chapter, I should like to describe what we are learning when we try to teach strategy professionals the framework that Hermon-Taylor has described as well as the skills that are required to implement it, especially in dealing with organizational defenses.

## A PUZZLE

Early in my observations of strategy professionals at work in case teams and with the clients, I discovered a puzzle. The strategies of reasoning that they used to develop high-quality technical work was the same type of reasoning that I believed was required to reduce the organizational defenses. The puzzle was that the strategy professionals were (initially) reluctant to use these reasoning skills when dealing with human and organizational defenses. Why should they resist using these skills?

Elsewhere I have tried to suggest two different but interdependent answers for the reluctance. First, most human beings are programmed from early life to deal with threatening issues by using reasoning strategies that are bound to be ineffective. Second, they create organizational cultures to reinforce these counterproductive strategies (Argyris 1982, Argyris and Schön, 1978). Hence when we ask the strategy professionals to transfer their technical reasoning skills to the human domain, they are acting as our theories predict they would act. Let us explore this in more depth.

## How Do Strategy Professionals Deal with Threat?

The material that I will use in this chapter was obtained over a period of three years in the early 1980s, when I observed strategy professionals in a consulting firm and several internal planners in large corporations. I shall draw primarily from my work with the former, the external consultants. They are, in my opinion, an extremely bright and highly competent group of professionals who have shown themselves to be fast learners in dealing with client (and their own) defensiveness.

The first illustration of how they deal with client defensiveness comes from a discussion among 25 consultants. I selected this case because the consultants describe the strategies that they use with their clients when the latter act defensively. Another value of the case is that in discussing among each other how to deal with client defensiveness the consultants began to make each other defensive. Hence, we obtained first-hand data revealing how they may unknowingly create defensiveness and how they act to reduce it.

The discussion began with a senior officer presenting the reactions of these clients to a report. Briefly, the clients had begun a new venture which they believed could become a $billion-plus business. The consulting team was asked to help the clients' position themselves to take advantage of the opportunity. The team worked cooperatively with the client organization. After several months of work and periodic lengthy discussions, the consulting case team presented to the client hard data to show that it was unlikely that the business would be more than a $75 million venture (at least in the immediate future). "As the presentation wore on," the officer stated, "we became aware that there was a lot of nit-picking of analytical points. For the first time we were asked questions such as, 'When did you get that number?' or, 'How do you know your assumptions are correct?' "

The officer then asked his colleagues how they would diagnose what was going on. An analysis of the tape-recorded discussion indicated that all agreed that the clients' nit-picking behavior was caused by the clients' defensiveness. "What would make the clients defensive?", asked the officers. Three reasons were given:

1   The consultants had come to a different and much more pessimistic solution than had the clients using the same data. The nit-picking was caused by the feelings of embarrassment on the part of the clients as well as the fact that they did not know how else to react.

2   The consultants have not only just told the client that their projections were wrong. They have also created the possibility that at least some of the people brought in to build the new business may not have jobs.

3   The surprise itself could be the cause of the client defensiveness. If the consultants had spoken with some of the key individuals before the meeting, they could have prepared them for the surprise.

As one consultant said: "Their nit-picking is a survival process to be expected by anyone who is threatened." (Many nodded their heads approvingly or said "yes," "correct," "right.") He added: "Would we not act in the same way if we had an outsider tell us that our practice was wrong?" Again, many nodded their heads approvingly and several said "yes." Hence, we have an example where the consultants agreed that the clients were acting defensively. They disagreed that the "causes" of the defensiveness were that the consultants had arrived at a different conclusion than that which the clients had expected and had done so using the very data the clients had used to develop the wrong conclusion.

The officer leading the discussion asked what actions would they recommend. The responses could be categorized as follows:

1   Ask the clients to "raise their sights . . . and help them to see the big picture."
2   Encourage the clients to examine "our numbers any way they wish and see what happens to the analysis. If we are correct they will eventually realize it."
3   Invite the clients to express all their views: "we then promise to think about them and promise to respond. In the meantime, let us get on with the presentation."
4   Begin the presentation with more positive findings and then ease into the negative conclusions.

The first feature about his advice is that it made sense to most of the participants. By making sense I mean that (1) they appeared to agree with the hypothesized positive impact of such actions on the client and (2) they appeared to know how to implement the advice.

There is a second feature about the advice that is more complex and problematic than the easy agreement implies. All these strategies assume that clients who are feeling defensive have the capacity to reduce their defensiveness either by asking them "to raise their sights" or by promising a response, or by beginning with some positive examples. It is as if human beings can distance themselves from their feelings of threat and then continue to focus dispassionately on the data that is causing the threat in the first place. There is also a plea for suppressing the defensiveness in order to overcome it. The clients are expected to place their defensiveness "on hold" and discuss threatening subjects impartially. These strategies are being recommended even though earlier many of the consultants had agreed that they too would have reacted defensively if someone had told them something that was equally surprising about their practice using their data to make the point.

A third feature of the strategies is that all of them attempt to bypass the defensiveness. There is no attempt to discuss it. Moreover, there is no suggestion that they should state to the client that this is what they are doing. This is understandable because to discuss a covert bypass strategy overtly is to violate its face-saving features. Hence, the defensiveness is undiscussable and the undiscussability of the defensiveness is also undiscussable.

During the discussion, Consultant A said that he would have asked the client, "to temporarily suspend disbelief, to focus less on the details, and more on the major pieces of analyses." Consultant B responded, "but that would be adding insult to injury. Moreover, the clients could experience A as acting in a patronizing manner." There were a few moments of awkward silence since this was the first time one of the participants had evaluated negatively the contributions of another.

The officer asked A how he felt about B's response. Consultant A said that he felt B had not understood him. The officer then asked: "If the conversation continued as it did, would you have felt that B and others would be nit-picking?" Consultant A responded "yes." He then pointed out that A had concluded that his colleagues were wrong, acted as if that were not the case, and continued to hold his views more strongly while discounting the views of his critics. B smiled when he heard A's comments and said: "To be honest and I guess that's the idea of these sessions, I would have probably reacted the same way as you did."

The point is that the moment the threat occurred in the seminar, the participants also acted in ways to bypass the threat and to distance themselves from it. These strategies make it unlikely that individuals will ever test publicly their inferences and attributions to understand the defensiveness or will ever obtain the cooperation they seek to overcome it. Hence the strategies that clients may use when they become defensive the consultants may also use when they too become defensive.

In this connection it is interesting to note how the consultants tended to react if the clients questioned their conclusions, analyses, or models in a way that did not begin with defensiveness. The fundamental strategy, as one consultant stated it, was "to up the level of proof and overcome them with evidence." The clients' reactions, at best, were of feeling the brilliance and rigor of the consultants (but not necessarily their sense of concern of compassion). At worst, they felt put down and ignored. Both consequences would tend to lead to defensiveness and then the consultants switched to the strategies described above.

Another illustration of the same problem comes from a team which had as its objective to collect valid financial data. They met with 15 key middle managers (line and staff). They were unable to get from them relatively clear and unambiguous answers about the meaning of the numbers. After many hours of frustration, they assigned tasks to various individuals and scheduled individual meetings to get the answers. When the team was alone, the members made comments such as "unbelievable," "they're all screwed up," "Have you ever seen such a defensive group," "No wonder the top management does not trust the planning process." After the catharsis was finished, they laid plans for the future meetings. The team leader admonished the members to deal "sensitively" with the client members because they and the organization were obviously defensive and "we don't want to get mired down in their organizational garbage."

What happened? The team members observed the reactions of the line and staff managers to their questions. The team members inferred that the clients and the client system were acting defensively; that they were "screwed up" and "defensive." These inferences were not made explicit, nor were they tested publicly. The only "testing" that occurred was when the team members met by themselves and evaluated the clients' actions, hardly a valid test.

The conclusion of defensiveness then became the premise for guiding the team's actions. The team members' design for dealing with the clients included such strategies as: do not discuss the defensiveness in order to test or understand it because that will most likely make the clients more defensive; therefore act as if the clients are not judged as being defensive and cover up the diagnosis with a bypass strategy.

There are several important consequences of this strategy. First, the consultants may never learn the extent to which their diagnosis may have been incorrect. Second, the clients may never learn the extent to which their defensiveness inhibits the formulation, development and execution of a strategy. Third, if the clients' reactions are indeed defensive, and if they are spontaneous and automatic, then they must have been used previously and they will probably be used in the future. If this is the case, then the players will tend to use these reactions automatically when they are asked to accept and implement the new strategy that the team may develop. Fourth, if the clients react defensively, and if the consultants bypass that defensiveness, then the consultants have been induced into an organizational routine for dealing with defensiveness which is to bypass the defensiveness and act as if this is not being done; hence, cover up the cover-up.

Some may say that the consultants would not have found themselves in such a predicament if they had involved the clients more in the process. But the example was precisely of a meeting where the team and the clients were working cooperatively to produce data. The case-team members were trying to act participatively and cooperatively from the outset. Indeed, the consultants would maintain that they dealt with the defensiveness as they did in order to protect and encourage a sense of cooperation and participation. The clients would probably maintain that they have learned to use their defensive actions because that is the way to survive as well as the best possible way to make the planning process work. They could provide examples of the actions of superiors which led them to develop these automatic defensive reactions for individual and organizational survival.

We have therefore a situation where the clients exist in an organizational context that makes it unlikely that they can detect and correct important errors in the planning process and important cultural constraints to learning. The consultants act in ways to bypass these conditions and to act as if they are not doing so. The clients' defensive routines are therefore protected. Hence the ultimate effective implementation may be inhibited.

Perhaps more importantly the client organization is not being helped to understand that its defensive routines designed for survival also inhibit it in learning how to learn. One consequence of this is related to the reactions of the executives at the top. They created the case team (an internal task force with outside consultants) precisely because they did not believe that the present organization could produce the analysis necessary for a sound strategy. They reached that conclusion after several years of experience with the planning process that resulted in all sorts of incomplete or incorrect plans which the top concluded were the result of the defensiveness of the organization. Like everyone else involved in this case, they too kept their diagnoses secret, they too covered up, they too covered up the cover-up, and they too bypassed the entire issue by hiring the outside consultants to work with the "best" individuals from within that they could identify.

To sum up: the automatic reaction to defensiveness in both cases is to ignore or bypass the defensiveness. But the act of ignoring reality is itself defensive because individuals who are charged with producing a new strategy eventually will have to deal with the existing organizational defensive routines because they will operate to reduce the effectiveness of the new planning processes. Bypassing and distancing do not encourage the production of valid information with which to formulate and develop a strategy, not to mention to implement it.

## WHY THE AUTOMATIC REACTIONS OF BYPASS AND DISTANCING?

The automatic reactions of dealing with defensiveness by such actions as bypassing and distancing are by no means limited to strategy professionals. Executives and managers that we have studied to date – in large or small organizations, of whatever structure, private or public, volunteer or non-volunteer – appear to act in the same way. Indeed, most individuals deal with defensiveness in the same way. There are two reactions most often used. The first is to bypass. The second, used most often when the first does not work, is to confront the issued head on in a way that usually produces the predicted defensiveness. In organizations this reaction is usually dealt with by asking the top "to take a stand," "read the riot act" and tell the people to "shape up or ship out" (Argyris, 1982; Argyris and Schön, 1978). These types of reactions are often accompanied by the firing or transferring of key actors who are believed to inhibit progress. The reactions may solve the problem temporarily, but they do not help the organization to gain control over its defensive routines, to help the organization learn how to deal effectively with defensiveness for whatever problem or whatever level.

Why is this so when most line executives and strategy professionals believe that reducing organizational defensive routines is a good idea and learning how to learn is a noble aspiration? The answer, I suggest, is *not* because they believe that the noble aspiration is not noble but because they believe it is not realistic. If the examples above are illustrative, then one could understand why there is the doubt. The threatening factors and defensive reactions were so interdependent and complex that it would be very difficult to figure out how to untangle them without, as one executive once said, "creating more problems." This fear is the most frequent one that is expressed by line executives. It acts to reinforce the distancing and the predisposition to bypass because having the fear is itself threatening.

If no one wants this state of affairs how come it is so prevalent? The answer to this question requires that we examine the reasoning processes people use to make sense of, and to remain in some degree of control over their own and others' defensiveness. We must also explore the impact of these highly skilled modes of coping with defensiveness upon the organization.

## Individual and Organizational Learning: A Theory of Action Perspective

Whenever actors are participating in economic decision-making processes, they are designing the consequences they intend to implement. The same is true when actors are participating in managing people. Whenever actors produce a match between intentions and outcomes, or whenever they detect and correct errors (mismatches), they may be said to be learning. Organizational learning is produced through the behavior of individuals acting as agents for the organization. A theory of individual and organizational learning can therefore be the basis for understanding actions, be they intentionally economic or human relationships, or both. (The major concepts and empirical findings are described in Argyris, 1976, 1982; Argyris and Schön, 1974, 1978).

Behavior is designed to achieve tacit or explicit intentions. It is not possible to design every action from the beginning, nor is it likely that actors will have all the knowledge that is relevant in every situation. Thus, individuals carry around with them beliefs and values about how they and others ought to behave. These beliefs and values can be stated in the form of propositions about effectiveness: "If I behave in such and such a manner, then the following consequences should occur." Since these propositions have the same structure as propositions in any scientific theory, we have called them *theories of action*.

We have found that individuals hold two theories of action: their espoused theory – describing the way they *say* they behave – and their theory-in-use, which describes the behavior they actually display. Although individual behaviors vary widely, and espoused theories of action also differ, we have found almost no variation among individual theories-in-use. This has enabled us to develop a theory-in-use model that is highly generalizable, which we call Model I. (These concepts are dealt with in detail in chapters 3 and 4.) A schematic summary of Model I theory-in-use appears in figure 10.1.

Human beings hold theories-in-use which make it likely that they will deal with threat by bypassing it. The bypass strategies will all tend to lead to escalation of defensiveness and error and hence are not genuinely corrective. Strategy professionals are in the difficult position of dealing with clients who could become even more defensive if the threat is not bypassed. Defensive clients might easily decide, for example, to deal with their threat by projecting all the blame on to the consultants for acting in such "obviously immature" ways. They are also in the difficult situation because whatever strategy they may devise, it is highly likely that it will be consistent with Model I, hence it too would lead to escalation of defensiveness and error.

## Organizational Learning and Learning how to Learn

Strategy professionals may not have to worry about these dilemmas if their strategies are not threatening and if the organization is capable of implementing them. But even when the strategies are accepted, if they are difficult for the organization to implement then the issue of dealing with threat becomes important.

| Governing variables | Action strategies | Consequences for the behavioral world | Consequences for learning | Effectiveness |
|---|---|---|---|---|
| Define goals and try to achieve them | Design and manage the environment unilaterally (be persuasive, appeal to larger goals) | Actor seen as defensive, inconsistent, incongruent, competitive, controlling, fearful of being vulnerable, manipulative, withholding of feelings, overly concerned about self and others or underconcerned about others | Self-sealing | Decreased effectiveness |
| Maximize winning and minimize losing | Own and control the task (claim ownership of the task, be guardian of definition and execution of task) | Defensive interpersonal and group relationship (dependence upon actor, little additivity, little helping others) | Single-loop learning | |
| Minimize generating or expressing negative feelings | Unilaterally protect yourself (speak with inferred categories accompanied by little or no directly observable behavior, be blind to impact on others and to the incongruity between rhetoric and behavior, reduce incongruity by defensive actions such as blaming, stereotyping, suppressing feelings, intellectualizing) | Defensive norms (mistrust, lack of risk-taking, conformity, external commitment, emphasis on diplomacy, power-centered competition, and rivalry) | Little testing of theories publicly. Much testing of theories privately | |
| Be rational | Unilaterally protect others from being hurt (withhold information, create rules to censor information and behavior, hold private meetings) | Low freedom of choice, internal commitment, and risk-taking | | |

**Figure 10.1** Model I theory-in-use

Another major issue concerns the ultimate purpose of strategy formulation and implementation. What if the purpose was to implement a strategy in a way that not only reduces the organizational defensive routines but helps the organization to learn how to deal with future threat? In order to accomplish this objective, the participants will have to learn how to reflect upon and reduce the organizational defensive routines. But, in doing this effectively they will also reflect on how they learned to detect and correct these defensive routines and the errors that they produced. If this occurs strategic formulation, development and implementation become even more important and comprehensive than described at the outset. It now becomes the vehicle not only for defining where the business is going but a new management process that encourages organizational learning and learning how to learn.

### *What can strategy professionals do to help client organizations learn how to learn?*

The first step is for strategy professionals to learn to deal with threat in other ways than Model I. They require an additional theory-in-use which may be called Model II. Briefly, this theory-in-use is designed to enhance the kind of individual and organizational learning to which we have been alluding. The Model II governing variables are: valid information, free and informed choice, and internal commitment to choices made in order to monitor the effectiveness of their implementation (see figure 10.2). Model II, therefore, is not the opposite of Model I. These governing variables, combined with stipulated action strategies, should lead to consequences where search is enhanced and deepened, where ideas are tested publicly, where individuals collaborate to enlarge inquiry, and where trust and risk-taking are enhanced. These consequences should lead in turn to an O-II learning system whose consequences are to reduce the dysfunctional aspects of Models I and O-I, hence, to reduce the dysfunctional features described by the critics of the economic theory of the firm.

Research is in progress to develop usable theories of intervention to help individuals and organizations bring about these changes. To date, the results are encouraging. It appears possible to teach individuals Model II action strategies in the service of Model II governing variables and to produce O-II learning systems. (Model II action strategies, if used in the service of Model I governing variables, would result in gimmicks and trickery. See Argyris 1976, 1982; Argyris and Schön, 1978.) In designing the intervention theories to get from here to there, Models II and O-II act as guideposts or criteria for the processes that would be used and the conditions that would have to be created. Models II and O-II are ideals. It is unlikely that anyone will ever have all the valid information required, that choices made will be completely free and informed, or that monitoring will be perfect. The models, however, can serve to keep the participants' eyes on the objectives to be attained, and to offer some strategies to use to work toward the ideal even though the attainment will never be perfect.

At the outset of this chapter, I described many of the consultants that I work with as fast learners. There is an important reason for their capacity to learn fast, a reason which in a few cases can be at the core of their having difficulty to learn.

First, why can strategy professionals be fast learners? The answer is related to the analytical and research skills they learned in order to be rigorous planners. For example, the group with whom I work has a high respect for valid and reliable data. They prefer quantitative data but understand the importance of qualitative data. The key criterion in deciding what type of data to use is related to what will describe the world most accurately and what will be best understood by the clients. Second, all the reasoning processes used are made as explicit as possible. The inferences they make, the conclusions that they reach are done in such a way that they encourage inquiry into them. Third, all the inferences and especially the conclusions are subject to public testing. No matter how much they believe in

| Governing variables | Action strategies | Consequences for the behavioral world | Consequences for learning | Consequences for quality of life | Effectiveness |
|---|---|---|---|---|---|
| Valid information | Design situations or environments where participants can be origins and can experience high personal causation (psychological success, confirmation, essentiality) | Actor experienced as minimally defensive (facilitator, collaborator, choice creator) | Disconfirmable processes | Quality of life will be more positive than negative (high authenticity and high freedom of choice) | |
| Free and informed choice | Tasks are controlled jointly | Minimally defensive interpersonal relations and group dynamics | Double-loop learning | Effectiveness of problem solving and decision making will be great, especially for difficult problems | Increased long-run effectiveness |
| Internal commitment to the choice and constant monitoring of its implementation | Protection of self is a joint enterprise and oriented toward growth (speak in directly observable categories, seek to reduce blindness about own inconsistency and incongruity)

Bilateral protection of others | Learning-oriented norms (trust, individuality, open confrontation on difficult issues) | Public testing of theories | | |

**Figure 10.2** Model II theory-in-use

and advocate a way of reasoning or a particular set of conclusions, these are formulated as hypotheses subject to being empirically disproved. Fourth, they are learners and experimenters and as such are almost always willing to be playful with technical ideas. They appear to be able to defend them vigorously while at the same time, they are capable of dropping them with minimal defensiveness if the case could be made that they do so. Finally, they are always seeking to conceptualize their ideas into patterns and the patterns into models, and whenever possible the models are related to known and tested models in such fields as economics of the firm.

I believe that these observations should surprise few readers who are planners. They represent ways of reasoning and acting that help planners to be rigorous and tough-minded. When I asked these individuals to explain why they used tough-minded reasoning, almost all responded that they wanted to do their utmost to make sure that they were not unknowingly kidding themselves or others. Embedded in this reply are, I suggest, three objectives: first, seek to obtain valid information; in order, second, to make an informed choice; and third, keep testing the validity of the choices especially as they are being implemented.

If we examine carefully the five action strategies and the three objectives, they are consistent with Model II. Thus the strategy professionals have the values and the skills to act consistently with Model II. But, they are also programmed not to use their skills, but to use Model I to deal with threatening issues. Those who are willing to use the above objectives and skills when they examine their personal strategies for dealing with threat become the fast learners. They recognize the importance of getting and examining directly observable data; of making their inferences explicit; of testing them, etc.

A key issue therefore is their ability to use, when dealing with threat, the reasoning processes that they have mastered in dealing with the technical side of their activities. So far it appears that the ones who learn fast are those who are willing to inquire into their defensive actions, to take risks, and to experiment with new ways of behaving. Those who are slower learners appear to be good at diagnosing their defensive actions but resist taking risks and experimenting (in training sessions) because they believe that Model II actions can produce defensiveness in clients. Their fear is of course well founded. Model II actions can make Model I clients defensive. However, it is this very defensiveness that can be used as a fulcrum for change and learning.

### Examples of Consultants Using Model II Strategies with Clients

We are just beginning to collect examples of how strategy professionals may use Model II interventions to solve strategy problems and to help the clients learn how to learn. For example, a strategy consultant was participating in a discussion on critical economic issues with the top management of a firm. As the executives spoke he noted three important inconsistencies in their reasoning processes. Before learning the new skills, he reported that his predisposition would have been to take note of the inconsistencies, think about them after the meeting, and bring back some kind of presentation as to how to deal with them. If the clients agreed with the ideas, he would gladly accept their praise and feel that he had built up his credibility with the client.

He behaved somewhat differently now than he would have previously. First, he noted the inconsistencies. Second, he waited for the opportunity to state them and ask if the client agreed. In this case they agreed and praised the officer for his insight. The new feature of his strategy was then to go into the mode of helping the clients learn how to learn. First, he said in effect, "I am glad that you found this valuable. I would like, if I may, to ask one further question. What is it in this context that prevented you from recognizing the inconsistencies in the first place?" There was a momentary silence. The CEO said, "That's an interesting question." Another client said: "Well, it sounds as if some of us did not recognize it. The inconsistencies have been known."

The consultant then asked: "And could you describe what would lead individuals not to act on what they have known to be inconsistent; indeed if I understand you correctly, to act as if they are not aware of an inconsistency?" There was laughter among some of the executives, one of whom noted that the consultant may be opening up a can of worms. The consultant responded that he thought it would be important to explore the can of worms and gave his reasons. However, he added if the group did not wish to discuss the issue he certainly was not trying to push them to do so. The CEO thought that a discussion should be held because the comments suggested that: "Our consensus decision-making process that we pride ourselves in having may have flaws in it. If so, then correcting that would be of as much value, if not more, than the present planning study we are doing."

The consultant took a risk which, in this case, added value to the relationship. The clients learned more about the intimate relationship between effective formulation, development and implementation on the one hand, and learning how to learn on the other. In other cases the clients may not respond as cooperatively. The key issue is how confident the consultant feels in dealing with client defensiveness including helping them to choose not to discuss the issues. As a behavioral scientist intervening in organizations, I am impressed with the power of using economic issues to open up the organizational defensive routines. It is difficult for the client to ignore issues of trust, "group-think," intergroup rivalries, when they can be connected directly to the way they reason, conceive and implement business plans as well as corporate strategy.

In another case, the CEO of a decentralized organization felt that he was not receiving adequate information from his immediate reports. He felt that unless he took some action he may not only become distanced from the operations but indeed disconnected. The immediate reports, on the other hand, felt that if the CEO trusted them he should leave them alone and act only if they did not meet their commitments. After several months of operating under these conditions the CEO decided to act. He requested that with the help of a consulting firm a new set of managerial processes be instituted that provided him an opportunity to know what is going on before it was so late that a change would upset the people below him.

The consultants who studied the situation concluded that they could with the cooperation of the relevant people, devise some useful reporting processes and forms. They also concluded that the effectiveness of the new processes could be blunted by the values and actions of the executives involved. For example, the subordinates may now believe that they were not trusted or that their superior did not really mean to run a decentralized organization. The superior, on the other hand, who genuinely wanted to decentralize could feel that subordinates are blind to the issue of distancing and disconnecting the superior. At the time of this writing, the CEO and his immediate reports have agreed to this analysis and have scheduled a meeting to discuss the issue with a larger group of senior executives. The idea is to involve most of the senior executives who are relevant in the design and implementation of planning in such a way that they discuss the existing behavioral features that get in the way of implementing an effective planning process and then to examine jointly and redesign the planning process.

Bourgeoiss and Brodwin (1982) have recommended a bottom-up process of strategy formulation and development where the relevant managers design and send to the top the new plans. If such a process were in place in this organization, there is the likelihood that the ideas would reach the top only to be "mangled" (as one subordinate described it) by the defensive behavioral dynamics at the top.

Indeed, if my experience is valid, defensive dynamics exist at all levels. Hence the distortions could occur in many places in the organization. If these distortions are covered up and the cover-up is undiscussable then it is unlikely that they will ever be corrected.

## Conclusion

Individuals and organizations tend to deal with threat in ways that will increase defensiveness and reduce the probability of learning to learn. These features will tend to make it difficult for strategy professionals to help clients implement strategies that are genuinely new and require frame-breaking. To compound the problem, strategy professionals are also humans hence they too have learned the same counterproductive ways to deal with defensiveness (the clients' or their own).

There are several reasons to be optimistic. First, we are developing concepts and skills to deal effectively with threat at the individual through the organizational levels. Second, the reasoning skills required to deal effectively with human defensiveness are congruent with those required to produce rational, rigorous strategy plans. Third, it may be easier to get clients to examine their defensiveness by relating them to economic and strategy issues than by arguing for the benefits of such features as openness and trust in the name of organizational effectiveness. The strategy professionals who learn to integrate the technical (e.g. economic) issues with the behavioral ones will, I believe, be at the forefront of practice.

## References

Ansoff, H. I., 1979, "The state of practice in planning systems," (ed.) Dill, W. R., and Popov, G. Kh., Chichester, John Wiley & Sons.

Argyris, C., 1976, *Increasing Leadership Effectiveness*, New York, Wiley–Interscience.

Argyris, C., 1982, *Reasoning, Learning and Action*, San Francisco, Jossey-Bass.

Argyris, C., and Schön, D., 1974, *Theory in Practice*, San Francisco, Jossey-Bass.

Argyris, C., and Schön, D., 1978, *Organizational Learning*, Reading, Addison-Wesley.

Bourgeoiss, L. J. III and D. R., Brodwin, 1982, "Strategy Implementation: Five approaches to an elusive phenomenon," Stanford University, mimeograph.

Lorange, P., and Vancil, R. F., 1977, *Strategic Planning Systems*, New Jersey, Prentice-Hall Inc.

Mason, R., and Mitroff, I., 1981, *Challenging Strategic Planning Assumption. Theory, Cases, and Techniques*, New York, Wiley–Interscience.

Naylor, T. H. (ed.), 1978, *The Politics of Corporate Planning and Modeling*, Research Series, Oxford, Ohio, Planning Executives Institute.

Pettigrew, A., 1973, *The Politics of Organizational Decision-Making*, London, Tavistock.

Yavitz, B., and Newman, W. H., 1982, *Strategy in Action*, New York, The Free Press.

# — 11 —

# The Dilemma of Implementing Controls: The Case of Managerial Accounting

The purpose of managerial functional disciplines, of which accounting is one, is to help managers govern. Each functional discipline is, in effect, a theory about how to master events over which managers are responsible. Accounting relates specified actions and performance to quantitative numbers whose meaning is determined by the theory and rules of accounting. The meanings, in turn, are organized so that they can be used to diagnose and to act. Understanding of reality, therefore, is developed or enacted with the correct use of accounting principles. Action is guided (or one may say derived) from the picture developed by using accounting principles.

In this chapter, I want to examine several dilemmas of implementation of accounting. They are dilemmas because, it appears, the correct use of accounting ideas can lead to productive consequences, and at the same time lead to counterproductive consequences.

## ACCOUNTING PRINCIPLES

### *The Reasoning Required to Create Accounting Is the Same as That to Implement It*

Accounting uses concepts that are primarily objective and quantitative. The use of the concepts is guided by a set of rules that are defined as rigorously as possible. Once formulated, the rules are intended to apply equally to all. The technical knowledge is constructed with the intention of being consistent with science (Ijiri, 1975; Solomons, 1986; Sterling, 1979; Yu, 1976).

Accounting, as is true for the other managerial disciplines, requires the use of reasoning. Reasoning includes defining premises, making inferences, and reaching conclusions. Embedded in the use of accounting is a set of rules about effective reasoning that I will label as rules to bring about productive reasoning. The rules advise individuals to make their premises and inferences as unambiguous and explicit as possible. They also advise that conclusions should be tested publicly with the toughest tests that are available.

Productive reasoning is important because the credibility of accounting is ultimately based on its abilities (1) to create new ways of framing problems in order to solve them, and (2) to create knowledge that is usable by managers to detect and correct errors (i.e. any mismatch between intentions and actual consequences). A third basis for accounting credibility is its ability to help practitioners to know when they may not be capable of detecting and correcting error. The effective implementation of accounting is therefore strongly dependent upon the capacity for organizational learning.

## Effective Implementation

If productive reasoning is produced by implementing accounting principles then, not surprisingly, the first step in implementation is to teach the accounting principles that are relevant to problems at hand. Implementation therefore often begins with a theory of instruction which assumes that: if humans beings learn the principles of accounting; if they understand them fully; if they wish to use them; and if they are permitted to use them, then they will go ahead and use them. As long as they use the ideas consistently with sound accounting principles, the consequences promised by accounting will result.

There are two consequences that follow from the enthusiastic application of this theory of instruction. The accountants can come to believe that effective implementation is largely implementing the theory of instruction just described. This belief assumes an organization relatively dedicated to following the accounting ideas, especially if it can be shown that they do solve the problems at hand. The assumption is probably valid as long as the effective use of accounting knowledge is not embarrassing or threatening. But, sound accounting knowledge can be embarrassing and threatening precisely when it is most needed, that is, when the organization is in real trouble.

The second consequence of the theory of implementation described above, is that the accountants are held responsible for producing and advocating sound concepts and principles. As a result accountants understandably turn much of their attention inward into their discipline in order to make sure that their discipline is correct. This inward orientation, in turn, may also become an orientation for defense against the outsider.

Non-accountants see this self-referential defense as signs that accountants are acting like techies. A techie is one who uses the technical ideas at his or her command to attempt to influence and control others. Techies' sense of competence, confidence, and self-esteem are wrapped up in accounting ideas and rules. The stronger the techie orientation the less likely is the individual going to deal competently with user disbelief because the techie deals with disbelief by upping the level of accounting evidence and proof which may have triggered off the disbelief in the first place.

A strong techie orientation can make it difficult for accountants to "bend" their ideas without losing their validity in order to communicate to non-accountants. For example, metaphors may be useful to explain quantitative analyses. It takes a lot of skill and experience to take a precise quantitative analysis and communicate it in ways that users who may be threatened by quantitative precision will listen.

Accountants, indeed most professionals, do not look forward to encounters where they are disbelieved or resisted. Such conditions lead to conflict with the potential for embarrassment or threat. As noted above, a techie response will tend to escallate the embarrassment and threat.

## The Reasoning Required to Deal with Embarrassment or Threat Is Antithetical to Productive Reasoning

We now come to the heart of the dilemma. Individuals have human theories of how to remain in control when embarrassment and threat occur. To our surprise, this theory of control is the same across cultures, and regardless of age, sex, education, or wealth. The behavior that they use to implement the theory may vary. For example, all human beings that we have studied use the same theory of face-saving. However, the actual behavior may vary widely. (Argyris, 1985; Argyris and Schön, 1974, 1978). Some features that do not vary are as follows.

1   The theory of control is primarily unilateral.
2   The action strategies are primarily authoritarian. They depend on "selling," "persuading," "fighting" designed to win and not to lose one's point.
3   This results in the creation of a behavioral environment characterized by defensiveness, error escalation, self-fulfilling prophecies, and self-sealing thinking.
4   Defensive reasoning predominates (i.e., premises are tacit, inferences are not made explicit, and conclusions are not falsifiable).
5   Threat or embarrassment is dealt with by striving to bypass them and by covering up the bypass. Social virtues of concern and caring are often defined to be consistent with being "diplomatic," "easing-in," and similar bypass actions.

There is a paradox in using a human theory of control that has these features. If I use a theory of control that is unilaterally controlling because I believe it is effective then the player at the other end must act in a dependent submissive mode if my unilateral dominant mode is to be implemented. The paradox is: in order for me to act effectively, I require others to use a theory of action that I consider ineffective.

These consequences make it more likely that the information produced will be distorted; that the players will be unaware of their personal responsibility for the distortion; while clearly aware of the other's responsibility. In short, human beings' theories-in-use (not the ones that they espouse) when dealing with embarrassment or threat, are anti-learning and overprotective.

The reasoning embedded in the human theory of control described above may be called defensive. The rules of defensive reasoning are: keep premises tacit, make inferences with covert logic, and subject conclusions to a private test; the test should be consistent with the logic used by the person reaching the conclusion. Such reasoning is contrary to productive reasoning. Yet both the accountant and the line manager will tend to use it. Ironically, defensive reasoning will be activated when it is least likely to be effective and most likely to inhibit problem-solving.

## Organizational Defensive Routines

Defensive reasoning is not formally sanctioned by organizations. As a result, human beings create organizational defensive routines that are consistent with their individual defensive routines. The defensive reasoning individuals use to defend themselves now becomes acceptable, if not required, by organizational practices and policies (Argyris, 1985).

Organizational defensive routines are any routine policies or actions that are intended to circumvent the experience of embarrassment or threat by bypassing the situations that may trigger these responses. Organizational defensive routines make it unlikely that the organization will address the factors that caused the embarrassment or threat in the first place. Organizational defensive routines are anti-learning and overprotective.

Organizational defensive routines differ from individual defensive routines in that (1) they exist even though individuals move in and out of the organization, (2) psychologically different individuals use them in the same ways, (3) the source of learning them is socialization, and (4) the trigger to use them is concern and being realistic rather than a personal anxiety (Argyris, 1985).

## Mixed Messages: A Dominant Organizational Defensive Routine

An example of a prominent defensive routine is mixed messages, which is discussed more fully in chapter 4 (see especially pp. 93–4). Briefly, the strategies embedded in the logic of mixed messages are: when dealing with organizational defensive routines, be inconsistent, yet act as if you were not being inconsistent; make the issues undiscussable and uninfluence-able, and act as if this were not the case; thus the undiscussability and uninfluencability become undiscussable.

Organizational defensive routines can lead people to feel helpless and cynical about changing them. This leads people to distance themselves from trying to engage the defensive routines in order to reduce them. As a result, organizational defensive routines not only become unmanageable (it is difficult to manage what is undiscussable), but they become the source of much distorted information. The distortion of the information is taken for granted because it is seen as necessary for the survival of the players as well as for the organization.

## Adapting: Organizational Defensive Routines

How does managerial accounting as a system of control ever work under the conditions described above? First, these counterproductive consequences occur primarily when the players are experiencing potential or actual embarrassment or threat. There is a large domain in managerial accounting practice where there is little disagreement and feelings of disempowerment. Second, where there are difficulties, individuals often strive to work out their differences, especially through upward delegation: take it to the boss and let him decide. If subordinates lose the fight they can maintain that they did their best and the superior is responsible.

Neither of these two strategies deals effectively with the double binds that actors experience when the accounting systems are used in accordance with best current practice yet they produce for the players varying degrees of embarrassment or threat. Under these conditions, organizational and individual defensive routines are activated by the players to protect themselves (Lawler and Rhode, 1976). Birnberg, et al. (1983) identified six methods used by subordinates to distort accounting information. They are smoothing, biasing, focusing, gaming, filtering, and "illegal acts."

What is common about all these activities is that they bypass the causes of the threat and that they cover up the bypass while it is being produced. These are the properties of organizational defensive routines. Hence, to deal with defensive behavior norms in the system, the players adapt by producing further defensive behavior. In doing so, the players subject themselves to further potential embarrassment or threat that arises if they are caught. After all, such actions violate formal organizational politics and espoused managerial stewardship. Defensive routines beget defensive routines.

To the extent that they are undiscussable and their undiscussability is undiscussable, the defensive routines will be difficult to manage. Under these conditions not only subordinates but superiors may feel a sense of helplessness and cynicism about reducing them.

## Adapting: Reducing the Potential Embarrassment or Threat

As I interpret the research by Merchant (1988) and Merchant and Manzoni (1988) it suggests that some superiors may be dealing with the problem by trying to reduce the likelihood of embarrassment and threat arising in the first place. The choice of strategy is partially influenced by the superiors' fundamental assumptions about their relationships with their subordinates and with the budgeting process. They seemed to behave as if (1) they had great difficulty in evaluating (profit center) managers' performance, (2) they believed that managers cannot be trusted to give fair evaluation of their performance, and (3) they felt ill-equipped to openly confront threatening issues (Manzoni, 1988, p. 2). All these conditions are normally not discussable as they are occurring.

One way to bypass these problems is to design budgets that the players agree are "very likely to be achieved." In a study of 54 profit centers from 12 corporations the subordinates and superiors agreed that the budgets were designed to be achievable – e.g., subjective probability of 80 or 90 percent given that the management team exerts a high level of effort (Merchant and Manzoni, 1988). Under these conditions the potential for embarrassment or threat is minimized.

However, there may be an unintended consequence leading to another dilemma. The dilemma is that success under these conditions may be self-limiting. It is possible, for example, that setting goals is a bargaining process where the superior is ultimately in control. This is not surprising given the personal theory of control described above. The subordinates therefore participate within the limits (personal and organizational) set by the superior.

To the extent that the superior is in control, the ownership or responsibility for setting the goals and the paths is ultimately the superior's. To the extent that the performance goals do not stretch old abilities or do not require new skills, successful performance is predictable as long as the subordinate works hard and there are no unforeseen externalities. Under these conditions, subordinates may also feel very good about reaching the easily achievable performance targets and a great relief from pressure. But the success will not strengthen the individual's self-esteem and confidence in learning new abilities, taking risks, and producing and successfully dealing with surprises (Lewin, et al., 1944).

Bandura's theory of perceived self-efficacy (Bandura, 1986), leads to similar conclusions in the world of organizational management (Bandura, 1988; Wood and Bandura, 1989). Briefly, perceived self-efficacy is the belief in one's capabilities to exercise control over events and to accomplish goals. Human beings with strong beliefs of self-efficacy are often in, or seek, situations in which they focus on mastering tasks that are challenging, that are central to their needs, and that they have some non-trivial responsibility to figure out how to achieve. They are not depressed by error; they see it as an opportunity for learning. They persevere and are resilient in the face of difficulties.

As I interpreted the research on setting predictably achievable goals, the profit center managers are not likely to strengthen their belief in their self-efficacy. Indeed, if these conditions become routine the individuals' self-efficacy beliefs may be eroded or limited to aspirations that are easily achievable. Under these conditions individuals will tend to shy away from difficult tasks, seek goals with a level of aspiration that is similar to previous ones, be committed as long as there are rewards, give up quickly, and come to blame themselves or the environment for failure.

What difference does it make as long as the targets are achieved? Individuals who succeed in achieving easily achievable budgets in the defensive world described above should report that they feel safe, secure, and in control. They should be observed to be dependent on and grateful toward their supervisor, to seek a world that is programmable so that it is easily manageable, to expect that competence is equated with the easily achievable, that a just world is one where objectives are easily achievable, where no surprises is a sign of credibility and trust. The same individuals should express concern and fear about developing objectives that stretch their minds (not their energy) that requires risk-taking, that produce uncertainty.

What may be happening is this: In order for superiors to feel confident that (1) earnings can be predicted correctly, (2) overconsumption of resources will be reduced, (3) meddling into the players' space will be reduced, (4) harmful earnings management practice will be reduced, and (5) the probability of ensuring a competitive compensation package will be increased (Merchant and Manzoni, 1988, pp. 16–22), they use strategies (like early achievable goals) that may simultaneously produce in subordinates feelings of fear of risk-taking and stretching their capacities, fear of questioning the status quo.

Simons (1987) describes a different form of adaption in Johnson and Johnson. Compensation is separated from absolute output performance. Hence the managers are shielded from the variability in outcome due to an uncertain environment. This encourages subordinates to make their efforts visible which, in turn, requires more knowledge by superiors than that required by simply rewarding performance on the basis of output. Simons' description suggests that Johnson and Johnson uses information as much, if not more, for the purpose of learning than for control. Or to put it another way, Johnson and Johnson sees control as an ongoing iterative process and hence requires learning to go on continuously. This practice leads to a reduction of embarrassment and threat. It would be interesting to study if embarrassment or threat does occur and how they are handled by the players.

## AN INCORRECT THEORY OF MOTIVATION

The argument embedded in the strategy of achievable budgets fundamentally assumes that implementation will be more effective if individual goals and organizational goals are congruent. By defining budgets that, within reason, assure success then both the organization and the individual are well served. This theory of implementation stems from expectancy theory: a theory of motivation popular in the psychological literature a decade ago (Lawler, 1973). The theory states that human beings will expand effort in a particular direction when they believe their actions will result in outcomes that they desire. This has led accountants to recommend goal congruence as the basis for motivating individuals to act consistently with the requirements of managerial central systems (Anthony, 1988, pp. 94–6)

Unfortunately the theory never included – nor to my knowledge was there any empirical research conducted – to explore the conditions that are at the heart of this analysis: actions that are simultaneously congruent *and* incongruent with organizational and individual needs.

For example, Jaworski and Young (1988) hypothesize that in governing behavior, the actors choose actions that achieve their "most favorable personal outcome regardless of the actions that the firms prefers" (p. 6). But our research suggests that choosing gaming behavior is often experienced as "most" and "least" favorable. "Most" refers to protecting one's self; "least" refers to having to do so and to cover it up. The choice is made because individuals believe they have no other choice (Argyris, 1985). The goal congruence theory is not very helpful in advising management how to design congruence between individual and organizational goals where, due to the layers of double binds, inner contradictions exist in each and between both.

There is second feature of the current ideas on motivation that appears misleading. Accountants are aware that managerial accounting systems can be threatening because they evaluate managers' performance. (Horngren and Foster, 1987, p. 10.) The authors often counsel patience and education, persuasion, and intelligent interpretation (p. 159).

These three activities should be put in the service of convincing subordinates that budgets are positive devices.

As I read such advice it contains the following logic: If accountants describe reality accurately; if the description is objective (quantifiable) and testable; if accountants communicate their descriptions accurately, then accountants have fulfilled a key feature of their stewardship. But fulfilling this feature is not enough as long as line management finds accounting information threatening. How should accountants deal with this problem? As far as I can tell the primary advice is to repeat the logic above with the line manager. The accountant sits down with the line and persuades and convinces the line managers that the accounting information is good for them.

Unfortunately, the accounting textbooks do not describe in concrete detail what accountants should actually say and do. According to our research, it is highly likely that accountants will use a theory-in-use that is unilateral and coercive, and they will be unaware that this is the case. Line managers will react by using a similar theory-in-use. The result will be escalating misunderstanding usually in the name of honesty and integrity (Argyris and Schön, 1988). The only transcript that I was able to locate illustrates our prediction. According to the footnote by the authors, versions of the transcript have been printed many times (Horngren and Foster, 1987, pp. 473–5).

In one of the more comprehensive text books on accounting (Horngren and Foster, 1987) one may read:

- Budgeting systems change human behavior in ways sought by top management (p. 139).
- Budgets compel managers to look ahead. This forced planning is by far the greatest contribution of budgeting to management (p. 141).
- Budgets force executives to think (p. 148).
- Budgets [help] to remove unconscious bias (p. 142).
- Budgets [help] to search out weaknesses (p. 142).

Budgets change, compel, force, remove and search out. Strictly speaking budgets do not do these things. It is individuals who implement these actions. If the authors mean that accountants should use budgets to compel, force, etc. line management then they are recommending a strategy of implementation that will probably backfire. Such unilateral and coercive activity will activate, as we have seen, individual and organizational defensive routines that are overprotective and anti-learning.

Human beings are capable of looking ahead, of planning, of searching for biases, weaknesses, and blindness. They are not likely to do so when the fundamental assumption is that they have to be forced or coerced to do so. The dilemma is how to implement accounting practice in ways that change, looking ahead, thinking, removing unrecognized biases that are produced through internal commitment rather than the external commitment implicit in the statements above.

## IMPLICATION FOR CORRECTIVE ACTION: TEACHING AN ADDITIONAL THEORY-IN-USE

The idea that implementation is enhanced by creating goal congruence, which is enclosed, in turn, by using appropriate monetary rewards, is not likely to be relevant where the implementation of managerial controls is embarrassing or threatening to the players. The challenge under these conditions is less one of motivating individuals. It is more one of dealing with their automatic reactions to use skillfully a theory of action whose consequence is to produce defensive reactions, to bypass a cover-up. It is also one of engaging organizational defensive routines that protect and exacerbate the individual defensive but highly skilled behavior.

In order to accomplish these consequences individuals will have to be taught a new theory-in-use, one that, at present, few have, although many espouse. Such a theory-in-use exists. It can be taught as a general theory of learning (individual and organizational) (Argyris, 1982; Argyris and Schön, 1974, 1978). Moreover, it appears that the most powerful way to teach the new theory-in-use is in conjuction with a technical (functional) discipline such as managerial accounting, strategy, or a human resources activity such as evaluating human performance in ways that lead to genuine pay for performance. The reason this is true is that this behavioral theory, like all theories that underlie the management disciplines, is a normative theory of how to achieve intended consequences. Most theories of human behavior are descriptive: their objective is to understand. They espouse that applicability is important. The theory-in-use, however, leaves much to be desired (Argyris, 1980).

This theory-in-use is pro-learning and against overprotection. The new theory-in-use solves other dilemmas, namely: being tough- yet inquiry-oriented; making compelling arguments yet subjecting them to test; evaluating performance yet being confrontable. With these skills individuals can begin to deal with challenges such as accounting as a score-keeping and evaluating function as well as instrument of coercion of managerial attention. To advise that it is possible to act as an interpreter of the technical features of the accounting system "and not be seen by line as an evaluator or as encroaching on line manager's decision-making process" (Horngren and Foster, 1987, p. 10) is to suggest something that, in my opinion, is not possible. It will place accountants in a defensive position of denying something which they and line often experience as true. The skills and competencies that line and staff should be taught is how to deal openly with being evaluative and with encroaching on line management space.

Another example is the predisposition of many accountants to see line management's predisposition to ignore valid feedback as a weakness on their part. A different interpretation is that this behavior, given the organizational defensive routines, is a sign of strength and skill that indeed does prevent features of the organization from blowing apart.

## CONCLUSION

Focus on the organizational defensive routines and not simply their consequences. Organizational defensive routines are created by actions that bypass embarrassment or threat and cover up that this is the case. The emphasis on bypass and cover-up has a distinct influence on what is considered to constitute a successful dealing with the problems that they create. For example, if gaming activity becomes public, management usually stops the gaming and sets new rules to reduce the likelihood that the gaming will continue. The rules could be to increase the rewards and punishments or, as in the examples described above, they could lead to a lowering of budget objectives so that they are easily achievable.

In none of the accounting literature cited above is it recommended that the players should engage rather than bypass the causes of defensive routines themselves. For example, what causes the general managers to mistrust profit center managers? If budgets are made easily achievable because general managers seek to reduce the likelihood that profit center managers will act in ways that are detrimental to the company's interest, why not explore what leads the profit center managers to act in these counterproductive ways in the first place? Otherwise, the strategy of designing easily achievable objectives is itself a bypass and cover-up of a more fundamental problem.

Otley (1988) describes how information is systematically distorted as it goes to head-quarters. He then writes, "it seems surprising that better formal methods of dealing with [uncertainty] in budgetary control systems have not yet been made" (p. 25). I asked Professor Otley what the likelihood is that representatives of headquarters and the relevant subordinates would explore face to face what leads the latter to distort the information and cover up that they are doing so. He replied that the likelihood was very low indeed. Such a strategy would be rare.

The time has come, I suggest, that we go beyond describing the gaming, distorting, etc. and beyond trying to find ways to bypass the causes of the necessity for such behavior. It is time that practitioners attempt to engage the organizational defensive routines. It is time that researchers and practitioners join to design interventions to accomplish the engagement of organizational defensive routines.

# References

Anthony, R. N., 1988, *The Management Control Function*, Boston, MA, The Harvard Business School Press.

Argyris, C., 1980, *Inner Contradictions of Rigorous Research*, New York, Academic Press.

Argyris, C., 1982, *Reasoning, Learning and Action*, San Francisco, Jossey-Bass.

Argyris, C., 1985, *Strategy, Change and Defensive Routines*, Cambridge, MA, Ballinger.

Argyris, C., and Schön, D., 1974, *Theory in Practice*, San Francisco, Jossey-Bass.

Argyris, C., and Schön, D., 1978, *Organizational Learning*, Reading, MA, Addison-Wesley.

Argyris, C., and Schön, D., 1988, "Reciprocal integrity: creating conditions that encourage personal and organizational integrity," in Suresh Srivastva and Associates (ed.) *Executive Integrity*, San Francisco, Jossey-Bass 1988, pp. 197–222.

Bandura, A., 1986, *Social Foundations of Thought and Action: A Social Cognitive Theory*, Englewood Cliffs, NJ, Prentice-Hall.

Bandura, A., 1988, "Organizational applications of social cognitive theory," *Australian Journal of Management*, 13, 2, Dec., pp. 275–301.

Birnberg, J. G., Turopoles L., and Young, S. M., 1983, "The organizational context of accounting," *Accounting, Organizations, and Society*, 8, 2/3, pp. 111–29.

Horngren, C. T., and Foster, G., 1987, *Cost Accounting: A Managerial Emphasis*, 6th edn, Englewood Cliffs, NJ, Prentice-Hall, Inc.

Ijiri, Y., 1975, *Studies in Accounting Research #10, Theory of Accounting Measurement*, New York, American Accounting Association.

Jaworski, B. J., and Young, S. M., 1988, "Goal congruence, information asymmetry, and dysfunc-tional behavior: an empirical study," University of Arizona and University of Colorado at Boulder, mimeograph.

Lawler, E. E., 1973, *Motivation in Organization*, Monterey, CA, Brooke/Cole.

Lawler, E. E., and Rhode, J. G., 1976, *Information and Control in Organization*. Pacific Palisades, CA, Goodyear.

Lewin, K., Dembo, T., Festinger L., and Snedden-Sears, P., 1944, "Level of aspiration," in Hunt, J.M.V. (ed.), *Personality and Behavior Disorder*, New York, Ronald Press.

Manzoni, J.-F., 1988, "Control systems and double-loop learning," unpublished paper, Harvard Business School.

Merchant, K. A., 1988, *Rewarding Results: Designing and Managing Contracts to Motivate Profit Center Managers*, Boston, MA, Harvard Business School.

Merchant, K. A., and Manzoni, J.-F., 1988, "The achievability of budget targets in profit centers: a field study," working paper, Boston, MA, Division of Research, Harvard Business School.

Otley, D., 1988, "Issues in accountability and control: some observations from a study of colliery accountability in the British Coal Corporation," University of Lancaster, mimeograph.

Simons, R., 1987, "Planning, control, and uncertainty: a process view," in Bruno, W. J., Jr and Kaplan R. S. (eds), *Accounting and Management: Field Study Perspectives*, Cambridge, MA, Harvard Business School Press, pp. 339–62.

Solomons, D., 1986, *Making Accounting Policy*, New York, Oxford University Press.

Sterling, R. R., 1979, *Toward a Science of Accounting*, Houston, TX, Scholars Book Co.

Wood, R., and Bandura, A., 1989, "Social cognitive theory of organizational management," *Academy of Management Review*, 14, 3, pp. 361–84.

Yu, S. C., 1976, *The Structure of Accounting Theory*, Gainesville, FL, Presses of the University of Florida.

# — 12 —

# Human Problems with Budgets

Budgets are accounting techniques designed to control costs through people. As such their impact is felt by everyone in the organization. They are continuously being brought into the picture when anyone is trying to determine, plan, and implement an organizational policy or practice. Moreover, budgets frequently serve as a basis for rewarding and penalizing those in the organization. Failure to meet the budget in many plants invites much punishment; success, much reward.

Because budgets affect people so directly, it seems appropriate to ask ourselves some questions about them. What are the effects of budgets on the human relationships in the organization? How well are budgets accomplishing their practical purposes? How can the use of budgets be improved to make them more effective? This article reports some of the results of a pilot study designed to suggest answers to questions like these.

## BACKGROUND INFORMATION

To keep the research problem within manageable limits, it was decided to focus primarily on the effects of manufacturing budgets (e.g., production, waste, and error budgets) upon the front-line supervisor. To this end our research group made a field study of three small plants (i.e., with less than 1,500 employees) manufacturing both "custom made" products and products "for stock" – all three of them unionized and covering the full range from highly skilled to nonskilled workers. (None of the plants, it should be noted, has a supervisory incentive system as part of its budget system.) In one plant we interviewed a 100 percent sample of front-line supervisors, in another a 90 percent sample, and in the third a 25 percent sample, using nondirective questions; and in addition we observed many of the same supervisors in action.

Just in case my observations suggest that I have little sympathy for budgets, let me say that any such impression stems from the negative reactions which the interviews themselves produced. This is perhaps inevitable, when one keeps the following points about budgets in mind.

- Budgets are, first of all, evaluation instruments. Because they tend to set goals against which to measure people, they naturally are complained about.
- Budgets are one of the few evaluation processes that are always in writing and therefore concrete. Thus, some of the supervisors tend to use budgets as "whipping

posts" in order to release their feelings about many other (often totally unrelated) problems.

- Budgets are thought of as pressure devices. As such they produce the same kind of unfavourable reactions as do other kinds of pressure regardless of origin. In fact, the analysis I shall make of the effects of management pressure upon supervisors is not necessarily limited to budgets. For example, a company "saddled" with a domineering executive but which has no budget may well be affected by the same factors as those reported herein.

## Preparation of Budgets

The process of preparing a manufacturing budget is much the same in all plants. It usually starts with a meeting of the controller, the assistant controller, and a group of top-management members to determine overall financial goals for the company in the forth-coming year. The controller's staff then translates the financial goals into the detailed breakdowns required for departmental budgets. This preliminary budget is then sent to all superintendents, who are asked to scrutinize it carefully and report any alterations they wish to make.

During their period of scrutiny, the superintendents (middle management) discuss the budget with their own supervisory group in a series of meetings. The first-line foremen do not usually take part in these discussions, although their ideas are requested when the superintendents deem it desirable.

Once the superintendents have their budget modifications clearly in mind, a meeting is held with the controller and his staff. Both parties come to the meeting "armed to the teeth" with "ammunition" to back their demands After the disagreements are resolved, all parties sign the new budget proposal. The superintendents return to their offices, awaiting the new budget and the expected drive to "put it over."

Some of the effects budgets seem to have upon people are problematic. Our discussion will be limited to five major areas: (1) the problem resulting from the fact that budgets are used as a pressure device, (2) the problem of the budget supervisor's success and the factory supervisor's failure, (3) the problem of department centered supervisors, (4) the problem resulting from the fact that budgets are used as a medium for personality expression, and (5) a case example of human problems related to budgets. In conclusion, some lines of action for management to follow in meeting these problems will be suggested.

## AS A PRESSURE DEVICE

One of the most common of the factory supervisors' assumptions about budgets is that they can be used as a pressure device to increase production efficiency. Finance people also admit to the attitude that budgets help "keep employees on the ball" by raising their goals and increasing their motivation. The problem of the effects of pressure applied through budgets seems to be at the core of the budget problem.

### Causes of Pressure

Employees believe that pressure from above is due to top management's assumption that most workers are basically or inherently lazy. Employees also believe that top management thinks the workers do not have enough motivation of their own to do the best possible job. And first-line supervisors have the same beliefs.

Interviews with top-management officials revealed that these employee beliefs were not totally unfounded, as a few quotations from some of the top management (both line and finance) make clear:

> I'll tell you my honest opinion. About 5 percent of the people work, 10 percent of the people think they work, and the other 85 percent would rather die than work!

> I think there is a definite need for more pressure. People have to be needled a but. Man is inherently lazy, and if we could only increase the pressure, I think the budget system would be more effective.

> There are lots of workers in this plant, hundreds of them, who don't have the capacity to do things other than what they're doing. And they're lazy! They might be able to develop some capacities, although I think there are a lot of them who couldn't even if they wanted to. But *they don't even have the desire*.

Such feelings, even if never openly expressed to the employees, filter through to them in very subtle ways. Once they sense that feelings of this kind exist in top management, they may become very resentful. Some supervisors, who apparently felt that budgets reflected this situation, expressed warnings like the following:

> The employees have an established conception of a fair output. Now, if you believe, like most financial people do, that the average worker is out to cheat the company all the time, I give up.

> Managements ought to change their attitudes that employees are out to get them.

> Well, I guess they think that we need this needling. But *I* don't think so.

## Effects of Pressure

How do people react to pressure? In the three plants studied factory supervisors felt they were working under pressure and that the budget was the principal instrument of pressure. Management exerts pressure on the work force in many ways, of course; budgets are but one way. Being concrete, however, budgets seem to serve as a medium through which the total effects of management pressure are best expressed. As such they become an excellent focal point for studying the effect of pressure on people in a working organization.

To help clarify what happens when management "puts on the pressure" let us think of a situation in specific terms.

For the sake of illustration, assume that the technical efficiency of a plant is at a maximum and that human efficiency, or effort, has to be increased if production is to be raised. The work force of the plant is producing at 70 percent of its efficiency. Since the level of efficiency is 70 percent, there must be certain forces which keep it from falling below 70 percent and certain forces which prevent it from going above 70 percent.

Some of the forces which keep it from falling below 70 percent are (1) budget talks to foremen; (2) red circling of poor showing of the departments in the budget results; (3) production drives; (4) pep talks by supervisors using budgets as evidence; (5) threat of reprimand if the budget is not met, and (6) threat of feelings of failure if budget is not met.

Some of the forces which prevent efficiency from going above 70 percent are: (1) informal agreements among employees not to produce more; (2) fear of loss of job if efficiency increases; (3) foreman (union) agreements against "speedups"; (4) abilities of individual employees; (5) abilities of work teams as a whole.

In our example the level of production is stable; therefore both sets of forces are equal in strength. Suppose that top management decides to increase production. Usually, thought is immediately given to adding more factors to those that help increase production. The logic is that if these forces can be strengthened, they overcome the forces which tend to prevent efficiency from rising, and thereby increase production.

Budgets play an important part in this new "push." Finance people are usually asked to scrutinize all budgets carefully. They are directed to cut out all "the lace and niceties" and "get down to essentials." In short, a new pressure upwards is expressed somewhere in the new budgets in terms of a "tighter" figure.

The results may be as expected. Human efficiency rises, say, 10 percent, and production is increased. A new level of efficiency is stabilized at 80 percent.

But actually something else has occurred concurrently with this new push – something which management may not perceive. Since the level of human efficiency has now been stabilized at 80 percent, presumably factors that keep production down also have increased until they equal the factors that tend to increase production. Therefore, coupled with an increase in production, the plant also acquires an increase in forces directed in the opposite direction. People and groups are now trying harder (consciously or unconsciously) to keep production at this new level and prevent it from rising again.

It is not difficult to see what happens. Tension begins to mount. People become uneasy and suspicious. They increase the informal pressure to keep production at the new level. Any new increase will have to be "paid for" by management in "free" tickets to football games, slowdowns, strikes, etc. (see Lewin, 1947).

Moreover, management has to work harder to keep the new strength of the forces which tend to drag down efficiency from overwhelming the forces which resulted in increased production. It will find itself constantly looking for new ideas, new methods to keep the production at the present level. Any slight decrease in pressure on its part will result in an immediate reduction in production.

Finally, this constant increasing pressure from top management for greater production may lead to long-term negative results. People living under these conditions tend to become suspicious of every new move management makes to increase production, particularly budgets.

### Creation of Groups

An increase in tension, resentment, suspicion, fear, and mistrust may not be the only result of ever stronger management pressures transmitted to supervisors and, in turn, to employees. We know, from psychological research, that people can stand only a certain amount of pressure. After this point is passed, it becomes intolerable to an individual. We also know that one method people use to reduce the effect of the pressure (assuming that the employees cannot reduce the pressure itself) is to join groups, which help absorb much of the pressure and thus relieve the individual personally.

The process of individuals' joining groups to relieve themselves of pressure is not a simple one. It does not occur overnight. The development of a group on such a basis seems to go through the following general stages:

1  First, the individuals sense an increase in pressure.
2  Then they begin to see definite evidences of the pressure. They not only feel it; they can point to it.

3   Since they feel this pressure is on them personally, they begin to experience tension and general uneasiness.
4   Next, they usually "feel out" their fellow workers to see if they too sense the pressure.
5   Finding out that others have noted the pressure, they begin to feel more at ease. It helps to be able to say, "I'm not the only one."
6   Finally, they realize that they can acquire emotional support from each other by becoming a group. Furthermore, they can "blow their top" about this pressure in front of their group.

Gradually, therefore, the individuals become a group because in so doing they are able to satisfy their need to (1) reduce the pressure on each individual; (2) get rid of tension; (3) feel more secure by belonging to a group which can counteract the pressure. Now, let us take a look at an actual example of the way this works out.

One of the plants we studied was under the "iron rule" of a top management executive known to the employees as "old thunder and guts" or "the whip." Many of the people interviewed in this plant mentioned what a terrible place it was in which to work. The pressure from above was high, and no one, reported the interviewees, knew exactly why it was high. Furthermore, they saw no sign that it would "let up."

As the pressure became intolerable for these people, some interesting things began to happen. Informal meetings between employees occurred with the pressure as the main topic of conversation. At first it was mentioned through jokes and "friendly gripes," but it soon became an increasing source of grievance. The private meetings expanded, and the groups became as high as eight in number. When asked why they attended these meetings, the interviewees answered: "It made me feel good to know I wasn't the only one." "If you're going through hell, it's nice to know that the others are also." And so on.

In due time the informal group feelings grew stronger, and the friendships created began to expand from the locker room to the members' homes, the local bars, and other social situations. Thus, out of these contacts there developed strong bonds which, although they were originally created by the pressure from management, had by now become reinforced and stabilized by many other social activities.

The end result, judging by the interview material, was that the new groups become extremely cohesive and "well-knit." This high degree of solidarity had the effect of permitting these people to feel that they were now free to gripe against management because they had the support and sanction of their group.

In short, new cohesive groups developed to combat management pressure. In a sense, the people had learned that they could be happier if they combined against it.

Suppose now that top management, aware of the tensions which have been generated and the groups which have been formed, seeks to reduce the pressure. The emphasis on budgets is relaxed. Perhaps even the standards are "loosened." Does this then destroy the group? After all, its primary reason for existence was to combat the pressure; and now that the pressure is gone, the group should, according to common sense, disintegrate.

But apparently the group continues to exist. Just why this is so cannot be stated conclusively. In matters like this, we must make use in part of inference. Conceivably one or more of three factors could operate to keep the group in existence. First, there may be a "time lag" between the moment management announces the new policy and the time the workers put it into effect. However, no direct evidence was obtained to substantiate this possibility.

Second, the individuals have made a new and satisfactory adjustment with one another. They have helped to satisfy each other's needs. They are, as the social scientist would say, "in equilibrium" with each other. Any attempt to destroy this balance will tend to be resisted even if the attempt represents an elimination of a "bad" or unhealthy set of conditions. People have created a stable pattern of life, and they will resist a change in this pattern.

This resistance to change is not unusual. Experimental evidence suggests that cohesive groups will tend to resist attempts which may destroy their solidarity regardless of where these attempts originate (i.e., whether they come from the members themselves or from people outside the group).

The top executives in two of the plants studied presented us with some vivid evidence of this factor. Under the influence of "high-pressure" leadership in these plants the employees seemed to become more suspicious of all management executives and at the same time more rigid and "harder to get along with." Issues which had never previously erupted were channeled through the organizational ladder as being "red-hot" grievances. Moreover, employees seemed to show great fear of any new changes. This was true even when they were assured that such changes would not occur until all their arguments had been heard and appropriate steps taken wherever possible.

The top executives summed up the situation with such phrases as: "Things weren't like they used to be." "We weren't as close as we used to be." "To be honest with you something smelled somewhere, but I was not sure what." When asked if they felt the union might be the cause of their problem, they were quick to reply that the plants were organized long before these unhappy developments.

Third, the individuals in the group may fear that pressure will come again in the future. Because of this feeling they will tend to create unreal conditions or to exaggerate existing conditions just so they can rationalize to themselves that pressure still exists and therefore that the need for the group also exists.

Here again we found substantiating evidence. Some of the employees admitted in their interviews that, while management had officially announced a new policy of less pressure and more participation, they were suspicious about the participation and considered it a new way to cover up the old pressure. Others admitted freely that they spread unverified rumors about management intentions. In short, employees were doing their best to create in their own minds the conditions that would permit them to feel that pressure was still present and the need for the group still strong.

### Pressure on Supervisors

But what about the supervisor, particularly the front-line supervisor or foreman? Strong pressures also converge upon him. How does he protect himself from these pressures?

He cannot join a group against management, as his work force does. For one thing, he probably has at least partially identified himself with management. For another, he may be trying to advance in the hierarchy. Naturally, he would not help his chances for advancement if he joined an anti-management group.

The evidence obtained from our study seems to indicate that the line supervisor cannot pass all the pressure he feels along to his workers. Time and time again factory supervisors stated that passing the pressure down would only create conflict and trouble, which in turn would lead to a decrease in production.

The question thus arises: Where does the pressure go? How do the supervisors relieve themselves of at least some of it? There is evidence to suggest at least three ways in which pressure is handled by the supervisors.

1   Interdepartmental strife. Some foremen seek release from pressure by continuously trying to blame others for the troubles that exist. In the three plants observed much time was spent by certain factory supervisors in trying to lay the blame for errors and problems on their fellow supervisors. As one foreman put it: "They are trying to throw the cat in each other's backyard."

2   Staff versus factory strife. Foremen also try to diminish pressure by blaming the budget people, production-control people, and salesmen for their problems.

3   "Internalizing" pressure. Many supervisors who do not complain about the pressure have in reality "internalized" it and, in a sense, made it a part of themselves. Such damming up of pressure can affect supervisors in at least two different ways.

(a) Supervisor A is quiet, relatively nonemotional, seldom expresses his negative feelings to anyone, but at the same time he works excessively. He can be found at his desk long after the others have gone home. He often draws the comment: "That guy works himself to death."

(b) Supervisor B is nervous, always running around "checking up" on all the employees. He usually talks fast, gives one the impression that he is "selling" himself and his job when interviewed. He is forever picking up the phone, barking commands, and requesting prompt action.

One type A supervisor made the following remark:

> I'm just about sick and tired of the damn pressure in industry. It isn't human; moreover it's unnecessary. I've learned my lesson. I'm going to do my job as well as I can and not let things bother me. Some of the men around here work with the speed of a man "hell bent for election." Not me. And to be quite honest with you, I think I get as much done as they do.

After some further questioning, the same supervisor admitted that he would "like to tell a few people off around here. Believe me, at times I'd like to tear into..." With a smile he speculated, "I wonder what they would think of me. I bet I'd surprise the daylights out of them." (There is little doubt that this supervisor would surprise those he threatens to attack. In fact, he would probably also surprise himself.)

Although we found quite a few examples of type A in our study, there were even more of type B. One budget man of the B variety, after substantial clinical interviewing, admitted that he was working too hard. But he quickly added that he *had* to overwork himself, and that, if he didn't, the organization would not be in as sound a financial position as it is now. He sadly lamented the "fact" that there was no subordinate capable of replacing him. He said that he didn't think any of the likely candidates would worry about the job as he does. Yet, interestingly enough, he seemed greatly relieved when, after his admission that he really did want to take it easy, the interviewer did not respond with astonishment.

Both of these types are expressions of tensions and pent-up emotions that have been internalized. People working under too much pressure finally are forced to "take it easy," or they find themselves with ulcers or a nervous breakdown.

But that is not the end of the problem. Constant tension leads to frustration. A person who has become frustrated no longer operates as effectively as he used to (Barker, et al., 1941). He finds that he tends to forget things he used to remember. Work that he once did with pleasure he now delegates to someone else. He is not able to make decisions as fast as previously. Now he finds he has to take a walk or get a cup of coffee – anything to "get away from it all."

## When Times Are Bad

Most finance people agreed that budgets are used with greatest force when times are bad. In their experience, as soon as sales and profits decrease and the economic future begins to look black, budgets are immediately emphasized and strengthened.

What happens in such a situation? The foreman, who is already living in a pressure-laden and tension-filled world, suddenly finds himself (with others) in a bad economic period. All the stresses and strains (at home as well as in the plant) which are associated with poor economic conditions are added to the already existing tension-creating factors in his life. To make matters worse, management usually adds a third set of such factors by applying all sorts of pressure on him through budgeting.

The results are immediately evident. Extreme application to work or extreme aggression become "natural," part of the "human nature" of the supervisor. His consequent attempts to alleviate some of the factors causing the tension may lead to quick, ill-conceived, confused, or violent action (see Leighton, 1946, especially the appendices).

Withdrawal, apathy, indifference are other results of such stresses and strains. Rumors begin to fly; mistrust, suspicion, and intolerance grow fast. In short, conflict, tension, and unhappiness become the key characteristics of the supervisor's life.

## Another Way to Raise Production

We have seen how, in order to increase human efficiency from 70 percent to 80 percent, pressure was applied through the medium of the budget. Adding to the forces which increase efficiency also strengthened the forces which decrease efficiency. Employees sought to relieve themselves of increased tension by combining into groups. Front-line supervisors, prevented from grouping, either "took it out" on other foremen or on the budget people, or else bottled it up within themselves. It seems possible that by such a procedure management has mortgaged the future to bring about an immediate increase in efficiency. This raises the question: is there any other way to increase production?

The necessity for constantly increasing efficiency is a basic fact of business life. Yet increasing efficiency generates forces which in the long run decrease efficiency, and the problem is still unsolved; it may be worse than ever. So perhaps more can be gained by concentrating on weakening those forces which tend to decrease efficiency. Basically, the only way out is to obtain the participation of the employees themselves in alleviating the factors that they have created to help keep production down.

To this end, conferences and interviews can be conducted where the employees have an opportunity to express their fears of increased production and their reasons for preventing production from rising. Needless to say, the executives in charge of such meetings should be sensitive to and aware of the factors that can cause resistances to changes. They should also be skilled in conference technique. For example, they may find it more profitable too prevent any vote by the group on a new idea, even a majority vote in acceptance. A vote in any group simply points up the fact that the group is divided. And since there may be employees who, as a result of the vote, are forced to do more than they consider a fair day's work, they are likely to have inner resistances to the changes and be the cause of further trouble. A more fruitful and lasting objective would be for the executives to help the group members define an objective upon which they all can agree.

In other words, the primary aim of such participation is to attempt to obtain acceptance of a new idea or change by removing the resisting forces within the individuals rather than by applying outside pressure.

## SUCCESS AND FAILURE

Students of human relations agree that most people want to feel a sense of achievement. We observe people constantly defining social and psychological goals, struggling to meet them, and, as they meet them, feeling successful.

Budget and factory supervisors are no exception. The typical budget or finance supervisor does his work as best he can. He hopes and expects just praise of this work from his superior. It is the "boss" who will eventually say "well done," or recommend a promotion. Most of his success comes, therefore, from his superior's evaluation. The situation is the same for the factory supervisor. He also desires success; and, like the finance supervisor, much of his success also derives from the comments and behavior of the "boss." In short, both finance and factory supervisors are oriented toward the top for an evaluation of how well they are doing their jobs.

But here is where the trouble comes in: success for budget supervisors means failure for factory supervisors.

### Role of Budget Supervisors

Our interviewers suggested that the budget people perceive their role as being "the watch-dog of the company." They are always trying to improve the situation in the plant. As one finance supervisor said: "*Always* there is room to make it better." Or as a controller said, when describing a successful budget supervisor: "The budget man has made an excellent contribution to this plant. He's found a lot of things that were *sour*. You might say a good budget man . . . lets top management know if anything is *wrong*."

In other words, the success of the finance men derives from finding errors, weaknesses, and faults that exist in the plant. But when they discover such conditions, in effect they also are singling out a "guilty party" and implicitly, at least, placing him in failure. Naturally, any comment that "things aren't going along as well as they could in your department" tends to make the particular foreman feel he is deficient.

To be sure, such an occurrence will not make every factory supervisor feel be has failed. Some of the foremen we studied apparently do not worry much about their jobs. The one who really feels the failure is the foreman who is highly interested in doing a good job.

The implications of this phenomenon are interesting. It means that management people need to think twice when they discipline their supervisors; they need to study the differential effects of discipline upon supervisors. Otherwise they may create a situation in which the supervisor who "doesn't give two hoots" about his job will be unaffected by the discipline while the supervisor who is loyal will suffer unduly.

Methods for rewarding supervisors may also need to be re-examined. The same objective increase in salary may tend to have different effects upon those receiving this increase. Thus a hard-working supervisor may feel hurt when he realizes that his "excellent" raise has also gone to supervisors who show in their work that they have no loyalty to the company.

### Reporting Foremen's Shortcomings

The way in which foremen's shortcomings are reported also is important. Let us assume that a finance man discovers an error in a particular foreman's department. How is this error reported? Does the finance man go directly to the factory foreman? In the plants studied the answer, usually, is no.

The finance man cannot take the "shortest" route between the foreman and himself. For one reason, it may be a violation of policy for staff personnel to go directly to line personnel. Even more important (from a human point of view), the finance man achieves his success when *his* boss knows he is finding errors. But his boss would never know how good a job he is doing unless he brought attention to it. In short, perhaps because of organizational regulations but basically because the measure of success in industry is derived from above, the finance man usually takes his findings to his own boss, who in turn gives them to his superior, and so on up the line and across and down into the factory line structure.

Taking the long way around has at least one more positive value for finance people. Those in middle and top management also derive some success in being able to go to the plant manager and point to some newly discovered weaknesses in the factory. Therefore, all the interested people up the entire finance structure obtain some sense of satisfaction.

But how about the factory people? The answer seems evident. In such a situation, the foreman experiences the negative feelings not only of being wrong but also of knowing that his superiors know it, and that he has placed them in an undesirable position.

Finally, to add insult to injury, the entire incident is made permanent and exhibited to the plant officials by being placed in some budget report which is to be, or has been, circulated through many top channels.

### Effects of Failure on People

One might ask: what effects has this kind of failure upon an individual? If the results were insignificant, obviously we would not be concerned. Unfortunately, such is not the case. Feelings of failure can have devastating effects upon an individual, his work, and his relationships with others.

Lippitt and Bradford (1945), reporting on some ingenious scientific experiments conducted on the subject of success and failure, state (pp. 6–10) that people who experience failures tend to:

- lose interest in their work;
- lower their standards of achievement;
- lose confidence in themselves;
- give up quickly;
- fear any new task and refuse to try new methods or accept new jobs;
- expect failure;
- escape from failure by daydreaming;
- increase their difficulty in working with others;
- develop a tendency to blame others, to be overcritical of others' work, and to get into trouble with other employees.

We found many instances of supervisors who were experiencing failure and who exhibited these characteristics. Some of them were apathetic and did not care much for their work; they would, however, break out into a smile when they talked about fishing, vacations, the company recreational events, or any other activity which took place outside the plant environment. Other supervisors blamed everyone but themselves for their problems and insisted that in the industrial world one had to "look out for himself, for it was dog eat dog." Still others expressed little confidence in themselves or their subordinates; they claimed they could trust no one, and that life in the plant was a pretty dismal affair. (Of course other factors than a sense of failure were also contributing to these attitudes, but the failure aspect was clearly important.)

### Wall between Finance and Factory

At least two more factors operate to place the finance people in the peculiar position which they hold. First, since the budget people are always looking for faults, they begin to develop a philosophy of life in which their symbol for success is not the error discovered but the very *thought* of the discovery of a possible new error. Second, the realization of the peculiar position in which they are placed leads budget people into a tendency to become defensive about their work. Though basically they may not like putting people in embarrassing positions, they have to. So they react negatively to queries about their methods, their language, their books. Sometimes they even use their technical know-how and jargon to confuse the factory people. As one budget man suggested: "After all, if the foremen don't know anything about budgets, how can they criticize them?"

Thus, the ignorance of the factory people concerning budgets may serve as a wall behind which the finance people may work unmolested, and one of the major causes of insecurity among factory supervisors concerning budgets (i.e., "we can't understand them") becomes one of the primary factors of security for the budget people.

There seems little doubt that the problem of success and failure is a major one. It needs further study. Present research has served merely to identify it.

## Department-centered Supervisors

We have already shown that supervisors are partially evaluated by budget records. The factory supervisor who desires to be known as efficient and effective must make certain that his daily, weekly, monthly, and quarterly results compare favorably with the predicted results defined by the budgets. In short, a factory supervisor will feel successful, other things being equal, when he "meets his budget."

This idea of meeting the budget is crucial. For the budget, measuring the effectiveness of a supervisor as it does, continually emphasizes to each supervisor the importance of his, and primarily his, department. The budget records he receives show his department's mistakes, his department's errors, and his department's production – all against the other departments.

Interviews with the factory supervisors left little doubt that they were department-centered in outlook rather than plant-centered. Typical comments were:

> The other day, I received an order to do a job, but no requisition. I called up production control and asked what was going on. I said to them: "Why didn't I get the requisition on that order?" They started to give excuses. Sure, they didn't worry. This was my job, just like I don't have to worry when the other departments stand still.

Each one of us gets *his* own picture when we get the budget results. Even if we got the total picture, it wouldn't mean much to us. We go right for our sheet. As I said, we might get the whole plant picture, but we're primarily interested in our own department.

I don't get a picture of the other people's budgets in this place, and I don't think I need one or even want one. My main responsibility is in this here outfit of mine. *Nowhere else.* So, let them worry about their problem, and I'll worry about mine.

The philosophy which budgets foster may be expressed this way: if every supervisor worries about his own department, there will be no trouble in the plant. Therefore, if each supervisor is made primarily responsible for the production aspect of his part of the whole picture, no problems will arise.

Such a philosophy overlooks an extremely important point. An organization is something different from the sum of the individual parts. The parts of an organization exist in certain *relationships* with each other, and it is these relationships which create the difference. One cannot conceive of "adding" together the parts of an organization any more than adding together the hundreds of pieces that make up a watch in order to make it run. The crucial problem is to place the parts in correct relationship to each other.

Without laboring the point it seems clear that important relationships between departments are disregarded by overemphasizing the individual departments. If everyone does his utmost to make certain that his own department is functioning correctly, but at the same time pays no attention to the functioning of his department in relation to others, trouble will still arise. And then, particularly in plants which make forceful use of budgets, with the supervisors trying to blame someone else so their departments are not the ones to be penalized, the conflict begins.

## Controlling Conflicts

But does not control of the relationships among departments rest with the plant manager or some higher authority? Is he not able, from his high position, to control the conflict among departments? The crux of the matter is that this is *all* the leader can do – *control* conflict. (He is unable to eliminate it, since its deep-rooted causes are not within his reach.) And because the supervisors know he controls conflict, they increasingly look to him to break up a fight or settle a dispute. Furthermore, the more successful the top leader is in this respect, the less the supervisors need to worry about cooperation. They soon learn that the leader will solve any interdepartmental problem, and become dependent on him.

Here is an example of the kind of situation that can develop. In one of the plants studied a mistake was made on a customer order. The customer returned the material to the plant, where the error was corrected, and the material was then sent back to the customer.

The cost of making the correction was nearly $3,000. The error, especially since it was so large, had to be entered in the budget records. Some department had to be charged with the error. But which department? That was the problem.

For two months supervisors of the departments most likely to be blamed waged a continuous campaign to prove their innocence. Each blamed the others. No one wanted the error on *his* record. They spent hundreds of man-hours arguing and debating among themselves. Emotions were aroused; people began calling each other names. Finally, two of the supervisors stopped talking to each other.

By this time the division manager was also in hot water. To charge any supervisor with such an error would certainly invite hostility from that supervisor – hostility which might have further effects in the future. Naturally, the division manager did not want to risk a weakening of his relationships with any of his supervisors. But he had to make a decision.

A meeting was held with the interested supervisors. The problem was discussed, and blame was placed on just about everybody and everything possible. The division manager finally gave up; he decided to charge the error to no department but rather to let the plant as a whole carry the stigma. As he himself explained it, "I thought it might be best to put the whole thing under general factory loss. Or else someone would be hurt."

This case shows that budget records, as administered, foster a narrow viewpoint. They serve as a constant reminder that the important aspect to consider is one's own department, not the over-all good of the plant.

## LEADERSHIP PATTERNS

The final problem to be discussed became evident only after a series of interviews with various controllers and top factory officials indicated that the ways in which people express their interest in budgets, and the ways in which they describe and use them, are directly related to the pattern of leadership they use in their daily industrial life. For example, when a rather domineering, aggressive, "go-getting" top executive was interviewed, his presentation of the problem tended also to be made in a domineering, aggressive, "go-getting" manner.

Therefore, although it is accurate to state that budgets are composed of "cold, nonhuman symbols" (i.e., figures), it is equally valid to state that once human beings use these "nonhuman figures," they project on to them all the emotions and feelings at their command. An incident which occurred in one of the plants studied may illustrate this point.

At the close of a particularly violent budget meeting in which a top executive had flayed his subordinates needlessly, he ended by saying: "Now, fellows, I'm sorry I got hot. But it's these budget figures – well, you know. I worry about them." The subordinates all nodded their heads to indicate that they understood. They left the meeting room thinking: "Those damn budgets again. They get the boss all upset."

But this kind of interpretation, although highly prevalent when such instances occur, is not at all accurate. It was *not* the budgets that got the boss "all upset." The budgets were merely a medium through which the boss could express the fact that he was upset. Obviously budgets per se can do nothing. It is the people who use them that cause the behavior observed. Budgets, then, can be used to express one's pattern of leadership.

Because budgets become a medium of personality and leadership expression, and since people's personalities and leadership patterns are different, our research study found a number of methods with which top factory executives used budgets. A few of these methods are illustrated by the following comments made by top factory supervisors:

> I go to the office and check that budget every day. I can then see how we're meeting it. If it's OK, I don't say anything. But if it's no good, then I come back here and give the boys a little – well, you know, I needle them a bit.

> I make it a policy to have close contact, human contact, with the people in my department. If I see we're not hitting the budget, I go out and tell them I have $40,000 on the order. Well, they don't know what that $40,000 means. They think it's a lot of money so they get to work. The human factor, that's what is important. If you treat a human being like a human being, you can use them better and get more out of them.

> You know it's a funny thing. If I want my people to read the budget, I don't shove it under their nose. I just lay it on my desk and leave it alone. They'll pick it up without a doubt.

Note how the different ways in which these men use budgets express different patterns of leadership.

## A CASE EXAMPLE

A case example may serve to illustrate the use of budgets as media through which the factory executive expresses his personality, and at the same time point up the problem of department-centered supervisors previously discussed.

A top factory executive called a meeting to discuss the problem of waste in his organization, especially the waste in two departments. Present at the meeting were the supervisors of the two departments in question, the supervisor of another department supplying the material to these two departments, two budget people, and the top executive whom we shall call the leader.

LEADER:      I've called you fellows down to get some ideas about this waste. I *can't* see why we're having so much waste. I just can't see it... Now, I've called in these two budget men to get some ideas on the subject. Maybe they can tell us how much some of the arguments you're going to give are worth.

BUDGET MAN:  (slightly red, apparently realizing he is putting the supervisors "on the spot") Well, uh, we might be wrong, but I can't see how. There's an entire 0.1 percent difference, and that's a lot.

SUPERVISOR X:  (to Supervisor Y, trying to see if he can place the blame elsewhere) Well, maybe – maybe – some of your boys are throwing away the extra material I sent back to your department.

SUPERVISOR Y:  (quickly and curtly) No, no. We're reworking the extra material and getting it ready to use over again.

SUPERVISOR X:  (changing his tack) Well – you know – I've been thinking, maybe it's those new trainees we have in the plant. Maybe they're the cause for all the waste.

LEADER:      I can't understand that. Look here – look at their budget – their waste is low.

The meeting continued for another 20 minutes. It was primarily concerned with the efforts of supervisors X and Y to fix the blame on someone besides themselves. The leader terminated the meeting by saying: "All right, look here, let's get busy on this – all of you – all of *us*. Let's do something about it."

Supervisor X left the meeting, flushed, tense, and obviously unhappy. As he passed through the door, he muttered to himself: "Those goddamn budgets!"

Supervisor Y hurried down to his area of the plant. He rushed into the office and called his subordinates abruptly: "Joe, Jim, all of you, get over here. I want to speak to you; something is up."

The subordinates came in, all wondering what had occurred. As soon as they had all assembled, the supervisor started: "Look, we've just *got* to get at this waste. It makes me look like hell. Now let's put our heads together and get on the ball."

His subordinates then set to work to locate the causes for the waste. Their methods were interesting. Each one of them *first* checked to see, as one of them put it, "that the group in the other departments aren't cheating us." A confidential statement finally came to Supervisor Y's desk from one of the subordinates to the effect that he had located the cause in Department X.

Supervisor Y became elated, but at the same time was angry at the fact that he had been made to look "sick" at the meeting with the leader. He warned: "I'm going to find out why they are making the waste. I don't mind the short end of the stick as long as it's me that's doing the trouble."

Supervisor Y roared out of his office and headed straight for the office of Supervisor X. The latter saw him coming and braced himself for the onslaught. Y started in: "I found out that it's your boys causing the waste You bastard, I want to know why..."

"Now you just hold on to your water," cut in X. "Don't get your blood up. I'll tell you..."

And so it went. In this cost-conscious plant, six people on the supervisory level spent many hours trying to place the blame on someone else.

## IMPLICATIONS FOR MANAGEMENT

This explanatory research has led to the tentative conclusion that budgets and budgeting can be related to at least four important human relations problems:

1   Budget pressure tends to unite the employees against management, and tends to place the factory supervisor under tension. This tension may lead to inefficiency, aggression, and perhaps a complete breakdown on the part of the supervisor.
2   The finance staff can obtain feelings of success only by finding fault with factory people. These feelings of failure among factory supervisors lead to many human relations problems.
3   The use of budgets as "needlers" by top management tends to make each factory supervisor see only the problem of his own department.
4   Supervisors use budgets as a way of expressing their own patterns of leadership. When this results in people getting hurt, the budget, in itself a neutral thing, often gets blamed.

Now, in the light of these findings, what lines of action should management take? Though the problems obviously are complex, and the research into them exploratory, there do appear to be two areas in which management action may prove fruitful.

### Participation in Making Budgets

The first is in the problem of getting an acceptance of budgets. Interviews with controllers suggest that this area is a crucial one. Time and time again our research group was told that the best way to gain acceptance is to have the supervisors all participate in the making of the budgets that affect them. In particular the controllers emphasized the need for participation of all key people in instituting any changes in budgets, plus the willingness on the controllers' own part to revise their budgets whenever experience indicates it necessary.

The typical controller's insistence on others' participation sounded good to us when we first heard it in our interviews. But after a few minutes of discussion it began to look as if the word "participation" had a rather strange meaning for the controller. One thing in particular happened in *every* interview which led us to believe that we were not thinking of the same thing. After the controller had told us that he insisted on participation, he would then continue by describing his difficulty in getting the supervisors to speak freely. For example:

> We bring them in, we tell them that we want their frank opinion, but most of them just sit there and nod their heads. We know they're not coming out with exactly how they feel. I guess

budgets scare them; some of them don't have too much education . . . Then we request the line supervisor to sign the new budget, so he can't tell us he didn't accept it. We've found a signature helps an awful lot. If anything goes wrong, they can't come to us, as they often do, and complain. We just show them their signature and remind them they were shown exactly what the budget was made up of.

Such statements seem to indicate that only "pseudo-participation" is desired by the controller. True participation means that the people can be spontaneous and free in their discussion. Participation, in the real sense of the word, also involves a group decision which leads the group to accept or reject something new. Of course, organizations need to have their supervisors accept the new goals, not reject them; however, if the supervisors do not really accept the new changes but only say they do, then trouble is inevitable. Such halfhearted acceptance makes it necessary for the person who initiated the budget or induced the change, not only to request signatures of the "acceptors" so that they cannot later on deny they "accepted," but to be always on the lookout and apply pressure constantly upon the "acceptors" (through informal talks, meetings, and "educational discussions of accounting").

In other words, if top-management executives are going to use participation, then they should use it in the real sense of the word. Any dilution of the real thing "will taste funny," and people will not like it.

Of course employees cannot participate in all phases of the plant budget. In the typical plant most of the overall goals of a plant or even a department cannot be set by the members of the plant or the department. But the ways in which these goals are to be accomplished can be decided upon cooperatively by the interested employees. In other words, if top management has set down a profit goal for the year, then there is not much sense in saying the people actually participated in setting that goal. Nor should management try to get them to feel this is *their* goal in the sense that they created it. But top management can try to make them feel that this is their goal in the sense that they participated in a decision to accept it.

We have found that goals are most often accepted if the individual members can come together in a group, freely discuss their opinions concerning these goals, and take part in defining the steps by which these goals will be accomplished.

## Training in Human Relations

The second area in which management action may attack these budget problems is that of training in human relations.

Our interviews with the top controllers constantly brought out the "figure-conscious," narrow-minded rigidity of most finance people. Here are some typical criticisms of accountants:

Most of them are warped and they have narrow ideas. That, incidentally, is one of the failures of our educational system. We give the fellows all the textbook stuff, but we never teach them how to "sell" accounting.

Most of our accountants are narrow and shortsighted. They have a narrow breadth of view. They are what I call "shiny pants bookkeepers." They're technicians. They don't know how to handle people.

I might add, right here and now, that I think one of the worst human problems we have is the poor job of "selling" that is done with cost records and budgetary control. I think our accounting people are very, very poor in ability to get along with people and to sell them correctly. In fact, I'd go as far as to say that the better the accountant, the poorer he is in human relations. I feel quite strongly about this.

Our findings indicate that, first of all, more instruction in human relations needs to be given to students of cost accounting and budgeting at the college level. We are not prepared to say in what form this instruction can best be integrated into the curriculum, though it appears that such instruction could well be fitted into the traditional case approach of accounting instruction. The accounting and cost-control cases usually present to the student some major technical problems for solution. At the end of each case the student is asked to answer certain questions, and these could well include some issues involving the human relations implications of the problem.

As far as industry's role in training is concerned, I doubt that its main function is to make budget people familiar with the factory people's tasks. To do such a job thoroughly would require a lengthy and extremely expensive training program. Moreover, wherever plants have attempted to have the finance people visit the factory departments and learn some of the factory people's problems, this training has helped but does not seem to have solved the underlying problem.

Rather, the training should be focused on the underlying problems, not on the superficial difficulties. In line, then, with the major problems identified by our analysis up to this point, the following specific suggestions seem appropriate:

1   The training should be focused to help the finance staff perceive the human implications of the budget system.
2   The training should help show the finance staff the effects of pressure upon people. Thorough discussions seem necessary to understand the advantages and disadvantages of applying such pressure.
3   The training should also include discussions concerning the effects of success and failure. The accounting staff should be helped to perceive their difficult position, namely, that of placing others in failure. They should also be taught the symptoms of people who feel they have failed. Most important, the course should include practical techniques which the finance staff can use to get along better with the factory people, knowing full well that they may place these factory people in failure.
4   Again, the human relations training should include thorough discussions of the human problems related to the department-centeredness of supervisors that is caused by budgets. The finance people should be helped to perceive this department-centeredness as a defense on the part of the factory supervisors rather than as the "narrow-mindedness" which many of them seem to think it is.
5   Finally, there needs to be some instruction in the basic content of human relations as a field of study. This includes the concepts of informal and formal organizations, industrial organizations as social systems, status systems in industrial organizations, and such subjects as interviewing, counseling, and leadership.

Throughout such training the emphasis should be placed upon these supervisors' learning to understand themselves (e.g., their feelings, their values, their prejudices). Once they have been helped to evaluate themselves as human beings, then they are better able to understand their human effects on the others with whom they deal as experts in their particular field.

As for training methods, it follows that the trainer should keep lecturing to a minimum. Case discussion (Roethlisberger, 1951; see also Andrews, 1951), role-playing (Argyris, 1952), and the member-centered conference (Argyris, 1951) are examples of methods which may be profitably used. The conference sessions should be so designed that the leader helps the trainees help themselves. Since the group members are to be the center of their own problem-solving conferences, the leader will take only such roles as a "summarizer of opinions," "clarifier of feelings," and "instigator of free creative thinking (Argyris, 1951)."

The emphasis upon understanding oneself is crucial. Time and time again, we found examples where the bases for many so-called organizational or technical problems were actually rooted in the feelings people held.

The end result is that the financial staff will become more aware of the human problems existing in organizations. Whatever specific steps they take or new attitudes they adopt because of their better understanding of themselves and others in the organization cannot fail to make their use of budgets more constructive, i.e., more effective in terms of long-run results.

# References

Andrews, K. R., 1951, "Executive Training by the Case Method," *Harvard Business Review*, September, pp. 58–70.

Argyris, C., 1951, "Techniques of 'Member-Centered' Training," *Personnel*, November, pp. 236–41.

Argyris, C., 1952, "Role-playing in Action," NYSSIRL Bulletin Ithaca, NY, Cornell University, April.

Barker, R. G., Dembo, T., and Lewin, K., 1941, "Frustration and Regression," *University of Iowa Studies in Child Welfare*, 18, 1, p. 314.

Leighton, A., 1946, *The Governing of Men*, Princeton: Princeton University Press.

Lewin, K., 1947, "Group Decision and Social Change," in Newcomb, T., and Hartley, E. L., (eds) *Readings in Social Psychology*, New York, Henry Holt & Co., especially p. 342.

Lippitt, R., and Bradford, L., 1945, "Employee Success in Work Groups," *Personnel Administration*, December 4, pp. 6–10.

Roethlisberger, F. J., 1951, "Training Supervisors in Human Relations," *Harvard Business Review*, September, pp. 47–57.

# — 13 —

# Bridging Economics and Psychology: The Case of the Economic Theory of the Firm

All theories require valid information for both testing and utilization. Useful theories also facilitate production of such valid information for self-testing. In this chapter, I will attempt to show how a social-cognitive-clinical theory of intervention can be used to increase the production of valid economic information in situations that previously generated information noise. Furthermore, I will suggest that one cause of this information noise has been the adherence to features of microeconomic theory, including the behavioral theory of the firm.

## NOISE AND VALID INFORMATION

Noise may be defined as distortion in the information being used. Psychologists studying the amount of noise in any system often differentiate between "hot" and "cold" variables that can affect the amount of this noise. Cold variables are related to cognitive processes, and hot variables are related to emotional and motivational factors. Let me also differentiate between individual and organizational (or system) variables.

In figure 13.1, I identify four possible causes of information noise. In the case of the first quadrant, Knight (1965) and Hayek (1945) have stated that the data required by the "economic calculus" implicit in economic theory could never be known by a single mind because of the limits of the information processing capacities of the human mind (Hayek, 1945, p. 519). Miller (1956) and Simon (1957) studied this assertion more empirically and confirmed the finite information processing capacities of the human mind. Turning to the second quadrant, Ackoff (1967) has suggested that information systems can produce so much information that it swamps the decision maker and reduces the likelihood that he or she will make informed decisions. Wagner (1971) has shown that many of the systems models used by operations researchers are not helpful to decision makers because they often require (1) the collection and analysis of more information than decision makers can use and (2) a level of precision that, even if achieved, is beyond use by decision makers under the pressures and complexities of everyday life.

Elsewhere (Argyris, 1979), I have suggested that the theory of control embedded in the use of most management information systems is consistent with top-down, unilateral control where those above seek to win rather than to learn. Accordingly, subordinates protect themselves by providing as valid information as they can while still protecting themselves. This can lead to the subordinates' systematically distorting information.

|  | Individual | Organization |
|---|---|---|
| Cold | Finite information processing capacities<br><br>1 | Management information systems<br><br>2 |
| Hot | 3<br>Individual defenses | 4<br>Organizational defensive routines |

**Figure 13.1**   Variables creating information noise

The motivational and personality literature has documented that noise can be created by individual psychological defensive mechanisms and emotions (quadrant 3 of figure 13.1). For example, Freud showed how psychological defense mechanisms such as suppression, repression, denial, and displacement can influence significantly how individuals view reality and the modes by which they cope with it (Maddi, 1980).

## Organizational Defensive Routines and Noise

Recent research (Argyris, 1985) suggests that organizations have defensive routines that can play an important role in producing noise (quadrant 4). Ironically, these defensive routines are most intrusive precisely when valid information is most needed: when substantive issues containing potential embarrassment or threat to the organization arise.

Organizational defensive routines are routinized policies or actions intended to prevent the experience of embarrassment or threat. However, they are unlikely to reduce the factors that caused the embarrassment or threat in the first place. Organizational defensive routines are anti-learning and overprotective.

Most participants in organizations can identify organizational defensive routines. Yet, the same participants appear to be unaware of using such routines themselves. Acting consistently with defensive routines is usually done skillfully, and skillful behavior is tacit. It is tacit because skillful behavior is automatic and taken for granted (Argyris, 1982; Polanyi, 1967).

Organizational defensive routines differ from individual defensive routines in that they exist even though (1) individuals move in and out of the organization, (2) psychologically different individuals use them in the same way, (3) the source of learning them is socialization, and (4) the trigger for use is concern and being realistic. Once operative, individuals bypass them and act as if they are not bypassing them. This builds up camouflage and further defensive routines. Soon, the network of camouflage and deception is so powerful that the participants think it is unrealistic to do anything but bypass it.

I will explore an example of a prominent organizational defensive routine that is often found in decentralized organizations, but is certainly not limited to such organizations.

## Mixed Messages and Decentralization

A persistent feature of genuine decentralization is the tension between autonomy and control among executive levels. Executives frequently deal with this dilemma by sending mixed messages: "You are running the show, but ..." (see chapter 4, especially pp. 93–4). These develop into organizational defensive routines characterized by unacknowledged inconsistencies, which, by remaining unacknowledged, become undiscussable and unin-fluenceable (which features themselves become undiscussable ...). Actors fail to recognize their own part in the cycle, blaming the organizational defensive routines and feeling powerless and cynical about change. Organizational defensive routines are, according to the senior executives that I studied as well as my own observations, a key cause of what the executives often describe as a monumental barrier to valid economic information (Argyris, 1985). The executives report that they violate their sense of stewardship when, in order to get the job done, they bypass this barrier. However, the thought of engaging and confront-ing the defensive routines seems to them to be impractical and unrealistic.

## ENTER APPLIED ECONOMISTS

Recently, I have studied the activities of internal and external economic strategy planners who use economic models (e.g., models of competition) and who conduct rigorous empirical research to produce economic plans for organizations. The professionals cooperated because the implementation of their economic strategies was being seriously impaired by organiza-tional defensive routines. They wished to reduce the noise related to all quadrant outlined in figure 13.1, but especially quadrant 4.

They believed that the implementation of their ideas required a world that was as noise-free as possible. Their belief was consistent with the fundamental assumption of classical economic theory. Thus, these applied economists, who often looked with disdain at classical economics, were seeking a behavioral world that approximated one of the theory's major assumptions. I will return to this puzzle later.

I conducted interventions in several management consulting firms but will describe my work with one of them: a leader in the field of strategy formulation and implementation. My colleagues and I discovered that they (a management consulting firm) had their own defensive routines concerning the management of their firm, the clients, the formulation of valid strategy plans, and the implementation of these plans. Thus, before we could help them to reduce the noise in the clients' contexts, we had to help them reduce the noise in their own management of the firm.

We discovered differential willingness to learn the interpersonal, group, and intergroup skills required to manage their own internal relationships or their relationships with their clients in ways that reduced the noise. In a population of 20 officers, about 10 thought the ideas were great, difficult, but worth implementing. About three thought they were foolish and dangerous. The rest wavered back and forth, usually seeking what their more senior colleagues would decide. Needless to say, there was also a differential ability to learn, although my own estimation was that over 80 percent of the officers could learn the new skills if they wished to do so. The theory and methods used to produce the learning required to reduce organizational defensive routines are described in Argyris (1982, 1985), Argyris, et al. (1985) and Argyris and Schön (1974, 1978).

The clients were ambivalent regarding hiring consultants to give advice. All agreed that organizational defensive routines inhibited the effective production of valid information. On the other hand, many wondered if the consultants had the intervention skills to tackle the defenses constructively. Shades of the monumental barrier!

In spite of all these problems, some officers did learn the new skills well enough to use them in managing their own case teams and their relationships with clients. These client-consultants proved that organizational defensive routines could be interrupted and reduced, that this in turn resulted in the reduction of noise (economic and behavioral), and that this in turn led to an increase in the amount of valid economic information given to and used by decision makers. Moreover, the clients not only learned to solve the immediate economic issues, they also began to develop individual and group skills to learn how to learn. This in turn necessarily changed the norms in the culture toward rewarding learning experiments (Argyris, 1985).

The cases presented below illustrate that the barrier to valid economic information produced by defensive routines can be broken without the client system's blowing apart and that better economic information can be produced that increases the probability of effective development and implementation of economic strategies.

The cases do not illustrate that these consequences necessarily lead to more profits. Profits are the result of more complex sets of factors than those being discussed in this chapter. Much more research is needed before we will be able to connect our results to such variables as costs and profits. The thrust, to repeat, is to illustrate that the monumental barrier to valid economic information when issues are complex and threatening can be reduced. (All cases are taken from Argyris, 1985.)

## Case 1

The first case is related to quadrant 1: creating groups whose members are able to act as external memories for each other and help to produce knowledge that was beyond the capabilities of the individual members.

A senior consultant who was an engineer and an applied economist by education was participating in a discussion of pricing policies with a top management group of a large business organization. At a particular point in time, he interrupted the discussion to review the policies and then to point out three inconsistencies embedded in these pricing policies. The group listened attentively, and when he finished, the following conversation took place:

CLIENT 1: That's interesting. I think you are correct in your analysis. As I listened to you, I realized that I had seen [a certain] feature of the problem, but not the rest of it.

CLIENT 2: I agree this is interesting. I did not see what you [Client 1] saw. I knew about [certain] features. I, like you, had not put the pieces together the way he did.

CLIENT 3: (Said the same, but pointed to a different part of the analysis about which he was familiar.)

After several more such contributions, the executives, with the help of the consultant, developed a pricing policy that was significantly more effective in that more sales were produced during the next two quarters.

After the new pricing policy was formulated, the consultant said:

CONSULTANT: I would like to revisit what happened during our meeting for a different purpose. If I recollect correctly, each of you was aware of different features of my analysis before I made it. Once we put them together, they led to a nonobvious change in pricing policy.

CLIENTS: Yes, yes...

CONSULTANT: I should now like to ask what it is about the dynamics of this group that prevented you from developing your individual views into a coherent economic picture without my intervention?
(Silence)

CLIENT:           As I said, I found your analysis superb. I am pleased with the new pricing policy. However, I am bewildered by your latest question. We did not hire you to be our shrink.

CONSULTANT:  I do not want to say or do anything that would cause me to lose you as a client. If you and the others wish me to stay away from the group defenses that inhibit your problem–solving, I will do so. However, I should like to suggest that if we do not deal with the organizational and group defenses, they will become activated and harm any new strategies that we develop.

After a lengthy and somewhat defensive discussion on the part of the clients, they agreed that they should explore the defensive routines that they used while making economic decisions. The result was that the level of trust among them was increased and the use of guile was decreased (Williamson, 1975). They began to question each others' data and to reason more effectively. They also tended to increase the frequency with which they became the external memories of their colleagues by providing needed data. Up to this point, they had not done so.

Working on these issues caused some degree of discomfort for all the members. Yet they preservered, not because they liked what they were experiencing, nor because the changes could increase the quality of their lives. The most powerful reason, they reported, was their sense of responsibility as economic stewards in a top management team. They framed their stewardship as taking any actions that would lead to decreases in organizational noise and increases in economic information, a frame that was consistent with the idealized assumptions of classical economic theory: namely a noise-free set of decision making processes.

## Case 2

The second case is related to the information systems that get in the way of producing valid information (quadrant 2). In this study, we focused on a large divisional management information system (MIS) that was designed to provide the management with economic information.

The senior consultant in this case listened attentively for several sessions as the MIS representatives described the financial numbers they collected. After several sessions, the consultant reported to me:

> I realized that the stuff they were presenting was not going to serve their purposes [to convince corporate decision makers], and judging from the little agreement among themselves, there was little commitment [at the functional group level] as to what was a valid economic picture.

> The clients were exluding important analyses of supply and demand, elasticity and impact on prices; it was subsumed and not made explicit. They had not reconciled their own financial statement to see what are the pieces of it and how well the pieces fit or did not fit into a consistent whole.

The consultant could have found ways to bypass the behavioral problems that led to poor economic information. These actions could have varied from diplomatically and indirectly communicating his views to the more likely action of withholding them, focusing on getting the economic numbers, and later producing a report to fulfill the consulting contract.

The consultant chose instead to focus on discussing the behavioral problems during the meeting. He accomplished this purpose by identifying inconsistencies and gaps in the economic numbers and reasoning. For example, as the consultant helped the clients to bring to the surface inconsistencies in pricing policies and economic forecasting, one client said that the problem did not lie simply with them and that the entire industry was thinking the same way.

As the discussion progressed, the consultant was able to get the clients to focus on the validity of the financial numbers. The MIS people began to describe the games that they said they had to play in order to survive. For example:

1   Even after we negotiate with each other about the meaning of the financial numbers, and even after we sign off on them, often they are changed.
2   In the real world, we have difficulty in producing valid numbers; although in our reports, we act as if every number is sound.

From these discussions, the consultant was able to develop a map of how the MIS produced poor information and poor plans (figure 13.2); how in turn, the MIS systems eventually became discredited in the eyes of the senior management; and how the MIS professionals became distanced from the very economic problem-solving activities they were supposed to help resolve.

The consultant was able to help the MIS players work through many of the problems described above. The result was an economic information system that produced numbers that were significantly more valid, which then were used in economic decision making, and which decreased the credibility and distancing problems described in figure 13.2. The case illustrates how changes in quadrant 4 (defensive routines) led to changes in quadrant 2 (information systems).

## Case 3

The third case represents issues that are related to quadrants 3 and 4. The chief executive officer (CEO) of a large organization disliked conflict. Whenever he felt that conflict would erupt, he would use a range of tactics to avoid it, including ignoring it, steering away from it, calling for a break, or delaying it by suggesting further study.

The planning people recognized this personal defense and did their best to bypass it. One strategy was to document heavily any idea that they thought was controversial. Another was not to present controversial ideas during the session or to water them down so that they would not appear to be controversial. Both strategies irked the CEO, who felt that the planners were "a bunch of pencil pushers and paper fillers." The planners also disliked their strategies. They felt that they were not being professional.

The consultants expressed the following dilemma: if the avoidance of conflict issue were not engaged, no new planning system would work. However, engaging this issue might represent a cure that made the illness worse: a CEO illness. The result could be dangerous to the client relationship and to the organization. After considerable work, the consultants felt they were ready to take the risk of engaging the CEO and others rather than bypassing the problem.

The initial reaction of the CEO was defensive. "I think you are in an area beyond your competence. You are not psychologists. You are strategy consultants." The consultants were able to respond to these and other defensive reactions constuctively as follows:

CONSULTANT:  We believe that we can develop a new strategic planning process. But, in all honesty, we also believe that the behavioral issues that we have just described will eventually torpedo the new planning process.

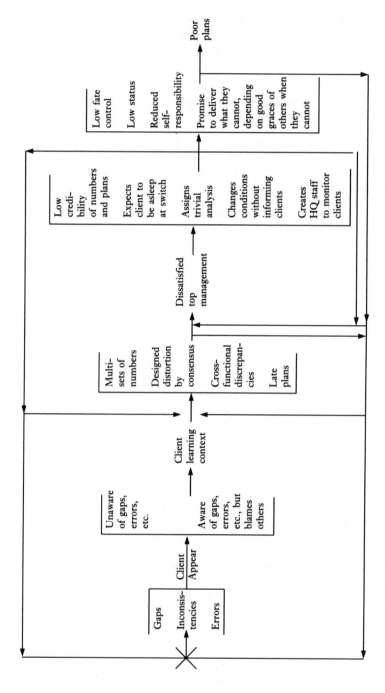

**Figure 13.2** MIS and learning

CLIENT:              I see your problem. But do you think you can deal with these issues
                     constructively?
CONSULTANT:   I believe that we can. I also believe that this group has much to contribute.
                     Why not start out slowly and monitor the process carefully?

Two sets of results occurred. First, the CEO and his top management team decided to
undergo some education in reducing these types of defensive routines. More importantly,
the planners then reduced their defensive strategies and produced reports that were more
hard hitting, forthright, and above all contained economic information that was more valid.

## Case 4

The fourth case deals with top management defensive routines that inhibited the production
of valid economic information (quadrant 4).
    In this case, a senior consultant attempted an intervention to interrupt the reasoning
games among a top management group. This is not easy to do; nor would the consultant
maintain that he did it in the best possible way. The point is that even with the errors made,
it led to important positive consequences. Further, the consultant may have had a greater
degree of freedom to err on the behavioral features (including his own behavior) because he
was dealing with economic issues that go to the heart of the stewardship of the top
administrators in organizations.
    The consultants had set two objectives for themselves during a meeting with the CEO
and his immediate subordinate: the first was to present an economic analysis whose
inevitable conclusion would seriously question several economic business plans made by
the top group. The consultants intended to assess the top's resistance to exploring the
possibility that their program was in error by careful attention to their reactions to the
analysis. The consultants' second objective was to help the clients explore the nature of their
organizational culture and the economic decision making processes that encouraged individuals to withhold information that permitted errors to occur.
    As the consultants presented their analysis, the CEO recognized the inevitable conclusion
and asked, in effect, if this conclusion meant that their present economic plan might be in
error. The consultant replied affirmatively, and added that the presentation was based on
data primarily obtained from their subordinates.
    A discussion then ensued in which the CEO asked if the members of his group, who had
recommended the economic decision, were aware of the data. The consultant replied that
they had heard many doubts expressed about the economic decisions from many different
levels of the organization.

CEO:                 I'm disturbed. Are you telling me that individuals at the lower levels
                     believe that whatever they recommend regarding economic decisions
                     will not be seriously considered?
CONSULTANT:   Yes, our team was told that many people at the top would be closed to
                     hearing things [that were contrary to present business plans].
CEO:                 If we were closed, you would not have been hired. We hired you because
                     we judged that you would tell it as you see it.
CONSULTANT:   It is because we believe what you have just said that we are behaving as we
                     are in this meeting.
                                        (Later)
CEO:                 I thought we had pretty open discussions up and down the line.
                                        (Later)

CEO:                    (To the consultants and subordinates): Have you found anyone who
                        thought [our economic decision] was a good idea?
                                (Silence)
CONSULTANT: It is interesting that most people who had doubts could recite accurately
                        how the decision was taken although they did not agree; they felt it was
                        expected that they wait [two years] before they could judge the decision
                        fairly.
CEO:                    Does this include people who made the recommendation?
                                (Silence)
CONSULTANT: Yes, it does.
                                (Later)
CEO:                    The implication is that some executives are proposing ideas that their
                        people do not agree with.

The consultant then described what he felt was a set of very subtle games that caused the problems. For example, functional representatives at all levels tended to be candid about their doubts. However, they felt little or no need to work through their doubts. The resolution of doubts was left to the top. In this structure, it meant that resolution was left to the CEO.

But, as we have seen, the players censored important economic information that went to the top and acted as if they were not doing so. As the discussion evolved superiors would push for consensus in order to communicate something to the top. The subordinates saw this as their cue to give in. They would then repeat their doubts in ways that were ambiguous and imprecise, but agree with the recommendation. As this process was repeated through several layers of the hierarchy, the differences were rounded out and the CEO received the final report that gave the impression of a strong recommendation.

CEO:                    This is important. If you are correct, we have more than an economic
                        problem. We have some very fundamental management problems.
                                (Later)
CEO:                    No one who works for me should feel afraid.
                                (Later)
                        This comes a shock. I urge you to stop [the economic analysis] and research
                        what you have stated carefully.
CONSULTANT: We are prepared to make a further presentation and some proposals.

This discussion was the most animated one that the top management committee ever had. It should be pointed out that one or two of the people close to the CEO felt that the issue of undiscussability should never have been raised. Galbraith (1967) would have found their comments heartwarming, because they were indeed acting to protect their technocratic empires.

However, most of the executives agreed with the CEO who, while he expressed disbelief and anger, simultaneously encouraged the consultants to be candid. He stated: "Don't let my reactions or anyone else's distract you from telling us what you believe to be the truth."

Two days later an executive from the financial department, who had not attended the meeting described above, remarked to another executive that something had happened to the CEO. It was the first time that he had seen the CEO ask sharp questions about economic issues. Three days later at another meeting that was taped, the executive continued his more proactive stance regarding economic issues. He appeared to no longer take anything for granted. The following are examples of the questions he asked:

Why do we carry so many different types of () [a practice carried on for years]?

How do you know that we are overpriced [after hearing that a product is bought for $5.00 and sold for $2.50]? What I am beginning to realize is that there is no coordinating between purchasing and sales.

What I now realize is that we really do not know our acquisition costs. I want to make sure we become much better at knowing our economic position much more accurately than is now the case.

These cases illustrate that the barrier to valid information, decribed by practitioners and scholars as monumental, can be reduced. The results include: (1) the flow of more valid economic information, (2) the development of group cultures whose members can help each other overcome inherent information-processing limits, and (3) the reduction of polarized win–lose dynamics between coalition groups.

To summarize the discussion so far, it is possible to help individuals in organizations produce more valid economic information related to nontrivial economic decisions. The enhanced valid information did lead to developing indexes of more effective economic performance (reduced costs) in the world of practice. However, this conclusion remains to be tested more thoroughly by further research.

## REFLECTING ON FEATURES OF MICROECONOMIC THEORY

The interventions described above lead to questions about some economic concepts in the behavioral theory of the firm. They also indicate another way by which features of social-cognitive–clinical psychologies can be interrelated with features of microeconomic theory.

First, Knight (1965) and Hayek (1945) are correct in suggesting that the human mind can never know all the data required by the "economic calculus" implicit in economic theory (Hayek, 1945, p. 519). From this it follows (Simon, 1957) that people do not have the wit to maximize or optimize. The most decision makers can do is to "satisfice," to take the alternative that seems best to them at a given moment in time (Simon, 1957).

Our research suggests that there is an important danger in using the concept of satisficing without exploring its relationship with defensive routines. For example, the clients who were unaware of the inconsistencies in their marketing and financial policies (Case 1) were ready to satisfice at a much lower level than they were after they explored their defensive routines as a group. Moreover, they were unaware of this possibility until the intervention. The consultant helped them to see that their defensive routines made it unlikely that they would detect and correct errors in their economic reasoning. They were not learners, and they were unaware that this was the case. Satisficing, as presently understood, runs the risk of reinforcing organizational defensive routines.

Let us turn to the behavioral theory of the firm as represented by Bower (1970), Cyert and March (1963), March (1981), and Williamson (1975). Cyert and March (1963) have pointed out that there are many important hot organizational factors that significantly affect the way decisions are made. For example, coalitions they studied fought each other in ways that only partially resolved the conflict, search was limited to satisficing choices, and organizational learning was importantly impaired (pp. 116–27). Bower (1970) has added more hot organizational factors in the form of organizational politics and maneuvering. Williamson (1975) has added factors such as opportunism (defined as self-interest with guile) that influenced the degree of honesty and trust that could be produced among the actors, which in turn influenced the quality of the economic information available to the participants.

In Cases 2, 3, and 4, we saw how conflict was, at best, only partially resolved and how search was limited. In Case 2, we saw how coalition groups can form between divisional and corporate levels in which the former produce invalid economic information to protect themselves. This in turn, gets them in trouble with the corporate hierarchy. The division then feels more threatened, and the noise in the economic information they produce increases.

Economic theory as represented by Cyert, March, Bower, and Williamson includes a tacit theory of human behavior and motivation that is self-fulfilling and self-contained. Partial resolution of conflict, problemistic search, and satisficing do exist. It is probably true, as Williamson (personal communication, November 30, 1982) has suggested, that guile and mistrust will not be reduced. The politics that Bower described are to be expected in a world dominated by organizational defensive routines. These authors have observed the world accurately.

The question that remains to be asked is whether the world must remain as they have described it. The concepts of the behavioral theory of the firm (such as satisficing, partial resolution of conflict, guile, politics, and mistrust) are consistent with and reinforce organizational defensive routines, including the collusion that is embedded in these defensive routines. Such concepts are therefore unintended creators and reinforcers of the very noise that economic theory requires be reduced.

The research that led to the interventions described here is based on a perspective that has been called action-science (Argyris, 1982; Argyris and Schön, 1974, 1978; Argyris, et al., 1985). A fundamental tenet of this approach is that social scientists should aspire to go beyond describing the world as is, for two reasons. The first is that by conducting research on changing the status quo, we learn much about how the status quo resists change. Such knowledge is necessary if we are to develop more complete descriptions of the world as it is (Argyris, 1980). Second, by developing models of new worlds (for example, those that would be lower in organizational defensive routines), it is possible to see how social scientists may unknowingly become servants of the status quo.

## CONCLUSION

A body of knowledge (initially motivated to make organizational life more humane), is being developed that can be used to reduce organizational defensive routines. The reduction of these routines, in turn, makes it possible to reduce many causes of noise in economic information in all the quadrants. The intervention processes do require individuals, groups, intergroups, and organizations to take behavioral risks. The commitment to persevere in this endeavor has come primarily from executives or applied economists who accept the fundamental assumption of classical economics: the importance of attaining as noise-free a world as possible. The classical economic assumption about information now becomes an ideal state never to be reached, but always to be approximated. The results of research on defensive routines and how to change them can become the vehicles for economists to strive to approximate their ideal. We may have discovered new ways by which issues about economic performance and quality of life can be genuinely integrated and enhanced.

## References

Ackoff, R. L., 1967, "Management misinformation systems," *Management Science*, 14, 4, pp. B147–56.

Argyris, C., 1979, "Some inner contradictions in management information systems," in *Proceedings of Symposium on Managerial Accounting*, Department of Accountancy, University of Illinois.

Argyris, C., 1980, *Inner Contradictions of Rigorous Research*, New York, Academic Press.

Argyris, C., 1982, *Reasoning, Learning, and Action*, San Francisco, Jossey-Bass.

Argyris, C., 1985, *Strategy, Change, and Defensive Routines*, Boston, Pitman.

Argyris, C., and Schön, D., 1974, *Theory in Practice*, San Francisco, Jossey-Bass.

Argyris, C., and Schön, D., 1978, *Organizational Learning*, Reading, MA, Addison-Wesley.

Argyris, C., Putnam, R., and Smith, D. M., 1985, *Action Science*, San Francisco, Jossey-Bass.

Bower, J. L., 1970, *Managing the Resource Allocation Function: A Study of Corporate Planning and Investment*, Division of Research, Graduate School of Business Administration, Harvard University, Cambridge, MA.

Cyert, R. M., and March, J. G., 1963, *A Behavioral Theory of the Firm*, Englewood Cliffs, NJ, Prentice-Hall.

Galbraith, J. K., 1967, *The New Industrial State*, Boston, Houghton-Mifflin.

Hayek, F. A., 1945, "The use of knowledge in society," *American Economic Review*, 35, 4, pp. 519–30.

Knight, H., 1965, *Risk, Uncertainty, and Profit*, New York, Harper & Row (original work published 1921).

Maddi, S. R., 1980, *Personality Theories: A Comparative Analysis* (4th edn), Homewood, Ill, Dorsey Press.

March, J. G., 1981, "Decisions in organizations and theories of choice," in Van de Ven, A., and Joyce, W. (eds), *Perspectives on Organizational Design and Behavior*, New York, Wiley, pp. 205–44.

Miller, G. A., 1956, "The Magical Number Seven, Plus or Minus Two: Some Limits on Our Capacity for Processing Information," *Psychological Review*, 63, pp. 81–96.

Polanyi, M., 1967, *The Tacit Dimension*, Garden City, NY, Doubleday.

Simon, H. A., 1957, *Models of Man*, New York, Wiley.

Wagner, H. M., 1971, "The ABCs of OR," *Operations Research*, 19, 6, pp. 1259–81.

Williamson, O. E., 1975, *Markets and Hierarchies: Analyses and Anti-Trust Implications*, New York, Free Press.

# Part III

## The Counterproductive Consequences of Organizational Development and Human Resource Activities

# — 14 —

# Good Communication that Blocks Learning

Twenty-first-century corporations will find it hard to survive, let alone flourish, unless they get better work from their employees. This does not necessarily mean harder work or more work. What it does necessarily mean is employees who've learned to take active responsibility for their own behavior, develop and share first-rate information about their jobs, and make good use of genuine empowerment to shape lasting solutions to fundamental problems.

This is not news. Most executives understand that tougher competition will require more effective learning, broader empowerment, and greater commitment from everyone in the company. Moreover, they understand that the key to better performance is better communication. For 20 years or more, business leaders have used a score of communication tools – focus groups, organizational surveys, management-by-walking-around, and others – to convey and to gather the information needed to bring about change.

What *is* news is that these familiar techniques, used correctly, will actually inhibit the learning and communication that twenty-first-century corporations will require not just of managers but of every employee. For years, I have watched corporate leaders talking to subordinates at every level in order to find out what actually goes on in their companies and then help it go on more effectively. What I have observed is that the methods these executives use to tackle relatively simple problems actually prevent them from getting the kind of deep information, insightful behavior, and productive change they need to cope with the much more complex problem of organizational renewal.

Years ago, when corporations still wanted employees who did only what they were told, employee surveys and walk-around management were appropriate and effective tools. They can still produce useful information about routine issues like cafeteria service and parking privileges, and they can still generate valuable quantitative data in support of programs like total quality management. What they do *not* do is get people to reflect on their work and behavior. They do not encourage individual accountability. And they do not surface the kinds of deep and potentially threatening or embarrassing information that can motivate learning and produce real change.

Let me give an example of what I mean. Not long ago, I worked with a company conducting a TQM initiative. TQM has been highly successful at cutting unnecessary costs, so successful that many companies have raised it to the status of a management philosophy. In this particular case, a TQM consultant worked with top management to carry out a variety of surveys and group meetings to help 40 supervisors identify nine areas in which they could tighten procedures and reduce costs. The resulting initiative met its goals one month early and saved more money than management had anticipated. The CEO was so elated that he treated the entire team to a champagne dinner to celebrate what was clearly a victory for everyone involved.

I had regular conversations with the supervisors throughout the implementation, and I was struck by two often-repeated comments. First, the supervisors told me several times how easy it had been to identify the nine target areas since they knew in advance where the worst inefficiencies might be found. Second, they complained again and again that fixing the nine areas was long overdue, that it was high time management took action. As one supervisor put it, "Thank God for TQM!"

I asked several supervisors how long they had known about the nine problem areas, and their responses ranged from three to five years. I then asked them why, if they'd known about the problems, they'd never taken action themselves. "Why 'Thank God for TQM'?" I said. "Why not 'Thank God for the supervisors'?"

None of the supervisors hesitated to answer these questions. They cited the blindness and timidity of management. They blamed interdepartmental competitiveness verging on warfare. They said the culture of the company made it unacceptable to get others into trouble for the sake of correcting problems. In every explanation, the responsibility for fixing the nine problem areas belonged to someone else. The supervisors were loyal, honest managers. The blame lay elsewhere.

What was really going on in this company? To begin with, we can identify two different problems. Cost reduction is one. The other is a group of employees who stand passively by and watch inefficiencies develop and persevere. TQM produces the simple learning necessary to effect a solution to the first problem. But TQM will not prevent a recurrence of the second problem or cause the supervisors to wonder why they never acted. To understand why this is so, we need to know more about how learning takes place and about at least two mechanisms that keep it from taking place at all.

As I have emphasized in my previous articles on learning in the workplace, learning occurs in two forms: single-loop and double-loop. Single-loop learning asks a one-dimensional question to elicit a one-dimensional answer. My favorite example is a thermostat, which measures ambient temperature against a standard setting and turns the heat source on or off accordingly. The whole transaction is binary.

Double-loop learning takes an additional step or, more often than not, several additional steps. It turns the question back on the questioner. It asks what the media call follow-ups. In the case of the thermostat, for instance, double-loop learning would wonder whether the current setting was actually the most effective temperature at which to keep the room and, if so, whether the present heat source was the most effective means of achieving it. A double-loop process might also ask why the current setting was chosen in the first place. In other words, double-loop learning asks questions not only about objective facts but also about the reasons and motives behind those facts.

Here is a simple illustration of the difference between these two kinds of learning: A CEO who had begun to practice his own form of management-by-walking-around learned from his employees that the company inhibited innovation by subjecting every new idea to more than 275 separate checks and sign-offs. He promptly appointed a task force to look at this situation, and it eliminated 200 of the obstacles. The result was a higher innovation rate.

This may sound like a successful managerial intervention. The CEO discovers a counterproductive process and, with the cooperation of others, produces dramatic improvement. Yet I would call it a case of single-loop learning. It addresses a difficulty but ignores a more fundamental problem. A more complete diagnosis – that is to say, a double-loop approach to this situation – would require the CEO to ask the employees who told him about the sign-offs some tougher questions about company culture and their own behavior. For example, "How long have you known about the 275 required sign-offs?" Or "What goes on in this company that prevented you from questioning these practices and getting them corrected or eliminated?"

Why didn't the CEO ask these questions of the supervisor? And why didn't the 40 supervisors ask these questions of themselves? There are two closely related mechanisms at work here – one social, the other psychological.

The social reason that the CEO did not dig deeper is that doing so might have been seen as putting people on the spot. Unavoidably, digging deeper would have uncovered the employees' collusion with the inefficient process. Their motives were probably quite decent – they didn't want to open Pandora's box, didn't want to be negative. But their behavior – and the behavior of the CEO in ignoring this dimension of the problem – combined with everyone's failure to examine his or her individual behavior and blocked the kind of learning that is crucial to organizational effectiveness.

In the name of positive thinking, in other words, managers often censor what everyone needs to say and hear. For the sake of "morale" and "considerateness," they deprive employees and themselves of the opportunity to take responsibility for their own behavior by learning to understand it. Because double-loop learning depends on questioning one's own assumptions and behavior, this apparently benevolent strategy is actually *anti*learning. Admittedly, being considerate and positive can contribute to the solution of single-loop problems like cutting costs. But it will never help people figure out why they lived with problems for years on end, why they covered up those problems, why they covered up the cover-up, why they were so good at pointing to the responsibility of others and so slow to focus on their own. The 40 supervisors said it was high time that management took steps. None of them asked why they themselves had never even drawn management's attention to nine areas of waste and inefficiency.

What we see here is managers using socially "up-beat" behavior to inhibit learning. What we do not see, at least not readily, is why anyone should want to inhibit learning. The reason lies in a set of deeper and more complex psychological motives.

Consider again the story of the 40 supervisors. TQM's rigorous, linear reasoning solves a set of important, single-loop problems. But while we see some effective single-loop learning, no double-loop learning occurs at all. Instead, the moment the important problems involve potential threat or embarrassment, rigorous reasoning goes right out the window and *defensive reasoning* takes over. Note how the supervisors deftly sidestep all responsibility and defend themselves against the charge of inaction – or worse, collusion – by blaming others. In fact, what I call defensive reasoning serves no purpose except self-protection, though the people who use it rarely acknowledge that they are protecting themselves. It is the group, the department, the organization that they are protecting, in the name of being positive. They believe themselves to be using the kind of rigorous thinking employed in TQM, which identifies problems, gathers objective data, postulates causes, tests explanations, and derives corrective action, all along relatively scientific lines. But the supervisors' actual techniques – gathering data selectively, postulating only causes that do not threaten themselves, testing explanations in ways that are sloppy and self-serving – are a parody of scientific method. The supervisors are not protecting others; they are blaming them. They have learned this procedure carefully over time, supported at each step by defensive organizational rationalizations like "caring" and "thoughtfulness."

The reason the supervisors fail to question their own rather remarkable behavior – the reason they so instinctively and thoroughly avoid double-loop learning – is psychological. It has to do with the mental models that we all develop early in life for dealing with emotional or threatening issues.

In the process of growing up, all of us learn and warehouse master programs for dealing with difficult situations. These programs are sets of rules we use to design our own actions and interpret the actions of others. We retrieve them whenever we need to diagnose a problem or invent or size up a solution. Without them, we'd have to start from scratch each time we faced a challenge.

One of the puzzling things about these mental models is that when the issues we face are embarassing or threatening, the master programs we actually use are rarely the ones we think we use. Each of us has what I call an *espoused theory of action* based on principles and precepts that fit our intellectual backgrounds and commitments. But most of us have quite a different *theory-in-use* to which we resort in moments of stress. And very few of us are aware of the contradiction between the two. In short, most of us are consistently inconsistent in the way we act.

Espoused theories differ widely, but most theories-in-use have the same set of four governing values. All of us design our behavior in order to remain in unilateral control, to maximize winning and minimize losing, to suppress negative feelings, and to be as rational as possible, by which we mean laying out clear-cut goals and then evaluating our own behavior on the basis of whether or not we've achieved them.

The purpose of this strategy is to avoid vulnerability, risk, embarrassment, and the appearance of incompetence. In other words, it is a deeply defensive strategy and a recipe for ineffective learning. We might even call it a recipe for antilearning, because it helps us avoid reflecting on the counterproductive consequences of our own behavior. Theories-in-use assume a world that prizes unilateral control and winning above all else, and in that world, we focus primarily on controlling others and on making sure that we are not ourselves controlled. If any reflection does occur, it is in the service of winning and controlling, not of opening ourselves to learning.

Defensive strategies discourage reflection in another way as well. Because we practice them most of our lives, we are all highly skilled at carrying them out. Skilled actions are second nature; we rarely reflect on what we take for granted.

In studies of more than 6,000 people, I have found this kind of defensive theory-in-use to be universal, with no measurable difference by country, age, sex, ethnic identity, education, wealth, power, or experience. All over the world, in every kind of business and organization, in every kind of crisis and dilemma, the principles of defensive reasoning encourage people to leave their own behavior unexamined and to avoid any objective test of their premises and conclusions.

As if this individual defensive reasoning were not enough of a problem, genuine learning in organizations is inhibited by a second universal phenomenon that I call *organizational defensive routines*. These consist of all the policies, practices, and actions that prevent human beings from having to experience embarrassment or threat and, at the same time, prevent them from examining the nature and causes of that embarrassment or threat.

Take face-saving. To work, it must be unacknowledged. If you tell your subordinate Fred that you are saving his face, you have defeated your own purpose. What you do tell Fred is a fiction about the success of his own decision and a lie about your reasons for rescinding it. What's more, if Fred correctly senses the mixed message, he will almost certainly say nothing.

The logic here, as in all organizational defensive routines, is unmistakable: send a mixed message ("Your decision was a good one, and I'm overruling it"); pretend it is not mixed ("You can be proud of your contribution"); make the mixed message and the pretense undiscussable ("I feel good about this outcome, and I'm sure you do too"); and, finally, make the undiscussability undiscussable ("Now that I've explained everything to your satisfaction, is there anything *else* you'd like to talk about?").

Defensive reasoning occurs when individuals make their premises and inferences tacit, then draw conclusions that cannot be tested except by the tenets of this tacit logic. Nothing could be more detrimental to organizational learning than this process of elevating individual defensive tactics to an organizational routine.

Yet whenever managers are trying to get at the truth about problems that are embarrassing or threatening, they are likely to stumble into the same set of predictable pitfalls. Asked to examine their own behavior or the behavior of subordinates, people in this situation are likely to:

- reason defensively and to interact with others who are reasoning defensively;
- get superficial, single-loop responses that lead to superficial, single-loop solutions;
- reinforce the organizational defensive routines that inhibit access to valid information and genuine learning;
- be unaware of their own defenses because these are so skilled and automatic; and
- be unaware that they are producing any of these consequences, or, if they *are* aware of defensiveness, to see it only in others.

Given all these built-in barriers to self-understanding and self-examination under threatening conditions, it is a wonder that organizational learning takes place at all. It is an even greater wonder when we realize that many of the forms of communication that management works so hard to perfect actually reinforce those barriers. Yet this is exactly what they do.

We have seen a couple of examples of management's "benevolent" censorship of true but negative messages. In addition, we have looked at the psychological mechanisms that lead employees, supervisors, managers, and executives to engage in personal and collective defensive routines. The question we still have to answer is precisely how modern corporate communications succeed in actually contributing to this censorship and these defensive routines.

They do so in two explicit ways. First, they create a bias against personal learning and commitment in the way they parcel out roles and responsibilities in every survey, dialogue, and conversation. Second, they open a door to defensive reasoning – and close one on individual self-awareness – in the way they continuously emphasize extrinsic as opposed to intrinsic motivation.

First, consider the way roles and responsibilities are assigned in manager–employee (or leader–subordinate) conversations, interviews, and surveys. There seem to be two rules. Rule number one is that employees are to be truthful and forthcoming about the world they work in, about norms, procedures, and the strengths and weaknesses of their superiors. All other aspects of their role in the life of the organization – their goals, feelings, failings, and conflicted motives – are taken for granted and remain unexamined. Rule number two is that top-level managers, who play an intensely scrutinized role in the life of the company, are to assume virtually all responsibility for employee well-being and organizational success. Employees must tell the truth as they see it; leaders must modify their own and the company's behavior. In other words, employees educate, and managers act.

Take the case of Acme, a large, multinational energy company with 6,000 employees. Under increasing competitive pressure, the company was forced to downsize, and to no one's surprise, morale was failing fast. To learn as much as possible about its own shortcomings and how to correct them, Acme management designed and conducted an employee survey with the help of experts, and 95 per cent of employees responded. Of those responding, 75 per cent agreed on five positive points:

- They were proud to work for Acme.
- Their job satisfaction was very high.

- They found their immediate supervisors fair and technically competent.
- They believed management was concerned for their welfare.
- They felt competent to perform their own jobs.

Some 65 per cent of the respondents also indicated some concerns:

- They were skeptical about management's capacity to take initiative, communicate candidly, and act effectively.
- They described Acme's corporate culture as one of blame.
- They complained that managers, while espousing empowerment, were strongly attached to their own unilateral control.

The CEO read the first set of findings to mean that employees were basically satisfied and loyal. He saw the second set as a list of problems that he must make a serious effort to correct. And so the CEO replaced several top managers and arranged for the reeducation of the whole management team, including himself and his direct reports. He announced that Acme would no longer tolerate a culture of blame. He introduced training programs to make managers more forthright and better able to take initiative. And he promised to place greater emphasis on genuine empowerment.

The CEO's logic went like this: My employees will identify the problems. I'll fix them by creating a new vision, defining new practices and policies, and selecting a top management team genuinely committed to them. Change will inevitably follow.

I think most managers would call this a success story. If we dig deeper, however, we see a pattern I've observed hundreds of times. Underneath the CEO's aggressive action, important issues have been bypassed, and the bypass has been covered up.

When the CEO took his new team on a five-day retreat to develop the new strategy and plan its implementation, he invited me to come along. In the course of the workshop, I asked each participant to write a simple case in a format I have found to be a powerful tool in predicting how executives will deal with difficult issues during implementation. The method also reveals contradictions between what the executives say and what they do and highlights their awareness of these discrepancies.

I asked each member of the team to write one or two sentences describing one important barrier to the new strategy and another three or four sentences telling how they would overcome that barrier. Then I asked them to split the rest of the page in half. On one side, they were to write an actual or imagined dialogue with a subordinate about the issue in question. On the other side, they were to note any unsaid or unsayable thoughts or feelings they might have about this conversation. I asked them to continue this script for several pages. When they were finished, the group as a whole discussed each case at some length, and we recorded the discussions. The ability to replay key sections made it easier for the participants to score themselves on candor, forthrightness, and the extent to which their comments and behavior encouraged genuine employee commitment – the three values that the CEO had directed the executives to foster.

All of the executives chose genuinely important issues around resistance to change. But all of them dealt with the resistance they expected from subordinates by easing in, covering up, and avoiding candor and plain speaking. They did so in the name of minimizing subordinates' defensiveness and in hopes of getting them to buy into change. The implicit logic behind their scripts went something like this:

- Hide your fears about the other person's likely resistance to change. Cover this fear with persistent positiveness. Pretend the two of you agree, especially when you know you don't.

- Deal with resistant responses by stressing the problem rather than the resistance. Be positive. Keep this strategy a secret.
- If this approach doesn't work, make it clear that you won't take no for an answer. After all, you're the boss.

Imagine this kind of logic applied to sensitive issues in hundreds of conversations with employees. It's not hard to guess what the response will be, and it certainly isn't buy-in.

What happened to candor, forthrightness, and commitment building? All the executives failed to walk their talk, and all were unaware of their own inconsistency. When I pointed out the gap between action and intention, most saw it at once. Most were surprised that they hadn't seen it before. Most were quick to recognize inconsistency in others, but their lack of awareness with regard to their own inconsistency was systematic.

I know of only one way to get at these inconsistencies, and that is to focus on them. In the Acme case, the CEO managed to ignore the fact that the survey results didn't compute: on the one hand, employees said they were proud to work for the company and described management as caring; on the other, they doubted management's candor and competence. How could they hold both views? How could they be proud to work for a company whose managers were ineffective and inconsistent?

The CEO did not stop to explore any of these contradictions before embarking on corrective action. Had he done so, he might have discovered that the employees felt strong job satisfaction precisely *because* management never asked them to accept personal responsibility for Acme's poor competitive performance. Employees could safely focus their skepticism on top management because they had learned to depend on top management for their welfare. They claimed to value empowerment when in reality they valued dependence. They claimed commitment to the company when in reality they were committed only to the principle that management should make all the tough decisions, guarantee their employment, and pay them fairly. This logic made sense to employees, but it was *not* the kind of commitment that management had in mind.

None of these issues was ever discussed with employees, and none was raised in the leadership workshops. No effort was made to explore the concept of loyalty that permitted, indeed encouraged, managers to think one thing and say another. No attempt was made to help employees understand the role they played in the "culture of blame" that they'd named in the survey as one of their chief concerns. Above all, no one tried to untangle the defensive logic that contributed so mightily to these inconsistencies and that so badly needed critical examination. In fact, when I asked the management team why they had not discussed these questions, one person told me, "Frankly, until you started asking these questions, it just didn't occur to us. I see your point, but trying to talk to our people about this could be awfully messy. We're really trying to be *positive* here, and this would just stir things up."

The Acme story is a very common one: lots of energy is expended with little lasting progress. Employee surveys like the one Acme conducted – and like most other forms of leader–subordinate communication – have a fundamentally antimanagement bias whenever they deal with double-loop issues. They encourage employees *not* to reflect on their own behavior and attitudes. By assigning all the responsibility for fixing problems to management, they encourage managers *not* to relinquish the top-down, command-and-control mind-set that prevents empowerment.

The employees at Acme, like the 40 supervisors who were wined and dined for their TQM accomplishments, will continue to do what's asked of them as long as they feel adequately rewarded. They will follow the rules, but they will not take initiative, they will not take risks, and they are very unlikely to engage in double-loop learning. In short, they will not adopt the new behaviors and frames of reference so critical to keeping their companies competitive.

Over the last few years, I have come in contact with any number of companies struggling with this transition from command-and-control hierarchy to employee empowerment and organizational learning, and every one of them is its own worst enemy. Managers embrace the language of intrinsic motivation but fail to see how firmly mired in the old extrinsic world their communications actually are. This is the second explicit way in which corporate communications contribute to nonlearning.

Take the case of the 1,200-person operations division of what I'll call Europabank, where employee commitment to customer service was about to become a matter of survival. The bank's CEO had decided to spin off the division, and its future depended on its ability to *earn* customer loyalty. Europabank's CEO felt confident that the employees could become more market-oriented. Because he knew they would have to take more initiative and risk, he created small project groups to work out all the implementation details and get employees to buy into the new mission. He was pleased with the way the organization was responding.

The vice president for human resources was not so pleased. He worried that the buy-in wasn't genuine and that his boss was overly optimistic. Not wanting to be negative, however, he kept his misgivings to himself.

In order to assess what was really going on here, I needed to know more about the attitudes behind the CEO's behavior. I asked him for some written examples of how he would answer employee concerns about the spin-off. What would he say to allay their doubts and build their commitment? Here are two samples of what he wrote:

> If the employees express fear about the new plan because the "old" company guaranteed employment, say: "The new organization will do its utmost to guarantee employment and better prospects for growth. I promise that."

> If the employees express fear that they are not used to dealing with the market approach, say: "I promise you will get the education you need, and I will ensure that appropriate actions are rewarded."

When these very situations later arose and he made these very statements to employees, their reactions were positive. They felt that the CEO really cared about them.

But look at the confusion of messages and roles. If the CEO means to give these employees a sense of their own power over their own professional fate – and that was his stated intent-then why emphasize instead what *he* will do for *them*? Each time he said, "I promise you," the CEO undermined his own goal of creating internal commitment, intrinsic motivation, and genuine empowerment.

He might have begun to generate real buy-in by pointing out to employees that their wishes were unreasonable. They want management to deal with their fears and reassure them that everything will turn out for the best. They want management to take responsibility for a challenge that is theirs to face. In a market-driven business, the CEO cannot possibly give the guarantees these employees want. The employees see the CEO as caring when he promises to protect and reward them. Unfortunately, this kind of caring disempowers, and someday it will hurt both the employees and the company.

Once employees base their motivation on extrinsic factors – the CEO's promises – they are much less likely to take chances, question established policies and practices, or explore the territory that lies beyond the company vision as defined by management. They are much less likely to learn.

Externally committed employees believe that management manipulates them and see loyalty as allowing the manipulation to take place. They will give honest responses to a direct question or a typical employee survey because they will be glad to tell management what's wrong. They will see it as a loyal act. What they are *not* likely to do is examine the risky issues surrounding their dependence, their ambivalence, and their avoidance of personal responsibility. Employees will commit to TQM, for example, if they believe that their compensation is just and that their managers are fair and trustworthy. However, these conditions, like the commitment they produce, come from an outside source: management.

This is external commitment, and external commitment harnesses external motivation. The energy available for work derives from extrinsic factors like good pay, well-designed jobs, and management promises. Individuals whose commitment and motivation are external depend on their managers to give them the incentive to work.

I recently watched a videotape of the CEO of a large airline meeting with relatively upper-level managers. The CEO repeatedly emphasized the importance of individual empowerment at all levels of the organization. At one point in the tape, a young manager identified a problem that top managers at the home office had prevented him from resolving. The CEO thanked the man and then asked him to go directly to the senior vice president who ran the department in question and raise the issue again. In the meantime, he said, he would pave the way. By implication, he encouraged all the managers present to take the initiative and come to him if they encountered bureaucratic barriers.

I watched this video with a group of some 80 senior executives. All but one praised the CEO for empowering the young manager. The singe dissenter wondered out loud about the quality of the empowerment, which struck him as entirely external, entirely dependent on the action of the CEO.

I agreed with that lonely voice. The CEO could have opened a window into genuine empowerment for the young manager by asking a few critical questions: What had the young man done to communicate his sense of disempowerment to those who blocked him? What fears would doing so have triggered? How could the organization redesign itself to give young managers the freedom and safety to take such initiatives? For that matter, the CEO could have asked these same questions of his senior vice presidents.

By failing to explore the deeper issues – and by failing to encourage his managers to do the same – all the CEO did was promise to lend the young manager some high-level executive power and authority the next time he had a problem. In other words, the CEO built external commitment and gave his manager access to it. What he did *not* do was encourage the young man to build permanent empowerment for himself on the basis of his own insights, abilities, and prerogatives.

Companies that hope to reap the rewards of a committed, empowered workforce have to learn to stop kidding themselves. External commitment, positive thinking at any price, employees protected from the consequences and even the knowledge of cause and effect – this mind-set may produce superficial honesty and single-loop learning, but it will never yield the kind of learning that might actually help a company change. The reason is quite simply that for companies to change, employees must take an active role not only in describing the faults of others but also in drawing out the truth about their *own* behavior and motivation. In my experience, moreover, employees dig deeper and harder into the truth when the task of scrutinizing the organization includes taking a good look at their own roles, responsibilities, and potential contributions to corrective action.

The problem is not that employees run away from this kind of organizational self-examination. The problem is that no one asks it of them. Managers seem to attach no importance to employees' feelings, defenses, and inner conflicts. Moreover, leaders focus so earnestly on "positive" values – employee satisfaction, upbeat attitude, high morale – that it would strike them as destructive to make demands on employee self-awareness.

But this emphasis on being positive is plainly counterproductive. First, it overlooks the critical role that dissatisfaction, low morale, and negative attitudes can play – often *should* play – in giving an accurate picture of organizational reality, especially with regard to threatening or sensitive issues. (For example, if employees are helping to eliminate their own jobs, why should we expect or encourage them to display high morale or disguise their mixed feelings?) Second, it condescendingly assumes that employees can only function in a cheerful world, even if the cheer is false. We make no such assumption about senior executives. We expect leaders to stand up and take their punches like adults, and we recognize that their best performance is often linked to shaky morale, job insecurity, high levels of frustration, and a vigilant focus on negatives. But leaders have a tendency to treat everyone below the top, including many of their managers, like members of a more fragile race, who can be productive only if they are contented.

Now, there is nothing wrong with contented people, if contentment is the only goal. My research suggests it is possible to achieve quite respectable productivity with middling commitment and morale. The key is a system of external compensation and job security that employees consider fair. In such a system, superficial answers to critical questions produce adequate results, and no one demands more.

But the criteria for effectiveness and responsibility have risen sharply in recent years and will rise more sharply still in the decades to come. A generation ago, business wanted employees to do exactly what they were told, and company leadership bought their acquiescence with a system of purely extrinsic rewards. Extrinsic motivation had fairly narrow boundaries – defined by phrases like "That's not my job" – but it did produce acceptable results with a minimum of complication.

Today, facing competitive pressures an earlier generation could hardly have imagined, managers need employees who think constantly and creatively about the needs of the organization. They need employees with as much *intrinsic* motivation and as deep a sense of organizational stewardship as any company executive. To bring this about, corporate communications must demand more of everyone involved. Leaders and subordinates alike – those who ask and those who answer – must all begin struggling with a new level of self-awareness, candor, and responsibility.

# — 15 —

# Reasoning, Action Strategies, and Defensive Routines: The Case of OD Practitioners

## INTRODUCTION

The focus of this chapter is a particularly thorny set of problems that organizational development (OD) practitioners face, usually with clients who have cooperated in the past but increasingly find it difficult to do so. Their cooperation takes the form of going along with *and* resisting; adhering to *and* violating the values and assumptions of OD. I believe that much of the ambivalence of the clients is due largely to the actions that OD practitioners use to reduce or overcome the client ambivalence in the first place.

I hope to show that the OD professionals studied used defensive reasoning processes to design and implement their actions when dealing with difficult issues, yet they espoused and counseled their clients not to use such reasoning processes. The defensive reasoning and actions produced consequences that were counterproductive by the OD professionals' own criteria. This, in turn, led to the OD practitioners having decreasing credibility with their clients, which in turn reinforced the OD professionals' use of defensive reasoning.

The clients also used defensive reasoning. I focus on the OD professionals, because they are the ones who are supposed to help others use productive reasoning, and it is unlikely that they will do so unless they first learn these skills.

## A Brief Description of the OD Group

An OD group in a very large high-tech organization sensed clues from their clients that their effectiveness and credibility with them was beginning to deteriorate. The deterioration was not severe, nor was it across all programs. Nevertheless, the OD professionals decided to examine their practice in order to make changes before the situation became more serious.

The story that I pieced together from what the OD professionals said is one that I have now heard in several organizations with a history of early commitment to the values of organizational development. In the early years, the major thrust of many OD programs was to emphasize such factors as involvement, participation, and ownership. The expression of feelings, the creation of trust, the reduction of defenses were high on their agendas. The early success of OD programs was related primarily to overcoming very difficult situations (e.g., highly authoritarian leadership, manipulative policies, and injustices such as the way minorities were dealt with).

As these programs succeeded, the support grew. The OD professionals were invited to redesign jobs, to redesign reward systems, and to redesign, or design from the beginning, new factories. As the scope of OD programs grew, the OD professionals began to confront traditional organizational dilemmas such as autonomy versus control, innovation versus no surprises, participation and ownership versus meeting deadlines, and job security versus excess employees, through job design. These dilemmas were there during the early years, but the programs did not face up to them because they took a back seat to authoritarian leadership, equal opportunities, and the like.

The OD professionals recalled the bewilderment they felt in dealing with these dilemmas. They were for involvement and ownership, and they knew how to produce these states of affairs. What they lacked was knowledge of how to deal with conditions where involvement and ownership were counterproductive, where unilateral control over employees was necessary, or where frustrating the needs of employees appeared necessary, or what to do when OD professionals designed programs that placed more demands on the employees than the employees expected. Too often they dealt with these dilemmas by bypassing them or by suggesting a short workshop to explore them.

Over time, the workshop strategy wore out its welcome. Line managers did not find the workshops helpful because most of them were designed with the assumption that line managers could solve these problems if they had an opportunity to think and discuss them. This assumption proved to be incorrect. The actions line managers took often expressed their bewilderment and ambivalence. For example, they would tighten up controls and hide their intentions by espousing the importance of increasing employee ownership. Others tried to give employees more influence, but kept to themselves that they would crack down if things got out of hand. In other words, when the OD programs ran up against these age-old dilemmas, the line management retrieved their old ways of exercising authority. Some OD practitioners reacted by confronting management for being two-faced. Others tried to work within the constraints by developing new concepts that could "organize people" and "energize efforts."

One frequently used concept in this organization was vision. If line management could only develop correct visions, they could manage these dilemmas more effectively. The different examples of visions that were found fell into two broad categories: one, visions of no-nonsense, back-to-the-basics approach that the OD people saw as regression to the old days; and two, visions of involvement and participation. When OD and line came up against the dilemmas described above, both "regressed" to the more traditional theories of unilateral control.

## The Action Science Program to Help the OD Professionals

A program was designed that combined inquiry and reeducation of the OD professionals. The first step was to obtain examples of nontrivial encounters and of how the OD professionals acted during them. They were asked to develop cases.

The case format is simple: first, a paragraph that describes the problem as they see it. This gives us insight into how they frame the problem. Next a paragraph or so as to how they would go about solving the problem if they had access to the people and systems they believe are relevant. This gives insight into the kinds of solutions they invent and the espoused theories of how to implement them.

Next they write a brief scenario of what they would say and expect others to say if the meeting they recommended actually took place. As they write the scenario, usually on the right-hand of the page, they are asked to describe (on the left-hand half of the page) any thoughts and feelings that they would have but, for whatever reason, would not communicate. They write the scenario for two to three double-spaced, typewritten pages. The actual conversation plus the material on the left-hand side of the page provides the data needed to infer the theory-in-use.

These cases can be used to develop quantitative and qualitative data about the frames, the espoused theories, the theories-in-use, and the self-censoring mechanisms of the writers. The results from the individual cases can be aggregated to produce findings about such organizational phenomena as defensive routines and culture (Argyris, 1985).

The next step was to use the cases as vehicles for reeducating the OD professionals and their clients. For example, they were distributed to the OD professionals in a workshop. The task was to help each writer understand more completely the problems identified in his or her case and to design ways to overcome them. Typically, the participants' discussions included (1) the extent to which the writer produced the intended consequences, (2) the gaps and inconsistencies, and (3) patterns of undiscussable issues and the way they were covered up.

The discussions were tape recorded in order to study the reactions of the person being helped as well as the quality of help being given by the other participants. As the diagnoses became clear, the individuals turned to the third step which was to redesign their actions and to practice producing the new designs. These discussions produce additional knowledge about the organization and the OD professionals because the new insights were generated as people moved from discovering to inventing to producing or implementing their ideas.

The fourth step was for the OD practitioners to use their new ideas and skills in actual client situations. They formed subgroups to help each other out, and they met as a total group to compare experiences.

### The Structure of this Chapter

First is a brief description of the theory that was used to design the action research and to intervene to help the OD professionals to increase their effectiveness. Second, the reasoning processes of Richard, an OD professional, are described in depth. Third, a map is presented of the organizational defensive loops that the OD professionals agreed resulted from their actions and the actions of their clients. Fourth, there is a discussion of the implications of the research for theory and practice.

## AN OVERVIEW OF THE PERSPECTIVE THAT INFORMED THE INQUIRY

The theory of action approach (Argyris, 1976, 1980, 1982; Argyris and Schön, 1974, 1978; Argyris, et al., 1985) begins with a conception of human beings as designers of action. To see human behavior under the aspect of action is to see it as constituted by the meanings and intentions of agents. Agents design action to achieve intended consequences and monitor themselves to learn whether their actions are effective. They make sense of their environment by constructing meanings to which they attend, and these constructions guide action. In monitoring the effectiveness of action, they also monitor the suitability of their construction of the environment.

Designing action requires that agents construct a simplified representation of the environment and a manageable set of causal theories that prescribe how to achieve intended consequences. It would be very inefficient to construct such representations and theories from scratch in each situation. Rather, agents learn a repertoire of concepts, schemas, and strategies, and they learn programs for drawing from their repertoire to design representations and action for unique situations. We speak of such design programs as *theories of action*. Theories of action determine all deliberate human behavior.

## Espoused Theory and Theory-in-use

There are two kinds of theories of action. Espoused theories are those that an individual claims to follow. Theories-in-use are those that can be inferred from action. (see chapter 3, pp. 81–3). Our distinction is not between theory and action, but between two different theories of action: those that people espouse, and those that they use. One reason for insisting that what people do is consistent with the theory (in-use) they hold, albeit inconsistent with their espoused theories, is to emphasize that what people do is not accidental. They do not "just happen" to act that way. Rather, their action is designed; and as agents, they are responsible for the design.

The models we create in action science are shaped by our interest in helping human beings to make more informed choices in creating the worlds in which they are embedded. Because we are interested in helping human beings to design and implement action, our models should have the feature of being connectable to concrete situations. We seek both generalizability and attention to the individual case.

## Modeling Theories-in-use

Models of theories-in-use can be constructed in the schematic frame shown in figure 15.1.

Governing variables are values that actors seek to "satisfice." Each governing variable can be thought of as a continuum with a preferred range. Human beings live in a field of many governing variables. Any action can have an impact on many governing variables. Agents typically must trade off among governing variables, because actions that raise the value of one may lower the value of another.

Action strategies are sequences of moves used by actors in particular situations to satisfice among governing variables. Action strategies have intended consequences, which are those that the actor believes will result from the action and will satisfy governing variables. Consequences feed back to action strategies and governing variables. Consequences may also be unintended and counterproductive. Consequences which are unintended may nevertheless be designed, in the following sense: action intended to achieve particular consequences may, by virtue of its design, necessarily lead to consequences which are unintended. For example, the questioning strategy of easing-in typically creates the very

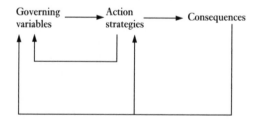

**Figure 15.1**   Model of theory-in-use

defensiveness that it is intended to avoid, because the recipient typically understands that the actor is easing-in.

## Single-loop and Double-loop Learning

When the consequences of an action strategy are as the agent intends, then there is a match between intention and outcome and the theory-in-use of the agent is confirmed (see chapter 3). If the consequences are unintended, and especially if they are counterproductive, there is a mismatch or an error. The first response to error is typically to search for another action strategy that will satisfy the same governing variables. In such a case, when new action strategies are used in the service of the same governing variables, we speak of *single-loop learning*. We do so because the change is in action but not in governing variables.

Another possibility is to change the governing variables themselves. For example, rather than suppress conflict, the agent might choose to value open inquiry. The associated action strategy might be to initiate discussion of conflictual issues. In such cases we speak of *double-loop learning*.

## Model I Theory-in-use

Argyris and Schön (1974) developed a model, or an ideal type, which describes features of theories-in-use which inhibit double-loop learning (see chapter 3). While espoused theories vary widely, research indicates that there is almost no variance in theory-in-use (Argyris, 1976, 1982). More precisely, the theories-in-use of virtually everyone we have studied are consistent with the master program called Model I, or with its mirror image, opposite Model I. There is considerable difference within Model I, in the weightings individuals give to particular governing variables, and in the particular strategies individuals favor; but these lower order variations appear to be governed by the Model I executive design program.

The four governing variables of Model I are:

1  achieve the purpose as the actor defines it;
2  win, do not lose;
3  suppress negative feelings; and
4  emphasize rationality.

The primary behavioral strategies in Model I are to control unilaterally the relevant environment and tasks and to protect oneself and others unilaterally. The underlying behavioral strategy is unilateral control over others. Characteristic ways of implementing this strategy include making unillustrated attributions and evaluations, advocating in ways that discourage inquiry, treating one's own views as obviously correct, making covert attributions and evaluations, and face-saving.

The consequences of Model I strategies include defensive interpersonal and group relationships, low freedom of choice, and reduced production of valid information. There are negative consequences for learning, because there is little public testing of ideas. The hypotheses that people generate tend to become self-sealing. What learning does occur remains within the bounds of what is acceptable. Double-loop learning does not tend to occur. As a result, error escalates and effectiveness in problem solving and in execution of action tends to decrease.

In claiming that human beings are programmed with Model I theory-in-use, we are making predictions about the kinds of strategies they will and will not use, and the kinds of consequences that will and will not occur. These predictions have been tested in dozens of client groups including thousands of individuals, and to date they have not been disproved (see Argyris, 1982, chapter 3 for a review). Most people hold espoused theories inconsistent with Model I, and when confronted with our predictions seek to demonstrate that they are not valid. At best, they are able to produce strategies consistent with opposite Model I.

The governing variables of opposite Model I are:

1   participation of everyone in defining purposes;
2   everyone wins, no one loses;
3   express feelings; and
4   suppress the cognitive intellective aspects of action.

The associated behavioral strategies include inquiry and minimizing unilateral control (Argyris and Schön, 1974).

The consequences of Model I theory-in-use, as we have described, include defensiveness, low freedom of choice, and self-sealing processes. If it is the case that Model I identifies features of theories-in-use that are common to virtually everyone, it follows that the behavioral worlds of groups, families, and organizations will have features that correspond to Model I. The interaction of people programmed with Model I theories-in-use generates pattern-building forces that create a characteristic behavioral world.

Argyris and Schön (1978) created a model of the behavioral world that is congruent with Model I theory-in-use. Model O-I ("O" signifies "organization") is a model of a *limited learning system*. The model states that when individuals programmed with Model I theory-in-use deal with difficult and threatening problems, they create primary inhibiting loops. That is, they create conditions of undiscussability, self-fulfilling prophecies, self-sealing processes, and escalating error, and they remain unaware of their responsibility for these conditions. Primary inhibiting loops lead to win–lose group dynamics, conformity, polarization between groups, and organizational games of deception. These secondary inhibiting loops reinforce primary inhibiting loops; together they lead people to despair of double-loop learning in organizations.

In a recent publication, these defensive loops have been called defensive routines. A defensive routine is any action or policy that prevents experiencing embarrassment or threat *and simultaneously* prevents reducing the causes of the embarrassment or threat (Argyris, 1985).

## Model II Theory-in-use

The action scientist is an interventionist, seeking to help members of client systems to reflect on the world they create and to learn to change it in ways more congruent with the values and theories they espouse. The normative perspective that guides the action scientist is described by a model of an alternative theory-in-use, Model II (Argyris and Schön, 1974). Model II as an espoused theory is not new; indeed most people readily espouse it. But as a theory-in-use it is rare. The action scientist intends to produce action consistent with Model II, because it is by so doing that the counter productive features of Models I and O-I can be interrupted. Just as action consistent with Models I and O-I creates threats to validity and inhibits learning, action consistent with Models II and O-II is hypothesized to enhance validity and learning. Model II provides an image of the theory-in-use that the action scientist as interventionist seeks to help clients learn.

The governing variables of Model II include:

1 valid information;
2 free and informed choice; and
3 internal commitment.

These are the features of the alternative worlds that action science seeks to create (Argyris, 1980). Creating conditions in which these values are realized is the primary task of the interventionist (Argyris, 1970; see also chapter 4).

The behavioral strategies of Model II involve sharing control with those who have competence and who are relevant to designing or implementing the action. Rather than unilateral advocacy (Model I) or inquiry that conceals the agent's own views (opposite Model I), in Model II the agent combines advocacy and inquiry. Attributions and evaluations are illustrated with relatively directly observable data and the surfacing of conflicting views is encouraged in order to facilitate public testing.

The consequences of Model II action strategies should include minimally defensive interpersonal and group relationships, high freedom of choice, and high risk-taking. The likelihood of double-loop learning is enhanced, and effectiveness should increase over time. Model O-II describes the behavioral world created by individuals interacting with Model II theory-in-use. Instead of creating primary inhibiting loops, when members of organizations deal with difficult and threatening problems using Model II theory-in-use they engage in Model II inquiry. Previously undiscussable issues will be surfaced, assumptions will be tested and corrected, and self-sealing processes will be interrupted. Both single-loop and double-loop learning can occur. Dysfunctional group and intergroup dynamics should decrease, and there should be less need for camouflage and games of deception.

At the espoused level, Models II and O-II sound like motherhood and apple pie. The trick is to produce them in the real world. This is quite difficult, both because people have been socialized to produce Model I and because the world continues to operate largely according to Model I even when some people try to act according to Model II.

Finally, Model I theory-in-use encourages the use of defensive reasoning and the O-I learning system culturally reinforces its use. Model II theory-in-use encourages also the use of productive reasoning and the O-II learning system culturally reinforces its use. Reasoning processes include all the "mind" activities that are used to produce premises, make inferences, and draw conclusions about any type of problem.

| *Defensive* | *Productive* |
|---|---|
| | Characteristics |
| • soft data | • hard data |
| • tacit, private inferences | • explicit inferences |
| • conclusions not publicly testable | • premises explicit, conclusions publicly testable |
| | Supported by |
| • tacit theory of dealing with threat | • (explicit or tacit) theory of strategy formulation |
| • set of tacitly interrelated concepts | • set of directly interrelated concepts |
| • set of tacit rules for using concepts to make permissable inferences, reach private conclusions, and private criteria to judge the validity of the test | • set of rules for using concepts to make permissable inferences, reach testable conclusions, and criteria to judge the validity of the test |

The fundamental assumption is that individuals programmed with Model I and embedded in an O-I learning system will use defensive reasoning for problems that are difficult and potentially embarrassing to them or to others. It is the defensive reasoning that leads to ideas or feelings that are counterproductive to learning and effective action. Let us turn to examining several cases written by OD professionals who were trying to learn how to minimize creating defensive routines while interacting with their clients.

## THE CASE OF RICHARD

"Richard" (a pseudonym) wrote a case to describe some difficulties he had with a line manager who liked the idea of using a vision to manage employees, but whose views of an effective vision were quite different from Richard's. The dialogue material is taken from a transcript of Richard's discussion with his fellow OD practitioners on how to deal with the problem.

The reasoning processes Richard used were similar to those I observed his colleagues using when they were dealing with difficult but different issues. Therefore, I could have selected any of the other 11 cases and illustrated the same underlying reasoning processes. Indeed, these results were replicated in discussions with another OD practitioner's group in the United States (a group of 20) and two groups in Europe (of 24 each). Note: all questions not otherwise identified are by peers or the author.

| *Conversation* | *Inferences I made during the conversation* |
|---|---|
| Q:   How certain were you by the time the session finished that you had explicit commitment (from your client)? | |
| RICHARD:  I think I had a commitment, but not an explicit one. He is fairly indirect in terms of making expectations explicit. Lots of politeness. Easing-in. He is a master at it. | Richard did not test this attribution about client commitment with the client. Richard appears to explain the reasoning behind not testing his attribution by creating another, namely that the clients prefer to ease-in. |
| | Making the easing-in attribution about the client and acting consistently with it is itself an act of easing-in. Thus the attribution Richard makes about his client may be also made about him. Richard appears unaware of this possibility. How does he know the easing-in he is attributing to the client is not partially caused by his own easing in? |
| | At another level of inquiry, how much of the attribution made by Richard is a projection? Why not test? |

(later)

| | |
|---|---|
| Q:   What was your reaction to his intended use of the video? | |
| RICHARD:  I am opposed to using a video in order to hook people into a vision in which they were not intimately involved (in creating). | How does he know the client intends to use the video tape to hook people in? |
| | How does he know that the use of a video tape must necessarily hook people in? Why cannot it be designed to get genuine involvement? |

If he thinks a video can be used in a way that is constructive, what prevented Richard from pointing out the difficulties with the client's views and how they could be corrected?

Again, Richard appears to be making attributions about the client's intentions that he does not test.

Q: Do you have ideas as to how to construct a good tape?

RICHARD: I've never done this before so I do not know what a good tape would look like. I do not even know how his would look.

What I do know is that if we have the right tape, everything will happen.

How can he then be so certain that a video tape will be harmful?

How would he know what is the right tape if he does not know what a good video tape would look like?

The tape must communicate the correct vision. I believe in the importance of having the right vision. I feel it in my bones and in my cells, but I do not know how to deliver it.

He believes strongly in the right vision. What leads him to believe so strongly? He feels it but is equally clear that he could not produce the right vision.

What is the nature of his knowing? What prevents him from communicating it to his client? What prevented him from testing the attribution with the client?

Q: Have you told the client that you oppose video tape as an exclusive media?

RICHARD: I think I've said it to him perhaps not in so many words. I do not know whether he buys that idea. I'm not sure that he would not be happy if we produced a tape that his staff could use to indoctrinate lots of people.

Again, what prevented him from testing the attribution?

## Richard's Reasoning: Reflection I

- Richard makes attributions about the clients' intentions which he does not test.
- Richard is unable to present the data in order to illustrate, nor is he able to make explicit the chain of reasoning that has led to his attributions about the client.
- Many of the attributions Richard makes about the client can be made about Richard.
- Richard believes that having the "right" vision is key to success. Yet he cannot define the features of the right vision to his own satisfaction.
- Richard judges the client's ideas about video tape as counterproductive yet he neither can state what makes them counterproductive nor does he discuss this with the client.
- Richard has little hard data with which to develop his premises about the importance and the practical value of having a vision. He is unable to make explicit the reasoning that leads him to conclude that he has the better or the more complete vision.

We may conclude that Richard's conversation so far was characterized by several patterns: (1) Untested and untestable attributions about the client. Yet the validity of his conservation and help were dependent on the attributions being valid. (2) Inconsistencies and gaps. Richard questions the effectiveness of easing-in yet does it himself. He laments client's unawareness yet he is also unaware. (3) Strategies of persuasion through ideology and faith. For example, Richard is sure that it is possible to produce an effective video tape yet he cannot describe its characteristics nor has he ever seen one. Richard asks the client to have faith that with genuine participative problem solving, a solution will be produced.

Richard's automatic reactions to the inconsistencies and gaps pointed out by his peers was a surprise. Instead of inquiring into the basis for his unawareness, Richard asserted that the problem would be resolved if the client and he engaged in a mutually productive problem solving process. The responses by Richard to his peers included untested attributions, distancing himself from his own unawareness, and trying to persuade his peers to have faith that the problems could be solved by a genuine joint problem solving process, a process that he has not yet been able to produce with the client. Richard dealt with his peers with the same type of defensive reasoning he used with his client. Moreover, until now, he acted as if this was not a problem about which he or they should be concerned.

Back to the discussion: as the discussion continues, Richard's peers begin to question more actively the reasoning behind and the validity of his attributions. For example, one asked him what he meant when he wrote, in his case, about the client: "That's what I was afraid of (about him)."

RICHARD: Yes, (but notice that I realized that my doubts may be unfair). You know why should I expect a left-brain analytically trained manager to have this (my) notion of vision and to be able to pick up on it like that quick in a conversation.

Richard "explains" the client's "inability to understand" Richard's view of vision by saying that the client was educated as an engineer and is left-brain dominated.

Note that Richard has presented no data that the client has an inability to understand; no data that this particular engineer was dominated by the left brain; nor any data that all engineers who are left-brain dominated cannot understand his notion of vision.

I mean I really believe that. It took me a year and I still cannot articulate it well.

Richard makes private attributions about the client's inability to understand his view of vision yet Richard does not understand it well enough to articulate it to his own satisfaction.
It is at least a plausible hypothesis that Richard's inarticulateness could be causally relevant in the client not understanding.
Richard's reasoning excludes him as a causal variable in the problem that he identifies and focuses on the client in ways difficult to test: he is left-brain dominated.

One of his peers questioned Richard about some features of the reasoning that were identified above.

Q:      It sounds like you're saying, well okay, this left-brain-trained manager doesn't know any better ... so you chose to teach him ... about what is a vision.

RICHARD: Well, in a way, I was trying to back off and not be judgemental and kind of accept him where he is and you know I was there too not too long ago.

By backing off (I meant) that I realized that it was maybe unfair for him to understand it so quickly. Recognizing my own struggle to understand this concept, I realize that it is going to take some time.

Instead of Richard exploring the possibility that he has prejudged the client as needing education, Richard "explains" his action to educate the client as an act of acceptance and tolerance. He will educate the uneducated.

Note phrases "in a way" and "kind of accept him." Questions arise: "In what way?" "What kind of acceptance?" I believe if Richard explained their meaning, he might begin to get insight into the gaps in his reasoning.

Richard implies that he understands the meaning of vision enough to communicate it and/or teach it to clients. So far, he has not illustrated this capacity with the client nor with his peers.

RICHARD: We're gonna have to work together for us to understand our meanings of the word (vision) and then to be able to engage in some kind of a mutual process around how are we going to do it together in this context.

Richard expects that through a mutual problem solving process the client can be helped to see what he now does not see.

## *Richard's Reasoning: Reflection II*

- Richard continues all the defensive reasoning processes described in Reflection I and adds a few more.
- Richard explains the client's difficulties to understand Richard's meaning of vision by (1) attributing that he has difficulties, and (2) attributing the cause of the difficulties to the "fact" that the client was educated as an engineer and is therefore left-brain dominated. Richard now assigns full causal responsibility to the client.
- Richard explains his attempt to educate the client in Richard's meaning of vision as an act of tolerance and patience with the client's limits.

Two additional patterns in Richard's reasoning appear in this episode:

1 Richard reacted to the client's questioning of Richard's beliefs by seeing the doubts expressed as signs of the client's limitations.
2 Richard acted as if the vague language that he used to explain his actions (e.g., "kind of accept him") was clear.

If Richard's language is vague and if he believes it is clear, then he must be unaware of its vagueness.

If we combine the first three patterns with these two, Richard's conversation, intended to help the client:

1 contained untested attributions;
2 contained inconsistencies and gaps;
3 contained reliance on ideology and faith;
4 deflected client questions by blaming him for his "ignorance;" and
5 used language that was vague.

Richard was not aware of these features while he was producing them with the client. His automatic reactions to his peers as they pointed out these problems was to use the same five defensive reasoning and action strategies just described. However, as we shall see below, when his peers were able to present further data and were able to discuss the consequences of these five defensive reasoning and action strategies, Richard began to see what his peers were trying to help him to learn.

There is a theory of intervention embedded in the five defensive reasoning and action strategies which is itself inconsistent and highly unlikely to be effective. For example, Richard is, in effect, maintaining: (1) "Although I (Richard) cannot articulate my meaning of vision, I will educate the client in my meaning of vision by engaging with him in a mutual problem solving process" (2) "It is possible for me to create a mutual problem solving process with a client who I consider to be unable to understand my meaning of vision, who has had an education that causes important blind spots, and with whom I have never tested my attributions and indeed kept them secret"; and (3) "It is possible for me to hide my untested negative attributions from the client so that they do not inhibit creating a mutual problem solving process."

Returning again to the discussion, when Richard denied his peers' assertion that he was communicating to the client that his (Richard's) vision was better, several of his peers questioned him closely by referring to the dialogue Richard wrote in his case. Richard finally said: "I guess I did back off when I said okay, you've got one meaning for the term vision. But you haven't got the one that I want you to get. (Your understanding) is the commonly accepted meaning of the term. It is, however, *wrong*" (emphasis his). Richard was surprised by what he identified as a slip. There was a silence. The silence was broken by laughter. Then he said "it's the unenlightened term" and laughed. His peers joined in the laughter and added terms like "the unwashed version," "the left-lane definition," each accompanied by heavy laughter.

> RICHARD:  I realize that I may come across (as if my version is better than his) but I really do believe that we need both.
> CHRIS:    Could you illustrate in the case where you say this?

Richard scans his case and nods his head negatively.

At one point in the conversation, I role-played a supportive client interacting with Richard.

> CHRIS:    Richard, it sounds to me as if you believe that if this company had the right vision, if it understood it, a hell of a lot of good things would follow.
> RICHARD:  That is essentially correct. Yes.
> CHRIS:    Could you tell me what is that vision.
> RICHARD:  No I can't. Because I do not know the vision for what the company ought to do. I do not believe there is one vision. (Visions vary at different levels of the organization.)
>                                         (later)
> RICHARD:  Once we are clear about the vision then I can help you find the appropriate people to discuss it and implement it.
> CHRIS:    And what is it that they will tell me?
> RICHARD:  A way of getting people involved in developing your vision.

I then turned to his peers and asked, "What is your reaction?"

I wouldn't let you (Richard) operate on me.

I think you know more than you're telling me. If you read these (outsider's stuff) then you must have some idea of what they would bring to the table.

Why do I need you? Are you the middle-man in this relationship?

Later:

RICHARD:  I have a very clear concept of what a vision is as a concept and as an outcome. I've seen visions work for individuals. What I have never seen or been part of is how do you do this with an organization. I've seen it work beautifully for individuals. I *know* it will work for organizations.
CHRIS:   In what way?
RICHARD:  It will provide a sense of purpose, a sense of clarity, a sense of direction, a sense of excitement, a sense of moving in a positive direction.

## Richard's Reasoning: Reflection III

As I listened to Richard, the following questions came into my mind. What is Richard's view of when he knows when he knows something? How does he know he knows what a vision is if he cannot produce it? How does he know it will work for organizations as it does for individuals when he has never seen that work?

Richard assigns to the successful use of a successful concept of vision all the outcomes that he wishes he could help produce in the organization. The reasoning behind what he is saying is instructive. I (Richard) conclude that all the good outcomes I promise will occur although I have never seen nor produced these outcomes. All I need to know is what is a successful concept of vision and a successful process to produce it. Yet, I do not know either. The logic appears more consistent with magic than with mutual problem solving.

What prevents Richard from admitting the gaps in his knowledge and, therefore, problem solving with the client? If we recall the early discussion of Richard's case, he acted toward the client as if he knew what the correct vision is and how to produce it.

We now enter a new phase where his peers are more openly critical of Richard's intervention as illustrated in his case. The comments included the following evaluations:

- You focus on what client is missing and not on what he is saying.
- You identify gaps in client's thinking and then you back off.
- You focus heavily on making sure the client would succeed by making sure he understood your view that you never got around to problem solving a solution that was acceptable to both.
- You create, right from the beginning, a win–lose situation.

Each of these comments focused on Richard's behavior and was easily illustrated by the speakers. In all cases Richard agreed. He stopped the group to say that he was finding the feedback difficult to hear but very helpful. "I see now that I made quite a few misses."

I asked: "Would you identify the misses that you have heard so far?" Richard responded that he missed the following: (1) he did not understand his own meaning of vision; (2) he tried to coerce the client to buy into his (Richard's) version of vision; (3) he persisted that his meaning of vision was better, and (4) he did not help the client to clarify his vision.

Richard then repeated his gratitude by saying: "This dialogue has been very helpful. It has helped me to clarify where the mismatches are right now between the client and myself." He then reflected further.

| *Richard's reflections* | *Comments on Richard's reasoning* |
|---|---|
| (I now remember) that the client talked about the importance of visions before I did. | This provides some data that contradicts Richard's assertion that the client, being educated as a left-brain engineer would naturally be uncomfortable with the concept of a vision. |
| My axe with the client was that he was using vision in a rather manipulative way to sell his ideas. | Richard used his concept of vision to manipulate the client. For example: "In a sense, I can now see that I am manipulating the client. I'm trying to parley his notion of a vision into something bigger which I believe would be more beneficial to the organization." |

## Reflection on Gaps in the Help being given to Richard

Richard reported that the discussion was very productive. He reported that he learned because he was helped to identify inconsistencies and gaps in his behavior. Neither he nor his peers, however, took the next step of exploring the reasoning behind his blindness. For example, during the conversations with Richard, none of his peers explored the questions raised about his reasoning on the right-hand columns. It is as if their view of help was equivalent to helping Richard become aware of his blind spots, gaps, and inconsistencies.

These are important and necessary learnings, but they are not sufficient. The argument for these not being sufficient has been made elsewhere and can be summarized as follows (Argyris, 1982, 1985; Argyris and Schön, 1974, 1978):

1   All diagnoses of reality and actions are designed. We are responsible for the designs that we produce. We cannot knowingly kid ourselves. As the Greek philosophers pointed out, it is not possible to knowingly lie to ourselves. To say to myself I am lying is to tell the truth.

    Similarly it is also not possible to knowingly produce mismatches or errors. If I say I intend to produce an error and do so that is a match.

2   However, it is obvious that people produce errors all the time. One way to explain the puzzle is to say that the individuals were unaware that they were producing errors while doing so.

    But if unawareness is action and all actions are designed then unawareness must be designed. This means that human beings have designs that keep them unaware of their errors and they are unaware of these designs. Although they cannot produce errors they can produce the designs that keep them unaware of their errors when they make them.

3   Productive reasoning requires that the part of the theory being used, the inferences made, and the conclusions produced be tested for validity.

    It is highly unlikely that defensive reasoning will lead to anything except defensive consequences. Unfortunately, the predisposition to use defensive reasoning under conditions of threat is widespread in most organizations. Hence when productive reasoning is most needed it is rarely found. One of the basic tasks of organizational development professionals is to help individuals and systems to use productive reasoning in their actions and policies, especially those related to threat.

4   How can individuals be unaware of the programs in their heads that keep them unaware? First, the lack of awareness could be due to the fact that the actions are highly skilled and therefore automatic. The very fact that they are skilled makes them

tacit. Second, the program that keeps people unaware may be related to the way they reason. The key to their unawareness is the reasoning that informed their actions. For example, if Richard were asked the questions about his reasoning processes that are described in the right-hand columns above, he would probably conclude that his reasoning was consistent with defensive reasoning. Defensive reasoning does not tend to encourage public testing or confrontation by others. The key to becoming aware of the defensive reasoning is to create a dialectic in order to question one's reasoning. This is unlikely because defensive reasoning acts to reduce the creation of a dialectic mode of inquiry. Third, as in this example, Richard is in a world where help includes identifying the gaps and inconsistencies but not the reasoning behind the gaps nor the consequences that flow from the gaps.

Returning to the discussion, one of Richard's peers advised him to go back to the client and create the mutual problem solving process that he had mentioned. I asked, given the analysis that we have made so far, what are the data and the reasoning that would lead the questioner to believe that Richard could create such a problem solving process. Richard replied, "Yes, well I think that is part of the dilemma. I don't think I know how to define vision well enough (that I can help the clients see the gaps in their views). Yet, I also feel this is a great opportunity (for us OD people). It is an opportunity to really address a real void (in line's thinking and action)."

Richard now introduces another important variable. The OD practitioners need to fill in voids in management's thinking and action. Thus, part of his pressuring the client may be related to the organizational requirement to show management how to perform more effectively. Yet, if the analysis above is correct, Richard will have difficulty in being effective because he is not able to bring to the helping relationship such critical features as knowing his concept of vision, being aware when he is evaluating and attributing, being aware of his self-fulfilling prophecies and self-sealing processes. Before this new organizational role dimension could be explored, another peer asked:

| | | |
|---|---|---|
| Q: | I was touched by your willingness to acknowledge that you do not know how (to define your wider view of vision). But I also wonder if you are not angry at the clients who do not have a vision? | |
| RICHARD: | The word hostility doesn't feel right for me. Frustration maybe. | Is Richard suggesting that the criterion for validity of the question is whether it feels right? How can his ideas then be genuinely disproven? |
| CHRIS: | You may be correct. Is there a way that we can test the different views? | |
| RICHARD: | Test? What is there to test? | What are the reasoning processes that lead Richard to say that there is no need for the test and at the same time admit that he feels highly frustrated? Could not his feelings of frustration lead to distortions? |
| CHRIS: | To test the extent to which anger may be relevant. | |
| RICHARD: | Well do we need to test it? I mean there is a lot of frustration for me around the topic. I have a lot of frustration about where our company is and where we are going to come out. | |

CHRIS:       Yes, and?

RICHARD: I think our ability to succeed has a lot to do with the ability of people who are in key leadership positions to be conceptual... around complex situations.

Richard believes his success is dependent upon line executives to be skilled at conceptualizing complex situations.

What frustrates me is the way the line managers handle complex, difficult situations. They analyze it and give it a quick and dirty, one, two, three answer. For example, I sent a memo (describes situation). I received a typical (simplistic) answer. That's not really a good answer. I don't like it. I expect more from them.

Yet he does not appear, so far, to have such reasoning skills himself. For example abstractions that are to be productive must be comprehensive yet explicitly connectable to a given situation. Richard cannot do it with his concept of vision.

We may now formulate the following diagnosis based on Richard's comments.

- I believe that our company and OD people are in trouble if we do not become better conceptualizers of complexity.
- I cannot meet this standard in my own work.
- I do not seem to be able to create mutual problem solving situations where we can produce new solutions.
- I get upset when the line sends me simplistic responses.
- I do not explore these responses with line because it may upset them and I could get rejected.
- I try as diplomatically as I can to get them to see the gaps in their thinking and action but, being left-brain dominated, they are unable to understand me.

This formulation provides a reasonable explanation for Richard's frustration. He is unlikely to be effective under these conditions. It is reasonable to expect frustration under these conditions.

One explanation is that Richard's reasoning leads him to place the primary responsibility for possible failure on the client: it is the client who is closed. But it is also the client who has power. Therefore, Richard has to be careful and diplomatic with these people lest they reject him.

The moment Richard takes on these protective actions he is violating his own theory of interpersonal openness and trust. Moreover, in his mind, he has to collude to do things that he believes are simplistic in order to get "good press" with the line, in order to have credibility to remain as an interventionist.

One source of the anger could be that Richard sees himself as forced to be supportive and cooperative with line executives who value and act differently but who have power over him. The support and cooperation take the form of saying and doing things that he (and others) call "shitty details."

But note that there is no evidence that the reasoning described above is valid. We do not know if the engineers are closed. We do not know if their view of vision is wrong. We do not know that they will fire Richard if he does not cooperate.

All of these fears could be valid or invalid. Richard never tests them. Moreover, they could be valid because Richard has in part made them so. That is, the line management may have come to believe that Richard holds concepts such as vision that he cannot define and that they do not feel are implementable. They could believe that Richard is closed to having his reasoning confronted and hence believe that they better ease in and be gentle with him.

Under these conditions they may ask Richard for help, but only to the extent that they can control him. In their view, this unilateral control is the only way they can protect themselves from Richard's use of unilateral control.

What unilateral control does Richard use? After all, he is against using such control. There are several levels at which the line could experience Richard as using unilateral control.

First, Richard creates win–lose situations and acts as if he does not. He asserts that his view of vision is better than his client's without saying what leads him to think so. Second, Richard prejudges the line with evaluations and attributions which he does not test and acts as if none of this is happening. Third, Richard insists that they should use his more encompassing view of vision which he cannot define and they therefore cannot independently reject. Fourth, Richard asks for mutual problem solving when he does little of it himself. Fifth, the only way the clients can continue to work with him is to act as if none of this is happening. It is as if they are controlled by the intention they attribute to Richard, which is if they believe any of the above is valid, they will, for his sake, not discuss it.

The clients are now in a double bind. If they discuss these issues, they could upset Richard and make it less likely that they can protect him organizationally. After all, why pay OD people who cannot perform by their own standards. On the other hand, if they do not discuss these issues, they have to collude in a game that makes it less likely that they or Richard will be as effective as they are capable of being.

Returning to the dialogue, several peers began to discuss their feelings of anger with clients. For example:

> I can identify with that. I do not know if that speaks to you or not. But the job that needs to be done is so much greater than the tools that I have to do it.
> Yes, I agree with that. A lot of my anger comes after working with an issue for a while and not making progress. And then I get angry at *them!*
> The issue is that we do not know how to deliver what we are selling. I want to understand that better.

We now add a new issue to explore. It may be that the OD professionals are aware of the gaps in their skills between what they wish to deliver and what they are able to deliver. Indeed as one of them said, she did not even know how to conceptualize what it is that they are delivering. The anger that they express about the client could then be as much related to their inability to deal with client defenses. But client defenses are basically defensive reasoning.

It is unlikely that these OD professionals are going to help clients examine their defensive reasoning if they are not able to examine their own. In order to examine defensive reasoning, the individuals must use productive reasoning under the conditions where they automatically use defensive reasoning.

Unless these OD professionals can learn to use productive reasoning they may eventually create a set of self-fulfilling, self-sealing processes that would mean a slow but sure disintegration with their clients.

## BARRIERS TO PRODUCTIVE REASONING IN OD

The defensive reasoning illustrated in Richard's case was also the predominant reasoning used by Richard's peers in their cases. This was true even though the nature of the problems reported in the cases varied widely, the location in the hierarchy at which they were working varied widely, and the degree of commitment of the clients varied widely.

Although the actions used by the OD professionals in the cases varied widely, the action strategies varied minimally and the reasoning almost not at all. The behavioral strategies were consistent with Model I or the opposite of Model I. The reasoning was defensive. For example:

- The OD professional was impatient with his client who kept seeing failure of performance by a manager as an individual problem. The cure, in the manager's mind, was therefore to fire or transfer the manager and bring in someone who can produce.
- The OD professional wanted to introduce systemic thinking. The failure of managerial performance is more accurately attributable to system variables than to individual ones.
- The way the OD professional dealt with his client and the way the client reacted (as recalled by the OD professional) created a problem at the level that he asserted was not important. For example, as the OD professional expressed his impatience, the client felt misunderstood, unfairly judged and under attack. The client interpreted this as an individual, not a systemic, problem. The OD professional, in the client's eyes, was creating the causal conditions that he was downplaying.

There is a puzzle embedded in the issue of individual and system. If systemic variables are causes of actions, then as long as individuals are acting as the agents of the system, they will experience advice or pressure by the OD professionals to change as a deeply individual, personal risk. One OD professional, for example, identified the following organizational rule that informed line managers' behavior: "Success in production schedules is always the priority. You can break any commitment to make the operations successful (short term)." The result, according to the OD professional, was a system which "had almost no integrity and so you're dealing with a shifting pile of sand."

The OD professional did not appear to appreciate the client's dilemma. The client was acting consistently within the rules of the system. The client realized that to violate the rules would bring down the wrath of the system. The client was being told that he was not thinking systemically when in fact he was. As the OD professional pointed out, the rules that the client followed were systemic.

To compound the problem, the OD professional explained the client's willingness to follow the systemic rules as "short-term oriented." Strictly speaking this is not true. The client was acting in his long-term interest when he was conforming to systemic rules.

The OD professionals considered the systemic rules as short-term oriented. They also considered themselves more long-term oriented. But to change the manager's orientation from short term to their view of long term, it would be their responsibility to help the client move toward the long-term perspective. In order for the client to do so, the OD professional would have to help the entire system change to a new state of affairs. But, by the OD professionals' own views, they did not know how to help systems move from where they are to where (the OD professionals) believed they should be.

In another case the dilemma identified by the interventionist was "how to help the clients take more responsibility for their future without forcing them to create the future of our choice." Again, the reasoning processes were defensive. The case began with the clients describing their situation much more positively than the OD professional thought was true. She noted, in the column designated thoughts and feelings not expressed: "We've really got a problem here of ownership." The attribution was never tested publicly with the clients.

The OD professional then attempted to help the clients see the error of their ways by using easing-in and other diplomatic strategies. The clients apparently sensed the covert negative evaluations. They responded by rejecting them, diplomatically of course. They kept insisting, "We're doing nicely right now."

As the dialogue continued, the OD professional wrote, "I'm so sick of this stuff." A couple of pages later, she asked, "What are you telling me? That you are perfect and do not need change?" The clients denied that this was their message, a denial that could be accurate. For example, they could have been saying that they did not trust the validity or the implementability of the future world that the OD professional was suggesting.

Interestingly, the clients agreed to be influenced by the OD professional in "accepting" that they may be wrong. Hence the clients ended up appearing to buy the future promulgated by the OD professional. This was the very consequence the OD professional wished to avoid.

A word about the apparent lack of awareness of the OD professionals. "Looking backwards everything seems obvious, embarrassingly so," was the comment made by one OD professional. If there are readers who may be somewhat bewildered by the unawareness and inconsistency of the OD professionals, they may wish to keep in mind that in every case that I have experienced to date where such individuals have expressed surprise, they have turned out to be equally inconsistent and unaware in their own practice.

A question that arises is what prevents the OD professionals from being more reflective of their practice while they are practicing? What prevents them from being on-line researchers or reflective practitioners? I believe that there are several important factors. First, defensive reasoning is anti-reflection for the purpose of discovering an error and correcting it. It is even less likely to encourage the kind of dialectical inquiry that is required for such learning (Argyris and Schön, 1978; Schön, 1983). Second, the OD professionals studied so far have used a Model I theory-in-use or the opposite of Model I theory-in-use. Neither of these theories of action will lead to the reflective inquiry required to learn to detect and correct error in an on-line manner. The defensive reasoning and the two theories-in-use combine to create inconsistency and unawareness as well as the unawareness of the program in their heads to keep them unaware.

There is also a systemic factor that is a very powerful causal agent of the inconsistency and unawareness. Elsewhere, we have shown that Model I or the opposite of Model I theories-in-use will lead to a learning system in organizations that does not encourage reflective practice, especially of the kind that re-examines governing values. We have called this double-loop learning (Argyris and Schön, 1974, 1978).

I should now like to turn to the map of the organizational learning system that existed in the heads of the OD professionals and the line managers that describes the organizational learning system created while the OD professionals were trying to make the company more humane and more productive. The map was developed by analyzing the tape recordings. It was then fed back to the OD professionals to check it for validity. I will discuss the issue of the validity of the map in a concluding section below.

## Two Orientations in OD Practice

All the OD professionals agreed that they were operating within an organization where the company was experiencing increased competition. This has resulted in pressures for meeting increased customer demands including quality and delivery schedules.

Pressures also have increased for the organization to become more cost conscious and to integrate many interfaces among departments that had hitherto not existed.

According to the cases and discussions with the OD professionals, I concluded that there were two dominant orientations to dealing with these contextual pressures. The control orientation was the most prominent and assigned largely to the line management. The learning orientation was the one advocated by the OD professionals and a few line executives who had been converted. These two orientations are shown in Figure 15.2.

The control orientation had at least six major components. First there was the commitment to respond to short-term rewards: "get the product out." The second component was to respond to crises. This led individuals to create crises in order to get individuals to pay attention. Understandably the greater the organizational status and power of the creator of the crisis, the more attention would be paid to that crisis. The third component was to seek diagnoses that could be dealt with by "quick fix." Motion and action were key strategies to keep superiors off subordinates' backs. A going metaphor was "apparent motion." As long as someone was seen as being in action, then the anxieties of the top would be reduced almost regardless of the relevance of that action (at least in the early stages of a crisis). A fourth component was the tendency of superiors to evaluate performance of subordinates privately and covertly. Performance evaluation was one of those public secrets while it was going on. After the superior has amassed the evidence and decided upon action, the fifth component, implementation was as swift and as face-saving as possible. The sixth component was the key criteria for the success orientation: the technology, the quality of the product, and the immediate performance. The learning orientation of the OD professionals acknowledged the importance of such criteria as technology, the quality of the product, and immediate performance such as shipment on time. They believed that it was possible to involve the employees in such a way that they would take on more causal responsibility to make sure that the criteria were achieved.

In order to accomplish the integration of people and organization, the OD professionals strove to help reduce the self-inflicted crises created by line. They attempted to make the more long-term rewards as powerful as the short-term rewards.

The OD professionals believed that a fundamental shift must occur from individual to systems level. It was simplistic to assume that major errors were made by individuals; major errors were systemic. Hence, if major errors were to be corrected, the focus should be on the system. The focus on the system was not initiated to exonerate the individuals. On the contrary, the OD professionals sought a more just distribution of responsibility for errors and for their correction.

The OD professionals sought to create a certain type of technological system that focused on excellence in quality, on timeliness of shipment, and on generating a sense of internal commitment among employees to continually monitor their performance in order to maintain the high standards that they had set.

### The Tension between the Two Orientations

It is not difficult to see that there are built-in tensions between these approaches. The degree of tension could vary widely with the problem, the individuals involved, the competitive pressures, and so on.

The point of the schema in Figure 15.2 is not to identify ahead of time the degree of each individual tension. That is a matter of empirical research. The point is to identify a pattern of variables that accounts for how the OD and line people dealt with the tensions, especially the more difficult ones. Once the pattern is identified, it too is subject to test.

The first response of the line was to maintain vigilance and pressure. In other words, they reinforced their control orientation. Second, they were willing to support experiments in creating learning orientations at the lower levels where "things can't get out of control."

Whenever the experiments were not producing the intended consequences, alternations were made in favor of the control orientation. The changes were justified in terms of competition and costs (the two governing variables identified in the first column). The result was that commitment to this system was ambivalent and often the ambivalence was covert and not discussable.

Like the line, the OD professionals' reactions were to continue to espouse their learning orientation. However, as the line appeared to be ambivalent or to resist, as we saw in the cases, the OD professionals reverted to selling or persuading through the use of metaphors such as "vision," "purposing," "ownership," and "energy."

Those metaphors made sense to the line managers. The line managers interpreted these metaphors differently than the OD professionals. The line wanted purposing, ownership, and energy to be produced in ways that were consistent with the control orientation which, in turn, violated the OD professionals' views.

Another strategy the OD professionals used was to develop technological instruments for selling the systems. For example, the OD professionals developed a systematic and thorough review of variance analysis that would be the envy of every production engineer. The OD professionals hoped to create employee involvement in designing and producing the variance analysis. More often than the OD professionals preferred, they found themselves selling and pressuring employees into using the new instruments.

The OD professionals also opposed the use of crisis management. They often found themselves in a win–lose combative relationship with management where issues were polarized in terms of wrong versus right, and so on.

To sum up, the line and the OD professionals tended to deal with the tensions by using their respective Model I theories-in-use and defensive reasoning. This would feed back to reinforce the tensions which, in turn, would feed back to reinforce and polarize more the control and learning orientations.

## Consequences of OD Reactions

The four major consequences of the OD professionals' reactions, as identified and confirmed by them, were unintended and counterproductive. First, the OD professionals tended to bypass dealing with the line's fears of things getting out of control. The OD professionals would attempt to assure the line that they were in favor of control. They simply wanted the control to be more self-control, embedded in every employee. The problem, according to the line, was that they doubted this self-control was producible, and that the OD professionals and employees often behaved in ways to make the doubt a self-fulfilling prophecy.

The line's anxiety about the systems was whether they were producible and whether the OD people could help the organization produce them. The more the OD professionals attempted to assure the line by using metaphors such as vision and purposing in ways that were disconnected from reality, the more the line became anxious.

Not surprisingly, the line dealt with their anxieties by reverting to and reinforcing their control orientation. They "bought" the systems only to the extent that they could control them. The OD professionals, in order to implement the systems, reluctantly accepted these constraints. Unfortunately, they tended to make the theory behind these systems less

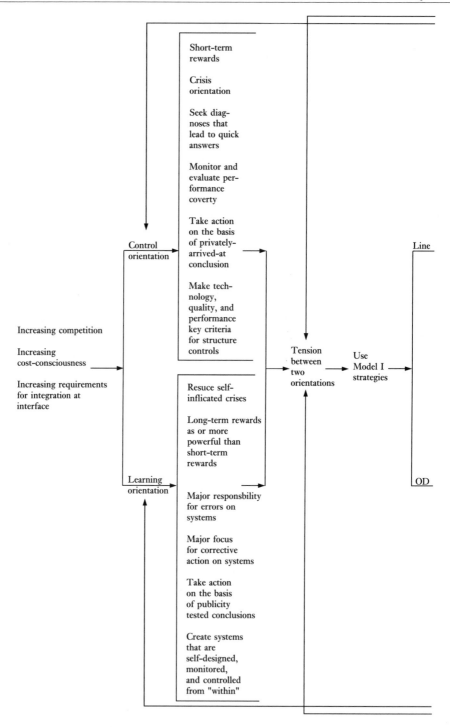

**Figure 15.2**   Learning versus control orientation patterns

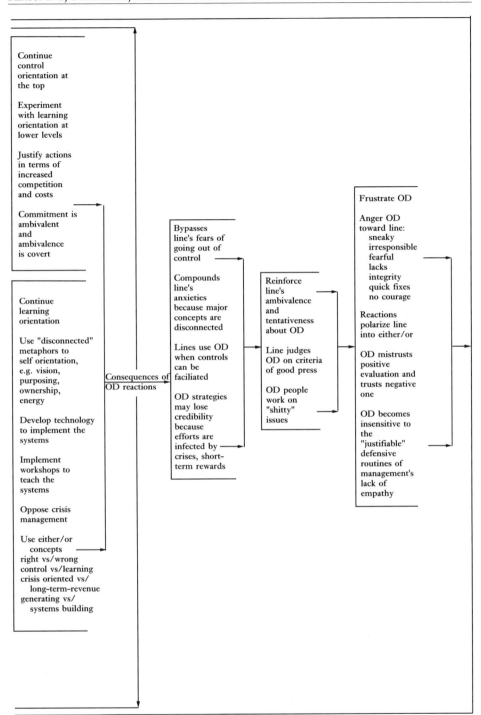

credible in the eyes of the employees. As the line continued its crisis and short-term orientation, it reduced the validity and credibility of the learning orientation.

The result of the these consequences was to reinforce the line's ambivalence about OD and about the systems. They sought to have their ambivalence reduced by seeking examples where the systems and OD professionals were to be trusted. This led OD people to act in ways that gave them "good press." Good press meant showing that their systems could operate under short-term rewards and meet immediate performance goals. Often the OD professionals helped the employees accomplish "good press" results by feeding upon or even creating their own crises.

These actions angered the OD professionals. "My personal sense of integrity is an issue. I want to do something significant. I do not want to get trapped in another petty issue."

Further consequences included OD frustration, with the frustration followed by anger. As one OD professional stated it: "My anger comes after having worked at an issue for a while, and not having made any progress."

The anger led the OD professionals to develop attributions about the line which came to the fore when they were reflecting on their frustration and anger. They described line managers, when under stress, as sneaky, irresponsible, fearful, lacking integrity, quick fixers, and lacking courage. It is interesting to note that the OD professionals found that they could make the same attributions about themselves when they were under pressure. Moreover, the attributions they made about the line managers that they believed they kept hidden actually came through in the reasoning they used to design and implement their interventions.

Under these conditions, it was difficult for the OD professionals to trust the positive evaluations made by line. It was easier to trust the negative ones. It was also more likely to exaggerate the negative and de-emphasize the positive evaluations.

The frustration, anger, and mistrust could combine to make it less likely that the OD professionals would be understanding of the line managements' defensive routines. I do not mean understanding in the sense of identifying the defensive routines. OD professionals were, as we have seen, quite competent at identifying the defensive routines. The lack of understanding is akin to a lack of empathy. It is illustrated by the inability of the OD professionals to have their "buttons pushed" by line defensive routines.

Finally, all the consequences reinforced each other and fed back to reinforce the tensions described earlier in the model. We now have a self-maintaining system that makes it less likely that errors will be detected and corrected and more likely that mutual trust will slowly deteriorate.

We can now see how the learning system encourage Model I theories-in-use and defensive reasoning. We can now hypothesize that some of the anger the OD professionals built up against the line could be related to the fact that the system of relationships that they helped to create caused them to behave inconsistently with their learning orientation while, at the same time, espousing that orientation as the preferred one. Not only were they being inconsistent but that inconsistency could lead to a deterioration in their credibility.

In a world locked into these counterproductive consequences, it is reasonable to expect the consequences described in the cases. It is also reasonable to predict the sense of deterioration between line and OD professionals. To the credit of the latter, they decided to explore these issues rather than ignore them.


### Mutual Problem-solving, Gap-filling, Ownership, and Energy

Richard, we may recall, provided explanations for clients' actions by making attributions. He did not test these attributions because he believed they were correct or he believed that testing them could upset the client. The latter was, in effect, a second attribution to make it unnecessary to test the first one. If we were to conceive of untested attributions as gaps in valid knowledge, then one primary pattern of Richard's reasoning is the creation of gaps, of further gaps to support the first ones, and of still further gaps to support the second ones.

A second pattern is to produce inconsistencies that he does not recognize as inconsistencies. For example, he judged the client's view of the video tape as incorrect, yet he admitted he neither knew the client's view of the video tape, nor did he have one of his own, nor did he know how to create it. These inconsistencies occurred almost one after the other in the same conversation.

There is another order of inconsistency that Richard produced; it became apparent as Richard interacted with the client over time. After making one untested attribution after another he then explained some of his behavior as his attempt to be nonjudgemental. It is as if he had not seen or kept track of the series of unilateral judgements that he had made. He seemed to have no sense of the patterns of history that he was creating.

Richard had two reactions to these patterns. The first was that he wanted to learn how to reduce them. The second was that he held the faith that if the client wanted to engage in genuine mutual problem solving, the negative consequences of his reasoning and actions could be reduced.

This reaction is one that I observed throughout these seminars as well as others. I suggest that one of the most fundamental working assumptions of current OD practice is the importance of mutual problem solving to close gaps, to identify and to correct errors such as inconsistencies. Moreover, an effective problem solving process will lead to a sense of ownership on the part of the clients to monitor the implementation of their decisions. Closely allied with ownership is the idea of energy for work. The assumption is that ownership causes the clients to have more energy to work the problem and to follow through.

Richard depends heavily on this working assumption in his dealings with the clients. Recall that Richard knew he did not know what was an appropriate vision for his client, he knew his client had the wrong one, and he believed if they could sit down and problem solve they would find a solution to the problem. The solution could include bringing in outside consulting professionals who knew how to produce effective visions.

From what we knew of Richard's reasoning and action strategies and from the contextual forces acting upon him and the clients, what can we say ahead of time about the likelihood that an effective mutual problem solving process can be established? We do not know the answer for the routine, simple problems but let us assume that the probability is high that he could help to create an effective mutual problem solving process. We do know, however, that the probability is quite low for creating a mutually satisfying problem solving process to deal with issues that contain threat to Richard or his clients. How do we arrive at this conclusion?

First, a word about the clients' states of mind. Many of them believed that the values underlying these concepts made good sense. Richard and the clients espoused some of the same values. Second, few of them realized how difficult it would be to design and implement a world consistent with their values. Their commitment was so high, however, that they not only invested thousands of dollars in the exercise, but they took major risks such as to delay the opening of new plants until the employees were adequately educated in the new theory of management and organization. Third, few of them realized the changes that would be necessary, not so much in their espoused values but in the values in their theories-in-use. Indeed few realized there would be much inconsistency. The degree of inconsistency they uncovered troubled and embarrassed them. Nevertheless, the clients persisted in their endeavors to learn. The conclusion is that the OD professionals were interacting with clients who were supportive of the changes to be made and the designs to be implemented. Thus the clients would probably come to the challenge of creating an effective mutual problem solving process with a good deal of concern and trepidation but a willingness to learn.

If the analysis above is correct, however, the clients are likely to frustrate the OD professionals leading the latter to reason and act in ways that will frustrate the clients and be unaware that this is happening. For example:

| *The OD professionals* | *What the clients can conclude* |
|---|---|
| 1  Tell the clients that the ultimate test of knowing is to be able to produce whatever ideas they espouse; and tell the clients that they know what their key concepts such as vision, ownership, energy mean but they have great difficulty in producing them. | 1  The OD professionals violate their own epistemology of knowledge. |
| 2  Define their key concepts by listing the outcomes they prefer to occur if the clients followed their advice. | 2  OD professionals use reasoning that is bewildering. They define their concepts by their outcomes but they cannot define how to produce the outcomes. |
| 3  Become impatient and angry with clients when they are seen as resisting; yet the resistance is predictable either from the attribution the OD professionals make or from the theory of action as described herein. | 3  The OD professionals are unfair. How can they get angry at us because we are acting consistently with their attributions? |
| 4  Make attributions about the clients that place the primary responsibility for lack of progress onto the clients. | 4  We are dealing with OD professionals who hold us responsible for slow progress. This will make it less likely that they will explore their responsibility with us. They are asking us to take ownership but they are not taking it themselves in certain crucial areas. |
| 5  Deal with persistent "resistance" on the part of the clients by either: | |
| (a) backing off which, upon reflection by the OD colleagues, is seen as putting down and pressuring; or | (a) Our OD professionals are unaware of important inconsistencies in their actions, at least while they are producing them. |
| (b) openly put down and pressure. | (b) When OD professionals are under stress and pressure, they act by creating the same kinds of defensive routines that they are telling us not to use. |

To the extent the above is valid, the clients may develop a second-order set of inferences. They are:

1  The OD professionals do not deal well with the inner contradictions in their theory in management and organization.
2  The OD professionals are unfair because they deal with us in the very ways they ask us not to use.
3  The OD professionals appear to be unaware of the first- and second-order consequences when they are producing them. They vary widely in their willingness to reflect on their errors after some time has passed.

If we examine these first- and second-order consequences in light of current OD practice, I believe we would have to conclude that the odds are low that these OD professionals can create a mutual problem solving process that is consistent with their own standards when dealing with threat.

It is important to add that this particular group came to this conclusion early in the seminars. They decided to learn the additional skills and knowledge required to begin to turn this around. Those with whom we are working have shown a great deal of progress. The point is that these defensive routines and loops can be interrupted and altered while the professionals are going about their practice.

## IMPLICATIONS

More empirical research is needed to assess the extent to which the findings described above are applicable in other situations. To the extent that the findings are applicable, then OD professionals should find it helpful to focus on the issues below.

Espoused theories, actions, and theories-in-use are key factors in the effectiveness of OD practice. OD professionals should identify the degree to which they produce inconsistencies and gaps among these three factors and the conditions under which they occur. A key feature of this inquiry should be the reasoning processes the OD professionals use to understand their world and to act in it. More empirical research, in turn, is needed to understand the relationship between defensive reasoning and organizational defensive routines.

OD professionals should learn how to develop maps of the behavioral worlds that they tend to create. The maps should especially focus on the organizational defensive routines and how they create organizational self-reinforcing, nonlearning patterns. Again, more research is needed on what the features of action maps are, how are they constructed, and how can they be used to inform OD practice and simultaneously test their theories.

More research is needed on why human beings appear to use a different set of reasoning processes when inventing solutions from those used to produce the solutions. What are the factors that cause the unawarenesses of the inconsistencies and gaps among espoused theories, theories-in-use, and action? What are the organizational processes by which the behavioral worlds feed back to reinforce defensive reasoning? What interventions can be used to reduce the limited learning features of the behavioral worlds in organizations?

What impact can structural factors have on producing double-loop learning? For example, what would be the features of management information systems or reward systems that could facilitate the use of productive reasoning when dealing with difficult issues, be they at the individual, group, intergroup, or organizational level? Can work be redesigned so that it encourages productive reasoning?

If management information systems, reward systems, and work can be designed to encourage productive reasoning, how will the existing defensive reasoning be overcome? Are individuals able to overcome their skilled defensive reasoning and use productive reasoning because the organization expects and rewards them for doing so?

# References

Argyris, C., 1970, *Intervention Theory and Method*, Reading, MA, Addison-Wesley.
Argyris, C., 1976, *Increasing Leadership Effectiveness*, New York, Wiley-Interscience.
Argyris, C., 1980, *Inner Contradictions of Rigorous Research*, New York, Academic Press.
Argyris, C., 1982, *Reasoning, Learning, and Action: Individual and Organizational*, San Francisco, Jossey-Bass.
Argyris, C., 1985, *Strategy, Change, and Defensive Routines*, Boston, Pitman.

Argyris, C., and Schön, D., 1974, *Theory in Practice*, San Francisco, Jossey-Bass.
Argyris, C., and Schön D., 1978, *Organizational Learning*, Reading, MA, Addison-Wesley.
Argyris, C., Putnam, R., and Smith, D. M., 1985, *Action Science*, San Francisco, Jossey-Bass.
Schön, D., 1983, *The Reflective Practitioner*, New York, Basic Books.

# — 16 —

# Inappropriate Defenses Against the Monitoring of Organization Development Practice

All professionals, especially those of us in the helping professions, are continually concerned about standards of conduct and practice. How do we monitor our actions as they occur while we are trying to be of help? How do we test the efficacy of our interventions as we make them? When faced with alternative hypotheses, diagnoses, claims for causality, or explanations, how do we decide which ones are credible and which ones are not?

I think one can fairly say the literature does not contain many discussions of these issues. Why is this so? I do not believe that we are not thinking about them, nor that we are incapable of writing about them. Instead, I believe that community norms are inhibiting our making such discussions public. I also believe that such proscriptive norms have risen over time because when we have tried to have discussions of these issues, they have often been unproductive and frustrating. In my experience, whenever such a dialogue has been more than superficial, it has soon become upsetting and threatening to those involved. This, in turn, has activated personal defenses – as well as community defenses – against attempts to press too hard on these issues.

This chapter presents three patterns of defenses I have experienced while engaging in such discussions. I believe that these patterns are not uniquely my own. Moreover, I myself have caused these defenses to be activated when, after becoming involved in dialogues on sensitive matters, I have pushed the discussion further than the other parties considered appropriate. Case 2 below especially shows that I behave in ways that are defensive, but also illustrates that I can be confronted regarding such behavior. I also believe that the cases illustrate how others act in ways to produce defensiveness.

## THREE PATTERNS THAT INHIBIT DIALOGUE

Case 1 illustrates the first pattern I have encountered, in which a person who asks questions about testing hypotheses and choosing among claims of causality is accused of being "too rational" or "too scientific." Those responding in this way typically describe themselves as intuitive, feeling oriented, and humanistic. This inhibits dialogue because many who deem these questions to be important also value intuition, are concerned about feelings, and consider themselves humanistic. They may therefore feel misunderstood and try to correct the erroneous impressions. But the reasoning of people acting defensively in such cases is complex. For example, those who claim that they are not – and need not be – concerned about the rational testing of their claims merely because they themselves are not rationally oriented tend to interpret inquiry into this position as itself being too rational. This is likely to result in a self-reinforcing process preventing people from addressing the original questions.

Case 2 depicts a second pattern, in which a person believes that rationality and logic are relevant, but maintains that dialogue should not be too rational when someone is upset and feeling highly emotional. To some extent, this makes sense: Many of us have difficulty thinking rationally when we are upset. When I have observed this pattern, though, I have seen it inhibit discussion in two ways. First, it often produces requests to "hold it" or "back off," which make it difficult to examine how one may have caused someone else to be upset, or the extent to which the upset individual contributed to the situation. Second, when I saw someone back off in response to such a request, the individual who was upset expressed feelings of caring and increasing trust, and the other person expressed happiness and a similar sense of increasing trust – yet three months later, when another difficult situation arose between the two, the increased levels of caring and trust did not appear to help matters and the dialogue was again counterproductive.

Case 3 demonstrates a third pattern, in which someone who questions the validity and appropriateness of a particular intervention is accused of being too evaluative, too judgemental, and punishing. Such responses are not only counterproductive in that they inhibit dialogue, but also logically inconsistent; the accusation that someone is too evaluative and judgemental is itself evaluative and judgemental, and charging someone with being punishing may itself cause that person to feel punished.

The purpose of this article is to reflect on – or "go meta" on, so to speak – conversations expressing disagreements on substantive issues of practice. The focus is not on the issues themselves, but on the ways we deal with them.

## Case 1. The Roles of Rationality and Intuition in Testing Our Theories of Practice

The dialogue in Case 1 occurred during a seminar with 24 senior organizational consultants. Slightly more than half described themselves as intuitive, existentially oriented, and humanistic. During the seminar, it became clear that the participants differed widely in general on issues of testing interventions, and specifically on claims of validity.

Those who labeled themselves intuitive judged the others to be too rational and too scientific, and maintained that practice is best dealt with from a humanistic, existential perspective. They considered it wrong to assess the validity of interventions heavily laden with feelings by using the types of activities required for tests of falsifiability or disconfirmability.

I pointed out to some of the members within the majority group that their cases showed they differed significantly on how they came to know what they said they knew, as well as on their strategies for helping clients. Were all of them correct? How could such a position be true? What criteria were needed to defend this position to the profession and to the society?

"There you go again, being too rational, too scientific," would be the dominant response of the majority. The following are examples from the discussion.

PROFESSIONAL A:  What I have wanted to say from the beginning is that we are not working with a scientific theory. Rationality, validity, testing. All these ideas are related to the paradigm of rationality and science. I don't buy that. In my experience, life isn't scientific.

PROFESSIONAL B:  I have difficulty in accepting the premise that we must state our ideas in ways that are falsifiable.

ARGYRIS:               How can we detect and correct unrecognized errors?
PROFESSIONAL B:  I think that there must be ways other than being scientific.
ARGYRIS:               What is your notion of testing?
PROFESSIONAL B:  All I'm saying is that I do not believe that the scientific paradigm is
                                absolute. I do not hold testing to be absolute.
PROFESSIONAL C:  What I do know is that when I'm around certain people I feel comfort-
                                able or good. It doesn't matter exactly what they are saying. I get
                                certain feelings that I am comfortable with.
PROFESSIONAL D:  The reason I bring this up is that I'm having problems [with the
                                discussion]. And the problem is that you cannot test effect.
ARGYRIS:               Well let's take your case. You say that Mary [the client] was manifesting
                                dependence and projection.
PROFESSIONAL D:  Yes.
ARGYRIS:               I would like to know what method you would use to test these
                                inferences. How would you discover mistakes in your diagnoses?
PROFESSIONAL D:  (silent, in thought) Well, I guess I don't have a method. It is not possible
                                to test effect.

The argument begins with the assertion that scientific testing is not appropriate. The individuals who say this cannot define what is scientific or what constitutes testing. When asked to state the source of their claim, they say it is their experience. But if experience is constructed by the professionals how can the validity of the assertion be independent of the professionals' perceptions? How can the professionals protect themselves from creating tests that are self-fulfilling?

When the professionals were asked to explicitly describe their concept of testing, they were unable to do so. Even more troublesome, those who held this view had not developed explicit guidelines for the means and limits of their testing, even though they had been active professionals for at least five years. Finally, statements such as "I do not accept the premise that our ideas should be stated in ways that are falsifiable" or "I do not believe that the scientific paradigm is absolute" are themselves absolute and likely to make dialogue more difficult.

The reader may wonder if the responses presented above were activated by my way of questioning and my persistence. I believe the answer is "yes – partially." I say partially because I find the responsibility to be joint.

In accepting only partial responsibility, I am not trying to exonerate myself from the responsibility to learn more. If some other way of questioning would likely be more effective under these conditions, I wish to learn it. In addition, the issue of persistence raises some questions: under what conditions is persistence justified? Why is my persistence in con-tinuing the dialogue seen as counterproductive, whereas the others' persistence in refusing to answer questions is seen as justified?

### Case 2. On-line Testing of Diagnosis and Intervention

During the first two sessions of a seminar, it became clear that another consultant – hereafter referred to as A – and I differed on when and how much to confront a client.

According to A, consultants should lean toward interventions that only minimally intrude on clients' thoughts and actions, and thus should carefully craft any confrontations to avoid making clients more inclined to be defensive. Many of us attending the seminar, including me, agreed with these criteria. The difficulty arose when we discussed ways to implement them. A wrote:

> My consulting model allows for emotional or logical "confrontation" in much the same way that Chris's does . . . We may differ on our timing and our criteria for when – [that is], what data do we react to in the client that would make us choose to escalate the emotionality of the inquiry, and when do we choose to make our hypotheses about what the client may be thinking or feeling public to the client (my definition of confrontation)?

I agree that we differ on timing and criteria, but these differences are not tactical. Rather, the differences stem from our having different theories of how to learn from defensiveness and how to test interventions. This can be seen in the example below.

A and I developed a defensive dialogue. We were discussing a case in which a CEO was pushing for an increasing emphasis on pay for performance. My colleagues and I had developed an action map of what facilitated and inhibited the likelihood of success for pay for performance. A was not certain such a map was necessary, and said he would begin instead by talking with the CEO.

All of us at the seminar agreed this provided an opportunity for role-play. A took the part of the consultant, and I acted as the CEO. Because A and I had been questioning each other's views, another seminar participant and I asked A if he preferred to have someone else play the role of the CEO. He responded that he had no problem with my taking that role.

During the role-play I felt that A understood me and was acting in ways consistent with his views on effective intervention. After five to ten minutes of role-playing, A stopped and said,

> Let me interrupt now and tell you what's on my mind. I'm now at a choice point. I think it's better to identify the choice point than to just keep the role-play, because you may not know what's going on in my mind. This is a client who is working very hard at not owning the problem. He's done every conceivable thing to get out from under it himself. He wants a quick fix, he wants somebody else to work it. Every opportunity I've given him to own the problem, he has shoved aside.

A then said that he was ready to continue the role-play. Several other seminar participants stated that they wanted to stop and examine what had just happened.

I was stunned by A's comments. I thought I had been acting as a relatively open-minded CEO who did not want a quick fix. Moreover, I felt perturbed that A had kept all these thoughts secret from me. If I were his client, I would have wanted him to share his evaluations and analyses of me to test their validity. If he – and the other seminar participants – could have helped me see that I was coming across in ways counter to what I intended, that would have provided an important lesson for me. Moreover, by exploring the issue, A might have learned to examine the validity of his diagnoses. I perceived, however, that A was acting as if his diagnosis of my actions as the CEO required no testing.

A argued that he would not test his evaluations publicly at this time, claiming that doing so might make the CEO – me – defensive. But could keeping these evaluations private, yet still acting on them, lead to unrecognized distortions? Moreover, if the basis for his decision to withhold his opinions is that they are private, then the logic for this choice is self-referential: that is, the test of its validity is limited to the logic of the actor. Such tests are susceptible to self-sealing reasoning. We advise our clients against the use of such logic. Therefore, why should we use it in our relationships with one another?

Immediately after we agreed to stop the role-play, another seminar participant, B, commented:

> I think [A] is on the verge of constructing an alternative theory of what's going on. He has formed a central hypothesis that [the CEO] refuses to take personal responsibility for what's

going on. What intrigues me is I would not have come to the same conclusion from the same data. The reason was that at a number of intervals [the CEO] said, "I realize my behavior is part of the problem. I realize I, too, would have to go through a change program if we had one. I'm not much better than they are.' So, I thought he was giving you offers; I read him as inviting you to change him. On the other hand, now that you [A] point it out, I think that it is true that he [the CEO] didn't respond to the failure of his nth attempt by going to the people and saying, 'You haven't done what I wanted.'

To be fair, the CEO did precisely that, although I may not have made that explicit in the role-play.

Two others (and I) overtly supported B's perspective. This suggests that A's analyses could be wrong. (Later I learned that at least three other participants disagreed with A's views.) Yet A had privately reached the conclusion that he should not test his evaluations of the CEO with the CEO, and had decided – also privately – that such a test could be counterproductive.

One other point deserves mention. B expressed his disagreement with A as follows. He said, in effect, that he had made a different set of analyses of the CEO. He then illustrated from his notes of the role-play what the CEO said that led him to differ with A's original inferences about the CEO. B differed with A, but expressed his views in a way that enabled others to see how he arrived at them. Therefore, in my opinion, he increased the likelihood of a constructive dialogue.

I acted using a similar strategy toward A. I asked him what I (as the CEO) had said or done that led him to make his evaluations of me and to decide he could not test the validity of them with me.

A responded, "There you go again." He said that I did not seem to realize that the difficulty that he had with my request for illustrations was that the request was "too cognitive."

"The problem of whether I can learn or not," he explained, "has to do with whether I can get my feelings under control. It is not a logical issue."

I empathized with that view. All of us have experienced moments when we are so upset that we cannot respond to requests that are primarily cognitive. Had A said that, I would have understood. But he continued by announcing I was "too competitive." I wondered how he had reached that conclusion. Was it because his actions were also "competitive"? How would this possibility be tested?

In reflecting on the episode, I suggest that A did to me – as Chris Argyris – the same thing he did to the CEO in the role-play. That is, he evaluated me as too competitive and declared this to be my problem in the sense that it was my behavior that was ineffective.

I was now feeling what I had previously been feeling in the role of the CEO. That is, judgements of me and my motives had been made unilaterally, and were protected from being tested by a set of evaluations about my competence and competitiveness. Thus, my efforts to learn where and how I was wrong were blocked.

I do not have difficulty meeting someone's request to "back off" until that person has come to grips with her or his feelings. Indeed, I would make a similar request in such circumstances. I do mind backing off, however, when doing so reinforces an action strategy with rules such as these: evaluate another person's intentions; do not attempt to test the validity of your evaluations; justify your thoughts and actions by asserting that the other person is acting incompetently; do not attempt to test this assertion.

With respect to the role-play, I believe that one cause of A's becoming emotionally upset was that after the role-play had ended – and after several seminar participants said they differed with his evaluation of the CEO – I told him I was stunned when I realized he had kept his judgements of me as the CEO secret, and added that I did not believe that consultants should make evaluations of clients without subsequently testing them.

A reacted negatively when I used the words "covert" and "secret," and described them as unfair and punishing. It was true, he agreed, that he had withheld his evaluations and his feelings of frustration and anger. But he claimed he did so because, according to his theory of intervention, this was effective consulting behavior.

Reflecting on the episode with the help of others in the group, I learned several things. First, I had automatically judged A as wrong because he was not acting in accordance with my theory, which prescribed testing one's evaluations of clients' intentions. If I had not made genuine inquiry so difficult, the dialogue about when one should and should not withhold evaluations being used to manage an intervention might have become more constructive.

But there was more to my error than that. I suspect that the tone of my voice and other nonverbal cues may have communicated my having made an emotional judgement of A that he was wrong. Thus, even if I had asked the correct questions, I might still have gotten into trouble because of my nonverbal cues. The tone, in turn, could have been driven by my using the word "secret." A objected to that word because it implied a cover-up. I did intend to refer to a "cover-up," but not as a deliberate, conscious act as much as a highly skillful, automatic, tacit reaction.

The following dialogue is an example of how the way I used my theory got me into trouble.

> A:        But you know what you are saying, which I think is important, is that you learn from confrontation. I'm not sure that I do, because I know that this is not helpful for me. [To give you an example of your confrontation that is not helpful to me,] when you say that large portions of [my] theory [are] covert, I find that hard to deal with. It may be true, but I do not learn from that.
>
> ARGYRIS: But if I could illustrate [these assertions]...
>
> A:        If I could hear you. But you see, I am caught in my own theory. Confrontational interventions are the last thing I'll try, because I know how I react to confrontation. Badly. I don't listen well. Therefore, I start with a projection that, if I am any kind of approximation of other people, I don't want to get them upset right off the bat by confronting them. I'll confront them when I know that it is safe. I experience you as being quite prepared to confront right away. And that probably works quite well with people who [do not become] defensive when they are confronted.

This raises another important issue. On the one hand, I believe many of us would agree that our biases and defenses influence the theories of intervention we create and the ways in which we implement them. On the other hand, I also believe that many of us agree that there must be a limit to this flexibility. Our biases and defenses can be counterproductive. This is why it is common practice for us to reflect on a difficult intervention to understand the extent to which we may have acted inappropriately.

How do we identify those rules of intervention that, if based upon our personal biases or defenses, ought to be changed? My answer is that behavioral rules permitting the rejection of inquiry into our actions should be highly limited. As professionals, we have an obligation to be able to be confronted, even if this makes us feel vulnerable.

For this assertion to be credible, however, I must define what I consider effective confrontation. I would suggest the following: in response to any statement of advocacy, evaluation, or attribution, it is acceptable behavior to request an illustration, an inquiry into the reasoning behind the attribution, and a test of the validity of the claims being made.

Moreover, such a test should not be trapped by the logic used to make the evaluations and attributions in the first place.

If at times someone cannot abide by this rule because that person is too upset, then it is legitimate to request empathy and support. Such a request should be accepted as long as the parties are committed to return to addressing the issues once the level of distress is reduced (perhaps with a third-party facilitator).

In the early 1950s, when T Groups typically worked together for three weeks at a time, we professionals used to state that participants could express any views and feelings as long as they did not try to inflict physical harm on anyone. Once feelings were expressed, everyone in the T Group was obligated to strive to work on them. It was considered inappropriate for anyone to walk out while the T Group was working because doing so could harm the members of the group, including the one leaving.

In the following case, one professional chose to leave while the group was working. Three others remained, and all three learned lessons they would not otherwise have gained if the dialogue had ended early (which might be the tacit intention of those who leave a context that they freely chose to enter in order to learn).

I see another problem related to keeping one's evaluations private until one decides it is safe to make them public. The problem is illustrated by an episode that took place in the seminar's group session.

X, another member of our group, intervened to help A and me. During the subsequent break, I learned from X the following.

> He privately perceived A as feeling isolated and alone in the group.
> He also privately perceived that Y, another participant, held views and feelings that, if expressed, would help A feel less isolated.
> He had asked several questions ostensibly of the group, to which Y responded as X had expected he would. Moreover, the questions led to a series of constructive conversations that produced the understanding between A and me that X had intended.

I asked X what prevented him from making his strategy public. He said he thought that doing so would have likely made A feel more defensive and perhaps even more isolated – the age-old dilemma of a cure that could make the illness worse. This is another point I consider worth exploring. Unless it was revealed, A would never know of the elaborate strategy X had designed to help A feel less isolated and less defensive. If A felt that X's actions were helpful (which I believe he did), he would never know he was helped by actions X had intended to be covered up.

This episode illustrates yet another issue. X seemed to be following several rules: first, make a private judgement of A's psychological state, Y's psychological state, the likelihood that Y will act as X wishes he would, and the likelihood that the group will let Y act in this way if he chooses to do so. Second, ask a question that will likely prompt Y to act, but do so in such a way that Y does not realize he is being used to help X (and others in the group) reach A.

In this case the intervention worked because of X's skills and the commitment of the participants to individual growth and to making the group become more effective. But what would happen if an executive learned such covert strategies and decided to use them in the service of "getting things done" in the organization without others' recognizing the executive's intentions? Moreover, what would happen to the others if the executive decided to back up these strategies with managerial power? When OD professionals use such strategies themselves, are they not modeling covert actions others could use to control people?

In sum, A and I both acted in ways that produced counterproductive dialogue. The experience of undergoing such dialogue, I believe, is a cause of why so few professionals in our field engage in active inquiry into the critical issues of monitoring the effectiveness of our actions. In my view, the dilemma in this case is that A acted in ways that prevented me from learning about my ineffectiveness, because he found my own actions unhelpful to him. Without the help of the other seminar participants, I doubt I would have learned about the moments when I acted ineffectively.

A second dilemma is that we both acted consistently with our own theories of intervention. Herein lies a critical issue. As I understand A's theory, it made him unable to be confronted when he was emotionally upset. Moreover, whatever I tried he judged as ineffective for him, because my actions violated his views and defenses.

I do not believe that we, as OD professionals, should hold theories of intervention that legitimize our being closed to learning. I do not object to our saying that at times when we feel highly upset we cannot learn, and agree that in such cases we should first try to reduce the degree to which any of the parties involved feel upset. But I suggest we adopt the rule that in such cases we will commit ourselves to returning to the discussion afterward. Otherwise we run the risk of encouraging professionals to design their thinking and act on reasoning that is self-protective and self-sealing.

## Case 3. Providing Space

"Providing space" for a client who is acting defensively and thus reducing her or his options to act freely seems to make sense. But two puzzles concern me. The first puzzle is the extent to which clients use this technique to divert the intervenor from threatening issues so that the clients can continue their counterproductive actions. The second puzzle is which strategies intervenors use to provide this space. So far, the majority of intervenors I have studied provide space in ways that do not communicate to the client what the intervenors are doing. That is, they cover up their strategy because making it overt may increase the client's defensiveness and hence reduce the space (see the example of X in Case 2 above).

Case 3 illustrates these puzzles in more detail. I was part of a team with C, D, and E that had begun working at the top of a multibillion dollar organization. I had introduced the team to the CEO, although the team members were chosen through a competitive bidding process.

During our work with the clients, I observed D making attributions and evaluations concerning the clients. In my opinion, he rarely crafted his judgements in ways that encouraged questioning or testing of them. C and E shared some of my concerns. They believed we should give D some space in this matter because they thought this would make him less defensive, and thus create the conditions for exploring these issues later. I doubted the validity of this hypothesis and said so to C and E.

The first time I told D about my concerns, the interchange became quite heated, just as C and E had predicted. In my view, D piled one unillustrated, untestable evaluation upon another. In turn, I believe he perceived my request for illustrations and testing as a means of backing him into a corner. C and E observed this interaction and tried to help us. I myself found some of their interventions helpful, although I winced at those that seemed to overprotect D.

Later the CEO told us that the firm had decided to ask that D be taken off the team and that the rest of us continue without him. C, E, and I then met to discuss the entire project, and at one point began addressing my relationship with D (D was not present by his own choice).

C began by describing the feelings he would attribute to a client who, when asked to examine the reasoning behind her or his actions, had difficulty doing this but did not intend to say so. C believed that this was the situation D underwent when I questioned him during a previous session. C said he thought the client would be feeling, "I'm terribly frustrated with the questions being asked of me. I'm frustrated with my inability to answer them. I'm welling up inside. I'm not succeeding in calming down."

C then said that if we considered such an evaluation plausible, he would role-play what he would have said to D or any other client in the situation. After E and I agreed that evaluation was plausible, C said he would probably say to the client:

> It's clear that you're very upset. I'm uncomfortable about that. I may have done something to upset you. Apparently your being so upset has something to do with me. I'd like to understand what I'm doing that makes it difficult for you. I'd like to come to the place where you are not so hurt or angry. What can I do? How do we move from here?

C articulated his reasoning as follows: "When I see that level of distress, I want to open up the space around the person . . . so that he can express whatever reality is for him." He later added, "[In effect I am saying] we made a little bit of progress. Let's move on. We will still have another chance."

I then role-played what I would have said:

> I'm sorry you are feeling upset. If you would like, we could stop the inquiry and return to it later. I would like to examine what I am saying to you in order to see if there is anything that I am saying or how I am saying it that may be upsetting you. At the same time, I would like to examine your actions and their impact on me and the others. I do not think that I or you will learn unless we examine our actions and the reasoning behind them. I am prepared to do it now or later. I am not willing to forget the episode. I am willing to include a third party to help us [in this case, C and E] should you wish.

C responded, "I'm going to use the word 'milk it.' You really are ready to work now." I then stated:

> Yes, I believe that D and I are causally responsible for our actions and our reasoning I also believe that it is a good idea to reflect on our actions as soon after our actions and thinking as possible. Finally, I believe that distancing or providing space can be of help. But the choice of providing space should be explicit and not covered up.

I felt that this was especially true when dealing with one another as professionals. The role-play continued.

| | |
|---|---|
| C: | We would say [to ourselves] let's move on. We will have another chance |
| ARGYRIS: | I would interpret that as bypassing unless the client [D] is involved in that decision. |
| E: | [I agree with C.] My fear is that if I did what you did, D might avoid expressing feelings in my presence . . . So I would like to build more of a therapeutic alliance before I jump into [your strategy]. You go at it immediately. I do not have the confidence that I could help a person to get to it. |

Both C and E felt that the approach of asking for illustrations, requiring that evaluations be tested, and the like could make a client feel like "being on the witness stand." I replied that I could see how the client might feel this way.

If I were to make an evaluation in such circumstances, I would state what I thought, illustrate it, and test it with the client. For example, if the client said, "yes, I do feel like I am on the witness stand," or "yes, and I resent it," or "yes, and it upsets me," I would not take such responses alone as evidence that my behavior was what led the client to feel this way. In the case of D, I asked him to craft his evaluations in ways that could be tested, a request I would also make of myself. Indeed, C, D, E, and I often made similar requests of our clients.

If I were acting consistently with the theory of communication we all held then, I would seek to examine the extent to which using the metaphor of the witness stand could be a way to avoid examining one's counterproductive behavior. For example, should I go along with a colleague (or client) who makes untested evaluations of others and then defends these evaluations merely by making more of them? C and E argued that if I gave D some space he might alter his actions. But if C and E were correct and D agreed he would find such space helpful, why not involve D explicitly in the decision to give him space?

In Case 2, A had difficulty learning from such confrontation. In my opinion, this does not necessarily mean he could not have learned at all from confrontation. In Case 3, C and E also defined my asking for illustrations and tests of evaluations as confrontational behavior. But, although they had felt pressured by my requests, they stated that these led them to develop insights they would not have had without my persistence. Perhaps the hypothesis is valid that OD professionals should not back off from this type of confrontation until the client requests that they do.

Professionals can still help clients who do not learn from such confrontations to design other ways of learning. In addition, conditions can be created to allow clients to cut off relationships with consultants. C and E chose the former alternative; D the latter. Commenting on D's choice, C said, "I told D that I can't understand his reaction toward you. He is still making attributions about your motives that make you [look like the villain]. I don't know where the hell he is coming from."

From this comment I infer that on other occasions C tried to resume discussing this issue, but was not successful because C's efforts to give D space and to care about him might have legitimized D's defense strategies that not only distanced him from the clients, but also from himself. C and I discussed this further.

C:              My sense of caring is to be more mothering. This is what he needed – someone to nurture him.

ARGYRIS:   In this case, I believe that your nurturing may collude with D's defenses. His actions say to you in effect "lay off" or "withdraw," but he never makes that explicit. You withdraw, and you never say that you are withdrawing, because of your attributions that (1) he is not likely to learn now, and (2) that there will be another time.

Toward the end of the discussion we addressed the witness stand metaphor described above. C stated that the CEO had implicit faith in me. I understood the word "implicit" to mean "tacit and unexamined." I did not think this was true, but thought that I could have misunderstood C, and that I could have been wrong.

ARGYRIS:   What have you seen the CEO do or say that leads you to believe that he has implicit faith in me?

C:              He told me that he wanted you at the meeting.

ARGYRIS:   And what is the reasoning by which you conclude that his saying that he wants me there is a sign of implicit faith in me?

C:              Well, it wasn't the only time.

ARGYRIS:   I understand that there may be several examples. Could we begin with this one?

C:              I am saying this because it was not the only case. It is a pattern.

Later the discussion went as follows.

> C:          [I remember a meeting] where the CEO sort of allied himself with your views.
> ARGYRIS:    [I do not understand two things.] One, what does "sort of" mean? Second, how
>             does allying himself with my view become an illustration of implicit faith in me?
> C:          I knew [you were going to ask that]. I'm going to answer. But I insist that you
>             accept [the reality] that [my judgements] are based on more than one behavior.
>             It is a pattern, and that is part of my reasoning process.

I responded that I wanted to understand the components of the pattern and the reasoning that C used for saying such a pattern existed.

> C:          I'm open to another construction, clearly I am.
> ARGYRIS:    To be honest with you, I believe that you believe that, but I do not believe it. Let
>             me illustrate how I arrive at that attribution and get your reaction. For example,
>             you crafted the assertion that the CEO had implicit faith as if you were correct.
>             To my knowledge, you never tested it with me or with him.
> C:          I think you are right.
> ARGYRIS:    [Would it also be fair to say that] when I said "I do not believe you," you would
>             categorize that as my acting in ways that reduce your space?
> C:          Absolutely.
> ARGYRIS:    Yet you do not appear to me to be closed to learning. I saw my saying what I did as
>             expressing concern and support for you and betting on your interest in learning
>             and in my learning.
> C:          Yes, when you said that, I said to myself, "I have to think about that."

I then remarked that although I was acting in ways that were consistent with the concepts of the witness stand, "being too rational," and "reducing his space," C was engaged in the activity and learning. This seemed to me to provide evidence that C was learning under the same conditions under which he had said D could not learn. That D might have found it helpful to learn under these conditions is illustrated by the reasons the executives gave for asking D to leave. In their opinion, D made evaluations of the executives that had questionable validity, and when they said so they felt that D responded by making more untested evaluations. They thus found him unreachable, and did to him what D had done to me – namely, they cut off their relationship with him.

> C:          And now, I understand.
> ARGYRIS:    [My problem was that] I doubted the examples that you gave, but I could not test
>             my doubts, nor could you test the validity of the assertion that you were sure of.
> C:          I agree, deeply, profoundly in a philosophical way.
> ARGYRIS:    Then I need to know . . .
> C:          (interrupting) How come I don't get these beliefs into the design of my behavior?

## IMPLICATIONS FOR PRACTICE

The three patterns of defenses discussed in this chapter inhibit because they stop discourse. I believe that, as professionals, we should strive to reduce these defenses as much as we can. Our credibility with clients and the long-term viability of our research and practice will be harmed if our professional culture allows and protects such defenses. I believe that the degree of help we can provide in the future will be self-limiting if it is constrained by such defenses.

I also believe that claims about validity and effectiveness are ultimately claims about causality. That is, if one acts in a particular manner, particular results will occur. To avoid ending up in the position of unwittingly deluding ourselves or others, our claims must be tested using logic and actions independent of our own.

I cannot see how we can fulfill these requirements without paying attention to logic and testing our evaluations publicly. I do not consider it inappropriate for professionals to introduce and test their feelings and perceptions as they are being formed. Indeed, most of us do so. The issue is whether they be addressed in a way that permits the reasoning behind them to be discussed and influenced.

The cases described above illustrate why this is not likely to occur if the three defense patterns are activated. Not only do those using these defenses make evaluations they do not test publicly, they also make judgements as to why it would be harmful or useless to test these evaluations publicly. The evaluations are "nested" and reinforce themselves, thereby making the actor less open to learning.

Framed as rules, the three defensive patterns described in this article offer the following instructions.

- Do not be too rational or too cognitive.
- Develop an intervention strategy that is consistent with your personal style of learning.
- Withdraw from dialogue with colleagues about substantive differences in your respective theories of practice if the conversation becomes too cognitive or requires that defenses be confronted.

Such rules, when applied, cause recursive patterns of thinking and action. They lead to a compulsive repetition of one's original strategy, because they do not permit any opportunity to interrupt it and explore it.

I find it interesting to compare these rules with the criteria and rules suggested by Habermas for producing authentic conversation or dialogue (Robinson, 1987). Habermas identifies four claims in every conversation that require inquiry. They are, first, what the speaker says is *comprehensible*. The players involved must agree on the essence of the communication. Second, what is being talked about is *true* for the individual speaking and for those he or she is speaking about. For example, if A asserts that B is defensive, and B disputes the claim, A cannot then say, "I didn't say you were defensive, I said that I felt you were defensive or that I experienced you as defensive." A has the obligation to join B in resolving their differences in perception. Both must be committed to exploring their personal views of reality. Both must be committed to reducing the gaps as much as possible. Both must be committed to not taking a live-and-let-live position. And both must be committed to persisting in this effort if they are seeking to create valid and authentic communications.

Third, the speaker has expressed her or his intentions and state of mind *truthfully*. This claim raises concerns about the issue of withholding. When individuals withhold attributions, evaluations, and strategies about others, yet design actions based on what they are withholding, they are not expressing their intentions and inner states truthfully. As professionals who value authentic communication, we must eventually deal with the dilemma illustrated in the examples above in which individuals withheld information because they decided this was in the best interests of the others and of progress in their work. Although at times human beings may require space, this model suggests that when one asserts that a person requires space, such decisions be shared with that person.

Fourth, the speaker's act of speaking was *right* or appropriate. Finally, this model of authentic communication requires speakers to test their experience. That is, if much of one's experience is a personal construction, one has an obligation to make explicit how one decided that the act of speaking was right or appropriate. The freedom to craft our meanings carries with it an obligation to examine the reasoning behind these meanings, which is the reasoning we use to construe reality as we do.

As shown in this chapter, asking people to state publicly their reasoning often produces strong feelings. Many of the professionals in the cases above felt strongly that asking them to reflect on their reasoning and make it explicit was "too rational." What leads human beings to become upset when they are asked to describe the reasoning they used to decide that their act of speaking was right or appropriate? I suggest that this is an important question requiring more research.

The position I recommend calls for us to use what I call productive reasoning (Argyris, 1982, 1990a). When using productive reasoning, people strive to make their premises, inferences, and conclusions explicit and to subject them to public tests that are genuinely independent. The reasoning illustrated in the three cases above is defensive reasoning (Argyris, 1985), for which the premises, inferences, and conclusions are either tacit, or, if explicit, subjected to no other tests of validity except those involving the personal biases of their creator.

Elsewhere, Donald Schön and I (Argyris and Schön, 1974) have shown that the reasoning an individual may espouse and that which one actually uses can be different and inconsistent. Moreover, the actor is often unaware of this inconsistency. To discover the reasoning actually in use, one must closely observe actual interactions and conversations and, if possible, tape record them. During the past two decades I have tape recorded most of the seminars I have held or attended.

In chapter 15 we looked at the case of Richard (see pp. 246–55), a man whose defensive reasoning illustrated, in my experience, what I consider to be the reasoning used by the majority of the professionals participating in the seminar he attended (this conclusion was confirmed by ten of the participants and rejected by two). Richard used the four nested strategies described above, with unintended consequences such as the following. Richard wanted a line manager to listen to him carefully, yet Richard himself did not listen to the manager. Richard advised the line manager not to develop prejudices against his subordinates, yet Richard himself developed prejudices against the line manager.

An example involving intra- and intergroup experiences comes from a study of 140 human resources professionals. An organization's vice president of human resources had learned that the majority of his professionals believed that line management acted in ways to disempower them. An experiment in learning was designed jointly and implemented whereby 20 professionals were selected to attend a five-day workshop designed to devise ways to combat the line's disempowering strategies. A simple diagnostic method to uncover nested strategies was devised using cases written by the participants. The writers described what they each would do to initiate efforts to reduce disempowerment. After some lively discussions, the 20 participants concluded that the cases they had prepared to reduce their disempowerment would actually increase it (Argyris, 1990b).

Another study, this one of 20 OD professionals in a large corporation, found that when line management acted toward these professionals in ways that were aggressive, manipulative, and unilaterally controlling (all posing threats of various degrees), the OD group created a set of patterned, systemic relationships with line managers at all levels of the organization that were counterproductive to the objectives the OD professionals espoused. Moreover, the OD professionals acted manipulatively and strove to be unilaterally controlling (Argyris, 1990b).

There is, I suggest, another important reason for developing OD theories of intervention that require the use of productive reasoning. Recent advances in strategy and financial accounting, to name two examples, seem to be based on logic that is not only more rigorous but more capable of being tested and withstanding confrontation. That is, these new advances are based on productive reasoning (Argyris, 1989, 1990a). If this is the case, then OD practices based on productive reasoning are more likely to be integrated with the other managerial functions, are less likely to be seen as "soft," and are more likely to assure clients that the quality of the implementation of the new technical managerial activities will be as high as the clients are capable of producing.

# References

Argyris, C., 1982, *Reasoning, Learning and Action*, San Francisco, Jossey-Bass.

Argyris, C., 1985, *Strategy, Change and Defensive Routines*, New York, Ballinger.

Argyris, C., 1989, "Strategy Implementation: An Experience in Learning," *Organizational Dynamics*, Autumn, pp. 1–5.

Argyris, C., 1990a, "The Dilemma of Implementing Controls: The Case of Managerial Accounting," *Accounting, Organization, and Society*, 15, 6, pp. 503–11.

Argyris, C., 1990b, *Overcoming Organizational Defenses*, Needham, MA, Allyn & Bacon.

Argyris, C., and Schön, D., 1974, *Theory in Practice*, San Francisco, Jossey-Bass.

Robinson, V., 1987, *The Nature and Conduct of a Critical Dialogue*, Department of Education, University of Auckland, New Zealand.

# — 17 —

# Do Personal Growth Laboratories Represent an Alternative Culture?

During the past few years the basic make-up of many cultures has been so questioned and confronted by its own members that a leading diplomat, in a speech at the United Nations, raised the possibility that the world may have entered an era in which nations may have more to fear from internal revolution than from attack by other nations.

One group raising serious questions about present American culture has been composed of behavioral scientists, especially those involved in laboratory education. Unlike many of the more militant protesters, they have been trying to design and field-test social technology that could bring about effective change. One such technology is laboratory education, and one subdivision of laboratory education is the personal growth laboratory.

Shepard (1970) states that personal growth laboratories represent an alternative culture to the present mechanistic, survival-oriented culture. These laboratories can provide learning experiences through which the participants can acquire a clearer vision of a better life, reasons Shepard. Shepard is careful not to claim that personal growth laboratories are a panacea, or that, in themselves, they provide all that is needed for the development of a new alternative culture. Indeed, he cautions that the probability of transfer from the laboratory to the mechanistic society is extremely difficult, because when the individual returns, he is confronted again with the society's self-sustaining, self-sealing system of truth (p. 264). Nevertheless, argues Shepard, one must begin – and one point of departure is the personal growth laboratory.

## METHOD

The purposes of this chapter are (1) to support the view that the present mechanistic society has many of the dysfunctionalities Shepard suggests, but (2) to question the extent to which the interpersonal processes in a personal growth laboratory are different from those in the mechanistic world; (3) to suggest that the personal growth laboratory (or, for that matter, other laboratory species) may teach their own brand of self-validating, self-sealing processes; and finally (4) to hypothesize that the processes learned in the personal growth laboratories, although basically similar to the ones in the mechanistic world, may be difficult to transplant to the back-home situation – primarily because the returnee believes that, acts as if, and at times, insists that they are different.

## System of Categories and Scoring Bases

The system of categories used in this study has been described in detail elsewhere (Argyris, 1965), and is presented briefly in table 17.1. Behavior categories above the middle or zero line are hypothesized to facilitate, and those below to inhibit, interpersonal relationships and problem solving. The further away from the zero line, the more difficult it is to perform the behavior. Thus, openness to the ideas (i) or feelings (f) of others is hypothesized to be more difficult than owning ideas or feelings (i.e., stating one's own ideas or feelings), and experimenting is, in turn, more difficult than openness. Each unit of behavior is scored on two levels. Level I represents the individual and the interpersonal; Level II represents norms of the group. For example:

| Sample statement | Would be scored as | |
|---|---|---|
| | *Level I* | *Level II* |
| 1 "I believe that we should reject the idea even though we are told not to." | Own i | Individuality f |
| 2 "I feel tense." | Own f | Individuality f |
| 3 "Would you please tell me more about your theory?" | Open i | Concern i |
| 4 "This is not easy for me to talk about. I feel as if my whole life has been a shambles. I feel frightened and bewildered." | Experimenting f | Trust f |

When both Level I and Level II scores represent categories above the zero line or below, the behavior may be said to be *consistent*. For example, in the four cases above the categories representing the personal and norms levels are all positive. If behavior was positive and negative, it would be viewed as *inconsistent* (e.g., owning i–conformity i or open i–antagonism i). Inconsistent behavior presents a special class of problems which are important determiners of individual or group effectiveness.

**Table 17.1**   Categories of behavior

| *Individual* | | *Level I* *Interpersonal* | | *Level II* *Norms* | |
|---|---|---|---|---|---|
| Experimenting | i | help others to experiment | i | Trust | i |
| | f | | f | | f |
| Openness | i | help others to be open | i | Concern | i |
| | f | | f | | f |
| Owning | i | help others to own | i | Individuality | i |
| | f | | f | | f |
| ...............................................................Zero line........................................................ | | | | | |
| Not owning | i | not help others to own | i | Conformity | i |
| | f | | f | | f |
| Not open | i | not help others to be open | i | Antagonism | i |
| | f | | f | | f |
| Rejecting | i | not help others to | i | Mistrust | |
| Experimenting | f | experiment | f | | |

## Pattern A and the Mechanistic World

As Shepard implies, it is possible to show empirically that the mechanistic world tends to contain a cluster of interpersonal relationships that may be characterized primarily as low trust, low openness, and the nonexpression of feelings. In a recent study of 28 different organizational settings, producing 45,802 units of interpersonal behavior, a pattern was uncovered which characterized mechanistic systems in this way. The interpersonal behavior found (Argyris, 1969) to be contained in what I call pattern A may be summarized as follows:

| Highly frequent behavior | Moderately frequent behavior | Infrequent or nonexistent behavior |
|---|---|---|
| Owning up to ideas | Openness to ideas | Expression of feelings |
| Concern for ideas | Individuality of ideas | Openness of feelings |
| Conformity to ideas | Antagonism to ideas | Experimenting with ideas or feelings |
| | | Helping each other to express |
| | | Trust (ideas or feelings) |
| | | Antagonism (feelings) |
| | | Mistrust (ideas or feelings) |

We have found, as Shepard states, that people who experience this pattern tend to report that they are in a world which they characterize as being low in openness and trust, where individuals are alone and compete with others, and where they are in danger of being exploited by others. As a result, individuals may take on impersonal roles, appearing to be what they are supposed to be, if they are to survive. Consequently, many persons have limited awareness of their feelings and often cover, with highly intellectualized denials, feelings that are readily apparent to others through nonverbal cues (Shepard, 1970, pp. 260–3). Pattern A is, therefore, a major cluster of behaviors causing interpersonal mechanistic relationships.

## Data Sources

Shepard (1970) states that the purpose of personal growth laboratories is to create an alternative culture: an "experience of a better order" (p. 259). A personal growth laboratory is an experiential test of the notion that mechanistic mentality and culture can be transcended. It is a resocializing institution, providing conditions that "disconfirm some mechanistic assumptions" (p. 263). The personal growth laboratory "creates an interpersonal world which disconfirms much of what people have learned in the world outside, affirms the possibility of a different world outside, and provides a partial model of what it could be like" (p. 260). Finally, "the alienating forces [which the participants] brought with them to the laboratory have largely disappeared" (p. 264).

What is the interpersonal behavior that leads to such learning experiences and to the accomplishment of these objectives? Unfortunately, Shepard has not presented systematic descriptive data concerning the events in personal growth laboratories that would permit the reader to judge for himself whether the above outcomes actually do occur. As a minimum, it would be helpful to have protocols of tape recordings, so that the reader would be provided the opportunity to relate the proposed outcomes to the actual behavior that presumably caused them.

Such descriptive material does not have to be highly systematic and rigorously obtained (although ultimately this will be necessary). Anecdotal data such as those found in the writings of Burton (1970) and Howard (1970) can be helpful.

For the remainder of this chapter I shall focus on Jane Howard's work because, in the tradition of a good journalist, she presents numerous vignettes in which she describes her recollections of what was actually said. Howard attended laboratory experiences designed and managed by Michael Murphy, William Schutz, George Bach, and John and Joyce Weir, all leaders in their field.

**Table 17.2**   Sample of vignettes from Howard (1970) and their scores

| Score | Example | Page |
|---|---|---|
| Own i | "Let whatever wants to happen happen . . . stay with the | |
| Conf i | feeling. Make whatever noises you want to make . . ." | 12 |
| Own i | "You don't mean that . . . you mean she should bring it | |
| Conf i | | 16 |
| Conf i | *right now* (italics Jane Howard's). | |
| Own i | "Take off your glasses," I was told. | |
| Conf i | | |
| Own i | "I'd rather not," I said. "I really need them. They're not just an | |
| Inter i | affectation. They're not emotional armor. I really do have lousy eyes." The other pairs of eyes in the room looked skeptical. | |
| Own i | "You're not going to be reading, *here*, this afternoon, are | |
| Conf i | you?" | |
| Own i | "I guess not," I said. "Hardly, at my first Esalen workshop." | |
| Conf i | | |
| Own i | "Well then, hand the glasses over. Don't you trust us?" | |
| Conf i | | |
| Open i | | |
| Conf i | | 38 |
| Own i | "I think I trust you," I said as I handed them over. | |
| Conc i | | |
| Open i | "*You think?* Whom aren't you sure you trust?" | |
| Conf i | I squinted around the room. "Him," I said, pointing at a man named Michael Kahn, who somehow resembled both Abraham Lincoln and Michelangelo's David. "He does't look at all that | |
| Own i | trustworthy." | |
| Conc i | | |
| Own i | "Don't tell me," said William Schutz, "tell him." | |
| Conf i | | |
| | "Keep your knees wide apart," said one of Doctor | |
| | Bach's assistants as I lay down, "as if you were having a baby." | 53 |
| Own i | "*What!* You've never *had* a baby. So much the better! | |
| Conf i | | |
| | Relax!" But seldom have I felt less relaxed. | |
| | "Don't be afraid to be a real shrew, a real bitch!" | |
| | Doctor Bach urged the first girl . . . "Get rid of all your | |
| Own i | | 54 |
| Conf i | pent-up hostilities! Tell them where you're really at! Let it be total, vicious, exaggerated hyperbole!" | |
| | "You goddam bitch," said Lloyd. "You're punishing me for no | |
| Own f | reason. I'd like to tear your hair out by the roots." | |
| Antag f | | |
| | Bindrim leaped across the room and grabbed from a box a Sears | |
| Own i | Roebuck Catalog, which he thrust at Lloyd. "Here's her hair," | |
| Conf i | he said, "Go ahead! Tear it out!" | |

Using the scheme described above (see table 17.1) and outlined in Argyris (1965, 1970), all the vignettes were scored by myself and Robert Barbieri, a research assistant. The interobserver reliability was 71 percent, which was deemed adequate for the purposes of the study.

In using the data, I should like to make several points clear. I am aware that my assistant and I could have unconsciously distorted the scores to favor a particular point of view. We do not believe this is the case, and include, in table 17.2, a lengthy sample of our scores versus dialogue, for readers to judge for themselves. (The entire raw data are available for the interested reader.) Nor do I claim that Howard's (1970) descriptions in *Please Touch* are reliable and valid. I have no way of making such judgements from her published work. I do infer from reading her book and from speaking to her, to Mike Murphy, and to Bill Schutz that she values many of her personal growth experiences and that the latter two regard positively her abilities as a reporter. Thus the raw data came from a "friend" of the personal growth laboratories. Though some may justifiably lament the use of such data, these were the only protocols I could find.[1]

More importantly, this article does not represent a systematic research study to prove or disprove any particular point. The objectives of this article are to present some data that may raise questions and hypotheses for the research that must eventually be conducted to illuminate the processes that go on in a personal growth laboratory and the processes involved when the individuals return home.

## RESULTS: SCORES FROM THE PERSONAL GROWTH LABORATORIES

The scoring results are presented in table 17.3. If one compares these results with those from previously published research (Argyris, 1966, 1969) one will find that, with two exceptions, to be discussed below, they are similar to the behaviors described earlier as pattern A. These results have been consistently found in such diverse but competitive groups as executives making decisions, executive T Groups (in the early phases), State Department problem solving meetings, and groups of scholars debating technical issues. Given the limitations of the raw data, the conclusion to be inferred is that the majority of the scores fit the behavioral pattern associated with the mechanistic, competitive world.

**Table 17.3** Scores of quotations from *Please Touch*

|  | N | % |
|---|---|---|
| Own i | 143 | 69 |
| Conform i | 90 | 43 |
| Open i | 38 | 18 |
| Individuality i | 35 | 17 |
| Owning f | 21 | 10 |
| Concern i | 36 | 17.3 |
| Antagonism i | 18 | 8.7 |
| Antagonism f | 12 | 6 |
| Individuality f | 10 | 5 |
| Conform f | 5 | 2 |
| (All others) | 8 | 4 |
| Total | 416 | 200.0 |

*Note*: N = 416. These scores combine two levels of analysis where the N is 208 for each level. Thus the percentage should total 200 percent.

The first exception is that the feeling scores were significantly higher than those typically found in pattern A. One possible explanation might be that personal growth laboratries were focused on exploring feelings, that participants were aware of this purpose, and that the trainers did their best to maximize its expression. Thus the high frequency of feeling scores would be attributable to the stated and understood nature of personal growth laboratories. (The same may be said for T Groups, where high feeling scores are also obtained.)

The second exception was the frequency of individuality scores. They were more frequent than was the case in most pattern As so far observed. One possibility is that these scores were caused by trainers' and members' coercing participants to remove their mechanistic facades and "tell it as they *really* felt it." This possibility could be investigated by noting the behavior immediately preceding the one scored as "individuality." If the participant had been asked, cajoled, or ordered to do something, then our hypothesis would be supported. Although this was found to be the case in a few incidents, a systematic test was not possible because, in the majority of cases, Howard had not included what had been said just before the unit in question.

However, there were some data that could shed light on this issue. It was an empirical fact that the relatively high individuality and feeling scores existed simultaneously with very high conformity and antagonism scores, relative to all other research results obtained to date. In previous studies, high conformity and antagonism scores have indicated a high degree of coercion, competitiveness, and stress (Argyris, 1965, 1970).

It is not possible to assign causality from the data available. It is possible that the individuality scores arose from the coercion and competitiveness which we inferred were present. Two very frequent interventions noted in the Howard book were (1) trainers' and members' coercing people (e.g., "speak up, don't be afraid, I don't believe that you can get angry") and (2) trainers' "asking" and ordering individuals to carry out specific exercises, both verbal and nonverbal. Both of these interventions could have influenced members to express ideas and feelings that would be scored as individuality. To be sure, such coercion could have tended to be high during the earlier phases and have decreased as the laboratory progressed. Also, it may be that the trainers are responsible for most of the coercion during the early phases and that the members continue to adhere to the pattern as they learn. Unfortunately, the data available do not permit such analysis. Research is needed to illuminate these possibilities.

These data suggest that individuality can arise out of, or exist simultaneously with, coercion and competitiveness. This may be a paradox, but it is not a new phenomenon. Researchers have reported that paradoxes such as these can exist, and can be productive for learning (Watzlawick, et al., 1967, pp. 192–229).

If the persons in the groups described by Howard were striving to be of help to one another (and there is little doubt of that in my mind), but were giving help in a coercive and antagonistic manner, then the individual might learn to experience help somewhat as the child does who has to take bad-tasting medicine: he may not like it, but knows that it is good for him. If help can be bad-tasting, and if it comes across that way from the trainer and the members, then the only person available to depend upon would be the individual himself (or any member whose behavior does not follow the pattern). Thus the person may be pushed into a position of defining and depending upon himself. Perhaps this is precisely what the trainer hopes to create. He may want the member finally to learn to stand on his or her own two feet, to be autonomous, to fight back, to realize that he will not be loved by others if he does not first know and love himself.

## Discussion: Do the Data Indicate an Alternative Culture?

The question relevant to our theme and to the Shepard article is: does the state of affairs described above illustrate a new order? The answer suggested by our data is that the order is not a new one. Competitiveness, coercion, antagonism, and conformity, coupled with low scores on the dimension of mutual help, are the essence of the mechanistic world.

If so, how may Shepard claim that the order inside the laboratory, as defined by the actual behavior, is different from the order outside the laboratory? Where is the behavior from which it can be inferred that the mechanistic culture has been transcended?

I should point out that many people have reported that their personal growth laboratory experiences *did* transcend the mechanistic world, *did* question some of their basic assumptions about mechanistic life, and *did* reduce the alienating forces so common in most groups outside the laboratories. How do we account for the voluminous anecdotal evidence that people have evaluated their personal growth laboratories as "fantastic," "great," and that the experience "opened up new insights," "gave me new inner strengths"?

One explanation is that Shepard's inferences (that personal growth laboratories transcend the mechanistic world and that they raise questions about the basic assumptions of present life) probably cannot be confirmed if we look at actual behavior but are clearly supported if we interview people about their feelings regarding the sessions. Perhaps personal growth laboratories provide a new consciousness and a new set of attitudes rather than new behavior. Perhaps behavioral change requires, as Shepard suggests, attendance at several laboratories. But then, we may ask, what is the logic and theory that would lead one to suggest (or hope) that behavioral processes that do not lead to behavior change in one laboratory session will lead to behavioral change in the second or third session? One may respond that behavior in advanced laboratories may be significantly different. Again, data are lacking to illustrate this possibility. In fact, after observing the behavior of trainers at many laboratories (observations made at Bethel during beginner and alumni laboratories) the author is convinced that their scores were as competitive as, and in some cases more competitive than, those of members. Whether trainers were "coerced" into this type of behavior because of the fact that some of the laboratories studied were for beginners is another moot question. Again research is indicated.

## The Blindness Phenomenon

In the research cited earlier, it was found that executives in the 28 organizations were aware that their interpersonal world was full of mistrust, competitiveness, closedness, and lack of risk-taking. Yet, however they may have lamented these processes, they tended to accept them as inevitable. Although they were clear about the mechanistic processes in their lives, they tended to be blind to their own impact on others and to other interpersonal processes. Any given level of superiors tended to see their relationships with their peers and subordinates in a much rosier light than did their respective peers and subordinates (Argyris, 1966, 1968).

In the cases illustrated by the Howard (1970) data, we may infer that the participants tended to have developed a new awareness of themselves and that they were probably relatively accurate predictors of their impact upon others (because these data were shared). However, if our data above are correct, they tended to be "blind" about the kinds of interpersonal processes which they had experienced and from which they had learned.

Thus, though they were *not* blind to their impact on others, and were self-aware, they were, we infer, blind to the interpersonal learning processes presented in the groups.

Why this interpersonal learning process "blindness"? Why were the group members apparently unaware of the discrepancy between their actual behavior and their reports that they had experienced a new and different world? One possibility might be that the people who attended these laboratories were prone to such blindness. Although empirical research is needed to test this hypothesis, we have pointed out that blindness to own impact on others, and to interpersonal processes has been reported among many people who have never attended laboratories of any kind (Argyris, 1968).

Another explanation might be that the trainers, the laboratory designs, the methods, and the culture of the laboratories interacted in some way to cause the interpersonal learning process blindness. This possibility may be worth exploring, because pattern A has been shown to be correlated with "blindness," and we have suggested that the behavior in personal growth laboratories may approximate pattern A. One hypothesis that suggests itself is as follows: the individuals who did learn under conditions of concern and warmth – along with conditions of antagonism and coercion – would experience the laboratory as a "new world" if they were genuinely able to connect causally the warmth and love *and* the antagonism and coercion to their increased expression of feelings and increased sense of individuality.

### Connecting Coercion–Antagonism with Concern–Warmth

In explaining this phenomenon, it may be that the individual causally connects the expression of feelings and individuality to coercion–antagonism and concern–warmth because he has come to believe that his closedness and defensiveness are the cause of his lack of effectiveness. The individual in the personal growth laboratory finds that people have to break down his defensive walls in order to help him connect himself with hitherto "unconnected" aspects of himself. The breaking down of his defenses may account for his reported coercion and antagonism score, while his view of others' intentions may cause him to report that his group activities were full of warmth and love.

One may ask whether there is any existing theory that would support this hypothesizing. One of the recurring themes in the book by Burton (1970) is that intensive group experiences seem to focus on helping people rediscover "dislocated" or "lost" parts of themselves. The groups are effective because the "missed subself, the unexperienced, is experienced" (pp. 19–20). Forer (1970, pp. 39–40) states that groups were successful as the person was helped to experience the "dissociated part of himself and simultaneously the shame, guilt, or anxiety related to the expected disapproval."

If an individual's defensive behavior is being partially caused by lost or dissociated aspects of himself, then he may be said to be controlled by those aspects of his self. A defensive wall has been built around these lost or dissociated parts over which the individual has little control. The first step in growth, therefore, can be viewed as breaking down the walls. Such breaking will probably have to be done by others; given the individual's present defenses, he would find it difficult, if not impossible, to break down the walls himself.

In breaking down the walls various kinds of confrontation, various modes of insistence that the person face himself may be used. Confrontation may be helpful when those doing the confronting and insisting also show a genuine *concern* for the person's growth and acceptance of his anger, his aggression, and his hurt, as he struggles to keep the dissociated aspects separate (in order not to experience the guilt and shame that is associated with them). As I read the vignettes in the Howard (1970) and Burton (1970) books, I am persuaded that the participants did manifest confrontation and insistence on the one hand *and* genuine concern and patience on the other.

Forer (1970, pp. 39–40) conceptualized the change process as follows:

1   The client must experience the dissociated part of himself and simultaneously the shame, guilt, or anxiety related to the expected disapproval . . .
2   The client must receive supportive feedback from the group. The group does not behave as the outside world does; they do not strive to reinforce the shame, guilt, or anxiety.
3   The client is helped to incorporate the new experience as valid.
4   The group members "use their power to convince the client that the newly exposed part of himself is not so bad or [is] even desirable and that his sharing of that part of himself with them was experienced by them as good . . .

There are at least two different levels of experience that could occur. The first level is the process, as when the client is being forced to experience dissociated aspects of self and his shame, or when he is convinced by the group that the behavior which he considered bad they consider good (or at least not bad). Such behavior will probably be scored by our scheme as "conformity," because the cause or the responsibility for the insight is "in" the others. As is the case in pattern A, the cause for growth (when it occurs) tends to be the responsibility of others. Personal causation is low in pattern A.

The second level of experience is the content that is being communicated with pattern A behavior. The content expresses love, concern, protection, and closeness. Such content (in the mechanistic world) rarely exists and is rarely associated with pattern A behavior.

To put this another way, I believe that the dynamics of personal growth laboratories described by Howard (1970) and Burton (1970) may operate as follows:

1   Most of us are imbued with pattern A behavior.
2   We will help Mr Dissociated experience aspects of his lost self by using the only behavior that we know, namely, that which is primarily mechanistic, pattern A behavior.
3   We will couple that behavior with a set of attitudes and motives which are *not* mechanistic, attitudes which *do* represent an alternative culture.
4   This will help batter down his defenses. During this process Mr Dissociated may get angry or hurt, but we will not hate him or condemn him because we expect this response when someone is struggling to keep dissociated aspects of self dissociated. Moreover, after it is all over, Mr Dissociated will finally sense our love, sense our concern, sense our commitment to break down his defenses without rejecting him, and he will feel closer to, and more genuinely accepted by, himself and us.

In an earlier article (Argyris, 1968), I have suggested that mechanistic, coercive behavior may be necessary when the individual is closed to learning. Groups whose major purpose is to re-experience the missed aspects of self have chosen to focus on the closed aspects of the individual. Thus the individuals are probably resistant to learning in these areas. Pattern A behavior would be functional under these conditions as a means for achieving pattern B behavior, which is found in groups in which feelings are expressed and risks are taken; in which helping others to own, to be open, and to experiment occurs; and in which the norms of conformity and antagonism become less potent, while the norms of individuality and trust become more potent (Argyris, 1969).

## *Unintended Consequences Due to Time Constraints*

However, there may be some unintended consequences related to the short time available in the laboratories (relative to the objectives to be achieved) and to the meshing of competitiveness–warmth–coercion behavior. If an individual is coerced into facing "bad" but dissociated aspects of himself *and* if he feels genuinely accepted by others as he comes to confront aspects of his self that have been, to date, so unacceptable to him that he has dissociated them from his awareness, then he may come to feel a special sense of gratitude toward and dependence on his group. "They" have shown themselves to be loving of him, especially when he is not loving of himself. If so, his gratitude, dependence, and resultant closeness could become so strong that they could act to help the individual to discount negative aspects of the coercion and competitiveness; indeed, as suggested above, he might see these behaviors as necessary if people were to help him penetrate his defenses.

It is no easy task to help individuals become aware of dissociated aspects of themselves, to become accepting of them, and to begin to integrate them into their conscious selves. One or two weeks' time is short for such learning, especially since all members seek such growth. Given these time constraints, it is understandable that trainers would tend to develop exercises that may push people a bit, that they would become somewhat coercive and competitive (indeed, executives also assign the lack of time as a cause of their coerciveness and competitiveness). But if an individual is helped to become aware of himself relatively quickly by the exercises designed by the trainers, then he will tend to assign a good deal of his success at facing reality to what others (trainers and members) have done for him, thereby blessing their mechanistic methods unknowingly and reinforcing further the feelings of gratitude and dependence.

May I interject that it is possible for an individual to be helped to gain insights too fast. For example, if A has been uncomfortable in expressing aggression, and through exercises (such as pushing others or punching pillows) he breaks through, lets loose, and is loved for it, he may be so elated that he may not stop to explore positive aspects of withholding aggression. Perhaps his overloving mother did mother him, but is he helped to see how she may have done so in order to keep herself intact while bringing up several children? Is there time for the individual to work through his fears of aggression so that he can explore the positive aspects of suppressing certain feelings? As I read the Howard vignettes, many of the staff imply (as John Weir has stated) that the expression of all personal feelings is good.[2]

Such an important generalization deserves some empirical research. But one need not wait for research to point out that such a position is constricting, not freeing. The more freeing position would be the ability to choose freely what feelings one will and will not express. Suppression is dysfunctional when it is coerced and not freely chosen. Under certain conditions love can be expressed and growth facilitated by the individual's choosing to suppress his feelings.

We may now summarize the conjectures so far: I believe that persons attending personal growth laboratories, though aware of themselves and their impact on others, nevertheless remain "blind" to the coercive aspects of the learning process they have gone through, mainly because of the reward involved in experiencing formerly dissociated aspects of self. The learner who experiences such positive results, when asked to evaluate his learning, tends to highlight the learning and the warmth and concern which accompanied it, while downplaying the coercion and antagonism involved (because he feels that they were necessary for him to grow). The coercive aspects of the learning process, which may have constricting effects (e.g., reducing the learner's freedom to express or not to express his feelings), go unrecognized.

## The Transfer of Learning to the Back-home World

Coercive pattern A behavior may be helpful in groups where (1) it is defined as a learning and growth-producing situation where (2) members learn to discount or ignore the coercive, antagonistic, hostile aspects of behavior, and (3) focus on the sense of concern and caring. But people outside the personal growth laboratories (in the back-home situation) will not tend to share such "tolerance." If the person who has gone to a laboratory and evaluates it as a "fantastic growth experience" (where he has learned to love and trust and to be loved and trusted) returns and behaves in a coercive, antagonistic, competitive manner (behaviors which he experienced in the laboratory), then the people in his world may understandably mistrust his claims. If he behaves confrontingly and "openly" (as he did in his group) and expects the concern and love from the outside world that he received in the group, then he will be in serious difficulty indeed.

Moreover, if group participants appear blind to the fact that, behaviorally speaking, the world inside the group is not too dissimilar from the outside world, they could develop a negative and hostile feeling about the "*non*understanding" that exists in the outside world. Such attitudes could tend to draw the individual closer to the group and make the group experience even more "fantastic," a reaction which would only serve to increase the probability that the individual would have difficulty when he returns to the back-home situation. If such difficulty occurs, it may confirm the prejudices which he has learned in the group and create even stronger feelings of cohesiveness with, and nostalgia for, his group. The people in the back-home world may sense his anger and prejudice. They may react with perplexity and hostility when he implies that they, as did his group, should make his growth a full-time occupation. This, in turn, could lead the individual to experience a new sense of dissociation from his society. Such feelings could feed back and create the beginnings of a new kind of internal personal dissociation. For example, the individual could come to feel an increasing sense of despair or anger toward his back-home world. He could become less tolerant of others who were apparently content with a mechanistic world.

Perhaps a key to the success reported by participants in personal growth laboratories is the fact that the learning situation has been so designed that they can have their cake and eat it too. Given the staff's commitment to be genuinely concerned, to care for, and to love the participants, no matter how difficult relationships may become, people are then placed in a situation where mechanistic behavior is accompanied by the growth feelings and attitudes of the alternative culture Shepard (1970) describes. This combination rarely exists in the noncontrived outside world. In that world, mechanistic behavior will tend to elicit the mistrust and closedness that Shepard describes. There may be, therefore, a greater degree of congruence between behavior and attitudes in the mechanistic world than in the personal growth world depicted by the data inferred from the Howard (1970) book.

This incongruence between behavior and attitudes may be the Achilles' heel of the experience. When such incongruence exists and "works" (i.e., people are helped), it may be because the people are in a setting where their growth is everyone's full-time concern, where the norms include loving people when they are not lovable (so that they can reconnect themselves with their dissociated aspects of self), and where competent experts design and manage the world to make sure that these growth-oriented, loving characteristics are maintained at the highest possible level. Such a world is not very probable when people are also at work, when tasks are being accomplished, or when products and services needed by a highly interdependent society are being produced under real-time conditions.

Some readers may agree, but reply that the trouble is with the present world. It should slow down and be concerned about people. But, do personal growth laboratory experiences show real concern for people, if they help them to "grow" while becoming more blind to the processes that produced the growth? I question whether we show concern for people by creating settings that tend to minimize personal causation and couple that with learning to value one's self. Indeed, I suggest that such action may be a source of narcissism. One operational definition of narcissism is the state in which an individual values himself highly, while minimizing his awareness of responsibility for his impact on others.

Some readers may object, pointing out that the end result of personal growth laboratories is not to increase interpersonal competence but to facilitate individual discovery and self-awareness. Individuals are not expected, in this view, to behave more competently, but it is hoped that they will have a deeper awareness of their own feelings. Indeed, perhaps they are helped to see that interpersonal relationships in a mechanistic world are basically "games."

These are valid objections, and if this is the position of the adherents to personal growth laboratories, they ought to make it explicit. If the comments above do represent their view, then we have helped to illuminate some of the more basic assumptions being made about human personality in these settings. However, having made the assumptions explicit, we must also recognize that they are supported by some research and seriously questioned by other research.

The basic issue is whether human personality exists apart from interpersonal relationships or the setting in which it is being studied. Subsidiary questions arise: Can one be aware of himself without being aware of others? Is it possible to gain meaningful self-awareness without also focusing on interpersonal competence? Can competence development be used as a criterion of self-awareness and self-mastery (if they have been accomplished effectively)? If not, we are in the position of suggesting that people may grow, even though they cannot continue to grow or even maintain the growth outside a special learning situation.

If we take such a position, then we have come full cycle back to the prevailing view of the mechanistic world. Human growth is presently relegated to nontask situations, such as bull sessions and personal confrontations. The challenge is to integrate personal growth and the task world, so that the values associated with growth can significantly influence the design and management of our workaday world.

## SUMMARY AND CONCLUSIONS

In closing, it should be emphasized that if the analysis is correct, the hypothesized consequences should occur in any learning situation in which the design of the experience, the trainer's behavior, and eventually the participants' behavior encourage the development of strong attitudes such as concern and warmth, while bringing about insight through pattern A behavior. This kind of world need not be limited to personal growth laboratories. For example, laboratory experiences designed to enhance interpersonal competence and the accomplishment of tasks could be designed in ways that match pattern A.

Finally, this analysis is congruent with Slater's (1970) view that the counterculture has certain correlative strains within it: namely, communality/individualism, violence/non-violence, and power and influence/noninvolvement in the established society. Personal growth laboratories, as illustrated in the Howard (1970) book, tended to focus more on individualism, violence (coercion and hostility), and noninvolvement in the mechanistic world. They seemed to de-emphasize the development of processes that would enhance communality in back-home settings that would help people to use power and influence constructively in order to begin to make changes in the mechanistic world. Personal growth laboratories, as Howard depicted them, also tended to de-emphasize the integration of tasks or "getting things done" with the enhancement of personal learning. Yet from an analysis of nineteenth-century new utopias, Kanter (1970) has concluded that only those utopias survived which were able to integrate self-awareness, competence in dealing with others, the development of rules and norms, and the accomplishment of meaningful tasks and objectives.

Most of the questions raised in this chapter depend upon data whose reliability, validity, and representativeness of the range of personal growth laboratories are unknown. Consequently, the conclusions are highly tentative. They are, first, that there is some evidence that behavior in a personal growth laboratory may not differ significantly from the behavior observed in the mechanistic world. A phenomenon of interpersonal blindness seems to be operating, leading the participants and staff to ignore certain behavioral similarities between the personal growth laboratory and the outside mechanistic and coercive world, and to report only the differences, namely, the concern and personal warmth experienced there.

Second, personal growth laboratories may, unintentionally, help to generate in their participants a sense of intergroup, win–lose rivalry between the inner world of the personal growth laboratory and the larger social and cultural context. Participants returning with these views could alienate themselves even more from their back-home mechanistic world, and could rationalize the estrangement by placing the responsibility on those who seem to accept the mechanistic world.

Finally, one important challenge facing all those who are attempting to create experiential learning is to find ways to integrate self-awareness, interpersonal competence, the accomplishment of meaningful work tasks, in such a way that the participants are helped to become more understanding and constructively confronting of their back-home mechanistic culture.

## Notes

1   Data from an intersting article by Haigh (1968) were not included here because the majority of the interaction involved the trainer and one member who had undergone several years of psychotherapy, was "relatively open to exploring the dark recesses of her memories," and was skilled "in free association" (p. 449). This focus tended to make the situation illustrative of a rather unique relationship.
2   Communication during a panel session at Bethel, Maine, summer 1968.

## References

Argyris, C., 1965, *Organization and Innovation*, Homewood, Ill., R. D. Irwin.
Argyris, C., 1966, "Interpersonal Barriers to Decision Making," *Harvard Business Review*, 44, 2, pp. 84–97.
Argyris, C., 1967, "On the Future of Laboratory Education," *Journal of Applied Behavioral Science*, 3, 2, pp. 153–83.
Argyris, C., 1968, "Conditions for Competence Acquisition and Therapy," *Journal of Applied Behavioral Science*, 4, 2, pp. 147–77.
Argyris, C., 1969, "The Incompleteness of Social Psychological Theory," *American Psychologist*, October, 24, 10, pp. 893–908.
Argyris, C., 1970, *Intervention Theory and Method*, Reading, MA, Addison-Wesley.
Burton, A. (ed.), 1970, *Encounter*, San Francisco, Jossey-Bass.
Forer, B. R., 1970, "Therapeutic Relationships in Groups," in Burton, A. (ed.), *Encounters*, San Francisco, Jossey-Bass, pp. 27–41.
Haigh, G. V., 1968, "A Personal Growth Crisis in Laboratory Training," *Journal of Applied Behavioral Science*, 4, 4, pp. 437–52.

Howard, J., 1970, *Please Touch*, New York, McGraw-Hill.
Kanter, R. M., 1970, "Communes," *Psychology Today*, 4, 2, pp. 53–7, 78ff.
Shepard, H. A., 1970, "Personal Growth Laboratories: Toward an Alternative Culture," *Journal of Applied Behavioral Science*, 6, 3, pp. 259–66.
Slater, P. E., 1970, "Culture in Collision," *Psychology Today*, 4, 2, pp. 31–2, 66.
Watzlawik, P., Beavin, J. H., and Jackson, D. D., 1967, *Pragmatics of Human Communication*, New York, W. W. Norton.

# Part IV

## *The Inhibition of Valid and Usable Information from the Correct Use of Normal Science*

# — 18 —

# Actionable Knowledge: Design Causality in the Service of Consequential Theory

I believe that the task of any theory of managing is to produce generalizations that are actionable by managers in everyday life *and* that as managers use such generalizations, they create opportunities for robust tests of their validity. The business of science and the business of managing are not separable.

I also believe that theories of managing are theories of effectiveness because they purport to define the activities through which intended consequences can be achieved in such a way that these consequences persist. Theories of management are normative theories because their ultimate basis is the values and goals selected by human beings.

Finally, I believe that the agents for managing are human beings. In our research, we have found that if these agents are to be effective, they must pay continual attention to five questions (Argyris, 1982; Argyris and Schön, 1996).

1   How do they know that they are producing the actions that they intended?
2   How do they know that the actions that they produced are having the intended effect?
3   How do they know that the answers that they are providing to the first two questions are not wrong?
4   How much confidence do they have that the answers they provided for the three questions above are not unrealizingly distorted?
5   To what extent are they acting in accordance with these questions in ways that permit and encourage other individuals (or larger social units) to answer the same questions?

A theory of managing enables answers to these questions in the following way. To answer question 1, propositions are required that enable individuals to select consequences and the actual actions required to produce them. Question 2 requires propositions and methodologies about how to monitor the effectiveness of the actions taken. Questions 3 and 4 require rules and methodologies about how to test claims of validity of the propositions while managing. Question 5 requires that the propositions used by actors to produce effective action should be equally usable by the recipients of the action. The propositions of any theory of managing should enable all actors to be effective.

Embedded in these requirements are three metavalues. They are competence, confidence in one's competence (self-esteem), and justice (the propositions that are used should not rule out the recipients from using the same propositions to be effective).

By metavalues I mean values that are fundamental to or behind the implementation of the questions above. For example, it is not likely that these questions can be answered if the actors do not have the competences required. Also, if they lack confidence in their competence, it could lead to their unrealizingly distancing while detecting and correcting errors. Finally, to detect and correct errors, it is often necessary to dialogue with others, especially to detect unrecognized errors. This requires that the actors create conditions where they can learn from others. This, in turn, requires that they create conditions that cause minimal conditions for defenses in self and others. Such conditions include that the rules an actor uses to act effectively cannot be denied to others as they seek to act effectively.

Managers are unlikely to be effective if they do not strive to increase the seamlessness between their designs for action and the actions themselves. They must be concerned about the validity of their claims. They must be concerned about the justice of the methods they use in managing.

These same metavalues are also key in the scientific community. Science requires human beings who are concerned about conducting competent research. Science thrives on scientists who are legitimately confident in their competence. Social science as an activity of inquiry will not last if social scientists are not concerned with justice.

I repeat that the bases for effective managerial theory and managerial practice are the same. The more each side attempts to see itself as distinct and different from the other, the more likely that bad science and bad managing will result.

## ACTIONABLE KNOWLEDGE THAT IS TESTABLE IN AN ON-LINE MANNER IN ORGANIZATIONS

The commonly accepted definition of theory is a set of logically interconnected concepts that are operationally defined and testable in the universe they purport to represent (Kaplan, 1964). These concepts are typically organized in the form of generalizations that purport to describe and to explain the universe. The claim that the generalizations are valid is tested through empirical research designed to falsify the generalizations. The key words in this view of theory are *to describe* and *to explain*. Science is descriptive and explanatory.

These requirements are necessary but not sufficient for managerial theory. The key activity in the universe called managing is creating or bringing about intended consequences. Description and explanation are in the service of creating.

The claim that managerial theory is about creating is central to the position that I am taking in this chapter. Creating is central because it is through the activity of creating that the universe called organizations comes about. It is not like the universe of biology or physics or chemistry where their basic features are not created by human beings. No individual created the brain or atomic structure or gravitation. Individuals may describe and construct these phenomena. But they are constructions of what scientists believe exists relating independently of their conceptual descriptions of these phenomena.

There are, at least, three differences between theories of description and explanation and theories of description and explanation in the service of creation:

1   The generalizations should inform the users not only what is likely to happen under the specified conditions but how to create the conditions and actions in the first place. Otherwise, the generalizations are not actionable. For example, there is much research in the empirical literature on the relevance of trust in managing. However, there is little attention paid to informing the reader on how to *create* trust. Actionable knowledge informs us how to create or produce what we claim has high external validity (Argyris, 1993; Argyris, et al., 1985; Argyris and Schön, 1996).

A generalization is actionable if it informs the user how to create it in settings beyond those in which it was first created. Actionability is different from external validity. External validity is about claims of relevance of the findings. It is not about how to create the relevance.

For example, let us consider a generalization about the impact of a specified set of reinforcements on learning and, in turn, on performance (Argyris, 1980). Years ago a world renowned learning theorist conducted studies in a large corporation to create appropriate reinforcement schedules that superiors could use to reinforce the desired behaviors of the subordinates. Subordinate A received a positive reinforcement on Tuesday morning; the next was not due until Thursday, and so forth. A was pleased with the reinforcement that he received. He told his colleague, who promptly told him that this was a great sign of his success. A then told his wife that evening, who again thought the event was important. Note that A received two reinforcements from individuals he valued. According to the schedule, he was not to receive such reinforcements.

Subordinate A's wife said, "I hope you thanked him." A replied that he was so pleased he forgot. He promised to do so the first thing the next day. The superior, describing all of this to the scholar and to me said that he found himself, the next day, in a bind. Subordinate A said, "Thank you." He replied, "You are welcome." Was that a reinforcement? If so, he violated the schedule because A was not supposed to get the next reinforcement until Thursday.

The story illustrates points that will be repeated in other examples. The implementation of the reinforcement schedule assumed that the superior was under full control of the reinforcements that the subordinate received; significant others would not intervene in the schedule. Finally, the implementation assumed that the purpose of the reinforcement schedule had to be covered up and the cover-up be covered up. Imagine the impact of the reinforcement schedule if the superior had said to Subordinate A, "I plan to reward you with following schedule in order to enhance your performance."

All these assumptions held during the experimental research that the scholar had conducted and upon which the field experiment was based. The experimental research was rigorously controlled by the scholar. The control mean that nothing would interfere with the schedule of reinforcement and that the existence of the reinforcement schedule would be covered up from the subjects. All these conditions, typical of sound experimental research, when emulated in the world of practice, require that the superior have the same control over the subordinates (and their control) as did the scholar. Such control is one of unilateral control and an authoritarian relationship. It often leads to the use of strategies whose sources require that they be kept secret.

The generalizations emanating from such research took the form, if such and such a reinforcement schedule was used in such and such a way, it would have the following impact on the subject's performance. This is typical of generalizations produced by descriptive research. What is also typical is that the conditions under which the generalization was produced were not included as part of the generalization. These are the conditions under which the generalization was created. Yet these are the conditions that must be created by anyone who wishes to re-create the findings, be they scholars or practitioners.

The problem is more complicated. To re-create the generalization, the user must be able to monitor what is going on, just as the scholars did when they were conducting their research. For example, Barker, et al. (1941) produced generalizations, such as frustration leads to regression and one consequence of regression is aggression. In the same studies, they also concluded that mild frustration caused creative responses. Such generalizations do not inform the potential user of what is required to create the conditions and consequences stated in the generalization.

For example, consider a manager who is interested in using this generalization, in real time, to generate creativity. He must therefore be able to remain below the threshold that, once pierced, would lead to frustration. How will he discover when the threshold point has been reached? How will he monitor the degree of frustration being produced? One way is to use the instruments the researchers used. But, how can this be done during a meeting? Will he interrupt the flow of events to pass out the instruments? Or, will he use a set of verbal questions that were formulated perhaps with the help of a human resources expert? But how is he to explain the introduction of the questions? Will the request to use the questions or the actual use of them add to the frustration? Or could such actions make the others feel manipulated and hence lead to anger? Would the others say so? If not, will suppressing the anger reduce the likelihood that the manager will get the knowledge that he requires?

These questions did not concern the researcher because the experiments that were created to produce the knowledge were highly controlled to keep the subjects ignorant of what was happening and how they were being studied. We are back to the previous condition, namely, that the experiments worked because the researchers were in unilateral control and the unilateral control was not discussible and the undiscussability was not discussible. The researchers would have had to deal with these questions if they treated actionability as important as they did validity.

The researchers, by following the rules of normal science, created conditions where crucial data were not surfaced and causal explanations were incomplete. Second, the research was consistent with value stances holding that superiors may use action strategies whose success depended upon their strategies being kept secret from those upon whom they were inflicted. This leads to ethical issues of unilateral secrecy, combined with acting in ways as if one is not behaving consistently with unilateral secrecy.

2   Propositions that are intended to be used in the world of practice, if used correctly, should lead to the predicted consequences and not to others that are counter to those predicted. For example, research in the social psychology of communication led to the proposition that if you are communicating to a smart audience, your message is likely to be trusted if you present several alternatives (Aronson, 1972). If the audience is judged not to be very smart, then present only one view forthrightly and accurately. Anyone using these generalizations will quickly realize that she cannot tell the audience that they were evaluated as smart or dumb and that this explains the communication strategy that is being used (Argyris, 1980). In other words, she must make this bit of critical knowledge undiscussable and the undiscussability undiscussable. Ironically, research on producing trust, if used as the researchers intended, requires cover-up and bypass of the cover-up.

3   The generalizations should be usable over time and under different conditions while, at the same time, usable in the individual case. The gap-filling between the many and the one should be as small or as seamless as possible.

The most common practice of producing generalizations is to conduct empirical research that leads to propositions that specify, let us say, a linear relationship between variables $X$ and $Y$. This practice is founded on the assumption that the key to explaining is to understand variance. One of the original proponents of this approach was Mills, who specified methods by which to understand differences or variance (James, et al., 1982; Kaplan, 1964).

Central to this view of causality is a view of the concept of "variable." For example, for James, et al. (1982), causality is understood as a particular kind of relationship between variables. Variables themselves are understood as named attributes extracted from the complexity of observed phenomena, and they are treated as essentially the same whatever the local contexts in which they occur. So, for example, James, et al. illustrated their concept of causality with the proposition that "role overload may be thought to cause state anxiety" (p. 28). They defined state anxiety, following Spielberger, as "subjective, consciously perceived feelings of tension, apprehension [and] nervousness, accompanied by or associated with the activation of the autonomic nervous system" (p. 110). They went on to suggest that role overload may be caused, directly or indirectly, by changes in expected quality or quantity of work (such as increases in demand for product) and that state anxiety may be a cause of "other psychological phenomena, such as performance and withdrawal behaviors" (p. 110).

Variables such as role overload, state anxiety, and withdrawal are considered to have the same meaning in each local context in which they appear. It is this presumed constancy of meaning that allows scientists to speak of variations in the local values and relationships of variables. Otherwise, whenever a variable took on a different value or relationship to other variables, they would have to speak of it as a different variable. This view of causality depends, in short, on an ontology according to which the complexity of observed phenomena is transformed into a collection of simple variables maintaining constant identity across local contexts.

Simon expresses this idea in another way when he says that each value of variables $X$ and $Y$, standing for cause and effect, defines a class of events and that each variable therefore "comprises a set of classes of events" (quoted in James, et al., 1982, p. 15). On this basis, it becomes possible to say that the same variable, $X$ or $Y$, may have the same or different values in different settings, a condition necessary for the discovery of general causal relationships between variables.

According to Simon's view, also adopted from James, et al. (1982), a causal relation is "a function of an effect ($Y$) on one or more causes ($X$s)" and takes the form $Y = f(X)$. Such a function is self-contained, which is to say that "one and only one value . . . of $Y$ is associated with each value . . . of $X$," or that "the values of $Y$ are determined completely by the values of $X$" (James, et al., 1982, p. 170). Self-containment implies independence of context. The researcher employing this view of causality seeks evidence to show that the values of $Y$ can be determined, given the values of $X$ and the knowledge that $X$ has occurred, independently of any other features of the contexts in which $X$ and $Y$ occur.

In this theory, causal functions are usually complex, in the sense that they involve many variables. They are asymmetric, because "it is impossible to reverse the direction of causation and still maintain unique determination" (James, et al., 1982, p. 118). And they must be expressed in quantitative terms, because one could not otherwise establish that one and only one value of $Y$ is associated with each value of $X$.

Causal inferences are usually expressed in probabilistic function equations, because variations in effects ($Y$) may be due to other causes ($X$) than those expressed in a given function equation, $Y = f(X)$. Self-containment is preserved in a probabilistic function equation if "the realized values of causes included explicitly in the equation determine the [conditional] probability distribution of the effect variable" (James, et al., 1982, p. 18). The thrust of these qualifications is to treat as noise the temporary, idiosyncratic influences of the local context on variables that are presumed to be causally connected.

At the core of all such designs is causality. Everyday life is not creatable without a concept of causality (Shoham, 1991). The nature of this causality may be stated in the form, given such and such conditions if A then B. This concept is akin to what Lewin (1935) described as the Gallilean mode of causal thought. The key feature of this form of causality is that one observed exception falsifies the causal proposition.

Like Lewin, I believe that this type of causality is at the heart of human beings designing causal consequences to achieve intended consequences. Lewin's writing is full of such examples. For example, there is the concept of the gatekeeper (Lewin, 1951). Briefly, Lewin claimed that if one individual is in control of the gate leading to the region that contains the goals of others, the others will find themselves dependent upon and submissive to the leader. This, in turn, will lead the subordinates to compete against each other to get through the gate. These prediction holds for any leadership situation that is consistent with the gatekeeper phenomenon, be it in organizations, homes, churches, schools, or trade unions. To my knowledge, there is no subsequent leadership research that has disconfirmed these hypotheses.

In this example, we see what Lewin meant when he said there is nothing as practical as a sound theory. His theory was based on Gallilean thought and on design causality (which is the essence of the concept life space). The concept is finite. It is easily storable in and retrievable from the human mind/brain. Indeed, Lewin's topological representation acted as a way to check the ideas so that they were within the finite information capacity of the human mind/brain. Variance among the variables (e.g., the number of subordinates, the strength of the gate, the variance in goals) will not alter the basic causal claims embedded in the concept of gatekeeper. This can be tested empirically. The concept of gatekeeper provides operational clues to how to answer questions 1, 2, and 3 given at the outset of this chapter.

For example, the concept informs the users that if they create gatekeeper conditions it will place the subordinators in a dependent relationship with the superior and a competitive relationship with each other. If they do not seek to create dependence and competitiveness, they can inquire about unintended consequences. Such a dialogue could set the stage for redesigning the relationship. Indeed, it is inquiries such as these that led to many practical articles and seminars on leadership.

## DESIGN CAUSALITY AND A THEORY OF ACTION PERSPECTIVE

An example of a theory based upon design causality is the theory of action perspective. Argyris and Schön (1974, 1996) claim that human beings have theories of action in their heads about how to behave effectively when dealing with others. There are two types of theories of action. The first comprises the theories that individuals espouse (e.g., values, attitudes, and beliefs). The second comprises the theories that they actually use (their theories-in-use). It is the latter theories that causally explain the action observed. These are the designs that they claim are in human beings' mind/brains, designs learned during acculturation.

These theories-in-use have been modeled and the model labeled Model I. They have the same structural characteristics as Lewin's gatekeeper concept described above. For example, as we shall see, they specify the governing values, the action strategies, and the consequences. The generalization can be applied over a wide variety of conditions as well as in the individual case. For example, studies were conducted in many different cultures, across all races, genders, and ages and all educational, economic, and social status positions (Argyris, 1982, 1990b, 1993; Argyris and Schön, 1996). Recently I was introduced to research that indicates that Model I may also be the design preferred by primates. To the extent that their claims are not disconfirmed, this is a basis for an important set of processes by which ambiguity and complexity are reduced (de Waal, 1982, 1989).

There is another way in which human beings reduce complexity and ambiguity. They create social systems and norms that are consistent with Model I. Model I contains three components. They are action strategies, consequences, and the values that govern the intentions of the actions.

Briefly, Model I values are (1) be in control, (2) minimize losing and maximize winning, (3) suppress negative feelings, and (4) act rationally. Three of the most frequent action strategies are (1) advocate your views, (2) evaluate, and (3) make causal attributions to explain. Do any or all of these three in ways that do not encourage inquiry and testing of your own views, evaluations, and attributions (to satisfice the governing values).

Model I predicts limited learning consequences. Argyris and Schön (1996) have shown how the use of Model I leads to organizational learning systems that also create limited learning systems. They are able to specify processes by which these organizational systems create limited learning systems and by which the feedback reinforces Model I theories-in-use. Finally, Argyris and Schön illustrate how human beings are acculturated with social virtues (caring, honesty, support, and integrity) that reinforce limited learning (Argyris, 1990b; Argyris and Schön, 1996).

## THEORY AND INTERVENTION RESEARCH BASED UPON DESIGN CAUSALITY

An example of intervention research based upon design causality has recently been published (Argyris, 1993). I will refer to it to illustrate many of the points made about research and theory whose generalizations are intended to be actionable.

A group of owner–directors came to see me with the following problem. Each had left a consulting or teaching organization because he did not like the quality of life in his respective organization. Also, each believed that effective consulting in the future would be founded upon learning, especially around difficult problems that were embarrassing or threatening. Their respective organizations had also failed this criterion.

About one year into the life of the organization, the owner–directors concluded that they were creating an organization that had all the negative features that they condemned. They also concluded that they were unable to correct these discrepancies.

The first observation is that the energy for change was based upon their sense of ineffectiveness. They were aware that they were producing errors ("we are doing something wrong"), but they were unable to correct them. The second observation is that the ineffectiveness was accompanied with a sense of low competence and confidence in their competence. The third observation was that they considered that continuing in this way violated their own sense of justice for themselves and others in their organization.

A theory of managing that is based upon design causality would immediately alert the interventionist in the following way. The behavior of the directors is designed. The errors and mismatches are the result of skillful actions. They are not the result of lack of skill. Moreover, these designs must contain components that designedly keep the directors unaware at the moment they are producing the counterproductive behavior. They are aware, however, of the others creating the undesired consequences, or they are aware of their personal responsibility after they have acted in counterproductive ways.

The first task is to discover the design that they use to create the undesired actions, wherever they exist in the organization. The first place to look is at the individuals' theories-in-use about managing others effectively (as well as themselves). The reason to begin with the theories-in-use (read designs) is that the source of the actions is in the mind/brain. If, for example, we were to find that organizational factors such as organizational defensive routines required such behavior (which turned out to be the case), we would still have to explain what went on in the directors' respective minds/brains to comply with these demands. We would also have to explain the processes by which they were unaware of their compliance.

Most importantly, we would have to explain how the organizational defensive routines arose in the first place. They are the owners and directors. There is no one with more power to coerce defensive routines upon their organization. Also, the organization is new, it has little history. But even if this were not the case, how would we explain the emergence of organizational factors as causal when the individuals do not intend to produce such organizational factors?

The consequences of Model I designs are to increase defensiveness, error, and self-fulfilling and self-sealing processes. To the extent that individuals use Model I, then they will necessarily create organizational behavioral contexts that are congruent with Model I. All these propositions are derived from Model I and Model O-I (organizational). They are all craftable in a form that can be tested in the organization.

For example:

- if individuals hold as governing values (1) be in unilateral control of situations or context, (2) strive to win and not to lose, (3) suppress negative feelings in self or others, and (4) be as rational as possible; and
- if they accompany these values with action strategies of advocating, evaluating, and attributing that are crafted to satisfice the governing values (e.g., craft the action in ways that do not encourage inquiry into and testing of the validity and effectiveness of these strategies);
- then they will create consequences that at best limit learning and at worst inhibit learning. For example, they will create consequences that encourage misunderstanding, self-fueling error processes, and self-sealing processes. These consequences will be created at the interpersonal, group, intergroup, and organizational levels. There should be no exceptions.
- These conditions will persist because this Model I theory-in-use is capable of correcting errors "within" routines (called single-loop learning) but not errors that require examining and changing Model I (double-loop learning).

The intellectual architecture of Model I is similar to Lewin's gatekeeper model. The causal predictions stipulated above will hold for any individual, group, intergroup, and organization where it can be shown that the individuals' theories-in-use are Model I. The type of organization (size, public or private, family or scout troop) should not matter. Nor should time matter. The predictions should hold forever as long as the conditions stipulated above exist. One observation to the contrary would disconfirm the prediction.

The predictions should be the same even if there is variance in the actual behavior (e.g., variance in the degree of evaluating or attributing), because the predictions are that there will be defensive antilearning consequences. The specific content is not specified. It is the features of defensiveness and antilearning that are specified.

One does not enhance actionability and the type of validity that accompanies actionability by specifying the degree of variance. The finiteness of the information processing capacity of the human mind/brain makes it unlikely that it can use such precision under everyday conditions. Also, as we have seen, it is unlikely that the flow of events will stand still while the evaluation that is necessary to assess the linear relationship is implemented. Finally, attempts to implement the variance generalizations (based on describing, not creating, reality) can lead to conditions that will inhibit or negate the very predictions made.

Returning to the hypothesis, the five-year intervention study provided many opportunities to test these hypotheses. For example, we tape-recorded many business sessions and found the actions of directors (and later others) informed by Model I. We also asked each director to complete a case designed to diagnose their respective theories-in-use. They were all Model I. We then showed them the map of the organizational defensive routines that their Model I actions created. Even though the map was not flattering of them, they validated it. The toughest validation came when they chose to go through the reeducation required to change it and to spread the change throughout the organization.

We tape-recorded the discussions around the feedback of all these findings. They were all Model I. When some directors vowed to change their actions, we predicted, in front of them, that they would be unable to do so because the only theory-in-use design they had was Model I. Some rebuffed these predictions. We collected more tapes (for ten months) before the change program began. They were all Model I.

The change program was based upon Model II and the organizational dialects to produce double-loop learning. Model II is also composed of governing values, action strategies, and consequences. Predictions that flow from this model are:

- if individuals hold as governing values (1) valid information, (2) informed choice, and (3) personal responsibility to monitor one's effectiveness; and
- if they accompany these governing values with action strategies of advocating, evaluating, and attributing that are crafted to satisfice the governing values (e.g., craft the action in ways that encourage inquiry into and testing of the validity and effectiveness of these strategies);
- then they will create consequences that facilitate learning (single- or double-loop) and that reduce organizational defensive routines in ways that the reduction persists.

It is not possible to provide a detailed description of the intervention research. A full description may be found in Argyris (1993), and a shorter version in Argyris and Schön (1996). Briefly, I observed the directors while they were in important meetings (e.g., director's meetings, case team meetings, performance evaluation sessions). The sessions were tape-recorded and then transcribed. The transcriptions provided the relatively directly observable data from which to infer their theories-in-use in dealing with others. Interviews were also held to capture the espoused theories as well as add another set of data from which to capture some features of the theories-in-use that could not be inferred accurately without some face-to-face inquiry.

These data were used to develop a model of the defenses (interpersonal, group, inter-group, and organizational) that produced the politics counterproductive to single- and especially double-loop learning.

The model was fed back to the directors during the second phase. The discussion that followed enriched the model. It also led the directors to ask the question, "What do we wish to do about this?"

The third phase was a two-day workshop. Each director was asked to write a specially designed case about an important problem that they faced related to their leadership, the effectiveness of the director group, and the creation of an organization that can produce double-loop learning. Each case was discussed by the entire group (about two hours per case). The first objective was to help the directors become aware of errors in their effect-iveness and to craft new ways to correct such errors. The second objective was to focus on errors the group members made as they attempted to help the case writer. For example, feedback such as "you are communicating in ways that are opinionated" is itself an opinionated statement. The third objective was to identify the causal processes by which these interpersonal strategies combined to cause the group, intergroup, and organizational features that inhibited double-loop learning. These discussions led to the correcting and enriching of the model of the organizational defenses.

Finally, there was a fourth or follow-up phase where each director selected an important and difficult session that he was to lead. He was helped (initially by myself and increasingly by his fellow directors) to design his actions to enhance the effectiveness of the session. The sessions were tape-recorded and provided a further basis for reflection and the development of Model II skills.

There were many consequences that were observed over the five-year period (now over ten years) that were consistent with Model II. For example, the directors defined at the outset several difficult issues (ownership, "stealing" consulting resources) that they doubted would ever become discussible. These issues did become discussible and continue to be so to this date.

The intervention program was implemented throughout the organization. Relationship directors especially focused on further learning. This, in turn, spread to the case teams. Finally, new products and services were created that are now sold to clients. One of the most challenging research activities going on within the organization is to develop methodologies by which to deliver services that genuinely integrate learning with accounting, finance, marketing, and so forth.

## SOME CONCLUDING THOUGHTS

The fundamental premise of this perspective is that a theory of management is a theory of managing. Managing means creating intended consequences. In a theory of managing, explanation, generalization, and testing are all in the service of creating managerial actions. To put it another way, the universe that social scientists study called management is created by someone(s) doing the managing. Our ultimate objective is to explain, generalize, and test propositions about creating.

Most social science research in this area has as its ultimate objective explanation and generalization. It is a science of after-the-fact. Social scientists observe what is going on, organize their observations into theories that explain, generalize, and predict. I believe that after-the-fact theory should be usable to inform before-the-fact, that is, usable to create what we observe.

The fundamental assumption of after-the-fact theory is that someday it will become complete enough to be used to inform before-the-fact phenomena. This assumption can be questioned on empirical as well as logical grounds. As to the former, I found little additivity in the field of organizational behavior that led to the completeness promised (Argyris, 1980).

More importantly, completeness may not be as helpful as suggested. For example, Naylor, et al. (1980) developed a relatively complete model to explain behavior in organization. By their own admission, the model was too complicated for practitioners to use in everyday life. They recognized that practitioners have to use what they label a more simplified model. Interestingly, they call the practitioner model one that degrades valid scientific description. From a design causality perspective, it is their model that degrades because it is not usable in an on-line manner by the human mind/brain. It is what they call the oversimplified nonscientifically based model that provides the key to explaining, predicting, and generalizing about how human beings create the universe they, as researchers, observe. What is the evidence that the model used by human beings to navigate everyday life is superficial? It may be nonscientific by their model of science. It is not unscientific to cognitive-social psychologists who spend their lives studying such models.

Another example of models that are not helpful in producing creating-type actions is the model Morgan and Smircich (1980) used to describe two research paradigms, interpretist and functionalist. They described each paradigm's assumptions about ontology, human nature, epistemology, metaphors, and research methods. The result is a 30-box table describing the different assumptions that accompany the different degrees of subjectivism and objectivism. I found the model helpful in organizing my thoughts about what I observe social scientists do when they conduct their research.

The unhelpfulness came when I attempted to apply the models to creating behavior. The model is well beyond the complexity that the human mind/brain can cope with. Actors would have to use the article (or parts of it) as an external memory. The moment they do that they will encounter, I believe, the same problem of interrupting the flow that was described in the frustration experiments.

More importantly, I never found myself using the model when, as an interventionist, I was in the creation mode. In creating, I was concerned about being effective. This concern focused around acting competently and justly. I was continuously focused on trying to answer questions such as the five stated at the outset of this chapter.

In reflecting on my actions as an interventionist, I could see how, in after-the-fact reflection on my actions, they could be categorized in terms of several of the boxes. But doing so was at best an exercise to please social scientists who created a model to organize what they observed, apparently so that they could argue for pluralism. I believe that the logic behind the model is self-referential to scientists' biases. There is no way that one can use it without standing outside of it. It is difficult to stand outside of it because its fundamental purpose is to support pluralism in research that purports to describe, explain, and generalize the universe as is. One way to stand outside of it is to conduct research where the ultimate goal is description, explanation, and generalization about creating universes, especially universes that are very rare (e.g., Model II universes). At that point, the model seems distant from the reality of creating a universe, the task of all actors in everyday life.

A theory of managing should include all the relevant disciplines. Examples of these relevant disciplines are the functional disciplines such as accounting, economics of the firm, finance, human resources, information technology, marketing, operations, and research and development. Ultimately we must find ways to integrate these disciplines with the ones focusing on the human side of the enterprise.

My first step in contributing to integration is to study the underlying intellectual structure of the functional disciplines to see if there are commonalities upon which to build the integration.

My first conclusion from examining the literature of the subdisciplines indicates that most are designed to meet the generic criteria of theory described at the outset. All of them strive to describe their universe as rigorously and completely as possible. All seek to develop generalizations in the form of causal propositions that are testable empirically. All are theories based on design causality. For example, accounting informs managers how to create an income statement (Argyris, 1990a). Marketing informs managers how to position their products in the marketplace. Corporate finance informs managers about using their cash flows effectively. In all cases, the generalizations are in the form of, if you do A then B will follow. This is akin to design causality.

All the theories of the functional disciplines are also normative theories because they are theories of creating or of making events come about that are chosen by the actors. Such theories make choices that are based on values, not on objective or "neutral" truths. For example, activity-based accounting is based on the idea that costs should be minimized to strengthen the contribution to the product or service which, in turn, should enhance organizational effectiveness. A key concept in activity-based accounting is to identify cost drivers. The behavioral steps required to do so are specified correctly and in detail. The intention is that the specifications are so clear and their connection with costs is so unambiguous that two individuals using the same data will arrive at similar conclusions. If they do not, there is so much certainty in the causal specifications that if two individuals traced back their steps they would eventually find where one deviated from the prescribed specifications. The specifications will also inform the individual as to how to correct the error.

I will call this ability to detect and correct such errors an indication of the internal validity of the theory. It is internal in the sense that it is related to the concepts of cost drivers that are part of the theory. The external validity is related to the degree to which the reduction of costs contributes, let us say, to profits. External and internal validities are first-order characteristics in the sense that they are related to the fundamental purpose of the theory of activity-based accounting.

Having a high degree of internal and external validity is no guarantee that the concepts and prescriptions will be implemented in a given context. For example, Argyris and Kaplan (1994) present illustrations where the top management agreed with the activity-based management analysis (internal validity) and with the actions to be taken (external validity), yet they did not implement the recommendations.

I will call this problem of implementability a second-order problem. It is second-order because the first-order requirements have been fulfilled, yet they were not applied in the context in which they were created. Another example is where the internal and external validities are high but those who commissioned the work do not agree with the prescriptions for action.[1]

Dealing with second-order issues is, I suggest, an exciting area for scholars to conduct integrative research. The integration can occur on at least two levels. First, knowledge can be developed to make implementability more effective. For example, Kaplan (a managerial accountant) developed a strategy for implementing financial recommendations. Argyris and Kaplan (1994) evolved a more comprehensive strategy that included such tasks as overcoming organizational defenses to implementing the financial ideas, which was not included in the first strategy.

A somewhat different path was being taken by Jensen and his colleagues (Jensen, et al., 1994) in formulating a theory of corporate governance and control. In this case, they modified several core concepts of their theory. For example, Jensen's concepts of the nature of human nature were altered. He developed a "pain avoidance model" to explain key phenomena that were not dealt with in the earlier versions of the theory.

On the other hand, the theoretical perspective that I use in my research and practice was influenced by working with Jensen and Kaplan. For example, I have associated creating liberating alternatives for more effective choice with creating double-loop learning. Employees, I claimed, could become more empowered by producing double-loop learning in this context. I have illustrated these claims (Argyris, 1982, 1990b, 1993) as have my colleagues Donald Schön (Argyris and Schön, 1996) and Putnam and Smith (Argyris, et al., 1985). Kaplan helped me to see ways in which employees could be empowered by the use of financial models. Indeed, the empowerment that appears to occur is more than I have observed in empowerment programs designed by human resources professionals (Argyris and Kaplan, 1994). The irony is that one such successful program was prevented from being spread to other divisions within the same organization by organizational defensive routines. Changing them would require double-loop learning.

The fundamental assumption of most functional disciplines is that if individuals learn their concepts, if they have skills to produce them, and if they then act accordingly, they will create the consequences predicted by the propositions in their respective theories. At the heart of this assumption is another that I will call willing compliance. It is compliance because the actors act as they are told by their discipline. The compliance is willing because the actors are, in their view, justly rewarded (in the broadest sense) for doing so.

There are, however, several ways where the willingness may be problematic or inadequate. First is where there is a gap in the effectiveness of the implementation. Second is when the first-order generalizations are, for any reason, inadequate to the specific context in which they are to be used. Gaps in effectiveness exist in both conditions. Such gaps are not uncommon because it is unlikely that a theory can a priori deal with all that is unique in a given situation. If a theory to comprehend a priori a concrete situation were possible, it would probably be too cumbersome to implement in real time.

The two conditions require that in addition to the first-order generalizations there is a continual need for a theory of gap filling. This theory of gap filling, to repeat, is required to harness appropriate motivations and to close gaps to produce effective action. Such a theory is importantly about leading and learning. Learning may be defined as the detection and correcting of error, where the error can be the use of inappropriate modes of motivation or the existence of gaps. Leading–learning occurs at all levels of the organization.

## Note

1 A third domain that inhibits implementability is when the concepts of activity-based accounting are incorrect. This means that the internal or external validities are questionable. To correct these gaps, one has to turn to the scholars who are developing activity-based accounting research.

## References

Argyris, C., 1980, *Inner Contradictions of Rigorous Research*, San Diego, CA, Academic Press.
Argyris, C., 1982, *Reasoning, Learning, and Action*. San Francisco, Jossey-Bass.
Argyris, C., 1990a, "The Dilemma of Implementing Controls: The Case of Managerial Accounting", *Accounting, Organizations, and Society*, 15, 6, pp. 503–11.
Argyris, C., 1990b, *Overcoming Organizational Defenses*, Needham, MA, Allyn-Bacon.
Argyris, C., 1993, *Knowledge for Action*, San Francisco, Jossey-Bass.
Argyris, C., and Kaplan, R. S., 1994, "Implementing New Knowledge: The Case of Activity-based Costing", *Accounting Horizons*, 8, 3, pp. 83–105.
Argyris, C., Putnam, R., and Smith, D., 1985, *Action Science*, San Francisco, Jossey-Bass.
Argyris, C., and Schön, D., 1974, *Theory in Practice*, San Francisco, Jossey-Bass.
Argyris, C., and Schön, D., 1996, *Organizational Learning II*, Reading, MA, Addison-Wesley.
Aronson, E., 1972, *The Social Animal*, San Francisco, Freeman.
Barker, R. G., Dembo, T., and Lewin, K., 1941, *Frustration and Regression* (University of Iowa Studies of Child Welfare I, pp. 1–43), Ames, University of Iowa Press.
de Waal, F., 1982, *Chimpanzee Politics: Power and Sex among Apes*, New York, Harper and Row.
de Waal, F., 1989, *Peacemaking among Primates*, Cambridge, MA, Harvard University Press.
James, L. R., Mulsik, S. A., and Brett, J. M., 1982, *Causal Analysis: Assumptions, Models, and Data*, Newbury Park, CA, Sage.
Jensen, M., Baker, G. P., and Wruck, K. H., 1994, *Organization Theory: Cooperation and Competition in Markets and Organizations*. Boston, MA, Harvard University, Graduate School of Business.
Kaplan, A., 1964, *The Conduct of Inquiry*, New York, Intext.
Lewin, K. 1935, *A Dynamic Theory of Personality*, New York, McGraw-Hill.
Lewin, K., 1951, *Field Theory in Social Science* (D. Cartwright, ed.). New York, Harper Collins.
Morgan, G., and Smircich, L, 1980, "The Case for Qualitative Research", *Academy of Management Review*, 5,4, 491–500.
Naylor, J. C., Pritchard, R. D., Ilgen, D. R., and Daniel, R., 1980, *A Theory of Behavior in Organization*, New York, Academic Press.
Shoham, Y., 1991, "Nonmonotonic Reasoning and Causation", *Cognitive Science*, 14, 213–302.

# — 19 —

# Field Theory as a Basis for Scholarly Consulting

About 45 scholars throughout the world met recently to celebrate the 50th anniversary of the Tavistock Institute. Many, including myself, left the conference with two impressions. There exists a wide variety of views on what is action research. When the participants questioned each other's views, the result was disagreement, conflict, and self-reinforcing defensive arguments.

As I reflected on the conference, I realized that the proponents were explicit about their respective theories; however, each showed little focus on two major features of any theory – causality and the testing of causal claims (Argyris and Schön, 1974; Kaplan, 1964; Pfeffer, 1997).

The participants, for the most part, did not have a meta theory – that is, a theory of how to build a theory. Lewin saw this as an important issue early on in his work. Indeed, he described field theory as a meta theory (Lewin, 1935, 1936; Cartwright, 1951, 1959; Gold, 1992; Metraux, 1992).

I believe that scholars are free to generate any theory about action research that they choose to develop. I also believe that they are not free not to make explicit what they believe are the features of sound theory.

Lewin did say, in effect, that there was nothing as practical as sound theory. He defined the properties of any sound theory. I will make some of these properties explicit and illustrate their implications for scholarly consulting.

## SCHOLARLY CONSULTING: DEFINITION

Scholarly consulting contains the following features:

- Propositions that are valid *and* actionable, that are generalizable *and* applicable in the individual case
- Propositions that can be produced by scholars or practitioners under real time, everday life conditions
- The effective implementation of these propositions leads to results that are consistent with what is intended; there are no inner contradictions, i.e., the effective implementation does not necessarily create effective *and* ineffective consequences.
- The claim of effectiveness is testable by methods that meet the most robust standards of disconfirmation.

## SCHOLARLY CONSULTING: PREMISES

- All understanding and explanation are in the service of action. The validity of the understanding or the explanation is ultimately established by the effectiveness of the action.

  *Implication*: All propositions about understanding and explanation are normative because the basis for effectiveness is chosen by those producing the propositions and those implementing them. These choices are not based on some objective truth.

  The method for testing effectiveness is through the implementation of prescriptions that are derived from the normative descriptions. Action research, as its core, is normative and prescriptive.

- All scholarly consulting activities are implemented by human beings in a context or situation.

  *Implication*: Scholarly propositions are crafted in ways that respect any systematic constraints imposed by the human mind/brain and by systematic features of the context in which the actions are being taken.

I will expand on the definition and the premises as I described some key features of sound theory.

### *Propositions that are Relevant to the Many and to the One*

Sound theory produces propositions that are generalizable *and* at the same time, applicable to the individual case. There is not one theory for the many and another for the one.

Lewin (1935, 1936) presented this feature in his description of the Galilean approach to explanation, as compared with the Aristotelian approach. The premiss of the Galilean approach is that a complete description should lead to predictions that do not admit to exceptions. If one exception is found, it can serve as the basis for disconfirmation *and* as a basis for further research. One cannot ignore or delay dealing with exceptions by labeling them as residual categories.

The criterion of what is complete is defined by the theory. This makes it especially important that the theory be confronted with robust tests such as those proposed by the Galilean approach.

I should like to illustrate by the gatekeeper concept developed by Lewin. For example, in the group climate and leadership research, Lewin proposed that an autocratic leader created the following conditions. There are four subordinates who report to the leader. The key feature of autocratic leadership is that the leader is in control of the gate through which any subordinate must go if they are to achieve their goals, whatever those goals may be. This places the subordinates in a situation where they will be dependent upon the leader. They have to learn how to deal with her if she is to let them through the gate to enter the region in which their goal exists. The subordinates will also be placed in a situation where they compete with each other in order to obtain the leader's permission to go through the gate.

The claim by Lewin and his colleagues is that these conditions and their consequences are valid for many contexts – be it a business organization, a government bureau, a union organization, a church setting, a school setting, or a setting where parents are trying to get their children to eat healthy food. Moreover, the claim is that these predictions will hold if the subordinates are female or male, young or old, better or less well educated, poor or wealthy, and regardless of race or culture. Finally, the claim is that this will be true from the day it was constructed until forever, as long as the conditions depicted in the diagram are not altered.

Exactly what words the actor uses to execute these actions may vary widely. But, whatever the variance, it is a difference that makes no difference in understanding and explaining. The words, in Lewin's terms, are phenotypes. Meaning and the concepts inferred from knowing it – such as gatekeeper, goals, and needs of the subordinates – are genotypes.

### Propositions that Can Be Produced by Anyone Under Real Time, Everyday Life Conditions

Propositions that are actionable must be producible in the universe being studied by the scholars and the practitioners.

In order to be producible, the propositions must contain causal claims crafted as statements – "If A, then B." Causality is the basis of effective action in everyday life (Shoham, 1990).

The ideas in good currency about how to produce valid descriptions of causality that should lead to effective action are largely based on the concept of variance. Many social scientists strive to produce causal explanations by using such perspectives as Mill's Method of Difference. This leads to the following consequences.

1  The research is organized around activities for the purpose of understanding. Understanding, at the outset, is in the service of understanding (explanation). The ultimate product is a valid description of the universe.
2  The rules for carrying out this activity include the following:
   • Produce as accurate and as complete descriptions as possible.
   • Take as much time as is necessary to produce these valid descriptions. Research time is different from time in everyday action. It is legitimate to study a one-hour group interaction for several months.
   • Develop causal analyses that describe the variables and their interrelationships as completely as possible.
   • Test the causal claims under conditions where unrecognized distortions that confound the claims are minimized.
   There are several consequence of these rules, when they are implemented *correctly*, that are counterproductive to producing valid knowledge in the service of effective action.

The causal models developed with an eye on completeness may not be actionable because they are not storable in and retrievable by the human mind under everyday life conditions. The human mind is a finite information system (Miller, 1956; Simon, 1969).

For example, Naylor, et al. (1980) developed a model to understand behavior in organizations. The model was described as being as scientifically complete as they could make it. When the authors were finished, they recognized that human beings were unlikely to use the model in everyday life because it was too complex. They argued that human beings will have to develop a more simple method in order to act. They lamented what they called the degrading of the model in order to act, but agreed that it was necessary.

There is another interpretation that can be taken if the requirements for actionability are considered as equal to the requirements of validity. It could be that the more simple model is the correct *scientific* model because this is what the human mind, being a finite information processor, can deal with. It is their model that degrades reality of science (Argyris, 1980).

A second counterproductive consequence that flows from propositions that are rigorously defined by the current ideas about rigor is that their "correct" implementation requires conditions which, if they exist, will *prima facie* lead to consequences that are counter-productive to the results.

The first example comes from the excellent research by Barker et al. (1943) on frustration and regression. Recall that they found that mild frustration leads to creativity, but beyond a certain threshold it led to frustration. Frustration, in turn, led to de-differentiation of the human personality which, in turn, resulted in regression.

Assume for a moment that a practitioner wishes to increase creativity by creating mild frustration. How would she do it? Would she tell her subordinates that she is about to generate mild frustration in them in order for them to act more creatively? Could doing so upset the subordinates and hence speed up the frustration?

How will she discover the threshold point? One answer is to use the instruments that the researchers developed to ascertain the threshold in their study. How could she use those instruments? Would she fill them out on-line? Would she have some observers fill them out? How could the results be analyzed in time to affect the on-line activity?

A second example comes from the research on communication (Aronson, 1972). The following advice flowed from the research findings. If the messenger and the message are to be trusted by an audience that is deemed to be bright, present several different messages. If the audience is composed of individuals who are not so bright, then only one message is effective. Nowhere in the publication is the practitioner told to make this reasoning explicit to the audience. That is not so surprising. Imagine telling the audience that they are getting one message because they have been judged as not being smart. Perhaps telling the bright audience that they are being given several messages could also activate mistrust – i.e., what are they driving at?

In both cases, the reasoning used to design the experiments followed the current rules for conducting empirical research. In the name of minimizing the confounding of results, the reasoning is covered up and the cover-up is covered up. If we are to be rigorous in the statements of the empirical results, these conditions should be included explicitly as part of the conditions under which the results hold.

If these "cover up" conditions are included explicitly, at least two consequences would occur that are consistent with stating the propositions rigorously. The first is that scientists would be clear about the conditions under which their results hold. The second is that the practitioners would be alerted to the conditions that they must create if the propositions are to be actionable.

These conditions are not neutral. They are based on a theory-in-use of unilateral, top-down control.

The counterproductive consequence is that the findings are usually organized around the specification of empirical relationships among variables such as a curvilinear relationship. The difficulty with such descriptions is that, to my knowledge, the human mind cannot produce them in the form of actual behavior in a specific situation or context. The results are not actionable.

How did the researchers produce this generalization? They followed the rules. They analyzed their data by using "research time." They crafted the generalization consistently with the rules that focuses on variance. Finally, they organized their findings in the form of a proposition about the empirical relationship. This proposition is so information rich that it is difficult to implement.

These examples illustrate, I suggest, that knowledge produced rigorously following the empirical methods based on variance is not user-friendly. The examples also illustrate that embedded in the generalizations are the conditions under which they were generated. In practice, these conditions are kept tacit. The difficulty is that, in keeping them tacit, they can lead to advice that, when carried out effectively, leads to consequences that are counter-productive to the claims made in the propositions.

### Predictions that are Tested Under the Most Rigorous Conditions of Disconfirmation

All tests should be crafted in ways that they can be carried out effectively under everyday life conditions by scholars or practitioners. Tests that cannot be carried out by practitioners render helpless those practitioners who are concerned about the validity and the action-ability of the propositions that they are using.

There are four types of tests that scholarly consultants can use. The first is the least robust. The last is the most robust.

1  Predict what will and will not occur under conditions that are consistent with the universe as it is – that is, the status quo.
2  Predict the conditions under which the above conditions will persevere.
3  Predict that if the solutions are to be implemented, they will require a context that does not exist in the present universe.
4  Predict the conditions under which 3 will persevere.

These modes of testing have important implications for establishing validity. For example, external validity is a necessary, but not sufficient, condition for actionability. External validity makes the claim that the results obtained in one setting (e.g., an experiment in the laboratory or the field) are *relevant* to other settings consistent with the conditions under which the research was conducted (Campbell and Stanley, 1963).

High external validity tells us little about actionability. Trust, for example, is a variable that has high external validity. But, most of the research that has established the external validity of trust specifies little about how to produce trust in the world of practice.

The most robust tests of validity are those that can be used to predict about universes that do not, as yet, exist. It is such tests that Lewin focused upon when he advised that, if social scientists truly wish to understand certain phenomena, they should try to change them.

Creating, not predicting, is the most robust test of validity–actionability. The criteria identified as 1 and 2 in the above list can be met by observing a universe that already exists. A more powerful test is if the scholarly consultants can show that they can recreate the universe that exists. This is an important distinction. Years ago, when the center research for the study innovations was created at Michigan, its primary focus was to seek out and study innovative examples. To my knowledge, there was little attention paid to creating such examples that already existed. If they had done so, they would have been able to show that their models not only led to predictions, but could also be used to create the conditions under which the predictions held.

Even more powerful is to fulfill conditions 3 and 4 when the conditions specified do not exist. To do so is to create rare events. Let us examine this claim in more detail.

### Knowledge that Can Be Used to Create Rare Events is What Drives Scholarly Consulting

All universes that we study are created by our subjects or clients. We may describe a universe, but we are always describing normative processes. Scholarly consultants keep reminding themselves that rigorously speaking description cannot be separated from normative activities and get at the causality that creates the universe being described.

The research on group climates and leadership contains many predictions about the impact of autocratic, democratic, and *laissez-faire* leadership on such variables as group productivity and cohesiveness. Lewin and his colleagues went beyond prediction when they attempted to reeducate the autocratic leaders to act more democratically. This is an act of creation. Such acts require much richer explanatory sequences than are required by straightforward prediction.

For example, autocratic and democratic leaders act on the basis of their respective theories-in-use about effective action. Lewin and his colleagues defined these theories-in-use on the basis of their theoretical perspective. They taught these theories-in-use to the various leaders until they were skillful at producing the leadership actions that they were assigned. Based on their theories, the researchers could predict the impact on specified outcomes.

In order to re-train the leaders to be more democratic, Lewin and his colleagues needed more information. How do they unfreeze the autocratic style with its accompanying skillful defenses and introduce a more democratic style? How is this done so that it not only perseveres but so that it can be monitored effectively in order to detect and correct any error or mismatches?

Experiments to change autocratic styles to democratic styles represented rare events in the leadership domain and in the organizational domain. Rare events are not likely to occur nor to persevere if the organizational context in which they occur is not also changed. How does one produce changes simultaneously in the leadership styles, group and intergroup dynamics, as well as the organizational context?

The hesitation by social scientists to become concerned about producing change creates a consequence that limits the power of our causal explanations because we do not include in the descriptions the causal reasoning that produced the patterns in the first place.

For example, social scientists may study organizations and develop patterns or generalization that organize their observations in the form of patterns and generalizations. They may observe actions that they categorize as "low trust," or "coalition group conflict," or "quasi-resolution of conflict." They may then claim, as do the behavioral theorists of the firm, that such phenomena are at the core of relationships in organizations (Cyert and March, 1963). A parallel program of inquiry called "action science" arrives at similar descriptions (Argyris and Schön 1974, 1996).

So far, these descriptions describe what the scholars claim to have observed. They do not, however, provide causal explanations of how the actors created or produced the behavior that the social scientists organized around such concepts as quasi-resolution of conflict, etc. What is lacking is causal explanations of what was in the heads of the actors that caused them to create the actions that were observed by the researchers. It is these types of causal explanations that are required if social science is to be actionable – that is, if it is to be used to create the universe that social scientists describe. This cannot be accomplished without focusing on the question, "How do the subjects produce and create the behavior that we observe and that we use to define our universe?"

There is another counterproductive consequence of research that describes reality and ignores how the reality was created in the first place. The research activity becomes the servant of the status quo.

For example, scholars associated with the behavioral theory of the firm create concepts that describe what they observe, but there is little attention paid to producing knowledge about how to change them. For example, several "relational concepts" are defined. These include limited learning, quasi resolution of conflict and intergroup rivalries. To my knowledge, the founders of this theory pay little attention to conducting research on how to reduce the dysfunctional features of limited learning, quasi resolution of conflict, and intergroup rivalries (Argyris, 1996b). They appear uninterested in changing the status quo, especially in creating rare events.

## A Theory of Action Perspective

An example of an approach that is concerned about changing the status quo is the one developed by Donald Schön and myself. The approach has been described in several publications and, hence, I will not repeat the description at length (Argyris and Schön, 1974, 1996; Argyris, et al., 1985; Argyris, 1982, 1985, 1990a, 1993).

The approach begins with the observation that individuals hold theories of action. The theories of action can be subdivided into the theories that they espouse and the theories that they use when they take action. Espoused theories are produced in the mind/brain in the activity described as understanding in order to explain. The theories-in-use are produced in the mind/brain in the activity described as understanding to take action.

So far, all the individuals that we have studied hold a theory-in-use that we call Model I. Gender, race, education, age, wealth, position in the organization and country culture appear to make no difference. The espoused theories vary widely, but they do not cause the actions the mind/brain produces. Also, the actual words used may vary. Thus, a Briton may speak of being civilized, an American easing-in, a Japanese of being respectful. The theory-in-use is the same. It is, in effect, "If you sense embarrassment or threat, in self or others, bypass it and cover up the bypass." Indeed, primates may exhibit Model I (de Waal, 1982, 1989).

The causal reasoning of all Model I designs is primarily defensive. Defensive reasoning is to use premises that are subjective and tacit, and to infer from the premises in ways that are also subjective and tact, and to test the conclusions reached by using logic that is the same as the logic used to reach the conclusion. The test therefore does not use independent logic. It is self-referential logic. "Trust me, I know what is really going on," is a frequently used example.

Productive reasoning focuses on making the premises explicit, making the inferences from the premises explicit also, and having the conclusions tested by logic that is independent of the logic used to create the conclusions in the first place.

This requirement has embedded in it a position about rigor. Rigorous, or what I call "productive" reasoning, is enhanced to the extent that causal relationships are specifiable at the conceptual level (e.g., the relationship between concepts of topology and methodology). Rigor also includes specifying the operational definitions and showing how they are connected to the conceptual domain.

Lewin spent many hours striving to be as rigorous as possible in his thinking, including where he thought gaps existed that someday had to be closed (Lewin, 1938). It is such hard work at theory building and connecting it to empirical reality that led to the asking of clear questions, because "nature cannot give clear and definite answers to vague questions" (Lippitt, 1940, p. 9).

Lewin's conception of theory-building illustrates a theory that is based upon productive reasoning. For example, his theory is composed of concepts and their logical interrelationships defined so precisely that hypotheses can be formulated about what is excluded and included. Lewin provides many illustrations in his early work (Cartwright, 1951; Lewin, 1935, 1936, 1938) of how topological and vector concepts can be integrated to provide a valid psychological science that permits the rigorous testing of hypotheses. Lewin's use of the concept's mathematical features is still open to question (Back, 1966), but this is not the point being made. The point is that his writings show that he was continually concerned with the use of rigorous productive reasoning.

For example, in his early writings (Lewin, 1935, 1936, 1938) Lewin published detailed discussions of what is required to translate topological vector concepts to psychological meaning. There are detailed discussions of the criteria used to coordinate a type of action to a place in the life space; the psychological meaning attached to the boundaries of regions and their degree of permeability; the psychological meaning connected to units of life space that are peripheral or central; to the path of locomotion through the life space.

I can recall providing, as concretely as possible, examples of what I had experienced in organizations to Roger Barker, Fritz Heider, and Herbert Wright. Their first step was to try to assess the richness of the examples. Consistent with Lewin's admonitions, they pressed their inquiry in order to see if my examples described the total dynamic structure. Instead of trying to abstract averages of as many historically given cases as possible, they sought to develop the full comprehensiveness of the situation.

> [Comprehending the]...actual situation as fully and as concretely as possible, even in its individual peculiarities, make the most precise possible qualitative and quantitative determination necessary and profitable. But it must not be forgotten that only this task, and not numerical precision for its own sake, give any point or meaning to exactness. (Lewin, 1935, p. 35)

Not surprisingly Barker, Heider, and Wright would spend hours coordinating the features of the examples to various topological and vector concepts. In order to produce valid coordination, they had to be as explicit as they could be as to what was occurring in the situation. They strove to be as comprehensive as possible and to minimize unexplained meaning (residual categories) because one empirical exception could disconfirm our hypothesis and features of our theory. Recall Lewin's claim that "Every psychological law must hold without exception" (Lewin, 1935, p. 23). Any exception found is a trigger for research and inquiry to modify the theory.

I noticed that another consequence of these discussions was that it prepared me for my encounters with clients. The clients rarely raised questions that were beyond those that we had raised. Or, if they did, it was psychologically easier to admit that I had not thought of the question and to present my reasoning behind this unrecognized gap.

It was also easier to engage in a dialogue with the client on how to close the gap. Not infrequently, I found myself questioning the client's reasoning. In most cases, they found the inquiry challenging and productive of important learning. Some realized early on that it would be useful for them to become skilled at productive reasoning.

As I have reflected on my experiences, I began to realize that productive reasoning was, at the heart of individuals and organizations, becoming more effective. I realized that one of the best ways to assure clients and myself that I was not unrealizingly leading them toward error was the vigilant use of productive reasoning. I learned that my confidence in myself and the clients' confidence in my competence was deepened and strengthened by becoming skillful at productive reasoning. This was not true in some cases. The client sought answers that did not require examining their reasoning process. I would do my best to show them why their quick fixes were not likely to work and, more certainly, not persevere. In those cases, I did not succeed and recommended that they look elsewhere.

I was bewildered to find that many organizational development professionals were not competent in productive reasoning. Some were not interested in it and some thought it was counterproductive. Many described the emphasis as too rational, too logical, and too scientific. I recall that I would push back for them to define "too rational" or "too logical" and to illustrate through the use of their behavior with me and others. They often became defensive and expressed emotions that they had just claimed would not be generated by this "too rational" approach. When I would focus on their *and* my here-and-now actions, they became more upset and closed off learning (Argyris, 1987, 1990b).

There is another feature of theory-in-use that is important. All theories-in-use are implemented through skillful actions. Such actions are rigorously programmed in the mind/brain. The features of skillful action include that it:

- works;
- appears effortless;
- is automatic, spontaneous, and tacit.

Once actions become tacit they are no longer at the forefront of the mind. It is precisely because the actions are skillful that there is little need for paying conscious attention to producing them. The ability to act skillfully depends on "designed ignorance." This designed ignorance leads human beings to be unaware of gaps and inconsistencies between their espoused theories and their theories-in-use. This unawareness is skillful. It is not based on incompetence or a hole in one's head.

The window into the mind/brain, therefore, is to begin with the actions human beings produce (e.g., conversation) and not espoused theories that is the basis of most paper and pencil instruments. Lewin and his colleagues were among the first to point out that observational data and transcripts of conversation were richer for producing and predicting than the many paper and pencil instruments that they used (Lippitt, 1940).

If we combine the existence of defensive reasoning and skilled unawareness, it is possible to explain why human beings often act in ways that can be described as skillfully incompetent. The actions are incompetent because they produce consequences that the actors do not intend. The actions are skillful because they are consistent with the actors' theories-in-use. This has important implications for the kind of behavior that is created in organizations.

For example, in our theory of action perspective, we causally connect Model I theory-in-use to producing contexts (in groups, intergroups, and organizations) that inhibit productive reasoning and double-loop learning (Argyris and Schön, 1996). A key concept is defensive routines. Defensive routines are any actions that are produced to prevent embarrassment or threat to the participants *and* simultaneously prevent getting at the causes of the embarrassment or threat.

Defensive routines are designed and implemented through the use of defensive reasoning. An example is mixed messages: "Joe, you run the department, but check with Charley," "Mary, be creative, but be careful." The reasoning embedded in the theory-in-use of mixed messages is:

- state a message that is inconsistent;
- act as if it is not inconsistent;
- make the above undiscussable;
- make the undiscussability undiscussable.

Under these conditions the effectiveness of learning is likely to be low. This feeds back to reinforce Model I theories-in-use which, in turn feeds forward to reinforce the organizational defensive routines. The result is an ultra-stable state that minimizes effectiveness.

Organizational defenses and theories-in-use are intimately related. Interrupting and changing the ultra-stable state just described should not be possible by making organizational changes that bypass the Model I theories-in-use and the defensive reasoning used by most human beings.

### The Preciousness of Human Beings and Their Institutions

Human beings are not likely to cooperate and seek help if they do not feel respected by those aspiring to help them. The first source of respect is for the scholarly consultants to realize that, whatever problems the clients produced, they did it because they believed it was the most effective way for them to act.

It follows from the above that whenever individuals act on the basis of their designs, the consequences cannot be errors if they produce what they intend. Such an outcome is a match, not a mismatch.

The second source of respect is the belief that individuals are capable of learning in order to detect error in their actions (single-loop learning) or in their underlying values (double-loop learning).

I believe that this is the basis for the respect scholars such as Lewin and Barker exhibited toward human beings regardless of race, gender, wealth, education, and culture. Human beings were to be treasured, otherwise neither they nor the scholars would be able to learn, especially in the case of double-loop learning.

The scholarly consultant is genuinely committed to help the clients build a better life. "Better" means having more effectiveness, more competence, and greater confidence in themselves and their institutions to provide enhanced learning that perseveres. Lewin, according to Deutsch (1992), exhibited these features in dealing with clients and with his colleagues. Caring for human beings is not unconditional. Indeed, unconditional caring may result in human beings who are over-protected and brittle (Argyris, 1985). Perhaps this is one reason why Lewin was caring but tough (Ash, 1992; Deutsch, 1992). The scholarly consultant is caring to the extent that the clients are genuinely interest in learning, in producing valid information, in encouraging informed choice, and in accepting personal responsibility for these actions.

This sense of the preciousness of human beings inveighs against the notion that scholars, in the interest of being objective, must distance themselves from those they study. By distancing, I mean acting in ways that separate or make the researcher appear remote, cold, and reserved.

There is another consequence of distancing that concerns me. The distancing leads to separating basic from applied research.

For example, Cronback and Suppes (1969) differentiate between "conclusion-oriented research" (basic) and "decision-oriented research" (applied). This distinction may make sense if the focus of research is upon diagnosis and invention (such as inventing policies). However, the distinction becomes problematic if one includes production and evaluation of human action as well as diagnosis and invention. Actors are forever reaching conclusions and making decisions about actions.

Moreover, Coleman's (1972) advice that self-correcting activities in present policy research are best done by independent studies, if carried out, undermines the personal responsibility of those who did the diagnosing and inventing of policies for implementation and monitoring their actions. True, this integrative approach is not easy for individuals or for organizations to implement. But this does not seem to be a valid reason to bypass the problem. It is a reason for conducting that research that leads to individuals or organizations that are capable of integrating diagnosis, invention, production, and evaluation.

Years ago, when the Ford Foundation began, it was genuinely concerned with supporting social science. I was a member of a small committee of scholars invited to brainstorm about methodologies for the financial support of research. My model was one of a high degree of decentralization with as much control of the funding at the local level (university, individual scholar) as possible. The idea was dismissed quickly by the senior officials of the Foundation (most of whom were former academics) and the committee (all of whom were academics). The reason, I was told, was that academics could not be trusted to be concerned about anything except their personal agendas. The Foundation officials expressed grave doubts that social scientists, left to their own devices, would care about producing basic and actionable knowledge that would help human beings and their institutions. When I pushed back, there was near unanimity that the reason that I thought academics might be trusted to change was that I was young and with little experience. As many of you know, the Ford Foundation executive eventually concluded that a radical change was necessary. They funded their own action projects.

This trend of distancing and mutual mistrust spread to the governmental agencies. They too began to define the research to be funded. Scholars who appeared before Congressional committees and who promised that researchers were centrally interested in actionable knowledge began to lose their credibility. This distancing continues. Congressman George E. Brown, Jr, known for being a supporter of social science research, recently publicly raised questions about researchers' credibility (Johnson, 1993).

## CONCLUSION

There are two key issues in studying organizations. They are establishing causality and the testing of the validity of causal claims (Pfeffer, 1997). Indeed, these two issues are key for social science inquiry in general (Argyris and Schön, 1974; Kaplan, 1964; Popper, 1959).

In examining the literature that contains reviews on action research (Bargal, et al., 1992; Eden and Huxham 1996; Elden and Chisholm, 1993; Gold, 1992; Susman and Evered, 1978), it is clear that there exists agreement that action research is intended to explain problems and, in many cases attempt to solve them, through the use of collaboration and participation. It is also clear that there exists a wide range of perspectives on how to accomplish these purposes and what methodologies to use.

As best as I can determine, the majority of the contributors do not focus explicitly on causality and how it is to be established. Indeed, there is a significant proportion who claim that it is not possible or necessary to make causal claims. Many of those typically decry positivism as being out of date and irrelevant. The same group substitute a more humanistic approach, subjective, postmodern perspective.

There are several problems with these claims. The researchers using the subjective and humanistic approaches can also distance themselves from the "subjects." They appeared unaware that they were creating the distancing that they decried positivism for creating (Argyris, 1995). Moreover, taking the position that causality is not relevant or testable is itself a causal claim. How can those who decry causality make arguments about more relevant ways to explain phenomena that are, themselves, based on causal reasoning?

Finally, there is increasing evidence from studies of the mind that much thought and all of action is based on causality (Shoham, 1990; Simon, 1969). Those who wish to eliminate causality are responsible to make it clear how they believe the mind works without causality.

Action researchers may define their respective perspectives as they wish. But, they cannot escape from defining what they mean by rigor (Heller, 1993; Peters and Robinson, 1984). Lewin's work and that of Schön and myself provide one meta theoretical perspective that is relevant to dealing with the issues of causality.

# References

Argyris, C., 1982, *Reasoning, Learning, Action*, San Francisco, Jossey-Bass.

Argyris, C., 1985, *Strategy, Change and Defensive Routines*, Boston, Pitman.

Argyris, C., 1987, "Reasoning, Action Strategies and Defensive Routines: The Case of OD Practitioners," *Research in Organizational Change and Development*, 1, JAI Press, Inc., pp. 89–128.

Argyris, C., 1990a, *Overcoming Organizational Defenses*, Needham, MA, Allyn-Bacon.

Argyris, C., 1990b, "Inappropriate Defenses Against the Monitoring of Organizational Development Practice," *Journal of Applied Behavioral Science*, 26, 3, pp. 299–312.

Argyris, C., 1993, *Knowledge for Action*, San Francisco, Jossey-Bass.

Argyris, C., 1995, "Knowledge When Used in Practice Tests Theory: The Case of Applied Communication Research," in Cissna, K. N. (ed.), *Applied Communication in the 20th Century*, Mahwak, NJ, Lawrence Erlbaum Associates, pp. 1–19.

Argyris, C., 1996b, "Unrecognized Defenses of Scholars: Impact on Theory and Research," *Organization Science*, 7, 1, pp. 79–87.

Argyris, C., and Schön, D., 1974, *Theory in Practice*, San Francisco, Jossey-Bass.

Argyris, C., and Schön, D., 1996, *Organizational Learning II*, Reading, MA, Addison-Wesley.

Argyris, C., Putnam, R., and Smith, D., 1985, *Action Science*, San Francisco, Jossey-Bass.

Aronson, E., 1972, *The Social Animal*, San Francisco, Freeman.

Ash, M. G., 1992, "Cultural Contexts and Scientific Change in Psychology: Kurt Lewin in Iowa," *American Psychologist*, 47, 2, pp. 198–207.

Back K., 1966, "This business of topology," *Journal of Social Issues*, 48, 2, pp. 51–66.

Bargal, D., Gold, M., and Lewin, M., 1992, "Introduction: The Heritage of Kurt Lewin," *Journal of Social Issues*, 48, 2, pp. 3–13.

Barker, R. G., Dembo, T., and Lewin, K., 1943, "Frustration and Regression," in Barker, R. G., Kounin, J., and Wright, H. (eds), *Child Behavior and Development*, New York, McGraw-Hill.

Campbell, D. T., and Stanley, J. C., 1963, *Experimental and Quasi-experimental Design for Research*, Skokie, IL, Rand McNally.

Cartwright, D. (ed.), 1951, *Field Theory in Social Science*, New York, Harper.

Cartwright, D., 1959, "Lewinian Theory as a Contemporary Systematic Framework," in Koch, S. (ed.), *Psychology: A Study of a Science*, New York, McGraw-Hill, pp. 7–91.

Coleman, J. S., 1972, *Policy Research in the Social Sciences*, Morristown, NJ, General Learning Press.

Cronback, L. J., and Suppes, P. (eds), 1969, *Research for Tomorrow's Schools*, London, Macmillan.

Cyert, R. M., and March, J. G., 1963, *A Behavioral Theory of the Firm*, Englewood Cliffs, NJ, Prentice-Hall.

Deutsch, M., 1992, "Kurt Lewin: The Tough-minded and Tender-hearted Scientist," *Journal of Social Issues*, 48, 2, pp. 31–43.

de Waal, F., 1982, *Chimpanzee Politics: Power and sex among apes*, New York, Harper and Row.

de Waal, F., 1989, *Peacemaking Among Primates*, Cambridge, MA, Harvard University Press.

Eden, C., and Huxham, C., 1996, "Action Research for the Study of Organizations," in Clegg, S. R., Hardy, C., and Nord, W. R. (eds), *Handbook of Organization Studies*, London, Sage, pp. 526–42.

Elden, M., and Chisholm, R. (eds), 1993, "Emerging Varieties of Action Research: Introduction to a Special Issue," *Human Relations*, 46, 2, pp. 121–42.

Gold, M., 1992, "Metatheory and Field Theory in Social Psychology: Relevance or Elegance?," *Journal of Social Issues*, 48, 2, pp. 67–78.

Heller, F., 1993, "Another Look at Action Research," *Human Relations*, 46, 10, pp. 1,235–42.

Johnson, D., 1993, "Psychology in Washington: Measurement to Improve Scientific Productivity: A Reflection on the Brown Report," *Psychological Science*, 4, 2, pp. 67–9.

Kaplan, A., 1964, *The Conduct of Inquiry*, San Francisco, Chandler Publishing.

Lewin, K., 1935, *A Dynamic Theory of Personality*, New York, McGraw-Hill.

Lewin, K., 1936, *Principles of Topological Psychology*, New York, McGraw-Hill.

Lewin, K., 1938, *The Conceptual Representation and the Measurement of Psychological Forces*, Durham, NC, Duke University Press.

Lippitt, R., 1940, "An Experimental Study of the Effect of Democratic and Authoritarian Group Atmospheres," in Lewin, K., Lippitt, R., and Escalona, S. K. (eds), *Studies in Topological Vector Psychology I*, Iowa City, IA, University of Iowa Press.

Metraux, A., 1992, "Kurt Lewin: Philosopher–Psychologist," *Science in Context*, 5, 2, pp. 373–84.

Miller, G., 1956, "The Magical Number Seven, Plus or Minus Two: Some Limits on Our Capacity for Processing Information," *Psychological Review*, 63, pp. 81–96.

Naylor, J. C., Pritchard, R. J., and Ilgen, D. R., 1980, *A Theory of Behavior in Organizations*, New York, Academic Press.

Peters, M., and Robinson, V., 1984, "The Origins and Status of Action Research," *Journal of Applied Behavioral Science*, 20, 2, pp. 113–24.

Pfeffer, J., 1997, *New Directions for Organizational Theory*, New York, Oxford University Press.

Popper, K., 1959, *The Logic of Scientific Discovery*, New York, Basic Books.

Shoham, Y., 1990, "Nonmonotonic Reasoning and Causation," *Cognitive Science*, 14, pp. 213–302.

Simon, H. A., 1969, *The Science of the Artificial*, Cambridge, MA, MIT Press.

Susman, G. S., and Evered, R. D., 1978, "An Assessment of the Scientific Merits of Action Research," *Administrative Science Quarterly*, 23, pp. 582–603.

# — 20 —

# Unrecognized Defenses of Scholars: Impact on Theory and Research

There is a body of literature, often identified as the sociology of knowledge, that includes the exploration of the ways by which interpersonal, group, and intergroup dynamics among scholars influence the development of scientific knowledge. (Bourdieu, 1977; Feyerabend, 1975; Kaplan, 1964; Merton, 1973; Mitroff, 1974; Watson, 1969). In the field of organization behavior, Herriot (1992) has examined how the psychometric subculture within organizational behavior can lead to its own demise and irrelevance.

I propose to examine how the theories used and research conducted by scholars can feed back to make them unaware of gaps in their theories. I hope to show that these counter-productive consequences are tacit and taken for granted. These factors combine to inhibit the production of valid knowledge.

I will focus primarily on my defenses as exhibited in my role in the development of the theory of action (TOA). I hope to illustrate that the assumptions and claims that I made, that only double-loop learning will lead to liberating alternatives and changing the status quo, were based on defensive reasoning. Defensive reasoning includes making premises and inference processes tacit; crafting conclusions in such a way that they are not falsifiable by reasoning external to the one used to create the conclusion. Such defensive reasoning not only produced gaps in the theory of which I was unaware. It also hindered seeing important connections with other relevant organizational theories, in this case the Behavioral Theory of the Firm (BTF).

For the sake of comparison, I will also focus on the reasoning and research of a few leading scholars of BTF, primarily James March. I hope to show that he too, used defensive reasoning which made it unlikely that BTF scholars will see certain important gaps in BTF, and that, in turn, hindered seeing important connections with TOA.

If my analysis is correct, these gaps are especially puzzling since both theories hold similar premises about the nature of organizational reality. For example, the human mind is a finite processing system; organizational life is often dominated by quasi-resolution of conflict and limited learning; that reality is constructed in the form of designs (Simon, 1969) or life space (Lewin: see Cartwright, 1951, p. 19,511); and societal cultures are constructed with features that are consistent with the designs (Berger and Luckmann, 1967; Geertz, 1973). How is it that two theories that exhibit similar premises lead to significantly different if not, at times, antagonistic views about the alterability and changeability of the universe that each purports to represent?

## SOME CONCEPTS OF TOA

First, a very brief review of some of the key concepts of TOA that are related to learning at all levels of organizations:

Learning occurs when a match between intentions and actuality is produced for the first time. The match is genuinely new to the actors producing it. Learning also occurs when actors detect and correct mismatches or errors. Single-loop learning occurs when the mismatch is corrected by changing the actions. Double-loop learning occurs when the underlying governing values or master programs are changed which, in turn, leads to changes in action.

Human beings manifest two kinds of theories of action. One that they espouse and the second that they actually use (theory-in-use). Human beings' studies to date hold varying espoused theories. However, their theories-in-use do not appear to vary across countries, ages, economic status, gender, race, or educational status. (Argyris, 1982, 1985, 1993; Argyris and Schön, 1974, 1978). For example, the theory-in-use formulation of face saving is the same: bypass embarrassment or threat and cover up the bypass. The actual behavior that individuals use to produce face saving varies but the theory-in-use from which it is derived does not.

The theory-in-use, called Model I, is fundamentally a theory-in-use that leads to limited learning, especially under conditions of embarrassment and threat. As Model I actions aggregate they produce organizational learning systems that are also limited. The most prominent examples studied so far are organizational defensive routines. (Argyris, 1985, 1990a, 1993). Model I theories-in-use and organizational defensive routines reinforce each other and make learning, especially double-loop learning, extremely difficult, if not impossible.

## GAPS TO BE FILLED IN AND TESTED IN TOA

Empirical research leads TOA researchers to conclude that Model I theories-in-use and organizational defensive routines combine to create quasi-resolution of conflict, coalition groups each looking out for its own interests and, at the same time, competing and condemning other groups, and limited learning. They also conclude that in order to alter these states, it is necessary to question the underlying governing variables or values of theories-in-use, at all levels of organizations, as well as behavioral routines that are consistent with these values.

It follows that changing the status quo is required if organizational learning is to be facilitated. It also follows that double-loop learning is key to achieving such outcomes. Single-loop learning and routines, although they dominate organizational life, are the enemy of organizations solving difficult problems that are embarrassing or threatening. It is variables such as these that disempower human beings and limit their commitment.

## FIELD RESEARCH THAT HELPED TO IDENTIFY LIMITS ON MY THINKING

About a decade ago, I began to explore the relationships between TOA and theories peculiar to various managerial functions, such as strategy, managerial accounting, microeconomics, manufacturing and product development, and information science. The impetus for this research came from several sources. First, as I tried to create interventions for double-loop learning in organizations I immediately encountered activities from executives using these managerial theories in ways that inhibited double-loop learning. Sometimes the cause of the inhibited was an error in the managerial technical theory. More often, the technical theory was not at fault as much as the way the human beings dealt with the embarrassment and threat generated by introducing these theories in everyday practice.

For example. Activity Analysis was introduced in an organization by a senior financial executive. By using analytical techniques associated with Activity Analysis he was able to document that the largest activities accounted for some 35 percent of the total costs. Yet, none of these activities were related to meeting the customer needs, an objective to which all top management were committed. To his surprise and dismay, he found that his study activated a hornet's nest of resistance on the part of other executives, even though these same executives did not question its validity. The resistance was predictable by the use of TOA concepts such as organizational defenses (Kaplan, 1991).

A second reason for seeking to connect with the managerial functional disciplines was my discovery that I could produce more powerful double-loop learning in organizations when I could combine it with more effective implementation of the functional theories. It is one thing to create an intervention to increase trust among a top management group. It is quite another to produce trust that overcomes organizational defensive routines which have been inhibiting the quality of rigorous thinking and problem solving around key business issues in the organization. The first type of trust was as one executive described it, "a human resources goody." The second intervention generated trust that was connected to the stewardship and responsibility that the executives had for all the people in the organization. The second type of trust turned out to be more humane and to generate reinforcement that caused it to persist longer than the first (Argyris, 1982, 1985, 1993).

In short, the first phase led me to become more interdisciplinary-oriented because I could use the ideas around double-loop learning to help other scholars implement their ideas more effectively (Argyris and Kaplan, 1994).

I was not prepared for another set of learning experiences that also occurred. I began to observe examples where technical theories that were implemented correctly reduced the likelihood of embarrassment and threat in the first place. The routine single-loop features of technical theories also created liberating alternatives. Although they did not create double-loop learning, it appeared that they prevented the need for double-loop learning in the first place.

For example. Steve Briely (Kaplan, 1989) expressed doubts about the efficiency of empowerment workshops created by his Human Resources organization. He believed that genuine empowerment would occur if his employees were in control over and responsible for their performance. The system would provide timely information on performance. This, in turn, would provide employees with the capability to detect and correct errors. The financial system would enable the employees to become a mini business unit to manage their activities.

Since the technical details are published elsewhere and they are not germane to the argument, I turn to the results from implementing these new financial procedures. The reported results included a doubling of profit, five new production records, a 50 percent improvement in quality as well as a new kitchen in the control room for the operators. The financial statements empowered the operators to act responsibly. They did so; and their performance persisted (Kaplan, 1989). Ironically, the concept did not spread throughout other departments in the same organization because of organizational defenses. This case illustrates that technical systems such as financial reports can empower people. It also illustrates that when the same routines are experienced as embarrassing and threatening they will tend to activate organizational defenses. Double-loop learning will then be necessary to overcome the resistance.

Being exposed to such situations, I began to see how relatively rigorous managerial technical theories (such as accounting, strategy, etc.) could create powerful empowering conditions for the employees. Elsewhere, I have discussed the feature of such rigorous technical theories. They include the specification of actions to be taken to achieve intended consequences. Moreover, the validity of the specifications can be checked. For example, if two individuals used the same financial numbers and procedures, arrived at different conclusions, it is possible to trace backwards the steps taken to identify the error and what created it (Argyris, 1990b). In focusing my research on difficult and ineffective implementation. I naturally focused on double-loop learning as the corrective activity. I did not focus on the introduction of routine technical theories which, if designed correctly, could reduce the likelihood of embarrassment or threat as happened in Briley's department.

The Steve Briley's story illustrates the likelihood that the implementation of "enlightened" technical managerial theories may still require the help of double-loop learning. The CEO attempted to get other divisional heads involved. Briley made a presentation. It was received, by the other divisional heads, with warm praise. Yet several years later they have not taken actions to implement the ideas. The organizational defensive routines are, apparently, quite powerful.

## WHAT ARE SOME OF THE CAUSES OF MY BLINDNESS?

Reflecting upon my experiences. I believe that there are several causes for my blindness.

1   The basis for the commitment to double-loop learning was to address the problem of resolving issues that were difficult, embarrassing, and threatening. It was rare to find organizations producing double-loop learning even when their survival depended upon it. My commitment was compounded by the fact that I often found that the players knew what had to be done and they were pessimistic, indeed cynical, that it could be done. For me, single-loop learning was necessary to get the every-day-job done; double-loop learning was necessary for the organization to have another day.

2   If double-loop learning is rare then in order to study it, one had to create it. In order to create it, one had to challenge two levels of status quo. First, executives were often quite threatened about cooperating to produce double-loop learning because they feared it would open up Pandora's Box.

The second level of status quo was related to the norms of the academic community; my primary community. In order to conduct research on double-loop learning, I had to develop normative theories; I had to intervene to produce universes that were not in existence. None of this, in turn, could be done without the genuine involvement of the participants. They would not take on such involvement without a commitment on our part that we would have as an objective of the research to help them resolve serious problems that were embarrassing and threatening.

All these conditions required intervention-type research that was, and still is, rare among scholars. The primary exception is Kurt Lewin. Intervention research focuses on conducting experiments to change the status quo with the intention of testing features of TOA. It also meant combining research with what I call scholarly consulting. Scholarly consulting, I suggest, could be used to produce basic knowledge as well as to solve important problems (Argyris, 1993).

Although I found few colleagues who would not disagree with my espousing this strategy, few of them made it part of their theory-in-use. And fewer encouraged their graduate students to learn the skills of intervention research.

Thus, scholars who may wish to conduct empirical research on changing the status quo and on conducting interventions will likely feel strong pressures against such a choice. In a recent conference in France, six senior scholars in first rate European and American universities said that they decided early in their careers not to focus on such research for that reason. I also hear that from doctoral students in many fine universities. Their advisors warn them to conduct research that is consistent with the norms of the scholarly community. They can explore intervention research intended to produce actionable knowledge for changing the status quo, after they have received their tenure.

These factors often lead researchers who are interested in intervention and changing the status quo to become more inward-oriented. They soon begin to see the very colleagues that they value, acting as enemies. They also fail to communicate effectively with these colleagues on issues regarding developing mutual understanding and respect. Shades of Kuhn (1970).

An interesting example of such inward-looking defensive behavior, in my opinion, is to be found in a debate between myself and Professor Herbert Simon (Argyris, 1973; Simon, 1973). I remember how surprised I was that several readers wrote to the editor saying that our debate was a good example of how two scholars can speak past each other and how apparently unaware they are when doing so. I also remember that I asked a colleague who had extended experience in working with Professor Simon and myself to give me his reactions to the readers' comments. He responded that he thought the readers made valid evaluations. Yet, he never told me of the possible defensive reasoning in my article when he read the draft.

## BEHAVIORAL THEORY OF THE FIRM

I now turn to the behavioral theory of the firm (BTF). I have selected that theory because, in my opinion, some of its proponents manifest a blindness that is complementary to mine. My blindness was around single-loop learning. I suggest that scholars of BTF manifest a blindness around double-loop learning. Their blindness was created by appearing to place their core concepts beyond the requirement of empirical falsifiability. They did so, as I hope to show by developing arguments that changes in their basic concepts are not likely to be successful. I hope to show that the arguments that were crafted used defensive reasoning.

Cyert and March (1963) define four relational concepts at the core of their perspective. They are:

1  quasi-resolution of conflict;
2  uncertainty avoidance;
3  problemistic search; and
4  limited organizational learning.

Twenty-five years later, in an introduction to a collection of his essays, March (1988) identified four key concepts of BTF which he now described as "heresies" in the eyes of many economists and students of traditional decision-making. They are:

1  the importance of allocating attention;
2  the omnipresence of conflict, politics, and coalition groups;

3   the conception that action involves rules that adapt to experience, rather than anticipatory choices; and
4   the importance of ambiguity, preferences, technology and history.

There is fundamental agreement here between BTF and TOA. Both perspectives agree that coalition groups, uncertainty avoidance, limited learning, quasi-resolution of conflict are central features of the universe. TOA includes these phenomena as part of Model I theories-in-use and organizational defensive routines. The concepts of allocating attention, rules that adapt to experience, and the importance of ambiguity, preferences and history are consistent with the TOA focus on design and action that is related to theories in use.

The divergence of views can be illustrated by the position March (1981) takes on concepts such as routines, control, loyalty and trust. March (p. 221) states that it is the standard operating procedures and routines that are causally responsible for much of the behavior that is observed in organizations. Mundane rules are at the heart of organizational activity. Rules, in turn, are based upon previous experience and history (p. 244). If change is to occur, it must be clearly linked to mundane rules (p. 222).

What is the meaning of "linked?" One reading is that all changes, if they are to persevere, have to be linked to routines and procedures. I agree. Double-loop changes, for example, will eventually have to be linked to routines and procedures if they are to persevere.

There could be another reading of the term "linked." This reading could lead researchers to focus so heavily upon routines that they pay little attention to research that is aimed at double-loop changes in the routines. The focus on routines leads to reinforcing the status quo. For example, if it works, don't fix it or question it. The routines are taken for granted. One of the most difficult learning problems organizations may face is to learn that they are not able to learn, *and* that the cause of this inability is the focus on what is taken for granted namely, routines.

If one claims that limited learning, quasi-resolution of conflict and competitive coalition groups are omnipresent and routine, it is not difficult to conclude that they are to be taken for granted and therefore not likely to be altered.

The point is not their skepticism that relational variables are not likely to change. The point is: why is not such a crucial claim subjected to empirical test? It may be, for example, that learning is limited by the finite information-processing capacities of the human mind. Such capacities are not likely to be altered.

However, learning can also be limited by organizational defensive routines and Model I theories-in-use. These have been shown to be alterable and that the changes persevere for, at least, seven years (Argyris, 1982, 1993).

I turn next to the concept of control. March states that control is a fundamental process in most organizations. I agree. Then, March links control and conflict in the following way. He suggests that control systems drive conflict systems because once measures are developed to evaluate performance and compliance they invite manipulation. Once the rules of evaluation are set, conflict of interest between the rule setters and the rule followers assures that there will be some incentives for the latter to maximize the difference between the rule setters and the rule followers. It assures that there will be some incentives for the latter to maximize the difference between their score and their effort. "Any system of accounts is a road map to cheating on them" (March, 1981, p. 220).

The reasoning appears to be as follows. Control processes are fundamental to organization. Controls require the evaluation of performance. People cope with such evaluations by manipulation and cheating. They create coalition groups to bring about and to protect these self-protective processes. If this self interest is not consistent with the organization's, then more manipulation and cheating will occur. This, in turn, results into more control. The processes can become self-reenforcing.

The basis for these claims depends on making explicit the causal processes that are not, to my knowledge, made explicit. TOA would predict that if such empirical research were conducted, we would discover that it is Model I theories-in-use and organizational defenses that are the processes by which control systems produce the cheating coalition group actions, and limited learning that he describes. This possible explanation is empirically testable. One test would be to observe organizations that are high and low on Model I and organizational defenses respectively. A more robust test would be to take an organization that is high on these variables; reduce them and see if double-loop learning is enhanced.

March uses similar logic in discussing trust and loyalty. Trust and loyalty, he asserts, are hard to find. The problems of trust is exacerbated by organizational politics. Organizational politics is a central feature of most organizations. "The first principle of politics is that everyone is rational and no one can be trusted." There may be a few who can be trusted but they are to be characterized as innocent and naive (March, 1981, p. 219).

The consequence is that the organizations are composed of winners and losers. The players will try to look trustworthy even though they are not, in order to be trusted by those people who might become winners. It is therefore, a palpable feature of organizational life, "that organizations may be validly characterized as individuals and groups pursuing their own interests by the manipulation of information" (March, 1988, p. 6).

This line of scholarly reasoning is similar to the reasoning often used by practicing executives. They too believe that low trust and high conflict are fundamental features of organizations. Hence the necessity to establish goals and objectives, to communicate priorities, and to monitor how well these are being implemented. Managerial controls play a central role in these activities.

It is not surprising that March concludes changes in the domains of conflict and trust ... thought the confrontation and resolution of conflict are not likely to be effective (March, 1988, p. 8). Cyert and March (1963) advise readers that the way too deal with conflict is by using local rationality, acceptable-level decision rules, and sequential attention to goals. If one examines these concepts there is little or no attention paid to how organizational and group defenses might be causally involved. It would be helpful to read research that provides descriptions of actual behavior involved in the conflict in order to assess whether conflict can exist so devoid of organizational defenses that rules such as local rationality, acceptable-level decisions rules, and sequential attention to goals are adequate explanations and a valid basis for advice. If TOA research is relevant, these rules should lead to incomplete resolution of conflict that should not persevere. This hypothesis can be tested.

To summarize, it appears that BTF is so structured that its predictions require the assumption of the non-alterability of the relational concepts. This will tend to focus attention away from empirical research on double-loop learning that can put the non-alterability feature to an empirical test. For example, Argyris (1993) describes the organizational defenses of a group of director-owners that is consistent with the BTF view that quasi-resolution of conflict and limited learning dominate organizational life. He also presents evidence, in the form of actual transcripts, where these variables are engaged or reduced. Moreover, issues that the directors identified, at the outset, as crucial *and* undiscussable (e.g. financial ownership) became discussible and were resolved.

To my knowledge, scholars associated with the BFT are not against double-loop learning. Indeed, they cite its relevance for organizational learning. (Cohen and Sproull, 1991, 1992; Fiol and Lyles, 1985; Huber, 1991; Levitt and March, 1988; Lant and Mezian, 1992; Slepian, 1990). The question is why it has not been taken seriously in their research programs.

## CONDITIONS FOR SURFACING THE DEFENSES OF SCHOLARLY
## COMMUNITIES AND THEIR MEMBERS

As a first step, it would be helpful if scholars replace and make explicit the values and assumptions of their research. For example, I hold a belief about the malleability of defensive behavior be it individual, group, or organizational. I infer that March is less sanguine about the malleability of defense. Not surprisingly, I conduct research on how to create double-loop changes. Most BFT scholars whose work I cite in this paper do not. Why not conduct joint research on these values and assumption to test their strengths and weaknesses?

The second implication is that descriptions of the universe should begin with the collection of observations that are as directly observable as possible (e.g., descriptions of actual behavior or tape recordings). It is not by chance, I suggest, that the work of Kurt Lewin almost always began with insights observed and experienced in everyday life. His work on experimental studies of leadership (Lewin, et al., 1939) began with ethnographic descriptions from which various kinds of qualitative and quantitative analyses were made.

The reason that relatively directly observable data are important is that these are the data that are produced by our subjects, in a manner that is relatively independent of our theories. Such data are produced by the subjects by using their respective theories-in-use. Such data provide therefore a robust basis for a process that questions our theories. They also provide a basis for scholars with competing theories to begin a dialogue.

The third implication may be more controversial. The dominant norm in research communities is to describe reality as accurately and completely as possible. But who created the reality that we are studying? As I have suggested above, it is practitioners, using their Model I theories-in-use and creating organizational defenses, that lead to a universe that can be characteristic as exhibiting limited learning, quasi resolution of conflict, and competitive coalition group.

Focusing on describing this reality is a normative decision because it is a decision to study the universe that the practitioners create. If we make this choice, do we not have an obligation to create universes where limited learning, quasi-resolution of conflict, and competitive coalition groups are less powerful? Such studies will provide *descriptive* knowledge of the conditions under which these variables could or could not be altered.

Such research focuses the practitioners' and scholar's personal responsibilities for going along with or changing the status quo. For example, if my analysis is correct, March and I have behaved in ways that were consistent with limiting learning, minimizing the resolution of conflict and, indirectly creating competitive coalition groups. Do we have no personal responsibility to conduct research to reduce the dysfunctional features of what we have helped to create? Are not we as responsible for creating new alternatives as we are for developing, let us say, new research procedures?

A deeper problem related to conducting empirical research that is primarily descriptive surfaces when researchers attempt to develop action implications from such research. For example, Feldman and Levy (1994) suggest that defensive routines such as gossip may maintain channels open. Being hypocritical may promote useful changes. Their conclusions are, I believe, empirically valid. But their existence depends upon a cover-up. For example, the fact that channels are kept open by gossip is covered-up or it would not be gossip. Being hypocritical to promote useful change may achieve the change and strengthen the hypocrisy. Do the authors have responsibility to state their position on such consequences? I think they do because practitioners can easily infer that cover-up is documented by social scientists therefore they (practitioners) take such a description as acting in accordance with norms of everyday life.

Randall and Baker (1994) document a case where a policy, on reproductive health in the workplace, was adapted without extensive consideration of alternatives. Yet, the authors state other options were available. The authors explain these findings by referring to the extensive descriptive research about the finite information processing capacity of the human mind and use of inferential heuristics. Thus they explain the lack of extensive consideration of alternatives as being related to the emprical findings that managers have limited information processing capacity and that their attentiveness was focused on the vivid cues.

The unintended consequence of these explanations is that they can be used by the actors to explain away their lack of personnel causal responsibility. They could say, in effect that they *are* limited information processors and they focused on the vivid cues just as social scientists say the human mind works. Hence it is understandable that they did not examine alternatives that were available.

In order to test double-loop changes emprically, scholars will have to define how to get from here to there. The definitions should not only be conceptual. They should also be operational so that they can be tested in the world of practice. But, in order to be tested in the world of practice they must be actionable in the world of practice.

In order for the knowledge to be actionable, it must specify the sequence of action required to achieve the specified intended consequence. Such specifications are causal in the sense that they state, if one acts according to A then B will occur. Such a specification informs the practitioners on how to act. It also becomes a disconfirmable proposition of the theory that can be tested. For example, Model I theory-in-use specifies that to the extent individuals craft their conversations when they are advocating their positions, making evaluations and attributions in ways that do not encourage inquiry into testing the ideas that they are advocating, and the evaluations and attributions that they are making, they will produce defensiveness, escalating error, and limited learning processes. Model II specifies that these dyfunctional (to learning) consequences can be reduced by combining inquiry and testing with advocating, evaluating, and attributing. These skills can be taught to practitioners who, if they choose to do so, can use them in every day life. They (and researchers) can observe if the dysfunctional consequences (to learning) actually occur.

We now have the conditions where the gap between knowledge and action is more seamless than is usually the case. Seamlessness, I claim, is in the interests of the practitioner because the knowledge is "actionable." It is also in the interest of the scholars because their theories can be tested in the universe to which they claim relevancy.

The research experiences that I have described above and continue to undertake suggest that there is another requirement for seamlessness. I refer to the limitation of each academic discipline. As I have suggested, I found my propositions for example, about organizational defenses could be more powerful if they were studied in the context of managerial disciplines such as managerial accounting economics and governance of the firm, manufacturing, and new product development.

There is a fifth implication of this inquiry. All the scholars of the adjoining managerial disciplines with whom I have worked (e.g., Professors Kim Clark, Michael Jensen, Robert Kaplan, and Steve Wheelwright) are scientists oriented toward describing their universe accurately. They became interventionists when they attempted to implement their propositions in organizations in order to test the validity and actionability of these propositions. The moment they became interventionists they also became scholars who are intending to be helpful to clients. Thus they became consultants *in addition* to descriptive researchers. But they are *scholarly* consultants. They are dedicated to empirical inquiry, to testing their theories and to a rigorous evaluation of the consequences when the theories are implemented. Kaplan (1993) for example (whose intellectual beginning was in operations research) has written about how scholarly consulting can be of help in testing and revising theories. Argyris (1980, 1993) and Schein (1987) have taken a similar position.

Lammers (1981) a leading organizational sociologist agrees that it is possible for scholars to be scholarly consultants and fruitful organizational scientists but, the combination is empirically rare. He then writes, "after all, not everyone is an Argyris who appears to be as effective a consultant as he is an organizational scientist! Consequently, why should not those less gifted mortals, who apparently are endowed 'only' with scientific capacities and inclinations" be permitted to stick to their strengths (Lammers, 1981, p. 370).

Needless to say, I was and am still grateful for Lammers kind words. The problem is that most social scientists who do not combine these skills control the graduate doctoral programs, the jobs, and the gatekeepers to the prestigious academic journals. The result is that there are few departments who consciously strive to provide such education. A self-sealing process results where the empirically rare individuals are kept empirically rare.

It is understandable that most social scientists have grown up differentiating consulting from research. Some scholars suggest that to be paid by clients places the scholar in the position of being influenced by the client values and needs. To my knowledge, if this is true, it is an evaluation of the weakness of the scholars. Why do scholarly consultants have to accept uncritically client values? One answer is that they are paid by these clients. But, this does not necessarily have to lead to scholars compromising themselves. They do not have to accept the job. Moreover, it can be shown that social scientists have conducted research that is consistent with managerial values and they were not paid by clients. For example, the works of Blau, Perrow, and Thompson fit comfortably within the values of the traditional administrative theories of practitioners (Argyris, 1972).

Robert Duncan, a scholar of organizational behavior, told me that he did not find his own work, or that of many of his fellow social scientists helpful in acting as provost. Indeed he found some of the "softer" less rigorous work more helpful. This does not mean, in my opinion, nor in Duncan's, that we should continue to develop less rigorous research. It means, I suggest, that we have to conduct rigorous research that produces propositions that not only have high external validity but that are teachable, learnable, and useable by practitioners in every day life.

Representative George E. Brown, Jr, who was described by Johnson, in *Psychological Science* as science's great champion for scientific excellence, wrote a report that raises serious questions about the credibility of scholars. Over two decades they promised to focus on reducing the breach between knowledge and action yet the breach not only continues, it is getting wider. The breach has worked to the detriment of both basic and applied science. A similar call was made in *Science* nearly 30 years ago. Johnson notes that this attempt to reduce the breach ended disastrously. Since Brown was in Congress at the same time, Johnson ends his article with a warning to scientists: let's be careful lest the implementation this time be very different (Johnson, 1993).

## CONCLUSION: CHALLENGE FOR FUTURE DIALOGUE

Reflecting on the chapter, it appears that scholars who are members of communities entitled Theory of Action and Behavioral Theory of the Firm appear to think and act in ways that they create a context that is consistent with many of their core concepts such as limited attention capacity, quasi-resolution of conflict, and limited learning.

Assume for a moment that a more systematic empirical study was made that included interviews of an appropriate sample of scholars as well as observations of their actions "within their respective communities and between them (e.g., at conferences). Assume also that such a study resulted in similar findings.

The question is: would it be accurate to conclude that their concepts were tested and not disconfirmed? I suggest that such a conclusion would not be valid. In order to make a claim that propositions are not confirmed, these propositions must, in principle, be falsifiable in the first place. But if BTF scholars (or any other group) argue that their core concepts are not likely to be alterable, then the possibility of being disconfirmed is not real. If so, we have a theory where key concepts are not falsifiable.

# References

Argyris, C., 1972, *The Applicability of Organizational Sociology Cambridge*, England, Cambridge University Press.

Argyris, C., 1973, "Some Limits of Rational Organizational Theory" and "Organizational Man: Rational and Self-actualizing," *Public Administration Review*, 33, 3, pp. 253–267 and 4, pp. 354–357.

Argyris, C., 1980, *Inner Contradictions of Rigorous Research*, New York, Academic Press.

Argyris, C., 1982, *Reasoning, Learning, and Action*, San Francisco, Jossey-Bass.

Argyris, C., 1985, *Strategy, Change and Defensive Routines*, Boston, Ballingar.

Argyris, C., 1990a, *Overcoming Organizational Defenses*, Needham, MA, Allen Bacon.

Argyris, C., 1990b, "The Dilemma of Implementing Controls: The Case of Managerial Accounting," *Accounting Organizations, and Society*, 15, 6, 503–11.

Argyris, C., 1993, *Knowledge for Action*, San Francisco, CA, Jossey-Bass.

Argyris, C., and Kaplan, R. S., 1994, "Implementing New Knowledge The Case of Activity-Based Costing." *Accounting Horizons*, 8, 3, pp. 83–105.

Argyris, C., and Schön, D., 1974, *Theory in Practice*, San Francisco, CA, Jossey-Bass.

Argyris, C., and Schön D., 1978, *Organizational Learning*, Reading, MA, Addison-Wesley.

Berger, P., and Luckmann, T., 1967, *The Social Construction of Reality*, Garden City, NY, Doubleday.

Bourdieu, P., 1977, *Outline of a Theory of Practice*, Cambridge, MA, Cambridge University Press.

Cartwright, D. (ed.), 1951, *Field Theory and Social Science*, York, Harper & Bros.

Cohen, M. D., and Sproull (eds), 1991, "Special Issue on Organizational Learning," *Organization Science*, 2, 1.

Cohwn, M. D., and Sproull (eds), 1992, "Continuation of Special Issue on Organizational Learning," *Organization Science*, 3, 1, 1–11.

Cyert, R. M and March, J. G., 1963, *A Behavioral Theory of the Firm*, Englewood Clifts, NJ, Prentice-Hall.

Feldman, M. S., and Levy, A. J., 1994, "Effects of Legal Context on Decision Making under Ambiguity," in Sitkin, S. B., and Bies R. J. (eds), 1994, pp. 109–36.

Feyerabend, P. K., 1975, "*Against Method*," in Radner, M., and Winokur, S. (eds), *Analyses of Theories & Methods of Physics & Psychology*, Minnesota Studies in the Philosophy of Science, IV, Minneapolis, MN, University of Minnesota Press.

Fiol, M. C., and Lyles, M. A., 1985, "Organizational Learning," *Academy of Management Review*, 10, 4, pp. 803–13.

Geertz, C., 1973, *The Interpretation of Cultures*, New York, Basic Books.

Herriot, P., 1992, "Selection: The Two Subcultures," *European Work and Organizational Psychologist*, 2, 2, pp. 129–40.

Huber, G. P., 1991, "Organizational Learning: The Contributing Processes and the Literatures," *Organization Science*, 2, 1, pp. 88, 115.

Johnson, D., 1993, "Psychology in Washington: Measurement to Improve Scientific Productivity: A Reflection on the Brown Report," *Psychological Science*, 4, 2, pp. 67–69.

Kaplan, A., 1964, *The Conduct of Inquiry*, New York, Intext 1964.

Kaplan, R. S., 1989, "Texas Eastman Company," President and Fellows of Harvard College. Harvard Business School Case, 190–039, Boston, MA.

Kaplan, R. S., 1991, "Maxwell Appliance Contros", President and Fellows of Harvard College, Harvard Business School Case 9-192–580, Boston, MA.

Kaplan, R. S., 1993, "Research Opportunities in Management Accounting," *Journal of Management Account Research*.

Kuhn, T. S., 1970, *The Structure of Scientific Revolutions*, 2nd edn, Chicago, IL, University of Chicago Press.

Lammers, C. J., 1981, "Contributions of Organizational Sociology: Part II: Contributions to Organizational Theory and Practice – A Liberal View," *Organizational Studies*, 2, 4, pp. 361–76.

Lant, T. K., and Mezian, S. J., 1992, "An Organizational Learning Model of Convergence and Orientation," *Organization Science*, 3, 1, pp. 47–71.

Levitt, B., and March, J. G., 1988, "Organizational Learning," *Annual Review of Sociology*, 14, pp. 319–40.

Lewin, K., Lippitt, R., and White, R. K., 1939, "Patterns of Aggressive Behavior in Experimentally Created Social Climates," *Journal of Social Psychology*, 10, pp. 271–3010.

March, J. G., 1981, "Decision Making Perspective," in Van DeVen, A. H., and Joyce, W. F., (eds), *Perspectives on Organizational Design and Behavior*, New York, John Wiley & Sons, pp. 205–44.

March, J. G., 1988, *Decisions and Organizations*, Oxford, England, Basil Blackwell.

Merton, R. K., 1973, *The Sociology of Science: Theoretical and Empirical Investigations*, Chicago, IL, University Press.

Mitroff, I. I., 1974, *The Subjective Side of Science*, Amsterdam, The Netherlands, Elsevier.

Popper, K. C., 1959, *The Logic of Scientific Democracy*, New York, Basic Books.

Randall, D. M., and Baker, D. D., 1994, "The Threat of Legal Liability and Managerial Decision Making: Regulation of Reproductive Health in the Workplace," in Sitkin, S. B., and Bies, R. J. (eds) 1994.

Schein E. H., 1987, *The Clinical Perspective in Fieldwork*, Beverly Hills, CA, Sage.

Simon, H. A., 1969, *The Science of the Artificial*, Cambridge, MA, M.I.T. Press.

Simon, H. A., 1973, "Applying Information Technology to Organization Design," *Public Administration Review*, 33, 3, pp. 346–53.

Sitkin, S. B. and Bies, R. J. (eds) 1994, *The Legalistic Organisation*, Thousand Oaks, CA, Sale Publications.

Slepian, J., 1990, "Organizational Learning and Information Acquisition in Changing Environments," mimeographed, New Haven, CT, Yale School of Organization and Management.

Watson, J. D., 1969, *The Double Helix*, New York, New American Library.

# — 21 —

# Seeking Truth and Actionable Knowledge: How the Scientific Method Inhibits Both

## THE STEWARDSHIP OF SOCIAL SCIENTISTS

Regardless of the particular theoretical bent or the bias each of us has for conducting research, all social scientists share, I believe, a common commitment to produce valid knowledge for understanding and explaining whatever universe of discourse we have chosen to study. The implementation of this commitment requires that we exercise three responsibilities. The first responsibility is to make as certain as we can that we are not unknowingly kidding ourselves or others about the validity of the knowledge that we produce. We continuously strive to approximate truth by producing knowledge that is as free of distortion and error as we know how to produce. The second responsibility is to push back the frontiers of knowledge. We strive to expand knowledge and wherever possible, to make it additive. A third responsibility is to monitor continuously the ideas in good currency about the nature of sound theory and the methods to conduct empirical research.

I believe that much progress has been made and continues to be made regarding these three responsibilities. The focus of this chapter is to ask, are there any ways in which the *effective* implementation of the above results in consequences that are counter-productive to the responsibilities just described. Are there inner contradictions in our practice?

I believe the answer is yes when we consider research whose objective is to understand some of the most fundamental processes used to control human beings in order to maintain social systems ranging from the family to organizations. Our research indicates that the theory of control used necessarily inhibits producing valid information if the subject matter is threatening; the very condition when valid information is especially needed. The connection with the conduct of empirical research is that social scientists often use a theory of control over subjects that is similar to the one used in the larger society. It too necessarily limits learning. For reasons to be discussed below, social scientists have not explored the possibility that this theory of control will also inhibit the production of valid information, a consequence that is opposite to what we intend.

I begin with a quick summary of some findings about how the internal systems of organizations maintain themselves from embarrassment and threat. Next, I will present, again in summary form, a theoretical perspective to explain the findings. Then I will use these examples to illustrate how the correct use of rules for rigorous research can have the unintended consequences just described.

## CONDUCTING RESEARCH ON ORGANIZATIONAL DEFENSIVE ROUTINES

Organizational defensive routines are policies and actions that prevent individuals, parts, or the whole organization from experiencing threat or embarrassment, and simultaneously prevent them from identifying and reducing the causes of the potential embarrassment or threat.

Organizational defensive routines differ from psychological defensive routines along four dimensions. First, we have collected data on nearly 5,000 people that show that they almost all behave consistently with their organization's defensive routines. Yet on the basis of personality research, we would expect a diversity of personalities in such a large group. Second, although individuals move in and out of organizations, the defensive routines do not change over time. Third, our research suggests that the source for creating these defensive routines are the social virtues taught to human beings early in life. Therefore, the organizational defensive routines are more likely a product of socialization. Finally because the actions used to create or to trigger organizational defensive routines are used by most people, their use cannot be attributed primarily to individual psychological anxiety.

Organizational defensive routines proliferate around dilemmas that contain important conflict. We have discussed organizational defensive routines in chapters 4 and 10. Essentially, the argument is that individuals, acting as agents for organizations or for themselves, produce defensive routines that prevent or distort valid information, that are undiscussable, and whose undiscussibility is undiscussable. All of these features are protected by both the internal and external cultures of the organization. Individuals express hopelessness, fears, and anxieties about changing these features.

Let us now suppose that we wish to conduct empirical research on organizational defensive routines. No matter what our bias, there are at least three rules that we must follow if we are to act consistently with the ideas in good currency about conducting sound empirical research. They are (1) describe the universe as accurately as possible, (2) minimize threats to internal and external validity, and (3) remain as neutral as possible. How is it that if we implement these rules correctly, we will limit our abilities to discover new knowledge, and we will increase the threats to validity?

### Rule I. Describe the Universe as Is

The first rule of normal science is to describe the universe as completely as possible and to produce explanations of what has been described. The modes of description and explanation may vary widely but not the requirement to produce descriptive knowledge.

My description of defensive routines above suggests that it is possible to describe them and to develop explanatory theories. The conclusion is only partially correct.

In order to provide a comprehensive description of organizational defensive routines, we must produce propositions about what happens when we try to change them. How do they respond to varying degrees of change? We must answer these questions in order to describe the universe as it is.

So far, we have found it almost impossible to study these questions by observing everyday life. Individuals do not strive to change them. This is not surprising if we recall (1) the societally taught logic that makes defensive routines undiscussable and their undiscussability undiscussable, (2) the sense of hopelessness, and (3) the sense of fear and danger about changing them. The world is not likely to offer us examples to study, for in order to do so, someone must have decided to violate powerful cultural norms.

If changes in defensive routines are to be conducted, social scientists will have to help to create and implement them in actual settings. What would be required to conduct such research?

1   A model of a universe in which defensive routines would be rare. This would mean a normative model of a universe that may be espoused but does not exist.
2   A theory of intervention of how to get from the present universe to a new one.
3   A theory of instruction on how to teach the new skills required; how to create a new culture; how to create organizational contexts that would reinforce the new skills and cultural norms. Also a theory of instruction on how to unfreeze the old variables and how to deal with the bewilderment, frustration, and anger that individuals will experience as they realize that some of their most cherished skills are no longer valid.

But even if we met all these requirements, we would have to gain the cooperation of the subjects. Usually, we find that the first requirement is that they be assured that neither they nor their organization will be harmed. As they come to realize how much they will have to expose themselves, they usually up the ante of what they require of us. In addition to not being harmed, they also want to be helped. In effect, they change their role from subjects to clients. That request has nontrivial consequences for how we design the research.

If we examine most of the leading texts on conducting research, we will find, I believe, almost no attention paid to producing normative models of rare universes; to intervention theories and methods; and to theories of instruction of the kind described above. Moreover, little attention is paid to how to create a psychological contract with subjects as clients. Little attention is also given to the clinical skills required to help individuals deal with their feelings of embarrassment, frustration, and anger. At most, the texts speak of debriefing the subjects.

## Rule II. Reduce Threats to Validity

Social scientists strive to reduce threats to validity by developing rules such as those formulated by Campbell and Stanley (1963). If we conceive of these rules as parts of a theory of action on how to conduct research, we may then ask what is the theory-in-use embedded in these rules as to how to manage subjects in ways to reduce threats to validity. Elsewhere I have suggested that there is embedded in these rules a theory of control that is highly similar to Model I (Argyris, 1980). For example, the researchers are advised how to reduce threats to validity by being in unilateral control of the research activities, by suppressing unwanted noise, by using face-saving devices whenever necessary in order that the subjects be kept appropriately in the dark about the experimental manipulation, the hypothesis being tested, and the modes of analysis.

The result is that we are using research methods whose theory-in-use is consistent with the one used by most individuals to create defensive routines in the first place. If this is the case, then the research methods should also create, for the subjects, limited learning systems such as those described in Models I and O-I. For example, the subjects are not supposed to inquire beyond that which the researchers design for them. The researchers design very little space for inquiry into the purpose, the experimental manipulation, who is in the experimental and control groups, etc.

What are the consequences of this for the study of how to reduce defensive routines? How would we create an experimental manipulation to reduce defensive routines without the subjects realizing that is our intention and hence knowing the nature of the experimental manipulation? If we tried to hide knowledge of the experimental manipulation, and if we acted as if we were not hiding that information, and if we made all of this undiscussable with the subjects (and all three ifs represent correct practice), then we are using defensive routines to conduct research on how to reduce them.

There is another problem. In order to gain the participation of individuals, the researchers would have to know how to produce a world where defensive routines are rare. They would also have to know the processes by which they could get from the Model I/O-I world to the new one and these processes would have to be consistent with the old world. If they cannot, then the clients have cause to be concerned about the credibility of the new world they try to create for themselves or for others.

## Rule III. Be Neutral

The third problem created by combining the theory-in-use embedded in our research methods and the one used in everyday life is related to the criterion of neutrality. Social scientists are not supposed to take positions favoring one point of view over another. Social science research is supposed to encourage the systematic inquiry into any position.

If a Model I theory-in-use is embedded in research methods, then the generalization produced by such research will have Model I as part of the conditions under which they hold. If Model I conditions are embedded in the generalizations, and if other models are therefore precluded, then social scientists are not neutral. I conducted a review of research from social psychology, sociology, and political science and found this to be the case (Argyris, 1980). I will cite a few examples briefly.

The studies on mass communication suggest that the presenter should present several alternative points of view if the group to be influenced is largely composed of people who are smart and one point of view if they are not (Aronson, 1965, pp. 47–88).

Assume this is true. Can you imagine the presenter giving the rationale to a "dumb" group or even to some smart groups? They would have to hide the rationale, act as if they are not hiding it, make the hiding undiscussable and its undiscussability undiscussable.

Let us take another example of the research on interpersonal touch and the foot-in-the-door effect. Research has shown that the foot-in-the-door procedure increases compliance for a desired request and that touch can also encourage compliance (Goldman, et al., 1985). The authors cite Bem (1972) to explain the results. "An individual (into whose door someone has placed a foot) observing his or her own behavior while granting an initial, easy request decides that he or she is a cooperative individual who is helpful to others. This altered self-perception induces the individual to continue to be helpful and to comply with a second larger request".

Assume that the explanation is valid. An individual using the foot-in-the-door technique would have this explanation in mind when acting in this way. But, he would *also* have in mind keeping the explanation secret. If the individual ever told the recipient, "I am going to put my foot in the door, because (and then recited the explanation)", it might result in the door being slammed. The reason is that the actor has a theory about how to induce someone to do something whose empirical validity is reduced if it is said openly. The point is that the reason social psychologists found that these actions succeed is that they are consistent with a Model I world of unilateral control and unilateral censorship.

Learning theorists speak of partial reinforcement schedules to motivate individuals. Consider the following scenario, supervisor A has a partial reinforcement schedule designed to motivate subordinate B. A gives the first reinforcement at the appropriate time. The reward surprises and pleases B. He tells some of his peers who assure him that he is "in" with the boss. This too is reinforcement but not part of the schedule. What if B remembered he did not thank A and returned to his office to do so? If he said thank you, what is A to say in return? If A said, "You are welcome. It was a pleasure", that would be another reinforcement but not on the schedule.

Or, consider the scenario where A tells B that he has a partial reinforcement schedule to reward him. Does he tell the schedule ahead of time? What is the impact of having this knowledge on B? Would he not feel that he is part of a designed, mechanical process? How is this psychologically motivating?

In the first scenario, the partial reinforcement process follows the logic of defensive routines (making them undiscussable and their undiscussability undiscussable). In the second, it makes the process public, but how discussable or influenceable is it? Can B alter it? If he cannot, will he not feel that his relationship with his superior is one-way?

None of this raises questions about the usefulness of learning theories. The point is that if they work, it is because the social scientists have embedded into their generalization a Model I world.

The lack of neutrality is also relevant for the inferences made by researchers from the data that they have collected. For example, Milgram explains the importance of unilateral obedience by saying it is required to maintain order in the universe (Argyris, et al., 1985). This inference may well be valid for a Model I world. But, it places the researcher on the side of not exploring worlds where unilateral obedience is not necessary in order to maintain worlds.

In the fields of organizational assessment, a central concept has been the fit between individual needs and organizational requirements. The assumption is that the better the fit, the more likely that individuals will perform better or have more positive attitudes, or minimize such behavior as absenteeism (Van de Ven and Joyce, 1981). There is a fundamental methodological assumption in such research. If individuals tell the truth about the fit as they experience it, the aggregate of such reports is a valid indicator of the fit.

The difficulty with this assumption is that we find many individuals hold beliefs about the fit that are incorrect, yet they are unaware of the gap. For example, most individuals do not see themselves as contributing to organizational defensive routines. Yet, when we observe them, they do. Hence their responses about the fit may be incorrect. If researchers are not aware of this systematic blindness on the part of the subjects, they may not only produce invalid descriptions of reality; they may create or reinforce injustices.

As an illustration, consider the study of several hundred young professionals. All had graduated at the upper levels of their respective business schools. They worked for a large management consulting firm. They lamented the fact that their superiors were unable to create conditions for genuine participation, openness, risk-taking, and trust. They had been taught to expect these capabilities from their superiors. Since the superiors were not acting in these ways, the subordinates concluded that their superiors were ineffective and should undergo training in leadership. An experiment was carried out where the subordinates conducted a study within their firm to illustrate their conclusions. They were then asked to feed back the results to the superiors. An analysis of the tape recording shows that the subordinates used the very behavior that they condemned while feeding back the results. For example, they described opinionated and unilateral actions on the part of superiors in ways that outside observers evaluated as opinionated and unilateral. The subordinates resisted this conclusion until they listened to the tape recording. They agreed and also reflected on their blindness (Argyris, 1982).

There is a second type of blindness that we have observed. Individuals are able to produce the actions they espouse but they are unaware that the actions are counterproductive to their own intentions. Again, the blindness appears to exist for most individuals. It is related to certain commonly accepted Model I norms.

For example, most of our respondents report that when dealing with organizational or individual defensive routines, they should act in ways that are supportive and show respect for others. Support is defined as communicating that which the others are able to hear without becoming defensive. Respect means not questioning the reasoning behind others' defensive actions.

The difficulty with these actions is that they can get people into trouble. For example, we have found that support gets translated into hiding negative judgements. People strive to communicate negative messages by being indirect and acting as if they are not. They may ease in by asking questions. "How do you feel the session went with your subordinate?" "How much do you think he heard when you talked with him?" The hope is that the receiver will answer the question in a way that he will realize that he did not do well.

In our research, we found that if the individual does not cooperate by learning from the indirect mode, the "helpers" switch to showing integrity (which means telling it as they see it) and strength (which means not giving in). In short, when support and respect do not work, people switch to integrity and strength. Usually those who have more positional power win out.

It is unlikely that we could discover these results unless we focused on the differences between espoused theory and theories-in-use. But helping people recognize the discrepancies is not enough in the sense that such awareness leaves them feeling helpless, bewildered, and frustrated. It is necessary for the researchers to help the clients overcome these problems. This requires a normative theory with different meanings of support, respect, integrity, and strength (Argyris, 1985).

## IMPLICATIONS FOR RESEARCHERS

More time and effort should be spent on learning how to produce normative models of rare universes that are empirically disconfirmable. In producing such models, researchers will find it necessary to make explicit the values that are embedded in their models and to provide a rationale for those values. All of us will find ourselves dealing with generating theories of morality.

In this connection, it is important to differentiate between normative theories and normative theories that become prescriptive for society. Researchers should focus on making their normative theories as comprehensive and as empirically valid as possible. Researchers should also study the processes by which individuals can use the theories in everyday life. The choice, however, as to whether or not the individuals will choose to use them is a citizen's choice.

Another implication is that the rules to reduce threats to validity will be refocused. For example, researchers would now make predictions about features of the theory-in-use and not about behavior. Researchers must study the actual behavior because the theory-in-use is inferrable from the behavior.

The refocus has certain interesting advantages. First, so far, most human beings use Model I and most limited organizational learning systems are consistent with Model O-I. Although the specific actions used may vary widely, if we make our predictions about action strategies and their consequences, then our sample task is greatly simplified. So far we have not found any difference in theory-in-use related to age, gender, education, economic position, or race; nor in organizations that are small or large, young or old, profit or nonprofit.

Second, if we focus on theory-in-use, then we are making predictions about behavior that cannot easily be altered by individuals. This, in turn, makes it possible to become more open about experimental treatments without running the risk of confounding the responses. For example, people who wish to alter their Model I theory-in-use, who understand Model II, who accept Model II, are still unable to produce it. This is predictable. It is not possible for human beings to change their theory-in-use because they wish to do so. Behaving according to a new theory-in-use requires new skills and new values. It is "do-able," but it requires at least as much education and practice as is required to play a decent game of tennis.

Third, if theories-in-use are not alterable by knowing a different one or by wanting to change, or by being rewarded to change, then issues such as learning or maturation cannot be threats to validity. It is not possible to produce that which they are incapable of producing (i.e., behavior inconsistent with their theory-in-use).

A fourth implication for reducing threats to validity is to provide the reader with samples of the observable data: that is the conversations people used. It is then possible for the readers to judge how the researchers made their inferences and drew their conclusions. It is also possible for them to challenge the validity of the research conclusion. The importance of this rule can be illustrated by recalling that almost all paper and pencil instruments that use abstract categories (and almost all do) bypass the directly observable data. For example, it appears that leaders who are judged as "considerate" are ones who have been scored as being close to their subordinates and who leave them alone (Argyris, 1976).

The fifth implication is for social scientists to realize that it is unlikely that we can be neutral and use the technology of rigorous research. The technology for rigorous research is biased toward Model I. Recall, for example, that the learning theorists and those producing the research on mass communication had embedded in their propositions conditions that were consistent with a Model I world. Scientists have a right to produce such generalizations. They also have an obligation to make the tacit choices explicit.

The sixth implication is that researchers should pay more attention to producing scientific generalizations that are reproducible under real time conditions by individuals who wish to do so. For example, let us assume that there is a curvilinear relationship between variable $A$ and $B$. Let us also assume that Mr X wants to have his action influenced by such a proposition. The problem arises as to how he would ascertain, in an on-line manner, where variables $A$ and $B$ are along a continuum. In order for human beings to use propositions, they must be producible under everyday life conditions. Otherwise, life will pass them by while they are trying to diagnose the situation.

Perhaps more important is the likelihood that practitioners could find themselves using our generalizations correctly yet producing conditions that are counter to the ones the generalization states will occur. For example, assume that Stodgdill's handbook on leadership contains valid and usable information. The first thing we can say about it is that leaders are not likely to store all the information in their heads and retrieve it when they need it. If leaders use the handbook as an external memory, then the leaders face a new dilemma. Let us assume that there is a chapter on intergroup relationships. What is a leader supposed to do when he suddenly realizes that he is faced with an intergroup situation? Does he turn to the chapter to refresh his memory? What does he tell his group to do while he is exploring the chapter?

# References

Argyris, C., 1976, "Problems and New Directions for Industrial Psychology," in Dunnette, M. D. (ed.), *Handbook of Industrial and Organizational Psychology*, Chicago, Rand-McNally.

Argyris, C., 1980, *Inner Contradictions of Rigorous Research*, New York, Academic Press.

Argyris, C., 1982, *Reasoning, Learning and Action*, San Francisco, Jossey-Bass.

Argyris, C., 1985, *Strategy, Change, and Defensive Routines*, Boston, Pitman Publishing.

Argyris, C., Putnam, R., and Smith, D. M., 1985, *Action Science*, San Francisco, Jossey-Bass.

Aronson, E., 1965, *The Social Animal*, San Francisco, W. H. Freeman and Co.

Bem, D., 1972, "Self-perception Theory," in Berkowitz, L. (ed.), *Advances in Experimental Psychology*, 6, New York, Academic Press.

Campbell, D. T., and Stanley, J. C., 1963, *Experimental and Quasi-experimental Design for Research*, Skokie, Ill., Rand-McNally.

Goldman, M., Kiyohare, O., and Pfannesteil, D. H., 1985, "Interpersonal Touch, Social Labeling, and the Foot-in-the-Door Effect," *Journal of Social Psychology*, 125, 2, p. 147.

Van de Ven, A., and Joyce, W. (eds), 1981, *Perspectives on Organizational Design and Behavior*, New York, Wiley.

# — 22 —

# Problems and New Directions for Industrial Psychology

Important reviews have been written about the state of research and knowledge in industrial psychology (Dunnette, 1962; Gilmer, 1960; Hinrichs, 1970; Owens and Jewell, 1969; Porter, 1966). These reviews have emphasized the importance of the development of more rigorous research methods, models to cope with complex situations, dynamic criteria, the eventual integration of industrial and organizational psychology, etc. Their suggestions make sense.

This chapter looks at other steps that may be taken to deepen the scientific validity of industrial psychology and enlarge the generalizability of its findings to the world of action.

The chapter is divided into two sections. In the first section some of the foundations of industrial psychology (such as selection, placement, job analysis and design, wage-system design, safety, and training) are explored. These foundations have produced much that is useful. However, they may have produced some unintended forces which constrain industrial psychology from enlarging its scope of scientific interests and applicability.

In the second section some possible courses of action are explored that may help industrial psychology enlarge its scientific domain, deepen its usefulness to the practitioner and hasten the day when it can integrate itself conceptually and empirically with sister areas of psychology.

## INDIVIDUAL DIFFERENCES: A FOUNDATION OF INDUSTRIAL PSYCHOLOGY

Nearly all industrial psychology textbooks leave little doubt that the study of individual differences is a major foundation of the field. They all begin with the fact that people differ greatly, that these differences are important, and that they "provide the basis of psychology, the science of human behavior" (Dunnette, 1966, p. 1). Indeed, if anyone were to question this foundation "it would seriously weaken the net effectiveness of psychological research in industry, and it should be strenuously avoided" (Dunnette and Kirchner, 1965, p. 7).

How did individual differences become so important?

There are several reasons that are generally accepted. First is the pressure placed on psychologists (especially during the two world wars and the post-World War II industrial boom) to select, place, and train soldiers and personnel for the new plants. The second reason follows from the technology needed to select, place, and train individuals. Effective personnel selection and placement requires that differences be measurable. Measurement is a "fundamental assumption when we set out to make sense of the chaos of variation present in the world around us" (Dunnette, 1966, p. 14). Measurement permits the psychologist to be precise.

How does the industrial psychologist use measurement? First he measures attributes characterizing people and uses them as predictor variables. Examples are IQ, social class, cognitive or motor abilities, attitudes, etc. Obviously, the attributes he chooses must show some degree of reliable variance in order that they be capable of being correlated with the criterion variables. Thus his task is to relate statistically the variance in the predictor variable(s) to that in the criterion variable(s).

What are criterion variables? Again this is a difficult question to answer. Schneider (1969) suggests that industrial psychologists went from situation to situation always asking what was adaptive behavior; that is, what was effective in that situation. In each situation, the operational definition for effective behavior was the criterion variable.

Several important consequences flow from this strategy.

- The primary focus of industrial psychologists becomes the documentation of the nature and variance of individual differences (Anastasi, 1965, pp. 1–2).
- The major methodological strategy becomes measurement. "Unless it can be measured it does not hold the attention of the industrial psychologist," a senior scholar recently told the writer. Guion (1965, p. 5) suggests that this set remains predominant in the thinking processes of industrial psychologists. They tend to ignore phenomena that are not quantifiable.
- The primary index of success becomes prediction. If one can accurately predict the criterion, the industrial psychologist has fulfilled his scientific and professional obligations.

### The Consequence upon Industrial Psychology as a Scientific Discipline

Are these three foci adequate to develop a scholarly field? Anastasi (1965, pp. 1–2) responds that they are not enough. In addition to measuring the nature and extent of individual differences and predicting criterion variables one needs to focus on (1) discovering causal relationships, (2) modifying individual differences, and (3) discovering relationships between variables (see Dunnette, 1972). Measurement, prediction, control, and understanding are equally important.

Prediction is possible without understanding. It is possible to predict accurately that there will be a traffic jam in New York City about 5 p.m. or that aspirin relieves headaches, etc. But accurate predictions tell us little about causes or how the variables can be altered.

When prediction is separated from explanation it is assumed that facts, such as individual differences, can exist "independent of theory" (Ghiselli and Brown, 1955, p. 5). The separation of facts from theory, supported by many industrial psychologists (Guion, 1965; Tiffin, 1946), is rejected by most philosophers of science (Braithwaite, 1956; Hanson, 1958; Kaplan, 1964) as well as by many psychologists. These people maintain that facts get their meaning from theory, that to separate facts from theory implies a theory, and that to separate facts from theory is to separate explanation from description.

Unfortunately, causal explanations and the processes by which these phenomena may be altered tend to be the central focus of scientists outside of industrial psychology. Industrial psychologists have not focused heavily on conducting research that explains their phenomena or shows how they can be altered because of the kind of pressures that have been applied, namely, fulfilling practical demands for effective selection, placement, and training. If they show that individual differences exist, if they measure their variance, and if they correlate the variance in the predictors with the variance in the criterion variables, then their objective is accomplished. These pressures are both real and heavy. It may be that individuals preoccupied with applications in specific situations may become so focused on the concreteness and complexity of these situations that it is difficult to generate interest in generalizing (Hinrichs, 1970).

Industrial psychologists have the right to define their field any way they wish. However, with that right may come an obligation to make explicit the unintended consequences of defining the field in the manner that they choose. Two unintended consequences are (1) it places the field primarily in what Lewin (1935) called the Aristotelian mode of thought; and (2) the field becomes focused upon stability, upon steady state processes, and upon the status quo. First a word about Aristotelian logic and industrial psychology.

## ARISTOTELIAN LOGIC AND INDUSTRIAL PSYCHOLOGY

In the Aristotelian mode of thought, explanation resides "in" the properties of the pheno-mena under study and not in the relationships among the phenomena (which would be Galilean mode of thought).

If the variables under study are attributes "in" people, or "in" situations, and if relation-ships are not sought, the natural consequence is to explain by finding the "cause" in the individual or the situation. Thus individual A is successful because he has certain attributes and because these attributes correlate with something in the situation. This is Aristotelian logic.

The folly of focusing on describing individual differences and then correlating those differences with some other phenomena that manifest variance is exemplified by looking at other fields and pondering where they would be if they had pursued such an avenue of investigation. If physicists, as they sought to understand the laws of falling bodies, had concentrated only upon describing differences in sizes and weights of falling objects and correlating such variables with whether the objects fall directly to the ground, roll down a hill, or fall down a ravine, the laws of physics relevant to falling bodies probably would have been quite different. If the biologist had used the industrial psychologist's paradigm he might have asked about the effectiveness of leaf sizes in, for example, creating shade (a very important practical question in farming). He might then have correlated the different sizes of leaves with the different amounts of shade (criterion variables). As a result, he might have been able to select with a respectable degree of precision, which leaves would give the greatest amount of shade. But, historically, biological scientists did not make these types of questions central to their discipline. The size of a leaf was much less important than understanding the processes by which leaves grew, turned green, turned yellow, etc. This type of knowledge is more explanatory. But initially, the knowledge was much more difficult to derive and the field was much less "practical." Eventually, however, answers about shade effectiveness were provided. Moreover, it led to knowledge about how to grow the leaves larger, how to hasten the trees getting leaves, and how to delay the loss of leaves. Thus the explanatory route can provide the basis for a wide range of applications regarding shade.

### The Emphasis upon Steady State and Status Quo

In Aristotelian thought there is little emphasis upon understanding causal relationships by explaining the interaction or transaction processes between the individual and his environ-ment. Thus as Forehand and Gilmer (1964), Pugh (1966), and Vale and Vale (1969) have pointed out, industrial psychology has not focused adequately on the interactions that exist in the environment. Instead, industrial psychologists emphasize the steady state.

## Organizational Processes as a Black Box

What is the primary environment within which the individual interacts or within which the individuals are embedded? The organization. Where is the environment – the organization – in the model used by industrial psychologists who select, place, and train individuals for organizations? The answer is, I believe, in a black box between the predictor variables and the criterion variables. Why? Because given the emphasis on prediction, the paradigm used in selection and placement must assume that the organizational environment is relatively static and benign and, therefore, need not be known. The paradigm assumes (1) that minimal or unimportant changes occur in the black box or (2) if important changes do occur they are random and cancel out each other (although importance and randomness may be contradictory), (3) that whatever changes occur they are benign to the interests of the industrial psychologists' activities, or more ironically (because the assumption is anti-individual differences) the contents of the black box have equal impact on all individuals.

The latter assumption was questioned early by Fleishman's (1953) study of supervisory training and later by Meyer, et al. (1965) in their study of management performance evaluation activities. Forehand and Gilmer (1964) have also written a systematic exploration of the importance of studying "organizational climate" which includes variables that have been relegated to a black box status.

As an example of the dangers in ignoring organizational processes there are the recent social psychological experimental studies which have suggested that organizational structure can influence leadership selection in hitherto unnoticed ways. Lowen, et al. (1969) suggested that the leadership studies based on the concepts of "initiation of structure and considera-tion" may have suffered by not taking into account the nature of the organizational structure, the nature of the task requirements, and the expertise of the superior or subordinate. First, they noted that initiation of structure and consideration may not be orthogonal, as was once assumed. A high use of initiation of structure can influence a subordinate's view of the superior's sense of consideration. This high use of initiation of structure, in turn, could be caused by the demands the organizational structure imposes on the participants. Moreover, initiation of structure did not show the predicted relationship with productivity. To explain these results the authors hypothesized that the very nature of organizational structure and the way information was handled in the system had to be understood. "It is perfectly reasonable that the productivity of a subordinate (an index of organizational effectiveness) will sometimes vary directly with the extent of imposed intelligent structuring of his activities by experts" (Lowen, et al., 1969, p. 248). If their findings are replicated and their theorizing found valid then the correlations reported between initiation of structure and indices of effectiveness " . . . must be understood as statements generalizable only to organizations in similar settings (Schneider and Bartlett, 1968). The data will not replicate in settings where the level of subordinate-anticipated structuring is markedly different, or where the new task and environment allow a greater or lesser contribution of imposed instructions to subordinate proficiency" (Lowen, et al., 1969, p. 249).

## Implicit Use of Traditional Management Theory

When one uses the paradigm described above, the major contact with organizational factors comes primarily when industrial psychologists attempt to relate their predictor variables to criterion variables such as production, quality of output, absenteeism, volume of sales, and turnover. The implicit assumption is that these factors are valid indices of effective organization. This assumption is based on principles of "scientific management" such as chain of command, unity of direction, and span of control and the concept of effectiveness embedded in these principles. However, they have been shown to be less principles and more rules of thumb (Argyris, 1957; March and Simon, 1958).

Industrial psychologists, then, actually do depend upon a theory. Unfortunately, the theory has been subject to little systematic test, indeed much less than the behavioral organizational theory that many industrial psychologists view with skepticism. Until recently, industrial psychologists have chosen to use this traditional management theory in spite of the increasing theoretical and empirical research regarding its dysfunctionality. The early works of Argyris (1957, 1964), McGregor (1960), and Likert (1967) were seen as too theoretical, overly anecdotal, or empirically primitive (Dunnette, 1962). Likert's (1967) empirical work was more acceptable although the theorizing was equally doubted.

## Consequences of Using an Implicit Organizational Theory

Organizational research increasingly supports the notion that the effectiveness of the whole organization cannot be understood by limiting the criterion variables to those that management would tend to see as relevant since most of those focus primarily on the formal aspects of the organization. Criterion variables tend to be those which management see as signs of effectiveness. Few studies focus on criteria that go beyond management's perceptions and fewer still focus on how the organization can become more effective by going beyond the present conception of effectiveness.

Yet such information is important, especially in light of recent research which suggests that organizations may have built-in forces that cause slow deterioration (organizational entropy) and make it difficult to produce valid information about important issues (Argyris, 1964; Likert, 1967). Gardner (1968) has predicted that our organizations will end slowly from the dry rot that permeates their make-up. Elsewhere, the writer has listed examples of organizational turmoil in organizations that have been considered to have exemplary personnel programs, for example, telephone and oil companies (Argyris, 1970).

Andrews (1967) contrasted an aggressive, expanding, efficient company with a sluggish one. He found that the first company was more likely to advance executives high on achievement and not to reward those high on power. The second company rewarded those who were high on power and low on achievement. Each company rewarded those leaders who were useful in its *present* make-up. The industrial psychologist may see this as an example of a fit between organizational demands and individual traits. The organizational theorist would agree, but also ask questions, about the long range dysfunctional consequences of such an equilibrium state.

In another study, it was concluded that a bank favored what its officers called a "right type" for promotion. Three of the more important qualities of the "right type" were passivity, non-confrontation of or withdrawal from conflict, and a lack of awareness of their impact upon the organization. The organizational theorist noted that a large number of such officers had dysfunctional consequences on internal problem solving, the growth of the bank, and the development of officers to meet the challenges of the next decades (Argyris, 1958). The result of the study created some argument and conflict within the top group. In a few years, because of normal retirement, officers who wanted to make changes came into power. One change they instituted was a new selection program that would identify men who were "non-right-typers." The first few "non-right-typers" had great difficulty; some even resigned in frustration (Argyris, 1958). However, as the number enlarged *and* as the bank changed its rewards to support the new behavior, the newer men began to be integrated into the organization. Thus organizational change and selection were integrated, resulting in a program that was, overall, better than either approach if used alone.

A study of the same bank by Alderfer (1971) suggests the need for even further organizational change and development. For example, there has developed a schism between the "right-typers" and the "non-right-typers." This schism is not being dealt with effectively. The "non-right-typers" have found themselves in the middle with "right-typers" at the highest and lowest levels. These findings emphasize the incompleteness of any organizational change that is not designed to monitor and correct itself. Unless an organization is able to develop competence in generating valid information, free choice, and internal commitment to decision, it may be unable to correct its own dysfunctional consequences (Argyris, 1970).

Some industrial psychologists would deny that many organizational environments produce conformity via the effects of individuals desiring promotion. Ambitious young men observe the behavior of executives and they learn much from observing. They emulate the successful executives and make that behavior their own. They conform to the organization's present standards and thereby perpetuate the status quo. It is these persons that the organization, its management, and its industrial psychologists reward with promotions.

The writer has interviewed executives and has 25 tape recordings of executive meetings in a particular organization (Argyris, 1965). The executives, during the interviews, emphasized that they promoted men who did not conform, who were open, and who took risks. Yet, the inferences made from the behavioral observations were quite different. The forces toward conformity were some of the strongest measured in any organization. Strong norms were found against open confrontation of important but threatening substantive or business issues and against risk-taking. Another relevant finding was that the individuals showed less conformity outside the business settings and that they were able to behave in many more ways than they exhibited during the meetings. Moreover, they tended to be unaware of how much they actually conformed. These comments are not included as proof of anything. They are included to legitimize the suggestion that industrial psychologists working on the identification and selection of executives have to focus more on specifics of on-the-job behavior.

To summarize, given the industrial psychologist's basic assumptions and his lack of interest in organizational processes, there may develop an unintended but powerful thrust toward the development of a point of view that supports the steady state. This, in turn, leads to the reinforcement of the status quo in organizations. I would question the position of Ryan and Smith (1954, pp. 5–6) that industrial psychologists have been captured by management because they are paid by management. Pay has little to do with the issue. Organizational theorists (McGregor, Likert, Bennis, Schein, etc.) probably have received as high or higher rates of pay from management than many industrial psychologists, and yet, they have been unwilling to accept the problems as defined by management.

There is another way in which industrial psychologists ignore the environment. They ignore the environment of the testing situation. Industrial psychologists have conducted little empirical research on the interpersonal relationships, group dynamics (in the case of large groups taking tests), and the organizational norms that may develop during the testing activities.[1] Indeed, when the industrial psychologist does talk about the tester-testee relationship he may become as much, and perhaps more, imprecise and anecdotal than the organizational behaviorists, whom he has ignored because of the imprecision and anecdotal nature of their data.

Blum and Naylor (1968) devote less than a page to the interpersonal dynamics of the testing situation. It is instructive to read carefully their message to the tester. They begin by stating: "Chances are that the inexperienced examiner underestimates his interference to the same extent that the subject overestimates it; the happy medium is somewhere in between. The experienced examiner takes pains to develop rapport. He is frank and interested and explains the purpose of the tests within the limits of the directions. He attempts to encourage relaxation or at least reduce the applicant's tension" (Blum and Naylor, 1968, p. 97).

Blum and Naylor (1968, p. 97) indicate that fear of tests (on the part of the person being tested) may be caused by the feeling that the test is unfair, that it may keep him from getting the job, that he may feel he is unable to estimate if he is doing well or poorly, and that the test may be experienced as an imposition. Their answer to these critical feelings is: "For all these reasons the attitudes of the person taking the test must be taken into consideration." There is nothing else that they say.

Several pages later Blum and Naylor (pp. 99–100) quote the major parts of the American Psychological Association's ethical code for psychological tests. None of the eight items mentioned deals with the interpersonal relationships created between the psychologist and the subject.

The reader might infer that the testing situation has little impact in the area in which a code of ethics might apply. Yet, later on Blum and Naylor cite impressive evidence of how an interviewer or interviewee can disort reality in an interview situation, such as a selection interview. Why is it that industrial psychologists have conducted impressive research on the unreliability of the selection interview, yet have not manifested the same intensity of research interest in the interpersonal relationships of the situations their technology creates? One reason may be that interpersonal relationships are difficult to measure. But this difficulty should also be true for the interpersonal relationships in the selection interviews. Another possibility is that the industrial psychologists have genuinely mistrusted the interview situation because of the potential for bias. Perhaps this has caused some industrial psychologists to unwittingly assume that one way to reduce bias in the testing situation is to de-emphasize the dynamics of that situation and emphasize the objectivity and rigorousness of the test. But how can they do this with so little intellectual discomfort? One hypothesis suggested by Storrs (1963) is that people design their interpersonal life around the fear of being overwhelmed or the fear of being rejected. Those who have the former fear as the primary one, tend to develop vocational interests where it is possible to deal with people at a distance (psychological testing, job analysis, etc.). Such individuals would prefer to collect data quickly from subjects and get their deepest kicks out of poring over the statistical analysis. Those whose primary concern is the fear of being rejected would spend more time on research techniques that emphasize interpersonal relationships (interviews, T-groups, etc.). The experimental and industrial psychologists would tend to be in the former category; the field researchers and clinicians would tend to be in the latter category.

## JOB ANALYSIS, JOB SATISFACTION, AND JOB ENLARGEMENT STUDIED
### WITHIN CONSTRAINTS OF TRADITIONAL MANAGEMENT THEORY

Conceptualizing their field in a way that relegates the internal organizational processes to a black box status and that accepts the traditional managerial assumptions (since they are the basis for the criterion variables) may lead industrial psychologists to conduct research without ever questioning its basis in traditional management theory.

For example, the industrial psychologist's focus on motion and time study, job analysis, and certain aspects of human engineering is very much in the tradition of scientific management and Taylorism. Job analysis is an accurate study of various components of a job. It concerns itself with fitting individuals to the jobs and with "testing" the fit through performance and reported employee satisfaction. The former is usually defined in terms of some organizational output, preferably objective, such as the number of pieces produced, the quality of the product, etc. The latter is usually measured by asking the individual to report his satisfaction.

One difficulty with using employee satisfaction as a test for the degree of fit between the individual and the job is that employees can be satisfied for many different reasons. They can be satisfied if the job is monotonous or complex and varied, because the work is involving or noninvolving. Information is, therefore, needed to help us understand what makes the individual satisfied. For example, Korman (1971) has shown that it is possible for individuals performing repetitive work to have high job satisfaction with the same job because their self-acceptance tends to be high.

On the other hand, Hulin and Blood (1968) suggest and Blood (1969) presents evidence that the individuals' degree of commitment to the "Protestant ethic" may influence their job satisfaction, and that the Protestant ethic is high in the rural areas and low in the urban areas. If the Protestant ethic has the impact that the authors suggest, how would they account for the attitude and performance changes *among city workers* reported in the literature when their work has been enlarged? For example, Banks (1960) notes that 33 percent of the employees reported higher fulfillment after they were assigned to jobs of greater interest, variety, or responsibility (pp. 24–5). Mann and Williams (1962) took two populations of employees for whom matched data existed before and after the introduction of new equipment. They reported that the employees with the more enlarged jobs reported greater fulfillment with the increased amount of responsibility, more variety, and change as well as greater tension and more job risk. These experiences, therefore, could lead some employees to feel satisfied with their jobs and others to become frustrated, tense, and dissatisfied, and still others to go through a change from dissatisfaction to satisfaction (Mann and Williams, 1962; Banks, 1960). The first condition could lead to increasing job involvement which, in turn, could feed back to strengthen satisfaction. The second condition could lead to decreasing job involvement, which, in turn, could feed back to strengthen the frustration, tension, and thus, dissatisfaction. The third condition would lead to ambivalence or sequential dissatisfaction to satisfaction.

The point is that in both studies cited above many workers "changed" their values. There appears to be little room for such changes in the views of many industrial psychologists, including Hulin and Blood. People seem to adhere to the Protestant ethic or they do not. The word "changed" above was placed in quotes because there is the possibility that no change occurred in the workers' value system. It is possible for workers to value the Protestant ethic but not adhere to it in a particular situation. Workers may become more oriented toward the Protestant ethic once work becomes meaningful. If one reads the early studies of workers on assembly lines (Argyris, 1957), or work by Goldthorpe et al. (1968), it should be clear that many workers value challenging work and being involved *if* the work is worth becoming involved with. When it is not, they do not value that particular work nor do they become involved in it, even though they may prefer a work world where this were possible. This is not to imply that all workers will seek enlarged jobs. It is to imply that we have offered such opportunities only to a very small fraction of workers who do prefer more meaningful work (as long as they aren't being forced to risk unfavorable economic conditions by accepting such work).

Another possibility apparently overlooked by the critics of job enlargement is the possibility that if it failed it may be a function of alienation from management. If the employees believe that the job enlargement is a trick or a gimmick created by management, they will mistrust the entire process. In some recent research Meyer and his associates have shown that job enlargement can lead to increased sense of "stewardship" and productivity (Sorcher, 1969). However, Sorcher also cautions that job enlargement programs cannot be based on a few mechanically applied gimmicks. They need to be based on genuine trust; otherwise, the programs will fail (pp. 9–10).

Finally, job enlargement may not be immediately and positively related to satisfaction. Indeed, Argyris (1964) predicted an initial decrease in satisfaction for apathetic, instrument-ally and deficiency-oriented employees, if they were offered enlarged jobs. Some would resist job enlargement for years (Argyris, 1960). Job enlargement was hypothesized to be related positively to increasing experience of psychological success or increasing the employee's control over his work or the use of more abilities. Job satisfaction may or may *not* follow. Thus, for Hulin and Blood to attempt to relate enriched or enlarged jobs to questionnaire items of job satisfaction may be a misreading of the complexity of the theory related to job enlargement.[2]

Returning to the concepts appropriate for understanding employee satisfaction, it may that the more appropriate ones are those suggested by the works of Lodahl (1964) on job-involvement, Koch (1956) and McReynolds (1971) on intrinsic and extrinsic orientation, and the concept of psychological involvement by Argyris (1960).

For those scholars who prefer the concept of the Protestant ethic, they could contribute more to the field if they would (1) be more explicit as to why they selected the Protestant ethic as a concept, (2) define conceptually the meaning of the concept, and (3) relate it to other concepts because the acceptance of a concept is partially a function of its relationship to a set of interrelated concepts, which, in turn, are evaluated by their ability to explain comprehensively, commensurate with greatest simplicity.

## Valid Instruments Reinforcing the Status Quo

If a field tends to be atheoretical, if it tends not to be primarily concerned about causal explanations and the development of knowledge about altering its variables, the very processes of developing valid instruments can also come to support the status quo and lead to the use of hidden or implicit theory.

To explore this consequence, let us focus on some aspects of the Ohio State Leadership studies because they had an important impact on the field and because much research has been generated about them. (For some reviews see Blum and Naylor, 1968, pp. 421–4; Korman, 1966.) In order to develop their leadership questionnaire, an original pool of 1,800 items was selected and studied empirically. Several factor analyses were made. The responses to the 150 items indicated two distinct groupings of supervisory behavior. They were labeled "Consideration" and "Initiation of Structure."

This inventory, like any other similar instrument, tells us where the individual "is" on these two dimensions. He could be high on one and low on the other, low on both, or high on both. So far, we have an accurate description of the status quo.

But what would happen if a supervisor wished to alter his behavior? Could he utilize the questionnaire to help him change? Recently, it has been suggested that, in order for the information to be helpful for change, it must, in addition to being valid, be given in terms of *directly observable* behavior. The more concrete and operational is the feedback, the more helpful it can be (Argyris, 1968). These suggestions should not be new to industrial psychologists. DuBois (1960, p. 232) has pointed out that, "the greatest achievements of psychological measurement have been reached where the behavior of interest has been actually worked into the testing situation." This is what is meant by directly observable behavior. The writer is aware of the situational leaderless group tests by Bass (1959) and the in-basket technique (Frederiksen, 1966). These do go in the direction that is being suggested and that may be one reason why they show (especially the in-basket) a relatively high degree of predictive validity (Bray and Grant, 1966). Both are situational exercises which attempt to simulate conditions of actual on-the-job behavior.

Returning to the supervisor, to be told he is high or low on "consideration" and/or "initiation of structure" is to give feedback that is typically not based on observable behavior. Even the Leadership Behavior Description Questionnaire (LBDQ) which is filled in by subordinates or others who have observed the supervisor is made up of statements that are inferences from behavior.

Let us assume the supervisor is able to obtain a copy of the Leadership Behavior Description Questionnaire and he examines the items with the highest loadings on consideration. The items are (Blum and Naylor, 1968, p. 422):

1    He expresses appreciation when one of us does a good job.
2    He is easy to understand.
3    He stresses the importance of high morale among those under him.
4    He makes those under him feel at ease when talking with him.
5    He is friendly and can be easily approached.

These items are not directly observable behavior. They are inferences. Thus, the category, consideration, is not composed of directly observable behavior. There is no feedback about how to change behavior from such categories. For example, no cues are given regarding the actual behavior involved in "expresses appreciation," "is easy to understand," "makes those under him feel at ease." The variance of behavior that could be perceived to accomplish these may be very great. In one study, "friendly and easily approachable foremen" (upon observation) turned out to be foremen "who left the men alone and rarely pressured them" (Argyris, 1960). In another study "friendly foremen" were men who took the initiative to discuss "difficult issues" with the men (Argyris, 1965).[3]

Lowen et al. (1969, pp. 246–7) have raised similar questions. In an attempt to prepare scripts related to consideration and initiation of structure they found it difficult to understand precisely the behavioral content of these categories, especially initiation of structure. They wondered about the applicability of the concepts in the evaluation and education of supervisors.

Recently, Dunnette and Campbell (1969) have conducted some through research in order to develop a new career index for a particular organization. After a systematic series of research studies, nine dimensions were chosen to describe the relative effectiveness of managers. The items are primarily of the inferred category variety. There are no items that the writer could find that described behavior in directly observable categories. For example:

Maintains harmonious relationship with sales associates.
Avoids and counteracts harmful turnover among sales associates.
Exercise tact and consideration in working with sales associates.

The question arises, how (in actual behavior) does an individual "maintain harmonious relationships"? Dunnette and Campbell are aware of these questions. They have attempted to make the instrument more operational by developing scales that have actual critical incidents defining the levels of effectiveness. For example, one such scale is reproduced in Figure 22.1. The questions raised above, however, still seem to remain unanswered. How

## Handling customer complaints and making adjustments

In his job as department manager, how well does this man handle customer adjustments? Consider not only his day-to-day or typical job behavior but also how he does when he's at his best.

Write BEST on the scale opposite the action that seems to fit him most closely when he's doing his best in handling customer adjustments

Write TYPICAL on the scale opposite the action that seems to fit him most closely when he's doing his usual or typical job of handling customer adjustments

|  |  |
|---|---|
|  | Could be expected to exchange a dress purchased in a distant town and to impress the customer so much that she would purchase three coats and three pairs of shoes. |
| Could be expected to smooth things over beautifully with an irate customer who returned a sweater with a hole in it and turn her into a satisfied customer. |  |
|  | Could be expected to be friendly and tactful and to agree to reline a coat for a customer who wanted a new coat because the lining had worn out in "only" two years. |
| Could be expected to courteously exchange a pair of gloves that were too small. |  |
|  | Could be expected to handle the after Christmas rush of refunds and exchanges in a reasonable manner. |
| Could be expected to make a refund for a sweater only if the customer insists. |  |
|  | Could be expected to be quite abrupt with customers who want to exchange merchandise for a different colour or style. |
| Could be expected to tell customer that a "six week old" order couldn't be changed even though the merchandise had actually been ordered only two weeks previously. |  |
|  | Could be expected to tell customers who tried to return a shirt bought in Hawaii that a store in the "States" had no use for a Hawaiian shirt. |

*Source*: Dunnette and Campbell (1969)

**Figure 22.1**   A job performance scale from the Penney Career Index

does a manager behave so that he impresses a customer to buy more than she would ordinarily buy? How does he "smooth things over beautifully"? How is he "friendly and tactful"?

Does he smooth things over by withdrawal or compromise? These can be significantly different behaviors. Thus, it would be difficult to use the Dunnette and Campbell instrument directly for purposes of behavioral change and individual development. Moreover, could not one raise questions about the effectiveness of compromise or withdrawal? Blake and Mouton (1969) would answer affirmatively. Moreover, they would contend that the strategies for being a successful salesman (as identified by Dunnette and Campbell, 1969) may lead to long-run difficulties. For example, maintaining harmonious relations could be done at the expense of quality of the openness; being tactful and diplomatic could lead to a lowering of the salespeople's levels of aspiration.

The time may be appropriate for industrial psychologists to explore these issues. As they integrate individual diagnosis with development and as they provide maps of possible new designs for organizational and customer relationships their work may become even more relevant and applicable.

The industrial psychologists may respond that they do not typically design such instruments for education; they design them for selection. But this is the issue that is being raised. Why is this the case? Must it continue to be the case? Isn't there some value to designing instruments that integrate selection and education, which would lead to change? Would not such instruments provide more valid knowledge about our understanding of human behavior, in addition to being of more practical value? Could not helping supervisors alter their leadership behavior also provide excellent field opportunities for predictive tests regarding consideration and initiation of structure? In medicine, cancer will be understood when the analysis developed explains the processes that cause cancer, can be used to create cancer, and can lead directly to a cure for cancer. Medicine does have some tests that identify illness but give no insight into cures (e.g., the Pap test for cancer). But these are seen as incomplete and temporary tests to be outdated as quickly as possible. Medical researchers are, therefore, not content to relegate the processes of cancer to a black box status. They place their heaviest emphasis on conducting research that will explain the processes within the black box.

Why should not this be the case in the study of human behavior? Why cannot instruments be developed that diagnose leadership styles and provide the basis for change? The argument often made that the instruments would be too cumbersome and not acceptable to management can hardly square with experience. The managerial grid, for example, is a program that permits diagnostic and educational functions. The diagnosis is followed by exploration of behavior in a group setting where directly observable feedback is possible. It has generated wide acceptance on the part of administrators of many different kinds of organizations throughout the world (Blake and Mouton, 1969). This is not to suggest that the instrument is perfect, indeed much more empirical research is needed. The point being made is that diagnosis and change are complementary. However, in order to integrate the two applications, one needs to develop knowledge about conflict, the nature of organizations, and the management of conflict in systems. Blake and Mouton have presented a theoretical framework about these issues and some empirical research. Some may wish to fault them on either or both counts but that would not be relevant to the point that they have shown it is possible to work on understanding these processes.

If more systematic knowledge can be developed from instruments that integrate selection and education, we may be able to shed light on why supervisors do not tend to be effective selectors. Based on data from assessment centers, supervisors tend to come off second best in their ability to predict who will be an effective supervisor (Bray and Grant, 1966;

DeNelsky and McKee, 1969). Why is this so? One reason may be that the supervisor may not know about the actual behavior of his subordinates on the job. Such a situation may be the result of supervisors not creating a climate where the subordinate exposes his behavior. For example, subordinates may tend to suppress their leadership styles in a meeting. Consequently, during an assessment center, or any evaluation situation, when the supervisor does observe non distorted behavior he has had little previous experience with such behavior and lacks a basis for making a prediction about its effectiveness.

If one decides to design questionnaires that individuals can use as a basis for their personal development, then another alteration of practice may become necessary. Given the criteria of analytic simplicity and comprehensiveness, it is routine to conduct factor analyses to reduce a larger set of factors to a smaller set which are relatively independent of each other. Thus, in the Ohio State Leadership studies nearly ten factors were reduced to two. However, if the questionnaire were to be used to facilitate individual learning it may be helpful for the learner to have all the factors that were collapsed into consideration and initiation of structure. This may help him become more aware of the behavioral requirements of each factor.

To put the issue another way, redundancy and overlap may be qualities of "poor" research; but they may be helpful as a basis for education and learning, *and* they may gain higher status as we realize that redundancy and overlap may be key processes in man's rational activities. This is not to ignore the scientific canon of parsimony. Parsimony means that, other things equal, the simplest explanation is the best. The question arises as to when one has an explanation and when one has a description. The writer would argue that psychologists who develop such instruments as the leadership questionnaire have been primarily interested in describing what the respondents say rather than why they say what they do or do what they do. An accurate description would include the original items and not the categories of higher level of abstraction. It is when one attempts to develop an explanation for the data that the law of parsimony applies.

A field that tends to ignore theory, but uses it implicitly, may unwittingly become tied to this implicit theory. Thus, those who utilize the leadership inventories may become tied to implicit theories that contribute little to validating, or correcting, or adding to existing explicit theory (Korman, 1966).

### *Rigorous Research Methods Compound the Focus on the Steady State*

Our intention to this point has been to suggest that industrial psychology, as an academic discipline, was greatly influenced in its development by the applied problems of developing selection, placement, and training activities. This tended to lead to minimum interest in theory-building and to explanations in terms of the Aristotelian mode of thought. The consequences of this were (1) to relegate the organizational processes (or the environment in which the individual was embedded) to the status of a black box, (2) to use implicit theories that were untested, (3) to undertake such actions as job analysis and job enlargement under unnecessarily extreme constraints, and (4) to develop valid instruments that tend not to be helpful in testing or developing new theory or in providing a basis for reeducation of individuals.

To these consequences we may now add another. It may be that the concepts of rigorous research accepted by industrial psychologists (and most other behavioral scientists) may actually compound the difficulties just described above. Recently, the writer has argued that rigorous research may not be achieved as fully as possible unless the concepts of what constitutes empirical methodology is altered (Argyris, 1968).

Rigorous research has two characteristics. One is related to the output, the other to the process. The output is usually viewed as empirically validated, publicly verifiable generalizations hopefully stated in quantitative terms. The process is usually conceived to be empirical research following the rules of the scientific method.

The process: the procedures of rigorous research and the methods of traditional scientific management are similar. For example, rigorous research and the pyramidal organization assume that rigor is obtained (1) by unambiguous operational definition and measurement of the relevant variables and (2) through control by the researcher (or manager) of the design of the research situation (production situation) in which data are collected (products produced). Control is obtained by the researcher (management) defining the subject's (worker's) role as rationally and clearly as possible (to minimize error) and as simply as possible (to assure understanding and performance). The researcher (manager) also provides as little information as possible beyond the tasks he wants the subject to perform (thereby creating a relationship of dependence and minimal time perspective). Finally, the researcher attempts to standardize the inducements for participation, the methods for scoring, and interpreting the data (Argyris, 1968).

The output: in testing, selection, and job analysis, the industrial psychologist strives to produce products that are (1) objective (minimal subjective influence in arriving at scores), (2) reliable and valid, (3) uniform in the method for interpretation of results, and (4) standardized. Moreover, there is an emphasis on techniques that reduce "error." Dunnette (1966), Guion (1965), and Ryan and Smith (1954) suggest that errors may be minimized by (1) obtaining adequate samples, (2) utilizing appropriate statistical techniques, (3) minimizing chance response tendencies, and (4) minimizing changes in environment and in persons taking the tests.

All these requirements characterize the essence of the management activity in pyramidal organizations. They strive to define jobs, to develop measures that are objective, reliably evaluated, standardized, etc. They strive to minimize system error through continual quality control which is based on adequate samples and appropriate statistical procedures. The industrial psychologist also strives to maintain control, to define the tasks clearly and to standardize them, to provide minimal opportunity for the subject to contaminate the results through conscious or unconscious distortion, and to score and evaluate the performance of the subject with little or no participation by the subject, etc. The subject, be he in a testing, placement, or job analysis situation, is being largely controlled by the professional. He is, therefore, in a dependent, subordinate situation to the professional and has a short time perspective.

To compound the problem the subject (employee) is usually told that he is being placed in such a situation for his own good. That is, if he is to be helped to find the best possible job for his talents, then he must accept these conditions. The same is true when he is being asked to complete a morale or satisfaction questionnaire. He is asked to fill out a questionnaire designed by the experts whose results could influence his work life, but whose make-up and rationale must be kept secret from him. Thus the subject is being asked to be open, manifest a spirit of inquiry, and take risks, when he is placed in a (testing or questionnaire) situation that has many of the repressive characteristics of formal organizations, which he has long ago learned to adapt to by not being open or taking risks (Argyris, 1968, pp. 190–92).

From previous research on organizational settings, it is possible to predict some of the probable consequences that the subjects will manifest. They can refuse to take the tests or keep putting them off. They can withdraw psychologically and thus give answers that may not be representative of their true feelings or views. They can express different types of covert hostility by knowingly, but carefully, giving false data. They can also resist overtly. These types of reactions are not new to industrial psychologists. Indeed, it is safe to state that our society has reached the point where the resistance is active and overt. The recent congressional hearings and the new constraints placed over the use of psychological tests may be an example.

## RESULTANT STATUS OF INDUSTRIAL PSYCHOLOGY IN THE
## EYES OF PRACTITIONERS

The use of models which relegate most of the living system to a black box status; the emphasis of static analysis over process; the acceptance of management values, pyramidal organizational structure, and administrative controls as given; the use of research methods and measuring instruments that place subjects in temporary systems that can be as constrictive as the formal aspects of organizations; the separation of selection from development; the apparent disdain of industrial psychology for raising basic questions about, or seeking to redesign crucial aspects of the working world – all these factors have important consequences for industrial psychology as an academic, scientific, and professional enterprise. Here are some of those consequences.

First, there is an increased probability that workers' perceptions of the industrial psychologist may tend to become similar to their perceptions of the earlier industrial engineers and time-study men. Employees may see industrial psychologists (the testers, the designers of performance appraisal programs, inventors of different wage schemes and incentive programs, the authors of job descriptions) as part of management's human control system (more diplomatically entitled personnel activities).

A further major perception of industrial psychologists may be that they are the measures of employee morale in order to keep management informed of employee attitudes and concerns. The reaction to the morale surveys may vary with the quality of the relationship between employee and company and the union (when that exists). In some cases, the industrial psychologists may be seen as a genuine link to the top. In other cases, they are seen as the gestapo. In both examples, industrial psychologists are seen as playing a linkage role; yet, industrial psychologists are rarely seen as having a significant influence in their areas.

Second, unions may fear and tend to mistrust industrial psychologists. They may be seen as being in the pay of management to use research technology to make management policies and practice "scientifically" valid. They may especially mistrust the wage and salary schemes and the incentive programs. The latter are seen as insidious attempts to place employees in competition with each other thereby pitting worker against worker. Such competition could have negative effects upon the union because its members would begin to compete and mistrust each other.

Given that the industrial psychologist is perceived as supporting the status quo, one may hypothesize that the people who will tend to support their services are those who themselves are oriented toward the status quo (e.g., "old time" top executives, *less* innovative and progressive supervisors, and personnel administrators). One would expect to find, as does Thornton (1969), that personnel administrators see industrial psychology as being useful. It is still the field from which they draw much of their technology. Some supervisors may seek the technology that the industrial psychologists develop for selection, testing, wages, etc. because, if the workers feel unfairly treated, the supervisors can blame "personnel." In short, the role of "personnel" as the keeper of the status quo may suit the less innovative supervisors, because they can transfer their problems to the personnel specialists. The old time executives may like the industrial psychologists because they help to make their management more "concerned" about people; yet, they rarely want studies which ask questions about the way jobs are designed, the organization is structured, the use of administrative controls (such as budget and production bogeys), and the interpersonal relationships among top executives. Such studies may threaten persons at the top.

This may seem like a harsh judgment but I believe it is an accurate one. The writer is acquainted with several key top executives in three organizations in the United States that have supported the largest, most systematic, and thorough top management identification and selection studies. Although these projects have made, and will continue to make, contributions to the firms and important copy for textbooks, the boards of directors and the top executive committees have relatively vague knowledge about them. Where the top line executive are enthusiastic, it tends to occur where the evaluation programs are not used to assess their behavior.

There is a third consequence that deserves special attention. During the past two decades a revolution has been going on in schools of business. With the impetus of the Ford report (Gordon and Howell, 1959), the schools redesigned and upgraded themselves. The changes were well timed because the schools became the largest producers of future top line executives. No longer were law and engineering the major sources of top executives. For reasons which will be discussed below, the schools of business tended to shun the traditional industrial psychologists and vice versa. Instead, they focused increasingly in the areas of organizational behavior, industrial sociology and psychology, and the research aspects of the human relations emphasis. The result was that several new generations of executives were fed into the system, many of whom are now in key positions.

These young executives are not as doctrinaire as their older predecessors. They tend to see less sacredness in maintaining the present technology, organizational structure, administrative controls, and in their own behavior. Indeed, many believe that these variables may represent the new leverage points for instituting changes. Thus, when they look into their organizations for help in the "people area" they are neither attracted to selection, testing, job analysis, etc., nor to the methods of study and analysis that industrial psychologists tend to use. Those methods may be more rigorous but, in the eyes of these young top executives, they are neither relevant for, nor applicable to, the problems that interest them. Unfortunately, the result may be that industrial psychologists could become, unintentionally, to the field of human behavior, what the shiny-pants, green-shade bookkeeper is to finance.

## THE INDUSTRIAL PSYCHOLOGIST REACTS

If these descriptions are accurate portrayals of trends, how are industrial psychologists reacting to them? There are two major reactions that the writer has been able to identify. One is to continue, with even more deliberate speed and conviction, the processes of developing more sophisticated methodologies. The other is to enlarge the interests to take on some of the activities traditionally developed outside of the field. Concerning the latter, those who have enlarged their interests and skills *and* integrated them with the previously learned ones bring to their job a unique combination of rigor and vigor that will probably make them extremely useful to their organizations. It is hoped that they will write conceptually about their achievements because by doing so, they can make important contributions to their field.

The larger number have reacted to the above by returning to their field to rework it and to develop more sophisticated empirical technology. Several years ago, the writer asked two of the highest ranking industrial psychologists in the Civil Service to identify a major innovation in industrial psychology produced by professional psychologists in the Civil Service. They immediately identified Primoff's J-coefficient approach to job analysis as an important breakthrough. Yet, that approach questions no basic tenets of job design. Indeed, one could argue that the time study engineers, when they establish standard times for new operations primarily on an a priori basis through the use of synthetic times for the various elements of the job in question, were doing what Primoff did for industrial psychology.

The point is that better empirical methods may actually compound some of the problems. If it is technically possible to track down multivariate relationships with bigger computers, moderator models with multiple discriminant analyses, etc., then the researcher may increase his investment in pursuing blind, atheoretical leads, which may reduce his openness to use theory to guide his activities. Another way to innovate with dynamic criteria and moderator variables is to develop a theory from which they may be derived. Likert (1967) is an example of a scholar who has succeeded in this way.

An excellent example of a more advanced selection model has been developed by Dunnette (1966, pp. 104–12). He asks industrial psychologists to look into the black box and begin to note the variance and dynamics of its variables. The model is too new to say with certainty what its impact will be. However, if Dunnette's own work is illustrative, the most effective use has been to differentiate populations within the organization. Ironically, the biggest barrier to the Dunnette model may be its complexity. The number of combinations possible among individuals, job behaviors, and situations may be too large for developing meaningful generalizations or for applicable results. As shall be argued below, the next step may not be to make the analysis more complex and dynamic.

## IMPORTANT RESEARCH QUESTIONS

The second objective of this chapter is to explore some possible courses of action that may be taken to reduce the unintended consequences. One major suggestion that flows from the previous analysis is that more emphasis should be placed on the construction of explicit theories that attempt to explain phenomena; more attention should be given to the interaction between the individual and the environment in which he exists; more research should be done on systematically changing or altering the variables to study their impact in other relevant variables; more concern should be held for studies about other states of individual–environmental interaction that do not exist in the present world; a greater integration should be made between systematic diagnosis (on the individual, group, or organizational levels) and the reeducation, development, or growth of these systems.

More specifically, there are five research questions, discussed below, that deserve increasing attention in the future.

### How Do Individuals and Organizations Optimally Reduce Individual Differences in Predictor, Moderator, and Criterion Variables?

One fruitful next step for some part of industrial psychology to take may be to ask how are individual differences "optimally suppressed" so that individuals and the organizations gain? In asking this question, we do not want to be understood as asking how can individuals give themselves up for the sake of the organizations. Such an oversocialized view of man is as incomplete and inaccurate as an overindividualized view (Wrong, 1961). The emphasis will be on the integration of man with system.

Tyler (1959) has raised a similar question. She concluded that the traditional way of dealing with individual differences, "shows signs of becoming completely unworkable because of the proliferation of dimensions" (p. 76). She had hoped that factor analytic methods might resolve the problems but she now doubts this possibility. Tyler then suggested that perhaps we need to accept the evidence indicating that no individual is able to actualize all his potential. The individual, through choice, selects the potential he wishes to express and organizes it into a meaningful pattern so that its expression becomes possible (p. 77).

The work in psychological ecology by Barker and Wright (1955) makes it clear that there are almost unlimited possibilities to determine individuality. However, people have to choose or they become immobilized. Indeed, one of the criteria of mature development may be whether the individual makes valid choices and develops patterns that encourage competence in life. This process of the conscious and (unconscious) narrowing down of individual differences to a meaningful pattern is part of the process to which I refer when I speak of "optimal suppression" of individual differences.

The second part of "optimal suppression" of individual differences is based upon the assumptions of reciprocity (Gouldner, 1960) and constructive intent (Buhler, 1962, pp. 36–9). Individuals manifest a willingness to be just in reciprocal relationships and intend to be constructive even if they do not succeed in many instances. Thus individuals coming to an organization may be willing to give of (but not give up) themselves if they believe that the returns are equitable and just (Adams, 1963; Homans, 1961). The employees may be aware of the dysfunctional aspects of formal organization. They may have learned to adapt by creating informal systems, unions, and attitudes toward work involvement that sanction psychological withdrawal (Argyris, 1968).

To be sure, these informal activities can have dysfunctional effects upon individuals. Psychological withdrawal may create internal forces within individuals to smother their own individual differences and to worry more about how much they are worth than who they are as human beings (Fromm, 1941). This could lead to functional smothering (Argyris, 1964). What we are seeking is that optimal relationship where the individual gives up aspects of self that would not harm him and that might, in fact, facilitate the growth of other aspects. The choice would be made out of responsibility for himself *and* the organization. Research is needed to specify the processes by which this could occur. One may hypothesize that if such choices are to be free and informed, individuals may need much more awareness of themselves, more knowledge of the needs of the organization, and more information about the benefits and costs.

Presently, individual differences are smothered in organizations but little attention is given to whether it is an optimal suppression of individual differences. In a series of observational studies of 28 different types of groups, ranging in duration from two to fifteen months some strong similarities among groups were found. In a total of nearly 46,000 units of behavior, the "typical" interpersonal relationships formed a pattern called A. Pattern A could be described as individuals tending to express their ideas in ways that supported the norm of conformity. Individuals did not, nor did group norms, support their owning up to their feelings, being open to their own and others' feelings. There was almost no experimenting with ideas and feelings, and also no trust observed in the groups. Rarely did individuals help others to own up, to be open with, and experiment with ideas and feelings (Argyris, 1969, pp. 894–5).

The result of such a world was to tend to make people "diplomatic," "careful," "not make waves," to credit conformity. Again individual differences, at the upper levels, tended to be smothered. As was reported in many of these studies, the executives learned to suppress many of their feelings and abilities in order not to upset the systematic equilibrium. Their individual differences did not dissipate; they could report them in a psychological test. They simply did not use them in their everyday working life.

These findings underline the importance of studying individual differences in such a way that we come "to grips meaningfully with the problem of the *interaction* of organisms and environments" (Vale and Vale, 1969, p. 1093). More knowledge is needed about what happens to individual differences under differing environmental settings.

To raise the question in another way, the more sophisticated selection model by Dunnette described previously assumes that if researchers had a more differentiated view of predictors, job behaviors, and situations, prediction of criterion variables would be more effective. Another possibility is to study how individuals create work worlds that reduce the variance of all these factors, including the criterion variables. How do individuals decide to conform to systematic demands? How do they get to the point where "don't rock the boat" becomes expected, and, indeed, is seen as competent behavior? How many organizations are designed so that the individual differences the individual gives up are those that are functional to his continued development and to the organization's effectiveness?

Another related issue is generated by the fact that the overwhelming number of executives report that they *do* express feelings; that they *do* behave in trusting manners, they *are* very open, etc., and they select executives who behave in similar ways. Yet, in every study reported above, almost none of that behavior was observed. That the researchers could be perceiving reality inaccurately was unlikely because the researchers were able to make more accurate predictions based on their view of the world than were the executives based on their view (Argyris, 1969). Thus the organizational world may be populated with executives who tend to be genuinely unaware of their own impact, unaware about what the factors may be that affect their own personnel selection strategies, and unaware that their subordinates and peers act to maintain the blindness. What is the impact of these consequences on selection research?

Finally, perhaps the attitudinal or behavioural variance being reported by psychologists represents variance "within" individuals which they do not tend or expect to use.

Is it possible that when attitudinal or behavioural variance is found to be great, the variables being studied may not be, organizationally speaking, the potent ones and that is why the variance exists? Perhaps organizations limit the variance in the potent variables.

Research is also needed to understand the causes and the content of performance variance in actual settings. Some hypothesize that there are at least two organizational forces that inveigh against the exposure of as wide a variance as is possible. First are the wage systems which provide the highest rewards for moderate performance (Argyris, 1964; Lawler, 1971; McGregor, 1960), and second is the design of organizational control mechanisms by the principle of "management by exception." This is one of the most central principles of scientific management. It defines as an acceptable level of performance the maintenance of performance that is close to an externally set standard. The performing individuals are checked only when their performance goes significantly above or significantly below the standard. If it goes below, they may be warned or punished. If it goes above, they may be rewarded and their peers or that individual punished (by a re-timing or redesign of the job to make it "tighter"). The consequence may be for individuals to play it safe. Indeed, the "rate busters" may be ostracized (Whyte, 1969). What is the meaning of the performance variance reported on criterion variables under these conditions?

*How May Organizations Be Designed to Reduce the Dysfunctional Suppression of Individual Differences in Human Capacities and Performance?*

Another task that industrial psychologists may find fruitful to consider is the redesign of organizations that encourages optimal use of individual potentialities. This is the position taken by Argyris (1964), Bennis (1966), and by Hackman and Lawler (1971).

The suggestion to encourage the optimal use of individual differences may seem contradictory to the previous discussion in which we argue that reduction of individual differences may be a necessary activity of life. I believe that the contradiction is more accurately a dilemma and that the dilemma provides a basis for problem solving and individual development. One might say that human self-expression or actualization would have little impetus or only vague meaning without the dilemma.

How do we arrive at this conclusion? First consider the work of Barker and Wright (1955), Tyler (1959) and Simon (1969). The first two document the proposition that man's social environment is extremely rich and complex. Simon's research supports this proposition and adds another important one about the nature of human problem solving capacity. He suggests that man's apparatus for problem solving is really quite simple compared to the richness of the environment. In order for man to use his simple capacities effectively he has to conceptualize and organize reality into more simple and more manageable units. As man does this he necessarily chooses aspects of his environment to organize. As he continues this process of simplification and organization, he stores up the successful attempts and throws out or represses the unsuccessful attempts. The strategies that he stores up become parts of himself. Indeed, they may be what we call individual identity and uniqueness. Man develops his identity by these sequential decision-making processes.

Implicit in this model is that the environment must be rich and complex (relative to man) *and* permit man to do the searching, choosing, and integrating. But, as we have seen, most formal organizations are designed and/or result in living systems that reduce the complexity and restrict greatly the processes of search and choice.

The organizations of the future, therefore, may require designs where complexity and richness can be increased. This will probably be encouraged by the computer science technology introducing much more complex information systems *and* the increasing interdependence among organizations in our society. As richness and complexity are returned to the internal make-up of organization, the processes of search, choice, and organization become paramount.

Research is needed to identify the conditions under which these processes are effective. One may hypothesize that the probability of effective search and free choice increases as individuals experience psychological success and feelings of essentiality. The opportunity for psychological success necessarily means less unilateral dependence, submissiveness, and more opportunity to express one's important abilities. The more these conditions exist, the higher the probability that individuals will experience increased sense of competence and confidence. These would, in turn, increase their need for new experiences of psychological success and essentiality.

On the organization side, one may hypothesize that as the above processes are set in motion the amount of energy for work and internal commitment to a decision would tend to increase. As internal commitment increases, the willingness to monitor one's own effectiveness in the decisions increases. This means that the individual is more open to being corrected and more motivated to work and perform.

If the above logic can be confirmed by empirical research, then organizations may find it useful to design for their employees experiences that provide the maximum possible opportunity for psychological success (individuals significantly influencing the definition of their goals, the paths to these goals, the degree of challenge, etc.) and feelings of essentiality. This does *not* mean that all employees will strive to reach the maximum possible. Some may find it too great a challenge. What we are suggesting is that the organization design itself in ways where the range of individual differences can be expressed.

I should like to take a moment to emphasize that the logic developed stems from a concept of man and his environment that is evolving from research in child development, personality, cognitive processes, clinical and social psychology. As such, it is not a middle-class concept as suggested by Strauss (1963). Argyris (1964) has cited several large studies while Herzberg (1966), and Tannenbaum (1968), have presented evidence that lower level employees prefer more control over their working world which would lead to their being less dependent upon management and more able to utilize their abilities (e.g., those involved in self-control). If the design of organizations is based on conclusions about man that he exists in impoverished environments, the organizations will create impoverished men, impoverished organizations, and impoverished societies.

If research is to be conducted on these questions of redesign, the descriptively oriented researcher is faced with the following dilemma: studies that require the testing of new designs that are contrary to existing norms will tend to be perceived as deviant ideas by the potential subjects. Such changes will rarely be permitted by subjects unless they have some degree of assurance that the change will be for the "better." To make such assurances (even very modestly) requires a cognitive map, or theory, of the new world and why it may be more effective. Such a map would be a prescriptive one and the development of such normative maps has hitherto been looked upon with disfavor. One of the reasons for this negative attitude has been the fear that to study normative questions and to develop maps with prescriptive implications necessarily means that the researcher must take a normative position about what the organization should look like. This is not necessarily the case. There are several strategies that researchers may take to understand these normative states of affairs.

The first strategy is to conduct research that increases knowledge about the alternatives open to the client and that provides him with an increasing opportunity for informed and free choice.

An example of such research may be the study of job enlargement under differently enlarged or enriched conditions. Such research may well provide insights into employee motivation, performance, and job satisfaction (Goodman, 1969; Hackman and Lawler, 1971; Scott, 1966). Moreover, such research may help industrial psychologists to preserve the importance and relevance of individual differences which tend to be suppressed in the highly specialized jobs designed by job simplification experts. As Cronbach and Gleser (1965, p. 143) have pointed out, the psychologist is competing with job simplification experts who are, in effect, treatment simplifiers. They are trying to make the job requirements so simple that selection would not be necessary. Their method is the more economical, for their changes may be more permanent while the tester must evaluate new employees forever.

Job enlargement may also provide a research setting where the alteration of individual differences may be studied. Tiffin (1946) has concluded that training "tends to increase individual differences in proportion to the complexity of the task in question" (p. 17). And later: "Whenever the effect of training has been to increase the magnitude of individual differences, a study of the task involved usually reveals it to be fairly complicated (i.e., it requires a fairly long learning period for the average individual to reach maximum level of performance)" (p. 17). In other words, if psychologists had a genuine scholarly interest in studying the alteration of individual differences, which could also lead to insights into their causal processes, the study of job enlargement would provide such an opportunity.

Such research may also have consequences for raising the ability levels in the total society. Apparently, the Russians have concentrated less on testing and differentiating students and more on developing the most efficient means of raising the total educational level of society. There is evidence that they are succeeding (Goslin, 1963, p. 37). Interestingly, Goslin suggests that such a program tends to generate high enthusiasm and motivation on the part of the students and faculty because it focuses on growth and development opportunities.

The second strategy is to conduct studies that identify inconsistencies between what the clients want for their system and what they are getting. The researcher does *not* decide what they should want; he helps them to see if they are accomplishing their goals. Part of the study may focus on discrepancies among individuals' goals or between individuals' and the systems' goals.

For example, the clients may say that they want employees who are committed to the organization, who take risks, and who are productive. The researcher may show them that the pyramidal structure, the administrative controls, and the style of leadership all tend to cause employee apathy, indifference, lower productivity, and to reduce risk-taking.

The third strategy is for the researcher to examine the validity of the criteria the client system used for defining success. For example, it may be that low turnover and absenteeism could be signs of system illness as well as health. In some cases it may be that the organization has minimal turnover and absenteeism because the people are not required to be responsible for being productive. In other cases, high absenteeism may be necessary because it provides the involved and committed people a periodic respite from extreme pressure. Without absenteeism they might quit or become less involved.

A fourth strategy is to conduct research which helps people to explore more meaningfully what they want their norms and criteria to be. For example, research on the nature of human self-acceptance could suggest criteria for designing work which have hitherto been unexplored. Studies of the source of human energy and its variability could shed important light on employee productivity.

In none of these strategies is the researcher telling the client what he ought to desire, what criteria of system success he should use, or what values he should accept or reject. This is the domain of the client.

There is one way in which such research could become normative; it could focus on the study of the many informal activities that exist in organizations as well as the interpenetration of the formal and informal activities creating the "living system." These factors, we have suggested, have been part of the industrial psychologists' black box. Moreover, to study the "living system" of organization is difficult and would require the organizing and guiding power of theory (an activity shunned by industrial psychologists) and the temporary emphasis on naturalistic observation (a focus not valued by industrial psychologists).

There is another sense in which the systematic study of job enlargement (whether it is successful or not in the practical sense) may be instructive for industrial psychologists to consider. If one examines the Blum and Naylor (1968) book, and we have selected a book that is more supportive of expanding the interests of industrial psychologists, one will find that they discuss job enlargement for only half a page. Job analysis, on the other hand, is given an entire chapter. Sadly, detailed descriptions of job analysis, the activity that describes the world of work as it is, receives a much more thorough treatment than job enlargement, the activity that describes the world of work as it might become or, perhaps, should be.

However, there is one area in which the researcher may have to become more normative in his relationships with the client. This is the area of how the information will be obtained, how a valid diagnosis can be made, how the client can be helped to make informed choices, and how clients can monitor their own decisions once implemented. Thus the processes of diagnosis and intervention will require a normative position.

Formidable as these challenges may be, I should like to suggest that we have no – or should not seek any other – alternative. Such research is necessary if the original, academic goal of understanding human behavior is to be achieved. Studies of this type are needed, for example, to develop valid knowledge about the interaction of individuals (and their individual differences) in environments (that are also different).

The second reason such research is necessary is that the universe of social sciences is an "ought"-oriented, normative universe. It is composed of what mankind considers how people ought and ought not to behave. This universe, unlike the universe of the physical sciences, is continually subject to change. The changes, until now, have been made by individuals and groups who are not utilizing social scientific knowledge. Therefore, the changes represent what the groups in a particular generation wish to alter.

Perhaps it is time that social scientists take more initiative to conduct descriptive research that sheds light on normative issues such as the design of more effective human relationships and the quality of life within complex systems. For example, it seems that experiential learning theory and technology could help to produce a pattern B world where openness, trust, and expression of feelings are high. Under these conditions dissonance reduction, attribution, and social evaluation could be so reduced that they would no longer play a central role in social psychological theory (Argyris, 1969).

To the extent that changes are created by non-social scientists, the social scientist relegates himself (and has been by society, gladly relegated) to a passive position of observing and documenting changes. In the course of human events, the social scientist becomes the keeper of the minutes, a scribe, a role which he would probably resist in most groups to which he belongs.

If one realizes that change is going on all the time, he should also realize that the issue becomes one of how much one wishes to influence such changes. I believe social scientists should wish to influence such changes, *not* by telling people what to do, but by providing relevant valid information and by creating conditions for open interchange, free choice, and the likelihood of internal commitment to the choices made (Argyris, 1971). They can help create a process of change that will help to increase the probability that the new behavioral requirements are as effective as was possible to design. They could also help to design monitoring systems to evaluate the changes made, and to continue designing changes.

Two other reasons that social scientists may wish to include themselves in the activity of redesigning the universe may be inferred from the research on interpersonal relations described previously (Argyris, 1969). People who live in a pattern A world do not tend to generate valid information about threatening issues. One example of a threatening issue is basic change in the system. Consequently, there is little monitoring of the system and much prohibition against change. The result is that those who are disaffected tend to withdraw or to become angry and aggressive. People who have psychologically withdrawn will rarely effect change. People who are angry and aggressive may effect change but in ways that reduce free choice and internal commitment to the people.

Moreover, under conditions of festering frustration, pent up hostility, and eventually open aggression, there is every reason to question whether or not the agents for change will seek or even recognize valid information. If they do not, the prognosis for any long-range effectiveness of the change cannot be an optimistic one. Indeed, the prognosis for even descriptive research is not encouraging if the subjects have difficulties in generating valid information.

*How Can Research Technology be Designed that Does Not Unintentionally
Require the Acceptance of the Status Quo in the Universe?*

A third area for exploration is how to design research methods whose nature is less congruent with the mechanistic pyramidal relationships and more congruent with organic relationships.

This will not be an easy objective to achieve. There is need for more emphasis on combining clinical and measurement approaches (Alderfer, 1967; Kahn et al., 1964; Porter, 1966) and longitudinal research and time series design (Alderfer and Lodahl, 1971; Argyris, 1965; Lawler and Hackman, 1969; Scheflen, et al., 1970). It may also be necessary to overcome the mistrust that people have begun to develop about empirical research (Argyris, 1968; Kelman, 1968). There may be some individuals who cannot be involved even if the research is designed correctly. For example, people with poor mental health may reject participating in research (Westley and Epstein, 1969).

Some dimensions that describe differences between mechanistic and organic research and may be worth empirical study are:

| *In a mechanistically oriented research* | *In an organically oriented research* |
|---|---|
| 1  The interventionist takes the most prominent role in defining the goals of the program. | 1  The subjects participate in defining goals, confirming and disconfirming, and modifying or adding to those goals defined by the professionals. |
| 2  The interventionist assumes that his relationship of being strictly professional is not influenceable by the clients. He maintains his power of expertise and, therefore, a psychological distance from the clients. | 2  The interventionist realizes that, in addition to being a professional, he is also a stranger in the institution. Subjects should be encouraged to confront and test relationships. His power over the subjects, due to his professional competence, is equalized by his encouragement to them to question him and the entire program. |
| 3  The interventionist controls the amount of client participation in the project. | 3  Both client and interventionist determine the amount of client participation. |
| 4  Interventionist depends upon the client's need for help or need to cooperate to be the basis for their involvement. Expects clients to be used as information givers. | 4  Interventionist depends upon the client's need for help to encourage internal involvement in the control and definition of the program. The client feels as responsible as the interventionist. |
| 5  If participation is encouraged, it tends to be only skin-deep, designed to keep subjects "happy." | 5  Participation is encouraged in terms of designing instruments, research methods, and change strategy. |
| 6  The costs and rewards of the change program are defined primarily by the interventionist. | 6  The costs and rewards of the change program are defined by the clients and the interventionist. |
| 7  Feedback to subjects is designed to inform them how much the diagnostician learned about the system, as well as how professionally competent was the diagnosis. | 7  Feedback to subjects is designed to unfreeze them, as well as to help them develop more effective interpersonal relations and group processes. |

It should be noted that the organic dimensions involve providing the subjects a greater opportunity for free choice internal involvement with the research so that they will help the researchers produce valid information. Organic research does *not* alter the value of such activities as constructing theory, developing operational definition, stating hypotheses, using control groups, or making statistical analyses.

The second challenge is to strive to collect data by the use of instruments that integrate diagnosis and change, analysis and development (individual or organizational). If instruments are designed to create temporary systems or settings for the subject which produces information in terms of directly observable categories, attributions and evaluations can then be made by the researcher or the subject. Each is then required to show explicitly how he progressed from the directly observable behavior to the inferences that he made. One example is in the use of tape recordings. A group meeting can be studied, individual behavior observed, and inferences made by the researcher. When he gives the feedback of his results, he presents the inferred categories (e.g., how much openness, trust, and risk-taking was observed) and connects these inferred categories to actual portions of the tapes. This permits the subjects to see unambiguously how the inferences were made by the professional. Dependency on the professional and the mystery–mastery relationship (Bakan, 1968) may be reduced. The subject is less likely to feel, as Blum and Naylor (1968, p. 97) have suggested, that the tests are unfair, that they are imposed, and that he is unable to estimate whether he is doing poorly or well. It may also help to reduce some of the "seven deadly sins" (Gellerman, 1958) of selection, such as overdependence upon expert opinion, careless treatment of candidates, and poor estimates of job requirements.

Some readers may wonder why these problems cannot be overcome by the use of unobtrusive measures. Have not Webb, et al. (1966) shown that instruments can be designed that do not interfere with ongoing life and, therefore, can generate accurate data?

Unfortunately, there are at least two difficulties with the accounts of unobtrusive measures published to data. First, they do not provide a direct basis for change. Thus, the observation of where the floor tiles were worn tells us much about the most popular paintings in a gallery, but they provide little insight into why this is so. A more damaging criticism is that unobtrusive measures raise serious ethical issues. Should people be aware that they are being studied? Should their consent be genuinely sought? If not, social scientists could create the same ethical problems created by those (especially in law enforcement agencies) who wish to "bug" rooms, telephones, etc. in order to obtain data. It is our hypothesis that subjects will be most highly involved in providing valid data about issues important to them *if* they are active participants in the research and have consented to the study.

A final point that needs to be made is related to the ethical issue involved in using the generalizations obtained from rigorous (mechanistically oriented) experimental research. Generalizations obtained from research ought to "work" (in the sense that they account for substantial portions of the nonrandom variance) only in life situations which are analogous to the experimental situations in which the original data were collected. In industry, the analogous situation to the mechanistically oriented experimental research is one that contains authoritarian relationships and provides for social isolation of the participants (Argyris, 1968). The ethical difficulties arise when individuals utilize generalizations obtained through mechanistically oriented research to change people's needs and to coerce them into making choices that reflect the researcher's choices.

An example is the recent work of Varela who utilizes generalizations and methods derived from mechanistically oriented experimental learning theories. If one analyzes his strategy, Varela treats his subjects exactly the way learning theorists treat their animal subjects (Zimbardo and Ebbesen, 1969). For example, Varela is continuously in control of the situation. He openly states that he is responsible for planning the "powerful manipulations" in order to make people buy (curtains) during a time period that they have never done so before, even though the country is in a depression and curtains are not urgently needed by the population. Varela keeps his tactics secret; if he succeeds he will do so whether the subject likes it or not – indeed the subject may even be manipulated into liking it. The subject has little opportunity for free choice to develop internal commitment to "his" decision. By using the theory of reactance (the view that a communication that is seen as attempting to influence will tend also to be seen as a threat to one's freedom to decide for one's self) and by continued reinforcement, Varela manipulates people into buying curtains in hitherto unheard-of quantites. For example, Varela manipulates the customer to expand "his latitude of acceptance" of buying. He then manipulates the customer into systematically altering his views of a rival company. Much of this is done in accordance with those experimental learning theories in which attitudes are changed by manipulating the individual to justify his behavior (because he put the salesman to the trouble of getting out the samples, an act Varela aimed at from the beginning).

Perhaps this is enough to make two points that are relevant to our analysis. Varela's paradigm may be neutral but his way of putting it into effect is theory X-indeed $X^3$. Varela gets into difficulty because he uses the experimental setting as his model for interpersonal relationships between the influencer and the influence. He uses the model because this is the type of setting in which the generalizations were developed (Argyris, 1966, pp. 189–90). The experimental setting is, as we have noted, based upon theory X. It is ironic that Miller (1969, p. 1070) recently cited Varela's work as an excellent example of applied research.

## How Can Systematic Knowledge Be Produced that Enhances the Competence of the Systems Being Studied?

Theoretically, a sophisticated selection system could reduce many management problems. If there were effective selection and proper job placement, presumably the organization difficulties might be reduced. But so may some of the challenges that face executives today. Moreover, individuals who believe that selection can be an ultimate solution could unintentionally lead to a psychological set that influences the individual to see fewer problems and less need for radical changes (Alderfer, 1972). Also, if the match between people and system is so perfect, there is a strong tendency for the system to resist, indeed to be unaware of the necessity for, change (Argyris, 1965; Culbert, 1969).

Another alternative that may be profitably explored is the extension of the applicability of knowledge. This will not be an easy task to accomplish.

The applicability of behavioral science knowledge has traditionally been based on identifying the relevant variables, studying them systematically, verifying them publicly, and incorporating them into increasingly comprehensive and logically consistent theories. Although all fields can improve on these activities, we have suggested that industrial psychology may have to focus especially on identifying the relevant variables and on producing theories that are empirically verified.

The applicability of behavioral science knowledge also depends on two other activities that to date may not have received the attention they deserve. The first is the development of rigorous research methods that take into account the nature of man (his needs, his defenses, the social mores, and cultural norms that he has internalized). As we have noted, such methods should probably fall toward the organic ends of the continua described above. The second factor is related to the usability of knowledge.

Usability of knowledge is partly a function of semantic clarity. Although this can be a difficult barrier because all groups (including practitioners) have their "jargonese," let us assume that the problem is solvable if the parties find it worthwhile to learn each other's language.

The more difficult and relatively unexplored aspect of usability is related to the form knowledge must be in if man is to be able to use it (even though he may understand it). The very nature of man may create constraints on the form and kind of knowledge that is usable. Man, as the applier, may need knowledge that is in somewhat different form than that which behavioral scientists tend to produce when they aspire to being rigorous.

Some behavioral scientists may argue that their responsibility is simply to generate valid knowledge. It is someone else's responsibility to put it in usable form. This position may make sense if the behavioral scientist takes on responsibility to train the "someone" else to do it and does it well. Unless knowledge does become more applicable, man may become so disenchanted with behavioral science that he may fight the development of further know-ledge or he may become so disinterested that he may withdraw from its development. In either case, the behavioral scientist would be in difficulty because the motivations associated with either stance would not, as a minimum, encourage people to give (consciously or unconsciously) valid data.

There is another argument, that presently may be less visible, but is worthy of considera-tion. If the researcher decides to separate himself from the problem of application, the resulting stance may create internal processes within the researcher that may tend to distort or constrain the kind of knowledge that he may obtain, and the kind of theories that he may create. For example, having separated the development of knowledge from its applicability, many behavioral scientists have stated that the objective of research should be primarily the development of descriptive knowledge. They have ignored, and in some cases openly condemned, normative research. There are at least two unintended consequences of such a stance. The first is a result of testing the theory by creating the variables being studied and then changing them systematically. But, if one is going to change variables systematically, society will probably permit the change only if it is in a "good" direction. What is a good direction? Who will define what is good? One possible answer is to leave that to the man on the street or to the politicians. Another possibility as for behavioral scientists to take normative positions based upon the existing descriptive research (as has been done with the issue of integration). The separation between research on "is" and on "ought" may be an artificial one if we keep in mind that the "ought" in human behavior comes from what "is." People behave at time $t_1$ or $t_2, \ldots, t_n$ like they behaved at time $t_0$ because they believe that the behavior at $t_0$ is good for them.

A second problem with separating descriptive and normative questions may be illustrated by a recent analysis of consistency and attribution theories currently popular in social psychology (Argyris, 1969). The theories were confirmed by the empirical data collected by the writer. However, certain data collected from normative research showed that if human beings behaved in accordance with these theories, they would tend to create and maintain ineffective interpersonal relationships.

When asking how systematic knowledge can be produced which enhances the com-petence of the system, it is profitable to examine the constraints on the use of that know-ledge. Two very important constraints are related to man's mechanisms for thinking and problem solving (Simon, 1969) and his mechanisms for seeking to enhance his sense of competence (White, 1956).

Beginning with the sense of competence, recent preliminary research suggests that man as an activist may tend to feel successful when he makes self-fulfilling prophecies (i.e., make things come true). In striving to make these self-fulfilling prophecies he marshals all the resources available to him. Also he may make his behavior redundant and overdetermined in order to increase the probability that he will succeed. He will be especially conscious that ambiguity will tend to be high while the time available to solve the problem will tend to be little.

To make matters more difficult, Simon's recent work on thinking suggests that man's machinery for thought is finite and relatively simple. It is the environment that is complex. Man may need much time to work out a problem because he has to go through a laborious process of examining his memory (which is in the form of lists) and matching the problem as he conceives it with the knowledge stored up in his mind. The relevance of this knowledge to our problem is that under conditions of ambiguity and complexity the time available is frequently inadequate. Under these conditions man's thinking capacities are most taxed. Given these constraints, how can knowledge be "packaged" so that it is most useful to man as an activist?

First, knowledge should be stated in the form of units that are usable by man. Research needs to be conducted concerning the size of unit with which man can deal. It is the writer's experience that much research is stated in units that are much more molecular than the human mind can use effectively. It is as if man is capable of thinking primarily in feet while much research is defined (in order to be rigorous) in inches.

Second, if we were to take seriously the aspirations to develop generalizations such as X varies monotonically with Y, then the number of such generalizations needed to accurately describe the complexity of the noncontrived world would probably lead to generalizations which would become as difficult to utilize and manage as (at least) a complex chess game. The reaction of the user will be, according to Simon, to develop heuristics which greatly simplify the generalizations without losing too much of their usability. If so, perhaps we should take more interest in developing the heuristics for the practitioner to assure their proper translation of the rigorous generalization. Developing these heuristics will be no easy task. However, as Simon indicates, it is possible to do so and can be systematically studied.

One may conjecture that such heuristics would be statements that take into account man's apparent capacity to overdetermine, and to be redundant, and to use variables that stand up under conditions of noise or ambiguity. The calculus of heuristics may turn out to be sloppy (compared to precise mathematical formulations). This conjecture may not be too unreal. As Von Neumann has suggested, the capacity to use sloppy categories and yet make accurate predictions may be a basic characteristic that distinguishes the human being from other problem solving unities, be they animal or computer (Von Neumann, 1958).

Third, scientific generalizations may have to be stated in a form in which man can utilize his capacity and need to make self-fulfilling prophecies. This means that man may prefer generalizations that specify the variables that are relevant more than the systematic empirical generalizations about relationships among the variables (e.g., X varies monotonically with Y). He may prefer a theory that specifies the possible relevant variables more than knowledge about the potency of the variables. For example, a group of executives preferred the following theoretical but untested generalization (i.e., an hypothesis): The higher up one goes in the organizational hierarchy, the more potent are the interpersonal relationships and the less the individuals tend to trust each other, to the generalization that was inferred from empirical research that specifying a quantifiable relationship between trust, on the one hand, and position in the hierarchy and length of time on the job on the other (Alderfer, 1967; Hall and Lawler, 1968).

The reasons for the preference for the less rigorously tested generalizations are that it apparently provided the executives with the knowledge that they needed in order to create their own self-fulfilling prophecies. The more they used generalizations that spelled out rigorously the relationships among the variables, the less they felt that they could attribute success to their efforts; therefore, the less the possibility of psychological success and of feeling competent.

Moreover, given the necessary incompleteness of most generalizations, the executives expect that most behavioral sciences generalizations will tend to be inadequate. Consequently, they may prefer decision-making processes where they design the sequence of steps and then elicit corrective feedback, and where they define the relationships among the variables so that they can but more overtly diplomatic in the way they handle their intragroup conflict. No one will gain if this happens.

## Notes

1 Recently, because of race issues, the impact of white and black testers has been studied. However, even in these studies the interpersonal dynamics have been only minimally explored (Sattler, 1970). For a recent study that focuses on interpersonal factors, see Alderfer and McCord (1970).
2 One way to judge the defensiveness of an article is to note if the writers utilize logic and argument that they condemn others for using. Hulin and Blood's (1968) article is full of such examples. They condemn the use of anecdotal evidence to make points, yet they state, with no evidence, that the experience of an assembly-line worker is significantly different from the experimental settings where vigilance decrements were reliably obtained. They decry the use of generalizations that ignore individual differences, yet they make generalizations about the influence the grandfathers and fathers have upon the present employees which ignore individual differences and which are not supported with empirical evidence. They hypothesize that workers may feel hesitant to admit that they are *not* dissatisfied with their work to interviewers when the overwhelming evidence is that workers freely make such statements (Argyris, 1960; Blauner, 1960; Goldthorpe, et al., 1968). They make inferences that interviewers can bias the results when the evidence for such biases come from selection interviews or marketing and public opinion studies. Even these studies recently suggest that verbal reinforcement does alter the responses *and* the responses turn out to be more accurate (Cannell, 1969).
3 Another problem with leadership inventories (and many other instruments that depend upon variance for their validity) is that the dimensions used are those that differentiate among respondents and not those that are common to all the respondents. Perhaps these results should be included because many insights may reside in the qualities or attributes in which there is little variance.

## References

Adams, J. S., 1963, "Toward an Understanding of Inequity," *Journal of Abnormal and Social Psychology*, 67, pp. 422–36.
Alderfer, C., 1967, "The Organizational Syndrome," *Administrative Science Quarterly*, 12, 3, pp. 440–60.
Alderfer, C., 1971, "The Effect of Individual, Group, and Intergroup Relations on Attitudes Toward a Management Development Program," *Journal of Applied Psychology*, 55, pp. 302–11.
Alderfer, C., 1972, "Conflict Resolution among Behavioral Scientists," *Professional Psychology*, 3, pp. 41–7.
Alderfer, C., and Lodahl, T. A., 1971, "Quasi-experiment on the Use of Experiential Methods in the Classroom," *Journal of Applied Behavioral Science*, 7, 1, pp. 43–70.
Alderfer, C., and McCord, C. G., 1970, "Personal and Situational Factors in the Recruitment Interview," *Journal of Applied Psychology*, 54, 4, pp. 377–85.
Anastasi, A., 1965, *Differential Psychology*, New York, Macmillan.
Andrews, J. D., 1967, "The Achievement Motive and Advancement in Two Types of Organizations," *Journal of Personality and Social Psychology*, 6, pp. 163–8.
Argyris, C., 1957, *Personality and Organization*, New York, Harper & Row.
Argyris, C., 1958, "Some Problems in Conceptualizing Organizational Climate: A Case Study of a Bank," *Administrative Science Quarterly*, 2, 4, pp. 501–20.
Argyris, C., 1960, *Understanding Organizational Behavior*, Homewood, Ill., Dorsey Press.

Argyris, C., 1964, *Integrating the individual and the organization*, New York, Wiley.

Argyris, C., 1965, *Organization and Innovation*, Homewood, Ill., Irwin.

Argyris, C., 1966, *Some Causes of Organizational Ineffectiveness within the Department of State*, Center for International Systems Research, Department of State, November.

Argyris, C., 1968, "Some Unintended Consequences of Rigorous Research," *Psychological Bulletin*, 70, 3, pp. 185–97.

Argyris, C., 1969, "The Incompleteness of Social-Psychological Theory," *American Psychologist*, 24, 10, pp. 893–908.

Argyris, C., 1970, *Intervention Theory and Method*, Reading, MA, Addison-Wesley.

Argyris, C., 1971, "Management Information Systems: The Challenge to Rationality and Emotionality," *Management Science*, February, 17, pp. 275–92.

Bakan, D., 1968, *Disease, Pain, and Sacrifice*, Chicago, University of Chicago Press.

Banks, O., 1960, *The Attitude of Steelworkers to Technological Change*, England, University Press of Liverpool.

Barker, R. G., and Wright, H. F., 1955, *Midwest and its Children*, Evanston, Ill., Row, Peterson.

Bass, B. M., 1959, "An Approach to the Objective Assessment of Successful Leadership," in B. M. Bass and Berg, I. A. (eds), *Objective Approaches to Personality Assessment*, New York, Van Nostrand, ch. 8.

Bennis, W. G., 1966, *Changing Organization*, New York, McGraw-Hill.

Blake, R. R., and Mouton, J. S., 1969, *Building a Dynamic Corporation Through Grid Organization Development*, Reading, MA, Addison-Wesley.

Blauner, R., 1960, "Work Satisfaction and Industrial trends in Modern Society," in Galenson, W. and Lipset, S. M. (eds), *Labor and Trade Unionism: An interdisciplinary reader*, New York, Wiley, pp. 339–60.

Blood, M. R., 1969, "Work Values and Job Satisfaction," *Journal of Applied Psychology*, 53, 6, pp. 456–9.

Blum, M. L., and Naylor, J. C., 1968, *Industrial Psychology*, New York, Harper & Row.

Braithwaite, R. B., 1956, *Scientific Explanation*, Cambridge, England, University of Trinity College.

Bray, D. W., and Grant, D. L., 1966. "The Assessment Center in the Measurement of Potential for Business Management," *Psychological Monographs*, 80, 17, Whole No. 625.

Buhler, C., 1962, *Values in Psychology*, New York, Free Press of Glencoe, pp. 36–9.

Cannell, C., 1969, "Interactions of respondent interviews examined," *ISR Newsletter*, Institute for Social Research, University of Michigan, Ann Arbor, 1, 4, pp. 5–7.

Cronbach, L. J., and Gleser, G. C., 1965, *Psychological Tests and Personnel Decisions*, Urbana, University of Illinois Press.

Culbert, S. A., 1969, "Organization Renewal Using Internal Conflicts to Solve External Problems", mimeograph, paper presented Annual IRRA conference, December 29, Graduate School of Business, University of California at Los Angeles.

DeNelsky, G. Y., and McKee, M. G., 1969, "Prediction of Job Performance from Assessment Reports: Use of a Modified Q-sort Technique to Expand Predictor and Criterion Variance," *Journal of Applied Psychology*, 53, 6, pp. 439–45.

DuBois, P. H., 1960, "Individual Differences," *Annual Review of Psychology*, 2, pp. 225–54.

Dunnette, M. D., 1962, "Personnel Management," *Annual Review of Psychology*, 13, pp. 285–314.

Dunnette, M. D., 1966, *Personnel, Selection and Placement*, Belmont, CA., Wadsworth Publishing.

Dunnette, M. D., 1972, "Research Needs of the Future in Industrial and Organizational Psychology," *Personnel Psychology*, 25, pp. 31–40.

Dunnette, M. D., and Campbell, J. P., 1969, *Development of the Penney Career Index: Final Technical Report*, mimeograph, Minneapolis, University of Minnesota.

Dunnette, M. D., and Kirchner, W. K., 1965, *Psychology Applied to Industry*, New York, Appleton-Century-Crofts.

Fleishman, E. A., 1953, "Leadership Climate, Human Relations Training, and Supervisory Behavior," *Personnel Psychology*, 6, pp. 205–22.

Forehand, G. A., and Gilmer, B. von H., 1964, "Environment Variation in Studies of Organizational Behavior," *Psychological Bulletin*, 6, 2, pp. 361–82.

Frederiksen, N., 1966, "In-basket Tests and Factors in Administrative Performance," in Anastasi, A. (ed.), *Testing Problems in Perspective*, Washington, DC, American Council on Education, pp. 208–21.

Fromm, E., 1941, *Escape from Freedom*, New York, Rinehart.

Gardner, J., 1968, "America in the Twenty-third Century," *New York Times*, July, 27.

Gellerman, S. W., 1958, "Seven Deadly Sins of Executive Placement," *Management Review*, 47, pp. 4–9.

Ghiselli, E. E., and Brown, C. W., 1955, *Personnel and Industrial Psychology*, New York, McGraw-Hill.

Gilmer, B. von H., 1960, "Industrial Psychology," *Annual Review of Psychology*, 11, pp. 323–50.

Goldthorpe, H., Lockwood, D., Bechhofer, F., and Platt, J., 1968, *The Affluent Worker: Industrial Attitudes and Behavior*, England, Cambridge University Press.

Goodman, R., 1969, "Job Content and Motivation: A Hypothesis," *Industrial Engineering*, May, 40–6.

Gordon, R. A., and Howell, J. E., 1959, *Higher Education for Business*, New York, Columbia University Press.

Goslin, D. A., 1963, *The Search for Ability*, New York, Russell Sage Foundation.

Gouldner, A. W., 1960, "The Norm of Reciprocity: A Preliminary Statement," *American Sociological Review*, 25, pp. 161–79.

Guion, R. M., 1965, *Personnel Testing*, New York, McGraw-Hill.

Hackman, J. R., and Lawler, III., E. E., 1971, "Employee Reactions to Job Characteristics," *Journal of Applied Psychology Monographs*, 55, 3, 259–86.

Hall, D. R., and Lawler, E., 1968, *Attitude and Behavior Patterns in Research and Development Organizations*, New Haven: Sponsored by Connecticut Research Commission and Department of Administrative Sciences, Yale University, May.

Hanson, N. R., 1958, *Patterns of Discovery*, England, Cambridge University Press.

Herzberg, F., 1966, *Work and the Nature of Man*, Cleveland, World Publishing.

Hinrichs, J. R., 1970, "Psychology of Men at Work," *Annual Review*, 21, pp. 519–54.

Homans, G., 1961, *Social Behavior: Its Elementary Form*, New York, Harcourt, Brace.

Hulin, C. L., and Blood, M. R., 1968, "Job Enlargement, Individual Differences, and Workers Resources," *Psychological Bulletin*, 69, 1, pp. 41–55.

Kahn, R. L., Wolfe, D. M., Quinn, R. P., Snoek, J. D., and Rosenthal, R. A., 1964, *Organizational Stress: Studies in Role Conflict and Ambiguity*, New York, Wiley.

Kaplan, A., 1964, *The Conduct of Inquiry*, San Francisco, Chandler Publishing.

Kelman, H. C., 1968, *A Time to Speak*, San Francisco, Jossey-Bass.

Koch, S., 1956, "Behavior as 'Intrinsically' Regulated: Work Notes Toward a Pre-theory of Phenomenon called Motivation," in Jones, R. (ed.), *Nebraska Symposium on Motivation*, Lincoln, University of Nebraska Press.

Korman, A. K., 1966, "Consideration, Initiation Structure, and Organizational Criteria: A Review," *Personnel Psychology*, 19, 4, pp. 349–61.

Korman, A. K., 1971, *Industrial and Organizational Psychology*, Englewood Cliffs, NJ, Prentice-Hall.

Lawler, E., 1971, *Pay and Organizational Effectiveness: A Psychological View*, New York, McGraw-Hill.

Lawler, E. E. III, and Hackman, J. R., 1969, "Impact of Employee Participation in the Development of Incentive Plans," *Journal of Applied Psychology*, 53, 6, pp. 467–71.

Lewin, K., 1935, *A Dynamic Theory of Personality*, New York, McGraw-Hill, pp. 1–42.

Likert, R., 1967, *The Human Organization: Its Management and Values*, New York, McGraw-Hill.

Lodahl, R. M., 1964, "Patterns of Job Attitudes in Two Assembly Technologies," *Administrative Science Quarterly*, 8, 4, pp. 482–519.

Lowen, A., Hrapchak, W. J., and Kavanagh, M. J., 1969, "Consideration and Initiating Structure: An Experimental Investigation of Leadership Traits," *Administrative Science Quarterly*, 14, 2, pp. 238–53.

Mann, F. C., and L. K. Williams, 1962, "Some Effects of the Changing Work Environment in the Office," in Lundstedt, S. (ed.), *Mental Health and the Work Environment*, Foundation for Research on Human Behavior, pp. 16–30.

March, J. G., and Simon, H. A., 1958, *Organizations*, New York, Wiley.

McGregor, D., 1960, *The Human Side of Enterprise*, New York, McGraw-Hill.

McReynolds, P., 1971, "The Nature and Assessment of Intrinsic Motivation," in McReynolds, P. (ed.), *Advances in Psychological Assessment*, Vol. 2. Palo Alto, CA, Science and Behavior Books.

Meyer, H. H., Kay, E., and French, J. R. P., 1965, "Split Roles in Performance Appraisal," *Harvard Business Review*, 43, pp. 123–9.

Miller, G. A., 1969, "Psychology as a Means of Promoting Human Welfare," *American Psychologist*, 24, 12, pp. 1063–75.

Owens, W. A., and Jewell, D. O., 1969, "Personnel Selection," *Annual Review of Psychology*, 20, pp. 413–46.

Porter, L. W., 1966, "Personnel Management," *Annual Review of Psychology*, 17, 395–422.

Pugh, D. S., 1966, "Modern Organization Theory: A Psychological and Sociological Study," *Psychological Bulletin*, 66, 4, pp. 235–51.

Ryan, T. A., and Smith, P. C., 1954, *Principles of Industrial Psychology*, New York, Ronald Press.

Sattler, J., 1970, "Racial 'Experimenter Effects' in Experimentation, Testing, Interviewing, and Psychotherapy," *Psychological Bulletin*, 73, 2, pp. 137–60.

Scheflen, K. G., Lawler, III, E. E., and Hackman, J. R., 1970, "The Long-term Impact of Employee Participation in the Development of Pay Incentive Plans: A Field Experiment Revisited," *Journal of Applied Psychology*.

Schneider, B., 1969, "Some Differences Between Students about to Study Industrial Organizational Psychology in Psychology and Nonpsychology Departments," mimeograph, symposium, American Psychological Association, August 31, Department of Administrative Sciences, Yale University.

Schneider, B., and Bartlett, C. J., 1968, "Individual Differences and Organizational Climate: I, the Research Plan and Questionnaire Development," *Personnel Psychology*, 21, pp. 323–33.

Scott, W. E. Jr, 1966, "Activation Theory and Task Design," *Organizational Behavior and Human Performance*, 1, 1, pp. 3–30.

Simon, H., 1969, *The Science of the Artificial*, Cambridge, M.I.T. Press.

Sorcher, M., 1969, *The Effects of Employee Involvement on Work Performance*, New York, Personnel Research Planning and Practices, General Electric Company.

Storrs, A., 1963, *The Integrity of Personality*, Baltimore, Penguin Books.

Strauss, G., 1963, "Some Notes on Power-Equalization," in Leavitt, H. J. (ed.), *The Social Science of Organizations: Four Perspectives*, Englewood Cliffs, NJ, Prentice-Hall.

Tannenbaum, A. S., 1968, *Control in Organizations*, New York, McGraw-Hill.

Thornton, G. C., 1969, "Image of Industrial Psychology among Personnel Administrators," *Journal of Applied Psychology*, 53, 5, pp. 436–8.

Tiffin, J., 1946, *Industrial Psychology*, Englewood Cliffs, NJ, Prentice-Hall.

Tyler, L. E., 1959, "Toward a Workable Psychology of Individuality," *American Psychologist*, 14, pp. 75–85.

Vale, J. R., and Vale, C. A., 1969, "Individual Differences and General Laws in Psychology: A Reconciliation," *American Psychologist*, 24, 12, pp. 1093–108.

Von Neumann, J., 1958, *The Computer and the Brain*, New Haven, Yale University Press.

Webb, E. J., Campbell, D. T., Schwartz, R. D., and Sechrest, L., 1966, *Unobstrusive Measures: Nonreactive Research in the Social Sciences*, Chicago, Rand McNally.

Westley, W. A., and Epstein, M. B., 1969, *Silent Majority*, San Francisco, Jossey-Bass.

White, R., 1956, "Motivation Reconsidered: The Concept of Competence," *Psychological Review*, 66, pp. 297–334.

Whyte, W. F., 1969, *Organizational Behavior*, Homewood, Ill., Irwin.

Wrong, D., 1961, "The Over-socialized Conception of Man in Modern Sociology," *American Sociological Review*, 26, pp. 183–93.

Zimbardo, P., and Ebbesen, B., 1969, *Influencing Attitudes and Changing Behavior*, Reading, MA, Addison-Wesley.

# — 23 —

# The Incompleteness of Social-Psychological Theory: Examples from Small Group, Cognitive Consistency, and Attribution Research

Recently experimental and field-oriented social psychologists, reviewing small group research, have suggested that more research about groups should be conducted in natural settings (Golembiewski, 1962; McGrath and Altman, 1966; McGuire, 1967; Ring, 1967). Two purposes of such research are to see the extent to which (1) the findings from the experimental laboratory can be substantiated in the field and (2) the existing theoretical models reflect the noncontrived world.

The purposes of this chapter are (1) to present some findings about small groups in their natural settings and (2) to raise some questions that stem from the findings about the completeness of attribution theory, theories of cognitive balance, and social comparison theory.

## MAJOR CHARACTERISTICS OF THE RESEARCH STUDIES

Small groups were studied in ten organizations; four of which represented business and industry; two represented research and development laboratories; two represented consulting firms; one a large governmental bureau; and one a university executive development program. Twenty-eight groups were studied over time periods ranging from two months to two years. The number of meetings studied for every group ranged from 3 through 20 with the total number being 163 (see table 23.1). The groups, when studied, were accomplishing a wide variety of tasks such as: discussion and solution of investment decisions, production planning, quality control, engineering, new pricing, personnel problems, foreign policy, long-range planning, new product development, sales promotion, marketing, organizational changes, executive promotions, relationships with the White House, and the development and introduction of mathematical models to the management of business problems.

Also having a probable influence on the group's behavior was the fact that each group had a past history, a future perspective, a membership that was earned and continually confirmed, and all were embedded in a larger social system.

**Table 23.1** Major characteristics of the research studies

| | Type of group | Type of organization | Number in group | Length of study | Number of meetings studied | Total number behavioral units observed |
|---|---|---|---|---|---|---|
| 1 | Top management, heterogeneous Group A | Attendees at university executive development program (AUEDP) | 16 | 2 months | 3 | 540 |
| 2 | Group B | AUEDP | 15 | 2 months | 3 | 540 |
| 3 | Group C | AUEDP | 16 | 2 months | 3 | 540 |
| 4 | Group D | AUEDP | 15 | 2 months | 3 | 540 |
| 5 | Group E | AUEDP | 13 | 2 months | 3 | 540 |
| 6 | Group F | AUEDP | 14 | 2 months | 3 | 540 |
| 7 | Group G | AUEDP | 15 | 2 months | 3 | 540 |
| 8 | Group H | AUEDP | 15 | 2 months | 3 | 540 |
| 9 | Top management | Appliance manufacturer | 15 | 1 year | 8 | 1,626 |
| 10 | Middle management | Appliance manufacturer | 15 | 1 year 3 months | 4 | 1,520 |
| 11 | Top management | Large R&D organization | 10 | 8 months | 6 | 3,116 |
| 12 | Middle management | Large R&D organization | 13 | 8 months | 5 | 2,080 |
| 13 | Middle management | Large R&D organization | 13 | 8 months | 5 | 2,080 |
| 14 | Top management | Small R&D organization | 8 | 1 year | 5 | 1,910 |
| 15 | Middle management | Small R&D organization | 16 | 1 year | 5 | 1,910 |
| 16 | First-level management | Small R&D organization | 14 | 1 year | 5 | 1,412 |
| 17 | First-level management | Small R&D organization | 15 | 1 year | 5 | 1,412 |
| 18 | Top management | Consulting organization | 6 | 2 year | 7 | 2,430 |
| 19 | Middle management | Consulting organization | 18 | 2 year | 15 | 2,050 |
| 20 | Top management | Manufacturer: heavy equipment | 10 | 1 year 3 months | 9 | 2,496 |
| 21 | Middle management | Manufacturer: heavy equipment | 15 | 1 year 3 months | 3 | 750 |
| 22 | Middle management | Manufacturer: heavy equipment | 16 | 1 year 3 months | 4 | 1,500 |
| 23 | Lower level management | Manufacturer: heavy equipment | 14 | 1 year 3 months | 4 | 1,300 |
| 24 | Top management | Food processor | 10 | 9 months | 8 | 1,520 |
| 25 | Middle management | Food processor | 21 | 9 months | 8 | 1,500 |
| 26 | Top executives | Governmental bureau | 11 | 1 year | 10 | 1,810 |
| 27 | Middle management | Governmental bureau | 20 | 1 year | 10 | 1,500 |
| 28 | Internal consulting organization | Very large chemical manufacturer | 21 | 1 year | 13 | 7,560 |
| | Total | | 400 | | 163 | 45,802 |

## Research Methods

Three research methods were used to collect data: semistructured interviewing, question-naires, and nonparticipant observation. The primary research method, and the one upon which this chapter is largely based, was the observational method. In all meetings except seven, nonparticipant observers were present and tape recordings were also made. In the remaining seven meetings only tape recordings were made.

The observational categories used in this research are graphically summarized in table 23.2.[1] The categories above the zero line are hypothesized to facilitate interpersonal relationships, those below the line to inhibit interpersonal relationships. Each category has an idea (i) and a feeling (f) component. The categories positioned closest to the zero line are the easiest to perform and those farthest away are the most difficult. For example, it is easier to own up to one's ideas or feelings (to express one's views and feelings) than it is to experiment with ideas or feelings (to discuss those ideas or feelings that, if wrong, would risk one's self-acceptance). There are two levels of analyses. Level I represents the individual and interpersonal. Level II represents norms of the group. Every unit of behavior is scored on both levels. For example:

|   |   | Would be scored as | |
|---|---|---|---|
| 1 | I believe that we should reject the idea even though we are told not to. | own i | individuality i |
| 2 | I feel tense. | own f | individuality f |
| 3 | Would you please tell me more about your theory? | open i | concern i |
| 4 | This is not easy for me to talk about. I feel like my whole life has been a shambles. I feel frightened and bewildered. | experimenting f | trust f |

**Table 23.2**  Categories of behavior

| Individual | | Level I Interpersonal | | Norms | Level II |
|---|---|---|---|---|---|
| Experimenting | i | Help others to experiment | i | Trust | i |
|  | f |  | f |  | f |
| Openness | i | Help others to be open | i | Concern | i |
|  | f |  | f |  | f |
| Owning | i | Help others to own | i | Individuality | i |
|  | f |  | f |  | f |
| ................................................ | | ..............Zero line.............. | | ................................................ | |
| Not owning | i | Not help others to own | i | Conformity | i |
|  | f |  | f |  | f |
| Not open | i | Not help others to be open | i | Antagonism | i |
|  | f |  | f |  | f |
| Rejecting experimenting | i f | Not helping others to experiment | i f | Mistrust | i f |

*Note*: Categories above zero line are hypothesized to facilitate interpersonal relationships, those below the line to inhibit interpersonal relationships. Each category has an idea (i) and a feeling (f) component. Categories positioned closest to zero line are easiest to perform and those farthest away the most difficult.

*Some Findings about the "Typical" Interpersonal World (Pattern A)*

A total of 45,802 units of behavior were recorded in 163 different meetings. Some of the relevant findings are as follows.

1   Only six categories (of the 36 available) were frequently observed. The categories used most frequently (i.e., they accounted for at least 75 percent of the scores in a given meeting) were (in order of frequency observed) own i, concern i, conform i. Categories that accounted for about 20 percent of the scores were open i, individuality i, and antagonism i. (The "i" means the behavior was observed to be intellective and not an expression of feelings.) The remaining 5 percent were spread variously over the other categories.
2   Rarely (and in most sessions, never) were individuals observed in groups expressing feelings, being open to feelings, experimenting with ideas or feelings. Rarely observed were the norms of concern, individuality, and trust related to feelings, the norm of trust related to ideas, and the norm of mistrust related to ideas or feelings.
3   Rarely observed were individuals in groups helping each other own up to, be open toward, and experiment with ideas or feelings. We will call this pattern of variables "pattern A."

Table 23.3 depicts a frequency distribution from 112 of the natural groups of pattern A representing 34,070 units and pattern B representing 3,610 observed units of behavior. At this point only the figures under pattern A are relevant to this discussion.[2] In the task groups (under A), in 56 percent of the meetings no feelings were expressed; in 24 percent of the meetings, 1 percent of the behavior were feelings. In one session feelings were 23 percent, and in another 35 percent, of the observed behavior. In both cases these represented sessions of great personal stress to the members. In the first one, the chairman of the board was insisting that he and half the board resign. In the second session the group was polarized about a major policy change. When the president gave the tape of the session to the researcher, he apologized for the "childish immaturity" and promised that it would never occur again. Three more board sessions were taped and scored. The president's prediction was confirmed (Argyris, 1965b, p. 95).

From these data one may infer that the interpersonal world of the individuals in the groups studied is one in which individuals tended to express their ideas in such a way that they supported the norms of concern for, or conformity to, ideas. They were significantly less open to ideas and expressed (slightly less so) their ideas in such a way that supported the norms of individuality or antagonism.

Individuals did not, nor did group norms, support their owning up to their feelings, being open to their own and others' feelings. There was almost no experimenting with ideas and feelings and also no trust existing in the groups. Rarely did individuals help others to own up to, be open with, and experiment with ideas and feelings. People rarely said what they believed about the important issues if they perceived them to be potentially threatening to any member. They preferred to be "diplomatic," "careful," "not make waves." Under these conditions, valid information about unimportant issues (task or interpersonal) was easy to obtain. It was very difficult to obtain valid information regarding important issues (task or interpersonal). It was very difficult to problem solve effectively about these important issues since people tended to cover up important information. Also, individuals rarely received valid information about threatening issues. For example, in a study of 199 important influence attempts (among a group of 20 executives over a period of a year), 134

**Table 23.3** Frequency of appearance of behavioral categories per meeting (percentage)

| Number of observations | Feelings except trust and mistrust | | Trust | | | | Mistrust | | | | Experimenting | | | | Helping others | | | |
|---|---|---|---|---|---|---|---|---|---|---|---|---|---|---|---|---|---|---|
| | | | f[c] | | i[d] | | f | | i | | f | | i | | f | | i | |
| | A[a] | B[b] | A | B | A | B | A | B | A | B | A | B | A | B | A | B | A | B |
| Up to 1 per cent | 56 | | 76 | | 1 | | 15 | | 15 | | 23 | | 23 | | — | 43 | — | |
| 1.1–2 | 24 | | 8 | | 8 | | | | | | | | 8 | | 23 | 16 | — | |
| 2.1–3 | 5 | | | | | | | | | | | | | | 30 | 12 | — | |
| 3.1–4 | 6 | | | | | | | | | | | | | | 23 | 9 | 46 | |
| 4.1–5 | 1 | | | | | | | | | | | | | | 23 | 3 | 54 | |
| 5.1–6 | | | | | | | | | | | | | | | | | | 3 |
| 6.1–7 | | | | | | | | | | | | | | | | | | 2 |
| 7.1–8 | | | 1 | | 1 | | | | | | 1 | | 1 | | | | | 2 |
| 8.1–9 | | | | | | | | | | | | | | | | | | |
| 9.1–10 | | | | | | | | | | | | | | | | | | |
| 13.1–14 | 1 | | | | | | | | | | | | | | | | | 2 |
| 14.1–15 | 2 | | | | | | | | | | | | | | | | | |
| 20.1–25 | 1 | 23 | | | | | | | | | | | | | | | | |
| 25.1–30 | | 15 | | | | | | | | | | | | | | | | |
| 30.1–35 | 1 | 8 | | | | | | | | | | | | | | | | |
| 35.1–40 | | 23 | | | | | | | | | | | | | | | | |
| 40.1–45 | | 15 | | | | | | | | | | | | | | | | |
| 45.1–50 | | 15 | | | | | | | | | | | | | | | | |

*Note*: Figures expressed in percentages.
[a] Pattern A: represents 112 meetings and 34,070 units of observed behavior.
[b] Pattern B: represents 13 T groups and 3,610 units of observed behavior.
[c] f = feeling component of category.
[d] i = idea component of category.

failed and 65 succeeded. In only two cases was honest feedback given about the failures. In all other cases the individual attempting to have the influence was assured that he had succeeded when, in fact, he had not. Of successes, 54 represented influence attempts made by the president. The observers reported that the influence attempts succeeded in that the president got the message across that he wanted. However, in 48 cases the subordinates felt hostile toward him. None of them communicated these feelings to the president (Argyris, 1962, pp. 77–98).

The game of telling people what they "should" hear and the consequent lack of valid information understandably led individuals to be blind about their impact upon others. However, they were able to be accurate (in an interview) about the impact others had on them (if they felt they could trust the researcher).

Several examples are presented below to illustrate the blindness individuals tended to manifest in the groups studied.

The study of Group 11 (see table 23.1) provided two examples of interpersonal blindness within the group and one between the group and the members' immediate subordinates. Group 11 (a top-management executive committee) was told, during the feedback of its results, that the researchers saw the members as not encouraging interpersonal risk-taking, openness, and owning of feelings, individuality, or trust. The executives disagreed. They admitted that negative feelings were not expressed, but said that the reason was that they trusted each other and respected each other (80 percent), that it was not in the interests of getting a job done to discuss feelings (70 percent). They described their climate as "friendly," "warm," "close relationship," and "mutual trust" (80 percent). The researchers concluded the opposite.

The executives and researchers agreed upon a field experiment. The next 25 executives would be interviewed, and among the questions there would be several on how they perceived the dynamics of the executive committee. These 25 were selected because they participated frequently in discussions with the executive committee. Table 23.4 summarizes the results. It shows that the subordinates were in strong agreement with the researchers' diagnosis.

**Table 23.4**  Subordinates' ratings of executive committee

| How would you rate the executive committee? ($n = 25$) | Low | | Moderate | | High | | Don't know | |
|---|---|---|---|---|---|---|---|---|
| | n | % | n | % | n | % | n | % |
| Openness to uncomfortable information | 12 | 48 | 6 | 24 | 4 | 16 | 3 | 12 |
| Risk-taking | 20 | 80 | 4 | 16 | 1 | 4 | | |
| Trust | | | 9 | 36 | 2 | 8 | | |
| Conformity | | | 2 | 8 | 23 | 92 | | |
| Ability to deal with interpersonal conflict | 19 | 76 | 6 | 24 | | | | |

The executive committee seemed surprised with the results. They asked for a meeting with the subordinates. The researcher was able to get the executive committee to agree that the invitation should be given so that the men could decline it. The researcher pushed for this alternative for two reasons. It would provide for another test of the analysis. If the researcher were correct, the subordinates would decline to attend. Equally important was the necessity for the subordinates not to be coerced into an embarrassing and potentially threatening situation. The results were as predicted. Only 3 out of the 25 subordinates agreed to come to such a meeting, with 2 abstentions.

Finally, the executive committee members gave contradictory statements during their interviews when they discussed their interpersonal relationships as well as their group's effectiveness. (The following display is an illustration of the contradictions. The first statement, numbered 1a, is an example of one statement made during one part of the interview; the second statement, numbered 1b, is an example of what was said later, in the same interview, etc. The percentages after each second statement represent the proportion of board members who manifested these apparent contradictions.) For example:

1a   The relationship among the executive committee members is "close," "friendly," and based upon years of working with each other.
1b   I do not know how my peers feel about me. That's a tough question to answer. (80 percent)
2a   I have an open relationship with my superior.
2b   I have no direct idea how he evaluates my work and feels about me. (70 percent)
3a   The strength of this company lies in its top people. They are a dedicated, friendly group. We never have the kinds of disagreements and fights that I hear others do.
3b   Yes, the more I think of it, the more that I think that this is a major weakness of the company. Management is afraid to hold someone accountable. They are afraid to say to someone, "You said you would do it, what happened?" (70 percent)
4a   We say pretty much what we feel.

4b   We are careful not to say anything that will antagonize anyone. (70 percent)

5a   The group discussions are warm, friendly, not critical.

5b   We trust each other not to upset one another. (70 percent)

6a   We have respect and faith in each other.

6b   People do not knowingly upset each other, so they are careful in what they say. (70 percent)

7a   The executive committee tackles all issues.

7b   The executive committee tends to spend too much time talking about relatively unimportant issues. (70 percent)

8a   The executive committee makes decisions quickly and effectively.

8b   One of the big problems of the executive committee is that it takes forever and a day to make important decisions. (60 percent)

9a   The executive committee makes the major policy decisions.

9b   On many of the major issues the decisions are really made outside the executive committee meetings. The executive committee convenes to approve a decision and have "holy water" placed on the decision. (50 percent)

10a   The members trust each other.

10b   The members are careful not to say something that may make another member look bad. It may be misinterpreted. (40 percent)

These results indicating interpersonal blindness were replicated in all our studies. Moreover, they extended in groups down the hierarchy (Argyris, 1965b). For example, members of Group 14 were unable to predict the feelings that their subordinates had about them; nor were they able to predict accurately their impact upon these subordinates. The subordinates, in turn, were blind to the impact of their subordinates, and so the findings continued until the first-line supervisor – where the research had ended (Argyris, 1965b, pp. 92–124).

An illustration of how strongly executives felt about, and yet feared the lack of, openness and trust came from a top executive group (which was an internal board of directors). They scheduled a meeting with their subordinates (in this case overriding the objections of the researcher) to discuss the research findings. When the meeting began, each executive was given a mimeographed set of results and asked to read them. A discussion was then held in which the researcher was to help engender an open exploration about the issues. The session was tape recorded. The majority of the subordinates carefully evaded all attempts to discuss the issues even when asked directly to do so. After three hours of futile attempts to discuss the subjects, the chairman called the meeting to a stop (Argyris, 1965b, pp. 113–21).

### Some Findings about the Atypical Interpersonal World (Pattern B)

It may be argued that the consistency of the findings may be due to the research method, which was the one consistent factor in all studies. This seems unlikely because groups have been observed to manifest a significantly different, but not discrete, pattern that may be called pattern B. Pattern B groups (see table 23.2) may be characterized as groups in which feelings are expressed and risks are taken; in which helping others to own, to be open, and to experiment occurs; and in which the norms of conformity and antagonism become less potent while the norms of individuality and trust become more potent (Argyris, 1965a).

For example, in 13 T (experiential) groups that were studied (column B in table 23.3), feelings were expressed in all meetings ranging from 20 to 50 percent of the total observed behavior.[3] Trust f scores represented up to 1 percent of the behavior in 76 percent of the sessions and up to 2 percent of the behavior in 8 percent of the sessions. In 23 percent of the sessions, 1 percent of the behavior was experimenting with ideas. The meaning of these scores is best indicated if it is recalled that no trust f scores and only 0.001 percent of experimenting with ideas were observed from nearly 35,000 units in the 112 tasks sessions.

It is also interesting to note that the only mistrust i or f scores were observed in T groups. These data suggest that T groups can produce much more "negative" behavior than regular task sessions. Finally, helping others to own up to, to be open with, and to experiment with feelings were only observed in the T groups. The T groups began with the typical pattern A and after several sessions, *if successful*, developed the atypical pattern B. The phrase "if successful" is emphasized because not all T groups become effective; indeed by our scoring methods a *minority* develop into pattern B. (This suggests empirical support for the criticism that T groups can become a new way to manipulate people according to the old [i.e., pattern A] rules). Task-oriented groups have also been changed to produce B inter-actions pattern. The development of pattern B therefore is not limited to T groups (Argyris, 1965b, pp. 174–9).

It may also be argued that the variables contained in our scheme are not central to individuals. If one criterion of centrality is the difficulty encountered in changing the behavior represented by the variables, then the data do not support this argument. For example, in the study just cited, a change to pattern B required a five-month change program. The studies of Groups 20 and 21 are also relevant to this issue. After receiving feedback of the diagnosis of their groups and discussing the findings for eight hours, the members decided that the diagnosis made by the researcher was accurate, that they wanted to change their behavior, and that they did not need any special reeducation to do so. They agreed to become more open with their feelings and to develop more trust. After two months of trying very hard, they gave up. They were frustrated with their own inability to keep all the "correct" behaviors in mind, especially when the discussion was a critical one that tended to cause regression to the original pattern. The members were also frustrated with the resistance of their subordinates who did not want to believe that their superiors wanted to change their behavior; who therefore resisted or ignored their superiors' attempts, which "proved" to the subordinates that they were correct about the superiors nongenuineness, which "proof" was further confirmed when their superiors "regressed" spontaneously during crucial decision-making meetings.

To conclude: We found in the "typical world" (pattern A) a tendency toward minimal expression of feelings, minimal openness to feelings, and minimal risk-taking with ideas or feelings. The most frequently observed norms were concerned for ideas (not feelings), and conformity (ideas). The norm of mistrust also tended to be high (but had to be inferred from other data than the observational scheme since individuals did not tend to show their mistrust openly).

The consequences of pattern A behavior were relatively ineffective interpersonal rela-tionships and ineffective problem solving of task issues that were important and loaded with feelings. When solutions were achieved, they did not tend to be lasting ones. The problems therefore seemed to recur continually. Finally, members seemed to be blind to the negative impact that they tended to have on others (partially because it violated the norms to give such feedback); they were accurately aware of the impact others have upon them, but careful not to communicate this impact openly or directly.

## The Individual as a Cause of Pattern A

Does this mean that individuals are part of interpersonal relationships in which their behavior is highly determined by factors "outside" themselves? The answer seems to be that individuals actually participate in, and reinforce the creation of, pattern A. The research suggests that human beings tend to hold values (defined as internalized commands) that would probably predispose them to create groups in a pattern A format.

During the research program several different methods were used to tap the values people held about effective interpersonal relationships. The simplest was a sentence-completion test. Examples of the sentences used are: "In a decision-making setting:

1   An effective leader is one who——.
2   The best member is one who——.
3   When disagreement erupts into personal feeling, the best thing for a leader to do is——."

The findings of the studies cited above show that in all groups (see table 23.1) more than 75 percent of the respondents completed the above sentences with answers such as:

1   is directive, controlling, leading;
2   is rational, objective, knows his topic;
3   avoid dealing with the interpersonal problem openly; get the members back to the task or subject of discussion.

These data suggest that individuals tend to hold three basic values about effective interpersonal relations.

1   In any given interpersonal relationship or group, the important behavior is that behavior that is related to the accomplishment of the purpose or task of the relationship or of the group.
2   Human effectiveness increases as people are rational and intellective. Human effectiveness decreases as people focus on interpersonal feelings and/or behave emotionally.
3   The most effective way to tap human energy and gain human commitment is through leadership that controls, rewards, and penalizes, and coordinates human behavior.

Individuals "programmed" with these values may be expected to focus on the rational and intellective, to suppress the emotional and interpersonal, and to employ norms that sanction conformity.

In *all* groups in which the majority of the members held these values, pattern A always resulted. In other words, a group populated with a majority of members with these values always created pattern A.

These findings are also supported indirectly by the published experiences of T groups (Argyris, 1962; Bradford, et al., 1964). These experiences are relevant because the purpose of the T group is not to develop pattern A. Thus in a situation in which pattern A is not desirable or required, individuals (who have never been in a T group before) frequently project onto the social vacuum created by the educator's initial withdrawal precisely the behavior that follows from the values above. For example, individuals begin to ask for (in some cases, demand) a task or an agenda; they urge each other to handle the vacuum with rationality; they admonish individuals to keep personalities out of the discussion; they ask that a chairman be appointed who will have power to control, direct, and coordinate.

These findings also suggest that the absence of feeling observed in the groups studied above is not due to the fact that all the groups were task-oriented groups, many of which were under pressure to make decisions. The fact that the same pattern of behavior occurs at the beginning of T groups indicates that pattern A is not significantly influenced by the task-oriented nature of the meetings.

If there is such a high correlation between these particular values and pattern A, then we are able to provide further data related to the generalizability of pattern A. For example, the writer has found that 350 undergraduates at his university tended to hold the values in the same proportions described above. Bolman (1967), who developed a more sophisticated instrument to study these values, has collected data from executives and from a range of respondents (housewives, YMCA workers, nurses, etc.) that support these findings. Steele (1968, 1969) has also collected data in his studies that support the above findings. His total sample was 413 and represented undergraduate and graduate students, top and middle management, executives, housewives, and professions such as nurses, teachers, and volunteer workers.

It is important to note that these values can be shown to be similar to the values implicit in formal organizational design. Apparently *any* organization that is structured in a pyramidal form, that uses the typical budgetary and accounting controls, that adheres to the concept of specialization, will tend to create a system whose values are identical to the ones described above (Argyris, 1964). Thus the organizations in our society support those values.

Where do these values come from? There are at least three answers. One answer is that the older people "program" the younger ones with these values. Another answer is that since schools, churches, businesses, and governmental and service organizations are designed according to these values, they reinforce the people in holding these values. A third answer is that these values can be traced back to the nature of industrialization, which is founded on rationality, task-orientedness, specialization, and control (Argyris, 1964). For our purposes the important point is that the values can be caused and reinforced by individuals, groups, intergroups, and organizations.

We may tentatively infer, therefore, that the "typical" interpersonal universe tends to be populated with individuals, groups, and organizations that tend to create an interpersonal world in which the conditions facilitating effective interpersonal relationships tend to be infrequent. Effective interpersonal relationships tend to be conceived in terms similar to the superior–subordinate relationship. At any given moment, A, if he is effective, is carefully and covertly diagnosing B (since openness is not sanctioned) and is acting on his unilaterally determined attributions about B. The individuals also tend to be blind to the negative impact of their relatively low degree of openness, expression of feelings, risk-taking, and the low potency of the norms of individuality and trust. Indeed, they tend to see these concomitants as "natural."

The theory by which to make explicit the processes of how pattern A helps to cause behavior already exists in social psychology. For example, it is suggested that perception is the gateway to behavior because it is through perception that we get our information about the environment toward which we behave (Newcomb, 1965, p. 85). Bruner (1957) has suggested that perception is a decision process in which the task is to find cues that can be fitted to categories available to the perceiver. A category is a set of specifications regarding certain events and the rules by which they may be grouped into organized patterns. Categories become more accessible as the expectancies of the individual increas the probability that the events will be encountered in the environment and as the search requirements are reduced. These conditions minimize "surprise value" and increase "veridical perception."

If our description of interpersonal reality is accurate, pattern A is significant in decreasing the surprise value and increasing the probability of veridical perception in social systems characterized by these patterns. The relevant interpersonal and norm variables stand out clearly. Moreover, the number of variables is small and thus the possibility for lengthy search activity is reduced. In short, given the assumption that individuals strive to perceive their world accurately, pattern A provides relatively clear cues on what is appropriate behavior. This should increase the probability that pattern A will be maintained over time.

The probability that pattern A will tend to be perpetuated may also be inferred from the Secord–Backman model (Secord and Backman, 1961, pp. 21–33). They propose that individuals tend to respect and perpetuate those interpersonal relations that were previously characterized by congruency. Also, the engagement of people in terms of these relations produces mutual effect that results in the further valuing of those relationships, which in turn increases the probability that these types of relationships will be selected the next time.[4]

## Relevance of Pattern B World for the Development of Social–Psychological Theory and a Psychological Conception of Man

There are four reasons why the understanding of human behavior may profit from the study of pattern B. First, the behavior in pattern B exists, it cannot be denied, and, as such, must be incorporated into any complete theory of human behavior. Also, a complete theory requires the development of propositions that specify the conditions under which pattern A behavior may be altered. As we have just shown above, the behavior sanctioned in pattern A tends to coerce self-fulfilling prophecies that prevent change in pattern A.

Change in pattern A requires behavior of the type that is sanctioned in pattern B. Second, intensive studies of pattern B behavior can lead, as we hope to show below, to re-examination of certain aspects of existing social-psychological theory. The third reason is related to research methodology in studying interpersonal relations. If our data are valid, there is a pervasive blindness in the interpersonal world on the part of individuals regarding the impact they have on others and a pervasive hesitancy for individuals to express many of their important feelings. These states of affairs combine to raise questions about research on interpersonal relations that do not use multimethods. For example, the responses to questionnaires and in interviews may be (unrealizingly as far as the respondent is concerned) incomplete or distorted. To develop a more complete picture observations are necessary, conducted by observers who can be shown to be competent in pattern B type behavior (Argyris, 1965b).

The fourth reason is related to the challenge of making social-psychological theory more relevant to some of the critical human problems of our world. The increasing importance of this purpose to psychologists is illustrated by the fact that the theme of the 1969 American Psychological Association Convention was the application of social science knowledge to critical societal problems. For example, studies of pattern B would lead to generalizations about how to create more settings in the ongoing, noncontrived, "real" world that encourage openness, trust, risk-taking, concern, and individuality. It should be emphasized, however, that this normative view, although valued by the writer, need not be accepted by the reader in order to give students of pattern B behavior a legitimate status in the world of scholarly research.

Finally, if one does not study the pattern B world, one runs the risk of developing a conception of man in which the "natural" behavior is hiding feelings, not taking risks, showing little concern, individuality, and trust. This will tend to occur naturally because individuals will turn to the descriptive research to develop their views about man. What *is* becomes what *ought to be*. Existing theory is used to explain existing behavior. Thus black militants have defended their aggressive behavior by citing psychological research that "proves" aggression is an expected response to frustration. The covert and silent analyzing of other people and unilaterally attributing motives to them can be shown to follow from present conceptions of attribution theory.

We may teach human beings, therefore, to be competent in ways that are congruent with pattern A. Yet pattern A represents a low interpersonal competence state of affairs. In abnormal psychology, abnormal behavior has been conceived of as the deviant behavior. In the social psychology of interpersonal relations the infrequent, deviant behavior may be the competent or "healthy" behavior.

Infrequent (pattern B) behavior is studied infrequently for two reasons. First, it is difficult to find. Second, in order to find it one has to create activities like experimental settings that make certain normative assumptions about "desirable" or "good" behavior. Such normative research, in the past, has been shunned by researchers. An example of a scholar who has conducted experimental research that is partly based on normative assumptions is Morton Deutsch. Because he has an interest in studying systematically the conditions under which cooperation can be increased, he has conducted laboratory studies that illuminate the concept of trust (Deutsch, 1962), which is a central one in pattern B.

Let us now turn to three social-psychological theories to illustrate some of the points suggested above.

## Cognitive Balance Theories

During the past two decades, several social-psychological theories have been developed that make two assumptions about cognitive consistency or balance. First, cognitive balance or consistency enables individuals to predict accurately and thus behave more effectively in their interactions with others (Deutsch and Krauss, 1965, p. 74; Secord and Backman, 1965, p. 93). Second, it is assumed that there is a basic tendency for individuals to strive to reduce such imbalanced states as cognitive dissonance and inconsistency. Brown (1962), in a review of several of these theories, concluded that they assume "human nature abhors imbalance" and "imbalance in the mind threatens to paralyze action (pp. 77–8)."

But why should imbalance (in our case *in interpersonal relations*) be so abhorrent? One possibility is that in a pattern A world, action to correct imbalance may be very difficult to take without violating the norms against discussing threatening issues. The individual who attempts to correct an interpersonal incongruency may find himself raising issues that have been hidden, discussing attributions that have been unilateral and covert, and experimenting with behavior, which in itself is not supported by pattern A norms. Under these conditions imbalance or incongruency in interpersonal relations may well become a state to be avoided or reduced as quickly as possible.

A second reason why imbalance may be abhorrent is also related to the finding above that in a pattern A world individuals tended to have a low frequency of interpersonal success. If interpersonal success is low, one might hypothesize that individuals, in those systems, will tend to have little confidence in themselves and others in solving interpersonal issues. If this is so, would not interpersonal imbalance, or incongruency, or dissonance tend to create anxiety within the actors? But since interpersonal anxiety is an issue loaded with feelings, and since expression of feelings violates the norms of pattern A, the incongruency will not tend to be resolved effectively and individual anxiety will not tend to be reduced; hence the abhorrence of imbalance.

Under these conditions the basic assumption of cognitive balance theories, namely, that given dissonant relations among cognitive elements, pressure will rise to reduce the dissonance and to avoid increase in dissonance (Festinger, 1957, p. 31), applies in interpersonal relationships. In other words, imbalance reduction theories are a valid model of how individuals in a pattern A world would tend to behave given the experience of imbalance in interpersonal relations.

This does not mean that individuals in a pattern B world will not tend to manifest needs for cognitive consistency in their interpersonal world. They will seek consistency, but their relatively immediate responses may be to increase the inconsistency or imbalance. Individuals in a pattern B world may tend to develop competence in prolonging and learning from dissonant experiences. Research on pattern B therefore may lead to insights into how individuals may develop optimal incongruity adaptation levels, research that Driver and Streufert (1966) recently suggested is lacking in the literature.

Again, systematic data are lacking but anecdotal evidence can be used to illustrate the point. Incongruities or imbalances form the basis for reeducation in T groups (Schein and Bennis, 1965). In effective T groups one can observe that imbalance-producing experiences are initially disliked by individuals; for example, A discovers he is perceived by others in ways that are opposite to his expectations; B discovers the behavior he believes is valued by others is inhibiting these individuals. A and B may attempt, as quickly as they can, to reduce the imbalance. However, as learning begins to occur, as attributions and social comparisons are reduced, as successful interpersonal experiences mount, as openness and trust become more prevalent, imbalance experiences take on a new meaning. Individuals begin to see them as opportunities to learn about themselves and others.

In a new method of self-directed change, one of the primary assumptions is that the individual should diagnose his own problems and do research on himself over a period of time (in this case a semester). The effectiveness of these programs is related to the degree to which the individual does not strive to reduce the dissonance quickly. Indeed, the research many do on their own problems can only serve to maintain or increase the dissonance for a period of time (Kolb, et al., 1968).

Valuing inconsistency in interpersonal relationships may also alter our present conceptions of how individuals maintain interpersonal stability. For example, instead of a "person with positive feelings toward himself resist[ing] the implication that he possesses undesirable traits or that traits he has are undesirable" (Secord and Backman, 1965, p. 93), the individual will tend to value the implication, exploring it fully to see what learning he and the others involved can generate from the imbalance. Also, instead of the basic assumption that individuals will tend to be attracted to those who have congruent views (Secord and Backman, 1965, p. 99), the individuals may also be attracted to individuals who hold divergent views.

Work by Rokeach (1968) supports our diagnosis of research activity in this field. First, he has criticized social psychology for emphasizing largely "the persuasive effects of group pressure, prestige, order of communication, and forced compliance on attitudes" (p. 15). These problems are consonant with the pattern A world. He also suggested that social psychologists have neglected reeducation. This neglect may be related to the fact that such studies require pattern B settings. It is not an accident that Kurt Lewin, one of the originators of laboratory education, also introduced the concept of reeducation into social psychology (Lewin and Grabbe, 1946).

Rokeach goes on to note that in his new thrust he is interested in dissonance induction that may "lead to larger and more enduring change than other types" (Rokeach, 1968, p. 20). Finally, he hypothesizes that one of the most powerful ways to do this is to help an individual see and experience inconsistencies between two or more terminal values (preferences about end states of existence). In discussing alternative approaches to inducing this experience, he describes three, two of which "are well known and the third is perhaps new." First, a person may be exposed to new information *from a credible source*. Second, a person may be induced to engage in behavior that is inconsistent with his attitudes or values. These two methods are consistent with a world identified as pattern A, and that is one reason social psychologists have focused upon them. The third is "to expose the person to information states of inconsistency already existing within his own value-attitude system" (Rokeach, 1968, p. 22). This is similar to the concept of dilemma creation identified above as a central activity of the T group staff member (during the early stages) and other members as the T group develops.

Rokeach's suggestions seem in line with those theorists who assume that man may value novelty, unexpectedness, change, and inconsistency. Maddi (1968) has recently reviewed the literature and concludes that inconsistency may be inherently satisfying and necessary for normal functioning and development.

If, as we maintain, researchers have been studying the pattern A world, which is correctly understood by cognitive consistency theories, how do we account for the research summarized by Maddi? An examination of this literature indicates that there are two major sources of data from which this view has been developed. First, it has come from studies of individuals performing such activities as solving problems and exploring challenges assigned to them by the researchers. In other words, the research settings are primarily individual, not interpersonal relations or group-centered.

Our interview material would support the notion that as individuals, people find variety, novelty, and inconsistency satisfying (Argyris, 1962, 1965b). Our position is that individuals tend to be programmed with values about effective interpersonal relations that lead them to create interpersonal worlds, groups, and organizations that will tend to prevent them from fulfilling what they may find to be intrinsically satisfying. Thus, like Maddi, our position is that human beings may strive for consistency *and* inconsistency. Our explanation, however, is different from those identified by Maddi (1968). It would begin with the postulate that individuals tend to seek, in interpersonal relationships, to increase their sense of interpersonal competence (White, 1959). A sense of interpersonal competence is a function partially of the amount of success the individual has experienced in the past, and partially a function of his expectations of how he should behave if he is to increase his sense of interpersonal competence. According to this analysis, the optimal strategy to increase one's sense of interpersonal competence in a pattern A world is consistency-seeking or imbalance-reduction. The optimal strategy in a pattern B world would be closer to striving for inconsistency and novelty.

This leads to the second major source of research for the variety view summarized by Maddi. Much of the research and theorizing has been conducted by scholars interested in understanding therapy and conditions for human growth. These conditions are consonant with a pattern B world.

Freedman's (1968) arguments that people are not particularly on the look-out for inconsistencies among their cognitions, that they are not aware of most such inconsistencies, and that they do not spend much time trying to find them may be also reinterpreted in the light of this analysis. Our data would support that in interpersonal and group settings, people are not aware of their inconsistencies. However, our data also suggest that individuals are constantly seeking for signs of inconsistencies in order to get cues about how people in the pattern A world are "really" thinking. Finally, Freedman's assertion that individuals are not terribly bothered by learning about their own inconsistencies may be valid for the types of cognitive situations that he describes. However, the assertion is clearly not supported in the world of interpersonal relationships that we have studied. Discovering inconsistencies tends to have a very potent emotional and intellective impact. As we have shown above, the impact is so great that it can provide the motivation to strive to change one's behavior even if it means months of personal struggle.

## Attribution Theory

A central concern of attribution theory is its attempt to account, in a systematic way, for a naive perceiver's inferences about an actor. "The perceiver seeks to find sufficient reason why the person acted and why the act took on a particular form" (Jones and Davis, 1965, p. 220). How is this done?

During the course of interaction, person A observes specific behaviors performed by person B. At the same time, person A has, from past experience, a storehouse of knowledge about behavior of people in general as well as personal knowledge. In order to be able to comprehend all the discreet bits of data about behavior, A has some scheme of organization that allows him to chalk up many instances of behavior as similar in some sense and to store them all under one category. The category may take the form of a trait that he attributes to a person who performs these acts consistently. Getting work done on time, meeting appointments, etc., may fall into the category of dependability, and anyone who performs these behaviors with high probability is seen as dependable. The attribution process is essentially a matching between observed behavior and categories or concepts supplied by the past experiences of the observer (DeCharms, 1968, p. 283). How is this process conceptualized in the work of Heider, Kelley, Jones and Davis? Jones and Davis (1965) state:

1 "The perceiver is imagined as a silent observer" (p. 223).
2 "The perceiver's fundamental task is to interpret or infer the causal antecedents of action" (p. 220).
3 "The actor is not conceived of as equal partner; as an 'active' information giver, interpreter, and inferer of the causal antecedents of his behavior. His primary responsibility is to behave. It is the perceiver's primary responsibility to perform the analysis and make the attribution" (p. 221).

This assignment of the roles is indicated by such statements as (italics added):

1 "When a person's actions have a certain consequence it is important for the *perceiver to determine* whether the person was capable of producing these" (p. 221).
2 "*The perceiver [has] the problem of assessing the* relative contribution of such or chance" (p. 221).
3 "The *perceiver assigns* intentions" (p. 221).
4 "The *perceiver makes certain decisions* concerning ability and knowledge [about the actor]" (pp. 221–2).

There are two links in these assumptions to the "typical" (pattern A) universe described previously. First, the perceiver–actor relationship is similar to the unilateral, "one way" relationship described in the pattern A world. It is the former's responsibility to "determine," "evaluate," "assign intentions," and "make decisions" about the subordinates' behavior. Second, the model of the "silent" perceiver going through the attribution activities is congruent with the consequences derived from pattern A. There is little openness, little sharing of motives, little expressing of feelings, little seeing others as resources for gaining knowledge about interpersonal relationships, etc.

Attribution theory, therefore, *is* a valid theory to explain behavior in pattern A that, as pointed out above, includes the overwhelming amount of observed interpersonal reality.

A final example of the congruence between attribution theory and pattern A is related to the concept of information value. "An event is informative if it is one of a large number of equiprobable events. It is uninformative if it is bound to occur" (Jones and Gerard, 1967, pp. 264–5). In-role behavior is not informative; out-of-role behavior is informative (p. 266).

The question arises: informative from whose point of view? If one conceives of the observer as the primary concern, as is the case in attribution theory, then this definition makes sense. However, it may have limitations if one wishes to understand the participant's behavior. People may behave the same way for different reasons. Thus an observer may report that ten subordinates behaved in a complaint, warm, and accepting manner every time they met with their superiors. From such observations one would make inferences that are different from those that would be made if the observer asked the subordinates and found that five subordinates hated and five liked the superior.

Some readers may point out that the congruence between the model of attribution activities and the consequences of pattern A is coincidental. The true cause of assigning the perceiver a more active but silent role is that the social scientists have cast him in the role of a researcher. Indeed, Heider, Kelley, Jones, and Davis would all agree, according to DeCharms (1968, p. 275), that: "When a person makes inferences about another person's motives he is acting like an amateur psychologists"

Two questions may be asked about this position. What empirical evidence is there that individuals in noncontrived settings use systematically the methods that are "analogous to experimental methods" (Heider, 1958, p. 297)? Do individuals use a simplified version of J. S. Mills' method of difference (the effect is attributed to that condition that is present when the effect is present and that is absent when the effect is absent)? Even in its more simplified form, individuals would have to examine systematically variations in effects in relation to variations on (1) entities, (2) persons, (3) time, and (4) modalities (Kelley, 1967, p. 194). Are individuals in the pattern A world able to do this? Research is needed to explore this question.

Some readers may object that too much is being expected of social–psychological theory. However, as Asch has suggested, every field of inquiry must begin with the phenomena that everyday experience reveals and with the distinctions it contains. Concepts of social psychology must be shown to apply to the ways in which the actors, who are often innocent of these notions, see their situation (Asch, 1959, pp. 375–9).

There is another more fundamental point that deserves examination. It has been suggested that the human conditions created by rigorous research methods are congruent with the conditions created by pattern A and formal pyramidal organizational structures (Argyris, 1968b). Thus, we arrive at the possibility that even though the social scientists did not have in mind the consequences described above when creating attribution theory, even though they selected what they believed to be, interpersonally speaking, a nonnormative model (the research model), they may have been blind to the fact that it was not. Is this blindness not similar to the blindness reported above to exist at all levels between superiors and subordinates? Thus, if social scientists who create these theories also hold the "pyramidal values," then they may create theories and models, and use research methods that are congruent with pattern A. Also, as in the case of the subjects in our studies, the subordinates (in this case the research subjects) may hesitate to tell the superiors (researchers) about their actual impact. If the subject perceives the researcher to be blind to his impact (say in any experiment) upon the subject, the latter may tend to follow attribution theory and (1) make an inference about the defensiveness of the researcher, (2) make the inference unilateral and keep it silent, (3) behave in ways that he perceives/believes are congruent with the experimenter's intentions. Thus, we have an interpersonal world where human beings learn to be silent perceivers making attributions.

## Social Evaluation Theory

The basic tenet of social evaluation theory is that human beings learn about themselves by comparing themselves to others (Pettigrew, 1967, p. 243). More specifically, the basic assumptions about man made by the theory are (Latané, 1966, p. 1):

1   People will seek to satisfy their need for self-evaluation through the use of social standards by comparing themselves with other people.
2   Comparisons can yield accurate and stable self-evaluations only when a person compares himself with someone similar to himself on the characteristic in question.
3   People will, therefore, seek out others who are similar to themselves or try to make the people who are near them more similar in order to allow accurate social comparison.

Several questions come to mind that are related to these assumptions.

If the world may be characterized as being composed of blindness on interpersonal issues, of low openness, of "silent" attributions, how accurate will individuals tend to be in perceiving others in terms of interpersonal attributes? How accurately will they be able to judge them as similar or dissimilar? How congruently will the others behave with whom they may be trying to compare themselves? If, as was reported, the individuals' confidence in their interpersonal skills tends to be low, then how much can they trust themselves to become their own base line for comparison purposes?

A second question that arises is: Could it be that in a world dominated by pattern B, the locus of comparison would change from others to oneself? For example, in a world of high openness, trust, and interpersonal competence, the probability of experiencing psychological success (Lewin, et al., 1944) will tend to be much higher. As an individual experiences more psychological success we can predict that he becomes more accurate in developing new levels of aspirations *and* that these more realistic levels of aspiration are created more by looking within one's self and less by looking to outsiders. The individuals with low psychological success use others more frequently for comparative purposes. Individuals with high inner confidence will tend to compare themselves more with their previous performance than with the performance of others.

Research is required to help us learn the answers to these issues. At the moment, all the writer can do is bring to bear some anecdotal evidence. It is common in a T group experience (i.e., effective) for individuals to report (early in the experience) three major learnings. These are: (1) many people they perceived as being different from themselves actually had problems similar to theirs; (2) many people they perceived to be similar to themselves were not; and finally (3) they were inaccurate in predicting the degree of inner confidence and self-acceptance individuals had in interpersonal activities.

Social comparison and evaluation may be a highly inaccurate process, and the individuals (1) may exist in a world in which they tend to "see" and/or receive feedback that they want, and therefore (2) may be blind to the degree of inaccuracy of their evaluations.

## SOME CLOSING COMMENTS

It follows from the above that as long as pattern B interpersonal relationships are rare, descriptive research will rarely study them. Research therefore will rarely discover knowledge that is representative of, and generate theories related to, high interpersonal competence and relatively effective interpersonal relations. Such theorizing may be significantly different. For example, recent competence theory suggests that one way to increase inter-personal competence (one way to increase the probability for pattern B) is to help individuals *minimize* their silent attribution activities. Instead of, for example, learning to observe another's behavior and check for consistency over time, over modality, the individual is encouraged to experiment with sharing openly the attributes that he is beginning to make with the individual concerned. Attribution becomes a joint interpersonal activity (Argyris, 1968a). This places attribution activities under the control of the individual to whom it applied and, therefore, increases the probability of his readiness to accept it or change it (Kolb, et al., 1968; Secord and Backman, 1964). "Silent" attributions would now be encouraged (1) when the other person is a stranger and one will not see him again; (2) when the individual may be psychologically hurt if he is told about the attributions being made; and (3) if the attribution is about an object. Attributions would still be made in other settings but they would be done publicly with the individual sharing the data from which he made the attribution as well as the attribution. Rogers (1964, p. 117) has called this "interpersonal knowing" which is possible in "a climate which makes it psychologically safe and rewarding for [you] to reveal [your] internal frame of reference."

Perhaps one reason that Maslow's humanistic psychology has not been so readily accepted is that it is based on a universe that is rarely available for empirical research. Also, humanistic psychology would alter the presently accepted criteria for rigorous research (Maslow, 1966). Koch (1965), after editing his volumes on the state of psychology, concluded that much psychological thought can become "ameaningful" because it tends to go on in a context of being "rule-bound," "rule-dependent," "rigid," and "emphasis on rote" – all consequences of pattern A.

How does one decide what "ought" to be? Maslow has suggested taking peak experiences as the basis for norms. What "is" in a peak experience becomes what ought to be in the everyday world (Maslow, 1963). A second strategy is to develop a theoretical framework for interpersonal relationships that is derivable from some commonly accepted properties of human nature and thus can be stated as an axiom. For example, in one recent attempt, a theoretical framework for understanding interpersonal relationships was begun with the axiom that all individuals have a need for increased self-awareness. If one accepts this assertion, it is possible to develop a theoretical framework of interpersonal relationships that includes such concepts as self-acceptance, psychological success, and information (about interpersonal relations) that is minimally attributive and evaluative with interpersonal communications being primarily in terms of descriptive, directly verifiable categories (Argyris, 1968a). As these theoretical views are developed, researchers will have to create settings in which these variables may exist because they will not be found in the "normal" world. Laboratory programs and T groups may be one such setting. But others are needed, especially in task-oriented groups. Natural groups of executives who go through laboratory education and return to apply their new skills and insight may be another useful setting. All these are examples of applied behavioral science. Thus, we have arrived at the point where applied behavioral science can be central to basic research in the social psychology of interpersonal relations.

## Notes

1  For a detailed discussion of the theoretical framework, the categories, their differential potency, interobserver reliability studies, and the major hypothesis tested, see Argyris (1965b).

2  Not included are Studies 13, 15, 17, and 24–27 listed in table 23.1.

3  In order to represent pattern B, we selected the last five sessions from two T groups (each of which lasted for nine sessions) and the last three sessions from one T group (which lasted seven sessions).

4 Selye (1956) has suggested that physical illness may be caused by the defenses the body produces to fight the illness. Bakan (1968) has suggested the same may be true about many psychological illness. We would conclude that the same causal processes may exist at the group and organizational levels. It is their defensive reactions to stress that may cause them to become more rigid, closed, and ineffective.

# References

Argyris, C., 1962, *Interpersonal Competence and Organizational Effectiveness*, Home-wood, Ill., Richard D. Irwin.

Argyris, C., 1964, *Integrating the Individual and the Organization*, New York, Wiley.

Argyris, C., 1965a, "Explorations in Interpersonal Competence – I," *Journal of Applied Behavioral Science*, 1, pp. 58–83.

Argyris, C., 1965b, *Organizations and Innovation*, Homewood, Ill., Richard D. Irwin.

Argyris, C., 1967a, "On the Future of Laboratory Education," *Applied Behavioral Science*, 3, pp. 153–83.

Argyris, C., 1968a, "Conditions for Competence Acquisition and Therapy," *Journal of Applied Behavioral Science*, 4, pp. 147–77.

Argyris, C., 1968b, "Some Unintended Consequences of Rigorous Research," *Psychological Bulletin*, 70, pp. 185–97.

Asch, S. E., 1959, "A Perspective on Social Psychology," in Koch, S. (ed.), *Psychology: A Study of a Science*, New York, McGraw-Hill.

Bakan, D., 1968, *Disease, Pain, and Sacrifice*, Chicago, University of Chicago Press.

Bolman, L. G., 1967, Managerial Experiences Questionnaire, unpublished manuscript, Department of Administrative Sciences, Yale University.

Bradford, L. P., Gibb, J. R., and Benne, K. D. (eds), 1964, *T group Theory and Laboratory Method. Innovation in reeducation*, New York, Wiley.

Brown, R., (ed.), 1962, *New Directions in Psychology*, New York, Holt, Rinehart & Winston.

Bruner, J. S., 1957, "On Perceptual Readiness," *Psychological Review*, 64, pp. 123–52.

DeCharms, R., 1968, *Personal Causation*, New York, Academic Press.

Deutsch, M., 1962, "Cooperation and Trust: Some Theoretical Notes," *Nebraska Symposium on Motivation*, 10, pp. 275–318.

Deutsch, M., and Krauss, R. M., 1965, *Theories in Social Psychology*, New York, Basic Books.

Driver, M., and Streufert, S., 1966, *The General Incongruity Adaptation Level (GIAL) Hypothesis II. Incongruity Motivation to Affect, Cognition, and Activation–Arousal Theory*, Institute Paper No. 148, Oct., Lafayette, Ind., Herman C. Krannert Graduate School of Industrial Administration, Purdue University.

Festinger, L., 1957, *A Theory of Cognitive Dissonance*, Evanston, Ill., Row, Peterson.

Freedman, J. L., 1968, "How Important is Cognitive Consistency," in Abelson, R. P., Aronson, E., McGuire, W. J., Newcomb, T. M., Rosenberg, M. J., and Tannenbaum, P. H. (eds), *Theories of Cognitive Consistency: A Sourcebook*, Chicago, Rand McNally.

Golembiewski, R. T., 1962, *The Small Group*, Chicago, University of Chicago Press.

Heider, F., 1958, *The Psychology of Interpersonal Relations*, New York, Wiley.

Jones, E. E., and Davis, K. E., 1965, "From Acts to Dispositions," in Berkowitz, L. (ed.), *Advances in Experimental Social Psychology*, Vol. 2, New York, Academic Press.

Jones, E. E., and Gerard, H. B., 1967, *Foundation of Social Psychology*, New York, Wiley.

Kelley, H. H., 1967, "Attribution Theory in Social Psychology," *Nebraska Symposium on Motivation*, 15, 192–240.

Koch, S., 1965, "The Allures of Meaning in Modern Psychology," in Farson, R. (ed.), *Science and Human Affairs*, Palo Alto, Science and Behavior Books.

Kolb, D. A., Winter, S. K., and Berlew, D. E., 1968, "Self-Directed Change: Two Studies," *Applied Behavioral Science*, 4, pp. 453–71.

Latané, B., 1966, "Studies in Social Comparison: Introduction and Overview," *Journal of Experimental Social Psychology*, Suppl. 1, pp. 1–5.

Lewin, K., and Grabbe, P., 1946, "Conduct Knowledge, and Acceptance of New Values, *Journal of Social Issues*, 2, pp. 34–46.

Lewin, K., Dembo, T., Festinger, L., and Sears, P., 1944, "Level of Aspiration," in Hunt, J. McV. (ed.), *Personality and the Behavior Disorders*, New York, Ronald Press.

Maddi, S. R., 1968, "The Pursuit of Consistency and Variety," in Abelson, R. P., Aronson, E., McGuire, W. J., Newcomb, T. M., Rosenberg, M. J., and Tannenbaum, P. H., (eds), *Theories of Cognitive Consistency: A Sourcebook*, Chicago, Rand McNally.

Maslow, A. H., 1963, "Fusions of Facts and Values," *American Journal of Psychoanalysis*, 23, pp. 117–31.

Maslow, A. H., 1966, *The Psychology of Science*, New York, Harper & Row.

McGrath, J. E., and Altman, I., 1966, *Small Group Research*, New York, Holt, Rinehart & Winston.

McGuire, W. J., 1967, "Some Impending Reorientations in Social Psychology," *Journal of Experimental Social Psychology*, 3, pp. 124–39.

Newcomb, T., 1965, "Aspects of the Acquaintance Process," in Farson, R. (ed.), *Science and Human Affairs*, Palo Alto, Science and Behavior Books.

Pettigrew, T. F., 1967, "Social Evaluation Theory: Convergences and Applications," *Nebraska Symposium on Motivation*, 15, pp. 241–315.

Ring, K., 1967, "Experimental Social Psychology: Some Sober Questions about Frivolous Values," *Journal of Experimental Social Psychology*, 3, pp. 113–23.

Rogers, C. R., 1964, "Toward a Science of the Person," in Wann, T. W. (ed.), *Behaviorism and Phenomenology*, Chicago, University of Chicago Press.

Rokeach, M., 1968, "A Theory of Organization and Change within Value-Attitude Systems," *Journal of Social Issues*, 24, 13–33.

Schein, E., and W. Bennis, 1965, *Personal and Organizational Change Through Group Methods: The Laboratory Approach*, New York, Wiley.

Secord, P. F., and Backman, C. W., 1961, "Personality Theory and the Problem of Stability and Change in Individual Behavior: An Interpersonal Approach," *Psychological Review*, 68, pp. 21–33.

Secord, P. F., and Backman, C. W., 1964, *Social Psychology*, New York, McGraw-Hill.

Secord, P. F., and Backman, C. W., 1965, "An Interpersonal Approach to Personality," in Maher, B. A. (ed.), *Progress in Experimental Personality Research*, New York, Academic Press.

Selye, H., 1956, *The Stress of Life*, New York, McGraw-Hill.

Steele, F. I., 1968, "Personality and the 'Laboratory Style,'" *Applied Behavioral Science*, 4, pp. 25–45.

Steele, F. I., 1969, "The interpersonal choices questionnaire. A measure of value orientation about interpersonal behavior in organizations," Administrative Sciences, Yale University, unpublished.

White, R., 1959, "Motivation Reconsidered: The Concept of Competence," *Psychological Review*, 66, pp. 297–334.

# — 24 —

# Dangers in Applying Results from Experimental Social Psychology

Argyris and Schön (1974) differentiated between espoused theories of action and theories-in-use. The espoused theories of action are those that people report as theories that inform their actions. Theories-in-use are the theories of action inferred from how people actually behave (taken from video or audio tapes or other instruments that focus on collecting relatively directly observable behavior). To date, most individuals studied appear to be blind to the discrepancies between their espoused theories and their theories-in-use, but are not blind to similar discrepancies on the part of others. People observe the discrepancies manifested by others, but they are programmed with theories-in-use that say: "If you observe others behaving incongruently with what they espouse, in the name of effectiveness, concern, and diplomacy, do not tell them". A model of the theories-in-use that we have found to account for much of the behavior relevant to this inquiry is given in detail in chapter 3.

There are several reasons that one may wish to explore new theories of action. First, theories of action are needed that help to reduce group and organizational entropy and to increase the effectiveness of problem solving at all levels. Moreover, a careful reading of Model I suggests that it is composed of inner contradictions. It requires rationality, yet it supports the suppression of valid information. It requires verification, yet it creates conditions for verification that are inadequate, hence the self-sealing processes. Another level of contradiction is illustrated by the fact that the actor is given the freedom to advocate his or her position while simultaneously preventing others from doing the same. Model I sanctions a world in which some people, usually those in power, have the right to control and manipulate others while simultaneously withholding information from the others. Unless social psychologists help to propose new theories of action, human beings will be informed by theories of action that facilitate inequality, injustice, and unilateral domination.

At the level of advancement of knowledge, all theories ought to have their limits explored fully. By researching other models of action we can define more clearly the conditions under which Model I holds and the conditions under which it does not.

## THE APPLICABILITY OF SOCIAL–PSYCHOLOGICAL EMPIRICAL RESULTS

What if we wanted to change the basically defensive consequences of Model I conditions (e.g., closedness to double-loop learning, deception, invalid feedback, private testing of ideas) to the opposite state of affairs? What does the social–psychological literature have to suggest? Again, in asking this question, the focus is primarily on social–psychological research that sheds light on human effectiveness (individual and group levels).

### Aronson: The Social Animal

Elliot Aronson (1972) has recently written a well-argued book about the applicability of experimental social–psychological studies. Of the eight major topics listed in the table of contents, all but two are topics that are central to Model I. We learn:

- The people most liked in groups are those who conform to group norms. The people least liked in groups are those who deviate from group norms (p. 15). Implication: if you wish to be liked, conform to group norms.
- Pressure to conform to judgements of others is effective if personal judgements have to be made publicly even though there are not explicit constraints against individuality (pp. 19–20). Implication: requiring people to make their personal judgements public will help to make them conform to these judgements.
- Pressures to conform to others' judgements have little (if any) effect on the private judgements (pp. 19–20). Implication: maintaining individuality may be best accomplished by keeping your judgements private.
- It is possible to increase group conformity (a) if members are seen as experts, (b) if members are friends, (c) if relationships with friends are insecure, and (d) if acceptance by the group is moderate (p. 21).
- It is possible to decrease the conformity to other's views by (a) having allies, (b) having high self-esteem, (c) having prior success in achieving tasks, (d) having secure relationships with friends, and (e) having total acceptance by the group (p. 21).

The pressure to conform may be decreased by becoming dependent on allies, by having success in tasks, and by having total acceptance in the group. But if the group tends to value those people who conform to its norms, then acceptance may mean high conformity. Also, having allies may require being dependent on or beholden to them. Succeeding in tasks focuses on the importance of productivity and assumes the acceptance of group goals. All of these conditions are congruent with Model I.

These illustrations could be expanded to show that research also suggests that someone can gain credibility: by using the advertising ploy of having big-name athletes or alluring women propound his views (select allies in order to win); by acting as if they have something to lose (deception); and by getting a message to individuals in a way that they cannot sense others are trying to influence them. For example, A can speak to B about a "hot tip" loudly enough so that C can hear it, and then C may be influenced (pp. 61–4) by the statement (deviousness in order to control others unilaterally).

### Zimbardo and Ebbesen: Influencing Attitudes and Changing Behavior

Zimbardo and Ebbesen (1969) also focused on showing readers how research results may be used to influence others unilaterally, mostly in a covert manner. For example, they advised that persuasion will work if the persuader is seen as an expert, as having good intentions, as being dynamic, sociable, and attractive, and as having an authoritative manner. They also provide interesting insights into how to design the communications (e.g., the order of presentation). The research in the field has focused on the following five questions that have relevance to practice and action.

1 Should the strongest arguments come last or first?
2 In a two-sided debate, should you present your case first or last?
3 Should you present only your position or your opponent's position as well, and then refute his?
4 Should the communicator draw the conclusions explicitly or allow the audience to do so from the arguments presented?
5 Should one use rational or emotional appeals with fear-stimulating properties?

(See Zimbardo and Ebbesen, 1969, p. 17.)

All of the questions are phrased to provide assistance to a communicator who wishes to influence others unilaterally. The action strategies therefore are aimed at controlling and winning over others. If one were to use such advice, he or she would be operating within the Model I paradigm.

If one examines Zimbardo and Ebbesen's comprehensive list of findings plus their implications for practice, it is not possible, I suggest, to find any principles that are not within the Model I paradigm. For example, they advised the following (as did Aronson, 1972):

1 Present one side of the argument when the audience is generally friendly or when your position is the only one that will be presented.
2 Present both sides of the argument when the audience starts out disagreeing with you.
3 There will probably be more opinion change in the direction you want if you explicitly state your conclusions than if you let the audience draw their own, except when they are rather intelligent (pp. 20–22).

The first thrust of these results is to provide the actor with insight into how to get others to do what the actor wants them to do. This thrust is related to the Model I governing variable of achieving the actor's purposes. The second thrust is to be an expert, which implies using knowledge to influence others, again Model I governing variables. Third, the advice to persuade others by acting as if the actor is willing to lose or not seeking to win is based on the assumption that the governing variable is win, not lose. All of the recommended behaviors are congruent with controlling others unilaterally and doing so, at times, by devious procedures.

McGuire (1969) explored the experimental literature and identified the major approaches to the problem of inducing resistance to persuasion:

- *Behavioral commitment* The believer takes some more or less irrevocable step on the basis of his belief, thereby committing himself to it. Commitment is presumed to make changing one's beliefs dangerous and costly (p. 194). This strategy relies on the Model I value of win, do not lose.
- *Anchoring the belief to other cognitions* Linking the belief in question to other cognitions may make it more difficult for the person to change his belief because such a change would require his changing all of the linked beliefs (p. 196). This strategy appears to focus on immunizing the person to double-loop learning and to keep him focused on single-loop learning.
- *Inducing resistant cognitive states* Inducing anxiety about the issue thereby induces aggressiveness and ideological preconditioning (p. 197). The strategy appears to maximize winning and to discourage double-loop learning.

- *Prior training in resisting persuasive attempts* Individuals are trained for selective avoidance or perceptual distortion of information that is at variance with one's beliefs (p. 199). Again, this strategy educates individuals to resist persuasion in a way that may reduce their predisposition for double-loop learning.
- *Inoculation* The person is typically made resistant to some attacking virus by pre-exposure to a weakened dose of the virus. This mild dose stimulates his defenses so that he will be better able to overcome any massive attack to which he is later exposed (p. 200).

All of these strategies assume that the way to deal with persuasion is to "plug into" the potential recipients of persuasion some skill and capacity to resist these persuasion attempts so that the recipients may remain effective at winning (i.e., maintaining their beliefs). Also, all of the strategies are covert. They do not recommend skills and capacities to openly confront the persuader with his attempts to induce change, nor do they provide insights into how the parties involved can create a relationship in which double-loop learning may occur (e.g., Why does the persuader strive to persuade through covert methods?). Finally, the resistance strategies are designed to be covert in order to reduce the probability of surfacing negative feelings between the parties involved.

## *Rubin: Liking and Loving*

Rubin (1973) has written a systematic, thoughtful, and carefully argued book about the research findings related to liking and loving. What is the reader told about the nature of liking, love, and interpersonal life? People spend energy seeking social approval. Individuals, if they are aware of social exchange theory and the experimental evidence, can: shape and manipulate the behavior of others by saying "mm . . . hm" or "yeah" or making approving sounds every time the other person states an opinion (p. 75). It should not be done too long because the other person can become satiated and he or she will stop being influenceable. Perhaps the best power leverage in personal relationships is to set the terms of the relationship by being the partner who is minimally involved. But there is a caveat. This principle may work best in unstable marriages. Stable marriages have equal partners, but exchange theory has little to say about equal partnerships (except how influence can be designed unilaterally by any given partner). Again, the use of power, the striving to control others, is central.

More results congruent with Model I principles are described in sections on how to gain social approval. The greatest success in getting social approval is to deny it to another person. For example, have him rejected by someone else, and then you come along and be accepting of the person (Rubin, 1973, p. 76). Another principle is: express dislike for the individual first and then express approval.

The readers are informed that if they want to use social–psychological knowledge to become liked by another, they are advised to reject the other person and then become more positive toward him or her. If the reader wants to reject someone, then he should say negative things about the other person after he is certain that the other person thinks the reader likes him or her (Rubin, 1973, pp. 77–8).

We like people who agree with us. Why is this so?

1  Agreement provides a basis for engaging in pleasurable activities.
2  It reduces the probability of feeling uneasy, of having to express hostility toward another, or of dealing with negative feelings.

3  "People have the egocentric habit of assuming that anyone who shares their views must be a sensible and praiseworthy individual, while anyone who differs with them must be doing so because of some basic incapacity or perversity" (p. 140).

4  Agreement tends to keep bickering and argument, and other such unpleasantries, to a minimum (p. 141).

Thus we learn that we can be liked if we agree with others (conformity); if we provide a basis for pleasurable activities and reduce uneasy, negative feelings (suppressing negative feelings); and if we acquiesce to people's egocentric habits of sharing their views (again, conformity).

## Conclusions to Date: Maintaining the Status Quo

If it is true that "real" life is dominated by Model I relationships, then social–psychological research does have a relatively high external validity: it is relevant to the noncontrived world. The research does provide results that can help individuals to increase their effectiveness within the constraints of Model I. For those who may be interested in reversing the consequences of Model I factors little advice is offered. The research unintentionally maintains the status quo.

Why is this so? Two reasons come to mind. The first is the time-honored norm that social scientists should describe reality. Their research should inform the reader about interpersonal and group reality as it is, a reality informed by Model I. But if one remains within the confines of Model I, it is difficult to offer new options for society to consider. Moreover, if new options are not available, what *is* becomes what *ought* to be. The meaning of the ought is not based on moral or ideological grounds; it is derived from the fact that what *is* becomes accepted as the nature of human beings. Consequently, what ought to be follows from, or is constrained by, what is. For example, if students read textbooks that purport to describe human nature and if these textbooks include dissonance and attribution theories, then the psychological processes that compose these theories may form the basis for the model of man implicit in these theories. We are told in these texts that human beings strive to reduce postdecisional dissonance or frequently make attributions of others. The student reading these generalizations may understandably come to conceive of human nature as including dissonance mechanisms and attribution activities. Such an inference would be supported empirically. But it does not follow that dissonance reduction and attribution are part of human nature in the same sense that $1/2\ gt^2$ is part of the physical universe. The latter is hypothesized to characterize an essential quality of the physical universe. The former can be shown to be an artifact, a convention that can be altered *if* other concepts of human nature are developed. But since most social scientists conceive of their task as to describe reality, the probability of discovery of new realities is very low (Argyris, 1969).

## SCIENTIFIC METHOD AS A THEORY OF ACTION

There is a second reason experimental social psychology will tend to produce results that are congruent with Model I. The requirements for internal validity are congruent with Model I. Rigorous research designs and practices are based on a theory-in-use that is consistent with the espoused theory (scientific method) and the espoused theory is consistent with Model I (Argyris, 1968). This is especially applicable to experiments that are designed to test hypotheses in which the experimenter is systematically manipulating the variables under conditions designed by him. According to Tajfel (1972), these conditions predominate in modern experimental social psychology (p. 70).

The true or pure experiment is basically exposing one or more experimental groups to one or more treatment conditions and comparing the results with one or more control groups not receiving the treatments. In true experiments, the selection of subjects, the assignment of subjects to groups, and the assignment of experimental treatments to groups are accomplished through randomization (Campbell and Stanley, 1963, pp. 13–30: Isaac, 1971, p. 24).

Much of experimental social psychology that attempts to test hypotheses by manipulating the conditions systematically attempts to maximize internal and external validity. Internal validity asks: did in fact the experimental treatments make a difference in this specific experimental instance? External validity asks: to what populations, settings, treatment variables, and measurement variables can this effect be generalized (Campbell and Stanley, 1963, p. 5)?

At this point, the focus is on internal validity, which is the sine qua non for experimental activity: it is the basic minimum without which any experiment is uninterpretable (Campbell and Stanley, 1963, p. 5). The degree of internal validity of experiments tends to be influenced by at least eight factors: history, maturation, testing, instrumentation, statistical regression, selection, experimental morality, and the selection X maturation interaction (Campbell and Stanley, 1963, p. 5).

Experimental social psychologists aspire to minimize the error variance due to any of these conditions. The greater the success, the greater the elegance of the experiment. Given the nature of social phenomena and its universe, no one can achieve perfection. The most that can be done is for social scientists to strive to approximate the state of experimental elegance.

What is the impact (intended or unintended) of striving for elegance on the applicability of the findings? An experiment is a peculiar "temporary" system. In order to obtain as unambiguous evidence about causation as possible and in order to control extraneous variables, the experimenter strives to gain as much control as possible over the design and execution of the experiment. Control is the name of the game.

If the experiment is to succeed, however, the subject must, at the moment of choice to act, be free not to choose in the way the experiment is designed for him to choose. The subject must maintain free choice not to act according to an a priori prediction made by the experimenter.

In order to ensure free choice, the purpose of the experiment, the meaning of the experimental tasks, the structure of the experiment, the assignment to different experimental treatments, etc., must be kept secret from the subjects. It is as if the experimenter is saying to the subject:

> I want to design the environment in such a way that when you enter it, I will have done my best to have induced you to behave as I predicted you would. However, I must be certain that if you behaved the way I predicted you would, it was because you wanted to, because it made sense to you to do so, because the choice was genuinely yours.
>
> In order to maximize this possibility, I must design the entire experiment rigorously and keep all of the key elements of the design secret from you until you have finished participating in it. Also, I cannot permit or encourage you to learn (ahead of time or during the experiment) anything about the experiment; I cannot encourage you to confront it, or to alter it. The only learning that I permit is learning that remains within the purposes of the experiment.
>
> The experimental conditions may be summarized as (a) high articulation and advocacy of my position (i.e., stating theory, deriving precise hypotheses) coupled with (b) high unilateral control over you (as subject) and (c) secrecy about goals, purposes, and design of the experiment leaving you a moment of free choice.

If the experiment is designed well, the choice is free in the sense that the subject makes it, but inevitable in that the experimenter designed the experiment to minimize other choices. This may provide an explanation for the paradox that Aronson and Carlsmith (1968) described, namely, that "experimental *realism*, internal validity, is achieved through *falsehood*" (p. 2). Under conditions required for internal validity, the only way that the experimenter can guarantee the subject free choice is to create a veil of secrecy about the design. The subject is placed in a position in which the tight security regulations are maintained for his own good, namely, to permit him free choice at the moment of choice.

In addition to the subjects' not being encouraged to confront and learn during the experiment, the experimenter is subject to the same constraints. Experimental designs or their execution cannot be altered without starting from the beginning. The theory of action imbedded in experimental procedure is high advocacy and high control over others with minimal real-time learning (that questions the basic purposes and design of the experiment) on the part of all concerned.

Generalizations produced by the experimental method will tend to have these conditions imbedded in them. They will be generalizations that will inform us how to make certain events happen under conditions in which the actor and the "recipients" will not confront each other to learn from their experience. To put this another way, empirically supported generalizations define the conditions under which they will tend to work; they do not define conditions for real-time learning of how to make the generalizations operative with the overt cooperation of the others. The cooperation the scientific generalizations require is of a particular kind; it is the subject who cooperates with the experimenter.

An experiment therefore makes certain assumptions about the nature of the involvement of the subject. The first assumption is that the experimental tasks must genuinely involve the subject. The tasks must realistically involve those aspects of the subject's psyche that are under study. The second assumption is that of defining the tasks simply enough so that any subject can perform them without a reduction in involvement.

The third assumption is that the subject's involvement and spontaneity will not be impaired by knowing that the nature of the experiment will have to be kept secret from them in order to ensure a genuine response from them; in other words, they will behave without acting. The fourth assumption is that the subject's response will not include "no response." Subjects are free to act, within the constraints of the experiment, but they are not free not to act. The fifth assumption is that subjects will not reflect upon what they are doing, as subjects. They will not question the design or credibility of the experiment or their role as subjects.

We may conclude that experiments that are designed to maximize internal validity tend to be designed in a way that maximizes the following probabilities: first, the experimenters will achieve their purposes – they will win and not lose, they will surface minimal negative feelings, and they will tap rational behavior. And second, the subjects will permit and accept being placed in an environment in which their behavior is controlled as completely as possible, the consequences are manipulated by the experimenters, no public testing or confrontation of the experiment is permitted, self-sealing processes are preferred and rewarded, and learning, if it is to occur, should remain within the purposes of the experiment, that is, single-loop learning.

Perhaps the above is one way to explain Zimbardo's (1969) statement:

> Control. That's what current psychology is all about . . . It has, in fact, become the all-consuming task of most psychologists to learn how to bring behavior under stimulus control . . . Laboratory studies of motivation and behavior control have typically been designed to render living organisms into passive subjects, who simply convert stimulus inputs into correlated response outputs. (pp. 237–8)

Elsewhere (Argyris, 1968) I have suggested that those subjects who do not find these conditions fulfilling or satisfying may (1) fight (covertly) the experiment, (2) withdraw (covertly), (3) modify the experiment (covertly), (4) up the price for their participation, or (5) require a predefinition of rules about the game of experimentation.

These consequences may be mitigated if subjects see their role as legitimate, for example, young children, individuals who prefer being dependent and manipulated, and people who have a price for participation that is payable by the experimenter.

If it is true that secrecy and free choice are combined in order to trust the experimental results, then a consequence follows for the applicability (not validity) of the experimental results. The practical advice derived from the experimental research will tend to work *if* the conditions of the experimental situation also exist for the person considering using the advice. For example, if A wants to use a particular reinforcement schedule to get B to behave in certain ways, (1) A must also be able to communicate the schedule, (2) B must be willing to accept it, and (3) A must not tell B why he is using the schedule.

Similarly, one cannot tell intelligent people that they are getting both sides of the argument because they are intelligent. Nor can one tell the less intelligent that they are being given one side of the argument because to give them both sides would confuse them. Nor can the strategy to immunize people against changing their views work if they are told the purpose of the strategy.

It is important to stress that the requirement of secrecy being discussed is related to the requirements for internal validity. It is a more pervasive problem than the deception that Kelman (1969) and others have discussed. There are many experiments that do not deceive subjects but nevertheless keep the experimental treatment secret.

Combining secrecy with free choice may also provide an explanation of why no literature was found on how to overcome conformity by means other than remaining within the constraints of Model I. To provide such data the experimenter would have to create conditions in which the security regulations of the experiment would be confrontable. For example, research indicates that adding one person who agrees that the lines (in the Asch-type experiments) are equal significantly reduces the conformity. But that solution is to increase the power of the subjects through rational knowledge to confront the confederate. The solution remains within the win–lose mode. It is a world of oscillating Model I in which each side tries to overwhelm the other. A different solution would be to confront the experimenter openly, to see if the others are confederates; to confront openly the validity of their perceptual processes, the way they make inferences from reality, their behavior within the group, etc. Is it possible to design an experiment with high internal validity that permits such confrontation? Would not learning that those who disagree are confederates reduce the conformity?

### Varela: Psychological Solutions to Social Problems

Next, let us consider several examples of applied social psychology in the "real" world. The first is the work of Jacobo Varela. He is an engineer by background who has studied social psychology thoroughly. The rigor and carefulness of his efforts are attested to by the fact that George Miller (1969), in a presidential address to the American Psychological Association, described him as an excellent example of the valid and judicious application of social–psychological research.

Zimbardo and Ebbesen (1969) described a case in which Varela, using social science knowledge, was able (1) to increase the sales of ready-made curtains to retailers in Uruguay (even though many windows in Uruguay are of different sizes); (2) to induce retailers to buy for inventory (a practice rarely followed); and (3) to accomplish these and other goals under conditions of spiraling inflation when the government froze all prices and wages, devalued the currency, and established severe penalties for infringement, which resulted in the virtual halt of all nonessential consumer buying and therefore all buying from wholesalers by retailers.

Varela developed two persuasion programs. The first program was designed on the basis of experimental research on commitment. In the first step the salesman skillfully piqued the storekeeper's interest and in the second step induced him into the wholesale showroom. The showroom, unknown to the storekeeper, was an experimental laboratory where even facial expressions were systematically observed. The sales strategy was designed on the basis of what experimenters had done to subjects in order to produce commitment. For example, whenever the shopkeeper responded that he was favorably impressed, he was asked to give his opinion about that product. To commit him further, he was encouraged to elaborate the reasons why he liked the sample.

Moreover, uncut yard goods were sold by indirectly influencing the shopkeeper to compare the new designs with older ones. When the shopkeeper asked about the fabric, the salesman hesitated but eventually agreed to show him bolts of the fabric:

> Once the retailer made this verbal commitment to see the material, and in addition put the salesperson through the work of presenting it, he had to justify his behavior. In such ways he very neatly *set himself up* for placing a big order. (Zimbardo and Ebbesen, 1969, p. 116)

The sales results were excellent. The wholesalers then trained the retailers to adapt these techniques to use in persuading their customers, the unsuspecting housewives with irregularly shaped windows.

The entire strategy was congruent with Model I governing variables to achieve purposes as Varela perceived them, win–don't lose, and remain away from negative emotions. The behavioral strategies were also consistent with Model I. The salesman manipulated and controlled the environment; whatever testing was done was covert, and no double-loop learning occurred.

Notice also that the entire strategy was kept secret and necessarily so. It is doubtful that the strategy selected by Varela would work if the unsuspecting retailers and later the housewives were told about what they were to be exposed to in the selling relationship. Because Varela followed faithfully the dictates of the experimental treatment, he naturally treated the retailers as "subjects." He therefore kept the experimental manipulation (sales strategy) secret from the subjects (retailers and housewives).

Some readers may believe that such a manipulation could not be repeated. After all, the retailers would now be less unsuspecting. Varela was aware that the retailers may have immunized their clients against further manipulation. He developed a second-phase sales strategy which was even more manipulative and secret than the previous one. It was based on reactance theory. Reactance theory states that the perception that a communication is attempting to influence will tend to be seen as a threat to one's freedom to decide for oneself. Varela educated salesmen to chat with retailers, to engage them in small talk, but to covertly obtain attitudes about business conditions. These data were then given to a different set of salesmen, who used them when they visited the unsuspecting retailers. For example, since most retailers felt (given the inflation) that times were bad, the salesmen were instructed to say: "Times are really bad, and I don't think it even pays to try to see what the new style trends are," in a way that implied sincerity. In order to maintain his freedom of choice, according to reactance theory, the retailer had to at least look at the materials. With carefully designed statements, the salesman was able to influence retailers to disagree with him. But in disagreeing with the salesman's statements, the retailer was forcing himself to buy (p. 118).

The sales techniques were effective with the retailers. The second phase, utilizing the showroom as an experimental laboratory, was also replicated with high ingenuity. The strategy included making buyers "yield," which involved bringing them into an unfamiliar environment, under the control of the salesman. The salesman had been taught to scan expressions and ask questions only of buyers who may be favorable, systematically rewarding the favorable comments and developing group pressure to persuade those customers who were not favorable to buying. The strategies were even differentiated to deal with highly authoritarian customers as well as customers who required "immunity against counter persuasion."

In a recent systematic book, Varela (1971) continues his application of psychological research. He cites how psychological research results can be used in organizations, in families, and with close friends. In one case a friend was covertly manipulated into going to a doctor for professional help. In another case, a son manipulated his mother into accepting a needed operation. The cases can be continued, but the exercise would produce the same unilaterally controlling Model I coupled with secret use of behavioral science principles.

Varela includes a discussion in his book about ethical issues. He realizes that his work raises questions about the ethics of people producing change in others, of invasion of privacy, of unilateral control by the powerful over the less powerful (p. 139). Varela's response to these questions may raise even more concerns. First, he correctly notes that all new methods have been feared and resisted. Next, he notes that the principles that he suggests need not be limited to despots. The ideas that Varela has published are available to the poor; indeed, suggests Varela, the ideas could give more power to the poor. This would be true if the poor had enough power to be in a position to manipulate others.

Moreover, the question may be raised, what are the ethics of implying that it is good for the poor to manipulate the rich, or the less powerful to manipulate the powerful (which is a contradiction in terms)? Wherever this has happened, be it at the community level (participation of the poor in community government) or the social level (socialist–communist countries), all that has been generated is a society of oscillating Model I relationships.

Varela warns the reader against the misuse of his principles. There have been cases in which salesmen sold much more than the buyer needed and there was a boomarang effect. Varela then advises:

> Size up your client, decide what is best for him, make a survey of his needs and possibilities and then design a persuasion to sell him those requirements. If he buys the amount and finds that he can sell it, then he will feel grateful, because at all times he will have the correct sensation that it was he himself who made the decision to buy. (pp. 140–41)

And so we find Model I advice tends to continue a Model I world, in a way that the client genuinely believes that he is making decisions when, in reality, it has all been managed by the persuader armed with results from experimental social psychology.

### Abelson and Zimbardo: Canvassing for Peace

The application of social–psychological findings to politics has been presented by Abelson and Zimbardo (1970). The pamphlet tells the canvassers: "We advise you on skills of interpersonal contact in order to reach people successfully [success was defined as supporting the peace candidate]" (p. 8). The advice given was designed to help them win, to advocate effectively, and to minimize client resistance. The possibility of a joint dialogue, the result of which may be that the canvassers might have their views altered, is not included. "Set firmly in mind exactly what you will want to obtain during your contact," advise the authors, "and look to your organization to tell you what the purpose should be" (p. 8).

The pamphlet advises the canvasser to be well informed (in order to be viewed as an expert), role play a call ahead of time, and especially practice being "the target person . . . experiencing the pressure to comply with your request" (p. 10). You must be confident and "you must be dedicated to winning, to making the 'sale'."

Sometimes the advice seems to place the canvasser in a dilemma that is neither acknowledged nor discussed. For example, the person must percieve that the canvasser cares about the person's views and his reaction as a person. Yet the canvasser is admonished to win and not to lose; he is told that attentive listening establishes him as an open person, yet his goal is to make the sale.

Finally, there is the advice that no matter what happens, strive to help the person feel that his self-esteem is greater because of the session with the canvasser. So we have a world in which the client is to feel genuinely better about himself as a human being because he has had an encounter with a canvasser who was schooled in winning and in controlling others.

## Zimbardo: The Tactics and Ethics of Persuasion

Two years later a chapter was written by Zimbardo (1972) that elaborated and went beyond the material in Abelson and Zimbardo (1970). For example, he recommends that those promoting an antiwar cause (1) impress the audience with their expertise concern (but in not too overbearing a manner), (2) make points against their interest, (3) have someone who may be respected by the "target" introduce them, (4) agree with what the audience wants to hear or with whatever they say first, and (5) minimize the manipulative intent until commitment is requested (p. 87) *and* keep the strategy covert.

Zimbardo continues his advice to the student by suggesting the student "individuate" the target person and "make the person feel you are reacting to his uniqueness and individuality – *which you should be*" (p. 87) and are not reacting in a programmed way to your stereotype of a housewife, blue collar worker, etc.

How can a process of persuasion that is identified as "tactical guidance" in a how-to-do-it manual (p. 51) individuate a person except in a somewhat perfunctory sense (e.g., Zimbardo suggests calling a person Mr or Mrs)? What is the meaning of individuation if the influence processes are kept secret and deliberate? How is it possible for the actor not to react in a programmed way if his behavior is guided by a program? How can the actor "individuate" another human being or "make the person feel you are reacting to his uniqueness" when the purpose is to win and sell (p. 85)?

That Zimbardo is aware that all of this may be an act on the part of the student is acknowledged a few lines later when he states: "Plan the organization of your approach well enough so that it seems natural and unplanned" (p. 88). Zimbardo also recommends that the student be flexible enough to modify his approach, yet he provides no insights nor generalizations on this issue nor any explanation of how an individual can be programmed with this advice and still remain flexible. Perhaps such advice is not included because social psychologists have yet to study such problems.

Zimbardo is aware that there are ethical issues involved. He asks: is it right to deceive someone, "hit him below his unconscious, . . . arouse [in other] strong feelings of guilt, shame, or even positive feelings of false pride?" (p. 91). Zimbardo responds that only each individual can answer that for himself or herself. Then Zimbardo tells the reader that when deception techniques are employed by a sophisticated practitioner the "victim" (his word) does not realize that he has been conned:

> But you always know what your intention was and that you "broke a man" thus. What effect does such knowledge have upon you? Do you respect yourself more because of it . . . ? If you are so ideologically committed to your cause or goal that any ends justify the means, then ethical issues will get a zero weighting coefficient. But that alone should give you pause. (p. 91)

I interpret Zimbardo as asking readers to think twice before they use manipulative techniques. But how about those who are so committed that they want to go ahead? Zimbardo continues: if after a searching search of one's self, "you still want to go for broke, then the time has come to go Machiavellian" (p. 92). Then he presents several pages of research evidence and experience (especially of cases of the police interrogators) that show the reader how to be an effective Machiavelli. Apparently Zimbardo is willing to recommend all these Machiavellian tactics because there are times when the poor, the subordinate, and the disadvantaged have to find ways to overcome those who maintain the status quo.

But will the advice work? I doubt it, because in order for the advice to work, the other person must be unaware of the principles and unaware of the fact that the actor is using the principles. If Zimbardo grants that his material should be available to all citizens then the power people vis-à-vis the poor, or the lower class vis-à-vis the students, will be immunized against the principles. The result of Zimbardo's recommendations may add up to a strategy of Model I persuasion processes oscillating between the sides involved. In practice the argument is weak because the power people are much more likely to learn these principles than the poor people, and by perpetuating Model I we perpetuate qualities that people tend to dislike in their lives.

### Langer and Dweck: Personal Politics

Langer and Dweck (1973) have shown that it is possible to learn principles about how to create happiness that are derived from psychological research. Their purpose was to help increase the readers' level of self- and situational awareness by making them skillful in obtaining and using information and "by emphasizing the *control* you have over yourself and your environment" (p. 2).

The focus is less on providing insight into possible causes of problems (a strategy they do not condemn) and more on how to deal effectively with situations and people. The basic underlying concept is control over the situation. For example:

> a firm understanding of the principles of reinforcement and a few other behavioral laws to be explained in a moment will equip you with the knowledge to give you the powers you desire (p. 20) . . . Direct thinking allows you to systematically exert your control over important situations (p. 66) . . . [The goal is to help the individuals develop competences that place them] in the driver's seat, determining the destination and planning the route. (p. 167)

Langer and Dweck (1973) cited an example in which Stu was unable to persuade Phil to stop eating fruit crunchies. Stu told Phil of an article which stated that fruit crunchies contain chemicals that may cause cancer. Phil responded that it was a lot of political bull. The authors advise that Stu should have known that Phil would have responded the way he did. Stu should have disclaimed Phil's objections in advance. For example, "Phil, I know everyday they say that another one of our favorite foods is no good, but this time it is not a lot of political bull." The strategy is how to win over Phil. What research is available to indicate that Phil will not soon learn that Stu uses disclaimers as a way to win him over?

The book is full of similar covert strategies with larger groups. For example, there are direct and indirect disclaimers. If you think the audience is actually thinking you are trying for personal gain, then disclaim openly that you are arguing the side you have chosen for personal gain (p. 67). If you are not sure about the audience, be quiet, otherwise you may be putting ideas in their heads that were not there (pp. 68–70). One example of an indirect disclaimer is initial agreement. Letting people know you agree with them from the very start is effective even if you later contradict yourself. This is true because it ensures that your message will be heard.

Concern for the other human being is developed in one of the last chapters. First, the reader is reminded that others may also have this knowledge. However, no advice is given as to what to do, for example, when both parties are using disclaimers to win; both are using the yes-but strategy; and each mistrusts the other. The authors also suggest that we should reward persons' actions that fulfill goals they have established for themselves. Again, they provide no discussion as to what we should do if the others' goals are to shape our behavior.

The model the authors present is that effectiveness increases as the individual is in control of the situation. The diagnoses about the other are conducted privately; the strategies are designed to achieve the actor's purposes, to win in spite of resistance, to be in the driver's seat while others are following your leadership and are under your control.


## Robert Mayer: Social Planning and Social Change

Robert Mayer (1972) has developed a framework for macroplanning that is based substantially on the research from experimental social psychology. For example, if the reader is interested in planning community units where prejudice can be reduced, Mayer suggests that the experimental work of Deutsch and Collins (1965) on prejudice can be very helpful. Deutsch and Collins, as a result of careful empirical research, concluded that prejudice was partially a function of contacts among individuals. The more frequent the contacts between blacks and whites, the less frequent the prejudice. The reason was that contacts helped people to see that blacks and whites were equally human. They had the same problems and the same potentialities.

It follows, for Mayer, that housing units should be planned to have a certain proportion of blacks and whites and, also, that black and white families should be situated near each other to foster contacts. How may this be accomplished? Mayer suggests inducing governing boards in housing units to require certain proportions of blacks to whites in every housing unit. The governing boards could also do their best to locate black and white families in such a way as to increase the probabilities for interracial contacts.

Mayer does not state whether the policy of selecting certain proportions of whites to blacks and the policy for location should be made public. Making public the motivations for the proportions and locations may be counterproductive. Residents may be willing to accept a rule that requires that blacks get their fair share of available housing units. Residents may even be willing to accept a mixing of families in terms of location. What would happen however if the residents were told that these policies were defined in order to decrease their prejudice? It seems likely that such openness could lead to defensiveness. The defensiveness, in turn, could immunize blacks and whites against reducing prejudice.

Thus we see again that the results from experimental research may have to be kept secret just as the experimental treatments were kept secret by Deutsch and Collins (1965). If the residents knew why the study was being conducted, the results might have been different and Mayer's suggestions would not be valid.

Another problem with applying the results of the study is that the operational measures used to measure prejudice reduction were responses to questions asked in questionnaires or in interviews. All such questions produced data at the espoused level. If whites say that they understand blacks better and vice versa, such answers do not give us insight into the theory-in-use. The credibility of the finding of reduced prejudice depends on the respondents' respective theories-in-use and not their espoused theories (which are what are tapped when one uses questionnaires and interviews).

If the data on espoused theories and theories-in-use collected to date are validated with larger and more comprehensive samples, then the Mayer policy may be questioned at another level. Our data show that at the level of theory-in-use, the black–white dichotomy is less pervasive a problem because a few blacks or whites deal with members of their own race on other than Model I terms. In other words, if blacks and whites were to become "fully integrated," they would still have problems of conformity, mistrust, and antagonism that would *not* be based on color. Thus integration represents progress, but our research would suggest an additional set of variables that would continue in effect to reduce the quality of life after integration is achieved.

A third problem with the application of the Deutsch and Collins findings is related to the fact that the original research did not consider the families as systems of human relation-ships. Many of the husbands were not included in the sample. Nor were discrepancies between husband and wife regarding prejudice explored. It may be possible, for example, that the action recommendations suggested by Mayer are more validly applicable to the black and white housewives than to the husbands, who may have significantly less contact with the male or female members of a different race *and* who may be influenced by norms in the work place that are biased against blacks.

A fourth problem with the application of the findings is that it may inhibit the need for double-loop learning. One might argue, for example, that whites and blacks, if they are to be coerced, should be coerced into exploring the reasons why they do not contact each other to explore their misconceptions of each other, etc.

In another study quoted by Mayer, he notes that "since the aged suffer from 'lower status' in the larger society . . . placing them in the position of neighbors with young people would inhibit the development of friendship" (p. 57). Another alternative is for young and old to be exposed to how their respective theories-in-use make life difficult for each other. If the problems could be overcome at the theory-in-use level, then there may be little need to make unilateral housing policies and to do so secretly.

As far as I can surmise, all of Mayer's suggested interventions are of the Model I variety. Someone in some centralized bureau is given the responsibility to change unilaterally the living patterns of the people, to do it secretly, and to keep the motivation secret, which means the controlling agency may have to lie if asked about its motivation.

To summarize: all human behavior is informed by theories of action. Theories of action exist at the interpersonal and technical level. Most of our subjects, to date, hold inter-personal theories of action that are congruent with Model I. The experimental method, as supplemented with the activities designed to maximize internal validity, represents a technical theory of action that is also congruent with Model I.

The research examined in this article was conducted by scholars whose primary purpose was to describe the world as it is. The implicit or explicit models of man and society used in this research appear to be congruent with Model I. The result is the production of generalizations, which when they are translated into statements about effective action become statements that remain within the constraints of and reinforce a Model I world.

There are several other plausible explanations for the phenomena discussed above. First, the thesis being advanced may be most relevant to experiments that are designed to test hypotheses. Many experiments are designed to be more exploratory. This suggests more data are needed on the theory-in-use of experimental social psychology. Such research may have the added payoff of producing insights into how to design experiments that are less controlling.

Another explanation is that the main cause of subjects' sense of dependency is primarily related to the act of joining the experiment. Once people have freely chosen to be subjects and once they feel that participation in the experiment is in their interest, the degree of control over them (the submissiveness to the experimental conditions during the experiment) has little psychological potency. It makes sense to say that there must be a difference if subjects choose freely to participate. To my knowledge, no empirical evidence exists that directly tests this hypothesis or that illuminates the potency of the experimental situation. Part of the difficulty is that to test the hypotheses experimentally places the experimenter in the paradoxical situation of using the technique to test the technique.

Finally, there is the possibility that it is the subjects who are programmed with Model I values and behavioral strategies who bring into the experimental setting the tendency to accept dependence and submissiveness. The experimenter does not create the control; the subjects seek it and perhaps magnify it. If this hypothesis is confirmed by research then it would suggest an added dimension that should be taken into account in selecting subjects and designing experiments.

If social psychologists wish to generate knowledge that informs society of effective behavior in other possible worlds (which, from a scientific viewpoint, would make more explicit the limitations of present generalizations) then research is needed to design experimental technology that still aims for publicly verifiable knowledge but that reduces the dysfunctional consequences of Model II technology (Argyris, 1968). Second, attention needs to be given to the formulation of new, empirically testable models of worlds that do not presently exist. The empirical verifiability of the models is emphasized, lest we be misunderstood to be recommending the unproductive practice of "futurizing" that generates abstract and incomplete models of new alternatives that lack operationalization, or when operationalized models turn out to be internally inconsistent or consistent with the very models they were destined to supplant, for example, alternative school models.

One possible model that has been suggested recently would lead to consequences that are the opposite of Model I; this model is identified as Model II (Argyris and Schon, 1974). The governing variables or values of Model II are *not* the opposite of Model I. The governing variables are valid information, free and informed choice, and internal commitment (see chapter 10). The behavior required to satisfy these values also is not the opposite of those of Model I. For example, Model I emphasizes that the individual be as articulate as he can be about his purposes, goals, etc., and simultaneously control the others and the environment in order to assure that his purposes are achieved. Model II does not reject the skill or competence to be articulate and precise about one's purposes. It does reject unilateral control over others as a way to achieve the purposes and to win in advisory relationships. Model II couples articulateness and advocacy with an invitation to others to confront one's views, to alter them in order to produce the position that is based on the most complete, valid information possible, to which people involved can become internally committed. This means the actor, in Model II, is skilled at inviting double-loop learning.

Every significant Model II action is evaluated in terms of the degree to which it helps the individuals involved generate valid and useful information (including relevant feelings), solve the problem in such a way that it remains solved, and do so without reducing the present level of problem solving effectiveness.

The behavioral strategies of Model II involve sharing power with anyone who has competence and who is relevant in deciding or implementing the action. The definition of the task, the control over the environment, is now shared with all the relevant action. Saving one's own or another's face is resisted because it is seen as a defensive nonlearning activity. If face-saving actions must be taken, they are planned jointly with the people involved. The exception would be with individuals who can be shown to be vulnerable to such candid and joint solutions to face-saving yet who need to be protected from others, and since it is done unilaterally, from themselves.

Under these conditions individuals will not tend to compete to make decisions for others, to one-up others, to outshine others for the purposes of self-gratification. Individuals in a Model II world seek to find the most competent people for the decision to be made. They seek to build viable decision-making networks in which the major function of the group is to maximize the contributions of each member so that when a synthesis is developed, the widest possible exploration of views has occurred.

Finally, under Model II conditions if new concepts are created, the meaning given to them by the creator and the inference processes used to develop them are open to scrutiny by those who are expected to use them. Evaluations and attributions are minimized. However, when they are used, they are coupled with the directly observable data that led to the formation of the evaluation or attribution. Also, the creator feels responsible to present the evaluations and attributions in ways that encourage that they will be confronted openly and constructively.

If the governing values and behavioral strategies just outlined are used, then the degree of defensiveness within individuals, within groups, and between and among groups will tend to decrease. Free choice will tend to increase as will feelings of internal commitment and essentiality. The consequences on learning should be an emphasis on double-loop learning where the basic assumptions behind ideas or present views are confronted, where hypotheses are tested publicly, and where the processes are disprovable, not self-sealing.

## CONDUCTING RESEARCH ON MODEL II WITH MODEL II
### RESEARCH METHODS

Research is needed on how to operationalize experimental methods that approximate Model II requirements. This will not be an easy task and much research is needed. Several steps may be suggested.

First, it will be necessary for social psychologists to develop new espoused theories about theories of action that presently may not exist. For example, in his book, Deutsch (1973) developed a theoretical framework of cooperation and trust (two variables that are infrequent in Model I). He then conducted extensive research to see under what conditions these factors could be increased. He tried to show that an increase of such factors might be one way to deal with the dysfunctional aspects of conflict and competition in our Model I world.

Deutsch also found ways to greatly reduce the need for secrecy by designing the experiments so that the subjects knew the rules of the games. They knew the kinds of choices that would indicate cooperation, competitiveness, trust, etc. Consequently Deutsch was able to infer the results about cooperation from the actual behavior of the subjects. He observed the processes of choice as well as the choices that were made. Data were also collected about how people were thinking and feeling while making their choices. In our terms, conditions such as trust were inferred from the theory-in-use of the participants as subjects and not simply their reports (espoused theories).

The work of Hackman and Morris (1974) and Kaplan (1973) also illustrates this attention to theories of new options and new designs of experimental research. Kaplan developed a concept of adaptive maintenance processes, which are congruent with Model II. Then he conducted research to explore what happened to problem solving and task accomplishment under conditions of adaptive maintenance processes.

Hackman worked on the problem of designing experimental group research that did not focus primarily on input–output relationships. He was interested in focusing on interaction processes. Moreover, the goal was to design studies that reduced the use of such inferred categories as "ask questions," "show agreements," which provided little insight into the behavior of the participants and rarely focused on the behavioral strategies which guided moment-to-moment communication among members.

The results present new insights into the conditions under which adaptive maintenance processes, which are presently rare phenomena in problem solving groups, could be used and how such usage might begin to decrease the phenomenon of "group think" so cogently described by Janis (1972).

Alderfer (1972) wanted to test certain hypotheses derived from Alderfer's ERG theory of personality. They designed the experiment in such a way that it could be a learning experience for the subject (learning that went beyond debriefing and could influence their theories-in-use). The authors obtained information from the subjects about the kinds of problems they faced as managers in their respective organizations. They designed the experimental treatments to be related to the problems identified by the subjects. The subjects were assigned to all the treatments and were told that it was necessary, for the sake of internal validity, that the nature of the hypotheses and the style of their subordinates be kept a temporary secret. The order of participation was counterbalanced for experimental control.

A series of three role-plays were conducted. (The role-plays were designed from the information gained during pre-interviews.) After each episode the experimental learner (subject) reviewed his behavior with a consultant who had observed him during the role-playing. The subject had the option of listening to a tape of his just completed behavior.

The consultants revealed to the subjects how well they performed as well as the performances of others (without identifying the others), etc. More importantly, they created a learning seminar in which the subjects could try out new behavior. In terms of our language, the authors involved the subjects heavily in the generation of knowledge that could be used in designing the nature of the experimental treatments (Model II). Then they assigned people to various treatments that were kept secret (Model I). Finally, all of the information was fed back; they accepted confrontation from the subjects and designed learning seminars so that the subjects could learn to behave more effectively in the kinds of problem situations that they had defined as crucial (Model II).

Although Alderfer, Kaplan, and Smith did not do this, they might have repeated the experiment with the same individuals. The subjects need not be told to what experimental treatment they were assigned. However, the assumption would be that most would now be able to recognize their tasks. Indeed, that might be an important learning experience for the subjects.

However, such knowledge on the part of the subjects could reduce the internal validity of the experiment. The authors could develop a new set of subjects and repeat the experiment as done originally. This new group would become the control group. In other words, if Model II conditions may reduce the internal validity, one alternative would be to test this possibility by an experimental design.

In the three cases just described, all of the researchers were interested in testing hypotheses as rigorously as possible, all had models of nontypical behavior with which they were experimenting, and two devised experimental treatments that were connected closely enough to the "real-life" problems faced by the subjects that learning experiences could be generated from the experiments.

It is conceivable however that further learning experiences could be designed. These learning experiences may not manifest the extreme control developed above, but this may not be as necessary as is believed, at least for research that illuminates Model II and the processes of moving toward Model II.

For example, 60 students were asked to develop two small personal cases about difficult and easy interventions designed to identify the degree to which they tended to behave in accordance with Model I or Model II (Argyris and Schön, 1974). On the basis of the data analysis, a priori predictions were made that no one in the group would be able to devise Model II consultancy relationships with a cooperative subject. The prediction was not shared with the group. The faculty member gave each member of the group a case to study for a week and told him to come prepared to help Dean Sylvan (a key actor in the case) learn to behave more effectively.

The next week, the instructions were repeated and time was given to answer all questions. Three observers were requested and three volunteered. They were instructed openly, in front of the class, to observe the faculty member's behavior to see if indeed he behaved as a cooperative Dean Sylvan.

The class members began their consulting. Each member role-played with Dean Sylvan for several minutes. After 30 minutes of such role-playing and after the observers reported that the faculty member was a cooperative Dean Sylvan, the faculty member reported that all interventions were of the Model I variety. (The class was aware of Model I, and most class members disparaged it as a model for effective helping behavior.) The faculty member encouraged confrontation of his diagnosis, especially the use of the tape recordings that had been made of the entire class.

Several students disagreed with the diagnosis but changed their position once the directly observable data (tapes) were used. The class response eventually was to agree with the diagnosis and to identify situational conditions that may have coerced them to behave according to Model I. For example, each person did not have enough time, there were too many consultants, and the Dean might have behaved in such and such a manner. Each suggestion that had support from at least ten members of the class was translated into a design of a new learning experience (e.g., a small group of four consultants and Dean Sylvan, played by a student; two consultants who had a week to think of their strategies; two consultants who tested out their strategies in front of the class; etc.). All of the experiments generated behavior that approximated Model I. Moreover, the behavior by the students toward each other was of a Model I variety.

Here is a situation in which little control was exercised by the faculty member yet the predictions were confirmed, even though the subjects were aware of everything about the experiment and were able to redesign it and even though many disclaimed Model I behavior. Why is this so? One reason may be that our categories are poorly defined and a more differentiated scheme would produce a different set of results. Empirical work has been and continues to be conducted on this possibility. The results, to date, are encouraging. First, we have been able to obtain a high degree of interobserver reliability in classifying cases of people's behavior as Model I or Model II (93 percent agreement with 100 cases). Second, we have taught 75 students who espoused Model II theories of action to re-examine their cases and score them in terms of Model I or Model II. All but six judged them to be completely Model I, five judged them to be largely Model I, and one judged his case to be about half and half. Finally, on the basis of the categories described above, we have been able to make a priori predictions as to how individuals will behave in the learning situations. These predictions have been confirmed, even when stated ahead of time to the subjects and even when the subjects did *not* wish to behave according to the prediction. (The subjects were free to behave contrary to the prediction: Argyris and Schön, 1974.)

These data support some previously published data that Model I theories-in-use predominate in groups and organizations (Argyris, 1969, 1970). Human beings, therefore, may vary in the degree to which they behave according to Model I (and vary according to the situation). They do not seem to vary as to how much they behave in accordance with Model II. Model II behavior, to date, is practically nonexistent.

Some may suggest that these results argue that Model I represents an innate aspect of human nature that is not significantly modifiable. This is a legitimate question and requires empirical research. To date, the only question that can be raised is that, empirically, many of our subjects *espouse* Model II theories of action. If Model I were innate why would people espouse Model II? Also, evidence is being accumulated that presidents of corporations (who tend to be high on Model I) can begin to develop irreversible changes toward Model II with the equivalent of four weeks of full-time education. If these results are substantiated, then Model I can hardly be said to be innate.

As pointed out above, the position in this is that much social behavior is not innate, that it is highly influenced by the environment, and that the environment (culture) is an artifact created by man to fulfill his basic predisposition to create orderly rule-dominated worlds (Israel and Tajfel, 1972). The time has arrived for social psychology to conduct research that provides mankind with insight into new cultures and new rules.

# References

Abelson, R. P., and Zimbardo, P. G., 1970, *Canvassing for Peace*, Ann Arbor, MI., Society for the Psychological Study of Social Issues.

Alderfer, C., 1972, *Existence, Relatedness, and Growth*. New York, Free Press.

Argyris, C., 1968, "Some Unintended Consequences of Rigorous Research," *Psychological Bulletin*, 70, 185–197.

Argyris, C., 1969, "The Incompleteness of Social Psychological Theory," *American Psychologist*, 24, 893–908.

Argyris, C., 1970, *The Applicability of Organizational Sociology*, Cambridge, England, Cambridge University Press.

Argyris, C., and Schon, D., 1974, *Theory in Practice*, San Francisco, CA, Jossey-Bass.

Aronson, E., 1972, *The Social Animal*, San Francisco, CA, W. H. Freeman.

Aronson, E., and Carlsmith, J. M., 1968, "Experimentation in Social Psychology," in Lindsey, G., and Aronson, E., (eds), *The Handbook of Social Psychology*, Vol. 2, Reading, MA, Addison-Wesley.

Campbell, D., and Stanley, J. C., 1963, *Experimental and Quasiexperimental Designs for Research*, CA, Rand McNally.

Deutsch, M., 1973, *The Resolution of Conflict: Constructive and Destructive Processes*, New Haven, CN, Yale University Press.

Deutsch, M., and Collins, M. E., 1965, "Inter-racial Housing," in Peterson, W. (ed.), *American Social Patterns*, Garden City, NY, Doubleday.

Hackman, R., and Morris, C. G., 1974, *Group Tasks, Group Interaction Process, and Group Performance Effectiveness: A Review and Proposed Integration* (Tech. Rep. 7). New Haven, Conn., Yale University, School of Organization and Management, August.

Isaac, S., 1971, *Handbook on Research and Evaluation*, San Diego, CA, Knapp.

Israel, J., and Tajfel, H. (eds), 1972, *The Context of Social Psychology: A Critical Assessment*, New York, Academic Press.

Janis, I. L., 1972, *Victims of Groupthink*, Boston, Houghton Mifflin.

Kaplan, R. E., 1973, "Managing Interpersonal Relations in Task Groups: A Study of Two Contrasting Strategies," unpublished doctoral dissertation, Department of Administrative Sciences, Yale University.

Kelman, H. C., 1969, *A Time to Speak*, San Francisco, CA, Jossey-Bass.

Langer, E. J., and Dweck, C. S., 1973, *Personal Politics*, Englewood Cliffs, NJ, Prentice-Hall.

McGuire, W. J., 1969, "Inducing Resistance to Persuasion," in Berkowitz, L. (ed.), *Advances in Experimental Social Psychology*, Vol. 1, New York, Academic Press.

Mayer, R. R., 1972, *Social Planning and Social Change*, Englewood Cliffs, NJ, Prentice-Hall.

Miller, G., 1969, "Psychology as a Means of Promoting Human Welfare," *American Psychologist*, 24, 1063–75.

Rubin, Z., 1973, *Liking and Loving*, New York, Holt, Rinehart & Winston.

Tajfel, H., 1972, "Experiments in a Vacuum," in Israel, J., and Tajfel, H. (eds), *The Context of Social Psychology*, New York, Academic Press.

Varela, J. A., 1971, *Psychological Solutions to Social Problems*, New York, Academic Press.

Zimbardo, P. G., 1969, "The Human Choice: Individuation, Reason, and Order Versus Deindividuation, Impulse, and Chaos," in Arnold, W. J., and Levine, D., (eds), *Nebraska Symposium on Motivation*, Vol. 17, Lincoln, University of Nebraska Press.

Zimbardo, P. G., 1972, "The Tactics and Ethics of Persuasion," in King, B. T., and McGinnies, E. (eds), *Attitudes, Conflict, and Social Change*, New York, Academic Press.

Zimbardo, P., and Ebbesen, E. B., 1969, *Influencing Attitudes and Changing Behavior*, Reading, MA, Addison-Wesley.

# — 25 —

# Making Knowledge More Relevant to Practice: Maps for Action

Elsewhere, I have tried to describe the conditions that tend to inhibit the production of valid and usable knowledge, especially when diagnosing and changing the status quo (Argyris, 1980, 1982a, 1983). In this chapter I should like to describe some concepts and research methods that can be used to develop usable knowledge that also adds to basic theory. In describing the methods in some detail, I also hope to show how they illustrate a more general perspective for making knowledge more relevant to practice.

## THE MEANING OF PRACTICE

Practice may be defined as the implementation of a set of ideas in order to achieve intended consequences in the world of practical affairs. The act of implementation may be at the level of formulating a policy or executing it. The focus of this chapter is on producing social science knowledge that practitioners can use in taking action, such as executing policies. The domain of focus is on human beings as they are interacting in order to achieve their intended goals. I take it as a given that it is individuals who will do the actual implementing, the acting, even though they may be serving as agents for an organization or group.

## MAPS FOR ACTION

If we are to be of help to practitioners as they act, we need to consider what kind of knowledge individuals require and use while acting. Fortunately, recent research provides many insights into how people make sense of their worlds in order to act. For example, they organize data into patterns, store these patterns in their heads, and then retrieve then whenever they need them.

Humans probably use several mechanisms to store these patterns. The one we will focus on here is called "maps for action." These maps represent the behaviors that people use to design and implement their actions. These maps are the key to helping us to understand and explain why human beings behave as they do, because they represent the problems or causal scripts that individuals use to inform their actions.

I want to emphasize that these maps are constructions formulated by researchers, and, as such, they are hypotheses to be tested. Further, action maps are never completed, because all the features of situations cannot be fully known. Ironically, then, maps are most useful if they contain designed ignorance. Or, to put it another way, a map for action may be viewed as the researcher's constructions of the actor's views of the strategic variables that determine the essential formulation of a solution (Ansoff, 1979, pp. 220–2).

One of the central arguments of this chapter is: if human beings use maps for action to inform their actions, then one way for social scientists to help ensure that the knowledge they produce will be usable is to organize, or package, it in the form of maps for action. I will present several examples of action maps that we have developed, discuss their underlying properties, and make explicit how they can be tested and how they add to knowledge while also making it more likely that the knowledge will be usable in action.

### Example I: Conflict Avoidance and Directive Control

The first map was developed by Diana Smith and me. We were trying to make sense of the data obtained during a weekend workshop attended by six senior members of a professional firm and their spouses. The objective of the workshop was to help the participants understand and cope more effectively with the pressures they were experiencing.

The map (figure 25.1) begins by identifying the factors that all participants agreed created the pressures and problems that they experienced. As indicated in column 1, these factors are related to work requirements (frequent travel, long and unpredictable hours at work, and so on) and home requirements (being with spouse and children, chores related to home, and so on). Next, the couples identified what may be called structural solutions to deal with the pressures (column 2). These consisted of a range of rules that were not to be violated, such as "Divide tasks" and "Define personal turf." At times these rules were effective, but at other times they were not, as any number of unexpected factors led to violations that, in turn, led to the difficulties that the couples were trying to solve. The frequency of rule ineffectiveness was high enough for the couples to agree that this was a major source of conflict. The couples identified two major patterns they used to deal with such conflict (column 3). Some spouses acted to avoid conflict (CA); others became aggressive and controlling (AC). Men were as likely to be in either category as women. Sometimes conflict avoiders acted aggressively but only when they felt there was absolutely no other recourse left to them.

In column 4 we note the most frequent reactions used by the individuals to deal with the conflicts and pressures. The CAs acted as if there were no problem and waited for the spouse to act. The ACs acted relatively quickly but usually tried to do so by hiding their exasperation and anger with disingenuous inquiry. The passivity of the CAs and the aggressiveness of the ACs tended to trigger automatic emotional responses. It was as if they had a psychological button that was pushed. In column 5 we note these typical reactions. As a rule the CAs would try to downplay their errors either directly or indirectly by saying that they had other chores or much higher priorities. The ACs would then express disbelief and outrage at such responses and question the CAs' sense of responsibility. This, in turn, would make it possible for the CAs to become angry and accuse the ACs of being hostile. The ACs would accept that they were acting in a hostile manner and then hold the CAs responsible (column 6).

In figure 25.1 we show that all these reactions feed back to reinforce the previous actions. The feedback processes in this system are not error-correcting but error-enhancing. Living under these self-sealing, escalating processes is difficult for all concerned. One way to live with these conditions is to formulate an explanation for the dysfunctional behavior of the other. The explanation becomes a dominant belief or assumption about the other. Hence, the CAs come to believe that the ACs prefer weak spouses and are uninfluenceable, and that

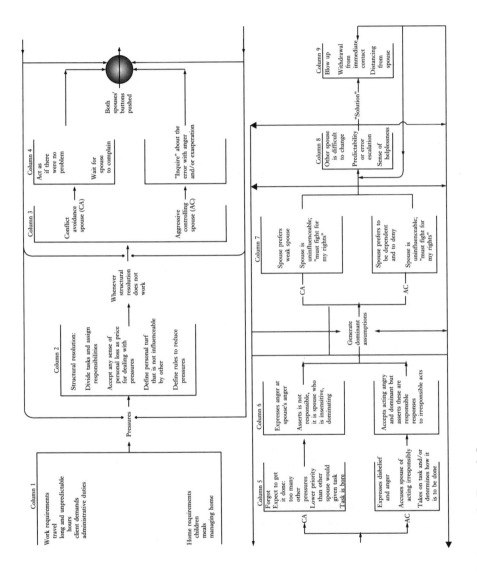

**Figure 25.1** Action map for Example I

they (CAs) must fight for their rights. The ACs, in contrast, come to believe that the CAs prefer to depend on them and to deny that this is the case. The ACs also come to see their spouses as uninfluenceable, so that they too must fight for their rights (column 7). These conditions lead all parties to conclude that the other spouse is difficult to change, that escalating error and a sense of helplessness are a way of life (column 8). The outcome of this state of affairs is either to experience blowups or to withdraw and distance from each other or both (column 9).

## Example II: Moving toward Genuine Matrix Management

In the second example (figure 25.2), we present a map of the operation of a top management group in a larger organization (developed primarily by Diana Smith). The group contained the 15 top executives of the firm, representing all the major functions. Its purpose was to act as the highest governing body for the important strategic issues of the firm. The members had committed themselves to creating group dynamics and a group culture that would make it possible for them to discuss issues that are typically undiscussable, to constructively confront one another's ideas, and to encourage risk-taking and new trust.

The members believed that if they were to succeed, two types of conditions would have to be developed. First, there were structural conditions. For example, policies would be developed to guarantee members organizational power to act forthrightly and candidly; rewards, including financial ones, would be available to those making important contributions to the development of the group; organizational policies would be implemented guaranteeing the job safety of individuals who, in acting forthrightly, might offend or upset members with more seniority; and finally, rules would be developed by which counterproductive actions by any members would be discussed. Second, group members would develop the skills required to produce actions consistent with the structural arrangements so that the structures would come to life and be put into practice as intended. Otherwise, if individuals were structurally protected to confront constructively – but when they did so, the actions themselves were destructive – then the structural arrangements would soon lose their credibility.

The top group met about once a month, usually for 12 to 15 hours, to deal with strategic issues. Tape recordings of sessions were sent to researchers whenever they were not present. After a year of operating, a good deal of concern was expressed that although important structural safeguards were in place, the actions of some members were counterproductive to the ideal of an effectively functioning strategic group that they were trying to approximate. The most pressing problem was that many of the younger officers felt that the four senior executives were not acting consistently with the collegial model. The president was seen as overcontrolling. He agreed that at times he acted this way because the others were creating a vacuum that he had to fill for the sake of the organization. The three other senior executives were seen as a good deal more passive, not confronting the president. As a result, the younger officers felt that they had to "play it safe." The metaphor in good currency was "run silent, run deep."

Turning to figure 25.2 the map begins with the conditions that all participants agreed were governing constraints.

The first column represents the conditions that all participants agree are constraints that cannot be ignored. All actions by the members must take these constraints into account. Six such governing conditions were identified.

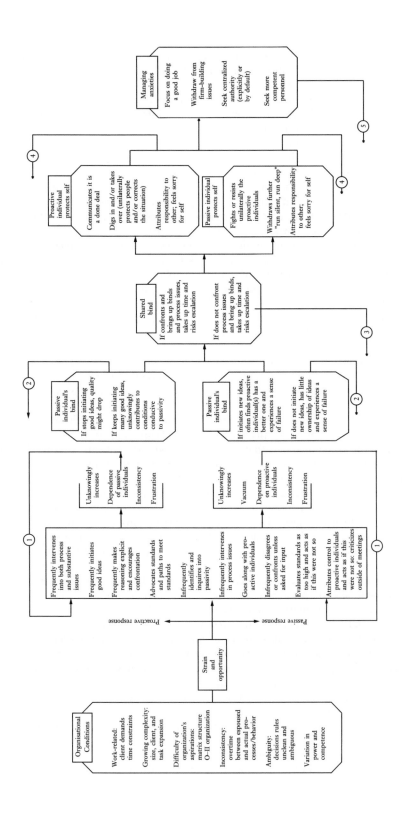

**Figure 25.2** Action map for Example II

1   High demands are placed on the professionals to meet clients' requirements. For example, the professionals typically work a 10 to 12-hour day and frequently work on Saturdays and part of Sundays.
2   The firm is growing so fast that the board of directors has asked the chief executive officer to reduce the pace of growth. The fast rate at which new clients are added places heavy demands on the professionals.
3   A third governing condition is the inconsistency between the participants' espousal of the ideal and their inability to produce such actions as often as they wish.
4   As a consequence of conditions 1, 2, and 3, the participants are faced with another governing condition, namely, they are having difficulties in creating a learning environment and group dynamics during the group meetings that are consistent with their ideal, which could be described as Model II. (For details of Model II, see chapter 10; Argyris, 1982a.)
5   There is a high degree of ambiguity around the decision rules related to the substantive features of the business as well as around the rules for moving toward the model of group functioning to which the members aspire.
6   Finally, the members agree, and the researchers confirm, that the individuals have different degrees of competence in skills as well as different degrees of power. An example of the latter is that the matrix includes the chief executive officer, three senior partners, and vice presidents.

These conditions create all sorts of strains and opportunities for learning. Individuals report that they respond (and they are observed to respond) to these governing conditions with varying degrees of proactivity. Hence, we show a continuum of passive to proactive responses.

Examples of the proactive responses include (1) intervening in both process and substantive issues that are critical to effective transition, (2) initiating and advocating ideas that are judged by the group members to be useful and good, (3) frequently making the reasoning behind actions explicit and encouraging confrontation of them, (4) advocating high standards both technically and in the management of the human processes within the group and organization, and (5) frequently identifying and inquiring into passivity.

The individuals who act more passively tend (1) to infrequently intervene in process issues, (2) to go along with proactive individuals' contributions, (3) to infrequently disagree or confront unless asked, (4) to evaluate standards as too high and act as if this were not so, and (5) to attribute control to proactive individuals and act as if this were not so, that is, to criticize proactive individuals privately.

In consequence, proactive individuals, who often make valid interventions, tend to facilitate dependence of passive individuals. These actions reinforce the inconsistency between the espoused aspirations and the actual individual actions and group dynamics. Finally, the proactive members feel frustrated with the lack of involvement by those who act more passively and who simultaneously condemn them for being more proactive.

The passivity tends to create a behavioral vacuum that the proactive members believe they must fill. The passive actions also reinforce the dependence on the proactive individuals, the inconsistency, and the frustration.

These two sets of consequences feed back to reinforce respectively the original responses. Hence, individuals who act more proactively defend themselves by maintaining or reinforcing their proactivity, while individuals who act more passively defend themselves by reinforcing their passivity.

In addition to respectively reinforcing the preferred response patterns of individuals, the actions and consequences described so far lead to a third order of consequences that are paradoxes. A paradox occurs when individuals are in a situation in which whatever response they make in order to be constructive is also counterproductive.

The paradox experienced by the proactive individuals is: if they stop being proactive with admittedly good ideas, the quality of the group's performance will drop. If they keep initiating good ideas, they will reinforce a passivity that will also lead the group's performance to drop, as well as inhibiting the move toward Model II and an O-II world (see chapter 10 and Argyris, 1982a).

The paradox experienced by the passive individuals is: if they initiate new ideas, they will often find that the proactive individuals have better ones, and hence they will feel disappointment or failure. Yet, if they do not initiate new ideas, they will experience little ownership of ideas and still experience failure in not producing their own ideas and not moving toward II and O-II.

This set of paradoxes reinforces the particular responses because the actors tend to continue their preferred ways of responding when dealing with the paradox.

These paradoxes, in turn, lead to another paradox that all participants have. When individuals confront the process issues, they are likely to take up precious time in an already full agenda and risk error escalation, particularly since they are apt to raise the dilemmas consistently with their predispositions. But if they do not confront the issues and bring up the paradoxes, the resulting dynamics will also take up time and lead to error escalation.

This shared paradox both reinforces the previous factors and leads to self-protective responses aimed at managing the paradoxes. Thus, the highly proactive individuals tend to become impatient with passivity, to take action and to take over, and to communicate that "it's done." If confronted, they tend to dig in and to place the blame for their unilateral actions on the passive actors. Finally, they tend to withhold their fears about the effectiveness of the matrix as well as the probable long-run failure of the experiment.

To protect themselves, the passive individuals tend to resist the proactive individuals, either covertly or overtly. Most often, however, they tend to withdraw even further, withholding their fears and holding the proactive individuals responsible for both their withdrawal and their fears (column 6).

These fifth-order consequences then feed back to reinforce the previous consequences and simultaneously lead to a set of final consequences related to how individuals manage the stress. They include (1) focus on performing one's own job very well, (2) withdrawal from firm-building and matrix-building issues, (3) seeking more centralized authority, and (4) seeking more competent personnel (column 7).

These consequences will help to produce high-quality individual performance but can also lead to an organization increasingly full of stress, which, in turn, may hinder the building of an organization that can ensure high performance over time.

## FEATURES OF THE MAPS

The maps purport to identify and to describe the interdependence of the variables that the actors define as relevant. By interdependence I mean how a given variable influences and is influenced by the other variables. For example, the passive actors and conflict avoiders have an impact on the proactive or aggressive actors, and this impact, in turn, has specified consequences on the variables that follow plus feedback consequences on the variables that precede it.

Embedded in the map is a microtheory of how the variables developed and how they are presently forming a self-maintaining and reinforcing system. Both these features contain what I should like to call "sloppy causality." The causal assertions are sloppy in that they are not formulated in rigorous and unambiguous terms. But it may be that sloppy causality is the most accurate causality that the participants will ever be able to use. If this is true, then the feature that social scientists will have to address is how human beings achieve "satisficing" accuracy by using causal theories that are sloppy.

The maps depict a story or drama that unfolds with predictable repetitiveness (Mangham, 1978) at different levels of analysis. The maps begin by specifying conditions that are external to couples' actions yet help to drive the actions. For example, the couples choose to have their professional careers, to raise children, to be active neighbors. The executives choose to design a top-level matrix group to administer their firm, they choose to make their firm a fast-growing one, they choose to create a world with many ambiguities, and they choose to be in a world where there is variation in power and competence. Yet, once created, these conditions come home to roost, requiring these individuals to take them into account.

The maps indicate the pressures and strains that these governing conditions create, followed by the ways the participants predictably and repetitively choose to act to deal with the pressures and stresses. Next are the second-order consequences of these choices as well as the way they feed back to reinforce the previous factors. The maps continue with third-order, fourth-order, and so on, consequences plus their feedback. Some of these lead to dominant assumptions and beliefs (Example I); others lead into paradoxes and then to dominant assumptions (Example II). The sequence in each map appears to start with governing conditions and then to go to strategies, behavioral consequences, norms, assumptions and beliefs, and further behavioral consequences. The exact nature of these conditions and sequences and of the feedback mechanisms depends on the context being studied.

Since participants, past or present, are able to identify the story embedded in each map, and since the story appears to exist over time and through the turnover of actors, the maps are also maps of social systems. The patterns they depict form a social system in the sense that the patterns exist even though the participants who wish to alter them appear unable to do so; and even as participants come and go, the essential components of the system depicted in the map remain.

These maps contain a frequently identified feature of "supra-individual" systems: they are created by individuals, yet once created, they become self-maintaining and it is difficult for the individuals to change them. They also contain another feature of supra-individual systems that is rarely emphasized: these maps cannot be changed directly by supra-individual factors. As we shall see, in order to help individuals we must first begin by altering their individual theories of action that lead them to produce the automatic responses (such as conflict avoidance or acting proactively) that, in turn, lead to the second-, third-, or fourth-order consequences that become supra-individual conditions.

Both maps suggest that there is a low probability that the system will become self-corrective or that the drama will change significantly. So far, almost all the maps developed, at the beginning of the relationship, have the features of feedback processes that inhibit the detection and correction of error, that escalate mistrust and defensiveness, that enhance self-fulfilling and self-sealing processes.

These general features of maps are caused by the theories of action that human beings use to deal with such problems. These theories-in-use appear to be the same for most participants; hence the similarities among systems, and hence the supra-individual features described earlier. But if most individuals have the same theory-in-use, then the individuals are the carriers of the supra-individual systemic features. In other words, (1) it is individuals who "cause" the supra-individual systems; (2) it is the supra-individual systemic features that "cause" the individuals to act and reason as they do; hence, (3) the system cannot be changed without altering the individuals' reasoning processes, which (4) are so protected by socially learned defenses that change must *begin* at the individual level; but (5) these changes are related to the theories-in-use, which are learned through socialization and hence are supra-individual variables.

It is this intimate connection between individual and supra-individual factors that makes these maps generalizable beyond the context in which they were developed. For example, "button-pushing" has been identified among senior-level executives (Argyris, 1976). Moreover, it appears that, in classes held in a university setting to help students learn Model II, the students act in ways that are consistent with the features of the map in Example II. Students are under time pressures during the classes or are constrained in how often they can meet in small sections outside class. They experience a growing complexity and ambiguity because they often act inconsistently between their espoused theory and their theory-in-use and feel stuck in their inability to change their theory-in-use. There are also varying degrees of power, the instructor and the teaching assistants having more than the students.

At the outset, the instructor is more proactive than the students. She or he frequently has important things to say and advocates high standards. In the classes, the number of participants is large (over 50), and hence the instructor does not often deal with passivity, because she or he is kept busy dealing with the issues by the more proactive students. The passive students tend to criticize the proactive students and, at the outset, the instructors outside class. They experience the sense of inconsistency and frustration that the passive members of the matrix team described in Example II. The paradoxes identified in the matrix example also exist in the classroom.

Finally, the maps do not identify how many individuals are members of the system, their age, sex, educational status, or social status, or many other demographic factors often studied by social scientists. The hypothesis is that the intimate connections among (1) the individuals' theories-in-use, (2) the systems depicted by the map, and (3) the operation of cultural factors through which the individuals learned their theories-in-use, are so powerful that many members in this system will act consistently with the system. If any are found not to do so, then we would predict that they would describe themselves as individuals who are bucking the system. The hypothesis of the powerful relationship is therefore disconfirmable, a topic discussed below.

## Creating the Action Maps

The first step in creating an action map is to describe the governing conditions that the players agree on. In Example I, all the couples agreed that the beginning of their problems was the pressure they were experiencing from work and home requirements. They then listed the features of these requirements that, up to that point, they had considered as givens, that is, as unlikely to be changed. In Example II, all the participants were able to agree on the governing conditions described in the first column that existed as they were trying to create an effective matrix organization.

The next step is to identify the strategies with which participants deal with the givens. For example, in Example I, we identified two strategies that the participants used to deal with the pressures. One was structural and the other behavioral. In the structural strategy, the couples tried to define rules and responsibilities that, if each spouse carried out, they hoped would reduce the pressures. The couples reported that the structural strategies worked for a while but did not solve the basic problems. After lengthy discussions, the basic problems, as they experienced them, turned out to be the behavioral strategies that individuals used to resolve conflicts. Example II illustrated the problem of an increasing discrepancy between the espoused theory of management (a matrix Model II) and the actualities plus the theory-in-use that produced the discrepancy. The logic was similar. We began with the governing conditions, then the behavioral strategies such as (1) the strain and opportunity, (2) the proactive and passive responses, (3) the consequences of each of these responses, (4) the separate binds that resulted for proactive and for passive players, as well as (5) the binds that resulted for both, (6) the ways individuals protected themselves, and (7) how they managed their anxieties.

Embedded in the maps is a theory of defense. For example, we hypothesized that the proactive and passive actions lead to dependence and frustration among the participants. Then we hypothesized that these effects lead to different sets of binds and a joint set. The binds could not be derived without a theory of human defensiveness. We then hypothesized how these binds lead to organizational consequences, such as the proactive individuals making decisions unilaterally, while the passive individuals go to meetings and withhold important views while acting as if they were not doing so.

Once the map was formulated, we then asked ourselves whether there were any episodes that contradicted it. If there were, then the map would have to be revised unless it could be shown that they were irrelevant to the map. The final map had to be acceptable to those involved as explaining all the relevant issues and problems that they were trying to solve. In fact, the first step in ascertaining the validity of the maps was to examine, discuss, and revise them with the players until they considered the maps authoritative descriptions of their context. These discussions were often time-consuming: most actors checked the causal relationships depicted in the maps; oftentimes they disagreed about the consequences; and individuals spent much time tracking themselves through the map. For example, some conflict avoiders went through all the consequences carefully. The proactive players sought data from the group to test the extent to which they produced dependence in others. Players also spent time discussing the content of the double binds.

In authenticating the map, the participants also set the stage for changing it should they wish to do so. Change cannot occur without having a map of the present state of affairs, including why the players remain boxed in even though they prefer a different state of affairs. If they did decide to begin to change the system, then an additional set of data became available to test features of the map. In Example I, for instance, a strategy for change that focused on changing the spouses' dominant assumptions without changing their own and/or others' automatic reactions and skills for dealing with conflict, we would predict, should fail. Or, in Example II, even if the group were to double the amount of time available in group meetings, the shared bind should not go away. Or requiring, cajoling, persuading the proactive to remain silent and the passive to become more proactive should not resolve the binds that each group experienced.

## Methods for Obtaining the Data used in the Maps

In obtaining the data on which the maps were based, the key requirement was to get as directly observable data as possible. (For detailed descriptions of how to execute methods for obtaining such data, see Argyris, 1982a.) Such data could be obtained through observations, backed up, if possible, with tape recordings. The exact number of observations depended on the nature of the conditions. For example, if the content and dynamics of the meetings were repetitive and routine, then the sample could be small. There might be as few as two observations of group meetings and probably not more than ten.

The second requirement was that the conditions for study be such that the actors would produce their everyday actions even though they might feel embarrassed or threatened. The third requirement was that they have the opportunity, with the help of the researchers, to reflect on their actions. Fourth, the actors should provide additional data that could not be collected by observations or tape recordings, for example, the reasoning processes that led them to act as they did and any thoughts and feelings that they suppressed.

The fifth requirement was that the data collection be repeated several times in order to check and recheck the actors' learning and their conclusions. The sixth requirement was to create an opportunity to explore what changes would have to be made in individual, group, intergroup, and organizational behaviors to reduce the counterproductive features. Such discussions could especially serve to test the participants' commitment to the validity of the maps.

### The Testability of the Maps

The maps represent the numerous variables, plus their interrelationships, that the actors use to make the problem manageable and to have a basis for a solution. The first test, therefore, is to obtain information on the variables included in the map. One way to achieve this is to show the map to the participants and obtain their reactions. As mentioned earlier, this step often requires at least several hours of discussion to examine differences and objectives and to redesign the map.

A second way to test features of the map is to make predictions about the future state of affairs. For example, we would predict that if the members of the couples group are left to their own devices, no actions will be observed over time that will alter the defensiveness and self-fulfilling, self-sealing, error-escalating processes even though the players have now confirmed the map as a valid description of their universe. The patterns in the map should be self-maintaining over the years. A third test is to predict conditions under which the players will leave the system or will consider it a failure.

A fourth type of test is to use the map as a basis for designing concrete and implementable learning environments to change the counterproductive features of the map. The theory of instruction to be used in these seminars can also be inferred from the map. The learning activity and change program, therefore, will be "derived" from the action map and hence can be used as a test of various features of it. For example, what individuals' attitudes, skills, and values will have to be unfrozen to help passive and conflict-avoiding individuals become more proactive and confront constructively? What skills and competencies do all the participants require in order to deal directly with paradoxes and double binds? Turning to the levels of group and intergroup dynamics, how can win–lose, competitive dynamics be reduced? How is it possible to create a culture in which the undiscussable becomes discussable and alterable?

None of these questions can be answered without specifying the processes by which individuals can unfreeze the old and produce the new. Once these processes are specified, they should be consistent with the relationships defined by the map. For example, the button-pushing in the couples group cannot be altered simply by altering the avoiding of conflict or acting less aggressively. The basic assumptions that each spouse develops about the changeability of the other must also be dealt with. In Example II, it is not enough to alter the passivity; one must alter the way the members deal with the double binds. Indeed, one cannot be altered without altering the other.

If educational experiences can be developed or structural arrangements implemented that alter the counterproductive features (for example, self-sealing processes, escalating error) without altering the variables identified in the maps, then the hypothesis that the variables and their interrelationships are both fundamental and strategic will be discon-firmed.

## The Nested Features of Maps for Action

I have been describing maps for action as constructions of what researchers hypothesize to be in the players' heads, both explicitly and tacitly, in order to explain their actions. The constructions are therefore hypotheses and are subject to testing. I have identified several tests that we have used, ranging from reworking the map with the players until all authenticate it to making predictions under the same conditions to making predictions under different conditions.

One way to create different conditions is to help the players change the social system in which they are embedded, including changing the actions that contribute to maintaining it. When individuals cooperate to produce change, gaps become evident in the maps that hitherto were often not realized. When the participants authenticate such actions as "inquires," "expresses disbelief," "acts as if there were no problem," "is proactive," they do so because they have experienced many situations in which those actions occured. They can illustrate the meanings for these terms with actual behaviors from their direct experi-ences or from the stories they have shared with one another.

But when participants wish to change the actions so that they can reduce the counter-productive features described in the maps, they do not have experience to use as a basis to create the new actions. Players who act primarily as passive may "know" what new actions mean, they may "know" what active behavior looks like from observing the more proactive, but they do not "know" how to produce it. Indeed, if they did know, they would have done so long before we arrived.

In order to begin to change actions, it is necessary to gain the cooperation of the other participants so that they are willing (1) to begin to change the system and (2) to help one another strive to change their individual actions. These conditions are usually met in our intervention programs, or else we could never go ahead with these programs. Nevertheless, these conditions are not adequate to produce change in individual actions; that is, even with system support and good intentions, these efforts fail. The insufficiency of the efforts shows that individuals must hold another program in their heads that leads them to produce the actions they wish they could eliminate or reduce. If they are unaware of that program, then a program must also exist that keeps them unaware. Hence, an additional map or set of maps is required if the systemic conditions described in the two examples are to be altered.

An example is the action of being "passive." One of the most frequently observed actions that passive individuals use when they try to act more proactively is "easing in." Easing in is used when individuals slowly unveil the information they wish to communicate in order to minimize making the other defensive. Often they ask questions in a nondirective mode such that, if the other answers correctly, he or she will realize what the hidden meanings are (Argyris, 1982a).

One way to help individuals change their easing-in actions is to help them generate a map for action that they probably use to produce such behavior. The following list states the master program that individuals probably have in their heads to produce easing-in. It begins with the rules (1 and 2) that the actors know how they wish the others would behave and that they do not intend to tell them. Next (3) is the rule that the actors should formulate any questions such that, if the others are able to answer them, they will figure out what the actors are hiding. Next (4–7) are the actors' expectations about the others' willingness to collude with them. Finally (8) are statements about how the actors will act if the others do not act as expected.

1   I know how I want you to behave, and I am not going to tell you directly.
2   I will not tell you that this is the case.
3   I will ask you questions such that, if you answer them correctly, you will understand my position.
4   I will expect that you will see all this without my saying it overtly.
5   I will expect that you will not discuss it.
6   I will expect that you will go along.
7   If you have questions or doubts about my intentions, I will expect that you will not raise them and will act as if you did not have doubts.
8   If you do not behave as I expect, I will:
    • give you more time to think "constructively" by continuing my questions;
    • eventually become more forthright about my views;
    • try to argue you out of your views;
    • conclude that your defenses are too high to permit you to learn or too difficult for me to handle;
    • compromise and/or withdraw and act as if I were doing neither.

Examining this map, we can identify some important assumptions embedded in it. First, the map focuses on how the actor should behave. It informs the actor to expect the others to behave as the actor expects them to. It does not tell the actor to test his or her impact on the others, especially for unintended consequences. Nor, therefore, does it encourage inquiry into the actor's actions. If the actor follows this program rigorously, and if the others do not behave as expected, then it follows that they are to blame. Hence, embedded in the program for being passive are rules that produce a high degree of unilateral control over the others and a high degree of blindness about the unintended consequences of one's controlling actions.

Using this map, the passive actors (easing in, conflict avoiders) can begin to gain insight into the reasoning processes that help them to create some of the systemic consequences of defensiveness, escalating error, helplessness, and distancing described in the models.

The actors can then help to alter the program by trying to master another program that, like the first one, has built into it the intent (1) to communicate difficult or threatening information and (2) to minimize the actor's responsibility for making the others defensive but adds some additional factors, such as (3) facilitating testing of, inquiry into, and constructive confrontation of the actor's actions. This new program is as follows.

1   I know how I believe that you (or I) should behave given the difficulties identified, and I will communicate* that to you.
2   I will act in ways to encourage you to inquire* into and to confront* my position.
3   I will expect* that you will inquire into and confront my position whenever you believe it is necessary and I will tell* you my position if you ask.
4   I will check* periodically to see whether you are inquiring and confronting. I will hold you responsible for continual designed congruence between your actions and your thoughts.
5   If I infer incongruence between thoughts and actions, I will test* it with you openly.
6a  If I learn* that the incongruence is unintentional, then I will act to help you by going back to number 1.
6b  If I learn* that the incongruence is intentional and you are knowingly hiding this fact, then I will feel that I cannot trust you and will go back to number 1.

Notice that several key words in the map are starred. These words are so general that they could be executed in a Model I or Model II manner. All should be executed in a Model II manner in this program. These words are key to producing the new program. Although the individuals may understand their meaning, we find that they are rarely able to produce the corresponding actions under on-line conditions. What they require, in addition to unfreezing the old program, is to learn a theory-in-use with which to communicate, inquire, confront, tell, and so on, so that they will not produce the unintended consequences in the two examples described at the outset. Once this new theory-in-use is mastered, it can be used to produce any actions that do not create the unintended consequences, as long as others aspire to the same conditions and the system permits alteration of the two conditions that I have suggested tend to exist with clients who are genuinely interested in correcting the dysfunctionalities of the existing system. This, in turn, requires both (1) examining and interrupting the old program and (2) something similar to learning the new program or skill. You need a map of the actions to take the opportunity to practice the actions depicted in the map repeatedly and to get frequent and accurate feedback on how well you are doing (Argyris, 1982b).

## CONCLUDING COMMENTS

I have tried to show that the practical problem of communicating scientific knowledge to practitioners in a form they can use is less a cosmetic issue and much more an issue of how we conceive of research designed to produce usable knowledge.

The approach embedded in this chapter and that embedded in normal science are similar in that both emphasize the importance of (1) describing and understanding reality as is, (2) specifying causal relationships that lead to explanations, and (3) producing generalizations that are subject to (4) public testing and refutation. The differences begin when we examine the source of the criteria for accomplishing these features. For example, in normal science objectivity, precision, and completeness are key features. Objectivity is often accomplished by distancing the researcher from those being studied. Precision is achieved through the use of quantitative language. Completeness is obtained through development of long-range research programs.

The approach embedded in this chapter does not ignore objectivity, precision, and completeness. It takes the position that the criteria for these should take into account the features of the way the human mind works when human beings try to use the knowledge that social scientists produce. For example, quantitative precision can lead to information-rich generalizations that either are not usable under on-line conditions or, if used correctly, could create conditions that would negate the predictions embedded in them. Distancing and objectivity may reduce some kinds of distortions and increase others. Moreover, if those being studied model their behavior after the researchers, they may distance themselves from the researchers when informants are distorting information. Finally, the aspiration for completeness may inhibit effective action in a given situation, because it is unlikely that one can know everything ahead of time; and if one aspires to being complete, one can create conditions of unilateral control over others that, in turn, may alter the validity of the data obtained.

Both approaches seek involvement by those being studied. But the nature of the involvement can be quite different. Social scientists using the normal science approach hope and expect that individuals will participate for the sake of producing valid knowledge. Those who are more applied have an additional hope that sound research will provide a basis for subject involvement.

The approach embedded in this chapter takes a view that builds on the one just described. It suggests that one is more likely to reduce distortion and enhance the production of valid information if the individuals see that participating in research will lead to important learning for them. By important learning I mean learning that goes beyond understanding and explanation to producing desired changes and, therefore, learning new values and skills as well as creating new kinds of social systems.

Take the idea of altering the actions of the participants in the two groups in this chapter. All their actions are highly skilled and often reinforced by the system in which they are embedded. Therefore, their sense of competence is related to their ability to continue to produce their actions. But altering their automatic, highly skilled actions requires time. More important, it requires that they become aware of the defenses of which they have been unaware; of unfreezing any defenses that exist that lead them to continue their actions even though those actions are counterproductive. Finally, it requires opportunities for the practice and iterative learning of new skills. All these conditions are rarely achievable under the condition of the participants' being subjects. The more appropriate metaphor may be the one of clients. Participants engage in research because in doing so they can be helped to act more effectively and to design and implement organizations that encourage new actions.

Finally, there is the issue of "ultimate" values, often recognized but rarely discussed. One such value is that we hold sacred the right – indeed, the obligation – of researchers to study whatever intrigues them. The constraints for researchers as described in books on research methods have been less in what to study and more in how to study. But if practice of rigorous research is based on a theory-in-use that is consonant with those used to manage hierarchical organizations, then adherence to these concepts may very well influence the choices social scientists make about what to study. For example, less attention may be paid to developing normative views, views that not only question the status quo but produce knowledge about how to alter it. Further, less attention may be paid to the possibility that research to produce understanding on an issue may be designed quite differently than research on the same issue intended to produce understanding for the purpose of action.

A second ultimate value is related to the kind of world that we prefer to support. It is not true, I believe, that social scientists are neutral about the kind of society in which they live. Even the most "anti" applied researchers value a society in which they are free to conduct research. Such societies would have to value experimentation and learning, which, if truly unfettered, would also require the valuing of risk-taking and trust. Such a society, in turn, is unlikely to come to exist without human beings who are willing to accept personal responsibility for their actions (Argyris, 1982a). If the maps we have developed as a result of our research are any indication, then understanding and effectiveness (individual or organizational) will not occur unless the players take seriously their personal causal responsibility for creating, maintaining, and changing those systems.

But this may be so because we choose to conceptualize the order of the universe in the way we do. Others may believe that individuals are not personally causally responsible for the universe in which they are embedded. For example, there are organizational ecologists (Brittain and Freeman, 1980; Hannan and Freeman, 1977) who are creating an ordered universe in which the individuals in organizations are seen as not responsible for the growth and death of their organizations. This view of the order contradicts our view, and vice versa.

The differences go beyond the issue of freedom to construe realities in different ways. All scientists believe that the universe that they are studying is ordered and that they key to understanding it is to specify the order. A second assumption is that a universe will not contain contradictory orders. Einstein believed that it was necessary and possible to unify Newtonian and quantum physics because nature would not play tricks on physical scientists by permitting two theories to be valid that contained fundamental views about physical reality that were contradictory.

Unlike the physical science universe, both orders I have described may be valid even though conflicting, because in the domain of human conduct different and contradictory orders may be possible. Physical nature may not play tricks, but human beings can create social universes that do.

But if several orders exist, if they contain contradictory values, then perhaps social scientists should be required to make explicit why they chose to develop the order they developed. The answer must go beyond the obvious, "because it is a valid view." The question to be answered is: "Of the several views that are valid, then why did you, as a social scientist, choose the particular focus?" For example, in my case, I am interested not only in understanding (explaining or predicting) a particular order but also in furthering, reinforcing, and supporting the world view that human beings are causally responsible, that they are the creators of the universe in which they are embedded. I am interested in furthering the probability that human beings will be in charge of their destinies. This does not mean that I should not make explicit how social systems may facilitate or inhibit human proactivity. Indeed, it is because they probably do both that they must be studied (that conforms to the requirement to study the universe as is). But, once having generated the map, I then seek to understand what it would take to change the status quo. The additional map of how to change the status quo not only tells us much about the status quo (a basic requirement of social science) but provides human beings with liberating alternatives.

## References and further reading

Ansoff, H. I., 1979, *Strategic Management*, London, Macmillan.

Argyris, C., 1976, *Increasing Leadership Effectiveness*, New York, Wiley-Interscience.

Argyris, C., 1980, *Inner Contradictions of Rigorous Research*, New York, Academic Press.

Argyris, C., 1982a, *Reasoning, Learning, and Action: Individual and Organizational*, San Francisco, Jossey-Bass.

Argyris, C., 1982b, "Research as Action: Usable Knowledge for Understanding and Changing the Status Quo," in Nicholson, N., and Wall, T. D. (eds), *The Theory and Practice of Organization Psychology*, London, Academic Press.

Argyris, C., 1983, "Usable Knowledge for Double-Loop Problems," in Kilmann, R., and others, *Producing Useful Knowledge for Organizations*, New York, Praeger.

Argyris, C., and Schön, D. A., 1974, *Theory in Practice: Increasing Professional Effectiveness*, San Francisco, Jossey-Bass.

Argyris, C., and Schön, D. A., 1978, *Organizational Learning*, Reading, MA, Addison-Wesley.

Athey, T., 1976, "The Development and Testing of a Seminar for Increasing the Cognitive Complexity of Individuals," unpublished doctoral dissertation, Graduate School of Business Administration, University of Southern California.

Brittain, J. W., and Freeman, J. H., 1980, "Organizational Proliferations and Density Dependent Selection," in Kimberly, J. R., Miles, R. H., and associates, *The Organizational Life Cycle: Issues in the Creation, Transformation, and Decline of Organizations*, San Francisco, Jossey-Bass.

Bryson, J., and Driver, M., 1972, "Cognitive Complexity, Introversion, and Preference for Complexity," *Journal of Personality and Social Psychology*, 23, pp. 320–7.

Driver, M., 1979, "Individual Decision Making and Creativity," in Kerr, S, (ed.), *Organizational Behavior*, Columbus, OH, Grid Press.

Driver, M., 1983, "A Human Resource Data Based Approach to Organizational Design." *Human Resource Planning*, 6, pp. 169–82.

Driver, M., 1987, "Cognitive Psychology – an Interactionist View," in Lorsch, J., (ed.), *Handbook of Organizational Behavior*, Englewood Cliffs, NJ, Prentice-Hall.

Driver, M., and Streufert, S., 1969, "Integrative Complexity," *Administrative Science Quarterly*, 14, pp. 272–85.

Hannan, M. T., and Freeman, J. H., 1977, "The Population Ecology of Organizations," *American Journal of Sociology*, 82, 5, pp. 929–64.

Jung, C. G., 1957, *Aion*, Princeton, NJ, Princeton University Press.

Mangham, I., 1978, *Interactions and Interventions in Organizations*, Chichester, Wiley.

# — 26 —

# Participatory Action Research and Action Science Compared

## THE DILEMMA OF RIGOR OR RELEVANCE

Whyte, Greenwood and Lazes (1989) frame their discussion of participatory action research (PAR) in terms of the desirability of pluralism in social science. They argue for the incorporation of PAR, along with normal science, in the social scientist's "kit of tools." We take a different tack. In our view, social scientists are faced with a fundamental *choice* which hinges on a dilemma of rigor or relevance. If social scientists tilt toward the rigor of normal science that currently dominates departments of social science in American universities, they risk becoming irrelevant to practitioners' demands for usable knowledge. If they tilt toward the relevance of action research, they risk falling short of prevailing disciplinary standards of rigor.

From the action researcher's perspective, the challenge is to define and meet standards of *appropriate* rigor without sacrificing relevance. And for this purpose, action research needs three things: a way of representing research results that enhances their usability, a complementary way of construing causality, and an appropriate methodology of causal inference.

In our review of the Whyte, Greenwood and Lazes paper, we shall explore the meaning of these three conditions. Let us begin, however, by defining "action research," "participating action research" and "action science." Action research takes its cues – its questions, puzzles and problems – from the perceptions of practitioners within particular, local practice contexts. It bounds episodes of research according to the boundaries of the local context. It builds descriptions and theories within the practice context itself, and tests them there through *intervention experiments*, that is through experiments that bear the double burden of testing hypotheses and effecting some (putatively) desirable change in the situation.

Hence, action researchers are always engaged in some practice context. In Geoffrey Vickers' phrase, they are "agents experient," and their research results tend to be couched in everyday language, often in metaphors of "optimal fuzziness," such as Kurt Lewin's "gatekeeper" or his distinction between "democratic and authoritarian group climates." Although action researchers may make claims to generalizability across local contexts, their generalizations are unlike the "covering laws" to which normal social science aspires; they do not describe relationships in which the values of a group of dependent variables are uniquely determined by the values of a group of independent ones. Rather, their generalizations tend to describe thematic patterns derived from inquiry in one setting whose valid transfer to other settings depends on confirmation there by further experiment.

Participatory action research is a form of action research that involves practitioners as both subjects and coresearchers. It is based on the Lewinian proposition that causal inferences about human behavior are more likely to be valid and enactable when the human beings in question participate in building and testing them. Hence, it aims at creating an environment in which participants give and get valid information, make free and informed choices (including the choice to participate), and generate internal commitment to the results of their inquiry.

Action science is a form of action research. It shares the values and the participative strategy described above, but it emphasizes certain tacit theories-in-use that participants spontaneously bring to situations of practice or research whenever feelings of embarrassment or threat come into play. These theories-in-use we call "Model I." They include strategies of unilateral control, unilateral self-protection, defensiveness, smoothing over, and covering up, of which their users tend to be largely unaware. (Argyris and Schön, 1974). And these strategies tend, in turn, to undermine attempts to implement inventions based on the discoveries of action research; indeed, they often distort the discoveries themselves – all in ways of which researchers and practitioners tend to remain unaware, not because of ignorance but because of a skillful adherence to Model I theories-in-use and virtues such as "strength" (construed as dominance, or unwillingness to be swayed by others) and "caring" (construed as unilateral protection of others) learned early in life.

In our commentary on the Whyte, Greenwood, Lazes paper, we shall use the action science perspective to point out certain practical limitations and conceptual gaps. We want to emphasize, however, that we see action science and PAR as members of the same action research family. In the broader world of social science, PAR and action science are aligned in a basic and consequential conflict with normal social science. What they have in common far outweights their differences. Nevertheless, as we shall try to show, an understanding of their differences illuminates both the potentials and limits of PAR and the future development of action research as a whole.

We shall illustrate these differences by reference to the Xerox case described in the Whyte, Greenwood and Lazes paper. We begin by reviewing its main features.

## THE XEROX CASE

The authors place the Lazes intervention within the framework of attempts by organizational researcher-consultants to bring workers and managers together to diagnose and solve organizational problems. Starting with the proposition that interventions "limited to the shop floor" tend to yield only marginal increases in productivity and quickly exhaust participants' interest, the authors ask: "How do you get from the conventional shop floor focus to the much broader sociotechnical economic focus?" and "How do you do so without opening up Pandora's box?" (Whyte et al., 1996, p. 6).

The break through occurred, the authors tell us, when Xerox proposed to close its wire harness division, outsourcing its production and eliminating some 180 jobs, in order to save $3.2 million dollars per year. Lazes proposed an alternative: creating a cost study team (CST) that would "study the possibilities of making changes internally that would save the $3.2 million and retain the 180 jobs" (p. 7). In order to gain the willingness of labor and management to participate in this venture, Lazes built on the "trusting relationship" he had previously established with them and on their prior experience as participants in regular meetings where management had invited union leaders to discuss its strategic business plans. Lazes interviewed labor and management representatives to draw out their sense of the risks involved in the CST venture and to help them "think their way through the costs and benefits of accepting his proposal."

Once the CST had been accepted by both labor and management, a joint team of eight people was set up and charged with the working on the problem over a six-month period. Lazes then operated as a "consultant/facilitator to identify the problems . . . caused primarily by blockages, the development of adversarial positions, turf issues, immobilization and a general loss of the sense of control and ownership of the organization's activities" (pp. 13–14).

> To address this "largely reactive behavior" he . . . emphasized "changing the shape of the box;" throwing out a broad array of options and tactics that temporarily disorganized the blocked system and might eventually lead to a sense of joint responsibility, openness and a sense of control and ownership, if properly handled. In a word, he attempted to facilitate a transition to a more reflective and action mode of organizational behavior. (p. 14)

Management offered the team access "to all figures they might require" (p. 12) and invited them to consider "any and all changes." Solutions were found, we are told, in two areas. First, the team discovered data that revealed the high costs of training new workers – in response to the "bumping" by seniority that was sanctioned by the labor contract – and was able to project a substantial savings through "stabilizing the work force . . . providing the parties would then negotiate contractual changes to make this possible" (p. 14). Second, the team discovered inappropriate allocation of overhead charges to the wire harness division whose removal would also achieve substantial cost reductions. The two measures, taken along with other changes, promised to achieve savings in excess of the required $3.2 million.

As a consequence, CSTs were established in three other units at Webster, resulting in productive changes that included worker participation in the R&D process and in plant redesign. These successes "made it possible for the union and management to work out a new labor contract providing employment security for workers in the bargaining unit" (p. 17) and led management to commit to establishment of a CST before any large-scale lay-offs were undertaken.

The authors note that this "powerful organizational learning process" did not spread to Xerox plants in locations other than Webster. They cite the "extremely favorable circumstances" at Webster: a history of labor and management relations "of mutual trust and respect built over years of joint problem solving" coupled with "urgent economic needs" that "had not reached the crisis stage" but "demanded quick and drastic rescue measures" (p. 20).


## THE XEROX CASE CONSIDERED FROM AN ACTION SCIENCE PERSPECTIVE

At least three kinds of important consequences are claimed for Lazes's intervention. They are (1) cost-savings to Xerox and retention of employee jobs, (2) restructuring of the cost accounting system and labor contract, and (3) an experience that would act to up the ante as to the kinds of changes that would be possible in the future. (This is what the authors refer to as "the intensification of organizational learning" at the Webster plants.)

We want to raise two main issues about these claims. The first has to do with the inferences, explicit and implicit, by which the authors link Lazes's intervention to its consequences. They do not consider alternative explanations and thereby miss an opportunity to demonstrate the kind of rigor appropriate to action research.

The second issue has to do with certain questions the authors do not ask: why was the "shape of the box" so narrow to begin with? Why was the organizational system so "blocked?" In short, why did the organizational learning system of the Webster plants have the features attributed to it prior to the intervention described in this paper? If this question were taken seriously, we believe, it would suggest important limits to Lazes' intervention and cast doubt on the likely durability of the organizational changes he facilitated.

There is a distinction between these two issues, but they are also interdependent in certain ways, as we shall try to show.

### The Authors' Treatment of Causal Linkages

We reconstruct the following causal chain associated with Lazes' intervention, drawing on explicit or implicit elements in the authors' paper:

1  Lazes intervention plus "favorable circumstance;"
2  intensified organizational learning process: breaking open the box, holistic, co-operative;
3  achieved (at least one-time) savings of over $3.2M at wire harness plant; saved 180 jobs; significant increase in organizational productivity;
4  established CSTs at three other Webster plants;
5  further organizational improvements: more efficient R&D cycles through worker involvement, more efficient plant redesign;
6  management commits to worker security at Webster, agrees to CST before lay-offs.

What we seem to have here is a threefold claim. First, important shifts in organizational learning occurred: hidden sources of data were opened up, participants' thinking was broadened to include the entire sociotechnical system of the firm, and cooperative problem solving took place among groups (especially labor and management) that were usually in an adversarial relationship to each other.

The second claim is that these shifts in organizational learning caused the favorable first-order results: cost-savings, job-retention, and the like.

The third claim is that Lazes' intervention, coupled with "favorable circumstances" – an impending crisis clearly visible to all concerned, and a prior history of labor–management relations characterized by "mutual trust and respect" – caused these shifts in organizational learning.

Let us take the first claim as given by observation, although even here we may wonder whether *all* relevant observers – other management and labor participants – saw the matter as Lazes did. We have no information on this point since the authors tell their story only from the interventionist's perspective.

With respect to the second claim, the causal attribution is supported in this paper only by the authors' claim. There is no consideration, as far as we can see, of other plausible causal accounts of the first-order effects. One such possibility is the following: "The change was really a political one; management made a decision to open up hidden data, and so on, in order to achieve labor peace. In other words, the story was really one of adversarial pressure rather than organizational learning." The authors may be easily able to refute this altern-ative on the basis of evidence available to them. (We shall suggest another version of it in the following section, when we have introduced some additional terms.) Our point here is that the authors do not try, on the basis of their special knowledge of the case, to construct and test plausible alternatives to their "organizational learning" hypothesis. Indeed, they do not treat it as a hypothesis at all but as an obvious interpretation of the data of the case. In this, we believe, they follow the practice customary in most published papers written in the traditions of organizational development and sociotechnical systems. We are not arguing that their interpretation is mistaken but that a failure to seek out countervailing evidence leads too easily to a belief in the efficacy of organizational learning – in effect, to an ideology of organizational learning.

With respect to the third claim, we are in worse shape. We know very little about what Lazes actually did. We are told that he proposed the structure of the CSTs within which the new organizational inquiry occurred, facilitated the process by which management and labor considered the risks and benefits associated with the CST venture, and thereby increased the likelihood of its acceptance. We are told that he facilitated the work of the CSTs through process consultation – that is, he "provided training in group methods and in problem analysis" and in the early stages of the intervention sat in as an observer in meetings of the CSTs but never intervened except to help the parties to resolve an impasse (p. 19).

We do not know, however, *how* Lazes trained the participants, or how he helped to reduce resistances or resolve impasses. Lazes' way of intervening remains, for the most part, a black box. And there is no attempt to present alternate accounts of his intervention and its role in organizational change at the Webster plants. In our experience, the several participants in and observers of an organizational intervention often see things in very different ways. The "Rashomon effect," whereby different observers tell internally compelling but incompatible stories of organization change, is a hallmark of organizational reality. The surfacing of such stories provides an opportunity for testing the interventionist's story, or reconciling it with others.

The authors make a brief reference to "quasi-experimental method" (p. 35) and to management's interest in testing claims made for intervention. But it is clear that at least what Donald Campbell describes as quasi-experimental method, which very much involves proposing and testing alternate causal accounts of phenomena, has not been carried through here, or at least, not recorded in the paper.

The issue of "appropriate rigor" is important from the point of view not only of research methodology but also of learning from the experience of the intervention. Prospective imitators of the Lazes intervention would need both an operational description of what Lazes did and a critical inquiry into the causal attribution of his achievements to certain features of his way of intervening.

We wish, finally, to comment on the theoretical advance the authors describe and attribute to the intervention. They were led, they say, to pose a new question and to propose a new theory in answer to that question. The question: "How come... no consistent relationships between participation and productivity have been reported in the literature, whereas in Xerox we could report participation leading to cost savings of 25% to 40%." And the answer: an interesting elaboration of various kinds and levels of participation, and a proposed shift in the definition of "productivity" from "productivity per worker" to "organizational productivity," meaning "the relationship between the total costs charged to (a) unit and the value of the output of that unit" (p. 45). The main thrust of the article, as far as Xerox is concerned, is really this shift toward a more broad-gauged, sociotechnical approach to participation coupled with the shift toward a more holistic definition of productivity.

This is certainly an interesting observation, with which we have no quarrel, except for the question of how we know that the shift toward "holism" really did account for the first-order effects described (as above), and how we are to understand the relationship of this theory-building to the intervention itself.

Was the new idea about productivity *suggested* by the intervention, or was its development an important part of the intervention itself? Surely there is nothing wrong with the former. But it is the latter that characterizes some of Lewin's best examples. In these instances, the development of the theory is critical to the effectiveness of the intervention, and it is the intervention that tests the theory. Did this happen in the Xerox case? The case might be made that it did, but we can't tell for sure. The issue seems to be important for what we intend by the relation between "action" and "research" when we speak of action research (or action science, for that matter). It is not merely a question of temporal priority but rather one of the function of "research" (theory-building and testing) within and in relation to "action" (organizational intervention). On one view, organizational intervention is said to be suggestive or evocative of theoretical insights. On the second, it is said to have a distinctive function as a context for theory-building and a means of theory-testing.

## Questions the Authors do not ask

As mentioned above, we do not have access to what Lazes actually said and did in the course of his intervention at Xerox. We do not have relatively directly observable data of what actually happened during the meetings. The reason we seek such data is that only by having access to actual behavior can we infer the interventionist's theory-in-use. At the moment, the most we can infer is what Lazes (and others) believed he did. To use our language, we can only develop a picture of Lazes's espoused theories. Moreover, if our knowledge is limited to espoused theories, we are also limited to the reasoning that underlies these theories. It is difficult to provide an independent test of causal relationships embedded in the case if we are limited to the ideas and reasoning espoused by the interventionist.

As we read the material, we find that we can piece together a more complex causal account than the one described in the case. This account, if valid, suggests that Lazes may well have produced successful first- and second-order consequences, as claimed, but that as he did so he bypassed the organizational contextual factors that helped to create the problem in the first place.

Since we do not have transcripts or notes of Lazes' actions, we will build our case upon the text provided by the authors. We hope to show that our conclusions are plausible by using their statements as our premises and by making inferences that they, and the readers, would find worth consideration. For example, the authors state, "it was obvious from the outset that such a plan would involve abandoning the rules that declared certain topics of study or discussion out of bounds" (p. 8). On page 12, they state that the CST was formed with individuals who were not handicapped by "pre-established interpersonal hostilities."

Abandoning rules that declared certain topics out of bounds makes sense. But we would wish to peel the causal onion by at least one more layer. What were the causal factors that made it possible to have rules whose effects were anti-learning? What rules existed in the organization that sanctioned making such topics undiscussable?

If it is possible to abandon the rules, as Lazes was able to do, we would wish to explore how he was able to accomplish this feat. Our inference is that he used the crisis situation to say to both sides, "OK, if you want to save jobs, or reduce unacceptable costs, then the undiscussables have to be discussed." This intervention "works" because everyone's back is against the wall, and is, in our terms, a "Model I" intervention. It does not require the players to explore how they got themselves into such a crisis in the first place.

What were the causal factors that produced the "pre-established interpersonal hostilities?" It makes sense to reduce these factors, as Lazes reports he did. The method used to reduce these factors was, in effect, to get rid of the old broom and start fresh – again, without leading the players to explore how the "old broom" (or the old "shape of the box" had been created and sustained.

Next, the team discovered that there were high training costs caused by the bumping procedures required by the existing labor contract. The team was able to show that these costs could be reduced by stabilizing the work force, which could be done by altering the contract. Moreover, the CST identified allocations of overhead charges that were inappropriate, and recommended their removal.

The question arises in both cases, what were the factors that had made these issues undiscussable prior to Lazes' intervention? What did management and labor do to make it likely that these discoveries would *not* be made and that solutions to discovered problems would *not* be found without the threat of an impending crisis?

In our own research, we find that whenever undiscussables exist, their existence is also undiscussable. Moreover, both are covered up, because rules that make important issues undiscussable violate espoused norms of managerial stewardship and union practice (in George Meany's terms, "helping management act more efficiently").

These cover-ups, and their cover-up, are indications of organizational defensive routines, which may be defined as any policy or practice that prevents organizations (and their agents) from experiencing embarrassment or threat *and* at the same time prevent them from identifying and reducing the causes of embarrassment or threat (Argyris, 1985). Defensive routines, at any level, are anti-learning.

Yet the Xerox case is described as one in which organizational learning occurred. The puzzle can be solved by introducing a distinction between "single-loop" and "double-loop" learning. In the former, the actions that produce errors are identified and changed. Thus, for example, the action, inappropriate allocation of overhead charges, was changed and costs allocated to the wire harness plant were reduced. Double-loop learning would ask: How come the inappropriate allocations were permitted to go on for years? Did the cost accountants know the allocations were unfair? If so, how did they get away with making them? Did the management sense that the cost allocations were arbitrary? If so, what led them to continue the practice?

In the case of bumping, what led the union and the management to continue a process that led to unnecessary and costly training? Was this due to a tacit labor–management agreement to keep the peace? If so, what theory of industrial relations served, if its propositions have to be renounced precisely when they are most needed, namely, during a crisis?

There is an interesting feature about organizational defensive routines that stems from their being undiscussable and the undiscussability being undiscussable. It is very difficult to manage them. They continue to exist and proliferate because they are relegated to the realm of "underground management" and all sides tacitly agree to this state of affairs. As a result, organizational defensive routines often are very powerful; yet there is, to our knowledge, no formal managerial policy protecting them.

Under these conditions, defensive routines can only begin to be managed if they are surfaced. To date, the most likely condition for surfacing them is a crisis that requires that they be engaged. Since it is difficult to get management or labor representatives to admit that they have been colluding in such activities, it is not surprising that in the Xerox case, the surfacing occurred when a new team was selected and when corporate management promised immunity.

Now back to Lazes' intervention. It is plausible that he succeeded in getting the two parties to discuss the undiscussables because of the impending crisis plus the apparently genuine commitment on the part of management not to punish local managers or workers for collaborating to solve the problems. If so, the basis for his success is an intervention theory that has been practiced for many years. Its premise is: "Wait until there is an undeniable and unhidable crisis; then bring in a fresh team; give them the power to look into the 'box' and change its shape if necessary." Lazes could apply genuine pressure on all sides because there was a crisis that no one could deny. But crisis management is not new (although the kinds of organizational learning described in this case are by no means the only or the usual response to crisis). Moreover, there is little reason to expect that changes effected in anticipation of a crisis would endure for very long beyond that crisis.

The authors frame Lazes' task as one of getting from the conventional shop-floor focus to the much broader sociotechnical economic focus "without opening up Pandora's box" (p. 6). It is our hypothesis that the moment Lazes chose not to open up Pandora's box, he chose to bypass the organizational defensive routines we have described above. From a single-loop learning perspective, this choice made some sense, because the players are probably not skilled at dealing with the challenges that arise when double-loop learning is attempted. The irony, in our view, is that double-loop skills can be learned so that the Xerox case could have been used by those involved not only to save jobs but to help the Webster plant, corporate management and union leaders to build an organizational system in which continued organizational learning – of single- and double-loop kinds – would be possible.

# References

Argyris, C., 1985, *Strategy, Change and Defensive Routines*, Cambridge, Ballinger.
Argyris, C., and Schön, D., 1974, *Theory in Practice*, San Francisco, Jossey-Bass.
Whyte, W.F., Greenwood and Lazes, 1989. In Argyris, C. and Schön, D., 1996, *Organizational Learning II*, Reading, Mass, Addison-Wesley.

# — 27 —

# Some Unintended Consequences of Rigorous Research

Rigorousness is to a researcher what efficiency is to an executive: an ideal state that is always aspired to, never reached, and continually revered. Much literature exists regarding the best ways to approach both rigorousness and efficiency. In the case of efficiency, executives have traditionally assumed that when organizations are not efficient it is usually because the members have not been adhering to an efficient organizational strategy. One of the contributions of organizational behaviorists has been to study how executives and employees actually behave (not limit themselves to how they say they behave). One major result of these studies has been to show that a good deal of inefficiency may occur precisely when and because the members are following closely the most accepted strategies for efficiency.

Literature has been and continues to be developed by scholars studying the research situation (Friedman, 1967; Rosenthal, 1966). They too have not limited themselves to what researchers say they do in conducting research. They have studied research in terms of how it is actually carried out. As a result, they have reported dysfunctions and opened up important new questions.

An exploration of this literature from the viewpoint of an organizational theorist suggests that his field may be able to make a modest contribution in terms of a theoretical framework to organize the existing findings and suggest other possible conclusions that have yet to be documented systematically. This framework conceives of the researcher–subject relationship as a systemic one, be it temporary. By borrowing from the established literature on research methodology, we shall attempt to show that the properties of this temporary system are remarkably similar to the properties of formal organizations. Moreover, many of the dysfunctions reported between experimenter and subject are similar to the dysfunctions between management and employee.

## UNDERLYING ASSUMPTIONS ABOUT RIGOROUS RESEARCH

Let us begin by asking what are the underlying assumptions for conducting rigorous research. The first is that rigorousness is an ideal state which one can only approximate. The second assumption is that rigorousness is more closely approximated as the researcher is able to define unambiguously his problem and the relevant variables. Moreover, the more easily the variables can be observed and measured, the greater the reliability, the greater the probability for future public verifiability, the more rigorous will be the research. The third assumption is that the more control a researcher has over his variables, the more rigorous will be his research.

## THE NATURE OF THE RELATIONSHIP BETWEEN RESEARCHER AND SUBJECT

These assumptions provide the basis for elegant research designs. Like management principles, the designs are expected to work if subjects cooperate. It is precisely at the point when people are brought into the picture that the difficulties arise. Why is this so?

In order to answer this question let us examine the basic qualities of rigorous research. Most methodologists agree with Edwards (1954) that rigorous research tends to occur when:

- the research is deliberately undertaken to satisfy the needs of the researcher and where the pace of activity is controlled by the researcher to give him maximum possible control over the subjects' behavior;
- the setting is designed by the researcher to achieve his objectives and to minimize any of the subjects' desires from contaminating the experiment;
- the researcher is responsible for making accurate observations, recording them, analyzing them, and eventually reporting them;
- the researcher has the conditions so rigorously defined that he or others can replicate them;
- the researcher can systematically vary the conditions and note the concomitant variation among the variables.

These conditions are remarkably similar to those top management defines when designing an organization. Top management (researcher) defines the worker's (subject's) role as rationally and clearly as possible (to minimize error) and as simply as possible (to minimize having to draw from a select population, thereby reducing the generalizability of the research findings); provides as little information as possible beyond the tasks (thereby minimizing the time perspective of the subject); and defines the inducements for participating (e.g., a requirement to pass a course, a plea for the creation of knowledge, or money). Indeed, if Edwards' description is valid, the rigorous research criteria would create a world for the subject in which his behavior is defined, controlled, evaluated, manipulated, and reported to a degree that is comparable to the behavior of workers in the most mechanized assembly-line conditions.

## THE UNINTENDED CONSEQUENCES OF RIGOROUS RESEARCH DESIGNS

If this similarity between conditions in organizations and those in research systems does exist, then the unintended consequences found in formal organizations should also be found, in varying degree, in the temporary systems created by research. These consequences have been discussed in detail elsewhere (Argyris, 1964). Briefly they are as follows.

1   Physical withdrawal which results in absenteeism and turnover
2   Psychological withdrawal while remaining physically in the research situation: under these conditions the subject is willing to let the researcher manipulate his behavior, usually for a price. The studies that show subjects as all too willing to cooperate are, from this point of view, examples of subject withdrawal from involvement and not, as

some researchers suggest, signs of subjects' high involvement. To give a researcher what he wants in such a way that the researcher does not realize that the subject is doing this (a skill long ago learned by employees and students) is a sign of non-responsibility and of a lack of commitment to the effectiveness of the research.

3   Overt hostility toward the research: Openly fighting the research rarely occurs, probably because the subjects are "volunteers." If they are not volunteers, they may still feel pressured to participate. If so, they would probably not feel free to fight the researcher openly.

4   Covert hostility is a safer adaptive mechanism: It includes such behavior as knowingly giving incorrect answers, being a difficult subject, second-guessing the research design and trying to circumvent it in some fashion, producing the minimally accepted amount of behavior, coercing others to produce minimally, and disbelief and mistrust of the researcher.

5   Emphasis upon monetary rewards as the reason for participation

6   Unionization of subjects

Organizational theory would suggest that the exact degree to which any of these conditions would hold for a given subject would be, in turn, a function of:

1   the degree to which being dependent, manipulated, and controled is "natural" in the lives of the subjects (e.g., research utilizing children or adults in highly authoritarian cultures may be more generalizable);

2   the length of time that the research takes and the degree of subject control it requires;

3   the motivations of the subjects (e.g., for the sake of science, to pass a course, to learn about self, for money);

4   the potency of the research (the involvement it requires of the subject);

5   the possible effect participation in research or its results could have on the subject's evaluation of his previous, and perception of his future, life;

6   the number of times the subject participates in other research;

7   the degree to which the research situation is similar to other situations in which the subject is immersed, about which he has strong feelings, few of which he can express. For example, in the case of students, the role in a lecture class is similar to the role of a subject in a psychological experiment. (The teacher controls, has the long-range perspective, defines the tasks, etc.) To the extent that he is unable to express his frustration in relation to the class, he may find it appropriate, if indeed he does not feel himself inwardly compelled, to express these pent-up feelings during the research.

Some may question if these feelings would come out in such research situations because participating in an experiment, being interviewed, filling out a questionnaire tend to take a short time. This view may be questioned. Has not the reader watched how quickly people become involved in parlor games and noted how easy it is for them to surface competitive needs, power aspirations, and fears of failure? Indeed, is it not the fundamental assumption of the researcher that an experiment is genuinely involving? Is it not accepted that the data would hardly be generalizable if the subjects could be shown to be involved only peripherally because of the shortness of time? As Sales (1966), a proponent of experimentation pointed out, the

"brevity" argument is not valid ... the entire science of experimental social psychology rests upon the assumption that experimental periods are sufficiently lengthy for treatments to "take," an assumption which is supported in every significant finding obtained in the experimental laboratory. (p. 28)

If experimental conditions "take" in short periods, then why should not the psychological conditions implicit in the researcher–subject relationship also "take"?

## ILLUSTRATION OF THE EXISTENCE OF ADAPTIVE STRATEGIES

The next question is, to what extent are subjects beginning to adapt in ways suggested by the theoretical framework? Mills (1962), Orne (1962), and Rosenthal (1963) have presented evidence that subjects are willing to become dependent upon and submissive to the experimenter and, as Kiesler (nd) suggested, overcooperative with the researcher. Unfortunately, little systematic research exists beyond these studies. Some anecdotal evidence was collected by the writer at his own institution. The students have increasingly emphasized the importance of being paid for participating in research. This trend can be predicted by an organizational theory. The "market orientation" (so common among lower level employees in industry) is an inevitable consequence of being in a formal organization (Argyris, 1964).

Second-guessing and beating the researcher at his own game may also be becoming commonplace, especially in dissonance experiments. Many experiments have been reported where it was crucial to deceive the students. Naturally, in many cases the students were carefully debriefed (although to the writer's knowledge few, if any, researchers have provided evidence which was collected as rigorously for this assertion as were the data directly related to the goal of the experiment). One result that has occurred is that students now come to experiments expecting to be tricked. The initial romance and challenge of being subjects has left them and they are now beginning to behave like lower level employees in companies. Their big challenge is to guess the deception (beat the management). If one likes the experimenter, then he cooperates. If he does not, he may enjoy botching the works with such great skill that the experimenter is not aware of this behavior. This practice is frequent enough for Burdick (1957) to make it the subject matter of an entire chapter in his best seller *The Ninth Wave*. He describes the hero who outguessed the experimenters and was eventually rejected by them. He also describes another subject who pleased the experimenters but who, it turned out, hated the experimenters deeply. In one major university a formal evaluation was made of the basic psychology course by nearly 600 undergraduates. They were given three topics from which they could choose one to evaluate thoroughly. The senior professor responsible for the course reported an overwhelming majority of the students focused on the requirement, in the course, that they had to participate as subjects. The students were very critical, mistrustful, and hostile to the requirement. In many cases they identified how they expressed their pent-up feelings by "beating the researcher" in such a way that he never found out (an activity frequently observed among frustrated employees).

These examples, incidentally, also serve to illustrate that students can generate strong feelings about experimentation in a very short time. They also raise the question, do we need systematic data showing that the briefing each subject received actually generated not only the correct cognitive maps but the proper psychological set upon which the experiment depends (Friedman, 1967)?

Another example of how students react like employees is illustrated by a request received by the writer from a senior social psychologist at Yale. He had concluded that to identify an experiment openly and honestly would lead to a set of attitudes among students that would be harmful to the experiments. He wanted to know if a place could be found for him to conduct his experiment in an organizational setting. He assumed that people in an organizational setting are not so contaminated as students (especially along the dimension of expecting to be tricked). As we shall see, this assumption is not necessarily valid.

A graduate student was recently able to design an experiment with no deception and one in which he could honestly advertise (as he did) that the students might learn about themselves as a result of participating in the research. His experiment was a ten-hour T group. In the first four sessions at least three hours were spent by the members trying to deal with the students' deep beliefs that the ad was phony, that they were to be tricked, and that the researcher didn't really mean what he had said.

Kelman (1967) raised similar issues. He doubts that the subjects will remain naive. He quoted one subject as saying, "Psychologists always lie!" He also suggested, and this would be predicted by an organizational theory, that the subjects may come to resent the experimenter and throw a monkey wrench in the experiment.

Brock and Becker (1966) attempted to prove that deception may not have the harmful effects suggested by Kelman (1967). Their work is open to serious question. Nowhere do they provide evidence that the subjects were not dutifully playing the role of subject and doing everything asked of them. One could argue that they signed the petition, after being told they had just ruined the experimenter's mechanical box (which was contrived to blow up when a button was pressed), because they saw through the hoax and went along with the game. An explanation for those who refused to sign the petition could be that since they did not blow up the box they saw little reason to go along with the researchers. One would predict that the subjects might openly resist if they were given a rational opportunity to do so. This turned out to be the case. There was high resistance to the experimenter when it was possible to connect the massive debriefing with participation in the second experiment.

Two points require emphasis at this juncture. First, these adaptive strategies are predictable by organizational theory because the relationship between the researcher and the subject is similar to the one between the manager and the employee in formal organizations. Moreover, the adaptive strategies may well lead to internal psychological states, on the part of the subjects, that can significantly alter their perception of the research and their response to it. If this is the case, then the generalizability of the results may be seriously limited unless the researcher can show "rigorously" that he has been able to control the existence of subjects' adaptive strategies.

One way a researcher may respond to the problem of controlling these adaptive strategies is to obtain a large sample of subjects. He may assume that these kinds of behavior are "noise" that can be partialed out. If our theoretical view is valid, then any increase in the sample may simply tend to increase the difficulties, not decrease them. Moreover, as the "noise" increases it may eliminate any "real" effect that might be there. Another response may be to increase the controls over the subjects' behavior. According to this analysis, the problems would then be compounded.

In another illustration of dysfunctions, some enterprising students at two major universities have begun to think about starting a student organization that would be similar to Manpower or, if this were resisted by the university, similar to a union. Instead of secretaries, they would offer subjects. They believe that they can get students to cooperate because they would promise them more money, better debriefing, and more interest on the part of the researcher (e.g., more complete feedback). When this experience was reported to some psychologists their response was similar to the reactions of businessmen who have just been told for the first time that their employees were considering the creation of a union. There was some nervous laughter, a comment indicating surprise, then another comment to the effect that every organization has some troublemakers, and finally a prediction that such an activity would never succeed because "the students are too disjointed to unite."

To continue the comparison with businessmen, is there not a strong similarity of the attitudes held by the early lumber kings and those held presently by many researchers? The lumber kings consumed trees without worrying very much about the future supply. Researchers (field and experimental) seem to consume subjects without worrying very much about their future supply. For example, as was shown above, simple debriefing may not be enough. Students who serve as subjects talk about their experiences with other students; they may even magnify them as they are prone to do a fraternity initiation rite. The impact upon future subjects can be deadly and difficult to overcome.

An experience the writer had several years ago illustrates how much the formal, authoritarian, pyramidal relationships are endemic in many social science generalizations even though they are never made explicit.

A world-renowned learning theorist met with a group of executives. To his surprise, one of these, a senior corporate officer, had attempted to utilize the learning theorist's views in his workplace. For example, he wanted to see what would happen if he related to his subordinates in a more systematic way, that is, by following a carefully thought-through reinforcement schedule of rewards. He reported a number of difficulties.

First, it was difficult to infer any guidelines or criteria as to what would be a valid schedule. Nevertheless, with the help of an advanced graduate student, one was developed. It was not too long before the executive found that he spent the majority of his time simply monitoring the schedules and giving the appropriate rewards according to schedule.

Although all subordinates seemed to respond favorably, there was an unexpected differential reaction. Many men, unlike the subjects in the experiment, reacted positively to their boss and to his rewards. They would say in effect: "Thank you, sir. I certainly appreciate your thoughtfulness." This genuine response tended to complicate matters for two reasons. First, being able to show gratitude toward a superior may in itself be gratifying. Second, such a warm response normally calls for an equally positive response from the recipient, such as: "It's always a pleasure, Smith, to reward excellent behavior." In either case the subject is experiencing rewards that would not be in the reinforcement schedule.

The executive, although pleased with the "subject's" reaction, strove to minimize the pleasure so that the original reinforcement schedule would not be confounded. In doing this he found that he was creating a world where his subordinates had a relationship to him that was similar to the one rats (or children) have to an experimenter. This relationship was one in which the subordinate was dependent and had a short time perspective. The schedule, if it were to work, required a fundamentally authoritarian relationship.

To make matters worse, the "subjects" were constantly having their lives bombarded with meaningful rewards and penalties from other employees as well as from such administrative procedures as budgets. The executive began to realize that if these were to be systematically controlled, he would have to become a little Hitler, control the world of his subordinates completely, to the point that they would be isolated from the system in which they were embedded.

It is important to note that nowhere did the learning theorist state these conditions in his generalizations. For example, he had concluded that a specified reinforcement schedule seemed to lead to a specific level of learning. He failed to specify that this generalization held only if the subject was in a specified relationship to the one doing the rewarding and penalizing, namely, one that is similar to that of an experimenter with a rat. Thus, we see that the nature of person-to-person relationships and the nature of the research situation can serve as potent moderators of the variable relationships we often study. If this is the case, the generalizations from rigorous research studies of the types described above ought to "work" (in the sense that they account for substantial portions of the nonrandom variance) only in life situations which are analogous to the experimental situations in which the original data were collected. The analogous situations are those that contain authoritarian relationships and provide for social isolation of the participants. These generalizations ought not to hold up (and indeed ought not to be expected to hold up), however, in those cases where a controlling party and the object of control are engaged in a relationship which is of a qualitatively different type from that of the experimenter and subject in the experimental situation which gave rise to the data, and where the characteristics of the situation (i.e., of the task and social environment) are substantially different in the life situation than in the experimental situation.

## RESEARCH IN FIELD SETTINGS

The problems discussed above also hold true for the researcher–subject relationship in field settings; indeed, in some cases the problems are compounded.

During the past several years, while conducting field research, the writer has interviewed 35 lower level employees and 30 upper level executives on the subject of how they heard about the research, how they felt coming to be interviewed or filling out the questionnaire, and how they felt while being interviewed or filling out a questionnaire.

The most consistant finding was the unanimity of responses. Apparently research conducted in organizations may create even deeper problems for subjects. Although the data are admittedly anecdotal, it seems appropriate to use them as suggestive of the problem. In doing so, it is important to keep in mind that in all the field studies from which these data were developed, the management at all levels had been briefed by the researcher in small groups with ample time for questions, and letters of explanation had gone to each employee from the president, as well as being displayed on all the bulletin boards.

Although the managers at the lower levels felt they understood the research program and were in favor of it, when it came to telling the employee such a seemingly simple thing as that he was scheduled to be interviewed the next day, many felt very uncomfortable in doing so. They did not feel they could honestly describe the research, nor did they feel they could answer employee anxieties, and more importantly, they reported, they did not want to try. This attitude is understandable because most managers tend to emphasize "getting the job done"; they rarely inquire about their interpersonal impact on the employees nor about interpersonal problems (Argyris, 1962, 1965). Thus to discuss a research project that could arouse emotional responses would place the manager in an interpersonal situation that would be uncomfortable for him.

Instead of running the risk of engaging impossible difficult conversation with an employee, most managers reported (and employees confirmed) that they simply went up to the employee and notified him that he would be interviewed the next day at a particular time. Over 75 percent of the employees reported that their superiors either ordered them to go to be interviewed or said it in such way that they implied that they did not want any "noise." Thus, most employees felt they (the employees) knew very little about the research. Few reported open resentment (after all, they were always being ordered to do something). Many reported feeling anxious.

The reasons for anxiety seemed to vary enormously. "Why did they pick me? Who picked me? Are they going to ask personal questions? Are they trying to get rid of me? Whose crazy idea was this? Will I be able to understand a professor or a researcher? Will the questions be too difficult? Will they ask me to write? How open should I be? Will it get anyone (including me) in trouble? What effect will this have on my wages earned for the day? What effect will my absence have upon others who are working and depend on me?" In some case the anxiety was compounded by informal employee kidding and discussion about the research. "Who goes to see the headshrinkers first?" "I hear they place a hot towel on your head and send electrical currents through you to make sure you don't lie." "They have a guy who can read your mind."

Few of these anxieties were openly stated and fewer were dealt with. Many employees, who came to be interviewed or to fill out the questionnaire with varying degrees of anxiety, attempted to cope with their feelings by becoming resigned ("They do things to me unilaterally all the time"), or by mild hostility and cautious withdrawal or noninvolvement.

The feelings of being controlled, or being pushed around, and of anxiety were reduced more quickly in the interview situation because the interviewer was able to answer many of their questions (without their having to raise them), helped them to feel that they did not have to participate, and encouraged them to alter the questions or the sequence in which they were asked, as well as to feel free to refuse to answer any questions. The negative feelings, reported the subjects, persisted over a longer period in the questionnaire situation. They reported that they felt more controlled, pushed around, and dealt with at a distance, while filling out the questionnaire. For example, many reported questions that arose in their minds but they hesitated to discuss them openly.

The reported feelings of being controlled, being dependent, and submissive to a researcher tended to decrease as one went up the hierarchy and with more participation people had in learning about the research and in deciding if permission was to be granted for its execution. Moreover, the fear of intellectual incompetence to participate was almost negligible. However, there were some anxieties about how open to be, how much risk to take, and how much to level with the interviewer. As in the case of the lower level employees, the (properly executed) questionnaire situation irritated a significantly higher proportion of the managers than did a (properly executed) interview. The executives reported that they resented the unilateral dependence that they experienced in filling out a questionnaire.

It seems that the research process, in a field setting, tends to place subjects in a situation vis-à-vis the researcher that is similar to the superior–subordinate relationship. This is not a neutral encounter for most people, especially for employees of organizations, and especially if the research is being conducted within the organization and during working time.

There is another impact that the research process tends to have upon people that has the effect of creating a double bind. Bennis (1966) has summarized the position of many scientists and philosophers of science that the underlying spirit of scientific research is the spirit of inquiry. It is the irresistible need to explore, the hypothetical spirit. The norm to be open, to experiment, is also crucial in the spirit of inquiry. Also there is a fundamental belief in the gratification derived from gaining knowledge for its own sake as well as the sharing of knowledge with all.

If we compare these conditions with those found in the living systems of organizations we find that the organizations tend to create the opposite conditions. For example, it has been shown that interpersonal openness, experimentation, and trust tend to be inhibited in organizations (Argyris, 1962). The same may be said for the concern for truth for its own sake. The sharing of knowledge is not a living value since that could lead to one's organizational survival being threatened. Thus, the subject is in a double bind. He is expected to be open, manifest a spirit of inquiry, and take risks when he is placed in a situation that has many of the repressive characteristics of formal organizations, which he has long ago learned to adapt to by not being open nor taking risks.

The degree to which this double bind exists probably varies enormously with the living system of the organization, the personal and organizational security of the subjects, their intellectual competence, their position in the system as well as the research methods, research style, and the interpersonal skills of the researcher. However, the position being taken here is that these forces and binds should be taken into account by the researchers in designing, introducing, executing, analyzing, and feeding back the data to the subjects.

To complete the picture we should mention the relationship between the senior researcher and the junior members of a research team. After all they too form a system in which superior–subordinate relationships exist. If our model is valid, we would expect that some of the adaptive mechanisms predicted above would be found in these relationships. Unfortunately, little systematic data exist on this subject. Recently, Roth (1966) presented some data that illustrate the writer's predictions. He presented evidence that the graduate students saw much of their work as being boring and tedious. In several cases the students adapted by withdrawing from work and by cheating. Observation time was cut, the number of observations reduced, and finally fake observations were submitted for full time periods. In other cases Roth suggests that guilt was reduced by becoming less able to hear what the people said and by reducing the richness of the observations on the (conscious) grounds that there was less going on. In still other cases, researchers who missed appointments or skipped questions, filled out their forms later by putting down what they thought the respondent should have answered. Of course, none of these informal behaviors was ever revealed to the senior researcher. As Roth correctly points out, the researchers acted pretty much like lower level employees in plants who perform repetitive tasks.

Recently, Rosenthal (1964) suggested another possibility which, if confirmed, is even more serious. He suggested that, in some cases, the junior investigator may be in such a dependency relationship to the senior investigator than he may, unknowingly, be more sensitized to instances that confirm his superior's views than to those that do not. These data raise serious questions about the standards usually accepted for checks on reliability and validity (i.e., the use of friends, colleagues, wives).

Before this discussion is ended, it may be helpful to note an important problem identified by research in organizations that social scientists may be faced with when conducting research in ongoing systems. The problem stems from the fact that in organizations, at the higher and lower levels, openness, concern for feelings, self-awareness, interpersonal experimentation, and trust tend to be suppressed. The reason for this, at the lower levels, is the technology which ties an employee to a highly molecularized and specialized job permitting little expression of self. At the upper levels, the technology decreases as a causal factor and the values executives hold about effective interpersonal relationships become dominant causal factors. In both cases therefore, organizational theory predicts, and to date the data support the prediction, that employees (lower and upper) will tend to be programmed to behave interpersonally more incompetently than competently, and to be unaware of this fact.

For example, in 35 different groups, with 370 participants, in 265 problem solving and decision-making meetings, tackling issues ranging from investments, production, engineering, personnel, foreign policy, case discussions, new products, sales promotion, to physical science research discussions, it was found that the participants were unable to predict their interpersonal behavior accurately. Ninety-two percent predicted that the *most frequently* observed categories would be owning up, concern, trust, individuality, experimentation, helping others, and openness to feelings. The actual scores (in a sample of 10,150 units) showed that their prediction was accurate only in the case of owning up to ideas. The prediction was moderately accurate in the case of concern for ideas. Trust, experimentation, individuality, helping others, and the expression of positive or negative feelings – all the behaviors that they predicted would be frequent – were rarely observed. Conformity, a category which they predicted would be low in frequency, was the second most frequently observed category (Argyris, 1966). These data have been replicated with groups of students, clergy, nurses, teachers, and physical scientists. If these data continue to be replicated, then the researchers who are studying interpersonal relationships may have to include observational data of the subject's actual behavior because the interview or questionnaire data could be highly (but unknowingly) distorted.

To summarize up to this point: organizational theory is an appropriate theory to use to understand the human system created by rigorous research designs. The theory predicts that the correct use of rigorous designs, in experimental or field settings, will tend to place subjects in situations that are similar to those which organizations create for the lower level employees. Also predicted is that the research assistants may be placed in situations that are similar, at worst, to the low-skill and, at best, to the high-skill employees in organizations.

These conditions lead to unintended consequences. The subjects may adapt by becoming dependent. They may also fight the research by actively rejecting a positive contributive role or by covertly withdrawing this involvement and thereby provide minimally useful data. The subjects may also band together into an organization that may better represent their interest. Finally, an organized society may unintentionally program people who may be asked to be interpersonally incompetent and unaware of the fact.

## SUGGESTIONS TO OVERCOME THE PROBLEMS

If the unintended consequences of rigorous research reside in the degree of control the researcher has over the subject and the subject's resultant dependence, submissiveness, and short time perspective, then theoretically it would make sense to reduce the researcher's control over the subject. It would also follow from the theoretical framework that it would make sense to provide the subject with greater influence, with longer time perspective regarding, and greater internal involvement in, the research project.

It is understandable that researchers resist these action suggestions. They argue that all research could be ruined if subjects had greater influence.

These arguments are almost identical to the reactions of many executives when asked to consider giving greater influence to their employees in administration of the firm. However, after much research the executives have begun to learn that the situation is not as bleak as they pictured it would be. They have learned that workers do not demand or desire complete control. They do not want to manage the entire plant. They wish greater influence, longer time perspective, and an opportunity for genuine participation at points and during time spans where it makes sense.

The same may be true of subjects. They would not tend to see the issue as one of complete versus no involvement. They would be willing to react reasonably if the researchers could show, by their behavior, that they assumed the subjects could be reasonable and are to be trusted.

Managers have developed from research an increasing number of guideposts regarding the conditions under which employee participation is helpful and harmful to the employee and to the organization. Unfortunately similar research is lacking in the area of conducting research. We have few data regarding when it is in the interests of the researcher and of the subject to invite the subject to participate in the design and execution of the research. It may be that, as a first step, much can be accomplished by having worker representative groups (in organizations) and student representative groups (in universities) to help in the design and execution of research as well as in the attraction and involvement of subjects in the research.

The most important fear expressed by researchers when considering subject influence is the fear of contamination of research. This is a legitimate fear. As we have seen, if subjects know what the research is about they may give the researcher what he wants. However, it should be noted in the studies where these results have been found they were *not* studies where the subject was to gain personally from participating (e.g., voting or marketing studies, Hyman, et al., 1954). One must be careful in generalizing from these studies to situations where the subject feels genuinely involved in the research.

There are further two points that may be worth considering about this position. Subjects *are* trying to please the researcher even when they are not told what the research is about. This means that much time and energy is being spent by the subject in second-guessing the researcher. If this is so, the researcher runs the risk of compounding the problem of unintended contamination.

The second point to be made about contamination is that it is inevitable. The issue therefore is *not* contamination versus no contamination. The issue is under what conditions can the researcher have the greatest awareness of and control over, the degree of contamination.

Is it possible to create a psychological set on the part of the subject so that he is involved in giving as accurate replies as he can *and* in keeping the researcher informed as to when he (subject) is becoming defensive or could become defensive? Can the subject be helped to become as objective and verb as he can about his subjectivity? Under what conditions can subjects be motivated to be so involved in the research that they strive to give valid data and warn the researcher when they (or others) may not be giving valid data?

Perhaps subjects will be motivated when they believe that it is in the interests to be so. Perhaps researchers may wish to consider designing research in such a way that the subject can gain from participating in the research (a gain that goes beyond simple feedback of results).

Motivating subjects by offering some possible help could make the situation more threatening rather than less threatening. For example, there are studies to show that people lie to their physicians when they describe their problems if they fear that there is something seriously wrong with them and they may be asked to undergo some stressful therapy like surgery. This is most certainly the case with employees who mistrust their management and would fear participation in research feedback and cooperating with management. In no case will valid research data be obtained where the subjects are fearful of the research or its consequences. If they are fearful, however, would it not be better to know this early in the relationship? Decisions could be made to drop the research or somehow account for the influence the fear would have upon the subjects' participation.

In field research, the biggest fear that we have discovered is that the research will not be relevant to their lives. They tend to see the researcher as someone who wants to use them as guinea pigs and who, at most, promises a feedback session to give them the results and leaves them with the more difficult problem (for them) of what to do about their feelings. For example, the writer interviewed about 50 employees in a bank to test certain hypotheses. As an expression of gratitude he wrote a nontechnical report to the officers, who liked it so much that they provided the support to enlarge the study. In enlarging the number interviewed, 25 of the original sample were reinterviewed. The results showed that many of their answers were drastically different from their original answers to the same questions. When the subjects were confronted they replied as follows: during the first study they saw the writer as a researcher who wanted to use them as guinea pigs; during the second study the officers had described the research as helping them to make the bank a more effective system. "Now," they continued, "you could really make a difference in our lives, so we had to tell you the truth!"

In our experience the more subjects are involved directly (or through representatives) in planning and designing the research, the more we learn about the best ways to ask questions, the critical questions from the employees' views, the kinds of resistances each research method would generate, and the best way to gain genuine and long-range commitment to the research (Argyris, 1958). Moreover, subjects have told interviewers why they felt the interviewers were biasing their answers, so that they wondered if giving an answer during an interview might not bias an interviewer in his observations (which they expected since they had participated in the design of the research). Or, they have hesitated to tell the researcher certain information in the interview because they thought it might bias his observations. In reading protocols of interviews where feedback and help in exploring their problems is promised to subjects, one can find a great number of comments that indicate the subject is trying to be very careful not to distort his responses. For example, subjects have told the writer when they were not certain about an answer, or when they were biased, or how we should check their views with certain individuals.

Researchers are also concerned about telling subjects about the research lest such feedback influence them to change their behavior. In our experience this fear is more valid when the subject does *not* perceive the feedback of the results as relevant to his life or when he is asked to provide data that he perceives as inconsequential and irrelevant. Also, the degree to which a subject can vary his response is much less if one is studying his behavior through observations rather than his reports of his behavior (either through interviews or questionnaires). For example, telling the subjects the plan of a study did not alter their behavior. The subjects were unable to alter their behavior even when asked, told, cajoled, required to do so (Argyris, 1965). In one case ten executives were observed for three months without telling them the variables that were being studied or the results. Their behavior showed no change during this period. Two men were then asked to alter their behavior in the direction that would make them more effective group members. They agreed to try and both were unable to do so. One man became so frustrated with himself that he wrote a large note to keep in front of himself with appropriate reminders (e.g., to listen more, to cut people off less, etc.). In the first ten minutes of a meeting a topic was raised that centrally involved him and he returned immediately to his original style.

In another case (Argyris, 1982) feedback was given to a group of executives about their behavior. After the feedback session, they spent three hours deciding what behavior they wanted to change. Three of them committed themselves to work together to change their behavior. The researcher acknowledged their constructive intent but told them he doubted they could change their behavior. They became annoyed and insisted they could. Subsequent research showed that their behavior patterns never changed.

These observations should not be surprising to anyone who has to help people change behavior that is internalized, highly potent, and related to their feelings of intellectual and interpersonal competence, as well as to their career survival. Put in another way, the more researchers study such behavior, the less they may need to worry about such contamination.

Even if this were not the case, the researcher still has many ways to check whether involving the subject and offering help contaminate the research. For example, if the analysis is valid, predictions can be made as to how subordinates will respond to a superior's behavior (or vice versa), or how people will behave under particular conditions. If these predictions are not confirmed, then one can doubt the validity of the diagnosis.

It should be emphasized that we are not suggesting that we must swing from little subject influence and control to total subject influence and control. The major suggestion is that research needs to be conducted to learn more about the conditions where subject influence and control are possible and under what conditions more rigorous research (in the sense that the researcher has greater awareness and control over contamination) can be accomplished.

We may also have to re-examine the meaning of our present concepts of rigorousness and preciseness. They may imply a degree of precision about the nature of our universe which may not be the case. Is not the universe of human behavior more accurately characterized by redundancy and over-determinedness? Human beings may design and build their inter-personal relationships the way engineers design and build bridges. The latter usually figure out precisely the stresses and strains and then triple their figures as a safety factor. Bridges are "over-built;" and behavior may be overdetermined. Human beings build their inter-personal relationships with the use of many imprecise and overlapping units. As Herbert A. Simon has pointed out, peoples' problem solving processes may be quite sloppy; they neither maximize nor optimize; they "satisfice." However, he has also shown that these sloppier processes are subject to systematic understanding.

This view is similar to von Neumann's (1958) thesis that one of the crucial differences between the computer and the brain is the brain's capacity to be accurate with a lot of noise going on in its circuits. The brain can operate relatively accurately with a calculus that, for the computer, is relatively sloppy. Indeed, the computer would probably break down if it had to use the calculus characteristic of the brain. Perhaps what social science methodology needs to do is take on more of the characteristics of human problem solving. It would then enter a realm of overlapping, redundant concepts and thus be able to operate and predict in the world in which we live even though it is full of noise.

In closing, it may be worth noting that high validity and reliability scores with these concepts are best obtained with observers who manifest a relatively high degree of competence in the variables being studied. For example, in the development of a system of categories in organization and innovation, observers with relatively high degree of inter-personal openness and trust were able to develop interobserver reliability scores with these variables ranging from 80 percent to 94 percent within eight hours of scoring. Two of these observers were able within two hours to reproduce the score of 74 percent agreement after one year of not using the scoring system. However, two observers with relatively low capacity to be open and trusting were never able to reach a higher observer interreliability score than about 50 percent. The possession of the higher level of interpersonal competence made it possible for the first pair to see the interpersonal world more accurately and reliably. These findings are similar to Meehl's (1965) and Barron's (1965). They have suggested that the most reliable and valid raters of "creativity" were people who themselves were creative. Reliable and valid observation of interpersonal phenomena may also require a certain level of interpersonal competence.

Research is needed to help us understand more precisely how social scientists can develop valid theories and rigorous operational measures in a universe which may be composed of overlapping and redundant parts; where interrelationships are so complex that concepts of steady state are needed to conceptualize them; where objective observations may be limited to researchers who already manifest a relatively high competence in the phenomena under study.

# References

Argyris, C., 1958, "Creating Effective Relationships in Organizations," *Human Organization*, 17, pp. 34–40.

Argyris, C., 1962, *Interpersonal Competence and Organizational Effectiveness*, Homewood, Ill., Irwin.

Argyris, C., 1964, *Intergrating the Individual and the Organization*, New York, Wiley.

Argyris, C., 1965, *Organization and Innovation*, Homewood, Ill., Irwin.

Argyris, C., 1966, "Interpersonal Barriers to Decision Making," *Harvard Business Review*, 44, 2, pp. 84–97.

Argyris, C., 1982, *Reasoning, Learning, and Action*, San Francisco, Jossey-Bass.

Barron, F., 1965 "Some Studies of Creativity at the Institute of Personality Assessment and Research," in Steiner, H. A. (ed.), *The Creative Organization*, Chicago, University of Chicago Press.

Bennis, W., 1966, *Changing Organizations*, New York, McGraw-Hill.

Brock, C., and Becker, L. A., 1966, "'Debriefing' and Susceptibility to Subsequent Experimental Manipulation," *Journal of Experimental Social Psychology*, 2, pp. 314–23.

Burdick, E., 1957, *The Ninth Wave*, New York, Dell.

Edwards, A. L., 1954, "Experiments: Their Planning and Execution," in Lindzey, G. (ed.), *Handbook of Social Psychology*, Reading, MA, Addison-Wesley.

Friedman, N., 1967, *The Social Nature of Psychological Research*, New York, Basic Books.

Hyman, H. H., Cobb, W. J., Feldman, J. J., Hart, C. W., and Stember, C. H., 1954, *Interviewing in Social Research*, Chicago, University of Chicago Press.

Kelman, H. C., 1967, "The Problem of Deception in Social Psychological Experiments," *Psychological Bulletin*, 67, pp. 1–11.

Kiesler, C., (nd), 1977, "Group Pressure and Conformity," in Mills, J. (ed.), *Advanced Experimental Social Psychology*, New York, Macmillan.

Meehl, P. E., 1965, "The Creative Individual: Why It Is Hard to Identify Him," in Steiner, H. A., (ed.), *The Creative Organization*, Chicago, University of Chicago Press.

Mills, T. M., 1962, "A Sleeper Variable in Small Groups Research: The Experimenter," *Pacific Sociology Review*, 5, pp. 21–8.

Orne, M. T., 1962, "On the Social Psychology of the Psychology Experiment; with Particular Reference to Demand Characteristics and their Implications," *American Psychologist*, 17, pp. 776–83.

Rosenthal, R., 1963, "On the Social Psychology of the Psychological Experiment: The Experimenter's Hypotheses as Unintended Determinants of Experimental Results," *American Scientist*, 51, pp. 268–83.

Rosenthal, R., 1964, "Experimenter Outcome-Orientation and the Results of the Psychological Experiment," *Psychological Bulletin*, 61, pp. 405–12.

Rosenthal, R., 1966, *Experimenter Effects in Behavioral Research*, New York, Appleton-Century-Crofts.

Roth, J. A., 1966, "Hired Hand Research," *American Sociologist*, 1, pp. 190–96.

Sales, S. M., 1966, "Supervisory Style and Productivity: Review and Theory," *Personnel Psychology*, 19, pp. 281–2.

von Neumann, J., 1958, *The Computer and the Brain*, New Haven, Yale University Press.

# Index